Martina and Babe Ciarlo

Charles Mann

Emma Belle Petcher

Clyde Odum

John Gray

Emily Lewis

Maurice Bell

Leo Goldberg

Anne DeVico (center)

James Fahey

Ray Pittmann

Tim Tokuno

Eugene Sledge (left) and his brother

Paul Fussell

Burnett Miller

Sam Hynes and his father

Waymon Ransom

Herndon Inge, Jr.

A THOUSAND VETERANS
OF THE WAR DIE EVERY DAY.
THIS BOOK IS DEDICATED TO ALL
THOSE WHO FOUGHT AND
WON THAT NECESSARY WAR
ON OUR BEHALF.

THE WAR

THE WAR

AN INTIMATE HISTORY

1941–1945

by GEOFFREY C. WARD

Based on
A KEN BURNS FILM

directed and produced by
KEN BURNS and LYNN NOVICK

written by
GEOFFREY C. WARD

With an introduction by
KEN BURNS

Picture research by
DAVID McMAHON

ALFRED A. KNOPF
NEW YORK
2007

This Is a Borzoi Book
Published by Alfred A. Knopf
Copyright © 2007 by American Lives II Film Project, LLC

All rights reserved. Published in the United States by Alfred A.
Knopf, a division of Random House, Inc., New York, and
in Canada by Random House of Canada Limited, Toronto.
www.aaknopf.com

Knopf, Borzoi Books, and the colophon are registered
trademarks of Random House, Inc.

Library of Congress Cataloging-in-Publication Data

Ward, Geoffrey C.
    The war : an intimate history, 1941–1945 / by Geoffrey C.
    Ward and Ken Burns.—1st ed.
        p. cm.
        Based on Burns' documentary, The war.
        Includes bibliographical references and index.
        ISBN 978-0-307-26283-7 (alk. paper)
    1. World War, 1939–1945—United States.   2. World War,
1939–1945—Social aspects—United States.   I. Burns, Ken,
1953–   II. War (Television program : 2007)   III. title.
    D769.W345 2007
    940.53'73—dc22   2007003640

Manufactured in the United States of America
First Edition

TEXT PERMISSIONS

Material from Ernie Pyle's war writing taken from *Ernie's War* edited by David Nichols (Random House, Inc., 1986) is used courtesy of Scripps Howard Foundation.

Grateful acknowledgment is made to the following for permission to reprint previously published material:

Brandt & Hochman Literary Agents, Inc.: Excerpt from *State of the Nation* by John Dos Passos, copyright © 1944 by John Dos Passos, copyright renewed by Elizabeth Dos Passos (Houghton Mifflin Company, 1944). Reprinted by permission of Brandt & Hochman Literary Agents, Inc.

Houghton Mifflin Company: Excerpts from *Pacific War Diary, 1942–1945* by James J. Fahey, copyright © 1963, and renewed 1991 by James J. Fahey. All rights reserved. Reprinted by permission of Houghton Mifflin Company.

Susan Lardner: Excerpt from "Okinawa" by John Lardner, from *The New Yorker Book of War Pieces* (Reynal & Hitchcock, Inc., 1947). Reprinted by permission of Susan Lardner.

Pen and Sword Books Ltd.: Untitled poem by E. S. Saunders from *Prisoners of Santo Tomas* by Celia Lucas, published by Leo Cooper, an imprint of Pen and Sword Books Ltd., South Yorkshire, Great Britain, in 1996. Reprinted by permission of Pen and Sword Books Ltd.

Pollinger Limited: Excerpt from *Eclipse* by Alan Moorehead, copyright © 1945 by The Estate of Alan Moorehead (Coward-McCann, Inc., 1945). Reprinted by permission of Pollinger Limited.

Presidio Press: Excerpt from *With the Old Breed* by E. B. Sledge, copyright © 1990 by E. B. Sledge. Reprinted by permission of Presidio Press, an imprint of The Ballantine Publishing Group, a division of Random House, Inc.

CONTENTS

Preceding pages:
Bougainville, Solomon Islands,
    March 1944
Geich, Germany, December 1944
Okinawa, 1945
Near Carentan, France, 1944
Near Hürtgen, Germany, 1944
Leyte, Philippines, 1944
Acerno, Italy, 1943
Bitche, France, 1945
Wöbbelin concentration camp,
    Ludwigslust, Germany, 1945
Pennsylvania Station, New York, 1943

INTRODUCTION
NO ORDINARY LIVES

THE GREATEST CATACLYSM in history grew out of ancient and ordinary human emotions—anger and arrogance and bigotry, victimhood and the lust for power. And it ended because other human qualities—courage and perseverance and selflessness, faith, leadership, and the hunger for freedom—combined with unimaginable brutality to change the course of human events. The Second World War brought out the best and the worst in a generation—and blurred the two so that they became at times almost indistinguishable.

In the killing that engulfed the world from 1939 to 1945, between 50 and 60 million people died, so many and in so many different places that the real number will never be known. More than 85 million men and women served in uniform, but the overwhelming majority of those who perished were civilians—men, women, and children, obliterated by the arithmetic of war.

The United States was relatively fortunate. More than 405,000 soldiers and sailors, airmen and marines died, but that figure represented proportionately fewer military casualties than were suffered by any of the other major combatants. American cities were not destroyed. American civilians were never really at risk. Without American power, however, and without the sacrifice of American lives, the struggle's outcome would have been very different.

The American economy only grew stronger as the fighting went on, and by the time it ended the United States would be the most powerful nation on earth, and a once-isolated and insular people would find themselves at the center of world affairs. The war touched every family on every street in every town in America: towns like Luverne, Minnesota; Sacramento, California; Waterbury, Connecticut; and Mobile, Alabama; and nothing would ever be the same again.

As World War II drew to a close in the spring of 1945, the CBS radio correspondent Eric Sevareid was troubled. He'd been reporting on the fighting for four years, had witnessed the fall of France, parachuted into the Burmese jungle, struggled to keep up with GIs as they battled their way toward Rome and then across southern France, and he had done his best to convey to his listeners back home all that he had seen and heard along the way. But he was haunted by the sense that he had failed.

"Only the soldier really lives the war," he told his audience.

The journalist does not. He may share the soldier's outward life and dangers, but he cannot share his inner life, because the same moral compulsion does not bear upon him. The observer knows he has alternatives of action; the soldier knows he has none. . . .

War happens inside a man . . . and that is why, in a certain sense, you and your sons from the war will be forever strangers. If, by the miracle of art and genius, in later years two or three among them can open their hearts and the right words come, then perhaps we shall know a little of what it was like—and we shall know then that all the present speakers and writers hardly touched the story.

This book—and the documentary series it accompanies—was created in that spirit. In it, nearly fifty men and women open their hearts about the war they knew—and which we, their inheritors, can only imagine.

We search our past continually for heroes, mentors, and guides and trust in their example to lead us through the most difficult of times. So many different things threaten the fragile coalition, the invisible and sometimes unspoken compact that binds us all together, that the resources of the present seem inadequate to our needs, and we turn to those distant figures to help us comprehend the whole. At no time is the need for this "advice" greater or the stakes higher than when our country is facing the daunting specter of war. Whether it is the revolution that made us or the devastating internal struggle of our civil war or the current actions in the Middle East, war sets our republic vibrating in often dangerous and unexpected and unintended ways. We seek desperately to understand the mysterious, inscrutable, sometimes even transcendent elements that force their way to the surface when human beings kill each other in great numbers—that is to say, when human beings go to war.

It is not enough to be against war. In a world where so much evil exists, where human nature itself propels people into aggressive action, there is no chance that war will simply disappear, just because we hope it will. Indeed, our history shows us that some wars *had* to be fought—and still the contradictions and paradox of armed conflict confound us at every turn. World War II was such a war, and there is much we can learn from it.

This project was born out of great reluctance. Seventeen years ago, we published a book and released an eleven-and-a-half-hour, nine-part film on the American Civil War. For years, those of us who were engaged with those projects struggled daily to understand the four horrible years in our national life, when, in order to become one, we tore ourselves in two.

Our series on the Civil War began with a short quote from Oliver Wendell Holmes, Jr. He had been wounded six times during that conflict and would go on to serve his country once more as a Supreme Court justice. He said: "We have shared the incommunicable experience of war. We have felt, we still feel, the passion of life at its top. . . . In our youths, our hearts were touched with fire." Holmes was struggling himself to put into words what every soldier who has faced combat knows in his or her guts: that, paradoxically, when your life is most threatened, when violent death is possible at any moment, *everything* is vivified, the intensity of experience heightened to a level not felt in ordinary life. War creates a terror—an excruciating, unbearable terror—that is not only repellent but undeniably and inexplicably compelling. It is an almost indescribable feeling that survivors of war from the beginning of recorded history have found overwhelming, intimidating, and haunting, yet also seductive and spellbinding.

Shortly after Appomattox, Walt Whitman, a Brooklyn journalist and sometime poet who had worked as a nurse in the appalling Union hospitals, warned posterity of what he had seen. "Future years," he wrote, "will never know the seething hell and the black infernal background of the countless minor scenes and interiors of the Secession War, and it is best they should not." "The real war," Whitman insisted, "will never get in the books."

That certainty, as so many soldiers have confirmed—as well as Eric Sevareid and Walt Whitman and countless other observers— that it is impossible to describe accurately the experience of war, has not kept novelists and writers, historians and documentary filmmakers from trying. But for years after our Civil War series was aired, we vowed we would not attempt another film about the subject, politely turning away the suggestions of strangers and colleagues that we take on this struggle or that one, usually the Second World War. Each protest cemented even more our resolve not to "go to war" again. At first, we didn't want to be typecast or seen to be exploiting the unexpected success of our Civil War film and book, but we also didn't want to descend again into the frightening—but also mesmerizing—parallel universe of war with its inevitable suffering, loss, catastrophe, and death.

But several years ago, two statistics began to erode that conviction for us. After years of deflecting requests that we do something specifically on World War II (usually from aging veterans or their children who were anxious that their parents' long private dramas

be shared), we learned to our alarm that one thousand veterans of the Second World War were dying each day in America; that we were losing, among our fathers and grandfathers, a direct connection to the deeds of that unusually reticent generation. It seemed clear that if we, the inheritors of the world they struggled so hard to create for us, neglected to hear them out before they passed away, we would be guilty of a historical amnesia too irresponsible to countenance.

Lt. Robert K. Burns, Jr.

In recent years, to be sure, there has been an increase in our popular culture in everything World War II that *might* have excused us. These manifestations have ranged from the ridiculous to the sublime, as in the superbly realized television series *Band of Brothers* and Steven Spielberg's *Saving Private Ryan,* with its extraordinary scene of the landing at Omaha Beach. And then there have been the books, each attempting to revisit and reinterpret the specific moments or grand themes of the Second World War. One of them, Tom Brokaw's *Greatest Generation,* became a phenomenon. It was as if, suddenly, that nearly lifelong reticence had dissolved, and brave soldier after brave soldier, liberated by the loose and essentially disconnected collection of stories in Brokaw's book, finally felt they had been given permission to speak, to tell their stories before they were gone. Their collective intimation of mortality provided a reminder that the "incommunicable experience of war" nonetheless *still* required them to try to express to those "future years" what had really happened to them when they were young men; what they themselves had seen and done, and how their individual stories connected to the larger issues and dramas of that war. Posterity, in a sense, beckoned. They had—*have*—to tell us. Their memory is their most valuable asset, and our inheritance.

Brokaw should be given a medal for helping to release this extraordinary energy, this outpouring of pure personal history, allowing us to understand, without artifice or false pieties, the real truth of war—that despite the leadership (or lack thereof) of politicians and generals, it is the bottom-up story of so-called ordinary soldiers that can fill in the fuller canvas for us, and remind us of the Union from which so many of our personal as well as collective blessings flow.

The second statistic was just as troubling as the first. Among a number of demoralizing facts about the continuing crisis in our schools over what our children know (and don't know), one item stood out. It seems that an unacceptably large number of graduating high-school seniors think we fought *with* the Germans *against* the Russians in the Second World War.

By the time these terrible statistics had fully sunk in, we found that we could no longer ignore the subject. We also noted that with the exception of a few excellent filmed efforts about specific battles or moments in that conflict, there had been no meaningful large-scale documentary film series on the Second World War for more than a generation. Six years ago, therefore, we committed to working on a film series and companion book that have just now been completed, a massive project that has consumed and transformed everyone who has worked on it.

The journey from the original outrage at those two awful facts—that we are losing both our soldiers and our historical compass—has been long and complicated. Taking on any war is risky, but taking on the biggest of them all is fraught with peril. Clearly, no book or film series, however long, can reflect the whole story. So, how would we limit our scope, then, while still providing the context so clearly lacking in recent works? How do you relate the reality of that war? What was it *really* like? Which battles do we *have* to cover? How do you do justice to the small moments, the quotidian details of ordinary happenstance, without sacrificing the larger sense and momentum of the struggle? How do you communicate the simultaneity of the two major theaters, European and Pacific, that we Americans were principally engaged in? How do you show the home front, from the radical and impressive transformation of American industrial might, in a country just emerging from the Great Depression, to the myriad personal moments of loss, worry, hope, and reunion? How do you show the larger aerial view of the war, the top-down version, alongside the bottom-up individual side we always try to champion? Where do you start? These were only a handful of the questions we asked ourselves as we began work.

To try to answer those questions for both the book and film, we traveled nearly around the world; conducted hundreds of interviews; drew on material from hundreds of archives; devoted thousands of man-hours to research and then organize the material we collected; edited that material for more than two years; wrote and rewrote and wrote again hundreds of pages of narration; engaged the services of Keith David to read that narration for the film (along with Tom Hanks and several other actors to read the diaries and letters, newspaper columns and other first-person material that punctuate our films); worked with a dozen talented musicians and one very great composer, Wynton Marsalis, to complement the pieces of classical, swing, jazz, folk, and other music from the period that form our joyous, sad, and eerie soundtrack; and collected the thousands of individual sounds of war to merge into an effects track that we hope will plunge the viewer uncomfortably *into* some of the battles we try to bring to the fore; and been *privileged* to be ushered into the lives and memories of nearly fifty men and women who brought the war—modestly, gingerly, with great emotion and pain, and no small amount of ambivalence—to our doorsteps; so that we, in turn, might try to work and re-work, massage and cajole, honor and celebrate, the bravery and heroism of these citizen-soldiers, who, when they were seventeen, eighteen, nineteen, and twenty years old, a time when most of us had the luxury of inattention and narcissistic self-involvement, happened to have helped save the world.

How fortunate it is that we in the United States are stitched together—as a people, indeed, as individuals—by words and ideas, but also by memory. And when, as it lawfully sometimes must, our magnificent tapestry becomes frayed and worn, we often lose that connection with one another, that which binds us back to the whole. In those moments, we look uneasily into the void that has, over the centuries, destroyed so many other promising experiments. In those moments, it becomes necessary to re-invigorate what we share in common, and to ignore those polarizing impulses that inevitably afflict us all.

One antidote to this misery of misunderstanding and division is memory. (One antidote, in a sense, is anecdote.) Memory is that deeply personal affirmation of self, that which calibrates and triangulates our sense of who we are, and yet it is also the ambassador of our own individual foreign policy—the agency that helps cement friendships, associations, and ambitions. In a larger sense, memory permits us to have an authentic relationship to our national narrative. These individual stories and moments, anecdotes and memories become the building blocks, the DNA, of our collective experience. Out of these associations we find the material, the glue to make our fragile experiment stick, permanent; "a machine," someone once said, "that will go of itself."

You will soon meet in this book (as in our film) fifty or so human beings who are about to descend into the madness of global war, all of whom you will know by the end of the last chapter, almost like family members. These will not be the traditional top-down heroes we are usually presented with—the generals, the presidents and statesmen, the prime ministers and field marshals who tend to recede from our understanding just as they ascend to the pantheon of Great Men. These are folks you might have had Thanksgiving with; men whose stories of war are just *now* being told. And most of the people who narrate our account of the most complex conflict in history come not from the centers of population and power in the United States but from four geographically distributed, to some extent isolated, towns: Luverne, Minnesota; Sacramento, California; Waterbury, Connecticut; and Mobile, Alabama.

Where our Civil War narrative focused primarily on the main players (while trying not to sacrifice an appreciation of what the privates were doing), *this* story is different, told almost exclusively from the perspective of those who did the actual fighting and dying, as well as those back home who waited for their loved ones to return. Through their eyes, it is possible, in moments, to sense how the whole country got caught up in that war (these towns could be any four towns, of course): how the nation reacted to the news of attack; how its sons were mobilized and sent off; how the progress of that war unfolded; what the battles were like from the ground up; how those who remained at home worked and worried and grieved in the face of the struggle; how innocent young men who had been turned into professional killers adjusted to a world without war; and how the four towns and their people were permanently transformed by the Second World War. By concentrating on the *specific* we hope we've made it possible to better receive the *universal*; to comprehend the whole because we are invested, deeply and emotionally invested, in the particular.

Over the course of these pages (and in the seven episodes of the film series), these brave individuals will take us on a tour of hell—not the "good war" of our sentimental imagination but the "necessary war" that gives our first chapter its title. Before the Japanese attacked on December 7, 1941, most Americans could not have found Pearl Harbor on a map. In the nearly four years that followed, they would have to learn a host of new names of the places where their sons would be fighting—Kasserine Pass and Monte Cassino; Utah Beach and Omaha Beach and Sainte-Mère-Église, Arnhem and Aachen and the Hürtgen Forest and the Ardennes; and on the other side of the world, Guam and Bataan and Guadalcanal, Saipan and Peleliu and Iwo Jima, Midway and Cape Gloucester and Okinawa. And young men from our towns would learn difficult, painful lessons in those places, lessons as old as war itself—that generals make plans, plans go wrong, and soldiers die.

Memory is imperfect, but its inherent instability allows our past, which we usually see as fixed, to remain as it actually is: malleable, changing not just as new information emerges but as our own interests, emotions, and inclinations change. In less than a generation, we can go from an almost obsessive interest in the guns and tactics of World War II to a profound apprehension of cause, heroism, loss, and even redemption. If history is accumulated memory, then war is a kind of *forgetting*, the worst kind of inattention to the flaws in our nature that repeatedly and foolishly propel us again and again into holocaust, magnifying and accelerating that loss but also uniting us, as a people, in that grief. The healing, if any, that can come from this, on both a collective as well as individual level, is sponsored by the corrective that cathartic memory and its authentic expression always is.

So what *did* we find out? Many things, of course. But perhaps the most important lesson to be learned from all the blood and horror and tragedy our witnesses recalled is that no nation should embark upon any war without first understanding what its cost will be and without being certain that its objectives are really worth the fearful price.

It is clear to us as well that the Second World War reverberates and echoes down the corridors of history, its lessons as fresh today—in our own difficult situation—as they were for those soldiers who struggled daily just to survive that horrible event. In the end, we have come to believe, in the presence of the young men whose stories we followed, that we did have one overarching theme we could not ignore. It is a truth, we think, as old as history itself, but one we always forget, especially in a society like ours, addicted as we are now to the breathless embrace of spurious celebrity, to the great tyranny those synthetic "heroes" have over the rest of us. It is a truth that this kind of nostalgia, and the mindless inattention that issues from it, prevents us from knowing. It is, however, the theme that issues out of every frame of our film and every page of our book—not so much from our own doing as from simply bearing witness to the stories of these remarkably brave young men. It is also an idea inherent in our country's great and often forgotten promise. And that is: *There are no ordinary lives.* By stepping into memory, by stepping into the great gift of memory these men and women have given us, we liberate ourselves.

The Second World War was fought in thousands of places, too many for any one accounting. This is the story of four American towns and how their citizens experienced that war.

Ken Burns
Walpole, New Hampshire

Much of the world was already at war in the first week of December 1941, and President Franklin D. Roosevelt was doing all he could to prepare the United States for the confrontation he believed was sure to come. But for most Americans, recovering from the Great Depression, events overseas still seemed very far away.

IN LUVERNE, MINNESOTA, the seat of Rock County, in the state's southwestern corner, the harvest was only a memory and the town's 3,100 citizens were well into the long annual winter wait until they could sow their fields again. Jim Sherman, the grandson of Luverne's general practitioner, was then six. "It was a pretty close-knit community," he remembered. "Everybody knew pretty much everybody else in town and there was a saying that if you don't want people to know about it, you don't do it."

Among the town's early settlers were immigrants from northern Europe: some Sunday services were still conducted in German and Norwegian as well as English. For many of their descendants, conflict in what they called the Old Country was none of America's business.

FARM TOWN: The stores and theaters on Luverne's Main Street (opposite page) did their briskest business on Saturdays, when farm families came to town to stock up on supplies. Rock County soil produced hogs (being auctioned at right) and supported dairies (below) as well as field crops.

IN SACRAMENTO, the capital of California, "Okies"—refugee families from the Dust Bowl—remained camped on the edge of town while their menfolk sought work in the fields and orchards and vineyards of the Sacramento Valley, where a different kind of crop needed harvesting nearly every month. The city had been the gateway to the Gold Rush and the western anchor of the transcontinental railroad, and it was home to some 106,000 diverse people—including Mexican, Italian, Portuguese, Chinese, Japanese, and Filipino Americans. But it still seemed like a small town to many of those who lived there. Earl Burke, who was then a junior at C. K. McClatchy High School, recalled that "you could go out on the streets at twelve o'clock at night and walk home in the dark. Nobody would lock the doors. Nobody even thought of it."

THE CAPITAL OF THE GOLDEN STATE (clockwise from opposite page): the statehouse dome; the home of Burt Wilson, who would watch the war through a child's eyes; the Esquire Theater, where adults witnessed their own version of it; and Japanese American rice farmers, who would soon find themselves denied the most basic rights of citizenship

WATERBURY, CONNECTICUT, on the banks of the Naugatuck River, had been known since the nineteenth century as "Brass City." Its skilled workforce, mostly immigrants and immigrants' children, turned out screws and washers and buttons, showerheads and alarm clocks, toy airplanes and lipstick holders and cocktail shakers. Ray Leopold, the son of a Jewish immigrant from Latvia, remembered the high standards of production the citizens of his city proudly maintained: "Waterbury was a center for high-quality craft. There were individuals there who could do one ten thousandth of an inch on anything—and if there was zero tolerance required, they could do that, too." Skill and precision had not been enough to defeat the Depression, and Waterbury had suffered terribly during the 1930s, but its residents would prove precisely what was needed by the new defense industries that were just beginning to transform their town.

BRASS CITY: Companies like Scovill Manufacturing (in the center of the overview, opposite page, top) helped turn the little New England village that once surrounded the green (opposite, bottom) into an industrial city (below), complete with refinements like the vast State Theater (above). Among its hardest-working citizens were immigrants from Italy like Tomaso Ciarlo (right), whose son Babe would find himself helping to liberate his father's homeland.

MOBILE, ALABAMA, once a center of cotton and the slave trade, was still best known for its annual azalea festival and leisurely southern air. "Daddy said Mobile made its living by taking in each other's wash," recalled Katharine Phillips, who lived with her younger brother Sidney and their family in one of the oldest parts of town. "And it was absolutely true. The pace of life was slow. There was no air conditioning, of course, so on a hot summer evening Daddy would load us in the car and we'd drive downtown to Brown's Ice Cream and he'd buy us an ice-cream cone, and then we'd drive out to Arlington and park out by the bay. We'd all sit there and enjoy the sea breeze. And when we'd cooled down enough, he'd bring us home and everybody could go to bed and go to sleep. Or we sat on the porch in the evening and the children played in the yard. It was a wonderful way to grow up. Down in Mobile we were completely away from the rest of the world."

By the winter of 1941, the rest of the world was closing in fast as President Roosevelt struggled to make good on his pledge to make the United States the "arsenal of democracy," and navy ship-building, which had flourished in Mobile during the Great War and collapsed during the Depression, began to boom once again.

SEAPORT OF THE OLD SOUTH: Visitors came to Mobile because romantic places like Bienville Square (far left) seemed untouched since antebellum days. When *Gone with the Wind* opened at the Roxy (above), it seemed only natural that local girls officiate in bonnets and hoopskirts. But there was another side to the city, symbolized by the shacks at the corner of Washington Avenue and Texas Street (left). When the time came, Eugene Sledge, the descendant of Confederate officers, who grew up in the ancestral home below, would find precious little romance on the battlefield.

But no one in Mobile, Waterbury, Sacramento, Luverne—or anywhere else in America—was prepared for what was about to happen to them and their country.

A NECESSARY WAR

I don't think there is such a thing as a good war. There are sometimes necessary wars. And I think one might say, "just" wars. I never questioned the necessity of that war. And I still do not question it. It was something that had to be done.
—SAM HYNES

SUNDAY MORNING, DECEMBER 7, 1941, began as most days do in Honolulu: warm and sunny with blue skies punctuated here and there by high wisps of cloud. At a few minutes after eight o'clock, the Hyotara Inouye family was at home on Coyne Street, getting ready for church. The sugary whine of Hawaiian music drifted through the house. The oldest of the four Inouye children, seventeen-year-old Daniel, a senior at William McKinley High and a Red Cross volunteer, was listening to station KGMB as he dressed. There were other sounds, too, muffled far-off sounds to which no one paid much attention at first because they had grown so familiar over the past few months. The drone of airplanes and the rumble of distant explosions had been commonplace since spring of the previous year, when the U.S. Pacific Fleet had shifted from the California coast to Pearl Harbor, some seven miles northwest of the Inouye home. Air-raid drills were frequent occurrences; so was practice firing of the big coastal defense batteries near Waikiki Beach.

But this was different. Daniel was just buttoning his shirt, he remembered, when the voice of disk jockey Webley Edwards broke into the music. "All army, navy, and marine personnel to report to duty," it said. At almost the same moment, Daniel's father shouted for him to come outside. Something strange was going on. Daniel hurried out into the sunshine and stood with his father by the side of the house, peering toward Pearl Harbor. They were too far away to see the fleet itself, and hills further obscured their view, but the sky above the harbor was filled with puffs of smoke. During drills the blank antiaircraft bursts had always been white. These were jet-black. Then, as the Inouyes watched in disbelief, the *crrrump* of distant explosions grew louder and more frequent and so much oily black smoke began billowing up into the sky that the mountains all but vanished and the horizon itself seemed about to disappear.

At that point, Daniel remembered, "all of a sudden, three aircraft flew right overhead. They were pearl gray with red dots on

Daniel Inouye (above) saw the war begin. Most Americans learned of it over the radio or from newspapers like those being peddled by the Redding, California, newsboy on the opposite page.

the wing—Japanese. I knew what was happening. And I thought my world had just come to an end."

He had no time for further reflection. The telephone rang. He was needed at the nearest aid station right away. A stray American antiaircraft shell had fallen into a crowded neighborhood. There were civilian casualties. "One haunts me every so often," Inouye remembered many years later. "It was a woman clutching a child. Her head was severed, but here she was with her arms around her baby. And so this is what I had to pick up. At seventeen."

Young Daniel Inouye's first experience of the war was like that of most Americans who lived through it. They would retain vivid memories of the things they actually saw. But each would also be affected by events they could not see, happening just over the horizon or thousands of miles away. The statesmen and strategists who moved so many of them from one place, one peril, to the next, were largely invisible, too. And most people were too busy trying simply to survive to be able to understand the parts that the battles they waged or watched or worried about were playing in the greater struggle. This is their story of the war, as some of them remember it.

NOTHING LIKE THE ATTACK on Pearl Harbor had ever happened to Americans before. In less than two hours, Japanese warplanes launched from carriers far out at sea had taken so terrible a toll on the Pacific Fleet that the War Department would keep the exact details to itself for years. Eight of the nine American battleships in the Pacific, including the USS *Arizona,* were sunk or severely damaged. So were three light cruisers, three destroyers, and four other naval vessels. (All three American carriers hap-

In this photograph, made from the cockpit of a Japanese warplane within a minute or two of the initial attack on Ford Island, in the center of Pearl Harbor, a torpedo bomber (center) can be seen veering away after hitting the battleship *Oklahoma.* Nine more torpedoes would follow, capsizing her and killing 415 of the men aboard. Meanwhile, two waves of enemy planes would sink or damage almost all of the other warships anchored along Battleship Row. "It was awful," one woman who watched the attack from shore recalled, "for great ships were dying before my eyes! Strangely enough, at first I didn't realize that men were dying, too."

While stunned crewmen survey the damage done by enemy bombs at Ford Island Naval Air Station (above), the USS *West Virginia,* her decks awash, has already sunk into the shallow muddy bottom of Pearl Harbor (below). Behind her looms the *Tennessee,* also damaged and now menaced by burning oil. "Hell," one sailor said as the last Japanese bombers flew away that morning, "I didn't even know they were sore at us."

pened to be away at the time of the attack, or they, too, might have been lost.) One hundred and sixty-four American aircraft—three quarters of those based around Pearl Harbor—were also destroyed, all but a few without ever having gotten off the ground. Two thousand four hundred and three Americans, servicemen and civilians, lost their lives. Some eleven hundred more were wounded.

It was around two-thirty in the afternoon when the first news of it reached ordinary citizens in the eastern United States. Katharine Phillips of Mobile, Alabama, was then a sophomore at Auburn University, in the east-central part of the state. She had just returned to her dormitory from church when she heard a scream from down the hall, then the sounds of weeping. "What's the matter?" she asked. "What's wrong?" Her housemates told her what they'd heard. Tears filled her eyes, too, she remembered, "but we comforted each other. The girls all cried and wept because they had boyfriends or relatives who were already in the armed forces. And we realized immediately that this would be war."

At about that same time back home in Mobile, Katharine's seventeen-year-old brother, Sidney Phillips, Jr., was perched on a soda fountain stool at Albright and Woods drugstore at the corner of Dauphin and Anne streets, drinking a nickel vanilla milkshake. It had an extra scoop of ice cream in it, courtesy of the soda jerk, Phillips's friend and former classmate William O. Brown. He and Brown—whom everybody called W.O.—had graduated from Murphy High School that June.

Suddenly, a distraught woman flew through the door. "Turn on the radio!" she shouted. Someone did. "It kept giving the same information again and again," Phillips remembered, "and we just all sat there quietly, listening." As the news crackled in, Brown kept wiping the same section of the marble countertop over and over again. Phillips just stared at the tiled floor; more than half a century later he could remember its distinctive black-and-white checkerboard pattern. "Everyone was very startled," he recalled, "excited, frightened, very serious. We knew this meant we were in the war. Some ladies started crying." After a time the radio announcer began repeating himself and the stunned customers at last began to talk among themselves. Phillips was the only one in the drugstore who had any idea where Pearl Harbor was; his uncle was a navy pilot and had once been stationed there.

W. O. Brown stopped wiping the counter and said, "Sid, let's go join the navy in the morning."

Phillips said, "Fine." He climbed onto his bike and pedaled home to tell his parents of his new plans. His mother was horrified: Sidney was too young for the draft, plus two of her brothers

Katharine (left) and Sidney Phillips and their family

were already in the navy—that should be enough sacrifice for any family. His father, a schoolteacher, felt differently. He had been wounded on the western front during the Great War and had seen how poorly replacements had been prepared for combat during the war's last weeks. Since his son was sure to be drafted anyway, it was best for the boy to go in early: he stood a better chance of surviving if he was well trained. Both his parents finally gave their permission for him to go, though his mother never really reconciled herself. "The story in the family," Sid's sister, Katharine, recalled, "is that the recruiting officer crossed the street any time in the next year that he encountered my mother, because she would give him a piece of her mind for taking her little boy."

When Sid and W.O. met outside the federal building in Bienville Square at eight o'clock the next morning, the line of volunteers in front of the navy recruiting office already stretched almost a block. The two boys sidled up to the head of the line to see how long the wait might be. A sergeant from the marine recruiting office next door took them aside.

"Do you want to kill Japs?" he asked.

They did. That's why they'd come down to join the navy.

Forget about the navy, the sergeant said. All sailors do is swab decks. Marines were guaranteed to meet the enemy "eyeball to eyeball." Besides, he said, "you can't get into the navy—your parents are married."

Sid Phillips and W. O. Brown laughed and signed on with the United States Marines.

BY THEN, THE RADIO WAS REPORTING still more terrible news. On the same day that the Japanese had attacked Pearl Harbor—December 8 west of the international date line—they had mounted simultaneous assaults on a host of other American and British targets in the Pacific region. Japanese troops had gone ashore in British Malaya. Japanese bombs fell on British strongholds in Hong Kong and Singapore, as well as on two U.S. outposts in the Pacific most Americans had never heard of before: Guam and Wake Island.

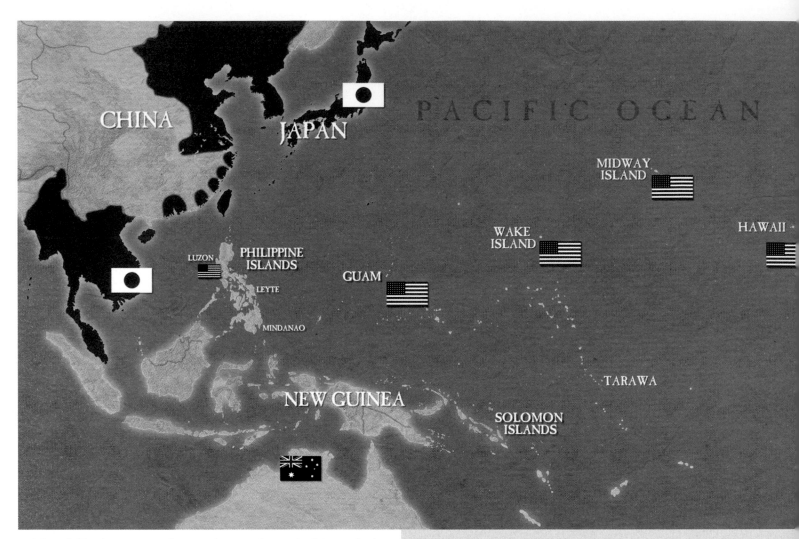

CHINA

JAPAN

PACIFIC OCEAN

MIDWAY ISLAND

WAKE ISLAND

HAWAII

LUZON

PHILIPPINE ISLANDS

GUAM

LEYTE

MINDANAO

NEW GUINEA

TARAWA

SOLOMON ISLANDS

The Pacific region on the eve of Pearl Harbor

The Philippines was under attack, too. The United States had never acknowledged possessing a Pacific empire, at least not formally, as the British and European powers did. And plans were already under way to grant the people of the Commonwealth of the Philippines their independence in four years. But the life many American civilians led in the islands the United States had occupied since helping to overthrow its Spanish rulers in 1898 mirrored the ease, comfort, and unexamined racial assumptions of colonial rule elsewhere in Asia.

Eight-year-old Sascha Weinzheimer lived with her family on the vast Calamba Sugar Estate, a little over an hour's drive south of Manila on the island of Luzon. The estate was owned by her grandfather, Ludwig Weinzheimer, a German American planter who now lived on a vast farm in the Sacramento Valley and left the management of his Philippine holdings to her father, Walter, and his brother, Conrad. She and her siblings—Doris, three, and Conrad, Jr., called Buddy, just six weeks old—along with two small cousins were the only American children on the estate. But it was in every other way "the most wonderful home a girl could

have," Sascha noted in a journal she began keeping about that time—a handsome bungalow surrounded by gardens filled with hibiscus and jasmine and ginger flowers. A Filipina amah named Esperanza kept her company. Jesus, the family cook, prepared the dishes she liked best. In the mornings, her mother taught her her lessons. In the afternoons, she galloped through the cane fields alongside the champion polo player who had taught her how to ride. At sundown, she was sometimes allowed to join her parents and their grown-up friends poolside at the Canlubang Golf and Recreation Club. Its membership was limited to American managers and their guests, whose glasses were kept topped up with beer or whiskey and soda by a phalanx of white-clad Filipino "boys."

The only intrusion on this idyll so far had been polio, which had affected Sascha's legs in infancy and required her to visit a physical therapist in Manila three times a week. There had been rumors of growing trouble with Japan for months now. Sascha's

In the years before the Japanese invaded the Philippines the sprawling Calamba Sugar Estate—its refinery is shown above—was home to the Walter Weinzheimer family. Sascha Weinzheimer, her siblings, and her young cousins (one of whom appears with her below) lived among lush formal gardens and cooled off in the Canlubang Club pool (right).

father had even written Ludwig to ask whether the family shouldn't come home to Sacramento but had been told to stay where he was; there would be no war.

Sascha's mother had learned of the attack on Pearl Harbor by breakfast time on December 8, but the physical therapy sessions seemed so important that she decided to send her daughter into town for her noon appointment anyway. That is where Sascha was at around half past twelve—lying on the therapist's table and undergoing the painful stretching of her leg muscles that was meant to help restore their strength—when the telephone rang. The therapist, a Jewish refugee from Nazi Germany, picked it up and paled: Japanese planes had hit Clark and Iba airfields and were bombing outlying neighborhoods of Manila as well. She said that Sascha must start for home right away; there was no time even to put her shoes back on. "There were many people on the streets walking, carrying bags and bundles," Sascha wrote. "All the people seemed so scared. They were trying hard to get to the provinces, where they would be safer."

As Benjamin, the family chauffeur, nosed the car through the frightened civilians who filled the road, he and Sascha's amah talked furiously in Tagalog. Sascha only dimly understood what they were saying, but when they finally reached home, she wrote, "Mummy was waiting in the driveway. She grabbed me, hugged me tight and said they were fools to have let me go to Manila that day." Sascha still didn't really comprehend what was happening; she was just glad to get home early, she remembered, "because that meant I could beg an extra swim before lunch."

THAT SAME MORNING, at about the time the automobile carrying Sascha Weinzheimer pulled up in front of her family's bungalow, Corporal Glenn Dowling Frazier of the 75th Ordnance and Supply Company was some forty miles away, standing on a forested hillside in Little Baguio, across Manila Bay on the Bataan peninsula, watching Japanese warplanes wheel and dive above Luzon and cursing his bad luck. After all, he had chosen to

Glenn Dowling Frazier (center), with a cousin and Rupert, one of his brothers

Manila dance hall, December 1, 1941: mounting talk of war failed to disturb the city's celebrated nightlife. "If the Japs come down here," one newspaperman reported, "they'll be playing in the big leagues for the first time in their lives."

come to the Philippines precisely because he had thought war would never follow him there.

One evening earlier that year, back home in the little farming town of Fort Deposit, Alabama, he found out that a girl he had known since the first grade and thought he loved was being courted by somebody else. The following day Frazier was still so angry and upset that when the owner of a juke joint in nearby Montgomery refused him service, he stalked outside, climbed onto his motorcycle, and roared back through the door, shattering bottles, smashing furniture, and leaving black skid marks on the dance floor. As Frazier raced away the bar owner chased him with a shotgun. The next morning, humiliated, scared, and unable to face his parents, he hurried to the nearest recruiting office. He was only seventeen, so he lied about his age, joined the peacetime army, and volunteered to serve in the Philippines. "I had no idea that we would actually be in a war," he remembered. But if there was to be one, "Germany was the most likely place," he'd thought then. "So, in my mind, I thought it'd be safe over there. I never thought Japan would be attacking us."

At first, he liked the choice he'd made. He was stationed in Manila, then known as the Pearl of the Orient for the beauty of its old buildings, parks, and broad avenues—and for the fleshly entertainment it offered to male visitors from everywhere. The city was a revelation to a country boy like Frazier. His unit was quartered at Fort Santiago, inside the thick-walled sixteenth-century Intramuros district. "It was like a luxury hotel," he remembered. Filipinos washed the men's clothes, cut their hair, shined their shoes, prepared and cooked their meals. Frazier spent his weekends with a young Filipina who helped him begin to forget the hometown girl he'd left behind. He hunted wild pigs in the forests of Bataan and prowled the city's bars with his buddies, sometimes brawling with sailors and marines just "because they thought the army was nothing." One night, he and his friends invaded a saloon that catered to Japanese sailors, picked a fight, wrecked the place, and escaped arrest only by out-running the MPs.

The task of Frazier's outfit was to truck ammunition and supplies from the Manila wharves to depots on Bataan and elsewhere on Luzon. He liked that, too. Filipino troops did most of the loading and unloading. He got to lead big convoys back and forth along the narrow, twisting roads that led out of the city, each truck with its own little red flag that signaled other traffic to get out of the way. The men knew that the countless tons of shells they carried were intended for the defense of the islands against a possible attack by the Japanese, but the official line in Manila was that no such attack was likely for months. "Stay," the American high commissioner told one anxious American resident that autumn. "Manila is the safest place in the Orient."

The United States had officially been pledged to defend the Philippines against the Japanese for nearly half a century. But almost from the first, the American military had realized it could not realistically fulfill that promise. Seven thousand miles of ocean separated the Philippines from the U.S. mainland. Pearl Harbor was just two thousand miles closer. There was simply no way to reach the islands before a determined Japanese force seized control of them. The best that American strategists could come up with was War Plan Orange: in case of attack, U.S. troops were to withdraw to the mountainous, forested Bataan peninsula and to Corregidor, the heavily fortified island at the entrance to

Manila Bay, and then hold out, doing their best to keep the Japanese fleet at bay, until American warships could steam to their rescue—a process sure to take months.

Then, in 1935, General Douglas MacArthur, the best-known soldier in the U.S. Army, had taken charge of the islands' defenses in his role as the top military advisor to the president of the Philippines, Manuel Quezon. A frontline hero of World War I and a former army Chief of Staff, MacArthur was as ambitious and self-absorbed as he was courageous. War Plan Orange was defeatism, pure and simple, he said. "I don't think the Philippines can defend themselves," he told Quezon. "I know they can." As the Japanese threat grew, President Franklin D. Roosevelt recalled MacArthur to active duty as army commander in the Far East, in charge of the Philippine army as well as all American forces in the islands. The general drew up plans for a new two-hundred-thousand-man army, to be made up of citizen conscripts trained and commanded by a core of regulars and guaranteed to hurl the invader back wherever in the islands he chose to strike. In late November, MacArthur had assured his civilian colleagues that there was no reason to fear a Japanese attack until late spring. By then, he promised to be ready for

General Douglas MacArthur (left) and Philippine President Manuel Quezon on Corregidor

Recruits belonging to the 41st Philippine Division head back toward their barracks after drill. Many Filipino soldiers would give a good accounting of themselves against the Japanese, despite the fact that they were hastily trained, poorly equipped, and spoke some twenty different dialects, so many that it often took five different translators to make the simplest orders in English understood. Despite these weaknesses, General MacArthur had assured Washington that under his command defense preparations were "progressing by leaps and bounds."

Smoke darkens the sky above Manila after a Japanese attack, part of what one city dweller called a "daily rain" of enemy bombs.

them, able to ensure the safety of the Philippines "until the end of time." Meanwhile, no one need worry, he said. "Destiny" had placed him in command.

Destiny was nowhere in evidence as Glenn Frazier watched from his hillside on December 8. MacArthur had known for nearly nine hours that the Japanese had attacked Pearl Harbor, but he had somehow failed to get his air force off the ground. The Japanese warplanes that flew in over Luzon had found American P-40 fighters and B-17 bombers still parked wingtip-to-wingtip on the runways. Most of America's air fleet in the Pacific was destroyed. At Clark Field, where fifty-five officers and men were blown apart along with their aircraft, one weeping, frustrated crewman threw his shoe at a low-flying Japanese plane.

Frazier and his outfit were ordered to race back from Bataan to Nichols Field, on the southern edge of Manila, with truckloads of five-hundred-pound bombs. Officers hoped they could still be used against the enemy carriers offshore. Air-raid sirens shrieked as the trucks approached the city. Antiaircraft shells exploded overhead. Frazier's truck passed beneath the body of a Filipino baby that had been blasted into the highest branches of a tree. As his convoy reached Nichols Field more bombs began falling, shaking the earth, blasting craters in the runways, killing ground crew, further damaging the wrecked American aircraft that would now never be able to employ any of the deadly cargo Frazier and his friends had risked their lives to bring in from Bataan. At about the same time, Japanese bombers hit the U.S. naval base at Cavite, south of the city, so hard—killing or seriously wounding at least five hundred men—that the admiral in charge ordered the few ships still intact to leave the Philippines. MacArthur's air and naval support had been eliminated.

When Frazier and his exhausted unit got back to their quarters in Fort Santiago the following morning, they found a Filipino soldier standing on top of the old wall, trying to shoot down enemy planes with a .50-caliber machine gun. His targets were far too high for him to hit. The gun was too heavy for him, too, and as he rocked back and forth trying to control it, his bullets first arced harmlessly over the river, then tore into nearby barracks, finally streamed down the street into civilian homes. To stop the gunfire, a sergeant had to clamber up a ladder and knock the soldier off the wall. It looked as if a full-scale Japanese invasion of the Philippines was about to begin—and no one seemed to know what they were doing.

ON MONDAY AFTERNOON, some 60 million Americans—in Sacramento, Waterbury, Luverne, Mobile, and everywhere else in the country—gathered around their radios to hear President Roosevelt ask a joint session of Congress for a declaration of war.

He did not mince words: "The attack yesterday on the Hawaiian Islands has caused severe damage to American naval and military forces. I regret to tell you that very many American lives have been lost." He went on to list some of the other places the Japanese had attacked over the preceding twenty-four hours. "There is no blinking at the fact that our people, our territory, and our interests are in grave danger," he said. But he also offered his assurance that victory would be won: "With confidence in our armed forces—with the unbounded determination of our people—we will gain the inevitable triumph—so help us God."

Three days later, Japan's allies, Germany and Italy, would formally declare war on the United States. Americans, who had hoped to stay out of the conflict overseas, now found themselves at war on both sides of the world at once.

The United States had not been attacked by a foreign enemy since the British burned the White House during the War of 1812, and despite Roosevelt's imperturbable voice, part of the country's first reaction was simple panic. The West Coast understandably saw the worst of it. Rumors spread that Japanese American fishermen were mining American harbors, that Japanese American truck farmers were lacing their vegetables with arsenic before taking them to market. A policeman in San Jose said he'd seen a flight of aircraft approaching from the sea. No one else spotted the phantom planes, but the report set off air-raid sirens up and down the coast. Antiaircraft batteries were established in the Hollywood hills. In San Francisco, a National Guard sentry on the Golden Gate Bridge shot and killed a woman who failed to stop her car as quickly as he thought she should. The organiz-

ers of the Rose Bowl ordered it moved from Pasadena to North Carolina—just in case.

In Sacramento, someone smeared "Down with Japs" across the door of the Japanese American Methodist church, police raided the Nippon Theater in "Japantown" and confiscated a carton of film canisters that turned out to be old newsreels, and the city council ordered that the municipal water tower at the corner of Thirty-third and J streets be camouflaged to confuse enemy pilots. ("I once asked somebody what it looked like from the air," remembered one man who had been a small boy then. "He said it looked like a camouflaged water tower.")

In Manhattan, the Metropolitan Opera announced that it would not present *Madame Butterfly* again until Japan had been defeated. In Washington, D.C., someone cut down four of the cherry trees around the Tidal Basin because they had been a gift from the emperor of Japan. The president himself had to veto a plan to have the White House camouflaged; he did allow antiaircraft guns to be set up on the roof, even though the Germans had no bomber that could reach the United States from Europe and possessed not a single aircraft carrier from which to launch bombers toward the capital.

A sound truck broadcasts President Roosevelt's call for a Declaration of War to students gathered outside Langdon Hall at Auburn University, where Katharine Phillips was a sophomore, December 8, 1941.

FRIGHTFULNESS

The attack on Pearl Harbor stunned Americans. History and geography had traditionally combined to keep them aloof from events overseas, and the horrors of the First World War, as well as postwar revelations about the role false Allied propaganda had played in whipping up fervor for it, had only served to deepen their suspicion of what George Washington had called "foreign entanglements."

But the threat of becoming involved in a new global war had grown steadily throughout the 1930s, as more and more of the world had found itself held hostage to the aggressive ambitions of the totalitarian rulers of Imperial Japan, Fascist Italy, and Nazi Germany, ruthless men who had crushed all opposition and whose power derived in part from their people's sense of grievance, real and imagined.

Japan had moved from medieval feudalism to the modern era in less than a century and had shown by defeating Czarist Russia in 1905 that it could more than hold its own against a European nation. But it remained too small and crowded to feed its own people, too dependent on other countries for the oil and rubber and steel and other raw materials needed to expand its power. With the complicit support of Emperor Hirohito, the generals and admirals who had come to dominate civil society determined to make Japan the master of what they euphemistically called a "Greater East Asia Co-Prosperity Sphere," comprising all the

Adolf Hitler surrounded by fervent admirers at Berchtesgaden in 1934 (below), and at his fiftieth birthday celebration in Berlin five years later (opposite). At the right, Benito Mussolini rallies his Fascist followers from horseback.

resources—and all the Asian peoples—then controlled by Western colonial powers. The rightful place of the Japanese, they believed, was as Asia's "leading race."

Benito Mussolini, the Fascist dictator of Italy, also believed his people were fated for great things. The flag of his party was emblazoned THE COUNTRY IS NOTHING WITHOUT CONQUEST, and he skillfully played on the desire of many Italians to see Rome reestablished as the center of a new empire

that would surround most of the Mediterranean and stretch from Somaliland to southeastern Switzerland.

Meanwhile, Adolf Hitler had built his monstrous Nazi regime in part upon the German thirst for revenge; revenge against the victors of the First World War, but also against those at home who, he claimed, had stabbed Germany's armed forces in the back: socialists, Communists, and the Jews—above all the Jews, who, he said, were at once evil and subhuman. The Germans, on the other hand, belonged to a superior race, and he had been chosen to lead them to their destiny, a Reich that would rule over the Old World and the New for a thousand years.

Between 1931 and August of 1939, all three countries went on the attack, and little was done to stop them. Japan invaded China. Mussolini's armies crushed Ethiopia. Hitler seized the Rhineland from France, annexed Austria, swallowed up Czechoslovakia, signed a nonaggression pact with the Soviet Union to protect his eastern flank, and then began to threaten Poland. He also promulgated laws denying Jews citizenship, and on the evening of November 9, 1938—*Kristallnacht*, the "Night of Broken Glass"—

Emperor Hirohito (on white horse, left) reviews the military, whose bombs brought about the death of the Chinese civilians (above), crushed in an air-raid shelter and left sprawled where frantic would-be rescuers dropped them in 1937.

unleashed a pogrom that left two hundred German Jews dead, twenty thousand under arrest, and ten thousand more confined to a concentration camp at Buchenwald.

America's initial reaction to the bloodshed overseas was to retreat further into itself. Congress passed three successive Neutrality acts aimed at keeping the U.S. out of the conflict. No American armaments were to be sold to any belligerent nation, invader or invaded alike, and nonmilitary goods could be purchased by them only on a "cash and carry" basis—no credit, no American vessels to bear them away.

Then, on September 1, 1939, Hitler's army stormed across the Polish border. Britain and France declared war on Germany. The Second World War was under way. "This nation will remain a neutral nation," President Roosevelt declared a few days later, "but I cannot ask that every American remain neutral in thought as well. Even a neutral has a right to take account of facts. Even a neutral cannot be asked to close his mind or conscience."

The Nazis went on to invade Denmark and Norway. They bombed Rotterdam, driving eighty thousand people from their homes. Rather than endure more of it, Holland surrendered. The Nazis called such bombing *Schrecklichkeit*—frightfulness. Belgium fell. French defenses collapsed. British troops were forced out of France and back across the English Channel. In June of 1940, German troops marched into Paris. Except for the neutral states of Sweden, Switzerland, and Spain, all of western Europe was now in Nazi hands. "The war is won," Hitler told Mussolini. "The rest is only a matter of time."

Britain alone held on. "We had a built-up resentment to Hitler," Katharine Phillips of Mobile remembered. "We had been watching the news, so we knew what Hitler was doing in Europe. The way he had attacked Poland, the way he tried to bring England to her knees with constant bombing. We just disliked Hitler and everything he was doing."

The overwhelming majority of Americans shared that dislike and wanted to help Britain, but most also still opposed U.S. entry into the war, and so, while FDR recognized the Nazi threat before many other statesmen did, he was forced to steer a

sinuous course, sometimes leading public opinion, sometimes seeming to lag behind it, in order to ready his countrymen to meet it. Barred by law from selling even disused destroyers to Britain, he swapped fifty of them in exchange for leases to British bases

German police torment an elderly Jew, Berlin, 1933.

On the rainy morning of March 15, 1939, stunned citizens of Prague look on as mechanized German troops splash their way through the city.

in the Caribbean. He backed passage of the first peacetime draft in U.S. history and pushed through the Lend-Lease Act, which allowed him to dispatch armaments overseas whenever he judged it would help in "the defense of the United States."

In August of 1941, he and British prime minister Winston Churchill met at sea off Newfoundland and issued what came to be called the Atlantic Charter, setting forth "certain common principles," including the promise of a world in which every nation would be free to control its own future once the "final destruction of the Nazi tyranny" had been achieved. After Hitler launched Operation Barbarossa in June of 1941, sending 3 million men eastward to attack the Soviet Union, Roosevelt extended Lend-Lease to the Russians, too. And when German U-boats attacked convoys carrying American matériel across the Atlantic, Roosevelt encouraged U.S. naval commanders to "shoot on sight."

By the fall of 1941, the United States and Germany seemed very close to war. Hitler professed to be unconcerned. "I don't see much future for the Americans," he told aides. "It's a decayed country. . . . America is half-Judaized, and the other half Negrified. How can one expect a state like that to hold together—a country where everything is built on the dollar?"

Meanwhile, as Roosevelt continued to focus on the German menace, tensions rose steadily in the Pacific. Germany's defeat of France and Holland in 1940, and its ongoing siege of Britain, provided Japan's military leaders with irresistible opportunities to seize the resources they craved in French Indochina (now Vietnam, Laos, and Cambodia), the Dutch West Indies (present-day Indonesia), and British Malaya. They signed a mutual defense pact with Germany and Italy; its specific aim was to keep the United States neutral rather than dare engage in a war on two fronts. Then, Japan stationed troops in northern Indochina. In response, Washington cut off the sale of aviation fuel and scrap metal until Japan withdrew its forces and ended its war in China as well. Instead, Japan invaded southern Indochina in July of 1941. At that, Roosevelt froze Japanese assets in the United States and cut off all shipments of oil. Without fuel, Japan's expansionist plans were doomed.

In October, when the relatively moderate prime minister Fumimaro Kone failed to reach a diplomatic settlement with the United States—he offered to pull Japanese troops out of Indochina but Washington continued to insist they also leave China—he was pressured by the army to resign. His replacement was the war minister, General Hideki Tojo, who had spent several years in the United States and did not believe a conventional victory over such a big and potentially powerful country was possible. But he was also an unwavering nationalist who saw war with the United States as unavoidable, and quickly convinced himself that by destroying the Pacific Fleet at one blow, Japanese forces might be able to demoralize the Americans long enough to seize Malaya and the Dutch West Indies and become so dominant in the region that they could never be dislodged. U.S. Intelligence had broken the Japanese diplomatic code and knew some kind of attack was coming. But no one had known where or when—until December 7.

Besieged allies: Prime Minister Winston Churchill inspects damage done to the House of Commons by German bombs, May 10, 1941 (left); seven months later, FDR signs the declaration of war. Most Americans believed his mourning band was meant to honor the dead at Pearl Harbor; he actually wore it in memory of his mother, who had died in September.

Every city and town in the country did its best to get ready for war. In Waterbury, Connecticut, an ordinance limited overnight parking to three hours to keep the streets clear in case of an enemy attack. In Mobile, rumors circulated that unidentified aircraft had been spotted off the coast at Pascagoula, Mississippi, and citizens were instructed to call Belmont 3781 to report suspicious Japanese aliens to the local office of the FBI. A wealthy businessman offered the city a 260-acre piece of land just west of the Mobile Country Club for an air-raid shelter; members of the County Defense Council expressed their gratitude but were embarrassed to admit that they had misplaced their only copy of the government pamphlet explaining how to build one.

The *Mobile Register* set out the city's blackout rules:

Any person leaving lights burning in a home at night when the entire family is away is subject to a $100 fine. . . . Only one 30-watt blue bulb may be left burning for every two rooms, provided all openings through which light may pass to the exterior are completely covered with light-excluding material. . . . Venetian blinds are not considered a material which will prevent the passage of light. . . . [If you must go out,] know where you want to go, think over how far it is, your route, how many streets you cross and what turns must be made to avoid being lost. . . . A flashlight may be used if the lens is covered with a blue cloth. Never point the flashlight upward nor on any object such as glass windows or a wet street which might reflect the light upward.

Luverne, Minnesota—more than 1,200 miles from the nearest seacoast—was taking no chances either. Al McIntosh, the editor of the local paper, was careful to reassure his readers that since "there are no members of any races other than the white and Negro living in the county . . . the problem of Japanese fifth column activities in Rock County should prove a light one." Still, he was pleased to see that "guards were immediately stationed at the Omaha Railroad Bridge east of the city. The men, Glen Ballmes, Albert Krahn and Claus Popkes, former section employees, are working eight-hour shifts straight around the clock. The men are parked in their cars with their heaters on, but some provision may be made soon for their comfort in winter months."

Luverne citizens patrolled the streets at night. "My dad was an air-raid warden," remembered Jim Sherman, a banker's son, who was six when the war began.

We'd have these blackouts. The siren would ring downtown. Then you had to turn off all your lights unless you had a blackout curtain that you could put over your window. The dads—my dad and these other guys—would go out and walk

Official Blackout and Air Raid Instructions and Information for the City of Sacramento

Prepared as a public service by the Sacramento Safety Council under authority of the Sacramento Civilian Defense Council.

Sources of information: Sacramento Police Bureau of Operations. Sacramento Fire Department and the Office of Civilian Defense.

The Sacramento Defense Council and the military authorities are taking every possible precaution for your protection and welfare in the event of an emergency. However, the full cooperation of every citizen in complying intelligently and cheerfully with these and subsequent instructions is absolutely essential for the safety of the whole community.

Herewith are basic instructions and information. Some of these instructions may later be subject to change. You are asked to watch your newspapers and the radio for such revisions.

If you have any questions, refer them to The Sacramento Safety Council, room 200, County Court House, telephone 3-8041, or your local air raid warden. The Safety Council has been designated by the Sacramento Defense Council as the official public informational agency in local civilian defense matters.

(Section 1)
BLACKOUT AND ALL CLEAR SIGNALS
BLACKOUT
At the present time (December 20th), Sacramento's blackout signal is three short whistle blasts, repeated at intervals. Watch the newspapers for a change in this signal system which will be made when special air raid sirens are installed.

ALL CLEAR
At the present time (December 20th), Sacramento's all clear signal is one long whistle blast, repeated at intervals. This signal also is subject to change when the new air raid sirens are installed. Watch newspapers for this change.

(Section 2)
WHAT TO DO IN THE HOME
WHEN THE BLACKOUT SIGNAL IS GIVEN:
1. Immediately blackout your home. This means that no light of any kind or degree shall show on the outside. Violation of this instruction makes you liable to maximum fine of $500 and, or, six months in jail.
2. Go to whatever room or area in the house you have previously prepared and remain there. (See section 5.) Do not move around in unlighted portions of the home any more than is absolutely necessary.
3. Remain in your home. Do not go out on the streets.

(Section 3)
IF YOU ARE IN A CAR
WHEN A BLACKOUT SIGNAL IS GIVEN:
(1) Immediately pull to the curb or the side of the road, stop and turn out all lights. Be sure no dashlights, tail lights, stop lights or other illumination is visible. Violation of this instruction is punishable by a maximum fine of $500 and, or, six months in jail.
(2) Leave your car and walk to a place of safety, such as a building or dwelling. Remain there until the all clear signal is given.

around the neighborhood to keep an eye out for enemy bombers. Now, I couldn't figure out how the Germans were going to fly all the way across the Atlantic Ocean and the Japanese were going to fly all the way across the Pacific Ocean to bomb Luverne. I mean, I just had no concept of what was going on. They wanted these guys to have guns, too, but they didn't have any guns for them. So my dad, the first couple of times he went out, he had a broomstick. He thought that was

A nervous homeland: (top left) dimmed lights in Times Square; (left) air raid instructions for Sacramento citizens; (above) San Francisco's Pacific Telephone Building shielded by sandbags against potential enemy bombs

kind of dumb, so after that he'd go out with his twelve-gauge shotgun. He had no shells or anything. And then it got to be where these guys would stay out awhile. And my mother finally figured out that they might be down at Doc Blake's or Ez Collins's or someplace, having a highball.

THE BATTLE OF THE ATLANTIC

On the evening of January 13, 1942, a German U-boat surfaced silently off Manhattan. Its commander was astonished but gratified to see that more than a month after Germany declared war on the United States, America's largest city was still ablaze with lights. Using those lights to silhouette his target, he sent a torpedo racing into the hull of an American oil tanker, then slipped back beneath the sea and moved south in search of further prey. Within twelve hours, he had sunk seven more unarmed vessels.

The United States was totally unprepared for this kind of war. The British pleaded for armed escorts to accompany the convoys that formed their lifeline, but there were not yet enough ships to provide them. By the end of January, U-boats would sink twenty-five tankers along the East Coast. Still, from Boston to Miami, city fathers stubbornly resisted the idea of blackouts. Turning off the lights would hurt tourism, they said. The last light would not wink out until May.

U-Boat War: On January 15, 1942, Mobilians learned that war had come within a few miles of the East Coast (as well as that Katharine and Sid Phillips's father had been appointed to a new job). It would be six months before planes flying from escort carriers began destroying German submarines like the one below, desperately maneuvering in mid-Atlantic to elude American strafing.

"Along the Gulf Coast," Katharine Phillips remembered, "and all along the shores of Mobile Bay, we could go sit on the beach, but we were not allowed to light a fire because of the U-boats. We heard that ships were sunk just as they went out of Mobile Bay. And we knew this to be true because the life preservers and the canned goods washed up on our beaches."

The impact of this murky warfare was felt all the way across the continent. Burt Wilson was nine years old that winter, a student at Theodore Judah School in Sacramento. One of his classmates, he remembered, was an English refugee from the Blitz named Murgatroyd Buchanan.

We all called him 'Royd. And we developed a great friendship. And one day, 'Royd came over to my house. I was upstairs and he called, "Burt, Burt!" And I looked out the window and said, "Hi, 'Royd, what's goin' on? And 'Royd said, "You know what a dirty German sub did to my father?" And I said, "No, what?" And he said, "It killed him." And I didn't know how to deal with that. Just to come out like that and say it. I went downstairs and we sat down under a tree and talked a while. But it was still something I never had had any experience with— one of my best friends telling me that his father was killed in the war.

The Germans continued to sink two or three merchant vessels every day; more than 230 Allied ships and almost 5 million tons of desperately needed matériel would be sent to the bottom of the sea in the first six months of 1942. With them went some 2,500 Allied merchant sailors. American beaches were black with oil, and for a time the waters from Jacksonville, Florida, to Galveston, Texas, were considered the most dangerous shipping lane in the world. "The only safe run," said one weary merchant seaman, "is from St. Louis to Cincinnati."

THE MOBILE REGISTER — STATE FINAL

VOL. 128—NO. 319   ESTABLISHED 1813   MOBILE, ALABAMA, THURSDAY, JANUARY 15, 1942   16 PAGES   PRICE: 5 CENTS

U-Boat Torpedoes Tanker Off Long Island

News and Views
By HOWARD BARNEY

Phillips Named Principal Of Mobile's Murpny High; Assure Term To Mid-April

Japs Use Nazi Terror Tactics In Philippines

Russian Pincer Drive Advances

War Is Brought Nearer To U.S. In Sea Attack

SASCHA WEINZHEIMER'S FAMILY ON LUZON was living with blackouts, too. The evening after she got home safe from Manila, the cook served sandwiches for dinner in her parents' bedroom, its doors and windows heavily draped so that no hint of light could be spotted from the air. "We kids thought it was fun," Sascha recalled. More fun followed two days later when a convoy of cars brought some two hundred American and British women and children from Manila in search of sanctuary from enemy bombing. "They were sad," Sascha wrote, "because they had to leave their homes carrying only their suitcases and also leave their daddies behind." But for the first time in her life she had a host of playmates. Room for the newcomers was found in the country club and the estate's bowling alley. Games and pool parties were arranged to entertain the children and keep their minds off the ominous news from elsewhere in the islands.

On December 22, more than forty thousand Japanese troops, most of them seasoned veterans of the fighting in China, came ashore north of Manila. General MacArthur breathed defiance over the radio that evening:

The enemy has landed scattered elements along the shores of Lingayen Gulf. My gallant divisions are holding ground and denying the foe the sacred soil of the Philippines. We have inflicted heavy casualties on his troops and nowhere is his bridgehead secure. Tomorrow we will drive him into the sea.

MacArthur was so convincing that the next day the *New York Times* headline read JAPANESE FORCES WIPED OUT IN WESTERN LUZON. In fact, neither American troops nor the thousands of ill-prepared Filipino reservists MacArthur had called up were able even to slow the invaders down. In some places the Japanese moved ten miles inland by nightfall. Not a single Filipino division in MacArthur's paper army was at full strength. Some troops had never learned to fire their antiquated rifles. When Glenn Frazier and his outfit reached the front with truckloads of ammunition, they found that at least one unit had until then been trying to fight back with blanks. Some Filipino troops, including the crack Philippine Scouts, fought hard. Many simply ran. The next night, ten thousand more Japanese troops would land south of the city. More than fifty thousand enemy soldiers were now converging on Manila from two directions.

Beneath a sky blackened by smoke from burning oil tanks, a sword-bearing Japanese officer leads his men toward Manila.

MacArthur's plan to defend the beaches had failed completely, but it took the general nearly forty more hours before he abandoned it in favor of the old War Plan Orange: he declared Manila a neutral "Open City" in hopes of sparing it further bombing, ordered his forces to retreat onto Bataan, and made plans to withdraw with his family and his aides to Corregidor and wait for rescue.

On December 23, Sascha Weinzheimer and some of her new friends were swimming in the country club pool when Japanese planes appeared suddenly overhead. The ground shuddered. Bombs were falling on the tracks of the narrow-gauge railroad that carried sugarcane to the mill. Mothers pulled their children from the water and made them lie facedown in the grass until the explosions stopped and the skies were empty again.

By five o'clock that afternoon, Sascha and her siblings were alone once more. All the refugees had headed back to Manila. Now that the war had followed them into the countryside, an Open City seemed the safer bet. At least there they could face whatever was to come alongside their husbands and fathers. "Mother was very nervous after that," Sascha wrote, but Christmas was just two days away and her parents were determined to celebrate it in their own home, just as they always had.

THAT SAME DAY, American newspaper readers learned that Winston Churchill had secretly crossed the Atlantic and was staying at the White House. It was the second meeting between the British prime minister and the American president. Together, they assessed the news that continued to come in from the Far East. All of it was bad. Off Malaya, Japanese bombers had sunk the *Repulse* and the *Prince of Wales,* the two biggest battleships in the British fleet. Japanese troops had now landed in Thailand and Singapore, Burma and Borneo and Hong Kong. They had taken Tarawa and Makin, Guam and Wake Island. There was no longer a single American base between Hawaii and the Philippines—where Japanese forces were only days away from seizing Manila. And the American public was clamoring for revenge against Japan for what it had done at Pearl Harbor.

Still, Roosevelt, Churchill, and their commanders had agreed well before Pearl Harbor that in the event of U.S. entry into a two-front war, Germany, with its vast armies and mighty industrial machine, would have to be defeated first. (The U.S. Army Chief of Staff, George C. Marshall, put it most simply: "Collapse in the Atlantic would be fatal; collapse in the Far East would be serious but not fatal.") Even the series of disasters that had befallen the Allies in the Pacific and southeast Asia would not be allowed to shake that resolve. It would take at least two years to

mobilize, train, and equip a force powerful enough to crush Hitler's armies on the European continent. Until then, they would have to remain on the defensive in the Pacific.

Behind the scenes, debate was often brisk between the American and British military chiefs. Some on the U.S. side feared American lives were about to be sacrificed to preserve the British Empire rather than protect American interests; the British, who had been at war with Germany since 1939, were scornful of the brash and inexperienced American latecomers. "As for war," wrote General Sir John Dill from Washington to a friend back home, "my own belief is that [the Americans] don't know the first thing about it. And yet as you know only too well they are great critics. How they have the nerve to criticize anyone beats me." The mood among British commanders was not improved when Churchill agreed that the Allied effort would henceforth be coordinated by a Combined Chiefs of Staff with headquarters in Washington, not London.

Still, there was far more uniting Americans and Britons that December than dividing them. On Christmas Eve, radio listeners tuned in to hear the traditional White House Christmas tree lighting ceremony. The president had insisted that there be a tree, over the objections of the Secret Service. People on both sides of the Atlantic needed this symbol of unity, he said, and he was eager to have Americans hear for themselves the voice of the man he introduced as "my old and good friend."

"This is a strange Christmas Eve," Churchill told the radio audience. But even though the whole world was at war, he said, "here, amid all these tumults," we should make "for the children an evening of happiness in a world of storm." He continued:

> *Here, then, for one night only, each home throughout the English-speaking world should be a brightly lighted island of happiness and peace.*
>
> *Let the children have their night of fun and laughter. Let the gifts of Father Christmas delight their play. Let us grown-ups share to the full in their unstinted pleasures before we turn again to the stern tasks and the formidable years that lie before us, resolved that by our sacrifice and daring, these same children shall not be robbed of their inheritance or denied their right to live in a free and decent world.*

AT CHRISTMASTIME IN PAST YEARS, Sascha Weinzheimer's grandparents in California had always sent her family big parcels of brightly wrapped packages and a tall, fragrant evergreen from Oregon. Nothing had arrived this December, so Sascha helped the gardener fashion a Christmas tree out of branches cut from

Under the constant threat of Japanese bombs, a Filipino waiter and a handful of guests in a Manila luxury hotel do their best to pretend nothing has changed.

Sandbags filled the lobby when the family checked in, and from the window of her room, Sascha could see distant fires and the damage enemy bombs had done to the dock area and the vessels that had been caught at anchor in Manila Bay. The gracious Federal-style residence of the American high commissioner stood across the boulevard, just as it always had. But no flag now hung from the flagpole; the high commissioner had taken it with him when he fled the city for Corregidor.

ON DECEMBER 29, as the Weinzheimers and their fellow refugees waited anxiously in Manila for word of the advancing Japanese, Sid Phillips of Mobile, his friend W. O. Brown, and eight other recruits boarded a train at the L & N station in Mobile and set out for marine boot camp at Parris Island, South Carolina. "We were in high spirits," Phillips remembered. "As with all seventeen-year-old young men, we already knew everything there was to know that was worth knowing." They sang "Chattanooga Choo Choo" over and over again, to the annoyance of their fellow passengers, and were "about as loud and obnoxious on that train as any young men could be."

Their first stop was Birmingham, Alabama, where they were housed overnight in a seedy hotel. Several bulbs were missing from its blinking neon sign, reminding the boys of all the detective movies they'd seen. When Phillips and Brown checked into their room and tried to hang up their jackets in what they thought was the closet, they opened a door into the next room instead. A naked prostitute was sitting on her bed. She screamed for help. Phillips slammed the door. A policeman turned up with a drawn pistol. Brown and Phillips managed to stutter out an explanation that satisfied him. A handyman came in to nail the door shut. Afterward, the boys lay awake for a long time, gazing up at the ceiling as the reflected light from the hotel sign came and went, wondering what they were getting themselves into.

The next morning, they and their new friends joined some forty more would-be marines on a day coach headed north. Three more cars filled with recruits from elsewhere on the East Coast attached themselves to the train at stops along the way. The men sang and played cards, swapped tall tales about home, and stuck their heads out the window to whistle at any girl who came in sight. "We were so young and so cocky," Phillips remembered, "and had very little idea what lay ahead."

That began to change at dawn on New Year's Day, as the train pulled into Yamassee Junction, the closest depot to Parris Island. Several marines in crisp green uniforms stormed into the car before the train had hissed to a full stop. They "immediately began screaming," Phillips remembered in an unpublished

the garden. On Christmas morning, the children of her father's Filipino employees lined up at the front door, just as they always had, so that Sascha could help hand out sweets to them. Their cook, Jesus, prepared the traditional turkey dinner, and the elder Weinzheimers bravely toasted each other with champagne. But the day was interrupted again and again by the mill whistle, warning everyone on the estate that enemy planes had been spotted overhead.

Even the Weinzheimers had to admit that it was time to leave for the relative safety of Manila. They set out two days later. As they drove toward the city, truckloads of grim-faced Filipino soldiers passed them heading in the other direction. Seven Japanese bombers swooped low over the road at one point, forcing them to take momentary cover. They passed what was left of Nichols Field, its broken runways strewn with black, twisted wreckage. In Manila they found lodging with some three hundred other American and British refugees in the nine-story Bay View Hotel. It overlooked the broad bay-front boulevard named after Admiral George Dewey, who had destroyed the Spanish fleet and staked America's claim to the islands forty-three years earlier.

memoir written for his children, "calling us morons, idiots . . . mallard-heads, stupid babies, and some unprintable names that I am not sure I had ever heard before. The old world [had] ended."

The new one did not look promising. Phillips and his fellow passengers were ordered to board buses. As they drove through the still dim light toward their new home, he recalled, a bellowing, uniformed marine told the newcomers over and over again that they were now nothing more than " 'boots,' the lowest form of humanity, in fact, maybe not even human . . . some sort of scum." And as the newcomers got down from the bus with their cheap suitcases and began filing into the barracks for breakfast, every marine they passed who was not in formation grinned and said, "You'll be sor-ree."

They *were* sorry, at least at first. They had numbers, not names, now: Sid Phillips became Service Serial Number 344263. Their heads were shaved. They were stripped of civilian clothing and personal belongings; everything except their wallets was tagged and sent home. Naked, they stood in line and were issued new shirts and pants and socks and underwear and a canvas seabag into which all these items and more had to be precisely folded. They were given a pair of dress shoes, too, and a steel bucket filled with toilet articles and a sewing kit, for all of which they were charged twenty-five dollars—four dollars more than they were to be paid each month.

Marine boot camp traditionally lasted twelve weeks, but Pearl Harbor had cut that time in half. Everything was accelerated. The result was what Phillips remembered as "a contrived nightmare," intended to transform "silly young men" into "serious, useful warriors," willing to die for one another. "We were all imperfect," another member of Phillips's platoon remembered, "and had to be torn down and reconstructed properly."

There was no privacy, another man in the outfit wrote: "rising, waking, writing letters, receiving mail, making beds, washing, shaving, combing one's hair, emptying one's bowels—all was done in public. . . . And always the marching, march to the sick bay, march to draw rifles slimy with [rust-proofing] Cosmoline, march to the water racks to scrub them clean, march to the marching ground."

Everything was under the control of the drill instructor (DI), a veteran sergeant whose loud bellow was the first thing the men heard when they flipped on the barracks lights at 4:45 a.m. and continued unabated until evening mess call (when his equally

Swedish American farm boys from Minnesota sign up to go to sea, 1942.

loud assistant picked up the slack). "The DI was never silent," Sid Phillips remembered, "and we were never still."

Chewing gum was forbidden, and if [the DI] caught you with gum in your mouth he would make you rub it in your short hairs. . . . If he caught you with an unbuttoned shirt pocket he would cut the button off and make you go get your sewing kit, sit down in the sand or mud, and sew it on . . . while . . . the whole platoon did push-ups until the sewing was finished. The DI of course reminded the platoon every minute that they were doing push-ups because a moron couldn't keep his buttons buttoned. . . .

If someone was caught smoking when the "smoking" lamp was out, he would make them smoke a cigarette with their bucket over their head and standing at attention, out in front of the platoon. No one ever did this without getting nauseated and vomiting. . . .

One day he decided we were not slapping [the leather slings of our rifles] loud enough so he marched us over to a stretch of black-top pavement, made us kneel down, [lay down] our precious rifles and start slapping the pavement in drill cadence. He would stop and examine our hands. If your hands were bleeding you could stop slapping and stand at rigid attention while he went back to counting. . . . You could hear our hands slapping from . . . two blocks away.

When an unauthorized box of cookies arrived, baked by some boot's fond but oblivious mother, the DI confiscated it, ordered the platoon to stand at attention, then made the men watch as he ate the cookies one by one. "Our natural human rebelliousness," Phillips wrote, "was being removed and replaced with unquestioned obedience to orders."

Boot camp ended with two rugged weeks on the rifle range, shivering in tents at night, and spending hour after maddening daylight hour struggling to master their weapons. Some boys—especially those who, like Sid Phillips, came from the South—were familiar with firearms and shot well almost from the first. Others, mostly those from the big cities of the North, had to learn everything from scratch. Drill instructors cursed and bullied and sometimes kicked them all, determined to make every marine into a marksman.

If you were "taken apart in those first few weeks," a member of Phillips's platoon recalled, "it was at the rifle range that they start[ed] to put you together again." And it worked. As they returned from their time on the range, the same marine remembered, "our path crossed that of a group of incoming recruits, still in civilian clothes, seeming to us . . . unkempt, bedrag-

Marine "boots" at the outdoor laundry rack: "All seemed chaos," one member of Sid Phillips's outfit wrote about boot camp, "marching, drilling in the manual of arms; listening to lectures on military courtesy—'In saluting, the right hand will strike the head at a forty-five-degree angle midway of the right eye'; listening to lectures on marine jargon—'From now on everything, floor, street, ground, everything, is 'the deck'; . . . shaving daily, whether hairy or beardless. It was all a jumble."

GREETINGS

When the Dutch army surrendered to Germany in May 1940, the United States moved up to nineteenth place on the roster of military powers, behind Portugal and Romania: only 174,000 American officers and men were on active duty, carrying rifles designed in 1903 and wearing tin hats and leggings issued during the Great War.

Congress federalized the National Guard. FDR increased the army's active-duty strength to 400,000. The War Department did its best to recruit more young men. But it quickly became clear that something more was needed. In September, Congress passed the Selective Service Act, the first peacetime draft in American history. Some 16 million young men between the ages of twenty-one and thirty-six were to register with one or another of 6,500 local draft boards on October 16. Those inducted were to serve for just one year and could be stationed only in the Western Hemisphere. (Later, the minimum age would be lowered to eighteen and men would be required to serve anywhere they were sent for the duration of the war plus six months.)

Nearly 50 million men would register for the draft over the course of the conflict and then watch anxiously each day to see if the mailman had brought them their "Greetings," the much dreaded official letter from the draft board ordering them to report for induction. To serve in the army they had to be five feet tall (and no taller than six feet six), weigh at least 105 pounds, have correctable vision, and at least half their teeth. Of some 20 million potential inductees examined by army doctors during the war, nearly a third were rejected for medical or dental shortcomings or on what was called "moral grounds"—usually because they'd given what the army considered the wrong answer to the question "Do you like girls?"

As time went by and the demand for men at the front steadily rose, standards loosened. At first, no one who'd been found guilty of even a trivial crime like shoplifting or making moonshine was considered fit to serve; by 1945, more than 100,000 convicted felons were in uniform, many inducted directly from prison. Missing teeth were initially enough to exempt a potential inductee; by 1942, he needed to possess only "sufficient teeth (natural or artificial) to subsist on the Army ration." Nearsightedness kept men out of the army in the early months of the war; by its end, the army had issued more than 2 million pairs of spectacles and thousands of one-eyed men were in uniform.

Servicemen also initially had to be able to read and write, but when hundreds of thousands were rejected on that score, the requirement was dropped—and the army set up schools to make some 800,000 citizen-soldiers literate, using specially prepared primers with titles like *Private Pete Eats His Dinner.*

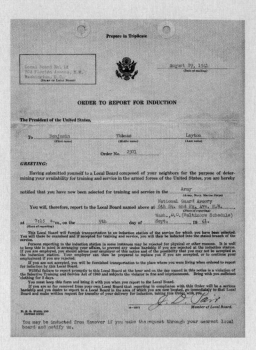

After appeals to patriotism like the posters that have piqued the curiosity of the Georgia farmer's son (below) failed to yield enough volunteers, local draft boards began sending out thousands of letters (above) requiring young men to report for induction.

gled. . . . As though by instinct we shouted with one voice, 'You'll be sor-ree!' " The DI couldn't help grinning with pleasure.

Washington was so eager to have more men ready for action that the traditional graduation ceremony was skipped: the brand-new marines simply shook hands with their DI and were shipped off to New River, North Carolina, to join the 1st Marine Division.

Boot camp had been rough, Phillips said, but looking back, he did not feel misused. What he called one's "selfish natural concern for . . . me and me only" had been at least temporarily obliterated, replaced by a reassuring sense of being part of something infinitely larger than oneself. "A strange feeling frequently came over me during the war," he remembered.

It is very difficult to explain in words. It was a feeling of armed might. I would get it often when marching in ranks like I was a leg on an invincible centipede. . . . I would feel it in a large convoy, or in landing craft under full power heading for the beach. There was danger all around you, but also a sensation of safety in what you were a part of. . . . It was, of course, associated with deep national pride. It definitely began at Parris Island.

Similar feelings shaped by basic training would provide badly needed strength for Sid Phillips—and for hundreds of thousands of other young men—in the months and years to come.

ON NEW YEAR'S EVE, as Phillips headed toward boot camp in South Carolina, Sascha Weinzheimer's father brought three exhausted American soldiers home with him to the Bay View Hotel in Manila. He had volunteered to serve with the Quartermaster Corps, driving Filipino laborers to Bataan to help prepare defense works for the coming battle. On his way back to the city he had found the three men plodding along the roadside and offered them a lift. He insisted that they be treated as honored guests at dinner. When their glasses had been filled with whisky and soda, a woman asked how they thought the fight against the Japanese was going. "Lady," one soldier answered, "we haven't got a chance."

Sascha's mother gently scolded him for his defeatism, but the next morning it was clear even to her that he had been right. A thick layer of sooty, foul-smelling smoke shrouded the city. The retreating Americans had blown the giant fuel tanks along the Pasig River, which flowed through the center of town. Flaming streams of oil had drifted down the river, setting on fire its banks and many of the piers and buildings that lined them. On the docks, the army quartermaster opened the doors to all his ware-

Walter Weinzheimer, Sascha's father

houses rather than have his provisions fall to the Japanese. Hundreds of Filipinos carried off everything left inside: chairs and spare truck parts, cigarette cartons and mattresses, bolts of cloth, bottles of liquor. When the mob had emptied the warehouses, it turned its attention to local shops, smashing windows, stripping shelves, fighting over the spoils. "I hope I will never see looters again," Sascha wrote. "Everything seemed to move so fast. I was glad to go to bed early and not beg to look out at the fires that night."

The next morning was January second. "Everyone was waiting for THEM to march into the city," Sascha noted. They didn't have long to wait. The *Life* magazine photographer Carl Mydans, also housed at the Bay View, watched the approaching enemy from the window of his room.

They came up the boulevard in the predawn glow from the bay, riding on bicycles and on tiny motorcycles, their little flags with the one red ball looking like children's pennants. They came without talk and in good order, the ridiculous pop-popping of their one-cylinder cycles sounding loud in the silent city.

Behind the motorcycles came tanks and trucks filled with Japanese troops shouting, "Banzai!" Hundreds of Japanese civilians waving Japanese flags turned out along the boulevard to greet them. Residents of Manila, they had just been released from the camps into which they had been driven after the first bombs fell. As Sascha watched, the Japanese troops hauled their flag to the top of the pole above what had been the home of the U.S. high commissioner and would soon become the official headquarters of the Japanese commander in the Philippines.

"After that, everything seemed to change," Sascha remembered. "The Nip soldiers were all around the building, in the lobby and at the desk. . . . Everyone was nervous." Guests were told to stay in their rooms. The Filipino hotel staff melted away. Sascha's father took his turn running the elevator. Her amah could not stop sobbing, fearing that the rape and murder that had accompanied the Japanese capture of Nanking might now be visited on the people of Manila. Instead, Japanese troops contented themselves with breaking into the cars in the parking lot, then honking their way up and down the street and across the lawns, learning to drive as they went.

At the hotel, a four-man "inspection" party led by an English-speaking officer began going from room to room. When the Weinzheimers' turn came, the soldiers poked through the family's belongings, then announced that Sascha and her father were to be sent to the new civilian internment camp being set up on the campus of the University of Santo Tomas. Her mother and the two smaller children could remain outside, the officer said, though they would have to find other quarters. The Japanese army was taking over the hotel.

Her father protested. Sascha could not get around without heavy braces, he explained, and needed her mother. The Japanese made Sascha walk back and forth across the room, then agreed that she, too, could remain outside the camp. But Weinzheimer himself would still have to be locked up. Sascha never forgot the day he was taken away.

> *After [Daddy] started to say goodbye I could just hardly stand it, and for the first time I was afraid. . . . I screamed and held on . . . until I had to be pulled away. Then he ran out and that was the last we saw of [him] for a few months. Mother had a hard time to get me quiet . . . but I couldn't help it, I just couldn't stop.*

She and the rest of her family found shelter first in the home of the hotel's owner and then, when her mother began to worry that the drunken Japanese troops whose shouts kept them awake at night might become more than a mere annoyance, within the walls of a convent. Wherever they were, they could hear the distant thump of the guns from Bataan and Corregidor continuing day and night.

BY THE END OF THE FIRST WEEK IN JANUARY, nearly twelve thousand Americans and more than sixty-five thousand Filipino troops had managed to make it onto the Bataan peninsula and take up positions there. On paper, it was an ideal place to wage defensive war: rugged and covered with thick jungle, it demanded that an invader fight hard for every inch of ground he gained. The combined "FilAmerican" force outnumbered the enemy almost two to one. Had combat alone settled the matter, things might have turned out differently.

But once again, MacArthur's grandiose plan to defend all the Philippine islands had ensured disaster. He had distributed his supplies and provisions to depots in Manila and elsewhere on Luzon; and despite the best efforts of men like Glenn Frazier, it had proved impossible to move all of it to the actual field of bat-

As American and Filipino troops struggle to hold on to the southern half of the Bataan peninsula (below), a GI who has run low on ammunition prepares to hurl a Molotov cocktail at the enemy.

tle before the fighting began. More than twenty-five thousand frightened, desperate civilians had accompanied the army onto the peninsula. They now had to be fed, too. On January 6, MacArthur ordered rations on Bataan cut in half; his men would have to fight on fewer than two thousand calories a day.

They did it. By early February, they had beaten back two Japanese assaults, fallen back to a new defense line halfway down the peninsula, and then successfully thwarted repeated Japanese attempts to land behind their lines. The enemy dug in and waited for reinforcements.

Through it all, behind the wheel of his truck, Glenn Frazier worked to keep the men at the front supplied with ammunition—and to destroy that ammunition to keep it out of enemy hands whenever the Americans were forced to retreat. Japanese fighters strafed his convoy. Sniper bullets smashed his windshield. Shards of shrapnel peppered his right side.

Frazier had been raised in "a real Christian family," he remembered, and "killing was not part of my training. That was a big hurdle for me to get over, because I'd been taught not to kill." A visit to the ammunition depot at Little Baguio during the fighting had changed that. A big red cross had been painted next to a field hospital there, marking it as off-limits to enemy warplanes. But that day, Frazier remembered, the Japanese paid no attention.

A couple of Zeros bombed and strafed the hospital. We got in a ditch and one of the dive bombers came back and strafed us and dropped one bomb and hit [my friend] direct and all I ever found of him was his left foot in a shoe. And when that Japanese pilot turned his wings right above the trees and started to fly away, I could see him with a smile on his face.

From that moment on, he remembered, "I had no problem with killing people. In fact, I got to the point where I hunted them. And if I didn't kill a Japanese in a day, I felt I didn't do my job. And that was commonplace in Bataan."

MacArthur repeatedly assured his men on the peninsula that "help is on the way," and that it was their duty to "hold until these reinforcements arrive." But no troops, no ships, no planes had ever actually been dispatched. To have sent to the Philippines the kind of naval force that might have blasted its way through the Japanese fleet, one official said, would have meant an "entirely unjustifiable diversion of forces from the principal theater, the Atlantic." "There are times," Secretary of War Henry Stimson confided to his diary, "when men must die."

Knowing none of this, the men on Bataan held on to the hope of rescue. "Day after day," one officer remembered, "the boys would scan the skies for the long-awaited Allied planes; lookouts never tired of watching for the convoy of ships that would bring us supplies and reinforcements."

ON FEBRUARY 19, 1942, as Americans continued their struggle to hold on to Bataan, President Roosevelt signed Executive Order 9066. Its tone was carefully neutral. It authorized the War Department to designate "military areas" in the United States and exclude from them anyone whom it felt to be a danger. But its real targets were some 111,000 persons of Japanese ancestry, citizens and aliens alike, living along the West Coast.

The worst anxieties of Japanese Americans were coming true. Young Daniel Inouye had reacted to the bombing of Pearl Harbor precisely as most other Americans had. His country had been attacked. That attack needed to be avenged. He was eager to do his part. But because of his ancestry he knew there was sure to be more to it than that. As he pedaled toward the Red Cross station that morning an elderly Japanese American had grabbed his handlebars. "Who did it?" he'd wanted to know. "Was it the Germans? It must have been the Germans."

Many other Americans had felt that way too at first. Myths about Japanese inferiority were widely held before Pearl Harbor. Japanese were said to be too nearsighted to fly well or fight after sunset; too small to face white men in combat on the ground; too childlike and unimaginative to have come up with warplanes or warships to match those built by Western powers. How, Americans asked, could the makers of cheap Christmas toys so flimsy they didn't last past New Year's Day have done such terrible damage to the United States? Even FDR had wondered aloud whether Germans hadn't somehow been involved in planning the attack.

Warning to Japanese Americans posted at the corner of Ninth and K streets, Sacramento: they have just a few days to prepare for relocation.

But no Germans had been involved, and as Inouye remembered, both he and the old man already understood that their loyalty was "certain to be called into question. . . . It took no great effort of imagination to see the hatred of many Americans for the enemy turned on us, who looked so much like him." Plans were in fact drawn up in Washington for a wholesale internment of all 158,000 Hawaiians of Japanese descent—nearly 40 percent of the total population of the islands. But the five wealthy families that largely controlled Hawaii's economy opposed it: without Japanese field-workers their sugar and pineapple plantations would suffer. As the weeks went by, the presence of overwhelming military force in the islands made the danger of an internal

threat there seem less and less plausible; in the end, Japanese Americans in Hawaii would be allowed to go about their lives more or less as they always had.

Meanwhile, the lives of their counterparts on the West Coast would be changed forever. There they represented a tiny proportion of the population and had always been targets of white hostility. State law and community custom barred Japanese immigrants from marrying whites, from eating in white restaurants, or living in white neighborhoods. Federal law prohibited them from owning land or becoming citizens. In 1924, Congress had cut off immigration from Japan altogether.

American-born descendants of Japanese immigrants, called nisei, were citizens by birthright, however, and some now owned the land their families had worked successfully for years—a fact many whites resented. The anti-Japanese frenzy that followed Pearl Harbor gave white growers and business interests an

Despite the bold declaration of loyalty that he nailed across his shop's windows, the owner of this Oakland, California, grocery was forced to sell his business before he and his family were sent off to a relocation center.

opportunity to agitate anew for the elimination of unwanted competitors. "We're charged with wanting to get rid of the Japs for selfish reasons," the head of the California Grower-Shipper Vegetable Association told the *Saturday Evening Post.*

We might as well be honest. We do. It's a question of whether the white man lives on the Pacific coast or the brown man. They came into this valley to work, and they stayed to take over. . . . If all the Japs were removed tomorrow, we'd never miss them . . . because the white farmers can take over and produce everything the Jap grows. And we don't want them back when the war ends, either.

Fears about the loyalty of Japanese Americans, and a handful of intercepted secret prewar messages that seemed to suggest the presence of enemy agents among them, provided the pretext for Roosevelt's extraordinary action. The FBI saw no need for it. Not a single documented case of espionage would ever be registered against a Japanese American. But politics won out, and the army was empowered to force Americans of Japanese ancestry from their homes and businesses into temporary camps and then ship them to inland relocation centers. Almost three quarters of those affected were American-born U.S. citizens (reclassified by the government as "non-aliens" to minimize any awkwardness). Most of the rest had lived in the United States for decades. It didn't matter. "A Jap's a Jap," said General John L. DeWitt, head of the West Coast Defense Command. "It makes no difference whether he is an American citizen or not. . . . I don't want any of them." (German and Italian aliens would be locked up, too, but German American and Italian American citizens remained free.)

The roughly seven thousand Japanese Americans living in and around Sacramento had feared something like this ever since the moment they'd heard about Pearl Harbor.

"What is going to happen to us?" Susumu Satow, a senior at Sacramento High School, had asked his father that day.

"It's not going to be good," his father answered.

Satow's father and uncle were berry farmers. They lived with their families just east of town on land they'd worked patiently for years and now partially owned. Susumu—"Sus" to his friends—knew only a few words of Japanese, loved playing baseball, attended services with his family every Sunday at the Mayhew Japanese Baptist Mission and was hurt when some of his white classmates suddenly turned "cold" toward him after Pearl Harbor. Federal agents soon turned up at the door of the family farmhouse and demanded to be allowed in to look for signs of disloyalty. They found a big book in Japanese on the mantel and demanded to know what it was. A Bible, the senior Satow explained, and when the agents saw a portrait of Jesus and a

Susumu Satow

reproduction of da Vinci's *The Last Supper* hanging on the wall, his son remembered, they backed off.

But it was only a temporary reprieve. The California congressional delegation unanimously called for the immediate removal of "all persons of Japanese lineage." The state dismissed all Japanese American employees. So did the city of Sacramento. Hand-lettered signs saying JAPS MUST GO went up all over town. Official notices followed, giving the Satows and their friends and neighbors just one week to wind up their affairs, pack a few belongings, and report for evacuation.

"We were allowed to bring whatever we could carry," Sus Satow recalled. "That's it." Everything else was to be left behind. "It was the middle of the harvest," he remembered, "but still we had to abandon it and leave. And so we made arrangements with our friends. 'Hey, come and pick the strawberries because they're ready to be marketed.' And so I imagine they did that." They did—and kept the profits. The Satows were more fortunate than many: they owned at least some of the land they farmed—purchased in young Susumu's name, since his elders were not citizens—and so hoped to have something to return to when the war was over. Many others lost everything, forced to sell off homes, shops, furnishings, even the clothes they couldn't carry with them, to white buyers happy to snap them up for next to nothing. The Satows' refrigerator went for three dollars; the family Buick fetched just twenty-five.

On Evacuation Day, armed troops stood guard as Sus Satow and his family climbed aboard one of the trains that helped carry Sacramento's Japanese American citizens out of town. With them went their neighbors: the Yamasakis and Kitadas, Matsumotos and Oganekus and Toguchis. Whole neighborhoods were emptied in an instant. One white Sacramento schoolboy named Burt Wilson years later remembered his bafflement:

We wondered what had happened. They took somebody out of eighth grade, a boy named Sammy, who drew wonderful cartoons. He was my friend, and one day he was there and the next day he was gone. And that was very difficult for us to understand because we didn't see Sammy or any Japanese American—at least I didn't—as the enemy.

Under the watchful eye of armed soldiers, a little San Francisco boy (above) awaits shipment to the Owens Valley, while other Japanese Americans (right) leave the train that has brought them to a temporary assembly center at the Santa Anita racetrack, where they will be forced to live in stables until permanent centers are readied for them farther from the Pacific coast.

As the train rattled southward out of town Susumu Satow wondered what would become of him and his family. "Maybe this is just the beginning," he remembered thinking. "They may very well send us back to Japan. And that, to me, was horrible. I, in my heart, knew my loyalty belonged to America. I went to school, pledged allegiance every morning in grammar school. And for me to think that I may be sent to Japan was horrendous."

The Satows and their friends were taken to the Pinedale Assembly Center near Fresno, one of sixteen makeshift centers up and down the coast that provided temporary shelter until more permanent camps could be constructed farther inland. Pinedale was a barren, featureless compound strung with barbed wire and guarded with machine guns. "To walk into a double-security fence with guard towers looking down into the crowd with guns," Satow recalled. "It's not a good feeling. You wonder, 'Gee, how could this be happening?' But it's happening. And so you kind of accept that, I guess."

Four thousand eight hundred men, women, and children from Sacramento, Oregon, and Washington would be locked up at Pinedale for months, jammed into barracks without privacy or indoor plumbing. The temperature often crept above one hundred, and whenever the slightest breeze stirred, fine dust sifted in through the banged-together walls. Pinedale, remembered one man forced to live there, was "a natural home only for rabbits."

The senior with the best grades at the University of California at Berkeley that year happened to be a Japanese American from Sacramento named Harvey A. Itano. When it came time for him to step forward and receive his diploma and special prize at commencement, the president of the university had to explain to the crowd that the winner of the University Medal could not be present. "His country has called him elsewhere," he said. By then, Itano and his proud parents, like Susumu Satow and his family, were locked away inside an assembly center, waiting to be shipped to a permanent camp somewhere still farther from their homes.

ON THE NIGHT OF MARCH 11, Douglas MacArthur, his wife, their four-year-old son, and seventeen members of his staff slipped out of Corregidor in a PT boat and disappeared into the darkness. Events elsewhere had forced him to flee. Japan was now poised to attack Java. Beyond it lay Australia, whose best troops were fighting alongside the British in North Africa. When the Australian prime minister threatened to bring them home to protect their own country, FDR agreed that the United States would guarantee Australian security and secretly ordered MacArthur to proceed to Sydney to take up new duties as Supreme Army Chief for the Pacific. A few days later, the general issued a brief statement from Australia: "I came through," he said, "and I shall return." His words were meant to reassure Filipinos that he would one day lead American forces back to liberate them. But to Glenn Frazier and the other men left behind on Bataan, they sounded like a death knell. "When MacArthur left and went to Australia," Frazier remembered, "that's what I called doomsday for Bataan, because he issued orders to fight to the last man. And that's when we knew what our fate was going to be."

By then, three out of four of Bataan's defenders were incapacitated in some way—wounded, starving, suffering from beriberi or malaria. There was little medicine on hand. One weary surgeon reported that his field hospital had eight operating tables—and 1,200 battle casualties in need of surgery. The men killed and ate horses and mules, water buffalo and wild pigs, snakes and iguanas, and finally the monkeys they'd once thought of almost as pets. "I can't hardly tell anybody how it is to shoot a monkey," Frazier recalled. "A monkey is just like a person. But when you get hungry enough, you'll do just that. At the end there was one can of salmon issued to thirty-five men and very little rice, so our situation was deteriorating and getting worse every day."

Meanwhile, the Japanese were being reinforced by sea. On April 3, they shelled and bombed American and Filipino positions so heavily that the jungle itself was set ablaze. Bataan's defenders began falling back toward the tiny port of Mariveles, on the peninsula's southern tip, destroying what little was left of their ammunition and supplies as they went. Glenn Frazier helped blow up the big depot at Little Baguio where he'd been standing when the bombing of Manila began. The top of the hill seemed to disappear, he said; "it looked like the biggest fireworks show ever."

From far-off Australia, MacArthur ordered the Americans and Filipinos to counterattack. The commander on the ground, Major General Edward L. King, was convinced it would be suicide: most of his men could no longer stand for long, let alone fight. On April 9, he sent a soldier forward with a white flag. It was the largest surrender by the United States Army in its history. Some seventy-eight thousand American and Filipino troops laid down their arms.

The news reached the United States that evening. Pearl Harbor, Wake Island, Singapore, Hong Kong, Manila, now Bataan—Americans who had once been dismissive of the Japanese now began to fear that they were invincible. In Mobile, Katharine Phillips remembered how "distressed" everyone was about abandoning the Americans on Bataan. "There was no way of rescuing them, we know now," she recalled. "But at the time we didn't know there were no ships. Remember, they didn't tell us how much had been sunk at Pearl Harbor. And we kept thinking, 'Why don't you go in there and get our boys out of the Philippines?'"

The next morning in Luverne, the surrender and its meaning was the only topic of conversation in the Main Street restaurant where Al McIntosh, the newspaper editor, downed the cup of coffee with which he started each day.

> *Walking back from the coffee shop we met Ben Padilla walking home from his night's work. The roly-poly baker was minus his customary infectious grin. . . .*
> *"What's the matter, Ben, lost your best friend?" we asked.*
> *"My brother was at Bataan," he answered quietly.*
> *What can one say at a time like that?*
> *Then, after we'd walked a few moments in silence, Ben said in a grim voice, "It's a hard thing to say but I hope Jake died fighting bravely rather than be captured by the Japs."*

Many of the men on Bataan would come to share that sentiment. "If we had known what was ahead of us," Glenn Frazier remembered many years later, "I would have taken death."

Before agreeing to surrender, General King had asked a Japanese officer just one question: Would his men be treated decently?

Yes, said the officer. "We are not barbarians."

Some of the seventy-eight thousand American and Filipino troops who were forced to surrender to the Japanese in and around Mariveles, at Bataan's southern tip

But the Japanese commander had expected only twenty-five thousand healthy, well-fed prisoners—not three times that many sick and starving ones—and hadn't enough supplies even for that many. He wanted to use Mariveles as the base from which to launch attacks on Corregidor and was determined to get his prisoners off the roads and out of the way as fast as possible. Japan had signed but never ratified the Geneva Convention governing the treatment of prisoners of war (the Soviets never signed it at all), and Japanese tradition held that those who surrendered rather than die on the battlefield were cowards, unworthy of respect.

The result was the Bataan Death March. The prisoners were to be prodded some sixty miles from Mariveles to San Fernando, then packed into trucks and railroad cars for the journey to their final destination, an unfinished Philippine army base in central Luzon called Camp O'Donnell.

As Glenn Frazier joined the endless procession plodding northward in columns of four the day after the surrender, the sun was merciless. April is the height of summer in the Philippines, and the air was thick with dust kicked up by the men. Just a few weeks earlier, Frazier had slammed his way up and down the same unpaved road in his truck, the red flag on the front forcing everyone else into the ditch. Now he and his comrades were at the mercy of an enemy whose apparent capriciousness they could not comprehend.

It was very, very difficult for us to understand what these people were all about because we had had no contact with the Japanese whatsoever. And what they were like. And they immediately started beating guys if they didn't stand right or if they were sitting down. We didn't know where we were going. We didn't know anything. And we were stopped on the way, some of us were, and searched and beat again. All our possessions were taken away from us. Some of us had rings so they just cut the fingers off. And took the rings. They poured water out of my canteen to be sure that I didn't have any.

Here and there along the road, water gushed from artesian wells. Some guards allowed men to pause long enough for a swallow or two. Others shot or clubbed or bayoneted those who tried. Food was a handful of rice, boiled in a roadside drum and eaten on the run. No one was allowed to lag behind or leave the line for any reason; men wet and soiled themselves as they walked. For Glenn Frazier, as for most of those who somehow survived, the sights and stench and random cruelty all merged in memory, until it was hard to tell one day's horrors from the next.

I saw men buried alive. When a guy was bayoneted or shot, lying in the road, and the convoys were coming along, I saw trucks that would just go out of their way to run over the guy in the middle of the road. And likewise the rest of the trucks, and by the time you have fifteen or twenty trucks run over you, you look like a smashed tomato. And I saw people that had their throats cut because [the Japanese] would take their bayonets and stick them out through the corner of their trucks at night and it would just be high enough to cut their throats. And I saw men beaten with a rifle butt until there just was no more life in them. I saw Filipino women [who tried to bring us food or water] cut. Their stomachs were cut open. Their throats were cut. I saw Filipinos and Americans beheaded just with one swipe of a saber.

Hissing vultures too engorged to fly battled over the blackening corpses sprawled along both sides of the road. The stench became unbearable. One officer thought it his duty to keep track of the number of cut-off heads he passed. He stopped counting at twenty-seven, afraid that further tallying would drive him mad.

For Frazier, it went on for six days and seven nights.

The Bataan Death March: Glenn Frazier believes himself to be the second man in line, wearing dark pants. Japanese, like the man at the right, lined the road, taking pictures, he remembered, and some of the villagers who tried to throw food to the weary, stumbling men were killed by their captors.

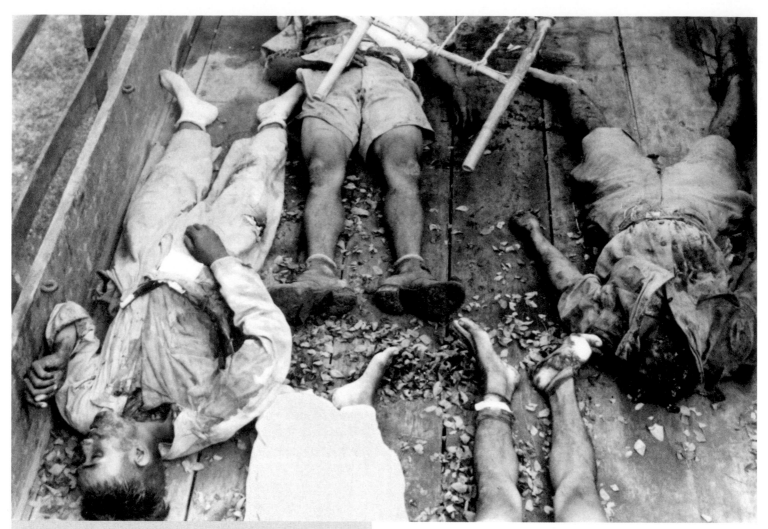

Filipino troops butchered on the way to Camp O'Donnell (above) and some of the sick, malnourished U.S. prisoners who managed somehow to get there (below)

I did not have but one sip of water and no food. Now, they say that you can't do this, but I did. When I got to the end of the march [at San Fernando] where they put us on a train, my tongue wouldn't even go back in my mouth. And if you talk to somebody about that, they'll tell you that's how close to death I was.

And still it wasn't over. The men were packed so tightly inside the airless, furnacelike iron boxcars that they had no choice but to stay on their feet for the three-hour train ride. Many suffered from dysentery. The floors of the swaying boxcars were awash in feces and urine. Some men died standing up before the doors were opened again and the survivors were pulled out and made to stagger the final six miles to Camp O'Donnell. No one knows precisely how many men perished during the Death March. Estimates run between six and eleven thousand Filipinos and Americans.

Camp O'Donnell offered precious little comfort to the men who managed to reach it. A cluster of half-finished nipa huts surrounded by barbed wire and machine-gun towers, with no trees to provide shelter from the sun, it would have to house more than sixty thousand miserable, desperate men. Standing on a little platform meant to make him seem taller, the commandant bellowed more or less the same unsettling greeting to each group of fresh arrivals. They were not prisoners of war, he told them, but "guests of the emperor," whose treatment would depend on the degree of obedience they demonstrated toward his uniformed representatives.

Most prisoners were ill but no medical facilities were provided. The few medicines American doctors had managed to carry with them quickly ran out. A single water spigot supplied the whole camp. Hundreds waited hours just to fill a canteen and sometimes, Frazier remembered, fought "like pigs" over their place in line. Food was nothing but *lugao,* watery rice soup filled with weevils and worms. It was best to try to swallow it after dark, one man recalled, so as not to have to look at it.

Conditions only got worse after Corregidor surrendered on May 6 and hundreds more desperate men flooded into the already overcrowded camp.

Some sixteen thousand Filipinos and Americans would die at Camp O'Donnell—of dehydration, malnutrition, malaria, beriberi, scurvy, dysentery, hopelessness. "Their bodies went by in an endless column," one sergeant remembered. "Day and night [they] were carried to the cemetery."

Glenn Frazier was one of those who helped carry corpses out of the camp for burial.

Some days we buried two hundred and fifty men. So I didn't know but what one day it might happen to me. I had two sets of dog tags. And so I said to myself, well, I think I'll just throw one of these sets of dog tags in the mass grave, so if I'm alive when the war ends, there's no problem. If I'm missing or dead, I wanted my family to know and have some kind of ending.

ON THE NIGHT OF MARCH 25, 1942, a lone B-25 bomber had landed at McClellan Field, just outside Sacramento. Aboard was Lieutenant Colonel James H. Doolittle, a daring, demanding flier charged with a mission so secret that none of the mechanics assigned to work on his plane or the fifteen others that soon followed it down the runway could be told where the aircraft were bound. Extensive modifications were demanded to extend the

One of Lieutenant Colonel James H. Doolittle's B-25s takes off for Japan from the tossing deck of the USS *Hornet,* April 18, 1942.

bombers' range, and a crew member stood by twenty-four hours a day to insure that nothing went wrong.

Everything did. New parts failed to arrive. Others did not fit. Jimmy Doolittle was not a patient man. On April 1 he ordered his men into the air: they could wait no longer. When a McClellan Field foreman asked him to provide a written evaluation of his men's work, Doolittle scrawled one word—"Lousy"—and proceeded on his clandestine mission.

The mystery of who he was and where he and his men were headed was solved less than three weeks later. In the hours following Pearl Harbor, FDR had let it be known that he wanted to retaliate against the Japanese mainland as soon as humanly possible. No plane then built could reach Japan from land. But it occurred to some naval officers that if an aircraft carrier could steal close enough, it could provide bombers with the boost they needed.

On April 18, eight days after the surrender on Bataan, Doolittle and his sixteen carrier-based bombers appeared suddenly in the skies over Tokyo and Yokohama, dropped their bombs, and then flew on to crash-land in China. They did little serious damage. Four American airmen were captured. Three were beheaded; the fourth died in prison after being tortured. Thousands of Chinese were butchered because a few villagers had gone to the rescue of the downed pilots. But a blow had finally been struck against the Japanese mainland.

The White House announced the raid in mid-May to an American public desperate for good news of any kind. The attack was not officially reported to the Japanese public at all, but one high-ranking Japanese naval officer remembered that news of it "passed like a shiver over Japan" nonetheless. And it came at a crucial moment in Japan's war planning.

THE BOYS OF BATTERY E

Almost a year before Pearl Harbor, 135 National Guardsmen from Rock County, Minnesota, had found themselves called to active duty. The whole town of Luverne turned out to see them off at the depot from which many of their fathers had left for the Great War in 1917. They were reorganized into Battery E, 215th Coastal Artillery, and eventually sent to Alaska to help protect Fort Greeley, on Kodiak Island. Back home, young Jim Sherman found this confusing: "I thought it was 'Kodak,' " he remembered, "and I couldn't, for the life of me, figure out why all these guys from Luverne were going to wherever they made cameras."

A Sioux City, Iowa, car dealer named Royal Miller visited the men of Battery E while on a hunting trip in the fall of 1941 and filmed them with an 8-millimeter camera. After he got back, he showed his home movies at the Pix Theater on Main Street. Families crowded in for a glimpse of how their boys were doing, then were encouraged to go down to city hall and write their Fourth of July greetings to their faraway friends on a wrapping-paper letter that

Lowell - JAN 1941 - Btry E - 215th CA.HA
Leaving Luverne

44

stretched 120 feet. The town barber, Kay Aanenson, helped organize the letter writing, and at least one serviceman sent his personal thanks.

Dear Kay and Everybody:
I wanted to let you know that the battery received the swell letter. . . . The boys are really having a time reading it. They're on their hands and knees and have the paper strung from one end of the barracks to the other. . . . It's things like this that make us feel pretty darn good. . . .
In case you don't remember me, I used to sling hash in the Gimm & Byrnes [café]. I was the tall slim fellow who used to work with Fred Gimm. Tell him hello for me. Well, Kay, I'll cut this off here. . . . We'll promise to get all the damned Japs that stick their noses in around here.
Thanks again from all of us.
As ever,
Vernon A. Fremstand

Although neither the townspeople nor the men themselves had initially believed the enemy would ever get anywhere near Kodiak, Japanese naval forces did occupy the barren Aleutian islands of Adak and Kiska in early June of 1942, apparently to discourage the United States from mounting an assault on Japan across the North Pacific. Both islands were liberated by U.S. troops the following year, in a little-known campaign overshadowed by the fighting on Guadalcanal.

Clockwise from bottom of the opposite page: Rock County boys receive a hometown send-off from the people of Luverne; Kodiak, Alaska, where they found themselves stationed; a booth on Main Street in Luverne, meant to collect funds with which to help provide them with some of the comforts of home; and their well-wishers' outsized Independence Day greeting.

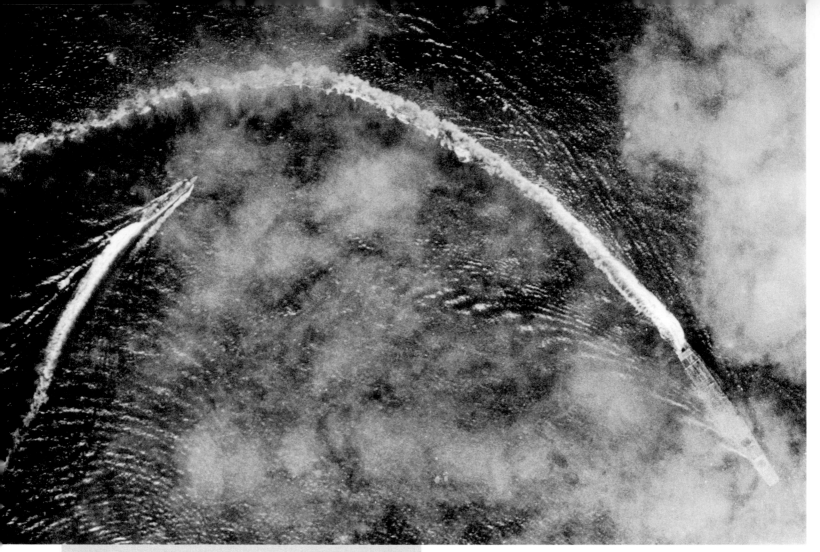

Revenge: During the Battle of Midway, the flagship of Japan's First Air Fleet, the carrier *Akagi* (right), and one of her destroyer escorts frantically seek to dodge the bombs being dropped by U.S. B-17s that would sink her by nightfall, June 4, 1942. A little less than six months earlier, Japanese torpedo planes had taken off from the *Akagi*'s flight deck to attack Pearl Harbor.

ADMIRAL ISOROKU YAMAMOTO, the architect of the Pearl Harbor attack, had always insisted that victory depended on the quickest possible conquest. "If we are to fight, regardless of consequences," Yamamoto had said before his planes attacked, "I shall run wild for six months or a year, but I have utterly no confidence for the second or third years of the fighting." If Japan slowed its advance, he was sure American industrial might would eventually overwhelm it.

Now he had a plan for a second lightning strike at sea. It had several objectives. First, to take Midway, the westernmost of the inhabited Hawaiian Islands. From there he thought Japan could threaten the whole Territory of Hawaii, hold its population hostage, and perhaps force the United States to sue for peace. Possession of Midway would also complete a picket line that would stretch more than twelve thousand miles, from the Aleutians in the north through Midway, Wake, and the Marshall Islands in the Central Pacific all the way to Singapore. Behind

that line, Japan would be free to occupy New Caledonia, the Fijis, Samoa, New Guinea, and the Solomon Islands, and then attack Australia. Finally, he believed that by moving on Midway, he would lure what was left of the American fleet with its all-important carriers into a great "decisive battle" that could finish the destruction begun at Pearl Harbor.

Before the Doolittle raid, some in Tokyo had thought Yamamoto's plan overly ambitious. Better to consolidate Japanese gains, they had argued, than undertake new adventures. But the American bombing of two Japanese cities by carrier-based aircraft drowned out the opposition. The homeland no longer seemed invulnerable. Taking Midway would help close the gap in her defenses.

In late May, Yamamoto ordered a Japanese armada—almost two hundred ships, including eleven battleships, six large fleet-class carriers, twelve cruisers, and forty-three destroyers, as well as seven hundred planes—to steam eastward toward Hawaii in secret.

At dawn on June 4, as Admiral Chuichi Nagumo ordered his bombers to attack Midway, everything seemed to be on schedule.

But American cryptographers had deciphered the Japanese plans, and a large fleet, with three carriers, was waiting just over the horizon. This time, the Americans had surprise on their side. The Japanese bombers hit Midway hard, and Japanese Zeroes easily outfought and outmaneuvered the inferior navy fighters that swarmed up to meet them. But the island held, and the Japanese commander sent his planes back to their carriers to be rearmed with fragmentation bombs for a second assault.

Admiral Raymond A. Spruance chose that moment—when the Japanese carrier decks were covered with aircraft and volatile gasoline—to order planes from all three of his carriers into the air. Forty-one American torpedo planes attacked the enemy carriers. Not one hit its target, and thirty-five planes were sent crashing into the sea. The Japanese sailors cheered what seemed to be yet another triumph.

But then, a flight of thirty-seven Dauntless dive-bombers from the carriers *Yorktown* and *Enterprise* swooped down—"like a beautiful silver waterfall," one pilot remembered—raining bombs onto the crowded decks. Three carriers sank quickly. The fourth was badly damaged and later sent below by another American torpedo.

The Americans also lost a carrier, but Admiral Yamamoto's plan had ended in disaster: the destruction of all but two of the six carriers from which he'd attacked Pearl Harbor. Midway marked the first defeat for the Japanese navy in 350 years. Over the next three years, Japanese shipyards would manage to produce just six more fleet carriers. Their American counterparts would turn out seventeen. Japanese warships would never again be able to "run wild" in the Pacific.

MARINE PRIVATE SID PHILLIPS OF MOBILE first heard about the big victory at Midway from a newsboy shouting about it on the dock at San Francisco. He and his friend W. O. Brown were then living aboard the USS *George F. Elliott*, a rusting World War I–vintage transport vessel that would soon help convoy part of the 1st Marine Division overseas. After three months of training at New River, North Carolina, Phillips and Brown were "stovepipers" (mortarmen), proud members of Gun Squad Number Four, H Company, 2nd Battalion, 1st Marine Regiment, 1st Marine Division. They called their eight-man outfit the Rebel Squad, because its members were all southerners except for one Vermonter, who belonged nonetheless, Phillips recalled, because he lived on the south side of the street in the southern bedroom of his parents' house.

On June 22, a little over two months after the American surrender on Bataan and eighteen days after the Battle of Midway, Phillips and his outfit set sail. Before leaving the dock, each man was given a postcard with a preprinted message telling his family

he was heading overseas. There was room for a signature and nothing more. No one was allowed to say where he was going. Most of the men didn't know anyway. As the *Elliott* moved past Alcatraz, one marine spotted a prisoner gazing out the window. "Hey, Lucky," he shouted, "want to trade places?" There was no answer from the Rock.

Major General A. A. Vandegrift, the commander of the 1st Division, did know where his men were going and what they would be doing when they got there—at least he thought he did. His orders called for him to establish a base in New Zealand and then see to it that his division got six more months of training in amphibious landing and jungle fighting before they were committed to combat. No American offensive action in the Pacific was expected until the beginning of the following year.

And as Sid Phillips and his friends adjusted to life at sea—seasickness, miserable food, cramped quarters, colossal boredom—secret Allied discussions in Washington seemed only to reconfirm those expectations. The war against Germany still had top priority, and in that struggle there was as yet little progress to report. Western Europe remained in Axis hands. In the east, 225 German divisions were advancing steadily toward the Russian oil fields in the Caucasus, and Joseph Stalin was demanding that the Allies immediately open a second front somewhere in the European theater to relieve the pressure on his forces. If he didn't get it, President Roosevelt feared, the Soviet leader might be defeated or forced to sign a separate peace with Hitler.

American military planners had a straightforward idea of how to beat the Germans: cross the English Channel and drive straight for Berlin. "We've got to go to Europe and fight," General Dwight D. Eisenhower had noted in his diary after Pearl Harbor. "And we've got to quit wasting resources all over the world—and still worse—wasting time." He and his fellow army commanders argued that nothing should be allowed to undercut preparations for an all-out Allied assault on France in the spring of 1943, to be followed by a relentless drive for the Rhine. Only if Germany suddenly crumbled or Russia really seemed about to collapse would they move faster and launch Operation Sledgehammer, sending a far smaller force across the English Channel in the fall of 1942 to gain at least a foothold on the French coast.

The British, too, wanted to invade France eventually, but they were wary of moving too fast. They had already been hurled from the Continent three times by the Germans since 1939, and the very idea of Sledgehammer made them nervous. A defeat on the French coast, Churchill warned, was "the only way in which we could possibly lose this war." Instead, the prime minister favored joint Allied action on the southern fringe of the Nazi

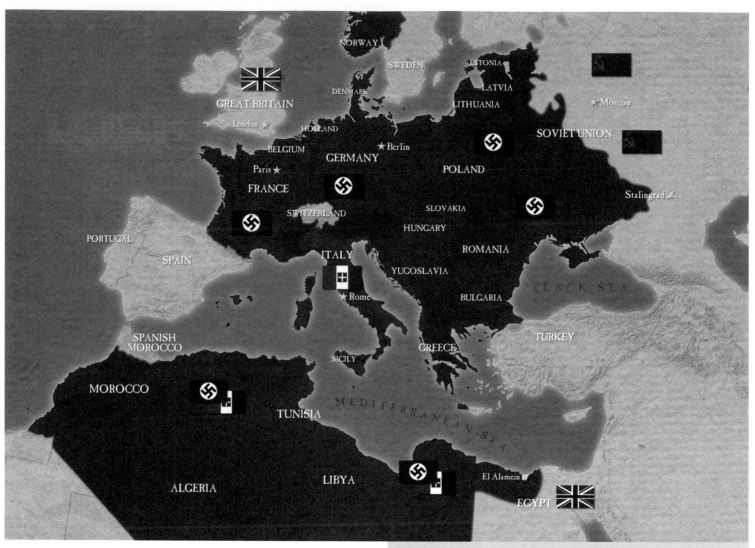

The situation in Europe and North Africa, mid-1942

empire, in North Africa. If American and British forces landed in Morocco, Algeria, and Tunisia, he argued, the Vichy French who ruled them might be persuaded to come over to the Allied cause. But more important, fresh troops could trap and destroy the German and Italian armies fighting the British in Egypt, safeguarding Middle Eastern oil fields and ensuring safe Allied passage through the Suez Canal to India.

Most of the American brass dismissed the British plan as "scatterization," a dangerous and wasteful diversion from the real task at hand. But congressional elections were coming up. American voters were eager for offensive action against the Axis somewhere, and Roosevelt was no less eager for them to understand that they had a serious stake in the war in the European theater as well as in the Pacific. He overruled his commanders. There would be no Sledgehammer. American and British troops under Eisenhower's command were to land together in North Africa in the autumn instead. A bitter General Marshall wrote privately that he and his fellow commanders had "failed to see

that the leader in a democracy has to keep the people entertained."

Admiral Ernest J. King, commander in chief of the U.S. fleet and chief of naval operations, was indignant, too, but for different reasons. He was convinced that the focus on defeating Germany was unnecessary; that the United States was potentially powerful enough to wage war simultaneously on both fronts; and that so long as the European war continued to come first, the navy would be denied the planes and ships it needed to strike back. Midway had halted the Japanese advance in the Central Pacific, but Tokyo still dreamed of fresh conquests in the South Pacific, where ships and planes based at Rabaul, on New Britain Island's eastern tip, were already harassing Allied shipping, threatening the Allied supply base at New Guinea's Port Moresby, and menacing Australia as well.

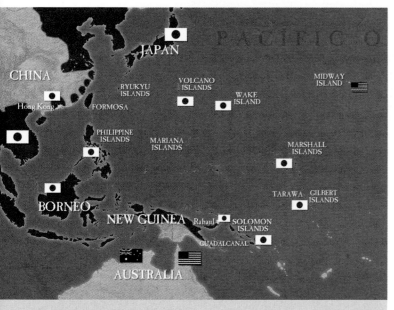

The situation in the Pacific, mid-1942

Admiral King and General MacArthur disagreed on almost everything. But both wanted the Japanese at Rabaul dislodged or neutralized, and a plan was eventually worked out that won the approval of the Joint Chiefs. MacArthur's army forces were to fight their way up the northeast coast of New Guinea from the east while the navy, under Admiral Chester W. Nimitz, destroyed the small Japanese seaplane base at Tulagi and took over adjacent islands near the eastern end of the Solomon chain.

The sense of urgency intensified when U.S. air reconnaissance spotted Japanese construction crews at work on an airstrip on Guadalcanal. If they were allowed to complete it, the enemy would be free to choke off shipping to Australia and make an eventual Allied counteroffensive across the Pacific far more difficult. To stop them, a naval task force was to move on the Solomons as soon as possible. And so, not long after General Vandegrift arrived at Wellington, New Zealand, with the first echelon of his division, he received new orders. There was to be no six-month training period for his men. Instead, he was to prepare to attack Tulagi and Guadalcanal by sea in a little over a month. Neither he nor most of his officers had ever heard of either island. There were no good maps. No one since the Allied disaster at Gallipoli during the Great War had ever made an amphibious landing on the scale that would be needed now. "I could not believe it," Vandegrift remembered. But he went right to work.

By the time Sid Phillips arrived at Wellington with the division's second echelon on July 11, preparations for the landing were well under way. The first order of business for Phillips's outfit was to carry everything packed into the vast hull of their warship onto

the docks and then reload it in "combat order." ("The essence of combat loading," a marine colonel once explained, "is not to put the toilet paper on top of the ammunition.")

It was winter in the Southern Hemisphere, and as the men labored day and night a cold rain fell steadily, drenching the men, dissolving the cardboard cartons in which foodstuffs were packed, washing the labels off cans of rations, turning the quays into a bog of cornflakes and candy bars, cigarettes and sodden clothing. There were no gloves. Wet crates of ammunition slipped through the men's hands. Bales of barbed wire tore at their numb fingers. "We were all young and strong and patriotic and eager to support our nation's war effort, and really worked our hearts out," Phillips remembered many years later, but "if anything in the armed forces ever needs correcting, it is the policy of the privates alone doing all of the manual labor."

Strict censorship governed the letters servicemen sent home from overseas, and the men chafed under its strictures. Before leaving home, Sid Phillips had promised to do all he could to get around the rules so that his family would know where he was, and so he wrote them a letter from Wellington saying how pleased he had been to hear that "Uncle Zeke is planting that new land for watermelons." Since Phillips *had* no Uncle Zeke nor any "new land," he assumed that the family would put together "new," "Zeke," and "land" and figure out his location. But just to make sure, he added that his extra set of car keys (he had none, was still too young to drive a car) was "beneath down under" his bed. "Everybody knew Australia as the land down under," he said later, and any map would show that New Zealand was the land beneath *that*. (His family didn't get it; they used a crowbar to pry off the baseboard beneath his bed, found nothing, and remained as mystified about his whereabouts as ever.) By the time his letter reached them, Sid and his fellow marines were on their way to Guadalcanal.

At dawn on August 7, 1942—eight months to the day after Pearl Harbor—American land forces went on the offensive for the first time in the Second World War. After a fierce naval shelling intended to soften up Japanese defenses, six thousand marines assaulted Tulagi and two other small but fiercely contested neighboring islands while Sid Phillips and eleven thousand of his comrades clambered down into landing craft and set out for Beach Red on the northern side of Guadalcanal. The island was ninety miles long and looked beautiful from out at sea: green, lush, mountainous.

Phillips's platoon was part of the second wave of marines to go ashore. "We had been repeatedly told that this would be the first ship-to-shore landing," he remembered, "and nobody could more than guess if such an idea would be successful. . . . We

The 1st Marine Division about to start inland on Guadalcanal; beneath a papaya tree, right, Sid Phillips can be seen relieving himself with his back to the camera.

braced ourselves. The landing craft slid up on the beach. We charged out, ready to do or die, and there was the first wave sitting there, laughing at us." The first U.S. casualty on Guadalcanal was a marine who cut his hand trying to open a coconut with a machete.

Marine commanders had believed some five thousand Japanese troops would be waiting for them. Actually, there were fewer than half that number on the island, and most were members of construction units who had fled the unfinished airfield as soon as the first American shells hit the beach.

Sid Phillips and his batallion moved off the beach as ordered and started toward what their crude sketch maps said was a "grassy knoll" just beyond the waterline. It turned out to be a full-scale mountain 1,500 feet high, extending several miles inland. A twisting tidal creek that was said to be shallow proved too deep to wade, so they waited in the open—"bunched up like a herd of stupid cattle," Phillips wrote—until an amphibious tractor could be found and driven out into the water to serve as the centerpiece of an improvised bridge. The men crossed it, then filed through coconut plantations, checkerboards of palms that would have provided little protection had there been an enemy force in position to open fire. They pushed their way through a patch of razor-sharp *kunai* grass that grew taller than their heads and finally entered the rain forest. Huge hardwood trees—some 150 feet tall and 40 feet around—formed a green, unbroken canopy that filtered out sunlight and trapped the humid heat. It was hard to see more than a few feet into the undergrowth. Unfamiliar birds called. Weeks at sea had reduced the men's strength. Thick vines curled around their ankles. Wet layers of rotting vegetation and slippery soil made some stumble and fall. Others collapsed from dehydration or the ill effects of swallowing too many salt pills too fast. Phillips, carrying a forty-six-pound mortar bipod across his shoulders, fell to his knees several times as he climbed.

At dusk they found themselves only halfway up the mountain. They spooned down C rations (so bad the men claimed they'd been made by a manufacturer of dog food) and spent a fitful night in foxholes hastily scraped into the slope. As they continued their climb the next day they heard explosions far below. Japanese torpedo bombers were attacking American ships offshore. The marines cheered as enemy warplanes went down in flames. When one crashed into the superstructure of the *George F. Elliott,* setting her ablaze, the men of Sid's company cheered that, too. "We won't have to ride in that old bastard again," one man said. They were so new to war that the distant loss of life wasn't yet real to them.

That night, from foxholes near the summit, they looked on as a great naval battle broke out all across the bay. In the darkness it was impossible to know what was happening, but every time there was an explosion and fire, the marines cheered again, assuming the U.S. Navy was winning. It was not. Japanese cruisers sent racing from Rabaul, six hundred miles away, had slipped in among the Allied ships and opened fire. Four cruisers—three American and one Australian—were sunk, and more than a thousand sailors were lost in what came to be called the Battle of Savo Island. It was one of the worst defeats in U.S. naval history.

By the time Sid Phillips's battalion made it back to the beach, on August 10, the waters offshore were empty of everything except abandoned landing craft and scattered wreckage. Medics were doing what they could for the badly burned survivors. The U.S. Navy had fled, taking with it most of the supplies and ammunition that had been meant to sustain the men on Guadalcanal. "We would have starved to death if there hadn't been a big supply of Japanese rice there," Phillips wrote. "We ate rice in a very measured amount twice a day for weeks."

While the 2nd Battalion made its way up and down the "grassy knoll," other marines had seized the unfinished airport, renamed it Henderson Field after a pilot who had been killed at Midway, and begun to prepare it for American planes with signs that read UNDER NEW MANAGEMENT. The 2nd Battalion took up defensive positions along the east bank of the Ilu River—mislabeled the Tenaru on marine maps—with the airstrip at their backs. "We were told to dig mortar pits and foxholes," Phillips wrote. "It seemed we were digging all the time."

The enemy now owned both the skies over Guadalcanal and the ocean around it. Japanese warplanes from Rabaul strafed and bombed the Americans at least once a day, often around noon, which the men took to calling Tojo Time. At night, Japanese warships moved in close to shore, switched on searchlights that lit up the target area so brightly that Phillips and his comrades "felt like we were in a shooting gallery," and then lobbed shell after shell in among them. All the marines could do was hunker down and hope for the best.

Some men could take it and some just physically could not take it. And the sheer terror of knowing that the next one is going to have your name on it. When that goes on and on and on and on, you get a strange feeling in which you seem to become detached and you just think, "Well, maybe this will end and maybe it won't and maybe we'll all be blown up and maybe we won't, but who cares?" And you learn to sort of live with it. And the initial wearing down begins to make you see that it is just a matter of fate. You will either survive if the Lord is willing or you will not. So there's really nothing you can do. And you just take it.

Phillips and most of his friends took it. But they were chronically hungry, low on ammunition, and starting to suffer from the illnesses that accompanied life in the jungle. "The typical marine on the island," Phillips remembered, "ran a fever, wore stinking dungarees, loathed twilight, and wondered whether the U.S. Navy still existed." They had also begun to wonder whether they, like the men on Bataan, had simply been abandoned. "We knew our country was not yet heavily armed," he recalled. "We understood that we might be expendable."

Looking back years later at photographs of himself and his smooth-cheeked friends in uniform, Sid Phillips marveled that America had ever "considered these young volunteers as her defenders. . . . They had the heart but not the experience." Nine out of ten of the men in his division really were boys (their average age was nineteen) and had no real idea before they landed what combat would be like. Luckily, as one officer recalled, there were veterans scattered among their ranks whose impact on them would be incalculable.

Sergeants from recruiting duty, gunnery sergeants who had fought in France, perennial privates with disciplinary records a yard long. These were the professionals, the "Old Breed" of the United States Marines. Many had fought "Cacos" in Haiti, "bandidos" in Nicaragua, and French, English, Italian,

A marine patrol wades the Lunga River in August. "It is impossible to describe the creepy sensation of walking through that empty-looking but crowded-seeming jungle," wrote a war correspondent who went along on one such mission. "Parakeets and cockatoos screeched from nowhere. There was one bird with an altogether unmusical call which sounded exactly like a man whistling shrilly through his fingers three times—and then another, far off in Jap territory, would answer."

and American soldiers and sailors in every bar in Shanghai, Manila, Tsingtao, Tientsin, and Peking.

They were inveterate gamblers and accomplished scroungers, who drank hair tonic in preference to post exchange beer ("horse piss"), cursed with wonderful fluency, and never went to chapel ("the God-box") unless forced to. . . . They knew their weapons and they knew their tactics. They knew that they were tough and they knew that they were good. There were enough of them to leaven the division and to impart to the thousands of younger men a share of both the unique spirit which animated them and the skills they possessed.

The men of the 1st Division now needed both that spirit and those skills. In Sid Phillips's outfit, it was Second Lieutenant Carl Benson—"Benny" to the men—who helped provide both. He had "tattoos up and down both arms," Phillips remembered, "knew all of the old marines in other companies, and had been all over the world. We all both hated and loved Benny, because he knew all our evil schemes but he also knew how to take care of us."

When a marine patrol was ambushed and search parties were dispatched to recover the bodies, Phillips and his outfit went along. "They came to the mortar platoon and chose our number for a gun squad," he remembered. "They always did that for dirty jobs. And so we carried our mortars and ammunition back out to the ambush site. It was about five miles." Phillips's squad came upon several Japanese corpses, the first enemy dead they'd seen. "The firefight had occurred the day before, and in just one day's time they had no faces, no hands, they were just masses of maggots. They were still in nice uniforms, but the jungle decomposes things in a rapid manner that you just can't understand elsewhere." In the end, Phillips and his friends found no dead Americans, but others did. When his squad met another unit coming back along the jungle trail, its veteran sergeant took his old friend Benny aside to tell him what he'd heard. The enemy had dismembered and beheaded the marine dead, he said, and then stuffed their genitals into their mouths. After hearing that, "our battalion never took a prisoner that I know of," Phillips recalled. "It was kill or be killed. Nothing more need be said than that."

The days on Guadalcanal were bad. Nights on the perimeter were worse. Benny helped with those, too. At dusk, he ordered

Members of Sid Phillips's outfit examine enemy dead after the Battle of the Tenaru. These Japanese had earlier overrun the marines on Guam. "We were up at dawn and began to gather souvenirs for trading purposes," Phillips remembered. "We found dozens of snapshots of marines and their families and girlfriends . . . which we carefully and almost reverently collected and burned right there on the beach."

his men to fall in, inspected their weapons, checked to see that their cartridge belts were filled and that each man had at least two bandoliers of ammunition. Between then and dawn, he told them, "anybody on top of the ground" was to be considered an enemy. On the other hand, no one should fire his weapon without being sure of his target, because the flash would give away his position. Benny would be in his own foxhole just behind theirs, he reminded them, so when the Japanese attacked, they'd better not "come back there looking for your mother," because he had a BAR (Browning automatic rifle) on fully automatic and promised to cut them in half.

With that, he left them alone, two men to a foxhole, peering into the darkness across the Ilu River, listening for the faintest sound. Feral cattle stumbled noisily in and out of the lines. Rats and iguanas scurried along the ground. Palm fronds rustled. "I wasn't going to be eighteen until September second," Phillips remembered. "If there had been such a thing as a meter that measured from Anxiety to Concern to Scared to Fear to Terror, many times mine would have been pinned beyond Terror."

Laughter sometimes helped. One night, Japanese scouts hidden in the darkness shouted, "Marine, you die," over and over again, hoping some crouching marine would answer and give away his position. Benny muttered, "Quiet, quiet," under his breath. But fifteen minutes of this was all one American could take. "Tojo eats shit!" he shouted back. The whole marine line erupted in laughter. Benny was furious.

In late afternoon on August 20, after thirteen harrowing days on the island, Phillips heard the sound of approaching aircraft and took cover as usual. But this time the planes were American: nineteen Wildcat fighters and twelve Dauntless dive-bombers, circling the field, waggling their wings in greeting, getting ready to land. The marines cheered. They were no longer alone. "It looked like Uncle Sam was going to fight for that miserable place after all," Phillips wrote.

The celebration didn't last long. Under cover of darkness two days earlier, the Japanese had landed a thousand troops from the crack 28th Infantry Regiment at the western end of the island, with orders to retake the airfield. Its men had already overwhelmed the marines on Guam. Many carried in their packs military insignia and family photographs taken from dead or captured Americans. Their commander, Colonel Kiyono Ichiki, was so certain his men were about to do it all again on Guadalcanal that in his diary he had already filled in the entry for the day: "21 August: Enjoy the fruits of victory."

Shortly after two the next morning, just hours after the first American planes skidded down the runway at Henderson Field,

Aftermath: the lesson of the Tenaru, wrote Marine Major General A. A. Vandegrift, was that while "yesterday, the Jap seemed something superhuman, a kind of mechanized juggernaut," his men now understood that their enemy was merely a "physical thing, a soldier in uniform, carrying a rifle and . . . charging stupidly against barbed wire and rifles and machine guns."

From the doorway of their reinforced dugout on the edge of Henderson Field, anxious marines scan the sky for enemy bombers.

Sid Phillips was awakened by gunfire. "At that time almost every night there would be some event that would keep everyone awake," he remembered. "But this night it was different. The whole world erupted, and the lines became just a wall of fire."

He and his mortar squad were positioned in gun pits some three hundred yards behind the front line that night, too far away to see everything that was happening. But green flares lit up the landscape. Enemy mortar shells arced overhead. And two hundred Japanese troops had come running out of the coconut trees and across the narrow sand spit at the Ilu's mouth, bayonets

fixed and shrieking, "Banzai!" The marines opened fire with everything they had: rifles, artillery, antitank guns. "Indian" Johnny Rivers—a young Native American machine-gunner from Pennsylvania, who had been a professional boxer in civilian life—poured fire into the advancing enemy until his own tracer bullets revealed his position. A dozen bullets hit him in the head. His finger froze on the trigger as he died, and his weapon poured two hundred more rounds into the darkness before his loader, Private Al Schmid, could shove his body out of the way and take over. Schmid, too, kept shooting, sweeping his muzzle back and forth and listening for the screams of wounded men, until a Japanese soldier got close enough to lob a grenade. Shrapnel ripped into Schmid's arm, his hand, his head, his left eye. Blood

The Japanese hit the airfield on Guadalcanal again and again. These American B-24 Liberators were set ablaze in early 1943.

blinded him. He drew his .45 and emptied it into the night, then went back to firing his machine gun until medics got to him and carried him to the rear.

Some attackers got hung up on a single strand of barbed wire and were shot before they could shake themselves loose. Others swam through the surf to get around the American line and into the marine positions. Hand-to-hand combat eliminated them. The handful that did manage to make it through were met by a reserve platoon rushed in to wipe them out.

Colonel Ichiki ordered a second assault. It, too, was shattered by American fire. Instead of retreating, the rest of his men dug in across the river.

Just before dawn, Gun Squad Four was finally ordered to move up. "We broke the mortar down and shouldered it and went stumbling off in the dim light, cursing our inability to see clearly," Sid Phillips remembered. Benny led the way, urging his men to stay close together and keep moving. They did, "falling into foxholes occasionally," until they reached a spot some 30 yards from the sea and 150 yards behind the marine lines. Phillips recalled:

As soon as it was light enough for us to see the bubbles in the sights we began to fire at three hundred yards . . . very close range for an eighty-one-millimeter mortar and we were firing at a very high elevation to clear the trees. . . .

The ammo was coming in trucks . . . from some dump in the rear and could be thrown out right by the guns. We could not open the canisters fast enough to keep up with the fire orders.

Phillips's squad fired some three hundred shells into the enemy across the river. "When we would sweep right or left the Japs would see the mortar fire coming toward them and try to move out of the path. When they got up to run, the riflemen and machine-gunners would cut them down." Several Japanese managed to set up a machine gun in an abandoned marine tank. Phillips's squad was ordered to knock it out. "We corrected range in a couple of rounds and then put one right in the tank," he wrote. "A loud cheer went up like a touchdown at a football stadium."

As the morning went on, American fighters from Henderson Field roared in to strafe the coconut grove, American artillery crashed through the trees, and the 1st Battalion slipped across the Ilu upstream and attacked the Japanese from behind. Trapped, outgunned, outnumbered, and disoriented, they left their foxholes and looked for a way out. Some fled into the sea and were picked off by marine marksmen. Four American tanks were sent beetling across the sand spit to finish off the rest. "It

was a slaughter," General Vandegrift reported. "Those they did not shoot they ran over. The rear of the tanks looked like meat grinders."

By the time it was over, 34 marines were dead. But so were 770 Japanese, Colonel Ichiki among them; he was said to have burned his regiment's colors and then killed himself. "The stench of bodies was strong," wrote the war correspondent Richard Tregaskis.

Many of them lay at the water's edge, and already were puffed and glossy, like shiny sausages. Some of the bodies had been partially buried by wave-washed sand; you might see a grotesque, bloated head or twisted torso sprouting from the beach. . . . We saw groups of Jap bodies torn apart by our artillery fire, their remains fried by the blast of the shells. . . . The tread tracks of one of our tanks ran directly over five squashed bodies, in the center of which was a broken machine gun on a flattened tripod.

Everywhere one turned there were piles of bodies; here one with a backbone visible from the front, and the rest of the flesh and bone peeled up over the man's head, like the leaf of an artichoke; there a charred head, hairless, but still equipped with blackened eyeballs; pink, blue, yellow entrails drooping; a man with a red bullet-hole through his eye; a dead Jap private, wearing dark, tortoise-shell glasses, his . . . teeth bared in a humorless grin, lying on his back with his chest a mess of ground meat. There is no horror to these things. The first one you see is the only shock. The rest are simple repetition.

The next morning, a plane arrived at Henderson Field, carrying the first mail the men had seen since setting out from New Zealand. "An almost churchlike hush fell over the area," one marine recalled.

Letters were arranged by postmark, read, fondled, and read yet again. The change in the men bordered on the miraculous. All swearing ceased and grim-faced men became almost boys again. Packages of Mom's brownies or a sweetheart's fudge would be proudly shared with buddies. The badly crumpled condition that thousands of miles and rough handling had exacted was overlooked. . . . One lad received a mashed cardboard box containing the crumbled remains of his nineteenth birthday cake.

Another marine got a letter from his draft board. He'd neglected to tell them he'd joined the marines, so they had had no choice but to declare him a draft dodger. He scribbled out a reply: he'd be glad to come right home and straighten things out, he wrote, if the government would arrange his transportation.

A sniper victim is carried out of a coconut plantation on Guadalcanal.

The misnamed Battle of the Tenaru had demonstrated to the men who survived it—and to newspaper readers back home—that despite all their earlier successes, the Japanese were not supermen, though they did seem to be a different kind of enemy from any Americans had faced before. "I have never heard or read of this kind of fighting," General Vandegrift wrote. "These people refuse to surrender. The wounded wait until men come up to examine them . . . and blow the other fellow to pieces with a hand grenade." The battle showed also that the newly minted U.S. Marines had become a formidable fighting force. As their commander wrote privately after the battle, "These youngsters are the darndest people when they get started you ever saw."

But it settled nothing on Guadalcanal. Japan still ruled the surrounding sea and would soon begin sending in reinforcements to try to take the all-important airfield back again. In late September, the first American reinforcements finally made it

through, but nighttime visits by fast-moving Japanese ships the marines called the *Tokyo Express* kept the enemy supplied and reinforced as well.

Sid Phillips and the 1st Marine Division would endure three more months of fighting on the island. Two more Japanese assaults on Henderson Field were beaten back; one came within a thousand yards of success. Bombing continued day and night. Phillips and his squad spent several weeks on the edge of the embattled airfield, living in what he called a "deluxe bomb-proof," a deep dugout roofed with coconut logs and dirt, which the men believed capable of resisting anything the enemy could throw at them or drop on them—unless it was a direct hit. That proposition was sorely tested one night in mid-October when two Japanese battleships poured fourteen-inch shells onto Henderson Field, more than nine hundred of them in seventy terrifying minutes. The shells sounded like freight cars as they came in. The explosions were beyond deafening. With each one, the log roof of Phillips's dugout leaped into the air and slammed down again, covering the squad with dirt. "We repeatedly died of terror," he remembered. "Grown men were sobbing like babies."

The U.S. Army—members of the 164th Infantry of the American Division—made it through to the island about that time, taking at least some of the pressure off the marines. The 2nd Battalion was shifted south to new positions on a treeless ridge so close to the enemy that, when the wind was right, the men could smell Japanese meals being cooked. When things were quiet, Phillips and his friends were sometimes assigned to work parties unloading supplies back on the beach. Returning from one of these, Phillips saw a sight he never forgot.

Two stacks of U.S. Army dead. Each stack was about the size of an automobile, and the dead were piled up like cross-ties. Their shoes had been removed and each body had a tag attached to a big toe. Most of the dead had their eyes open, and we knew they were army by their fatigues and longer hair. They seemed to be fresh troops in new clothing.

Thousands of flies buzzed around the bodies. Phillips and his friends hurried back up the ridge.

BY THEN, AMERICAN SOLDIERS on the other side of the world were facing enemy fire as well. In the early morning hours of November 8, Operation Torch began, as three Allied task forces began landing some hundred thousand U.S. and British troops at nine beachheads along the Moroccan and Algerian coasts. Things did not go smoothly. Behind-the-scenes diplomatic activity aimed at persuading Vichy commanders to surrender before the men went ashore had failed. Loudspeaker announcements in French—"Don't shoot. We are your friends. Don't shoot"—were met with gunfire. Landing craft turned over in choppy seas or deposited men on the wrong beaches. Scores of tanks and thousands of rounds of ammunition failed to make it ashore. Communications failed. Frightened, trigger-happy troops shot civilians and sometimes one another. Frantic officers drove up and down the unfamiliar roads in commandeered limousines, searching for their scattered men.

More than 1,100 U.S. troops were dead by the time the outnumbered, halfhearted French finally surrendered two days later. Still, some GIs were giddy with victory: They had survived their first battle, and they'd won. "There is a confidence and enthusiasm among the troops that didn't exist [before]," wrote the Scripps Howard correspondent Ernie Pyle, "and now that they sort of feel like veterans, they are eager to sweep on through." American commanders on the ground were more realistic. "Had the landings been opposed by Germans," General George S. Pat-

ton, Jr., said later, "we would never have gotten ashore." And it was the Germans who were waiting for them in Tunisia, with more and more reinforcements arriving from occupied Europe every day.

THAT FALL, THREE MORE NAVAL BATTLES were fought in the waters off Guadalcanal; so many ships were sunk that the area came to be called Ironbottom Sound. During the night of November 12–13, just a few days after the landings in North Africa, Sid Phillips and his squad had ringside seats for the beginning of the largest and most momentous of them: the three-day Battle of Guadalcanal. The Japanese had sent two battleships and a screening force of destroyers toward the island with orders to shell Henderson Field into submission and provide cover for eleven transports filled with twelve thousand fresh troops. As the ships emerged from behind Savo Island a much smaller American force steamed right into them, firing as it came. The twenty-four minutes of point-blank battle that followed were among the most furious of the war. In the darkness "you could see the salvos of the ships, and you could see the naval shells going through the air like lightning bugs," Sid Phillips remembered.

You could see ships explode. We didn't know if they were American or Japanese. We didn't know who was winning or who was losing. Sometimes when a ship would explode, the concussion would actually flap your clothes, miles and miles away. But we did know that our fate was being decided, and we would sit there sort of mystified and horrified by what was going on because we knew thousands of sailors were dying on one side or the other.

Two American admirals were killed. An American cruiser and four destroyers were sunk. More than seven hundred American sailors were lost. But Henderson Field was not bombarded by battleships again, and marine pilots sank seven of the Japanese transports the next morning.

That night, American losses were again heavy in a second naval battle, but when one of the two Japanese battleships sank, most of the enemy fleet steamed away. The next day, the desperate Japanese who remained deliberately beached the four surviving transports in hopes of getting at least some of their men safely ashore. American planes from Henderson and the carrier

After twenty-one straight days of jungle combat, exhausted GIs plod toward the rear. Within days, the battle for Guadalcanal would finally be over.

AL McINTOSH'S WAR
December 1941–November 1942

Throughout the war, in a weekly column called "More or Less Personal Chaff," Al McIntosh, the owner and editor of the Rock County Star-Herald, *chronicled its impact on the people of Luverne, Minnesota, and the farming communities that surrounded it. He was not a Luverne native: he'd been born in Park River, North Dakota, in 1905, the son of a Presbyterian minister. His vivid reporting for the* Lincoln [Nebraska] State Journal *caused William Allen White, the celebrated editor of the* Emporia Gazette, *to make him a handsome offer to join his staff. But McIntosh had always wanted a small-town paper of his own, and in 1940, he bought the weekly* Rock County Star. *When the owner of the rival* Herald *died in a car accident in 1942, he bought it, too, and merged the papers. He lived with his widowed mother on the second floor of a house at 403 North Kniss Street in Luverne. Nothing seems to have escaped his eye.*

DECEMBER 18, 1941. You're right. Mrs. Etta Dehmlow did look as if she wanted to dance in the streets for joy. She just received one of those Navy censor cards from her son, Larry, crewman on a submarine. It didn't carry any postmark but it was the message that thrilled Etta—"Okay" [was all it said but] that's enough to gladden the heart of any mother. It was dated December 8. . . .

• • •

Most of us are letting our daily cares and worries obscure for us the beauty that is around us—ours for the asking. It would pay us to look up—not down. The frost-laden trees and shrubbery last Sunday morning presented a picture so beautiful that there isn't a living artist who could do the scene justice.

And the lights of Christmas that are beginning to blaze from so many Luverne homes. It kindles the warmth of Christmas in your heart—no matter how cynical you may be. Take a few minutes off to cruise around and revel in the beauty of the lights. And give a moment's thought to the fact that we are privileged, by virtue of Rock County's "isolation," to be still able to enjoy this sweet beauty. There won't be any Christmas lights for the homes on the East and West coasts this year.

JANUARY 8, 1942. Jess Frakes, the contractor whose log of travel with the navy [a few years back] reads like the itinerary of a world cruise, has sadly resigned himself to the belief that his contribution to national defense will be "hoeing corn" next summer. Jess did three years, nine months and ten days with the Navy—winding up in 1930 as a first class yeoman. The other day he tried to get back in . . . but the Navy wouldn't take him although Jess will fight if you say he's not as good a man as he ever was. Trouble was—he's short some important teeth. He offered to stand the expense of having some plates made but "no dice" said the recruiting officer as Jess still fell short of dental and optical standards.

JANUARY 15, 1942. In the mail comes a . . . letter from Private A. O. Bierkamp—"Buck" to the thousand assorted friends he has in Rock County. Now at Camp Robinson, "Buck" will take twenty-below Minnesota weather anytime in preference to ten above in Arkansas where the cold knifes through you. His hope is to move soon to a pyramidal tent with five other fellows as the gas heater in his present tent was evidently designed for Florida. . . .

FEBRUARY 12, 1942. Many a person gave prayerful thanks that Rock County men serving in the armed forces were spared in the Japanese attack on Pearl Harbor that black Sunday. . . . But now—over two months later—comes word that a Rock County man was injured that day. It was Walter Rockman, formerly of Steen, who was a member of the Marine Corps. Rockman was off duty at the time he was wounded so he must have been hit at the very outset of the attack. [He] lost two fingers and his arm was badly injured. . . . Rockman was placed in a San Francisco hospital. Infection set in and it's believed it may be necessary to amputate the arm.

APRIL 3, 1942. In case you're one of those men being inducted into the military forces . . . it is suggested that you equip yourself as follows:
1) A full suit of civilian clothes . . .
2) Three or four bath towels.
3) Half a dozen pairs of light wool socks.
4) Extra underwear and plain white dress shirts.
5) Plain-toed oxfords . . .
6) For the soldier's own protection, a pair of shower shoes.
7) Plenty of handkerchiefs.
8) A few extra coat-hangers.

9) Every soldier is expected to supply his own toothbrush, shaving equipment, sleeping garments and any other toilet accessories which he may wish.

APRIL 30, 1942. A lot of people who patriotically hammered their fingers to a pulp and ruined their tempers straightening out old tin cans breathed a sigh of relief when they learned that the government isn't greatly interested in them right now. . . . It seems that the tin percentage is so small that nothing much will be done with the drive until more efficient methods of reclaiming the tin can be devised.

That belated news doesn't bring any happiness to Louis Ahrent for he had been one of the busiest toilers in the tin can drive staged by the cub scouts. . . . He had loaded the collection of tin cans into a borrowed trailer [that came] unhitched and the tongue rammed into the rear of his car. . . . So the score now stands "To Cub Scout treasury from sale of tin cans $2.45," and a local garage bill reads, "To Louis Ahrent, repairs on car, $10."

June 4, 1942. When it comes to family war records you have to go a long way to top that of the Smook family. Back in World War I days there were six Smook brothers all wearing this country's uniform. Lee and Joe were wounded in the battle of the Argonne. Six brothers who fought for this country a quarter century ago.

But the story isn't ended yet. Over at Ellsworth lives their sister, Edna, who is Mrs. Peter DeBoer. She now has four sons in service and by July she will have two more boys in. John and Jake are in the Navy; Harm and Henry are at Kodiak; Pete is joining the naval reserve as soon as school is out and Hilco expects to go in the selective service call in July. Top that one!

JUNE 11, 1942. Reading the item in last week's [paper] about Mrs. Peter DeBoer . . . prompted a phone call about the claim that

Mrs. Jake Wahlert can make. She has three sons in the army now. . . . Seven other sons and four sons-in-law are registered and prepared to enter service when called. Who can beat that record? asks the caller.

JULY 30, 1942. There's been a rumor going around that ought to be brought up short right now. It was to the effect that Louis Shelby, who is married and has four children, has been given a 1A classification and was to leave with the next selective service contingent.

Several men rushed home and told their wives, "Well if they take Shelby, who isn't any spring chicken and probably was in the other war, anything can happen."

The draft office admits it was a mistake and regrets the error. . . .

How did Shelby take it?

"Oh," he said, "I wasn't worried—I figured it was all a mistake so I never went up to see about it."

He might have been unconcerned but a lot of other chaps were in a dither.

SEPTEMBER 17, 1942. If you want to get a real thrill go down to the railroad yards and see the carloads of scrap [metal] rolling out of Rock County headed for the steel mills. It's tangible evidence the local scrap rally committee did a marvelous job. . . . It's estimated that 250 tons were collected . . . about a 50 pound average for every person in the county, man, woman and child. . . . But we can't rest on our oars when we remember that the Nebraska average per person was 105 pounds. There's a mark to shoot at and we've got to get busy again.

OCTOBER 22, 1942. Recalling pioneer days in Rock County, E. A. Brown said he wasn't worried by coffee rationing. When the family settled here they couldn't afford coffee, a lot of the time, even though it was selling for only ten cents a pound. So they would take their coffee and mix it with something else, just to capture the flavor. Dried peas, Brown

recalls, were the most satisfactory. . . . If worst comes to worst . . . he plans to mix his coffee with soy beans. A lot of the "Ten O'Clock Coffee Club" members won't agree with him, but the grain dealer maintains that if you hold your nose, so you don't get any aroma, one can't tell the difference between tea and coffee. . . .

• • •

Tallak Vegge is blaming careless hunters for killing a 700-pound steer at his farm south of Luverne. The animal, when noticed at noon Sunday, had been dead apparently for some time and could not be used as meat. The animal, said Vegge, apparently dropped in his tracks in an open, plowed field and must have been in plain sight of the hunter. "I'm still a good sport," Vegge said, "and don't mind hunters on my farm if they are careful." But now that meat is on the list of commodities to be conserved, he thinks it was criminal not to make use of the meat.

NOVEMBER 5, 1942. A few months ago Andrew Olson was holding his head and saying, "woe is me" about business at the Manitou [Hotel] because of the restrictions on travel. But Andrew had no idea what a "ten-strike" lay ahead for the hotel business here.

He's been putting up cots—when some boys [visiting from a nearby air base] get up and go to early church service Andrew rents the rooms again to those who have been a bit tardy in "getting in." They were even sleeping in the lobby Sunday morning. . . . A year ago you would have been a "bad boy" if you had spoken loudly after midnight, but now snake dances and "community sings" are the order of the day—or rather early morning.

Marines splash through their flooded encampment during the rainy season on Guadalcanal. Foul water and the men's inability to keep dry spread fungal infections and acute dysentery through their ranks.

Enterprise swarmed after them, bombing and strafing. All four began to burn. So many bodies and parts of bodies bobbed in the surf or were blasted into the sand that pilots diving down to hit the transports again vomited in their cockpits.

After more than three months of struggle simply to survive on Guadalcanal, Sid Phillips and his friends had no such ambivalence.

I recall there was no wind that day and the smoke from the burning ships went straight up in columns. When our planes would make their strafing runs on those burning transports we would jump up and down with joy. . . . We actually began to feel like we were winning at last, and that we might live to get off the wretched island.

The Japanese had not been their only enemy. The stench of rotting vegetation and decomposing corpses hung in the hot, lifeless air, clung to the men's clothes, remained as a taste in the mouth, day and night. Torrential rains turned campsites into swamps, jungle paths into rivers of mud. By mid-November, according to the 1st Marine Division Final Action Report, more than 3,200 men were incapacitated by malaria, rendering the division "no longer capable of offensive operations." Sid Phillips recalled that "everybody had lost at least twenty-five pounds. Our clothes were in rags and our skin was orange from taking all that [anti-malarial] atabrine all that time. We were covered with sores. And we had nearly starved to death two or three times."

On December 22, the 1st Marine Division was finally taken off the island. Sid Phillips, like many others, found himself too weak and weary to clamber up the rope nets on the side of the transports sent to carry them away. Lines had to be lowered to haul them aboard.

The enemy would continue to fight on Guadalcanal until the last starving Japanese troops were spirited off it the following February, but by the time the 1st Marine Division left, it was clear even to the Japanese top command that the Americans would eventually prevail. More than 7,100 American marines, sailors, and soldiers died in battle in and around the island. But the Japanese had lost well over 30,000. Midway had ended Japan's dreams of seizing Hawaii and forcing a negotiated peace upon the United States. Guadalcanal had now destroyed her hopes of expanding farther into the southwestern Pacific.

As the exhausted marines steamed away from Guadalcanal, one member of Sid's platoon took a deep breath and asked another, "What's that strange smell?"

"You dumb bastard," his friend said, "that's fresh, clean air."

SID PHILLIPS HAD SURVIVED. His mother's brother, Charles Tucker, a navy pilot who had flown in and out of Henderson Field, had not. The family back home took it hard, as Katharine Phillips remembered.

[Charlie] just did everything well and we just never thought anything would happen to Charlie. If anyone would come through the war, it would be Charlie. So, when the news came that he was missing in action, at Guadalcanal, we were devastated. We kept thinking that maybe his plane had gone down someplace where he could get ashore and be saved. But you know, the wonderful thing [in our minds], he stays twenty-two years old.

When we lost Charlie it made it very real to all of us. And by that time, we had started losing boys in the neighborhood. The boy up here on the corner was a Navy pilot and he was killed. The boy down the street was an Air Force pilot and he was missing in action. They started disappearing all around us. And my mother spent her time going to visit the other mothers consoling them. It was a very fearful time.

That fear was now being felt all across the country. Luverne had been lucky so far. No local family had lost a son in the war, though two men had been reported missing after the fall of Bataan. But in Sacramento, Mrs. Lillian Cole had received news that her son David had died aboard the USS *Arizona* at Pearl Harbor; she was asked by the War Department "to keep secret for the present the name of the ship on which he served." Another Sacramento native, airman Tom Burke, died on a training mission in Puerto Rico, leaving his younger brother, Earl, devastated. And in Waterbury, the family of Marine Private Albert Boulanger learned that he had been killed on Guadalcanal, not far from

Charles Tucker, 1939

where Sid Phillips of Mobile had been fighting.

The previous summer, *Holiday Inn* had opened in movie theaters all across the country. In it, Bing Crosby introduced the Irving Berlin tune "White Christmas." It was an instant hit, and by holiday time it was being heard by homesick Americans wherever they happened to be stationed. Japan had been halted at Midway and Guadalcanal, they knew,

Holiday greetings from Guadalcanal, 1942

but its Pacific empire still stretched for thousands of miles. On the other side of the world, the Red Army had stopped the German advance at Stalingrad in a titanic battle that would eventually cost more than a million lives. Allied troops had finally landed in North Africa in November but had yet to face the full might of the German army. And the Germans were still sinking Allied shipping and killing Allied merchant sailors; still occupied most of Europe; still had designs on Britain and dreamed of one day controlling the New World as well. For Americans in uniform, a hometown Christmas seemed very far away.

WHEN THINGS GET TOUGH

EARLY IN 1943, A TELEGRAM FROM the Selective Service Board arrived at 1032 North Main Street, a triple-decker house in the immigrant North End neighborhood of Waterbury, Connecticut. Three Ciarlo brothers from the little mountain village of Pontelandolfo in the Benevento region of Campania, in central Italy, had bought the house together. Rocco and his family occupied the top floor; the first belonged to Nicholas and his brood.

The family of Tomaso, the oldest brother, lived on the second floor. He had come to America before the Great War and worked as a ditchdigger, quarry worker, and stonemason in Vermont before moving to Waterbury. There, he and Nicholas had taken over a bar and done well enough to open their own grocery store and butcher shop called Ciarlo's Market. In 1919, he sent for his wife, Martina, and two children. Three more children were born in Waterbury. Then, in 1937, Tomaso died at fifty-five. His widow was devastated. "For years after my father died," her younger daughter Olga remembered, "my mother would take the bus and go up to the cemetery all by herself. She couldn't speak a word of English. And all she could tell the man on the bus was 'Cemetery.'"

Martina Ciarlo had known the Selective Service telegram was coming. She had three sons. Two were exempt from the draft: Dom, married with one child and another on the way; and Tom, just sixteen and therefore still too young to go. But the middle son, Corado—known to his family and friends as Babe—was nineteen and single, a perfect candidate for the service. He'd wanted to join the navy as soon as he turned eighteen, but his widowed mother had talked him out of it, telling him he should at least wait until he was called up. When he was, she'd persuaded him to apply for a six-month deferment on the grounds that he was engaged

Farewells: Babe Ciarlo (above) visits his mother before going overseas, while (opposite) an Indianapolis GI says goodbye at the bus station.

in indispensable defense work. Waterbury Steel Ball, where he worked, now made essential parts for aircraft, after all. But when the time came for him to request a second deferment, he wouldn't hear of it. "He wanted to go," his younger brother remembered. "That was it."

After he made his decision, Olga Ciarlo remembered, his mother, still grieving for her husband, "cried forever. My mother was very, very heartbroken already. And then to know that my brother was going off to war—she was scared. She didn't want to go through this all over again. So it was hard times, very hard times."

Babe Ciarlo loved his mother and always did his best to avoid adding to her anxiety. His letters to her from overseas would be filled with admonitions not to fret about him. But his concern for her feelings was trumped by his eagerness to get into uniform. Friendship was part of it: many of his friends from the neighborhood—including his best friend, Eddie Meccariello—were going into the army, and he wanted to be with them. Patriotism was important, too.

But there may have been more to it than that. Pearl Harbor had united the country, but just beneath the surface old divisions remained raw. There were some 5 million Italian Americans in the United States, most either born in Italy or the children of immigrants born there. During the 1920s and '30s, many of them, in Waterbury and elsewhere, had admired Mussolini and believed him when he said he was merely seeking to reestablish Italy's rightful "place in the sun." After FDR denounced the Italian dictator in 1939, thousands of Italian American voters had deserted the Democratic Party rather than support him again for president the following year. Republican handouts in Connecticut in 1940 had warned that if the United States went to war with Italy, "life for us of Italian origin will be very painful because we will have to bear daily the insult of being called a traitor." During the weeks following Pearl Harbor, those predictions had seemed to be coming true: Waterbury's 8,400 Italian-born residents were declared enemy aliens, fingerprinted and photographed, forced to carry special papers, and forbidden to own shortwave radios or to change jobs or shift from one address to another without notifying the authorities. The requirement was lifted in late 1942, but resentment smoldered, and to many young men in immigrant neighborhoods like North Hill, service overseas seemed the best way to demonstrate to the rest of the country that their first allegiance was to the United States.

The city held a farewell ceremony for each batch of boys. The mayor, John Monaghan, remembered every one of them as grim and "wrenching."

> *The selectees reported at 6:00 a.m. to the City Hall, where they were checked off by the draft board, were given their kits and prayer books, and then marched . . . to the railroad station about 7:30. There, the families were massed to say farewell. The Zindah Grotto [Shriners] cigarettes were presented by a veterans' organization official, and I said a few words of farewell. It mattered little what I said. . . . The emotion was too deep for words. Sometimes the draftees would listen and applaud. At other times they would stand with their backs to me, facing their families. On occasion, an old Italian grandmother might start wailing. Many would cling together, young girls with tears streaming down their cheeks. Many of these young men had never been away from home before. . . . Finally, the train conductor would cry, "All aboard," and the inductees would mount the last cars and move off to their new lives.*

When Babe Ciarlo's turn came, eleven of the fifteen young men with whom he climbed aboard the train bore Italian names. By then, decisions had already been made on the other side of the globe that would eventually require them to demonstrate their loyalty to the country their parents had chosen by helping to liberate the land they'd left behind.

MOST AMERICANS LEARNED HOW THE WAR WAS GOING from three sources: nightly radio reports, local newspapers (there were more than eleven thousand in the country then), and the newsreels that preceded the movies at their local theaters. In Waterbury, the movie houses included the Strand and the State. It was the Crest and the Alhambra in Sacramento. In Mobile, the Roxy and the Pike catered to white and black patrons, respectively. Even little Luverne boasted two theaters: the Pix and the Palace, on opposite sides of Main Street.

When Roosevelt and Churchill met again, in mid-January of 1943, at a seaside resort near Casablanca, in French Morocco, they made sure moviegoers saw vivid evidence of Allied unity. Generals Charles de Gaulle and Henri-Honoré Giraud, rival leaders of the Free French Forces, were persuaded to shake hands for the cameras, even though they loathed each other. When the American president told reporters the Allies would insist on

nothing less than unconditional surrender by all three of the Axis powers, the British prime minister quickly concurred: Roosevelt and Churchill were determined to prevent the Nazis from offering separate peace terms to any one of the Big Three and also wanted to reassure the Soviets that they were in the war for the duration. The official communiqué spoke of "complete agreement . . . between the leaders of the two countries and their respective staffs upon war plans and enterprises to be undertaken during the campaigns of 1943 against Germany, Italy, and Japan."

But away from the cameras, out of earshot of the press, agreement had been hard to come by. Stalin had been too preoccupied with the struggle in the East to come to Casablanca. His Red Army had stopped the enemy invaders along a front that stretched for more than a thousand miles and was about to take the offensive against those he called the "German occupationists." But his losses had been staggering, supplies were still dangerously short, and he was sure Hitler could be counted on eventually to counterattack. The Soviet dictator continued to demand that the Allies open the second front in France he'd been calling for since Hitler's mechanized legions had stormed into Russia two years earlier and which he believed he had been promised for the spring of 1943 "at the latest."

American and British leaders were not agreed on how to respond or what should happen next. General Marshall still insisted that all their energies should be focused on preparing a cross-Channel invasion for late summer. Further adventures in the Mediterranean—"periphery-pecking," he called them— would only serve as a "suction pump," draining resources, straining manpower, and further delaying the great battle on which the European war's outcome would ultimately depend. If the British did not agree, he warned, the Americans would be forced to turn more attention—and manpower—to a Pacific counteroffensive.

But the British argued that a cross-Channel invasion before the year was out was simply impossible. German submarines were still sinking more ships in the North Atlantic than U.S. shipyards could replace. The Allies had no prospect of having the number of landing craft they would need to storm the French beaches. There were forty-seven German divisions in France and the Low Countries, with eighteen more in reserve, while the Allies would not be able to muster more than twenty-five in Britain before the rough seas of autumn made a successful crossing impossible. And the North African campaign, which had already slowed the preinvasion buildup in Britain, was turning into a protracted struggle. Hitler, unwilling to give up an inch of territory, had reacted to the landings in France's North African

Prime Minister Churchill and President Roosevelt meet the press at Casablanca, January 24, 1943.

colonies by occupying Vichy France and reinforcing his armies in Tunisia.

Churchill offered an alternative. "Why stick your head in the alligator's mouth at Brest," he asked, "when you can go to the Mediterranean and rip his soft underbelly?" Once the North African coast was cleared, the Allies should take Sicily. A swift victory there might knock Italy out of the war, he believed, and would lure German divisions away from the eastern front and northern France as well. Meanwhile, the best the Allies could do for the Russians was to concentrate on eliminating the U-boat menace that continued to choke off supplies and begin round-the-clock bombing of Germany itself.

The Americans finally agreed to put off the invasion of France once again and land in Sicily. (In exchange, the British agreed to support more aggressive action against Japan.) But before they

could mount an assault, they had to finish the job they had started in North Africa. Eisenhower promised Roosevelt that victory there would be his by mid-May.

Casablanca afforded one more opportunity for the newsreel cameras: a presidential visit with the troops. Twenty thousand American soldiers of the 9th Infantry Division were positioned every few yards along the city streets and the fifty miles of coastal road that led north to Medhia and Port Lyautey. Security was tight. No one was told who was coming; one rumor had it that Shirley Temple had flown in to visit her fans. Nor were the troops standing at attention allowed to look right or left as Roosevelt's convoy rolled by. But as his car passed, one GI could not contain himself. "I saw him!" he shouted. "He waved at me."

Twenty-two-year-old Corporal Charles Mann of Luverne didn't happen to be among the men who stood and waited for the mysterious dignitary that day. He belonged to the 9th Infantry, too, but his unit—part of the 60th Combat Team—was camped too far back from the road along which the president traveled to see him pass by. But he'd already endured the first and fiercest fighting Americans had experienced in the European theater. During the initial Torch landings in French Morocco, in November, his unit had been aboard the battered American destroyer *Dallas* as she shot her way up the Sebu River in the dark to seize the airport at Port Lyautey. The ship ran aground several times under Vichy fire and

Charles Mann

had fired back with three-inch batteries that had so much concussive power, Mann remembered, the paint on her decks cracked and peeled.

Mann was born at home on his father's four-hundred-acre farm north of Luverne and had been part of the first batch of Rock County draftees to leave for the war after Pearl Harbor. Since the landing, he'd mostly remained behind the lines, helping to guard the border against an invasion through Spanish Morocco that never came, and trying to accustom himself to a world about as different from the green, flat, fertile countryside back home as it was possible to imagine. Morocco was brown and hilly and arid. The men camped in groves of olive and cork trees. Arab children darted in and out among the tents, giving the "V for victory" sign, asking for chocolates and chewing gum, peddling figs and eggs that the men boiled in their helmets. "After all those C rations," Mann recalled, "they were pretty darn good."

As Mann and his unit performed their routine duties more than a thousand miles from the nearest Axis soldier, two Allied columns—one mostly British, one American—had pushed eastward into Tunisia with orders to take the deepwater ports of Tunis and Bizerte, more than four hundred miles away. Everything seemed to go wrong. Eisenhower, who had never commanded men in battle, was too preoccupied with the politics of working with the French to pay attention to battlefield details. There were too few supplies and too few vehicles. The single east–west railroad line was antiquated and in disrepair. The unpaved roads were worse. British and American commanders

A U.S. Ranger battalion moves toward the Tunisian front.

quarreled. Allied equipment proved no match for what the enemy could bring to bear against it: the splendid German Mark IV tanks with their big .88-caliber guns set so many American tanks ablaze that GIs began to call them Ronsons, after the cigarette lighter that was advertised as "guaranteed to light up the first time, every time." German warplanes dominated the skies, too, while inexperienced American pilots did so much damage among their own troops on the ground that in at least one sector GIs were ordered to fire at every plane that flew into range, no matter its markings: "If it flies, it dies." Then a cold, relentless rain had begun to fall, turning grass-covered airfields into bogs and making roads all but impassable.

The Allies had still outnumbered the enemy at Christmastime but were scattered through the treeless mountains, often uncoordinated, unable to make progress. With fresh Axis troops

pouring into Tunisia every day and Field Marshal Erwin Rommel's veteran Afrika Korps approaching through Libya to the east, Eisenhower abandoned hope of advancing further before the winter rains ended. He admitted privately to a friend, "Our operations to date have violated every recognized principle of war, are in conflict with all operational and logistical methods . . . and will be condemned, in their entirety, by all . . . War College classes for the next twenty-five years."

There was little he could do until March except build up his forces for a renewed assault. The Germans saw no reason to wait. Beginning in late January, they mounted a series of fast-moving attacks that seized Faïd Pass and sealed off eastern Tunisia, took the crossroads village of Sidi Bou Zid in a sandstorm, and then stormed through Kasserine Pass, overwhelming the untried, poorly led Americans of the II Corps. Rommel, who launched

The proud American crew on the opposite page stopped to pose with its medium General Lee tank after U.S. forces had overwhelmed Algeria's Vichy defenders during the first, heady days of the North African campaign. They would soon confront the far more formidable Germans, commanded by

Field Marshal Erwin Rommel (above), as part of an Allied pincer campaign (below) in which American and British forces were meant to come at them from the west while General Bernard Montgomery's British forces pursued them from the east.

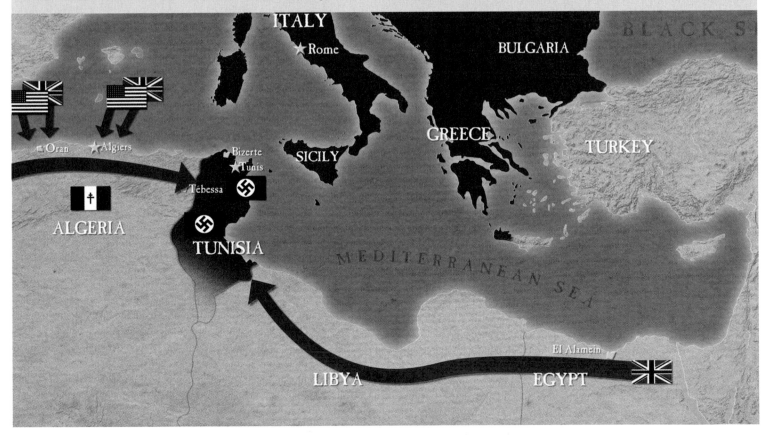

ITALY
★Rome
BULGARIA
BLACK S

Oran ★Algiers
Bizerte
★Tunis
SICILY
GREECE
TURKEY
Tébessa
ALGERIA
TUNISIA
MEDITERRANEAN SEA
El Alamein
LIBYA
EGYPT

Fresh American graves in Tunisia

the third attack, did so, he said, to instill in the Americans "an inferiority complex of no mean order." He succeeded, at least for the moment. The Americans, one reporter wrote, were "swamped, scattered, consumed by the German surprise." Sergeant John Goeske from Luverne never forgot his first glimpse of German tanks advancing "with the purpose of exterminating us. . . . You just can't believe they're mad at you." An officer described the aftermath of one German strafing, early in the three weeks of battle, that left fifty dead or wounded.

It was the most terrible thing I had ever seen. Not the bodies and parts of bodies near smoking vehicles, some sitting, some scattered, some blue from powder burns—it was the expressions on the faces of those [who] wandered listlessly around the wreckage, not knowing where to go or what to do, saying, "This can't happen to us."

Some men held. Others panicked. Survivors fled westward across the open plain. Some did not stop for nearly sixty miles. Six thousand Americans were lost. Nearly three thousand more surrendered before massed U.S. artillery made the Germans hesitate and a shortage of fuel and fear of an attack on their rear by British General Bernard Montgomery's Eighth Army forced them to fall back again.

The British were appalled. Americans simply didn't know how to fight, one commander said. They were "soft, green, and quite untrained"; if they didn't shape up quickly, they "will be quite useless and play no part whatsoever." Privately, some British officers dismissed GIs as "our Italians."

Ernie Pyle was with the stunned Americans during what he called the "awful nights of fleeing, crawling and hiding from death." He saw it as his duty to convey to American families as much as the censors and his own sensibilities would allow of what life for their sons was really like. "You folks at home must be disappointed at what happened to our American troops in Tunisia," he wrote after Kasserine Pass. "So are we here." He continued:

Correspondents are not now permitted to write anything critical, or to tell what we think was wrong. The powers that be feel that this would be bad for "home morale." So you just have to trust that our forces are learning to do better next time.

Personally, I feel that some such setback as this—tragic though it is for many Americans, for whom it is now too late—is not entirely a bad thing for us. It is all right to have a good opinion of yourself, but we Americans are so smug with our cockiness. We somehow feel that just because we're Americans we can whip our weight in wildcats.

ON MONDAY, FEBRUARY 15, as the Germans in Tunisia were driving the Americans from their positions at Sidi Bou Zid, Sascha Weinzheimer, now ten years old, her mother, her sister, Doris, and her baby brother, Buddy, had reported to the gate of the Santo Tomas Internment Camp in Manila. Her father was waiting just inside to greet them; he'd been a Japanese captive for almost fourteen months, so long that his infant son wasn't exactly sure who he was. He'd insisted that his family stay out of the camp the Japanese had established for enemy aliens as long as they could, so they had taken shelter first in one convent and then in another. But after several disturbing incidents—a Japanese soldier had grabbed at Sascha's mother at the vegetable market, a family friend was taken in for questioning and beaten so badly he could barely walk, and Sascha herself reported that just outside her physical therapist's house several soldiers had drowned a Filipino boy—her parents decided they would be safer in the prison than outside it. "Anyway," her mother said as she bowed to the Japanese sentry and led her children inside, "the next time we go through these gates we will be free."

"Everything was such a rush and hurry with crowds all around us after that," Sascha noted in her journal. More than 3,500 prisoners crowded the dusty fifty-three-acre compound, closed off by high masonry walls on three sides and barbed wire on the fourth. Three quarters of the internees were American. Twenty percent were classified as "British," though there were Canadians and Australians and a handful of Indians and Burmese among them. But there were also people from Holland, Norway, Russia, Poland, France, Egypt, Nicaragua, China, Mexico. Men and women were strictly segregated at night: Sascha's father slept amid some seven hundred other men in the gymna-

sium; Sascha, her siblings, and her mother were assigned to a small classroom in the wooden annex that already held seven women and nine children. "Mother got all mixed up," Sascha wrote. "There was so much to do. Buddy wouldn't go out of her arms. . . . Besides, it was so noisy, just like a carnival all day long."

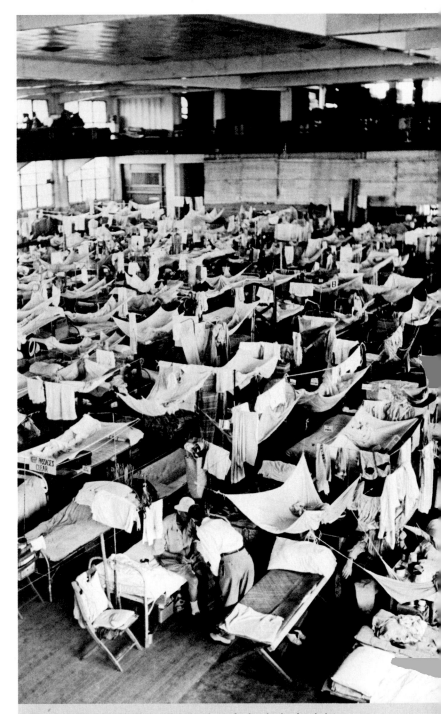

The gymnasium at Santo Tomas, nighttime home for hundreds of male internees: "Those who could sleep snored and choked, ground their teeth and cried and talked in their sleep," one resident remembered. "One man sang regularly. Every half-hour or so, someone would have a nightmare."

Early in their captivity, internees at Santo Tomas were allowed to publish a mimeographed newsletter, the *Internews*. Its editors also printed up this mock

diploma making light of some of the trials through which the captives had already passed. Before long, those trials would no longer be a laughing matter.

The family was permitted to spend the daylight hours together in one of some six hundred tiny, open-sided bamboo-and-thatch shanties that prosperous internees eventually built in miniature "districts" to which they gave all-American names: Hollywood and Glamorville, Toonerville and Jerkville and Jungletown. The Weinzheimers' shanty stood between Garden Court and Froggy Bottom on the edge of the camp's vegetable garden.

"We had to stand in line from early morning till night," Sascha noted.

You had to start right in when it got light and go like sixty or you would be left behind. We got up about six every morning, dressed fast, Daddy would already be in the chow line with our meal tickets and tin cans. Mother would try to get the beds made with Buddy in one arm, sweep and mop up our space, and get us out to the shanty where daddy would have breakfast ready. . . . Mother said that no matter what happened we would eat off our bridge table with a table cloth

with our colored dishes and small bowl of flowers so long as we could. . . . We kept it up when later there wasn't much to put on the plates.

There were lines for everything: dishwashing, bread, laundry, the understaffed clinic, and the inadequate toilets (just one for every one hundred internees). Everyone was expected to work, Sascha wrote. "It was funny to see bank presidents and other men like that cleaning toilets and garbage cans. There were all kinds of people in camp. Some were hard workers, like Daddy, others were gripers who liked to talk a lot and goldbricks who didn't do anything at all." Her father helped oversee the cleaning of the kitchen. Four times a week, Sascha and her mother took their turn on duty in one of the bathrooms, handing out sheets of toilet paper—four per visitor initially, then two, then one. There were no stalls in the bathrooms, no partitions in the showers. A sign read IF YOU WANT PRIVACY, CLOSE YOUR EYES.

Despite it all, Sascha noted, "Doris and I liked it a lot at first. The family was together again and it was fun seeing so many kids

I used to know. . . . At this time there was still enough food so some people could give some away and you could buy peanuts, peanut brittle, and chocolate and chocolate fudge."

The Japanese had initially refused either to feed or to clothe the foreign civilians they'd rounded up. They were not prisoners, their captors claimed; they were merely being kept "in protective custody" and therefore expected to care for themselves. (It was never clear just who they were being protected from, of course, and they were undeniably prisoners; when three internees tried to escape shortly after Santo Tomas opened, they were brought back, severely beaten within earshot of the whole camp, and then shot without trial as a warning to anyone else who might consider running away.) The American Red Cross had done what it could for the internees in the early days, and the Japanese-sanctioned Philippine Red Cross that replaced it had tried hard, too. Only when its funds ran out—it was also responsible for feeding eighty thousand Filipino civilians in Manila—did the Imperial Army grudgingly agree to provide money with which the internees could purchase food for themselves.

An Executive Committee made up of prominent business-men among the captives saw to the buying and did its best to ensure that everything else went smoothly as well. "Americans are fiends for organization," one man recalled. "We had committees within committees for the purpose of organizing further committees to delegate work": Discipline, Gardening, Lost and Found, Music, Public Relations, Recreating, Religious Service, Suggestions and Complaints, and more. Every room had an elected monitor. Each shantytown had a mayor. A Committee on Order was empowered to jail troublemakers, a twelve-man liquor patrol ferreted out smugglers, and a "morality patrol" struggled to keep teenagers from disappearing together into dark corners. Adult men and women were supposed to be kept apart, too, and when several women got pregnant anyway, the Japanese jailed their husbands for thirty days as punishment.

The anxiety and overcrowding at Santo Tomas brought out the best in some internees and the worst in others. "It was human nature condensed," one recalled. One man spent his days repairing the wooden sandals everyone wore and refused to take a penny for his work. Another made a small fortune renting out his bed on the third-floor landing of the Education Building to interned prostitutes and their clients at one peso a go; when he got caught, he lightened his punishment by betraying to the Japanese several servicemen who had been posing as civilians. There was sometimes hard feeling between those internees who lacked the money to build themselves shanties or buy extras from outside and those they called "the Manila people" and the "shanty aristocracy," who nearly every day received packages of food and supplies lovingly packed by friends and former servants. "It used to aggravate a lot of us to smell their pork chops frying," one shantyless man remembered, "while our tin can 'dishes' held nothing but musty, moldy, and bug-peppered 'line chow.' "

Members of the Executive Committee came under criticism, too. They used their connections to raise funds that benefited the whole camp, but they were also accused of favoring friends and sometimes denounced as overly cooperative with the Japanese commandant, Colonel A. Kodaki. Stateside prejudices were reflected at Santo Tomas, as well, and at least sometimes were transcended. When the Executive Committee asked the fifty-odd African American internees if they wanted their own committee, they declined. "We do not wish to stand apart," they said. "We are all Americans here."

Behind walls, "your world becomes very small," Sascha Weinzheimer remembered many years later. "And you don't think beyond your little environment, because everything that's important to you is right there. It's not in the States, it's not back at the plantation, it's right there. So you have to make do with what you can in this small sphere." She found solace reading in the shade provided by the thick planting her father had placed around the family shanty. "I would lie under the leaves," she remembered, "and feel safe."

Her grandfather in California blamed himself for having encouraged his sons and their families to stay in the Philippines until it was too late. Ever since Pearl Harbor, he had peppered the State Department and the Red Cross with letters and telegrams pleading for some word of them:

> Can you furnish me with the exact status of my two sons Walter Weinzheimer and Conrad Ludwig Weinzheimer who were American citizens but resided in the Philippines at the outbreak of the war stop Are they military or civilian prisoners, dead or alive or missing stop

A handful of Britons at Santo Tomas had received letters and been able to send replies by the time the Weinzheimers were reunited inside the camp, but Americans as yet had no way to communicate with the outside world. When the old man eventually did get indirect word that his sons and their families were alive and interned in Manila, he frantically began seeking some way to have them released and repatriated. Again he got nowhere.

When 127 American internees were eventually released and sent to Shanghai, many of those left behind were outraged. "The [U.S.] government sent a list of names of people they wanted [mostly diplomats], which was only about 65," Sascha wrote.

Camp O'Donnell, spruced up for a Japanese propaganda photograph. Out of camera range, scores of prisoners were dying every day.

The rest were supposed to be picked from the sick people. . . . I know there were many angry people in camp because only a couple of the sick ones were chosen . . . the rest were perfectly well people. . . . These people were friends of the Nips, I guess, especially of Mr. Kodaki, the commandant. He liked the ladies very much. That's why he allowed some healthy, but very good-looking young women to go on that ship. Mother said I'd better not put down their names.

When it came time for Commandant Kodaki to turn Santo Tomas over to his successor that fall, he would formally thank the internees for their cooperation over the past months and urge them to continue in that spirit. Then he offered an under-

stated but chilling warning: Remember, he said, they would be treated magnanimously only *"so long as Japan is winning."*

WHETHER JAPAN WAS WINNING OR LOSING made little difference to the treatment Corporal Glenn Frazier and his fellow prisoners of war were receiving at Japanese hands. By the time Sascha Weinzheimer entered Santo Tomas, Frazier had already been living in Japan for three months, an inmate of POW Camp #1 at Osaka, on the southern coast of the main island of Honshu.

His journey there had been a continuation of the neglect and brutality he'd first experienced during the forced march from Mariveles to Camp O'Donnell, and he'd come close to death so many times he'd lost count.

Back in June of 1943, he thought he'd found a way to escape the nightmare of Camp O'Donnell, where some fifteen hundred Americans had already died of wounds, disease, and neglect, and scores more were dying every day. When the Japanese called for men to serve on work details away from camp, he eagerly volunteered.

My idea was to get out of there, because it was a hellhole. They didn't tell us where we were going or what we were going to do. But they asked for three hundred, approximately three hundred men. So all the guys that wanted to go on details lined up, and they came through and picked us out. And they took us by truck and train and another march of about twenty-something miles into the jungles of southern Luzon.

There they were to carve a road through dense jungle linking the northern and southern parts of the island so Japanese forces could speed from one to the other in case of Allied attack. No provision had been made for their care. They camped out in the open on the bank of the Basaid River. There was no shelter from the sun. Drinking water was fouled by Japanese cavalrymen and their horses, camped just upstream. Leeches hung from the men's ankles and left ulcerating sores when burned off. Their clothes became rags. Their faces and hands were perpetually black from the charcoal they ate to fight off the dysentery that steadily thinned their ranks. Guards forced the ten-man crews to race one another with their wheelbarrows filled with earth and rocks, shouting, "Speedo! Speedo!" and slashing at their legs with bamboo staves when they thought them too slow.

"Guys started dying within the first week," Frazier remembered. "And we got so weak we couldn't hardly work. It was the worst detail, I think, that was ever arranged." By the time the rains halted work in midsummer and the Japanese got ready to truck the Americans to Bilibid Prison in Manila, only some twenty-six men in Frazier's group were thought strong enough to make the trip. The U.S. medical officer on the scene helped scratch out a shallow grave for the handful who would have to stay behind, then administered to each a fatal dose of morphine so they could simply sleep their lives away.

Frazier and his companions were so weak that they had to be helped onto the truck. One man died during the long, rattling road trip, and when the truck finally reached Bilibid, Frazier and the rest fell to the ground while trying to get off. By then, they

were so covered with their own excrement that navy corpsmen refused to carry them inside the compound until Filipinos with a firehose could be summoned to wash them down.

Bilibid was a ninety-five-year-old prison, condemned by the Philippine government before the war as unfit even for criminals. The Japanese packed it with more than a thousand POWs. Frazier spent almost two months there. He recovered from dysentery but grew so thin he could no longer stand and developed sores wherever his protruding bones contacted the bare concrete floor on which he was forced to sleep. Then, he and forty-seven other prisoners from Bilibid were trucked to the Manila waterfront and prodded aboard a rusty, rat-infested freighter called the *Totoru Maru*. Also aboard were nearly three thousand other POWs on their way to Korea and Japan to serve as unpaid laborers for the emperor. Sixteen men died en route and everyone aboard the ship might have perished had two Allied submarines not boiled harmlessly past her sides. (During the war, some fifty thousand Allied POWs were shipped to Japan aboard similar so-called hellships. Eleven thousand of them are thought to have died on the way to Japan, most sunk by Allied pilots and submarine commanders who had no way of knowing who was aboard.)

Frazier's new home at Osaka had seemed to promise a better life, at least at first. Wooden barracks provided shelter. There were straw mats to sleep on and there seemed to be a little more food on hand than there had been in the Philippines. But the treatment the men received was no less brutal. Beatings were routine. The six days of hard labor that Frazier and his fellow prisoners were made to perform on the wharves and in Osaka's foundries each week sapped their strength. And they never knew when something they did would trigger a violent reaction by their captors.

One day that February, Frazier remembered,

I was coming back from a detail on the street in Osaka. Japan's cold in the wintertime. And I put my hands in my pockets and I'm walking along with everybody else in this formation. When we got to the gate and they checked us in, this guard called me out and said, "Why did you have your hands in your pockets?"

And I said, "Because I was cold."

So they took me into the commanding major's office. He said to me through the interpreter, "That's against the military code. Soldiers do not walk with hands in pockets."

And I said, "Well, I'm not a soldier, I'm a prisoner of war."

The major banged his fist on his desk, shouted something in Japanese, then drew his sword and held it against Frazier's throat. "He's going to make an example of you," the interpreter told Frazier, "so the other men will understand they have to obey orders."

> *So he nicked me a little bit, and I could feel a little bit of blood coming down.*
>
> *The interpreter said, "He's going to execute you."*
>
> *So he asked me if I had any last words to say. And I looked him straight in the eye and I said, "He can kill me, but he cannot kill my spirit. And my spirit's going to lodge in his body and haunt him until the day he dies."*
>
> *The interpreter told him what I said. The major frowned and took three steps backward and lowered his sword. I had never seen a Japanese back down in front of anybody until that particular time. Because once they got to that point, they went through with it regardless of the results.*

The major ordered Frazier thrown into solitary confinement, a covered five-by-five-foot pit in the middle of the yard. The top was bolted down, and he was forced to spend seven days and nights in total darkness, subsisting on handfuls of rice and sips from a bottle of water. To keep from going mad, Frazier focused on thoughts of home.

> *I would think about the things that I missed most, like ice cream and potato salad and some ambrosia that my mother used to make for Christmas. And of course I had always thought we would get back home. But I got to the point where I was so weak I couldn't even remember whether I had sisters or brothers. I couldn't even remember their names. And it comes a time when you think, "Did I have a home, did I have a family?"*

At that point, he began to think more and more about the hometown girl whose courting by another had driven him to join the army in the first place.

> *The thing that really kept me going was to come back and see if that girl was still there, and see if I still in my heart was crazy about her. And also the fact that I wanted to live. I did not want my body pushing up Japanese daisies. And I just felt that-a-way, and I thought, "They gonna have a heck of a time getting me in a casket."*

Neither Glenn Frazier nor Sascha Weinzheimer nor anyone else in Japanese hands as yet had much realistic hope of rescue. There had been important victories on Guadalcanal and New Guinea, and at Casablanca the Allies had agreed in principle that 30 percent of their resources would be devoted to defeating the Japanese. But forces in the southeastern Pacific were still too small to destroy the big air and navy base at Rabaul, no progress at all had been made in the Central Pacific, and more than a year after Pearl Harbor, there was still no fully worked-out plan to defeat the Japanese or take back the Philippines. At this rate, one newspaperman said, "we won't get to Tokyo until 1960."

"POWERFUL ENEMIES MUST BE OUTFOUGHT and outproduced," President Roosevelt had told Congress and his countrymen less than a month after Pearl Harbor. "It is not enough to turn out just a few more planes, a few more tanks, a few more guns, a few more ships, than can be turned out by our enemies. We must outproduce them overwhelmingly, so that there can be no question of our ability to provide a crushing superiority of equipment in any theater of the world war."

Industries already engaged in defense work expanded. Others, like the automobile industry, were transformed completely. In 1941, more than 3 million cars were manufactured in the United States. Only 139 more were made during the entire war. Instead, Chrysler made fuselages. General Motors turned to fighter planes. Packard made Rolls-Royce engines for the British air force. And at its vast Willow Run plant in Ypsilanti, Michigan—sixty-seven acres of assembly lines under a single roof—which Charles Lindbergh called "the Grand Canyon of the mechanized world," the Ford Motor Company performed something like a miracle, twenty-four hours a day. The average Ford car had some 15,000 parts. The B-24 Liberator long-range bomber had 1,550,000. One came off the line at Willow Run every sixty-three minutes.

The chronic unemployment that had haunted America for more than a decade ended. Personal income nearly doubled. Eight million women entered the American workforce. The whole country seemed to be on the move. Sixteen million men left home to enter military service. Twenty-four million more moved in search of defense work: eight million from one state to another, four million to a wholly new region. Between 1940 and 1945, the populations of Washington, Oregon, and California grew by more than one-third. With unprecedented prosperity came growth, change—and dislocation.

The disruption caused by the war, the loneliness experienced by men and women forced apart, the feeling that the next day might be one's last, the opportunities for sexual adventure afforded to young men in their prime—all affected the most

On December 7, 1942, the first anniversary of the Japanese attack on Pearl Harbor, the brand-new battleship *New Jersey* slips down the ways at the Philadelphia Navy Yard.

From coast to coast, American industry performed miracles of manufacturing during the war. At a Hartford, Connecticut, aviation plant (left), a banner exhorts workers to keep turning out propellers at the same frenetic pace, while workers at Douglas Aviation in Long Beach, California, swarm over an unfinished B-17 (above) and polish gleaming Plexiglas noses (right), intended for more bombers being assembled nearby.

intimate aspects of American life. The birthrate rose for the first time in two decades as a generation of "goodbye babies" was born. The marriage rate climbed steadily, until the draft began to cut into the supply of eligible bachelors. The divorce rate soared, too.

The rate of female alcoholism rose fivefold. Arrests for female juvenile delinquency rose by many times that rate, and newspaper editors worried aloud about teenaged girls who seemed willing to sleep with anyone in uniform. They were "khaki-wacky," "patriotutes," "Victory Girls."

A serviceman's joke went, "I'm going to Walgreens to meet a girl."

"What's her name?"

"How should I know?"

The War Department did what it could to scare men into celibacy. Then it gave in, providing "prophylaxis stations" that distributed 50 million condoms a month. Some commanders even set up brothels for their men. According to one survey, three out of four servicemen sought female companionship—and found it.

EARLY IN THE WAR, the novelist John Dos Passos began a fact-finding trip across America to see what the conflict was doing to his country. He traveled from Detroit to New Orleans and from Portland, Maine, to Portland, Oregon, in search of signs of change. As soon as his bus pulled into Mobile in mid-March of 1943, it was clear to him that no city he had seen so far had been so completely transformed.

> *The mouldering old Gulf seaport with its ancient dusty elegance of tall shuttered windows under mansard roofs and iron lace overgrown with vines, and scaling colonnades shaded by great trees, looks trampled and battered like a city that's been taken by storm. Sidewalks are crowded. Gutters are stacked with litter that drifts back and forth in the brisk spring wind. Garbage cans are overflowing. Frame houses on treeshaded streets bulge with men in shirtsleeves who spill out onto the porches and trampled grassplots and stand in knots at the street corners. . . .*
>
> *And all the while, by every bus and train the new people, white and black, pour into the city. As fast as a new block of housing is finished, it's jampacked. As soon as a new bus is put into service, it's weighed down with passengers. The schools are too full of children. The restaurants are too full of eaters.*

In early 1940, Mobile County had had fewer than 142,000 citizens. Less than five years later that figure would climb to 231,000. The War Manpower Commission declared Mobile "the most congested shipyard center in the country."

The war was the cause of Mobile's hectic growth, but the Honorable Frank Boykin was the catalyst. He was a flamboyant millionaire politician whom one Washington columnist called "Mobile's brass-drum congressman." When he learned, long before Pearl Harbor, that General Henry "Hap" Arnold, commander of the army air forces, planned to establish a supply depot and bomber-modification center somewhere on the Gulf coast, he outmaneuvered boosters from Tampa, Florida, to win his district the $26 million defense contract that transformed the dusty municipal airport into Brookley Field. It would eventually provide seventeen thousand civilian jobs and an annual payroll of nearly $90 million. Then, under further pressure from Boykin, the War Department had gone on to sign multimillion-dollar contracts with local shipyards. In 1940, Gulf Shipbuilding had had 240 employees; by the time Dos Passos came to town, 11,600 men and women were at work there, building destroyers and minesweepers, cargo carriers and the big crude supply vessels called Liberty Ships. In the same period, Alabama Dry Dock and Shipbuilding Company—known to those who worked for it as ADDSCO—went from one thousand workers to almost thirty thousand. Hank Williams, the future country music star, was one of them; so was the father of the future home-run hitter Hank Aaron.

Mobile had become a magnet for people from all over the South. Dos Passos watched them stream through the bus station.

> *Soldiers, sailors, stout women with bundled up babies, lanky backwoodsmen with hats tipped over their brows and a cheek full of chewing tobacco, hatless young men in light-colored sport shirts open at the neck, countrymen with creased red necks and well washed overalls, cigarsmoking stocky men in business suits in pastel shades, girls in bright dresses with hair carefully piled up on their heads and highheeled shoes and bloodred fingernails, withered nutbrown old people with glasses carrying ruptured suitcases, broad-*

Emma Belle Petcher

shouldered men in oilstained khaki with shiny brown helmets on their heads, negroes in flap jackets and pegtop pants and little felt hats with turned-up brims, teenage boys in jockey caps, here and there a flustered negro woman dragging behind her a string of white-eyed children.

Seventeen-year-old Emma Belle Petcher had arrived in Mobile the previous year. Otherwise, she might have been part of that throng. She was from the little Alabama town of Millry. "When I got out of high school, everyone had gone to Mobile to work," she recalled. "So I packed my little cardboard suitcase and got on the bus to Mobile and went to the armory, where they was giving the tests and exams to see where they would place you." She was a beautiful young woman—airmen at Brookley Field later sometimes mistook her for the film star Ingrid Bergman—and she had a mind of her own. Most of the girls with whom she'd gone to school came to Mobile hoping to land a secretarial job. "But that wasn't my cup of tea," she said.

I'm creative, so I liked the challenge of finding what's wrong with things. Growing up, I always fixed my own appliances at home. If the washing machine got a nail in the pump, I didn't have the patience to call in a repairman who couldn't come for three days and then wouldn't tell you morning or evening. So I'd empty the washing machine, turn it upside down, take the screwdriver and get that nail out of the housing myself. I knew how to do all this stuff. And even if I didn't know how to do it, I experimented. My neighbors would bring me things to fix, like mixers and irons or heating pads or small appliances. And I enjoyed doing it.

So they put me in a school to learn airplane accessories: starters, generators, alternators, and some other things. We did those little instruments, over and over and over until we could almost put them together blindfolded. We couldn't

BUY A BOND TODAY

Over the course of the war, the U.S. government would spend more than $321 billion—well over $3 trillion in today's terms, twice as much as it had spent in the previous 150 years. The national debt rose from $49 billion in 1941 to $259 billion in 1945.

Greatly increased income taxes provided much of the needed revenue. When the war began, fewer than 4 million Americans paid federal income taxes; by its end, more than 40 million did. But the government also borrowed some $185 billion through the sale of war bonds. Banks, insurance companies, and corporations bought up the bulk of them, but millions of ordinary citizens took part in the series of eight war loan drives as well. "There are millions of people who say, 'What can we do to help?' " Treasury Secretary Henry Morgenthau, Jr., explained to the press as he introduced the first campaign; investing in war bonds would give every American not fighting overseas "a chance to do something." Madison Avenue enlisted in the effort: movie stars and radio entertainers toured the country; Hedy Lamarr sold kisses at $25,000 each; over the course of one sixteen-hour marathon radio broadcast, the

Bonds for sale on payday in a Mobile shipyard (opposite page) and being advertised at Chicago's Union Station

singer Kate Smith collected some $40 million in called-in pledges.

In Mobile, a worker at Brookley Field named John Cottingham invested all but eight cents of his paycheck in bonds each month, and the local Negro League baseball team, the Black Bears, staged a double-header that raised $100,000. The citizens of Sacramento were asked to buy $16 million worth of bonds during one drive—and were told it would pay for ninety-six minutes of the war. In Waterbury, bonds were sold from a "Liberty House," set up on the site in the middle of the town green where similar bonds had been sold to help defeat Germany during the First World War.

And in Luverne, Mrs. Maude Jochims, who owned and ran the Palace movie

theater with her husband, played an important part in local sales. Shortly after Pearl Harbor she helped arrange to have an automobile that had been riddled with machine-gun bullets during the Japanese attack parked in front of the marquee to stimulate bond buyers. In October of 1942, she took a still more active role. "They can send all the movie stars they want on country-wide War Bond sales drives," Al McIntosh wrote then, "but for our part we'll take Maude Jochims as the best bond salesman, or saleswoman, of them all. We stopped in at the Palace Wednesday afternoon. They were going to fall $8,000 short. Then Maude—as a one-woman campaign—waded in to canvass Rock County patrons. The bond orders poured in and the total was boosted over $48,000."

Bonds were available everywhere: at movie theaters in Washington, D.C. (opposite),
at the Beaver Creek post office just west of Luverne (opposite, above),
and at a workers' rally at the Scovill Manufacturing plant in Waterbury.

MAKING THE BEST OF IT

By September of 1942, some 110,000 people of Japanese ancestry, citizens and aliens alike, who had once lived along the Pacific coast, had been rounded up and shipped to ten inland relocation camps: Manzanar and Tule Lake in eastern California; Minidoka in Idaho; Topaz in Utah; Poston and Gila River in Arizona; Heart Mountain in Wyoming; Amache in Colorado; and Jerome and Rohwer in Arkansas. Wherever they were sent, however they were made to live, the internees acted like the Americans they were.

The sign at the left stood just outside Tule Lake, where the high schoolers (opposite page, bottom right) found themselves attending classes in a tar-paper shack they had yet to name and the young men beneath the flag registered for the draft. At Amache (opposite page, top and bottom center), enterprising women set up a hair-dressing salon in one of the flimsy barracks that were typical of those at all the camps. Camp housing was so cheaply built, National Director of the War Relocation Authority Milton Eisenhower told the Senate, that "frankly, if it stands up for the duration we are going to be lucky." The little girl and her music teacher below performed their patriotic number at Topaz.

Saturday afternoon softball
at Amache, 1943

would always go toward the black section. But they would turn me around and put me in the white.

Hawaiians, Kashiwagi continued, were unused to any such restrictions and "acted like they were at home." When they went into Hattiesburg, the nearest town, they drank from whichever water fountain they fancied, used whatever restroom happened to be empty, and, as Susumu Satow remembered, refused to be bullied by white soldiers at the USO.

There were a lot of people there that were very frustrated to see the Japanese individuals dancing with the white girls. And so they would start a fight. And naturally, those fellows from Hawaii, they acted like a wolf pack, and they just wouldn't be pushed around. And they would take these people down. They just ganged up on these taller, bigger white people and kicked their faces in. And there was one prejudiced bus driver that was very pushy. And so these boys stayed in the bus until the end of the run and then they pulled that bus driver out and almost killed him. And then our commanding officer got us together and gave us a rude awakening. He says, "You boys will need to straighten out. And if you continue something like this again," he said, "we're going to return you all back to camp and throw those keys away." And so then after that we had to kind of quiet down a little bit.

For a time, kotonks and buddhaheads continued to keep their distance from one another, Inouye recalled.

And this caused a great problem for our officers. At one point, they even considered disbanding the regiment because they felt we could not serve together as brothers. And that's when somebody had the great idea to choreograph a situation where some of us who were from Hawaii were invited to go to one of the [relocation] camps in Arkansas. I was invited to go to Rohwer.

Inouye and his friends clambered onto a truck. It started out as a lighthearted trip. The men played ukuleles and sang. There was talk of the girls they hoped would be waiting to dance with them. Then they swung around a bend in the road and got their first look at a relocation camp: block upon block of barracks surrounded by swampland; men, women, and children who looked like members of their own families, trapped behind barbed wire by armed men wearing the same uniforms they were wearing.

The laughter and the singing stopped. The internees made them welcome. There was food and music and dancing. But when the men climbed back into the truck for the return trip to Camp Shelby, Inouye remembered, there was absolute silence.

On our way back, something haunted me, and it's haunted me forever. Would I have volunteered if I were in that camp? And I think all the other fellows who were in that truck must have asked themselves the same question. Because it's easy to volunteer when your neighbors are good to you, America's good to you, and no one discriminates against you. And here are a group of men who look like us and their families and their little sisters and brothers, all in the barracks. You know, I can't answer that question. I don't know if I would have volunteered. But when we got back to the camp, immediately, [the mainlanders] became our brothers. You know, these guys were special that they would, even under those extreme conditions, volunteer. They were better than us.

In June 1943, the men of the 100th Infantry Battalion set sail for the European theater. The 442nd was to remain in training in Mississippi until the following spring.

IN NORTH AFRICA, not long after the American debacle at Kasserine Pass, Charles Mann's outfit, the 60th Combat Team, finally made it to the Tunisian front. "Our first Americans had done a very poor job," Mann remembered, but prospects now looked brighter. Supply and transport problems had been resolved: Mann's unit moved in a seemingly endless column of brown-painted military vehicles filled with men and matériel, and when it went into battle, it was provided real air cover by American planes.

Eisenhower had restructured the Allied top command, too, and placed in charge of the battered II Corps General George S. Patton, whose son-in-law had been captured by the Germans at Kasserine Pass. Patton was a swaggering showman—he wore gleaming cavalry boots and twin ivory-handled six-shooters into combat—but he was also a master of tank warfare. The men resented the discipline he insisted on imposing—a soldier could be fined twenty-five dollars for failing to wear his helmet—but they were reassured by his repeated pledge to "kick the bastards out of Africa."

"We had faith in him that he would eventually get it done and beat them suckers," Mann recalled, and by the third week of March, American, British, and Free French Forces were once again on the offensive, shoving the enemy back toward the sea as Montgomery's Eighth Army attacked their eastern flank. "We were so thankful for the training we had," Mann continued. "Even though we hated it when they made us do the same thing over and over a thousand times. You were afraid but you were

American wounded in North Africa: "They hadn't been paid and they couldn't get trace of their friends and they didn't know where they would be sent," one correspondent wrote after visiting a field hospital, "but still they didn't complain much, and they said calmly that they guessed it was enough just to be alive."

thinking pretty clearly. Otherwise, somebody else would have lost their lives because you didn't perform your duties."

Mann was thinking especially clearly on the morning of March 24, when he and his company were assigned to help take the treeless heights overlooking the village of Maknassy, in central Tunisia. As they climbed, two Germans in a machine-gun emplacement sent two of the distinctive stick grenades the Americans called potato-mashers clattering down toward them. Moving fast, Mann knocked them both out of the way before

they could hurt anyone. "You do what you have to do," he remembered. Then he threw a grenade of his own, "like you would a baseball." The German gun fell silent. But as he started up the hill again, a sniper to his left opened fire. A bullet tore through the stock of his rifle, hit metal, and shattered. Fragments ripped through two fingers. Another tore into Mann's neck, just missing the carotid artery. He "bled like a stuck hog," he remembered, until he could make it back to a medic, who managed to stanch the flow. He was airlifted out of the battle zone the following day. As the plane flew back over the Atlas Mountains, the officer in charge of the wounded asked the men if they'd like to hear some soothing music. "It was purely classical," Mann remembered. "That was music I'd hated all my life. But I enjoyed it then."

Blasted by U.S. artillery and tank fire, abandoned German armor burns in the Tunisian sun after the battle of the El Guettar valley, March 30, 1943. The victory won there, Omar Bradley would later write, was "the first, solid, indisputable defeat we inflicted on the Germans in the war," and it made a national hero out of the II Corps's new commander, General George S. Patton.

Below him, the Allies pushed on and eventually penned up the German and Italian armies on Cape Bon. On May 7, Tunis and Bizerte finally fell. On May 12—three days ahead of the deadline Eisenhower had set for himself at Casablanca—the last Axis troops in North Africa surrendered, a quarter of a million of them, in a line that stretched for nearly fourteen miles.

The lessons the Allies learned in North Africa came hard: some seventy-two thousand men had been lost in the six months since the Torch landings. But "one continent had been redeemed," as Churchill said. North Africa could now become a staging area for further action in the region, and the Allies had begun to demonstrate that they could work together in the field.

Had the U.S. Army that first failed in Tunisia tried to invade France instead of North Africa, as American commanders had initially wanted to do, wrote General Omar Bradley, it would have "resulted in an unthinkable disaster." Now, the hundred thousand men who made up four U.S. divisions understood firsthand what victory would require of them. "The most vivid change" among GIs since the Torch landings, Ernie Pyle wrote, was "the casual and workshop manner in which they now talk about killing."

They have made the psychological transition from the normal belief that taking human life is sinful, over to a new professional outlook where killing is a craft. To them now there is nothing morally wrong about killing. In fact it is an admirable thing. . . .

In this final phase of the Tunisian campaign we have yet to hear a word of criticism of our men. They fought like veterans. They were well handled. We had enough of what we needed. Everything meshed perfectly, and the end was inevitable. So you at home need never be ashamed of our American fighters. Even though they didn't do too well in the beginning, there was never at any time any question about the Americans' bravery.

It is a matter of being hardened and practiced by going through the flames. Tunisia has been a good warm-up field for our armies. . . . The greatest disservice you folks at home can do for our men over here is to believe we are at last over the hump. For actually—and over here we all know it—the worst is yet to come.

Thousands of Axis troops file into a prisoner-of-war compound at Mateur, just west of Tunis. The compound soon overflowed, a correspondent wrote, so "the Germans and Italians simply hung around the outskirts waiting to be taken in. A German band, complete with its instruments, had arrived. The bandsmen stood in a square and played soothing Viennese lieder."

ON TUESDAY MORNING, MAY 25, 1943—thirteen days after the last Axis soldier surrendered in Tunisia—the racial storm that had been building for months at the Alabama Dry Dock and Shipbuilding Company shipyard in Mobile finally broke. Nearly seven thousand African Americans worked at ADDSCO, all at unskilled jobs. For six months, management had avoided complying with the FEPC directive to upgrade those who were qualified. Then, on Monday evening, without a word of explanation to anyone, it promoted twelve black men to welding jobs and sent them to work on one of the shipways on Pinto Island. They acted as a separate crew, everything went peacefully, and when their shift ended, they went home without incident. But wild rumors were flying through the yards as they left: thousands of black workers were on the way; white women would be forced to work alongside them; one of the black welders had already killed a white woman.

Clyde Odum was supervising work in a machine shop on Pinto Island in Mobile Bay that morning when he heard angry voices outside. "What in the world's going on here?" he asked. "There's a big fight out front," someone answered. He rushed up onto the fantail of an unfinished hull to get a better view. Below him, Odum recalled, thousands of whites had turned on their black fellow workers, who were fleeing the shipways and trying to get back to the mainland.

It was war right there on that island, I'm telling you. It was real rough. I saw men and women, some of them with their shirts snatched off, bleeding, blood running down their face and their backs. And I said, "What in the world's going on here?" I never saw people so mad and agitated in my life. Men and women. And they had sticks three feet long. They would knock them down to their knees. The blacks didn't stand a chance coming down that gauntlet, with men and women on each side, beating them with sticks. They didn't attempt to fight, because they were outnumbered.

Whites were wielding wrenches and lengths of pipe as well as sticks. ADDSCO security guards did nothing to stop the attacks. Some even joined in. When a white worker who had been a football star at the University of Alabama tried to intervene, he was clubbed to the ground. Some men and women jumped into the bay to escape the mob and had to be rescued by the coast guard. At least eighty were injured before troops arrived from Brookley Field to stop the attacks. Only four whites were arrested; three of those were never even charged. When the editor of the *Mobile Register* criticized a local judge for letting the fourth off with a fine, the judge cited him for contempt and ordered him to jail for six hours.

Until their safety could be guaranteed, African American workers refused to return to ADDSCO. "They were afraid to go back," John Gray remembered, "because there would be a bunch [of whites] standing outside, and in their cars they'd have monkey wrenches and tire irons." More than a thousand approached the War Manpower Commission formally to request transfers to other defense jobs. The requests were denied. Some left Mobile altogether. But in the end, Clyde Odum remembered, most did come back, "because we begged them to come back. We needed them."

The shipyard itself was then formally segregated. Four separate shipways were created where black men and women were free to hold every kind of position—except foreman. Those working elsewhere at ADDSCO would remain confined to the kind of unskilled tasks they had always performed. Walter White, executive secretary of the NAACP, denounced the compromise as "the surrender of Mobile." The Pittsburgh *Courier* called it a victory for "Nazi racial theory and another defeat for the principle embodied in the Declaration of Independence." But peace had been restored, the shipyard resumed production of the ships the Allies desperately needed, and some seven thousand African Americans made more money than they had ever made before.

There were racial confrontations in forty-seven cities around the country that year: in Springfield, Massachusetts, and Port Arthur, Texas; in Hubbard, Ohio, and Newark, New Jersey; and in Detroit, where thirty-five people were killed and more than

The Mobile Compromise: following the race riot at ADDSCO, guards enforce strict segregation on the company ferry.

two hundred were wounded. But despite the bitterness, beyond the violence, the war was profoundly altering life for African Americans. More than half a million left the South in search of better lives during the war, and more than a million joined the industrial workforce for the first time. New hopes were being raised—and some, at least, were being fulfilled.

The same hopes would eventually affect the armed services as well. The Selective Service Act expressly forbade the intermingling of "colored and white" draftees, and despite the argument made by the NAACP and others that "a Jim Crow army cannot fight for a free world," the War Department refused to overturn that policy. Blacks were barred from frontline combat, at least at first, and asked instead to perform in uniform the menial tasks many had performed as civilians. Some men refused to serve in the segregated armed forces—and were imprisoned for it. There were frequent and sometimes bloody confrontations between black troops and white civilians, black troops and white ones.

Maintaining separate units was wasteful and demeaning, undemocratic and absurd—even blood plasma was stored separately. But Washington did its best to defend the indefensible. The script for a film aimed at recruiting African Americans to serve as navy stewards, the highest rank open to them in the early part of the war, tried to make segregation seem not only reasonable but patriotic:

> *Responsibility for having the ship in the right place at the right time, and for the efficiency and safety of her crew, rests upon the [white] officers aboard—officers who, because of their duty, must carry many operating details in their mind, must be ready for any emergency involving danger to ship or crew, day or night. This is where you, the Navy Steward, play an essential part in the operation of our fleet. By relieving officers of some of the routine tasks of daily living, you give them more time for their duties, you make a direct contribution to the effectiveness of your ship. The way you carry out your duties can, in great measure, make your ship a good ship, a credit to the Navy. . . .*
>
> *After everything is as ship shape as you can possibly make it, take out any cleaning or laundry, and shine the shoes that need shining. . . .*
>
> *If your station is in the galley or the pantry, your jobs may be doubly important. General Quarters sometimes last for many hours. Under the stress of battle conditions, feeding is just as vital as any other job aboard the ship. Hot food and steaming coffee add much to the morale of fighting men, giving them the extra endurance they need.*

Under unrelenting criticism from civil rights organizations and the African American press, some concessions were eventually made to black protest. A single ship, the USS *Mason*, was manned entirely by African Americans (except for the commander). An army air force training camp was set up at Tuskegee Institute, in Alabama, whose graduates, the 332nd Fighter Group, would eventually hold a unique distinction: They were the only American fighter-escort group never to lose a bomber to an enemy fighter. And in 1943, under intense pressure from the White House, the marines reluctantly began to accept volunteers to serve in all-black units.

John Gray was not working at the ADDSCO shipyard when the violence began. He had just joined the marines. He explained many years later:

> *Our attitude was that if the Germans or the Japanese won the war, the white folk would get on their side and we'd have to fight the Germans, the Japanese, and the white folk. So what we [wanted to do] was go over there and win the war and then come back up and pick up the gauntlet where we tried to get our civil rights. That was the feeling. When I went in, they had a recruiter with a stamp pad: "Eyes: Negro. Hair: Negro. Color: Negro. Complexion: Negro. Race: Negro." Everything was Negro except height and weight.*

Gray was sent to Montford Point at Camp Lejeune, North Carolina, where he joined the only black unit being trained for combat in the Marine Corps: the 51st Defense Battalion. Its commander was Lieutenant Colonel Floyd Stephenson, a veteran of the attack on Pearl Harbor, who won his men's loyalty by declaring, "There is *nothing* that suitable colored personnel cannot be taught." That, John Gray recalled, was a great improvement on the commandant of Camp Lejeune, General Henry L. Larsen, who told the men he had been "out in the jungles [on Guadalcanal] and he had fought this and he had done that and he came back to find *women* marines and *dog* Marines and then '*You* people.' We didn't like it when people said 'you people' instead of referring to troops as troops," said Gray. "We resented that."

Nineteen-year-old Willie Rushton joined the marines from Mobile that spring as well. Born in Nadawah, Alabama—a town so small it's not on most maps—and raised in Atmore, which was not much bigger, he had moved to Mobile and was working in the local Coca-Cola bottling plant when his draft number came up. "I was sent to Fort Benning, Georgia, for my physical," he remembered.

Newly arrived African American recruits brace for their first inspection at Mumford Point at the Marine Barracks (later Camp Lejeune), New River, North Carolina. A few weeks of training would turn them into the crisply turned-out marines shown below, strolling through Harlem in June 1943.

And when they got through with that exam, one of the colonels came over and started talking to us. He said, "Do you know why you're over here?" And I said, "No." And so he said, "The Marine Corps and the navy do not recruit too many black young men, so we're giving you a chance to go in the Marine Corps or the navy if you want to." And so he started passing out some photos of different uniforms and everything. So I looked at that marine uniform and I loved that uniform.

The colonel said, "I'll tell you right now, son, you got to go through some strenuous training if you're going to be a marine." And I said, "Well, I think I can take it." They had been talking about the Marine Corps and how tough it was, they didn't just take everybody. And even the white boys that was going in the Marine Corps, they had to be real physical. I always wanted to be in something that's really special. That really meant a lot to me, because my mother and father, they always told me whatever you be, be the best.

Marine boot camp was never easy, but it was made especially arduous for these first African American recruits. "I'm going to make you wish you had never joined this damn Marine Corps," one drill instructor told them. John Gray and Willie Rushton

Willie Rushton

took it all without complaint. "A lot of people just thought the black man just wasn't up to it," Rushton remembered. "Because you had to be *something* to be a marine, you know. And a lot of them didn't think the black man had the ability. My job in the marines was to prove to them that I could withstand whatever they could withstand."

John Gray and his battalion were eventually sent to the South Pacific. They had been trained as expert gunners on 90- and 150-millimeter guns and were so skilled, he remembered, that "we could shoot the sting off a bee. After we got tired of practicing on the target, we'd hit the cable and the target would just float away." But white commanders never saw fit to send them into battle—the men took to calling themselves "the lost battalion," because they had so little to do—and white marines resented their presence, Gray recalled, especially when women were involved.

> *We were down in American Samoa, and when we got a chance to dance or something, there was friction. Those girls were told that we had tails. The whites said we were like monkeys, see. So when a girl would dance with you, she would reach down and try and see if you had a tail. But those girls would be so glad to have the treatment they extended "separate-but-equal," into the armed services.*

Gray would spend nineteen months overseas and never come close to the serious combat for which he and his comrades had trained so hard. "It's funny," he remembered, "how people won't even let you die for your country."

Willie Rushton would also soon find himself in the Pacific, a member of the 11th Depot Company, providing support for the 1st Marine Division, the same outfit with which Sid Phillips had served on Guadalcanal. The company's assignment was simply to serve as stevedores, loading and unloading supplies. Like John Gray, Rushton sometimes brooded over why his country had bothered to send him so far from home if it believed there was so little he could do. His son had been born just before he went overseas, he remembered, and he yearned to be with him.

> *Sometimes I'd be lying up there in my tent at night and say, "I wonder, did I do the right thing? Wonder if I'll ever get the chance to see my son." And then I'd say, "Well, one thing about it, they can always tell him that I was over here trying to make a better place for him to live in the United States." So then I stopped worrying about that. I said, "I'm over here to make things better. That's what I'm doing over here."*

EVEN BEFORE VICTORY WAS WON in North Africa, Roosevelt and Churchill and their commanders had met again in Washington. There was real progress to report. British cryptologists had broken the German Enigma code and were now able to decipher enemy communications. In the Atlantic, the hunters had finally become the hunted: long-range B-24 Liberators flying from the decks of American-built escort carriers now prowled the skies, swooping down to destroy German U-boats whenever they rose to the surface. (Forty-three enemy submarines would be sunk in May alone.) Meanwhile, American shipyards, at Mobile and elsewhere, were turning out tonnage so fast that, by autumn, all the Allied ships lost since 1939 would be replaced.

But the Allies still differed as to how to proceed. The invasion of France remained the Americans' top priority, though it was now clear that the Allies would not be ready to undertake it until the spring of 1944. Stalin, whose Red Army was still facing nearly two hundred German divisions on its own soil, sent message after message expressing his bitterness that the long-promised second front was still so far away. Churchill continued to be wary of the invasion plan—"I see the Channel filled with corpses," he would confess to a colleague—and he feared that Stalin might abandon the Alliance if British and American troops were to remain idle in Europe for nearly a year. He therefore urged more action in the Mediterranean: an immediate assault on Italy once Sicily fell. If the Allies continued to engage the enemy, Stalin would be encouraged to hold on, he argued, while the German people might be made to see in the collapse of their chief ally "the beginning of their doom."

Roosevelt approved an assault on Italy. But he also set two conditions: the invasion of France would go forward no later than May 1, 1944, and the commanders in the field would have to be confident that Italy could be taken with a smaller force than was currently based in the Mediterranean before they could go forward. Seven divisions were to be shifted to Britain after Sicily was taken; nothing would again be allowed to interfere with the buildup for D-day.

THE INVASION OF SICILY—called Operation Husky—was set to begin on July 10. A few days beforehand, the men of the brand-new 82nd Airborne Division had a surprise visitor at their dusty staging area near the holy Tunisian city of Karouan. The 82nd was about to take part in the first large-scale Allied airborne operation of the war, dropping behind the enemy lines to keep the enemy from reinforcing the beaches. It was something new in warfare, and General Patton, who was to command the American forces in Sicily, had asked to speak to them.

Among the men lined up to hear him was twenty-five-year-old Dwain Luce of Mobile. A graduate of Hunter High School and of Auburn University, where he had undergone ROTC training, Luce was married, with one child and another on the way, a first lieutenant in the 320th Glider Field Artillery, charged with providing 105-millimeter howitzer support for the paratroops. As always, Patton's speech was crude and colorful, meant to

As Sicilian women look on, a medic administers plasma to a GI wounded by shrapnel in the lane outside their village home, August 9, 1943.

Dwain Luce

inflame his men against the enemy. "We all loved Patton," Luce remembered.

We loved Ike, too. But I mean, we loved Patton. He was something. I probably shouldn't repeat some of the things he said, but I remember he told us, "Now, some troops can move and some troops can shoot. But when you can move and shoot at the same time, then you and Napoleon are pissing through the same straw."

The 150,000 Allied soldiers who came ashore in Sicily would quickly prove that they could both move and shoot. But the landings were a disaster for the airborne troops. Inexperienced pilots missed their targets in the dark. High winds scattered paratroopers all over the southeastern end of the island. One hundred forty-four British gliders fell into the sea. The next night, inexperienced U.S. Navy and shore gunners, believing themselves under attack by enemy planes, shot down twenty-three American transports carrying members of the 82nd Airborne; 229 men were lost. Dwain Luce ended up being ferried by boat to Sicily, where his unit remained in reserve.

The Mediterranean theater on the eve of the invasion of Italy

It took thirty-eight da[y]
of Vermont. Thousands
fight. Sicilian villagers
Rome, with the suppo[rt]
King Victor Emmanuel
and named Marshal P[étain]
to get Italy out of the
greatly outnumbered
or air—used the i[s]
advance of 450,000 A[llied]
than 40,000 of their own men and 60,000
their arms and equipment, across the narrow Strait of Messina
the Italian mainland. By then, Eisenhower had decided to go ahead with the attack on Italy, though no one was sure whether or not Badoglio—or Hitler—would try seriously to defend it.

NIGHT AFTER NIGHT SINCE 1939, British bombers had been crossing the English Channel to attack the Germans. There was little else the Allies could do to damage the enemy in western Europe until the much-delayed invasion of France could be mounted. They'd tried daytime bombing of industrial targets at first but lost so many bombers to enemy fighters that they'd switched to night raids. Aerial surveys showed that only one in five British bombs had fallen within five miles of its intended target. The prime minister ordered a virtual halt to bombing and appointed a new commander, Air Chief Marshal Arthur Harris—"Bomber" Harris to the newspapers but "Butcher" Harris to his men because so many of them died following his orders.

Under Harris, British policy shifted to what was euphemistically called area bombing: remorseless, repeated night raids on German cities, intended to destroy whole neighborhoods and "break the spirit of the people." An assault on Cologne by more than a thousand bombers in May of 1942 had destroyed six hundred acres of housing, smashed or damaged some 250 factories, and driven forty thousand people into the streets. Bomber Harris was knighted for his apparent triumph. But within a month, Cologne's factories were once again functioning twenty-four hours a day.

Something more was needed. "By bombing the devils around the clock," Harris told Churchill, "we can prevent the German defenses from getting any rest." To do that, it had been decided at Casablanca to divide up the bombing task.

The British would continue to batter German cities at night. The Americans—who initially resisted the idea of bombing civilians, in part because they believed American public opinion would recoil from it—would target German defense industries

German civilians pick their way through the ruins of Hamburg during the summer of 1943. More than a third of the city's dwellings—thirty-five thousand residential buildings—had disappeared under Allied bombs.

by day. They believed the B-17, their big, four-engine bomber, superior to anything their allies or the enemy had. It was called the Flying Fortress because it bristled with thirteen .50-caliber machine guns, so much firepower that its most enthusiastic champions believed that formations of B-17s would be able to "shoot their way in and shoot their way out" of any situation. And because they flew so high, they would be impervious to antiaircraft fire from the ground as well. Each fully loaded Fortress could transport six thousand pounds of bombs some two thousand miles and was fitted with the top-secret Norden bombsight, said to be so accurate it made it possible to "drop a bomb in a pickle barrel" from twenty thousand feet. The joint aim of the new bombing campaign, set forth by American and British planners in a secret memorandum, was not only to destroy the enemy's military and industrial power but also to undermine "the morale of the German people to a point where their capacity for armed resistance is fatally weakened."

In late July, British bombs would set off a whirling firestorm that burned or asphyxiated at least forty thousand German civilians in and around Hamburg—taking almost as many lives in

one week as the German Luftwaffe had taken in eight months of bombing Britain. Many terrified survivors fled the city. A woman who had been a fifteen-year-old girl then recalled walking the desolate streets the next day:

Four-story-high blocks of flats were like glowing mounds of stone right down to the basement. Everything seemed to have melted and pressed the bodies away in front of it. Women and children were so charred as to be unrecognizable; those that had died through lack of oxygen were half-charred and recognizable. Their brains had tumbled from their burst temples, and their insides from the soft parts under the ribs. How terribly these people must have died. The smallest children lay like fried eels on the pavement.

Smaller firestorms set off by British bombs engulfed Kassel, Würzburg, Darmstadt, Heilbronn, and other towns. But the

German will to resist only intensified—just as the will of Londoners had intensified during the Blitz—and Hamburg's factories were soon back in business.

THE REQUIREMENTS OF OPERATIONS Torch and Husky had slowed the buildup of America's air arm in Britain. But by midsummer 130,000 men of the Eighth and Ninth Air Force were in place in the east of England, scattered among more than a hundred bases—so many that one British official wrote that East Anglia had been transformed into a "mosaic of aerodromes five miles apart." (By the following spring, there would be more than three times that many fliers and support staff in England—426,000 of them.) Each base was a self-contained little America. Most had their own PX and servicemen's and officers' clubs, their own movie theaters and baseball fields and bottomless supplies of Coca-Cola. "The Americans are not relying on this country for even the smallest items," one British newspaperman marveled; "they have actually brought with them their own dustbins—'garbage cans,' they call them."

Technical Sergeant Earl Burke of Sacramento was stationed at Grafton Underwood, home of the 384th Bomber Group. He had reached Britain in June with thousands of other air force service personnel aboard the fast-moving passenger liner the RMS *Queen Mary,* now painted gray and serving as a troopship. A family tragedy the previous year had moved him to enter the army air force. He'd been at home one evening when the telephone rang.

My uncle Earl said, "I want you to come over to my house." He was only a couple blocks away. So I went over there. And he showed me an article in the newspaper that said there was a crash in Puerto Rico. And my only brother, my older brother, was listed as killed. We tried for twelve hours on the telephone to try to get to Puerto Rico to confirm that this was indeed my brother. Finally, somebody said, "Yes, it was a Tom Burke from Sacramento." Well, five days later, we got the telegram telling that he had been killed. So that's how my war came to us.

Burke's father was away, working at a defense job in Washington state, when the bad news came. He boarded a train for home right away.

What he went through, coming down on that train, I'll never know. Because he never said anything, [but] we know that he was kind of tore up. He came home and we met him at the train station. My mother and he held each other for a while, [but] *there was no talking about what had happened. My parents were very stoic. They didn't break down and cry, wail, or whatever they do nowadays. I only heard my mother cry once, and that was not in my presence, it was in her bedroom. She never cried in front of me.*

It was a tough thing for those two people. For me, I lost a brother. Yeah, dammit! We gonna do something about it. So we moved up to Seattle, Washington, and I got the crazy idea that I was going to enlist. And win the war. It was kind of "for Tommy." In a way. Not so consciously. I didn't say, "This is for you, Tom." No, I never did that. But I enlisted. Glad I did.

As a member of the 854th Chemical Warfare Company, Burke helped load bombs onto B-17s for their early morning missions over Germany and occupied Europe. The number and intensity of those raids increased steadily that summer. So did American losses.

The indestructibility of the "self-defending formations" of big American bombers had quickly proved a myth. The planes were powerful and so ruggedly built that they could absorb a good deal of damage and still return to base. But they were all too vulnerable to attack, and no American fighter plane was yet able to fly far enough to provide an escort beyond the German border. There, fast-moving enemy fighters most often came at them from the front, where only Plexiglas protected the pilot and co-pilot, or raked their sides with rockets and machine-gun fire. Each American airman was meant to fly no more than twenty-five missions before being withdrawn from combat. In 1943, only one in three would ever reach that number. Statistically, it was safer to be a marine fighting in the Pacific than a member of a B-17 crew over Europe. Twenty-six thousand Eighth Air Force crewmen would die in action between 1942 and the end of the war—one in eight of those who flew. Forty thousand more were wounded or shot down and taken prisoner.

Earl Burke (right) with his mother and brother Tom

Burke's bomber group lost two planes on its first mission. By the sixth mission, thirty-five of its original thirty-six B-17s had been destroyed. After the tenth, a whole seven-plane squadron failed to return to Grafton Underwood. Determined to stem such fearful

losses, Allied commanders began targeting German aircraft production with special urgency. On August 17, 376 Fortresses ventured deeper into Germany than they'd ever gone before to blast an aircraft factory at Regensburg and a plant at Schweinfurt that turned out ball bearings, the frictionless mechanism required by tank and airplane engines. The raid was a disaster: sixty bombers failed to return, six hundred crewmen were lost, and the production of aircraft and ball bearings was only briefly interrupted.

Replacement planes and crews arrived regularly, but commanders could not always keep up with such catastrophic losses and began casting about for service personnel who might be trained to fill in for missing crew members. "At that time," Burke remembered, "they were taking anybody. They were taking cooks. They were taking truck drivers. Mechanics. Anybody they could get into an airplane."

He was having a beer in the enlisted men's club one evening late that summer when he came across two old friends, Robert and Richard Egger, identical twins from his hometown. Burke had been loading bombs for weeks now. It was hard, unglamorous work, performed in the predawn dark and complicated by frequent rains, which turned much of the base into a bog and inspired the men to rename it Grafton Undermud.

"We were having a good time," Burke remembered, "when one of the twins said, 'Well, why don't you up and get with us?' They were tail and ball-turret gunners on a B-17. It sounded like fun. What the heck, you know? I was nineteen! They seemed to be having a lot of fun. They were not scared at all. So I says, 'OK.'"

Perils of flight: At left, a B-17 struggles to keep up with its formation over a German city despite the loss of half its tail section, sheared off by an errant bomb dropped from above. Below, a wounded ball-turret gunner is gently lifted out of his plane and into an ambulance at an airbase somewhere in England.

He filled out an application, took a crash course in gunnery at a school run by the air force on England's northeast coast near an inlet called the Wash, and before dawn on September 16, found himself climbing aboard a B-17 for the first time as a full-fledged member of the crew. As the plane lumbered into the air and began to climb toward its place in the big formation heading eastward, Burke moved down into the ball-turret, a retractable sphere with Plexiglas windows that hung below the belly of the plane and allowed the occupant to spot danger from below as well as all sides. It was not a comfortable place, Burke recalled.

You put your knees up against your ears almost like a fetal position. You're up in there, jammed in that little thing, and you've got these horrendous machine guns in front of you—fifty-millimeter, two of them. And you've got a radio in there. You've got oxygen. And you can hook up your electrical suit to keep warm. That was it. But it didn't pass my mind that I was getting into trouble until the first mission.

The target that day was enemy shipping anchored in the harbor at Nantes, on the French coast. Burke was understandably nervous about how he'd do when and if the shooting started.

We're flying about twenty-eight thousand feet, and I tried my turret for the first time to see whether I could do a reasonable job of tracking a fighter plane. But I learned I didn't know my right foot from my left foot. I wanted the gun to go one way, and I'd push with the wrong foot and it'd go the other. I didn't know where it was going. I was so scared because I couldn't perform properly for the rest of the people in the airplane. I was not doing my job. But pretty soon, before we got to the bombing area and the fighters started to come out, I did learn my right foot from my left foot.

German fighters swarmed up to meet them. One B-17 exploded. Three crew members died instantly; the rest parachuted into enemy territory and were captured. Another bomber was forced to ditch in the English Channel, where a French fisherman rescued all ten men aboard. The German fighters did not happen to hit the plane below which Burke hung. It is unlikely his shooting damaged any of them either. "I couldn't hit the inside of a barn with a handful of oranges if the doors were closed," he remembered. "But I was up there, firing two fifty-caliber machine guns, shooting rounds half an inch in diameter out of two barrels. Lots of lead in the air." Most of the ships the B-17s had been sent to destroy survived as well, and a second raid on the same target six days later would have little more effect. Missions like these had reduced French coastal towns to rubble. Not a dog or a cat survived in them, said Grand Admiral Karl Dönitz, commander in chief of the German navy, but shipping continued to come and go, and no serious harm was ever done to the reinforced-concrete pens that hid his U-boats. German construction skill had something to do with that. But so did the clouds and fog that often blanketed the countryside and kept the Norden bombsight from working as well in Europe as it had when being tested back home. "The accuracy of our bombing left much to be desired," Burke admitted.

They said you could drop a bomb into a pickle barrel. We couldn't drop a bomb in France. In the beginning we just couldn't hit 'em! We would fly over, drop tons of bombs, and a P-38 would come in and check to see where the bombs had fallen for an after-action report. He'd come back and say, "Where'd you guys drop 'em?" Out in the field somewhere, some muddy field. And the minute they hit, they went down in the mud.

The B-17s kept flying nonetheless, and whenever he was needed, Earl Burke would keep flying, too.

FROM THE MOMENT MARTINA CIARLO'S MIDDLE SON, BABE, had left Waterbury for the army in the spring of 1943, he was the central focus of her thoughts. "She would go to St. Lucy's church every single morning," her daughter, Olga, remembered. "She used to go and meet some of her lady friends. And of course they would pray for everybody." Then she would hurry home to wait for the postman.

And he would go by sometimes and he would say, "Mrs. Ciarlo, not today." So the following day she'd wait again, and finally she would get a letter. She'd be so happy. She'd run upstairs and she'd let us read the letter because my mother couldn't read English. And we would read the letter to her and she'd be happy just knowing that she heard from him.

Wherever Ciarlo was stationed, whatever he was doing, he urged his mother and his aunts and uncles who lived above and below her in the Ciarlo house on North Main Street not to worry about him. Nearly every letter began with the same reassuring line: "I am feeling fine and I hope to hear the same from all of you." Few specific details of his army life were ever offered, but his family knew that he had gone through basic training at Camp Croft, in South Carolina; lived for a time at Camp Shenango, in Pennsylvania; then was shipped to Camp Patrick Henry, in Virginia (part of the Hampton Roads Port of Embarkation, through which some 1.6 million young Americans would pass before the war was over) and sailed from there for somewhere overseas. "I

V-MAIL

Few things mattered more to the men serving abroad than getting letters from home. "Mail was indispensable," one infantryman remembered. "It motivated us. We couldn't have won the war without it." At first, delivery was slow and erratic. Too bulky to be given precious space aboard aircraft, sacks of mail were loaded into the holds of cargo ships and often took more than a month to reach the front.

Then, in the late spring of 1942, the military began encouraging Americans to use V-mail, a simple but ingenious space-saving system devised by the British—who called their version the airgraph. Letters were addressed and written on a special one-sided form, sent to Washington where they were opened and read by army censors who blacked out anything they thought might give useful information to the enemy, then photographed onto a reel of 16-millimeter microfilm. The reels—each containing some 18,000 letters—were then flown overseas to receiving stations. There, each letter was printed onto a sheet of 4¼- by 5-inch photographic paper, slipped into an envelope, and bagged for delivery to the front.

A single mail sack could hold 150,000 one-page letters that would otherwise have required thirty-seven sacks and weighed 2,575 pounds. Between June 15, 1942 (when the first V-mail station began operation in North Africa), and the end of the war, anxious families sent more than 556 million pieces of V-mail to their sons overseas—and received some 510 million in return.

know you didn't receive mail from me for over a week but circumstances kept me from writing," he wrote after he had reached his first foreign destination in late September.

Yes, that's right, I took a little boat ride and I didn't even get sea-sick. Well, I suppose you're wondering where I am. I think that if I wouldn't tell you, you would never guess it. Okay, I'll tell you because I know you will want to know in the worst way. I am somewhere in North Africa. Surprised? Well, I am too, but I am very safe so don't worry.

He really would have been very safe in North Africa, but it is unlikely he spent more than a day or two there. The Third Infantry was already fighting in southern Italy, and he was on his way to a replacement depot near the town of Battipaglia to join it.

The Allied invasion of Italy was a gamble. It had no serious strategic goal. Instead, it was intended at least in part as a symbolic campaign, aimed at impressing the impatient Soviets with American and British willingness to engage the enemy somewhere on the European continent until the real second front could be opened in France. Success depended on a swift Italian surrender, followed by a German retreat from all but the northern region of its former ally's territory. But Marshal Badoglio, the old soldier who had replaced Mussolini as head of state, proved an inept statesman. Equally fearful of the Germans and the Allies, he dithered for more than a month rather than surrender and fled Rome on September 8 rather than announce the armistice he and the Allies had finally worked out.

Eisenhower announced it over the radio anyway, and five divisions of Allied troops already approaching the southern Italian coast aboard a fleet of more than five hundred warships cheered themselves hoarse. "Speculation was rampant, and it was all good," a British officer recalled. "We would dock in Naples harbor unopposed, with an olive branch in one hand and an opera ticket in the other."

"Italy is like a boot," Napoleon once said. "You must enter it, like Hannibal, from the top." The Allies, under the overall command of Sir Harold Alexander, were trying to take it from the bottom. The invasion was in two parts. Montgomery and his British Eighth Army had already made a diversionary landing at the toe's tip and were making slow progress northward along roads blasted apart and heavily mined by the retreating enemy.

GROWING UP

To Burt Wilson, a Sacramento second-grader at the time of Pearl Harbor, the war at first seemed just another game, to be captured in his family's home movies (right). "All kids played war when we were seven, eight, nine, ten," he recalled:

It started off with cowboys and Indians, and then, if the world wasn't at war, it went into the Foreign Legion vs. the Arabs or something like that. Then when the war came along, of course it was us against them—U.S. soldiers against the Axis. And we all played war to a certain extent. But it's interesting the way we played war because nobody ever died. If you got shot, somebody came to your aid and fixed you up and then you could rise up and shoot again. You could get hit five or six times and they'd come and fix you up and you would rise up and shoot again. And that was the way we felt it really was, that you couldn't die in war, really. Some way you could keep on going.

Movies and comic books helped reinforce that impression.

"We couldn't wait for the next war film to come out because it was filled with heroism and everybody sacrificing for the war. One I particularly liked was a Ronald Reagan film with Errol Flynn called *Desperate Journey*, in which they were always wisecracking to the Nazis, and we loved to see that. But the biggest audience response came from a movie like *Flying Tigers* with John Wayne. When he shot down a Japanese plane the Japanese pilot would hold his hands to his face and the blood would come out of his fingers, and we would jump up and cheer because the good guys were winning." But even in the newsreels, he remembered, "You never saw anything really horrible happening to any American soldier or for that matter to many enemy soldiers."

Actual death, Wilson remembered, remained unreal. But as the war went on, that slowly began to change.

We thought comic books were one way of keeping up with the war. There were a lot of stories in comic books about Guadalcanal. One story in particular I remember was about when we launched an attack against the Japanese and it said in the comic book that the enemy lost 200 soldiers and we only lost eighteen. And I took that story to my father and I said, "Isn't that great? Isn't that great?" He says, "Not if you were one of the eighteen." That made me think a little bit.

And then, what amounted to a surrealistic feeling about the war came to an end one day when our neighbors put a gold star in the window and pulled all the blinds down. Their oldest son had been killed in Italy. Now I knew the youngest son. I didn't know the oldest son that much, but I really grieved for the whole family. And in Sacramento in those days, the way you dealt with something like that was pulling all the shades down and never coming out of the house. And so every time you walked past that house, the whole idea of death was brought home to you because of the shades drawn and the gold star in the window.

Now the Fifth Army, under General Mark Clark, would land along a thirty-mile beachhead near Salerno, at the ankle of the Italian boot. Clark would prove one of the war's most controversial Allied commanders. Only forty-seven, he'd helped plan Operation Torch and gone from lieutenant colonel to lieutenant general in just over two years. Admirers spoke of his resolve and quickness of mind; Eisenhower called him "the best trainer, organizer, and planner I have ever met." His detractors thought him careless with the lives of his men, needlessly hostile to the British, and a shameless self-promoter. Once the 170,000 men under his command were all ashore, they would represent a cross-section of the Allied cause: about a third were Americans; roughly a sixth were British; the rest were New Zealanders and Indians, Gurkhas from Nepal, Poles, Brazilians, and French-speaking colonial troops from North Africa. Clark insisted, however, that every press release issued by his public relations staff of nearly fifty refer to them as Clark's Fifth Army at least three times on the first page and once a page after that.

The initial landings, starting on September 9, went well. Only a single, thinly spread German panzer division held the hills that overlooked the long pebbly beaches. But over the next few days, German reinforcements poured in faster than the Allies could come ashore, and on the fourteenth, an armored counterattack threatened to split the Allied force in two and drive them into the sea. In one sector, believing the enemy had already infiltrated their lines, panicky GIs opened fire on one another, and American ack-ack gunners shot down at least three British fighters. "What we saw," one British witness wrote, "was ineptitude and cowardice spreading down from the command, and this resulted in chaos." Cooks and truck drivers were issued weapons. The 82nd Airborne was flown in from North Africa to help. Clark considered withdrawing his men. But American artillery held its ground, and thunderous volleys—eleven thousand tons of shells—fired by Allied warships that risked running aground to creep in close to shore finally stopped the enemy advance. The British writer Norman Lewis, then an officer with British Intelligence, saw the impact the naval shelling had on German tanks that had been poised to break through: "Several of these lay near, or in, tremendous craters. In one case, the trapped crew had been broiled in such a way that a puddle of fat had spread out from under the tank and this was quilted with brilliant flies of all descriptions and colors."

The German counterattack had failed, but the Allies had suffered twice as many casualties as had the enemy: nine thousand men lost, with three thousand more taken prisoner.

Dwain Luce of Mobile was among the 82nd Airborne troops who had been brought in to help hold the line.

They put us in to get the beach fixed, and we helped them. Everybody worked together to get off the beach.

I had a really dear friend named Shug Eddington. He and I were kids growing up together. He and I had roomed together at Auburn. I knew he'd been in Africa and I knew his APO number, but I never could find him. Well, when we crossed the beach, in Italy, I saw his outfit. And I thought, gee, when we get this thing under control, I'm going to come back here and see him. And in a few days we did get the area under control, and I borrowed a jeep and went back to see him, and he had been killed on the beach. Probably around the time I crossed it. And so naturally I wrote my wife. I was quite upset about it. And in those days sometimes your V-mail went through quickly and sometimes a month later, you never knew for sure. And as it worked out, this letter went through immediately. My wife got it and went right down to see Shug's parents. But they hadn't heard anything, and so it happened that it was she who announced to them that he was killed. And it was a bad experience for her and an unfortunate thing for everybody.

On September 18, two days after Earl Burke's first bomber mission, the Germans began a carefully staged withdrawal up the peninsula from Salerno. What was left of Naples after American bombing and the fearsome damage done by the retreating Germans fell to the Allies on October 1; amid the rubble, its people were reduced to picking dandelions and netting pigeons for food, and women sold themselves on the streets to feed their children.

General Clark was elated by his progress. He believed he had the enemy on the run, that they now would not stop until they reached the Gothic Line, heavily fortified positions well north of Rome. Eisenhower agreed: he thought the Italian capital would be safely in Allied hands within six weeks, then revised that estimate to less than a month.

They were dead wrong. The Allies were about to lose their gamble. The loss of Sicily and a simultaneous Soviet victory at Kursk that ended Hitler's dream of regaining the offensive on the eastern front helped convince the German dictator that Italy had to be held as long as possible. He transformed Italy from an Axis ally into an occupied country overnight. More than a million Italian soldiers were disarmed at German gunpoint. Most simply stripped off their uniforms and melted into the population, but more than seven hundred thousand were shipped off to serve as slave laborers for the Reich. Meanwhile, a daring Nazi commando raid rescued Mussolini from captivity and set him up as head of a puppet regime in northern Italy.

German commanders had used the long delay caused by Badoglio's bumbling to funnel sixteen fresh divisions into Italy. But the Italian landscape would prove their best ally. The rugged Appennines ran up the spine of the peninsula for more than eight hundred miles. A series of rivers and deep ravines twisted their way down out of the mountains toward both coasts, too, providing Field Marshal Albert Kesselring, the German commander in the Mediterranean, with ideal natural lines of defense. Movement along the narrow, zigzagging mountain roads was made possible only by scores of bridges and culverts. The Germans blew them up one by one as they fell back, and established strong points on nearby slopes to pour fire down on anyone who dared try to make repairs. "Italy was one hill after another," one infantryman recalled, "and when it was wet, you were either going up too slow or down too fast, but always the mud. And every hill had a German gun on it. They were choosing the ground, and they were always looking down on us."

Weather, too, worked against the Allies. The autumn rains had begun. Allied aircraft were kept from the sky, tanks and artillery were mired in yellow mud when they tried to leave the road, and no landing craft were on hand to mount amphibious landings behind enemy lines. Supply problems also slowed things down: two different weapons systems had to be maintained, and soldiers of different nationalities demanded different diets.

Every hour the Germans could delay the Allied advance gave them more time to complete the centerpiece of their defenses: the Gustav Line, sixty-five miles north of Naples. There, thousands of soldiers and conscripted Italian civilians were at work, under orders from Kesselring to make it so strong that "the British and Americans would break their teeth on it."

SOMETIME DURING THE FIRST WEEK IN OCTOBER, Babe Ciarlo landed in Italy with a shipload of other replacements and was rushed to the front, assigned to take the place of a man lost from G Company, 2nd Battalion, 15th Regiment, 3rd Infantry Division. By the time he caught up with his new outfit, it had fought its way past the town of Caserta to the top of a ridge that overlooked the fast-moving Volturno River, the first of the series of defensive lines the Germans would establish as they moved north. Kesselring had ordered the German Tenth Army to hold the Volturno until at least October 15. General Clark was determined to get at the Germans in the mountains beyond it before the Gustav Line could be completed and reinforced and rain made the roads worse than they already were. Six Allied divisions were about to try to fight their way across the Volturno along a forty-mile front.

Because Babe Ciarlo was so determinedly unforthcoming about the details of his life in the infantry, any description of what he saw and survived must be pieced together from the memories of others who shared those experiences with him. In the sector with which his battalion had to contend, the coffee-colored Volturno was less than 150 feet across and no more than six and a half feet deep. But two bridges that had spanned the river had been destroyed, and its banks lay open to German guns hidden on two conical hills on the opposite side. Those guns would have to be silenced.

At 2:00 a.m. on October 13, after a full hour of intensive shelling of enemy positions—"the shells sighed over us in a ceiling of sounds," one witness remembered—and beneath a dense blanket of silvery smoke meant to mask their movements from the enemy, the men of the 3rd Division joined the attack. The 160 men of Babe Ciarlo's company crossed along with the rest. There is no way to know whether he was among the relatively fortunate few who made it across in rubber rafts or assault boats or whether he was forced to wade the icy river, holding his rifle above his head with one hand while clutching a guide rope with the other to keep from being swept away. But however he was ordered to advance, bright tracers crisscrossed above his head. Men sank around him, ripped by bullets. Wounded men splashed helplessly in the shallows. The smoke made it impossible to see more than a few yards in any direction. Ciarlo and the other wet, frightened men of his company clambered up the slippery bank into fire from German machine-gunners and mortarmen dug in just one hundred yards or so beyond the river. Somehow, most of them managed to get through it, bypass the enemy positions, avoid the mines scattered beneath the mud that covered the valley floor, and begin to move toward the guns firing down at them from both hills. More men fell. Some screamed for help. Ciarlo and the others did their best to ignore them, reached the bottom of the slopes, and began to climb, firing as they went. As more and more Allied troops streamed across the river, the Germans chose to withdraw, joining their comrades in a staged retreat toward their next defensive positions.

As the sun rose, Ciarlo and the other men of the 2nd Battalion paused on the ridgeline to reorganize, bring up ammunition, and see to the wounded who were being borne back across the river on the same rubber rafts on which some had crossed it a

American infantrymen climb a hillside near Caserta, Italy, in early November of 1943. "The hills rise to high ridges," Ernie Pyle wrote. "You can't go around them through the flat peaceful valleys because the Germans look down upon you and would let you have it. So you have to go up and over."

British troops on their way to the front pass through the ruined village of San Clemente, near Monte Camino. "There is no doubt that the Italians are paying a stiff price for their past sins," the infantryman-cartoonist Bill Mauldin wrote. "The country looks as if a giant rake had gone over it from end to end, and when you have been going along with the rake you wonder that there is anything left at all."

few hours earlier. Then they started down the other side of the hill in pursuit of the enemy.

A week after this first taste of combat, Babe Ciarlo took the time to write another letter home, its tone utterly unchanged by anything he'd experienced. As always, Ciarlo was careful to keep the details of what he was doing from his family so as not to alarm his mother. But he couldn't resist providing clues intended to let everyone in the family know he'd made it to Italy.

I am feeling fine and I hope to hear the same from all of you always. I know I haven't written to you for a long time and I hope you understand that the army has been keeping me pretty busy. . . . I think of all of you every day.

I suppose you have been keeping up with the news lately and by the way we are beating the Germans. The war won't last much longer.

Eddie [Meccariello, Ciarlo's high school friend, now serving in the 3rd Battalion of the 7th Infantry Regiment] and I are dying for some nice raviolis and I don't think it will be long before we get them. . . . Will you please send me Mom's brother's address [in Rome] in your next letter. I haven't got much more to say except to take care of yourselves and give my love and regards to all, especially Mom.

As he sat writing, Ciarlo was less than twenty-five miles from the little town of Pontelandolfo, where his late father and his uncles had been born.

ON THURSDAY, OCTOBER 14, the day after Babe Ciarlo and the 3rd Infantry Division made it across the Volturno, Earl Burke found himself back in action in the skies over Germany. The disastrous August raid on Schweinfurt that had cost so many lives and destroyed so many planes had also failed in its mission: the

Men of the 16th Engineers carry a wounded officer out of the Volturno River. Behind them on the opposite bank are abandoned rafts and sections of the bridge they were attempting to put in place when he was hit.

THREE UNITS OF FREEDOM

In the September 20, 1943, issue of *Life* magazine, on newsstands as the Fifth Army fought its way northward from Salerno, the editors published a photograph taken ten months earlier on a New Guinea beach in the South Pacific. It was the first image of dead American servicemen that American civilians had been allowed to see in the twenty-one months since Pearl Harbor.

Here lie three Americans.

What shall we say of them? . . . Shall we say that this is a fine thing, that they should give their lives for their country? . . .

Why print this picture anyway of three American boys, dead on an alien shore? . . .

The reason is that words are never enough. The eye sees. The mind knows. The heart feels. But the words do not exist to make us see, or know, or feel what it is like, what actually happens. . . .

Last week, President Roosevelt . . . and the War Department decided that the American people ought to be able to see their own boys as they fall in battle; to come directly and without words into the presence of their own dead.

And so here it is. This is the reality that lies behind the names that come to rest at last on monuments in the leafy squares of busy American towns. . . .

The camera doesn't show America . . . and yet here on the beach is America, three parts of a hundred and thirty million parts, three fragments of that life we call American life: three units of freedom.

So that it is not just these boys who have fallen here, it is freedom that has fallen. . . . It is our task to cause it to rise again.

ball-bearing factories were back in action, and the bomber crews now had to contend with more enemy fighters than they did when they had set out to destroy Germany's ability to produce them. And so the Allied command had determined to hit the factories a second time. "They thought, well, we'll go back and do it again," Burke remembered. "We were briefed, and you could have heard all the people groan and moan, swear, cuss. . . . Nobody wanted to go back to Schweinfurt." The men's anxiety was intensified by the knowledge that in the last six days alone the Eighth Army had lost eighty-eight bombers and their crews in raids over Germany.

That morning, 291 B-17s took off from their bases in East Anglia, one every thirty seconds, vanishing into the fog. Fighter escorts shielded the formation all the way across Belgium, then turned back before their fuel ran out.

Within moments, Burke remembered, hundreds of German fighters and fighter-bombers appeared as if out of nowhere.

They came in ten abreast. You see these little things wink along the wings. And as they wink you know what's coming— about a quarter pound of lead coming at you every time you saw one of those winks—twenty-millimeter shells. Then they would stay off, say a thousand yards, and they would lob rockets at you. You couldn't reach them, because your fifty-caliber machine gun wouldn't reach that far. They'd sit there and fire, and we couldn't touch them. So that's why we needed the fighter escorts. Without them, we were sitting ducks.

The B-17s were forced to run this gauntlet for nearly three hours, rumbling steadily toward their targets as here and there bombers burned, blew apart, fell out of formation and spiraled from sight. Crewmen's parachutes dotted the sky.

Burke's Fortress shook as all its guns fired at once. Empty shells blanketed the floor inside the plane and piled up around Burke's feet. He and the rest of the crew communicated through

AL McINTOSH'S WAR
January 1943–October 1943

JANUARY 7, 1943. "You ought to start one of those 'rumor clinics' in the *Star-Herald* to run down and disprove rumors," said Ray Ronlund. He was referring to the story circulated here that "all the boys on Guadal-canal had to eat for Christmas dinner was horse meat." The loophole that proves the story nothing but a vicious rumor, obviously untrue, is that no letter from any boy in that area written on Christmas Day could ever have been received here so soon.

JANUARY 14, 1943. How many of you have ever extended an invitation to any of the soldier boys you see almost every day in Luverne to come to your home for dinner? [Dr. F. W. Bofemkamp], on the spur of the moment, invited a couple of men because he thought of all days Christmas was the loneliest to be away from home, tramping the streets of a strange town, thousands of miles from home.

Did the boys love it? A couple of times the boys nearly "choked up" when the conversation veered to "home and mother" but they enjoyed every minute of the stay. One of the boys returned to Luverne and called again for a brief visit. He was so anxious to be "part of the family" that he kept suggesting things he could help do, like taking down the tree trimmings, wash-ing the dishes. That gives you a measure of how lonely some of the boys are, behind their mask of indifference, and how much it would mean to them in the way of happi-ness if you would extend an invitation to them.

APRIL 1, 1943. The marines and soldiers fighting the Japs have appealed to the folks back home for knives, not "penknives" but "pigstickers." Ed Hillebrand was exhibiting one made by his father. Made of saw steel,

long, wicked and curved, and with a deer horn fitted for a handle, it should be highly prized by the jungle fighters. If any of you with mechanical ability want to volunteer to make the type of knives needed, the *Star-Herald* will pay all the costs of seeing they get to their destination.

APRIL 15, 1943. Mr. and Mrs. Norman Steine have proved the truth of that biblical quotation that runs something like this: "Cast thy bread upon the waters for thou shall find it after many days."

They have entertained soldiers from the Sioux Falls air base from time to time, but one apparently was more appreciative of the hospitality. He wrote his mother who lives in Vermont about the Steines' kindness. The other day Mrs. Steine received a letter from the Vermont mother, expressing her appreci-ation. . . . In her letter she admitted she didn't know much about Minnesota condi-tions, but that there evidently was a real shortage of sugar, so "maybe a half-gallon of pure Vermont maple syrup will come in handy." Mr. and Mrs. Steine are now enjoy-ing the finest maple syrup they've ever tasted in their lives.

APRIL 29, 1943. He used to be one of those light-hearted, laughing youngsters that was always cutting didoes with his car (the kind of kid you sometimes shook your fist at because of his highway antics). And his car fairly groaned under the added weight of extra horns and the signs and lights made it look like a carnival midway.

It had probably been ten months since I had seen him . . . [and] I hadn't been particularly aware that he had been gone until he walked in the office wearing the dark green uniform of a U.S. Marine Corps private.

"Hello," we said, "where did you come from?"

And his low-voiced, matter of fact, one word answer accounted for that drawn, haggard and prematurely aged appearance.

"Guadalcanal."

It was Private Virgil Meeker. . . . He doesn't make any claim of bravery or having done anything wonderful. He immediately made it plain that he wasn't in the first wave of Marines. . . . He "caught it twice," he said, but he thinks he was "lucky, very lucky," and his biggest worry, next to whether or not the doctors will reverse their decision and let him return to combat duty again, is how much gas the ration board is going to allow him for his car during the leave.

MAY 27, 1943. "Absenteeism" wouldn't be a national problem if all workers in defense plants could match the record of Floyd Grout. Home on a visit from a west coast shipyard plant, where he has been working the "grave yard shift," Grout proudly wears a medal which signifies that he hasn't missed a single shift in a two year period.

JUNE 3, 1943. How times have changed! It was but three years ago that an item about a girl driving a farm tractor was big enough news that the city dailies ran pictures of Anne Nelson, daughter of Mr. and Mrs. Pete Nelson, driving the [family] tractor.

Now, on more than one farm, girls are doing a real "man's job" by helping in the fields. William Rogge says that four Hills girls are operating tractors this year: Dorothy Nelson, Frances Bakk, Joan Madison, Charlotte Larson. Any other nominations?

JUNE 10, 1943. The four grim lead lines of the newspaper seemed so tragically cold and bare.

"Staff Sergeant Richard E. Mueller . . . is reported missing with seven others following the crash of a medium bomber in the

Atlantic near Columbia, S.C. Saturday. All are believed dead."

Four grim lines of newspaper type—that tell so much and yet so little. . . .

But for us, and thousands of other friends, none of the usual information, or even a picture, is needed to help us remember "Red of the A & P," because that is the way he will be remembered here, not as Staff Sergeant Richard E. Mueller.

With hair as vivid as a June carrot, and a grin that had the power of a locomotive headlight, this boy never walked down the street, or round the aisles of the store. He fairly danced or ran and you knew that here was a chap that was going places.

"Red" did alright for himself in the army. . . . I don't know exactly what his job was . . . [and] nobody will ever know what happened. . . . But we'll gamble that even though they were pitching straight down to the dark blue water that "Red" never once looked up but fought right up to the last second to find, and right, trouble. And we'll never think any different but that if there was just a split second left—and a buddy was struggling to get free of the plunging plane, that Red, to use the old phrase of his "clerking" days, called out, "Can I help you?"

JULY 22, 1943. Just a few postmortems on the latest scrap drive. . . . Down at the S. S. Birkeland farm, one crew was told they could have anything they could salvage in a vacant house on an adjoining [lot].

Brave Hugo Moeller and Ed Storaker climbed up a ladder to the second floor to be scared half out of their wits by a squirrel. All of a sudden Hugo saw "something" so terrible he was afraid even to speak so he descended in a hurry. Ed turned around to say something and saw Hugo vanishing. "What's the matter," he asked. And then he saw "it"—a skunk had already gone thru the motions of "Ready! Aim!" and was ready to "Fire!" Nobody will ever equal Ed's record in dropping down that ladder . . . and

as far as they are concerned, any junk in that house will stay there. And to top it off, Lloyd Beatty's car in which they were riding caught on fire . . . and they all had to bail out and throw sand on the blaze. The fire was caused by overheated brake shoes and they probably would have noticed it sooner except, in the words of one chap, "burning brakes and Ed's cigars smell just the same."

SEPTEMBER 9, 1943. All of us use the phrase "after the war" so much it almost becomes meaningless. . . . The motorist uses it when he thinks of new tires, a new model car, and the right to drive as fast and as far as he pleases. But for all of us, although the words aren't often spoken, it means the day "when you boys come home." It means, if you had witnessed it, a portion of a little drama as we did this week, the ecstatic happiness and the wild gladness of thousands of family reunions.

The other morning an unshaven, weary uniformed man, with a string of gaily colored ribbons on his breast, slipped off the morning train and was driven to his home. Instead of going in the front way, he went around the back, un-noticed. Probably he just wanted to feast his eyes on "home." . . . His children were watching at the front, their noses almost boring holes in the window panes, as they watched the street for a sign of "daddy." Nobody needs to describe their shrieks of joy when he walked in from the backdoor to surprise them. If you could have seen them later, hanging on to his hands for dear life as though they could hold him home forever, you couldn't have helped getting a bit misty yourself.

It was Jess Frakes we're speaking of, "carrot top" himself, the chap who used to start so many arguments at the morning coffee shop sessions and who we used to tease so unmercifully when he was breaking in his "new teeth."

Jess knows what it is to undergo a torpedo attack on ship, to be shelled and bombed on an island, and to hear the Jap radio announce that . . . the Americans on that particular spot had been "wiped out."

SEPTEMBER 30, 1943. One boy came home on leave, the first time in three and a half years, and another boy left to join the navy. That's the way things happen at the Peter de Boer home in Ellsworth.

And if any family in Minnesota can beat their family record we want to hear about it. When they hang out a service flag at that house there are seven stars on it now. And the father, not to be out-done, joined up and worked on the Alaskan highway.

OCTOBER 21, 1943. Although critical Bible students will hasten to set me straight, I still think, even though there is no similarity in the subject matter, that the words in Luke 15–24 are in themselves fittingly descriptive. They read, "for this my son was dead, and is alive again, he was lost and is found."

Those were the words uttered by the father of the prodigal son but probably were not far from the fervent rejoicing uttered up this week at the H. O. Hansen home. There's great rejoicing in that household for their son, Lt. Lloyd Hansen, who was feared dead is reported alive and safe in a German prison camp.

The analogy, as I said, ended with the words for Lt. Lloyd Hansen is no prodigal son. Rather he could well be called the . . . Man with Nine Lives . . . for like a cat he seemingly, and literally, lands on his feet. . . .

Now comes thru the Red Cross to the bombardier's wife that he was captured by the Germans after the bomber, on which he was a member of the crew, was shot down in flames. His capture followed by exactly two months another crash—one which ended in the English Channel after their bomber had been shot down.

headphones: "You heard nine voices, almost at once, talking to each other. And they was not saying nice things. They were saying things like 'Holy shit! Look at that sonofabitch! No way that guy's gonna shoot me!' And you're pressing the little red button and hoping that the enemy flies into it."

As the battered formation reached the outskirts of Schweinfurt, the German fighters withdrew—and some three hundred 88-millimeter antiaircraft guns opened up, filling the sky with puffs of greasy black smoke and millions of deadly shards of metal.

We're flying about twenty-eight thousand feet over Schweinfurt when, BANG! the Plexiglas on my left-hand side exploded. A twenty-millimeter shell had come up through my turret, hitting me in the left arm. Not breaking the arm but smashing the bone and tearing my jacket off. And went up into the waist window on the left-hand side, hit the stanchion of the fifty-caliber gun, and blew up. Killed the waist gunner. I remember him lying on his ammunition boxes. I remember the tail gunner bleeding over everything.

Despite his own injury and the flak that continued to rattle against the sides of the plane as it slowed over its target, Burke found himself thinking about his parents.

I realized that they did not know what I was doing. They did not know I was in the air force flying in a B-17 over enemy territory. I didn't want to tell them that, because I knew what it would do to them if they knew I was doing it. I thought I'd get away with it. I thought I would go through the entire war and nobody ever know it. When I got hit, I says, "Oh, goodness! My parents will get another telegram telling them either I was wounded or dead." At that point I didn't know which. That was the first time I ever thought what my being in the service did to my parents. And I had second thoughts then. But it was too late.

Burke and the rest of the crew were relieved, as they always were, when they finally dropped their load of bombs and the sudden loss of weight made the Fortress lift, the signal that they were now free to wheel around and start toward home. German fighters resumed their attack on what was left of the

Emily Lewis

formation, tearing at the bombers again and again, all the way back to the Channel. More Fortresses burned. More fell from the sky. The rest of the bombers headed for home, not in battle formation, one veteran remembered, "but in a straggling line, like geese after a shotgun volley." They landed at airfields scattered all across England.

Emily Lewis, a twenty-one-year-old volunteer from Little Rock, Arkansas, was one of the nurses who met the returning American planes.

We first were sent to a bomber base to meet the B-17s coming in shooting off red flares, which meant there were wounded aboard. So the first day we were there, thirteen B-17s shot off red flares. The first one came in just right over the treetops. We thought it was going to crash. Right outside. Skidded on the runway, sliding down. And I was in the ambulance. We ran over there and ran in. You had to crawl, you know. There was no way to get back into a B-17 standing up. Everything was crowded. The copilot and the pilot had been in a fire. The tail gunner was dead. He'd been shot right through the head. And the belly gunner was hurt. They were all injured. The German plane that fired on them just riddled the whole plane. But fortunately, they came back.

Sixty Fortresses had been shot down; 138 more were damaged, some beyond repair. Six hundred men were lost, and dozens more, like Earl Burke, had been wounded. The second raid on Schweinfurt had little more long-lasting impact than had the first. Fighter production dipped briefly, then rose again, and long-range American bombing missions were suspended until some way could be found to protect them better over enemy territory.

THE CROSSING OF THE VOLTURNO had been just the beginning for Babe Ciarlo and the 3rd Division. The Allies would have to battle their way through two more heavily fortified German positions—the Barbara and Reinhard lines—before they could begin their assault on the still unfinished but far more formidable Gustav Line, which blocked the road to Rome. As the U.S. and British armies entered the Barbara Line over the next month, fall became winter, the terrain grew more and more forbidding, and the weather turned steadily more ugly. The men learned to sleep while marching (it was "a kind of coma," one remembered), and when they got a chance to lie down, they preferred rocks to bare ground because rocks were relatively dry. Mountain tracks and likely bivouac areas were mined and otherwise booby-trapped. At night, the retreating enemy sent patrols doubling back to infiltrate Allied positions and reoccupy their old ones.

It was a scattered kind of warfare, waged at close quarters by small isolated units with grenades and mortars and machine guns, working their way up and down and across rocky hillsides. Hundreds of mules had been requisitioned to carry supplies up to the men and to carry down the dead and wounded. But the mountains grew too steep even for sure-footed animals, and carrying parties of supply troops had to be organized to haul up water, food, and ammunition on their backs; both hands were needed for climbing.

Still, boulder by boulder, hill by hill, the Allies continued slowly to fight their way through the German defenses. Babe Ciarlo's regiment helped lead the way, fighting past piles of rubble that had once been villages with names like Liberi and Dragoni and Presenzano, driving the enemy off hills Allied maps designated simply as "437" and "450," and finally joining forces with the 30th Regiment to capture Monte Lungo and Monte Rotundo in clouds of cold mist and fog that made it all but impossible to see more than twenty feet ahead.

By November 15, they had broken through the Barbara Line. Two days later, battered and weary, Ciarlo's 3rd Infantry Division was finally pulled out of the line to rest. It had lost 3,265 men, roughly one-fifth of its full strength: 683 had died in battle, 2,412 had been wounded, 170 were missing. The night his outfit was relieved, Ciarlo wrote again to his brother. He apologized for having been silent for so long and gave no indication of what had really kept him from putting pen to paper.

The reason why I didn't write is because I don't have much to say and I am a little lazy. . . . I hope you have a good time over the holidays and I hope you eat up [at] Mom's house for Christmas so that Mom might be happier.

> *Your loving brother, always,*
> *Babe*

Winter rains stall a jeep—and slow the American advance toward the Gustav Line. "The war in Italy is tough," one newspaperman reported. "The land and the weather are both against us."

A DEADLY CALLING

BY THE TIME BABE CIARLO and the 3rd Infantry Division were pulled from the line in Italy in mid-November of 1943, the Allies had begun to move in earnest on the other side of the world. American forces had driven the Japanese from Attu and Kiska, footholds in the Aleutian Islands off Alaska that the enemy had won just before the Battle of Midway. In the South Pacific, Allied troops under the overall command of Douglas MacArthur had launched Operation Cartwheel, winning control of a large part of New Guinea; pushing north through the central Solomons to seize western New Georgia, Vella Lavella, and Bougainville; bypassing and isolating enemy garrisons at Rendova and Kolombangara; and beginning the process of cutting off and neutralizing the main Japanese base at Rabaul as well.

Meanwhile, in the Central Pacific, a second, parallel campaign was finally under way. American shipyards had not only replaced all the warships lost at Pearl Harbor and in subsequent battles but had built a new navy larger and more powerful than all the other combatants' navies combined. Now, commanded by Admiral Nimitz, the Allies were to move steadily northwest toward Japan, through the Gilberts, the Marshalls, the Carolines, the Marianas. The Americans would face brand-new challenges. Distances between targets were vast. The islands of the Central Pacific were small, for the most part, and had no jungles to slow the fighting. But they were strongly defended nonetheless. The battle to take each of them would be short, costly, and astonishingly brutal. The first, to begin at dawn on November 20, was to be for Tarawa in the Gilbert Islands.

"Going back through the letters written to me at college during the war," Katharine Phillips remembered,

> *I find almost every letter will mention we had a V-mail from my brother Sid. He was the main concern of the entire family. Daddy would try to anticipate where he thought Sid would be sent next. And when the Battle of Tarawa occurred, we lived in horror for five days. We thought Sidney was in the battle, and the news reports of Tarawa were terrible from the first.*

Sidney Phillips, who had endured four months on Guadalcanal, was actually in New Guinea that November, training for a planned assault on the western end of New Britain at Cape Gloucester. Once U.S. warplanes could use the airstrip located

there, they could complete the neutralization of Rabaul. The struggle to take it would be another rugged jungle campaign like Guadalcanal. "All of Cape Gloucester was a jungle except the airfield," Phillips recalled. "And it was raining and it was muddy. It rained the entire time we were at Cape Gloucester. Everything rotted. Your clothes rotted. Your shoes rotted. Your shoestrings rotted."

But for all the misery he would experience on Cape Gloucester, Phillips could count himself lucky not to have been among the marines ordered to take Tarawa. It was a coral atoll—a ring of thirty-eight tiny islands around a blue lagoon—that marked the easternmost edge of the perimeter Japan had marked out to shield its new empire.

The main American target was the island of Betio, at the atoll's western tip. Flat, featureless, and less than half the size of New York's Central Park, Betio had its own airfield and was defended by some 4,800 Japanese, hidden within hundreds of rifle pits and trenches, pillboxes and blockhouses, all heavily reinforced with concrete and steel, sandbags, and coconut logs. A log and coral seawall three to five feet tall had been built just back of the beaches, and a coral reef six hundred to eight hundred yards offshore provided still another line of defense.

Tarawa was to be the test case for a new theory of amphibious warfare: *any* island, no matter how strongly defended, could be taken by an all-out frontal assault.

In the early morning hours of November 20, a fleet of nearly two hundred warships moved toward Betio. The heavy cruiser USS *Indianapolis,* flagship of the Fifth Fleet, was part of the invasion force. Midshipman Maurice Bell was watching from topside. He was a Mississippi-born carpenter who had been making a dollar an hour at a

Maurice Bell, before shipping out. At mail call (opposite), a GI finds something to smile at in a letter while his buddy improvises fudge from ingredients freshly arrived from home.

Mobile shipyard when he received his draft notice and joined the navy rather than the army because, he said, he didn't want to sleep in a hole in the ground.

> *We had Admiral Spruance aboard, and he always wanted to get what he called a ringside seat to every battle we went into, get just as close as he possibly could. When we pulled in there and started bombarding the island, there were ships all around the island just as far as I could see in every direction. And of course we was bombarding the island and it just tore the island up, the pretty palm trees were just tore up.*

The official version was that it had all gone smoothly. "Everything went like clockwork," the narrator of one War Department film would intone. "When the navy guns stop firing, the navy planes take over. Bombing. Strafing. We were a team, working together."

The team clearly needed more practice. The first few shells missed the island entirely. American warplanes arrived half an hour late and dropped many of their bombs into the sea. Still, more than three hours of bombardment did seem to set the whole island ablaze. The marines would "go in standing up," said one navy officer. "There aren't fifty Japs left alive." Aboard one transport the marines were so encouraged by all the damage being done to Betio that one green lieutenant assured the men of his platoon there was now "no need to worry"; no heroics would be needed; it was unlikely his men would be lucky enough to fire a shot. But all but a few of the Japanese troops huddled in their thick-walled positions rode out the firestorm, and the shelling eventually yielded so much smoke and coral dust that the fleet's view of the island was obscured. Firing was stopped for half an hour to clear the air—plenty of time for the Japanese to get ready to defend the beaches.

Next, it became clear that American planners had misjudged the tides. The first wave of marines from the 2nd Division made it to the beach aboard eighty-seven brand-new amphibious tractors equipped with mechanized tracks that allowed them to crawl over the reef. But most of those who followed had to be ferried toward shore in Higgins boats, landing craft that needed four feet of water to clear the coral barrier. They got only one foot. Many hung up on the reef hundreds of yards from shore, easy targets for machine guns and howitzers, antitank guns and antiaircraft guns fixed to fire horizontally.

Landing craft blew apart, burned, floated helplessly. The marines who made it safely into the water had to wade shoulder-deep toward shore into the face of still more enemy fire. Holding their rifles above their heads, they could not even shoot back. Eight out of ten men in some companies were lost. "The water

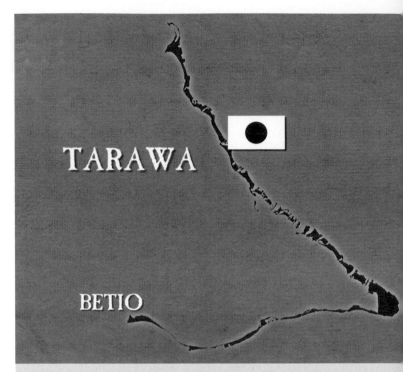

On his way toward the landing beach on Betio, the largest island in the Tarawa atoll of the Gilbert chain (above), a marine ignores the smoke and chaos that preoccupy most of his comrades and finds inspiration in his favorite pinup.

was red," one survivor said. "It takes a lot of blood to make water red." Another recalled, "Those who were not hit will always remember how the machine gun bullets hissed into the water, inches to the right, inches to the left." When they saw what was happening along the reef, some navy coxswains refused to take their landing craft anywhere near it and dropped their passengers into deep water, where many drowned, dragged under by heavy packs and ammunition.

"We were Americans and invincible," a coastguardsman remembered thinking after he found himself wading toward the island that afternoon as part of the seventh wave.

We had a huge armada of warships and a division of marines. How could this be happening? I kept as low as possible in the water and tried to pull my body up inside my hel- *met. . . . I discovered the rows of marines along the beach weren't lying there waiting for orders to move. They were dead. There were dead all over.*

By nightfall, five thousand marines had somehow made it to the narrow beach between the sea and the seawall. Some fifteen hundred of those were dead or wounded. Most of the rest could go no farther, crowded together behind the log barrier and pinned down by enemy fire. The beach commander, Colonel David M. Shoup, was hit nine times but remained on his feet. Communications failed, and at least two dozen men carrying messages between him and other officers up and down the beach were cut down. Had the Japanese counterattacked that night, the marines might have been annihilated. But American bombs had killed their commander and most of his staff. No one was left to give the order.

The beginning of the following day was a ghastly repetition of the last half of the first day. During the night, a handful of Japa-

Around noon on the second day of the struggle for Tarawa, marines battle their way over the log seawall and off the beach, on their way to take the Japanese airstrip that had been their initial target.

A marine demolition team dynamites a Japanese blockhouse on Tarawa.

Concealed within a pillbox on Tarawa, these Japanese soldiers shot themselves rather than suffer the shame of surrendering to the Americans.

nese troops had managed to swim out to several of the wrecked landing craft bobbing along the reef and set up machine guns in them. When the first marine reinforcements arrived and started wading toward the beach, trying not to notice the stench of dead bodies drifting toward them, they were caught in enemy fire from two sides. By 8:00 a.m. more than three hundred more men had been hit.

Around noon, the tide finally rolled in. Higgins boats could now carry men and guns and tanks over the reef and directly in to shore. Here and there, marines started to make their way over the seawall and move inland. They seized the airstrip and cut the island in two. More men and more supplies came ashore. At four o'clock that afternoon, Colonel Shoup issued a terse battle action report: "Casualties: Many. Percentage dead: Unknown. Combat efficiency: *We are winning.*"

In the early hours of the next morning, the Japanese mounted a series of counterattacks. Some were silent rushes by fifty men or less, discovered and destroyed only at the last moment. In other cases, hundreds of screaming men ran directly into the American guns. In the eerie light cast by volleys of star shells

fired offshore, the marines killed them with artillery, machine guns, grenades, bayonets, and finally bare hands. "They told us we had to hold," one marine told his colonel when the fury had subsided, "and by God, we held."

The following day, the marines went about the brutal, methodical business of eliminating the survivors. They sealed bunkers and blockhouses with bulldozers and light tanks, then burned or blew up everything and everyone inside.

Betio was declared "secured" at 1:12 p.m. on November 24. In an effort to inspire his men before the battle, the Japanese commander had told them "a million men cannot take Tarawa in a hundred years." Ten thousand marines had done the job in less than seventy-six hours, but at a fearful cost: 1,085 of them had been killed—nearly half so mangled they could not be identified before burial—and 2,233 more were wounded. All but 17 of the 4,800 Japanese on the island were dead as well. There were bodies everywhere: floating at the shoreline, heaped on the beaches, blasted into the sandy soil. One marine remembered that "you couldn't dig a grave for one body without uncovering another."

The green lieutenant who had assured his men before they landed that they needn't be concerned about their safety had made it through the battle unhurt. Twenty-six of the thirty-nine men in his platoon had not: thirteen were dead, and another thirteen were wounded. After he returned to the transport ship that had brought them to Betio, he remembered, he sat for hours in the wardroom, writing "over and over again the names of the dead and wounded, as though somehow putting their names on paper would make them alive and well."

It took the War Department ten days to compile and release the casualty lists. Americans were horrified. A comparable number of marines had died on Guadalcanal, but that campaign had dragged on for six months. When Marine Major General Holland "Howlin' Mad" Smith unwisely told the press that Tarawa had been taken only because so many young Americans had

been "willing to die," grieving parents accused him in the press of murdering their children and demanded his resignation.

Tokyo was still nearly four thousand miles away, and Washington worried that civilians did not yet understand the resolve of the enemy their sons were facing or the kind of sacrifices they would continue to be called upon to make before the war in the Pacific could be ended. To help clarify things, a film called *With the Marines at Tarawa*, compiled from footage shot under fire by fifteen marine cameramen, was rushed into theaters all over the country. It gave American moviegoers their first close-in look at what combat was really like. Marine recruitment plummeted for a time after it was shown, but sales of war bonds rose.

"When we saw those first pictures of Tarawa, we were overcome, just overcome," Katharine Phillips remembered.

Those American boys' bodies floating in the surf. It was just devastating to us. We just sat around and cried, and I know that's why they had kept it from the American public for so long. Our dislike for the Japanese was very violent. That they would do this to us. And would kill our boys like that. And of course the idea was "Kill the Japs." I'm ashamed to say it, but that's the way it was. We just had to get that war over with.

American dead strewn along the beach at Tarawa. Photographs and film footage of scenes like this helped cause an outcry all across the United States. "The truth was that many Americans were not prepared psychologically to accept the cruel facts of war," the correspondent Robert Sherrod wrote. "On Tarawa . . . there was a more realistic approach . . ."

THANKSGIVING FELL ON NOVEMBER 25 IN 1943, and President Roosevelt and Prime Minister Churchill found themselves in Cairo, on their way to Teheran for their first joint meeting with Stalin. FDR had brought turkeys with him and insisted on carving them for some twenty guests with what the prime minister called "masterly, indefatigable skill." The president also held forth on the holiday's history and said how pleased he was that American soldiers were now "spreading that custom all over the world." Churchill recalled the occasion as filled with the spirit of "warm and intimate friendship."

The talks at Teheran would turn out to be considerably less congenial. The Big Three discussed the outlines of a postwar world. They all supported the creation of some sort of successor to the League of Nations and agreed that, once defeated, Germany would be divided into separate Allied zones of occupation. But Stalin also made it clear, in discussions over the future of Poland, that the Soviet Union intended to remain in control of most of the eastern European countries through which its armies moved as they drove toward Germany, beginning with the Baltic states of Estonia, Latvia, and Lithuania. Roosevelt and Churchill felt powerless to intervene. Defeating Germany was their primary goal. The Red Army was bearing the brunt of the fighting. (In the battle of Moscow alone, more Soviet troops died than the combined total of American and British Commonwealth battle dead throughout the war.) And nothing short of military threat against their ally had the slightest chance of changing Stalin's mind. What made this war different from all others, he had recently told the Yugoslav Communist Josip Tito, was that "whoever occupies a territory also imposes his own social system. Everyone imposes his own system as far as his army can reach. It cannot be otherwise."

There was disagreement about the conduct of the fighting as well. Churchill entered the talks still clinging to the hope that more forceful Allied action in Italy or fresh assaults elsewhere in the Mediterranean—through German-occupied Yugoslavia or Greece, perhaps—could somehow both provide the second front Stalin continued to demand and delay or perhaps even make redundant Operation Overlord, the massive cross-Channel invasion that so concerned him and his commanders. The Soviet premier would have none of it. There were 260 enemy divisions on his country's soil, he said; such "diversions" would do little to drive them off. "If we are here to discuss military matters," he said, "then Russia's only interest is in Overlord." Roosevelt agreed, and reiterated that the invasion would go forward no later than May of 1944, and that it would be combined with a separate but simultaneous attack through southern France. Churchill went along reluctantly. "I realized at Teheran for the first time what a small nation we are," he would later write. "There I sat with the great Russian bear on one side of me, with paws outstretched, and on the other side sat the great American buffalo, and between the two sat the poor little English donkey who was the only one, the only one of the three, who knew the right way home." For his part, Stalin said he would consider joining the struggle against Japan once the Germans had been defeated.

THE CITIZENS OF WATERBURY did their best to celebrate Thanksgiving as they always had that year. But the war intruded upon even the most familiar holiday rituals. Those who'd waited too long to buy a turkey for the family dinner had to settle for chicken or duck; many of the bigger birds had been bought up by the War Department to serve to men and women in uniform wherever they happened to be. At Municipal Stadium that afternoon, Wilby High School upset Crosby 19–14 to win the annual schoolboy football title, but at halftime the six thousand boosters of both teams were asked to stand in silence while a bugler blew taps for two former Wilby players, Johnny Barnes and Bagio Pandolfi, both killed fighting in the Pacific.

The *Waterbury Republican* was filled with war news that week. The marines had taken Tarawa. The British Eighth Army, trying to fight its way up the eastern side of the Italian peninsula, had crossed the Sangro River and then stalled in the mountains. The Red Army continued to drive the Germans back across the Ukraine. The Royal Air Force had carried out a massive nighttime raid on Berlin: HITLER'S HOME ABLAZE, the headline read, BERLIN WHICH TOURISTS KNEW CEASES TO EXIST. A "very highly ranked American officer" was quoted as saying that "Bombing, plus Russia's magnificent victories, may crush Germany before any great battle." A nameless British counterpart begged to differ. "I've fought Germans in two wars and I don't think there's any cheap way to beat them—and I am convinced that the crack will come in this war as it came in the last, at the front, not at home, and only after the German army has been thoroughly whipped."

Waterbury went back to work on Friday. The city's

Leo Goldberg

Brass mills in Waterbury's south end

peacetime industries had now all switched over to defense work, and newcomers continued to stream into town in search of jobs. "Waterbury had become a humming city," Babe Ciarlo's younger brother, Tom, remembered.

You could almost compare it to a miniature Times Square. It was never quiet, because there were so many factories and each factory had three shifts so they're going around the clock. You didn't have cars, because there were no gasoline stamps, so you had to take buses. We had buses running up and down from the center of town to different streets all over the city, going constantly. The restaurants downtown were always booming. So were the bars. Theaters were always full. There was always something going on.

Leo Goldberg had been renting an apartment in his native Brooklyn when he first heard about the opportunities offered by the Brass City.

The landlord's son on a visit from Waterbury told me about how easy it was to get a job in a defense factory, and there I was working in a gas station at twelve dollars a day. So I went

up there looking for work. There was one memorable morning when I got on a bus, sat down next to a stranger, who turned to me and said, "Good morning." And I looked at him as if to say, "Who are you to say good morning to me." After all, I'm from Brooklyn, New York.

But the impact was very great. The friendliness that I found in Waterbury was something I was not accustomed to. I found a room at some rooming house. Having a job and no attachments, you don't have to answer to anybody. It was a burst of freedom.

The Scovill Manufacturing Company, where Leo Goldberg found work sharpening big circular brass-cutting saws, produced so many different military items, according to the *Republican*, that "there wasn't an American or British fighting man . . . who wasn't dependent on Scovill for some part of the food, clothing, shelter, and equipment that sustained him through the struggle."

Mattatuck Manufacturing gave up making upholstery nails in favor of cartridge clips for M-1 rifles—and turned out 3 million of them a week. Chase Brass and Copper made 52 million mortar shells and cartridge cases and more than a billion small-caliber bullets. And three times a day, buses lined up on the Waterbury green in the center of town to ferry workers to and from the big, new factory that the Waterbury Clock Company had built for itself in neighboring Middlebury. Put together in just eighty-eight days, it had trees, water, and grass painted on the roof to deceive enemy bombers, as well as an elaborate system that would have flooded the whole structure without damaging it if there was sufficient warning of an air raid. There, Waterbury Clock stopped producing the dollar watches that had made it famous and began turning out gyroscopes and artillery and anti-aircraft fuses—as well as some three hundred thousand alarm clocks, which, Washington insisted, were essential to ensure that people got to their defense jobs on time.

Anne DeVico had been just sixteen when Pearl Harbor was attacked. She never forgot walking down to the Waterbury green that afternoon and finding it crowded with people, "some screaming, some crying, some numb." Like her friend Babe Ciarlo, she was the child of Italian immigrants and lived in the North End. A half brother served in the air force in Italy; her old-

At the Chase Case Shop of the Waterbury Manufacturing Company on North Main Street, women inspect artillery shell casings (above), while a few miles to the west (opposite), inside the new plant the Waterbury Clock Company constructed for itself in Middlebury, workers bused in from Waterbury assemble antiaircraft fuses that could be set to explode at a certain time or altitude.

SALVAGE FOR VICTORY

The Office of Civilian Defense called upon each American family to become a "fighting unit on the home front." Everyone was asked to collect scrap metal from which armaments could be made. In one year alone, Mobile's citizens amassed 22 million pounds of it. "All the old iron beds were pulled out of the garages," Katharine Phillips recalled. "The city took up the old streetcar lines on Government and Dauphin streets, and they were added to the scrap pile. Everyone took part in World War II down to the youngest child. They could save something, or stomp a tin can. There was something for everybody to do, and we all did it."

In Sacramento, twenty-two big "Victory Bins" painted red, white, and blue were set up on downtown street corners for the duration, even though some people thought them unsightly. And in Waterbury, 281,135 pounds of tin were collected during the war, along with 65,000 pounds of rubber, 225,458 pounds of rags—and 372,733 pounds of kitchen fat, from which glycerin could be extracted for the manufacture of explosives.

Luverne had been founded by Civil War veterans, but the town council volunteered to melt down the cannonballs that formed part of the memorial to the Union dead to make munitions for the new conflict.

There, as elsewhere, children like Jim Sherman and his brothers were the most avid scrap collectors. "I think Luverne was cleaner during the war than at any time in its history," he remembered, "primarily because we kids would go out and we'd go to the alleys, back roads, ditches, anywhere to find something made out of metal."

Patriotism was only partly responsible. It cost eleven cents to get into the Saturday matinee at the Palace, but any boy or girl

who amassed twenty pounds of scrap could get in free.

My two brothers and I went out one time and made a horrendous haul, much more than enough to get into the theater, so we're handing it out to the kids who don't have enough. You know, "What do you need? Need a tire? Here's an old rim. Here's an old piece of metal." Then the manager of the theater came down and told us, "I don't want you doing this anymore. These kids have to get their own stuff."

The Sherman brothers competed with other Luverne children in gathering another unlikely commodity: milkweed floss for use in making life jackets for the navy.

They told us two pounds of milkweed would make one life vest. So we would go out looking for milkweed. And we got twenty cents a bag. We would each have our special patches that we wouldn't tell anyone else about. The one I remember was at the Olson's Dairy out toward the Blue

Mounds, along the old Rock Island Railroad. We'd go out there after dinner and crawl down among these weeds and brambles collecting these god-awful milkweed pods. In one year, I think there were 1,300 bags turned in. Now I could never understand how they were going to take this little bit of stuff and save some Navy pilot who ended up in the Pacific Ocean, but that was the story we got.

Scrap drives were in large part children's crusades. From southern California (opposite, top) to Waterbury (opposite, bottom) to Luverne (above right), boys and girls stripped their neighborhoods clean. Milkweed collecting (above) was a small-town specialty. The impressive parade of old tires below (more than eighty tons of them) was led by the Boy Scouts of Stevens Point, Wisconsin.

Anne DeVico (center) and friends

est brother went into the army and became an MP. She worried about them both, of course, but she also remembered wartime Waterbury as a lively place for young people. "Soldiers and sailors were everything, and when guys came home, you did whatever you could for them. We would have them come to the house for dinner, go to the USO dances with them, anything to make them happy."

At one dance, she met a boy from New York City named Angelo D'Agostino, who had a job at Waterbury Manufacturing. They went out together for a while. He was more serious about her than she was about him. "I was having a lot of fun," she said. "There were lots of guys around—always someone home on furlough that we had to go out with." After he was drafted and went into the army air force, she was astonished to get a letter from him from Italy, asking her for a photograph. He'd named his bomber *Waterbury Anne* in her honor, he wrote, and the rest of the crew wanted to see what she looked like. By then, she was dating a local boy named Art Grasso; he eventually went into the navy and died in a U-boat attack off the New Jersey coast. Then one of her brother's closest friends was killed, and "it began to get worse. Every day in the paper there were pictures of boys who were missing and who were killed."

She and her friends wrote to as many boys as they could, prayed for them at church, sent them Christmas parcels. "They loved hearing from us, because they said at mail call they wanted their name to be called over and over. We told them where we went last night: we went for a hot dog or we went to the USO and we saw so-and-so there."

On December 31, 1943, several of DeVico's girlfriends asked her to go with them into Manhattan to see in the New Year in Times Square. She had to get her mother's permission. It wasn't easy. Mrs. DeVico was convinced that only bad girls went to New York; it was where Waterbury boys went to try to "get something," after all. Anne argued that there was safety in numbers. Her friends and their mothers backed her up.

Finally we all cried, and my mother said, "Okay. You can go because there's eight of you going. How could eight of you do something wrong?"

So we were at the Times Square Hotel and we said, let's walk down toward where the ball drops, and on the way let's find an automat. As we're walking we're talking about the automat and all of a sudden this big, tall, good-looking dreamboat comes by with a whole bunch of sailors and says, "Hey, we're looking for the automat, too, why don't you look with us?" And I said, "Fine." So that was my future husband, Bob Swift. And he was so tall and had golden curls . . . he was just handsome. So I thought, "Wow. How could I be so lucky?"

And as he's walking with me he said, "Here, the ball is going to come down." So he turned and kissed me and said, "I'm going to marry you." And I said, "Oh, right."

When I came home, I'm thinking, "How could it be that I'm from a small city, Waterbury, Connecticut, and how could I meet somebody from Valparaiso, Indiana, in New York City, and how could we fall in love?" It was as if fate had just said, "You're going to meet somebody." Whoever thought it would be like that?

Bob Swift took the train up to Waterbury to see DeVico a week later. She had to pretend he was a friend of a friend's boyfriend before her mother would even allow him to call. "I was Italian, East Coast, Catholic," she remembered. "He was midwestern, tall, blond, Protestant. But somehow it just worked." Before he returned to the navy, they agreed to write to each other. After that, knowing that the man she loved was at sea in the Pacific, she began to trace the daily progress of the war.

I never was really following it until I started going out with Bob. I knew he was out there somewhere, but I certainly didn't know which battles he was in. I didn't know that, because they didn't say which ship was in which battle. So every time there was a battle, I would say, "I hope Bob's ship isn't there." But I didn't know.

He did call me once. He was in Honolulu, and it was just wonderful to hear his voice. We couldn't even talk that long, and we couldn't even hear each other that well. But it was just so nice to hear him say, "I'm fine. I'm coming home to you. I love you." And that was the one time I wasn't worried.

Bob Swift

When I'd get a letter from him, somebody'd say to me, "Oh you can get a letter and he still could have been killed." So then I would think, "You know, you're right. I could be reading this letter and it's two or three weeks old." So it did scare me. And especially when it was somebody that you were going to marry when he came home. That's all he talked about was getting married. So I'm thinking, "Gee whiz. He could be out there in the thick of it. And I don't even know," but you're always uncertain until you actually hear from him that we were in this battle, but we survived. He would say something like that and I'd say, "Well, he's safe for now," but it was a terrible time.

DESPITE EVERYTHING, THE INTERNEES at Santo Tomas in Manila had also done their best to have a festive New Year's Eve. After dinner, there was an open-air production of *Cinderella* performed by a cast of 150, mostly drawn from the camp's children. Afterward, a few men continued to sit out on the lawn. As one recalled:

At midnight, it was clear that the people of the Philippines were not in a celebrating mood. Not a ship's whistle blew; not a bell rang from any of the hundreds of churches in Manila. No searchlights illuminated the dark sky. The streets around Santo Tomas were entirely quiet. What little noise was to be heard came from the main building in the camp, where several small parties were in progress.

During the past few months, the internees had experienced both lows and highs. In November, a three-day typhoon had lashed the camp "like a spiked waterfall," one man recalled. Trees, shanties, canned goods floated away. Drinking water was fouled. Everyone was forced to take shelter in the main building. Two weeks later, the ground was still too spongy for the Thanksgiving football game. In December, a shipment of Red Cross parcels arrived. "Even though the sentries poked their bayonets through many of the kits and damaged what was in them, it seemed like a wonderful Christmas gift from America," Sascha Weinzheimer noted.

Many people we knew didn't like the Red Cross before that, but they sure changed their minds when they got Spam, corned beef, butter, cheese, chocolate, crackers. . . . Mother and Dad stored away all the cans that would keep a long time for a rainy day.

Even though Mummy and Daddy kept telling us kids to eat everything on our plates because the day would come

when we might have very little to eat, we didn't really believe them.

Christmas itself had been a disappointment. More than two thousand friends and family members had gathered outside the gate, assuming they would be allowed in for the holiday as they had been the year before. This time, the Japanese turned them all away. The holiday crackdown turned out to be only the beginning. On January 10, the Japanese let it be known that the camp was about to be taken over by the War Prisoners Department of the Imperial Army.

"If we thought we had reason to complain about how awful our life was," Sascha wrote, "we soon changed our minds and knew we had been on a picnic till then. From now on, we would be the same as military war prisoners and not civilian prisoners. . . . It seemed as if almost everything was taken away from us at once." Soldiers with bayonets now patrolled the camp. Men, women, even children were ordered to bow to every sentry they encountered and were sometimes slapped or kicked for failing to follow shouted orders they could not always understand. The gates were permanently barred. No one could visit family members outside the walls; no one from outside could come in. No more food was to be brought in for purchase; prisoners were to grow their own. Adult rations were reduced to less than fifteen hundred calories, half what a healthy man needed simply to maintain his weight. Children were expected to subsist on half that. Meat was cut off; fish would provide protein. "We all thought this would be fine for a change," Sascha wrote, because "the carabao meat [we'd been having] wasn't always fresh, and such a little bit you couldn't always see it in the gravy." But the fish turned out to be *sapsap*, the same dried, foul-smelling, finger-length fish the Weinzheimers had once fed to their cat. "Fish gravy made with them was pretty awful. The garbage cans were filled with them; even the cats turned up their noses." The elected Executive Committee that had been allowed at least limited powers to run things within the walls of Santo Tomas was replaced by an appointed three-man Internee Committee. When it complained that rations were inadequate, the new commandant responded that he had personally inspected the camp's garbage cans and found scraps of food in them. "Evidently you are not hungry yet," he said.

One morning, he brought a visiting delegation of Japanese officers past the long tables at which women sat, cutting worm holes out of the limp greens that were all they had for the evening stew. Among them was Mrs. Willie Brown Sanders, an elderly African American woman well over six feet tall. The widow of a 9th Cavalry soldier who had died fighting the Philippine Insurrection, she had stayed on in Manila to run a boardinghouse that catered to visiting Americans. She was almost as tall sitting down as the Japanese colonel was standing up. He had never seen anyone like her.

"You Canadian?" he asked.

She just kept cutting away at the vegetables.

He asked again. She said nothing.

The colonel turned to the others and said, "She's a Canadian."

That was enough for Mrs. Sanders. "No, I'm not a Canadian," she said, banging her knife down on the table and rising to her feet. Towering over her visitors, she said, "I'm an American Negro. I was born in Texas, and I'm proud of it. And while you're here telling me, I've got a few things I want to tell you. Now, come along with me." The commander and his followers meekly fell in line behind her as she strode through the camp, loudly pointing out its shortcomings: the crowding, the filth, the ragged clothing that was all anyone had left to wear. Edgar Kneedler, the former manager of the Bay View Hotel, where the Weinzheimers had stayed when the Japanese marched into Manila, happened to be in the kitchen when she got there. "I want you to taste this pig food you've been feeding us," she said to the Japanese. She demanded a ladle, dipped it into a pot of moldy cornmeal, and insisted that each officer take a mouthful. "Nothing but crap and corruption," she said. The officers backed away. Afterward, prisoners crowded around Sanders to congratulate her for her courage. "Call *me* a Canadian!" was all she said.

There was one bright spot for families like the Weinzheimers. To relieve crowding in the buildings that served as dormitories—there were now nearly four thousand internees at Santo Tomas, more than ever before—those families that had shanties were permitted to sleep in them overnight. Children were delighted. "Our shanty, like the others, had only one room," Sascha remembered, "but it seemed like Heaven to us because it was our own little place." Husbands and wives liked it, too; they'd been forced to sleep apart for months. The morning after the Shanty Edict, the internee who picked the daily wake-up music to play over the camp loudspeakers chose "Happy Days Are Here Again."

Santo Tomas lived on rumors of liberation. Some were based on stories in the Manila *Tribune,* the daily four-page Japanese propaganda sheet that was handed around among the internees. In its columns, Japan was always triumphant, but the shifting sites at which it claimed to be winning its victories suggested that the Allies were on the move against them. Other rumors were based on garbled versions of authentic war news that had crackled in from San Francisco or Brisbane or Delhi over the two radio receivers hidden in the camp. Internees knew that Tarawa had fallen, and when U.S. forces moved on to take Kwajalein and

Sascha Weinzheimer and her young brother, Buddy, dressed up and photographed at Santo Tomas for Japanese propaganda purposes

Eniwetok, in the Marshalls, they learned that, too. They'd heard that the Allies were ashore in Italy and that the Russians were driving the Germans back on the eastern front. Some took a kind of comfort from the thought that their captors' ever-increasing harshness was a product of their growing fear of invasion by the Allies. But other tales that raced through camp were just wishful thinking. A British internee scribbled a poem about what he called the camp's chronic "rumortism."

I heard it stated yesterday by a man who ought to know,
That by tomorrow afternoon we can pack our bags and go.
This information came to him from a most authentic source
Via his house-boy's cousin's aunt—and verified of course.
Ten thousand flying fortresses flew over town last night,
It's too bad we couldn't see them, because of their great
   height,

But they dropped a million leaflets, one of which would have
    been found
If some Japanese civilians hadn't just then come around. . . .

Somewhere in the Pacific (near the Marshalls we presume)
A naval battle is being fought; from which one can assume
That the Russians, Poles and Slovaks with twenty million
    more
Have joined forces in the Ukraine and retaken Singapore.
This may all sound like a rumor,
But to me it looks all right,
So why wait until tomorrow?
Let's pack our bags tonight.

IN JAPAN, GLENN FRAZIER had long since been allowed to climb out of the dark pit into which the commander of Osaka POW Camp #1 had thrown him for daring to keep his hands in his pockets. But there were times, looking back, when he wondered whether he would have been better off if he'd been allowed to stay there. The brutality with which he and his fellow prisoners were treated was relentless. Small boys followed them through the streets as they walked to and from their work details, he remembered, jeering and spitting and shouting that they were "American cowards, dishonored by our country and unable ever to go back to America." The Japanese winter continued to be cold and damp. There was no heat in the barracks. The men, wearing what was left of their summer clothes, slept in heaps to stay warm. Prisoners thought guilty of the smallest infraction were made to hold railroad ties over their heads until they collapsed; when they did, the guards beat them.

The prisoners did what they could to sabotage the Japanese war effort. Told to move brand-new captured British-made heavy machinery from railroad cars to military trucks, they managed to loosen or break off most of the handles. They poured sand into the oil tanks of unattended trucks, jabbed holes in the bottoms of barrels, and carried bits of sharpened bamboo to poke holes into bags of rice or beans, from which they filled their own pockets. They also fought with British prisoners housed nearby who somehow managed to obtain marginally more plentiful rations than they had.

Their keepers continued to insist that the prisoners would never see their homes again, that it would be best for them if they learned to speak Japanese and follow Japanese orders on the parade ground. When Frazier failed to lift his feet high enough to suit one drillmaster, a guard with a fixed bayonet ran forward and shoved its point deep into his knee. The wound was slow to heal.

"We knew nothing about how the war was going," Frazier remembered, "except that it was lasting much longer than we had expected it to last." Then a box from the Red Cross arrived. Inside was a letter from his family, marked up but not entirely obliterated by the Japanese. There were photographs of his mother and father, sister and cousins, in the box, too, and a five-cent candy bar that made Frazier's whole depleted body burn when he ate it. In weak moments he had begun to believe that his country really might have abandoned him again, just as it had on Bataan. The Red Cross box with its reminders of home made him hope again.

THE END IN THE PACIFIC could come only after Germany surrendered, and the end in Europe could come only after the Allies finally mounted the long-delayed invasion of France. Everyone knew 1944 was going to be a decisive year. "The war is now reaching the stage," FDR had warned in his 1943 Christmas message, "when we shall have to look forward to large casualty lists—dead, wounded, and missing. . . . War entails just that. There is no easy road to victory. And the end is not yet in sight."

In January, the men who would lead the invasion that had been named Operation Overlord met for the first time in London to draw up the final plans. Dwight Eisenhower had been picked to be supreme commander of the Allied Expeditionary Force. Three Britons would serve directly under him: General Bernard Montgomery, in charge of ground troops, Admiral Bertram Ramsey, who was to command the navy, and Air Chief Marshal Trafford Leigh-Mallory.

Five divisions—150,000 men—were to land along a fifty-mile front in Normandy on a single day, with hundreds of thousands more to follow. Nothing on anything like this scale had ever been attempted before. Nearly 3 million Allied military personnel would have to be assembled in Britain. A fleet of more than five thousand vessels had to be put together. The Germans had fortified every Channel port to block reinforcement and resupply. To help solve that problem, Allied engineers had to devise and construct two floating artificial ports, called mulberrys—fifty thousand tons of steel, a million tons of concrete, 120 miles of steel cable—that could be towed across the Channel in sections, then reassembled off the invasion beaches. Elaborate schemes were undertaken to convince the Germans that the attack would come somewhere other than Normandy—in Norway or at the closest point to England, the Pas-de-Calais. D-day would have to offer clear skies for air support; moonlight to insure visibility and reasonably calm seas; and a low tide at sunrise, so landing craft could make it through the obstacles the Germans had set up offshore. The original May 1 date for the landing had to be abandoned; there would still not be enough landing craft on hand by then. So thirteen American shipyards were put to work producing nothing else—one every three and a half days—and the invasion was eventually rescheduled for June 5. Any further delay would leave the Allies too little time to engage the enemy before winter set in; the assault would have to be put off for yet another year. Everything had to be ready on time, every part of the plan had to mesh with every other part—and all of it had to be kept a secret from the enemy.

The planning for Overlord affected everything, including the battle for Italy that had started with such promise nearly four months earlier. During the last two weeks of November the Fifth Army had made no progress at all toward Rome. The men had simply been too exhausted to go on. In early December, they began inching forward again, trying to batter their way through the Reinhard Line toward the Gustav Line despite stiffening German resistance, still colder and more frequent rains—it would be the worst Italian winter in memory—and more and more forbidding terrain.

"Where are we going?" one weary artilleryman asked a colonel.

"To another goddamned mountain" was his answer.

Alan Moorehead, an Australian correspondent working for the London *Daily Express,* watched the struggle for a single hill called Monte Camino. The men he described happened to belong to the British 56th Infantry Division, but for the Americans struggling to take similar mountains just a few miles away the landscape and the suffering were the same.

An earthen track zig-zagged up the sheer face of the mountain. . . . There were no trees, only coarse grass, and so the enemy on top had a perfect field of fire. Rain water was cascading down the track at such a pace that it unseated boulders and loose rocks and these went careering to the bottom. There were two processions in the track, one going up, the other coming down, and the whole of this human frieze was under shellfire. You could see it all from the bottom if you arched your neck. The upward travelers were mostly Italian mule teams carrying blankets and boxes of ammunition. Then there were single soldiers, each one with a heavy box of rations on his back, and they were bent double by the incline. As they lifted themselves upward step by step their faces were only inches from the mud. And then there were the reinforcements, the infantry in their camouflaged waterproof gas-capes, the rain streaming off their steel helmets,

their hands gone blue with cold. They climbed numbly, contemplating each few yards in front of them, since no one there could comprehend the whole battle or the worse discomforts that were to be added. Each man found it enough merely to contain himself, to keep himself alive and moving. . . .

Every minute or two a shell came down. They hit first on one side of the track, then the other, in the angles of the sharp bends. Whenever a shell hit the track itself a gap would open up in the procession. At first this gap was filled with smoke. Then as the smoke cleared, you would see the fallen men scattered about on the steep grass and the mules stampeding. And the gap would close again as others came down and others came up.

At the top on the exposed slopes . . . men lay in slit trenches and these were half-filled with water. There comes a time when the mind will react no more to cold and danger. Those who had been exposed up there for two days and nights slept waist deep in the water. In utter weariness they lost all sense of time and place and even perhaps the sense of hope. Only the sense of pain remained, of constantly reiterated pain that invaded sleep and waited for the end of sleep to increase. For these soldiers the risk of war had passed out of conscious-

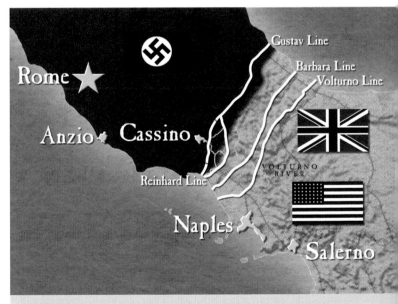

In order to advance up the Italian peninsula, the Allies had to battle their way through one German defensive line after another (above), often forced to fight over terrain as rugged as this slope (opposite) overlooking the Volturno in January 1944. "Our troops were living in almost inconceivable misery," Ernie Pyle wrote. "They dug into the stones and slept in little chasms and behind rocks and in half-caves. They lived like men in prehistoric times."

ness and was replaced by the misery and discomfort of war, which in the end is worse than anything.

By early January, the Allies had captured all the high ground that faced the Gustav Line. They had advanced fifty miles since landing at Salerno fourteen weeks earlier, but the last seven miles had taken them nearly half that time and cost them sixteen thousand casualties. At that rate it would be years before they reached Rome. And before they took another step they would have to find a way to get through defensive positions far more formidable than anything they'd previously encountered. The Volturno and the Barbara and Reinhard lines had all been meant to slow the Allies. The Gustav Line was meant to stop them cold. For a year, the Germans had been forced to give ground in Russia and North Africa, Sicily and Italy. Hitler had now declared "the end of withdrawals" and ordered the Gustav Line defended with "fanatical will . . . in a spirit of holy hatred not only against the enemy, but against all officers and units who fail in this decisive hour."

The Gustav Line was really a system of interlocking barriers, natural and man-made, that stretched for fifty miles across the narrowest part of the Italian peninsula. Most of it was mountains, their slopes meticulously sown with mines and blanketed with barbed wire. Every cave and hidden crevice seemed to harbor a bunker or pillbox, gun pit or steel-reinforced nest for machine guns whose crisscrossing zones of fire covered every likely approach.

Allied commanders looked for some way through it. West of the Appennines just two roads led to Rome. Highway 7, the ancient Appian Way, which skirted the Tyrrhenian coast, was the most direct route, but it threaded its way through miles of marshland that had been flooded by the Germans. Highway 6 looked more promising. It ran through a ten-mile gap between mountain ranges and then up the broad Liri Valley, ideally suited for the columns of Allied armor that had been of little use in the mountains. Field Marshal Kesselring and his commanders understood that the breach formed by the Liri Valley was the most likely point of Allied attack and did everything they could to make a breakthrough there impossible. Two fast-moving rivers, the Garigliano and the Rapido, provided a natural moat. Kesselring flooded both by destroying dams, turning the surrounding countryside into a vast bog; then filled dry areas with thousands of mines; and felled trees and blew up farmhouses to

American shells hit Castle Hill above the fortified village of Cassino. Still higher stands the ancient abbey of Monte Cassino, which Allied troops, trapped in the valley below, were convinced provided the Germans with a prized vantage point from which to direct fire down upon them.

give his gunners unobstructed fields of fire for every likely crossing point. On the right side of the valley's entrance, Highway 6 twisted through the little village of Cassino, transformed by the Germans into a fortress. Looming above what was left of the village was 1,715-foot Monte Cassino, capped by a vast white Benedictine abbey. Founded in the sixth century by St. Benedict himself, it was held sacred by Roman Catholics all around the world. The summit on which it stood and the surrounding hilltops afforded German observers a clear view of every inch of the terrain the Allies would have to cross to get at them.

"The stagnation of the whole campaign on the Italian front is becoming scandalous," Churchill told the British Chiefs of Staff in January. He demanded action, something new and daring to break the deadlock: "Nothing less than Rome could satisfy." The result was Operation Shingle: British and American troops under Major General John B. Lucas were to make a surprise amphibious landing behind the German lines at the resort towns of Anzio and Nettuno, some thirty miles south of Rome. There they were to establish a beachhead; advance toward the Alban Hills, overlooking the ancient city; capture highways 7 and 6; and cut off Kesselring's communications with his armies at Cassino. Meanwhile, the Fifth Army would storm across the Garigliano and Rapido, push past Cassino into the Liri Valley, and race northward, driving the Germans before them. A week or so later, when Mark Clark's forces advancing from Cassino linked up with the men who'd landed at Anzio, they would together trap the enemy and destroy it.

It was an audacious plan. No one thought much about how the Anzio force would be supplied and reinforced should the Fifth Army fail to break through the Gustav Line. And it had to be undertaken by January 22, when most of the landing craft needed to ferry men and arms from Salerno to Anzio were to be sent to England to take part in Overlord.

At Cassino, Mark Clark wanted the 36th Infantry—the unit that had replaced Babe Ciarlo's 3rd Division in November—to lead the main attack across the Rapido and establish the beachhead through which the 1st U.S. Armored Division was to race into the Liri Valley. But the 36th was not to move until it got help from the units on its flanks. First, the Free French Expeditionary Force was to cross the river north of Cassino, then fight its way over the mountains behind it to neutralize German positions on the heights above the right side of the gap. On the left, the British X Corps was to cross the Garigliano and establish three beachheads to the south, drawing off as many German defenders as possible from the mouth of the valley and taking the heights that overlooked its left side. Only then, with both flanks protected, would the American attack through the center go forward.

The French—two divisions of Algerian and Moroccan troops—jumped off first, on January 12, made it across the river, and began fighting their way up the slopes. The British were to begin their three-part assault on the fifteenth. The Americans would attack on the twentieth—two days before the landing at Anzio. The Allies had started their campaign in Italy with one gamble. They would try to end it with another.

PLATOON SERGEANT WARD BRYAN CHAMBERLIN III was now with the Fifth Army, waiting for the assault to begin. Despite his rank, Chamberlin was not a soldier, though he'd tried hard to become one. And although he was an American—raised in a handsome old house on the outskirts of Norwalk, Connecticut—he was attached to a British unit.

He almost hadn't made it to the front at all. When the war broke out, he was captain of the Princeton soccer team and eager to do his part, he recalled, just as his father had during the Great War.

He was at Belleau Wood, and he was wounded twice, got the Distinguished Service Cross, second-highest medal you can get. After he died, I was walking by St. Patrick's Cathedral, and I saw Father [Francis Patrick] Duffy out there, the famous chaplain from World War I. I'd met him with my dad a couple of times, so I went up to him on the steps of the cathedral. And I said, "Father Duffy, my name is Ward Chamberlin." He said, "That's a wonderful name." He said, "Your father's one of the bravest men I ever knew." That would break your heart. I had a lot to live up to.

But there was a problem: as a small boy, Chamberlin had lost his right eye to meningitis. Neither the army nor the navy would have him, and so he signed on in November of 1942 as one of nearly 2,200 men who volunteered to serve as ambulance drivers for the American Field Service (AFS). Formed during World War I by American college students in Paris eager to aid the French, it had performed superbly under fire at Ypres and Verdun and in the Ardennes. When World War II began, a new generation of American college students rushed to sign up. Some, like Chamberlin, had been kept from military service by some sort of disability. Others were conscientious objectors. But all wanted to do everything they could to help the Allied cause. They served in France until it fell to the Germans, then joined British forces in North Africa and the Middle East.

Chamberlin believed he was at last on his way to war when he was posted to Syria and Lebanon with the 485th AFS Company. But the British campaign through Turkey for which he and his

Ward Chamberlin (right) and a fellow AFSer in North Africa

men were training never materialized, and in June of 1943, he came down with a mild case of polio that sent him to the hospital for six weeks.

Meanwhile, his comrades moved on to Italy. As soon as Chamberlin got back on his feet, he recalled, "I got orders to report back to the AFS headquarters in Cairo. I read them, and they said you're supposed to have desk duty for a year, so I just tore those up and never gave them to anybody. Ten days later I was in Italy. Exactly where I wanted to be—exactly. Wasn't so sure once I got there."

In Chamberlin's platoon there were thirty-two Dodge ambulances equipped with four-wheel drive, which allowed them to maneuver through the Italian mud when their British counterparts could not. The platoon's task was to gather wounded men from collection points as close to the front lines as they could get and then drive them to the crude field hospitals the British called advanced dressing stations. It was dangerous, delicate work, best done under cover of darkness and without headlights to avoid enemy artillery, which could pinpoint anything that moved during the day. Roads were slithery with mud. Their shoulders were often mined. Drivers had to take care not to jar unduly the bleeding men they carried. Thirty-six AFS volunteers would be killed before the war ended; sixty-two more were wounded, and thirteen were captured.

Chamberlin joined his platoon at the front not long before the British X Corps began its drive across the Garigliano. The first two attacks—across the river's western end—went so well that, to keep the British from making further progress there, Kesselring rushed in two divisions that had been resting and refitting near Rome. One part of the great gamble seemed to be paying off: German defenses near the invasion beaches had at least been temporarily thinned.

But a third assault, by the 46th Infantry, that was meant to capture the heights overlooking the left side of the Liri Valley failed completely. Mines destroyed some men before they ever reached the Garigliano. The Germans had opened the sluice gates of still another dam, deepening the river by six feet and turning it into a torrent that snapped the cables meant to hold rafts and ferries. Scores of men were sent whirling helplessly downstream. Enemy artillery began to zero in on the rest. The single brigade that managed to make it to the other side was hastily withdrawn.

Ward Chamberlin was waiting when the first wounded were brought out.

We were in a forward position probably half a mile from the actual front line, if you could call it that. And the first guy that they brought in was so badly shot up that after we got him into the ambulance on a stretcher—I don't think I've ever said this to anybody—I went around the side of the ambulance and just let everything out. I was just sick, sick as I could be, for about thirty seconds. It was just that I'd never seen a body cut up as badly as that guy was.

Under threat from German artillery, British troops hurry across a hastily built pontoon bridge on the Garigliano.

Far worse was to come. General Clark insisted that the 36th Infantry cross the Rapido on the evening of January 20 precisely as scheduled, even though the high ground on both flanks remained in enemy hands. (The French, too, had now been stopped.) Unless the attack went forward and succeeded, the men already filing aboard transports at Naples for the short voyage up the coast to Anzio would soon find themselves alone and in great danger.

The 36th Infantry, made up initially of National Guardsmen from Texas, had already been mauled twice in Italy, during the landing at Salerno and again as the Fifth Army ground toward the Gustav Line. It was still at less than normal strength; many of its officers and men were green replacements, and its veteran commander, General Fred L. Walker, was doubtful of the whole enterprise. "We might succeed but I do not see how we can," he confided to his diary.

> The crossing is dominated by heights on both sides of the Valley where the German artillery observers are ready to bring down heavy artillery concentrations on our men. The river is the principal obstacle of the German main line of resistance. I do not know of a single case in military history where an attempt to cross a river that is incorporated into the main line of resistance has succeeded. So I am prepared for defeat. The mission should never have been assigned to any troops with flanks exposed. Clark sent me his best wishes; said he was worried about our success. I think he is worried over the fact that he made an unwise decision.

Every one of Walker's fears was about to be realized. A daylight assault would have been suicidal. Just to reach the river, his men would have to advance across two miles of boggy floodplain, totally exposed to German fire that was sure to come not only from both flanks but also from the fortified town of Sant' Angelo, which stood straight ahead of them atop a forty-foot bluff, as well as from a belt of slit trenches and machine guns, well back from the Rapido. Mud kept vehicles from reaching the river, so the men would have to carry into battle their own footbridges, rubber rafts, and boxy 412-pound plywood-and-canvas assault boats. The enemy had hidden thousands of mines on the Allied side of the river. Engineers did their best to clear safe paths through them, marked with white tape so the men could find their way in the darkness.

The attack began at 7:30 p.m., with an American artillery barrage. The Germans responded instantly with a bigger and far more accurate barrage of their own. Shells tore men apart, splintered their boats, shattered the footbridges, ripped the engineers' tapes or blasted them into the mud. Terrified men stumbled into minefields. Thick fog rising from the river made it almost impossible to see, but German guns, preregistered to cover the likeliest crossing points, killed so many men that those coming along behind had to climb over their bodies to reach the river. Riddled boats sank or capsized. Men drowned. Some refused to get into the boats and ran away. Those who managed to make it to the other side dug foxholes, which quickly filled with water. All most of them could do was hunker down and hope that the machine-gun bullets that played constantly just overhead and the hail of shells whose concussion made their ears and noses bleed would come no closer.

The next morning, Clark ordered the attack renewed—and in the full light of day this time. He was still hoping somehow to break through before the Anzio landing began. One soldier remembered that his battalion commander had tears in his eyes as he ordered fresh troops on toward the killing field along the river. They fared no better than the men who'd tried to cross the night before. A sergeant remembered one of the young men he led being hit by so many machine-gun bullets that they pushed his body along the ground "like a tin can." It was all over by eight o'clock that night.

So easily had the Germans ripped apart the units sent against them that their commanders on the ground never realized that they had repulsed what Clark had intended as an all-out attack on their positions. At least 1,681 Americans were lost. A few days later, a three-hour truce would be arranged so the dead could be gathered up. To avoid revealing their positions, Germans helped carry corpses to collection points. "At the river, Germans and Americans labored side by side," one GI remembered. "A stack of eighty bodies was piled up along the bank, to be recovered later; these had received direct hits from mortar shells while standing in their fighting holes and had no heads, shoulders, or arms." No one, the veteran realized, would now ever know who any of those men had been.

"How anybody could have sent people through that I just can't imagine," said Ward Chamberlin. "They were shot to pieces. I saw them come out of the line, walking down the side of the road, eyes shut, just plodding ahead, one foot after the other. They looked like they'd been through the worst stuff. They had been."

Survivors from the 36th Infantry stagger back from the Rapido disaster. "The great losses of fine young men during the attempts to cross the [river] to no purpose and in violation of good infantry tactics are very depressing," their commander wrote. "All chargeable to the stupidity of the higher command."

As Chamberlin watched the survivors stagger back from the Rapido on January 22, British and American troops were coming ashore at Anzio and Nettuno. Babe Ciarlo was with them, part of the 3rd Infantry Division. The landings could not have gone more smoothly. The Germans were caught by complete surprise. Two hundred were taken prisoner, some still in their pajamas. In Anzio, a GI spotted a door marked KOMMANDANT, took a piece of chalk, and scrawled RESIGNED across it. By midmorning, 36,000 men and 3,200 vehicles were safely ashore. By nightfall, the 3rd Division had moved three miles inland.

The initial beachhead was fifteen miles wide and no more than seven miles deep. A narrow, boggy coastal plain that had been reclaimed for agriculture by the Fascist government, it was dotted with clusters of stone farmhouses and crisscrossed with irrigation ditches and canals. The British held the left side, the Americans the right.

Only two German battalions stood between the beach and Rome, and Churchill assumed that the invasion force would dash inland right away, perhaps even march into Rome itself. The startled Germans assumed the same thing. But General Lucas had been told by Mark Clark not to "stick your neck out" too far, as Clark thought he himself had done at Salerno. Lucas needed no such cautioning. He had been at Salerno, too, and remembered how close a call the landing there had been. He was sure there would be a German counterattack, and before he tried to push farther, he wanted to be certain he had enough men and supplies on hand to stop them. "I must keep my feet on the ground and my forces in hand and do nothing foolish," Lucas wrote in his diary. "This is the most important thing I have ever tried to do and I will not be stampeded." And so, while more men and supplies came ashore each hour, and engineers turned the waterfront into what would soon become the seventh-busiest port on earth, he made sure that his troops only gingerly probed German defenses.

Nine days went by. Kesselring used them to rush the better part of eight German divisions into place along the Allied perimeter, with five more on the way. When Lucas finally gave the signal to move farther inland in the early morning hours of January 30, he had two objectives: the 3rd Division was to take Cisterna and cut off Highway 7 while the British fought their way up the surfaced road that led from Anzio toward Albano and the

Men and supplies stream inland from the undefended beach at Anzio, January 22, 1944. "The incredible had happened," an officer recalled. "We had got one thing we had never bargained for, utter, complete surprise." By week's end, some seventy thousand troops were ashore, along with all the guns and tanks and twenty-eight thousand tons of supplies they needed.

Alban Hills. The British managed to move two miles in two days and two nights of battle before exhaustion and heavy losses forced them to dig in and try to hold on to what they'd gained. But the Americans met almost immediate disaster. Two lightly armed Ranger battalions—767 men—were sent to lead the way into Cisterna and walked into an ambush; only six got safely back to U.S. lines. The Germans marched several hundred American captives through the streets of the Italian capital the following day. "The Rangers have at last entered Rome," said Axis Sally, the failed American actress who purred Nazi propaganda over the radio every night, "but they have come not as conquerors but as our prisoners." For two days, the 3rd Infantry inched its way toward Cisterna in the face of resistance far more serious than anyone had expected. Babe Ciarlo's battalion got within 1,500 yards of the town by nightfall on February 1, when the exhausted division was ordered to go no farther.

Since the landing at Anzio, each side had lost nearly 5,500 men. The Allied advance had failed. Some one hundred thousand Americans and Britons dug in as best they could on the flat, crowded Anzio plain, exposed to enemy fire. The Anzio opera-

German artillery constituted a constant threat to the Allies at Anzio: men from the 3rd Infantry Division (above) dig in for protection along the bank of the Mussolini Canal, while American artillerymen fire back from a 155-millimeter "Long Tom" howitzer beneath a web of camouflage netting. "We fired all day, from dawn until dusk, without a break," a gunner remembered. "We had stacks of ammunition, but we still had to send out for some more. . . . I never did see what we were firing at, but I'm sure that those guns did a lot of damage."

Field hospitals at Anzio were located along the coastline where German shelling and bombing were concentrated. Shrapnel tore hundreds of holes in this hospital tent (top); it also killed five patients and wounded eight more. Army nurses like the two shown taking a breather above shared the danger with their patients. Six of them were among nearly one hundred medical personnel killed in the Anzio-Nettuno beachhead.

tion had been meant to break the deadlock at Cassino but it had turned into a liability, an additional drain on already strained resources, and might itself soon be in need of rescue. "We hoped to land a wild cat [at Anzio] that would tear out the bowels of the *Boche*," Churchill wrote. "Instead, we have stranded a vast whale with its tail flopping about in the water."

Babe Ciarlo said nothing to his family about what he'd been through at Anzio. But another private in the 3rd Division, a replacement who got there just after the failed offensive, did leave a firsthand account of his nighttime arrival in the line of foxholes and dugouts that ran along the Mussolini Canal, where Ciarlo and his outfit were trying to survive.

The squad leaders took two of us to a two-man foxhole. We could just barely see a couple of boys rounding up some equipment. They climbed out and said, "Here it is. You're welcome to it." Then we climbed in.

The bottom was squashy. It wasn't a very big hole, about chest deep. . . .

The squad leader came around a few minutes later and said that one of us had to be awake at all times, and for Christ's sake if we heard or saw anything in front of us, not to challenge too loud or hesitate to shoot if we didn't get the right answer. . . . All through the night there were flares going up from the Jerry lines. Once Jerry threw in a terrific artillery barrage, which landed about five hundred yards behind us. . . .

It was just plain hell through the day, and the nights were worse. We had five days of rain. The hole got about six inches of water, and you couldn't do anything but try to bail it out with your helmet. We wrapped shelter halves and blankets around us, but they didn't do much good. They got soaked with rain, and then you sat on a piece of wood or something and shivered and cussed. . . .

Jerry threw in a lot of artillery and mortars. The best thing to do was pull in your head and pray. Some of that big stuff would cave in the side of a wet foxhole like it was sand, and a couple of the boys got buried right in their hole fifty yards away from me. We had two or three casualties every day. . . . If you got hit at night you were lucky, because they could get you out right away. God help you if you got hit in the day-time, because you might have to lay there all day before some-body could get to you. A couple of our medics got Silver Stars for going out in the daytime to help wounded men. One of them got his posthumously.

Icy rain and water-filled foxholes, cold K rations and the constant fear of enemy shells, were nothing new to men like Babe Ciarlo. But in the Italian mountains they had always been on the attack. Now they were about to become the targets of the all-out German counterattack General Lucas had feared from the beginning. The signs were everywhere during the first two weeks of February. German patrols probed Allied defenses at night. Artillery fire intensified. Enemy forces attacking on the left began driving the British back from the forward positions they had just won. "If we can wipe them out down there [at Anzio]," Hitler told his generals, "then there won't be an invasion any-where else."

ELEVEN DAYS BEFORE VALENTINE'S DAY, the young fighter pilots training at Harding Field, just outside Baton Rouge, Louisiana, were given a chance to celebrate it at a special dance held in their honor at a local nightclub called Rock's. Its sponsor was the Fifinella Club, made up of women who worked on the base and wanted to entertain the boys. The club was named after a mischievous female gremlin designed by the Walt Disney Studio, which later became the official mascot of the WASPs (Women Airforce Service Pilots).

One member of the club, a high school principal's daughter named Jacqueline Greer, who did secretarial work at the Harding Field supply depot, remembered that she hadn't much wanted to be there that evening. "I wasn't really feeling too well," she said, "but I wanted my boss to see me there, to make sure she knew that I came." Then someone announced that a number of the men they'd been expecting wouldn't be coming after all. Since the women would now outnumber their potential dance part-ners, it would be up to them to do the choosing. That suited Greer fine: "I talked to my girlfriend who was with me and I said, 'I'm going to stand here and watch, then I'm going to find the best dancer on the floor and I'm going to tag in. After the boss sees me dance, I'm going home.' And we watched and I spotted him." Dressed in a new Valentine's formal with red and white stripes, she crossed the dance floor and tapped a young pilot on the shoulder. His name was Quentin Aanenson, and he was from Luverne, Minnesota. "The band was playing a song called 'Paper Doll' that was famous at that time," he remembered. "And as I took her to dance I said, 'Hello, paper doll.' " She smiled up at him, and at that moment, as Aanenson recalled, "a major new dimension" was added to his life.

The war had already dramatically expanded his world. He was born in 1921 on a farm five miles south of Luverne, the grandson of Norwegian immigrants who had begun working the flat black lowlands watered by the Rock River in the 1870s. Aanenson was the second youngest of six children. He attended a one-room school with the children of his German, Dutch, Norwegian, and Swedish neighbors, fished for carp in a nearby creek in the spring, and helped his father and older brother in the fields. The most exotic place he'd seen as a boy was Sioux Falls, South Dakota, thirty-six miles away.

His father and mother had a hard time of it during the Great Depression. The bank foreclosed on the family farm, and when a sudden hailstorm the following year destroyed the family's oat crop and with it any hope of freeing the family of debt, Aanen-son remembered, his father was "too broken up to cry." He told his sons that "farming is a crapshoot," and he urged all of his children to find some way to avoid relying on the land.

Quentin Aanenson needed little urging. "It never entered my mind that I was going to stay on the farm," he said. "I always had something on the horizon that I looked forward to." Flying formed a big part of his dreams. In 1931, when he was ten, a barn-storming air show touched down just a few miles from the Aanenson farm. He never forgot watching a big Ford tri-motor repeatedly clatter into the cloudless sky, circle overhead, and

POSTERS MOBILIZE A NATION

The war was fought in waiting rooms and store windows, on the walls of post offices and factory floors and on big-city billboards—anywhere a poster could help individualize the struggle for ordinary citizens. "Ideally," a spokesman for the Office of War Information said, "people should wake up to find a visual message everywhere like new snow—every man, woman and child should be reached and moved by the message." Federal agencies issued a flood of brightly colored posters. Labor unions and big corporations printed up their own, aimed at turning defense workers into "production soldiers." Advertising directors, laboring at a dollar a year, helped lay down ground rules. No casualties were to be shown. Abstraction wouldn't work. It was best to appeal directly to the emotions: Norman Rockwell's painting at the top right of the opposite page, part of a quartet depicting the Four Freedoms spelled out in the Atlantic Charter, was widely distributed, but nothing compared with the demand for the lonely spaniel below it. Some posters were intended for special markets: "Keep Us Flying" featured a portrait of the Tuskegee airman Robert Deiz and was meant to sell bonds to African Americans.

Westinghouse War Production Co-Ordinating Committee, 1942

Railroad waiting room, San Augustine, Texas, 1943

Douglas Air Craft Company, 1942

Keep us flying!

BUY WAR BONDS

U.S. Treasury Department, 1943

SAVE FREEDOM OF SPEECH

BUY WAR BONDS

U.S. Office of War Information, 1944

...because somebody talked!

U.S. Office of War Information, 1943

GROW IT YOURSELF

PLAN A FARM GARDEN NOW

New York City WPA Art Services for the Rural Electrification Administration, U.S. Department of Agriculture

come back to earth again to spill out dazzled passengers who couldn't find words to describe what their little world looked like from the heavens. Aanenson didn't go up himself—the five-dollar fee would have covered the family's expenses for a week—but he was soon losing himself in books about the combat aces of the Great War. "Sometimes," he remembered, "I would be on a piece of farm machinery behind a couple of horses, plowing corn, and a lonely airplane would fly over and I would look up and my spirit would soar. 'That's where I want to be sometime,' I thought. 'I want to live that way. I want to do those things.'"

Pearl Harbor gave him his chance. He left the University of Minnesota after his sophomore year in 1941 because his tuition money had run out, and hitchhiked to Seattle, where he got a defense job building airplanes on the graveyard shift at Boeing and studied speech at the University of Washington during the day, thinking he might make radio broadcasting his career. When he got to the plant on the evening of December 7, he found armed guards at the gate and machine guns set up on the roof. "It was eerie," he remembered. "We were in a war zone, even though Pearl Harbor was two thousand miles away." He was determined to get into the fighting—and into the air as well. But color blindness kept him out of the U.S. Army Air Force until he was able to take the test enough times to memorize it.

He attended preflight school and underwent intermediate fighter training at California airfields, took two months of advanced training in Arizona, won his pilot's wings, and was commissioned a second lieutenant and then, "by the luck of the draw," was assigned to Harding Field to master precisely the kind of airplane he'd hoped most to fly. The Republic P-47 Thunderbolt was the biggest, heaviest, fastest single-seat fighter that had ever been built. Originally designed to escort American heavy bombers to and from their targets, it was soon to undertake a new mission: attacking German armor, troops, transport systems, and airfields in support of the men who would be advancing across France.

We knew that we were going to be the point of the spear, and we knew that the guys on the ground would be needing us, because they were down there having to fight this dirty war in the foxholes and the artillery barrages, and we could help them. And so there was that sense of the spirit we all had, that we're going to count for something.

The Thunderbolt would help make them count. It had a 2,300-horsepower engine, Aanenson recalled, could carry two thousand pounds of bombs beneath its wings, and was armed with eight .50-caliber machine guns "that had a rate of fire of seven hundred fifty rounds a minute per gun. So in a second we could throw a

Quentin Aanenson and Jackie Greer

hundred shells on a target and just devastate anything that was in front of us."

Fighter training was exhilarating. Aanenson and his fellow trainees spent hours practicing combat maneuvers over Lake Pontchartrain—rolling, looping, diving, climbing. The P-47's official top speed was 439 miles an hour, but it could reach 600 going straight down. They practiced bombing and strafing, too, churning up the bayou near the little town of Hammond. But training was also dangerous: five members of Aanenson's group of forty trainees would die before they got a chance to go overseas. One was killed when he tried to buzz the football stadium at Louisiana State University.

When Jackie Greer sought Aanenson out at the Valentine's Day Dance, he had been at Harding Field for less than two weeks. "After we danced to three or four tunes the music stopped to let the band rest, and I went home," she remembered. "And when I got home that night, my sister was already in bed, asleep. I woke her up and I said, 'Nelwyn, tonight I met the man I'm going to marry.'"

The next night, Jackie drove her father's car to another, bigger dance, for all the boys on the base, not just the pilots. Aanenson was there, and this time he tapped her on the shoulder. Afterward, he insisted on driving her home in her father's car and then got a bus back to Harding Field. "We had ninety days to work with from the time I met her until the time I shipped out," Aanenson recalled. "We would go to parties, and we saw each other almost every night, and we knew within a matter of just a short time that this was something serious. And everything was sort of on fast-forward. You lived your life realizing that you didn't have a lot of time."

AFTER THE FAILED JANUARY ASSAULT on the Gustav Line, Ward Chamberlin was promoted and reassigned, asked by Lieutenant Robert C. Bryan of Platoon C to become his second-in-command. Their ambulances were now attached to the 2nd New Zealand Division, newly arrived from Italy's Adriatic side and based in a field some four miles from Monte Cassino in what the press had come to call Purple Heart Valley.

There had been no lull in the fighting. Just two days after the disaster on the Rapido, Mark Clark ordered his men to try again to break through the German defenses. They had been unable to do it. A French force captured two positions on the northern end of the Monte Cassino promontory, but without reinforcement it was forced to call a halt. One regiment of the U.S. 34th Infantry tried but failed to dislodge the Germans from the village of Cassino. Two more regiments fought their way up the slopes and onto the ridge around and behind the abbey. They got to within four hundred yards of it and could look down on Highway 6 and the Liri Valley, but after three weeks of hideous hardship and savage small-unit combat amid the exposed ridges and ravines, they could go no farther. The 34th Division lost 2,200 men in three weeks. When the survivors were finally relieved, fifty had to be

A refugee mother and her children, driven from their home by the battle for Cassino: "The adult world," one British veteran of the Italian campaign remembered, "should forever hang its head in shame at the terrible, unforgivable things done to the young."

carried down the mountainside; still willing to fire their weapons, they could no longer move their legs.

As weeks went by with little progress, the men on the mountaintops and those crouched in slit trenches far below became more and more convinced that the battle against them was being directed from the vast white abbey that overlooked everything. "You began to have the feeling the monastery was watching you," a British soldier remembered. "It is like being stripped of your clothes. We were being watched by eyes in the monastery every inch of the way."

When Clark finally decided to send in the New Zealand Corps—made up of men from the Indian army as well as New Zealanders—to relieve the Americans, its commanders insisted that the abbey be destroyed before they resumed the attack on the high slopes. Clark was against it. He did not wish to be responsible for obliterating a great religious monument, had no firm intelligence that any Germans had ever been inside the abbey, and feared its ruins and thick-walled foundation would become enemy ramparts. The commanders warned Clark that if

he did not agree to destroy the abbey and the attack on Monte Cassino failed, he would have to bear the blame. Clark left the final decision up to General Alexander, commander in chief of all Allied forces in the Mediterranean. He sided with the New Zealanders. The abbey's destruction was "necessary more for the effect it would have on the morale of the attackers than for purely material reasons," Alexander explained later; his men would have settled for no less.

At nine-thirty on the morning of February 15, Ward Chamberlin watched from his tent as the first wave of 135 Flying Fortresses appeared above the abbey and began to drop their bombs. A good many missed the mountain on which it stood altogether; one landed near the AFS latrine and lightly wounded one of Chamberlin's friends in the rear. But most hit their target. "As wave after wave came in the smoke began to rise," a New Zealander remembered. "The vapor trails grew and merged, the sun was blotted out, and the whole sky turned gray." Thousands of men stood and cheered. One GI shouted, "Touchdown!" An hour later, there was a second cascade of bombs. A total of 453 tons fell in and around the abbey. Its roofs were blasted or burned away. The cloisters collapsed. More than one hundred Italian refugees who had sought sanctuary within its walls were crushed.

In fact, the Germans never had used the monastery as an observation post, though it was at the center of their defense line and troops had sometimes been stationed not far from its walls. Its destruction provided the Nazis with a propaganda triumph. And, just as Clark had feared, the Germans quickly turned the rubble into a new stronghold from which they were free to direct fire against anyone sent against them. When the 4th Indian Regiment attacked three days later, it was torn apart. Six hundred more men were lost. The summit remained in German hands. The fighting went on. Stretcher bearers continued to carry wounded men down the mountainside—a trip that could take eight hours—and the men of Ward Chamberlin's AFS platoon continued their perilous after-dark ambulance runs from the foot of the hill to the aid station.

You got a guy in and he looked okay. But there'd be a medical guy with me and a little further on he'd say, you know, "This guy's going." And I said, "Should I stop?" He said, "Yeah, why don't you stop for a minute." So I went back and held his hand, and he just looked up and kind of gave a sign of recognition and he was gone. It was quick, quick. It's hard to describe what it's really like. You can remember the moments, but when you see some guy leaving this world, it's not a lot of fun.

On the morning of February 16, the day after the abbey was bombed, the Germans launched their long-delayed counterattack at Anzio with a thirty-minute barrage. They now outnumbered the Allies on the beachhead 125,000 to 100,000. They attacked all along the line. South of Cisterna, the men of Babe Ciarlo's 3rd Division fought from their foxholes, peering through the cold drizzle and firing back whenever they spotted the men in long gray-green overcoats advancing toward them. But the main focus of the enemy assault was the Albano–Anzio road on the left. There, the attack was spearheaded by the Berlin-Spandau Lehr Division, handpicked by Hitler for the honor of lancing the Anzio "abscess" because it had performed so well on the drill field and was made up of dedicated Nazis. It had never been in battle, however, and when veterans of the U.S. 45th Division began shooting it up, the Lehr Division's frightened troops broke and ran. Still, the Germans kept coming, and over the next five days they shoved the 45th back one and a half miles to what General Lucas had declared the "final" beachhead line. It held, thanks to the tenacity of the men on the ground and the rain of bombs and shells—from Allied gunners and aircraft and from offshore warships—that fell among the attackers massed along the hard-surfaced road that was the only path their tanks could travel. On the twentieth, the Germans suspended their offensive.

The Allies still occupied their tightly packed beachhead. Each side had lost nearly twenty thousand men since the landings in January. Both armies were now too weary and depleted to mount another serious assault. General Lucas was replaced. General Lucian K. Truscott, Jr., former commander of the 3rd Division, presided over the bitter stalemate that followed and would stretch on for nearly three months. The constant danger was made more maddening by its randomness. Hundreds of German guns, some just three miles away, still targeted the beachhead. "Some days they shelled us hard," Ernie Pyle wrote, "and some days hours would go by without a single shell coming over. Yet nobody was wholly safe, and anybody who said he had been around Anzio two days without having a shell hit within a hundred yards of him was just bragging." The men had nicknames for the most fearsome German weapons, a pair of 280-millimeter guns that slid out of caves in the Alban Hills on railroad flatcars, fired their enormous shells, and then rolled back into the hill again to keep Allied planes from spotting them. They were Anzio Annie and the Anzio Express. When men like Babe Ciarlo had to leave their holes in daylight, they scurried across the ground, helmeted heads down, shoulders up, trying to keep their eyes and ears open for incoming; the men called it the Anzio crouch.

"There wasn't any rear," Bill Mauldin wrote.

There was no place in the entire beachhead where enemy shells couldn't seek you out. Sometimes it was worse at the front, sometimes worse at the harbor. Quartermasters buried their dead, and amphibious duck drivers went down with their craft. Infantrymen, dug into the Mussolini Canal, had the canal pushed in on top of them by armor-piercing shells, and Jerry bombers circled as they directed glider bombs into LSTs and Liberty ships. Wounded men got oak-leaf clusters on their Purple Hearts when shell fragments riddled them as they lay on hospital beds. Nurses died. Planes crash-landed on the single air strip. . . .

You couldn't stand up in the swamps without being cut down, and you couldn't sleep if you sat down. Guys stayed in those swamps for days and weeks. Every hole had to be covered because the "popcorn" man went over at night and shoveled hundreds of little butterfly bombs down on your head by the light of flares and exploding ack-ack. You'd wake up in the morning and find your sandbags torn open and spilled on the ground.

So far as possible, life at Anzio was lived underground. Ernie Pyle reported:

Around the outside perimeter line, where the infantry faced the Germans a few hundred yards away, the soldiers lay in foxholes devoid of all comfort. But everywhere back of that the men dug underground and built themselves homes. On that beachhead there must have been tens of thousands of dugouts, housing from two to half a dozen men each.

Wine cellars and ancient caves became barracks and command posts. Men turned emptied hand grenades filled with gasoline into lamps, with bootlaces for wicks. Bulldozers packed mounds of earth around precious supplies, fuel, and ammunition. One division built two subterranean theaters where two hundred men at a time could see movies. But nothing could guarantee anyone's safety. After one prolonged shelling, a mess sergeant

Misery was shared equally at Anzio: these Germans, left to die in a water-filled ditch, were photographed in March of 1944.

fell to his knees and began loudly to pray. "God, help us," he said. "You come yourself. Don't send Jesus. This is no place for children."

German aircraft and special artillery shells littered the beach with propaganda leaflets, urging Allied solders to surrender. Those meant to shake the morale of British soldiers charged that American GIs were sleeping with their wives and girlfriends in Britain. Leaflets aimed at Americans claimed that Jews back home were profiting from their misery. Those meant for both featured a drawing of a skull and the legend THE BEACHHEAD HAS BECOME A DEATH'S HEAD. Axis Sally began calling Anzio "the largest self-supporting prisoner of war camp in the world."

The men facing the Gustav Line at Cassino also remained captives of a kind, unable to move forward or to find shelter from the rain, sleet, and snow. On March 15, Mark Clark tried for a third time to smash through with simultaneous assaults on the ruins of the monastery at the top of Monte Cassino and the town at its foot, both held by the elite German 1st Parachute Division. First, 435 bombers flew over the mountains in successive waves. This time, their intended target was the town. The earth shook for five miles, but less than half of the two thousand bombs they dropped actually landed among its stone houses. Stray bombs killed or wounded 142 Allied troops and an unknown number of Italian civilians. Then, before ground troops from the New Zealand II Corps began to move toward Cassino, Allied gunners battered it and the abbey with two hundred thousand more shells. The town was reduced to rubble. Its defenders, huddled within concrete bunkers, deep tunnels, and underground sewers, were badly shaken. But when the assault force began moving into what remained of the little town, the Germans emerged with mortars and machine guns to hurl them back. Allied tanks were unable to provide much support because bomb craters and mountains of debris made the streets impassable. The fighting went on for a week before Clark again called a halt. Little had changed: the Germans still held most of Cassino, still occupied the ruins of the abbey. Looking back on the failed attacks that had left so many of his men sprawled on the murderous slopes around Monte Cassino, the commander of the 4th Indian Army wrote that "these battles . . . were military sins, no less."

New Zealanders with fixed bayonets struggle to drive Cassino's stubborn German defenders from the wreckage of the town. "Entering Cassino was a vision of the end of the world," one veteran remembered. "It was like some ghastly warning. Would this, then, be the fate of Rome, or for that matter, Paris, or London, or Berlin, or even Auckland?"

THE TERRIBLE LOSSES SUFFERED by the U.S. Eighth Air Force during the second assault on Schweinfurt, during which Earl Burke had been wounded, back in October of 1943—and other raids that week in which eighty-eight more American bombers had been shot down—helped persuade the Allies to cut back on daytime raids over Germany until they could assemble enough fighters capable of escorting bombers all the way to their targets and back again. Thousands of American-made P-51 Mustangs with powerful British-made Rolls-Royce Merlin engines were rushed into production. Able to fly to Berlin and back when fitted out with drop tanks beneath their wings, they could outmaneuver and outrace most of the German fighters they might encounter along the way.

Strategy was changed, too. Bombers continued to hit cities and batter war industries, but destruction of the Luftwaffe itself soon took top priority. "This is a must," General Hap Arnold told his European commanders. "Destroy the enemy air force wherever you find them—in the air, on the ground, and in the factories." In January 1944, the Germans lost 1,300 planes; they lost 2,121 in February and 2,115 more in March.

Raids remained perilous. The Egger twins, who had encouraged Burke to become a ball-turret gunner, were shot down in January and spent the rest of the war in a POW camp. But American aircraft were now being produced far more rapidly than the Germans could shoot them down.

Despite the relentless Allied air assaults that spring, German aircraft production actually increased—"We are virtually drowning in aircraft," one German flier would write—but the Luftwaffe was losing trained crews far faster than they could be replaced. "The time has come when our force is within sight of collapse," the chief of the German fighter wing told his superiors. And as Albert Speer, the Nazi minister for armaments and munitions, later admitted, the relentless bombing was doing serious damage to the German war effort.

The real importance of the air war consisted in the fact that it opened a second front long before the invasion of Europe. That front was in the skies over Germany. The fleets of bombers might appear at any time over any large German city or important factory. . . . Every square meter of our territory became a front line. Defense against air attacks required the production of thousands of antiaircraft guns, the stockpiling of tremendous quantities of ammunition all over the country, and holding in readiness hundreds of thousands of soldiers.

As D-day approached, Allied fliers were given still more targets. They began by blasting Germany's synthetic-oil plants,

reducing the Luftwaffe's fuel supply from 180,000 tons in April to fewer than 50,000 in June. They also undertook what D-day planners called the Transportation Plan, systematically destroying roads, river crossings, and railroad yards across Belgium and France to keep the enemy from reinforcing and resupplying their forces. Some twelve thousand civilians lost their lives in these raids, but eighty marshaling yards and fifteen hundred locomotives were blown to pieces. So were countless bridges, thirty-six airfields, forty-five gun batteries, and forty-one radar installations. When the time finally came to invade France, the Allies would own the skies and had disrupted much of the enemy's ability to move on land as well.

Earl Burke was no longer flying. He'd been wounded in the lip by a bomb fragment in late February. The wound healed fast enough, but by mid-March a secondary infection had settled into the upper part of his left arm, the site of his earlier injury. He was diagnosed with osteomyelitis, the bacterial bone infection that killed thousands of wounded men in the Great War, and was sent for surgery to an army hospital on the Welsh border. There was no hope for his arm, doctors told him; it would have to come off. He was lying on a gurney about to be wheeled into the operating room when the chief surgeon happened by, took a look at his injured limb, and decided to try something else. Burke was put into a body cast with his left arm bent out in front of him. (It made it hell going through doors, he remembered, though "my beer-drinking mastery increased substantially.")

Then the surgeon cut a hole in the cast.

He put a little wire net across it. I said, "What are you doing?" He says, "I'm making a little home for somebody." I said, "What is that little home going to do?" He says, "I'm going to keep these little guys on your arm so they can eat all that stuff out of your bone." And I said, "What kind of things are they?" He says, "They're little white things, you know, like this." He had a handful of maggots. Flipped them in there. And put the wire cage back on it. Says, "Now, those little guys are gonna eat that stuff out of you, because we can't get it out of you. No way we can get that out of you." So there I was, watching those guys having a meal.

Burke would spend two months in a stateside army hospital, where the maggots did their work, supplemented by injections of the new drug penicillin. He saw no more combat but spent the rest of the war working with an Air Sea Rescue squadron off the California coast, trying to save the lives of men like his brother, Tom, who'd gone down during training flights.

March 27, 1944

I just got through with chow. . . . We are having beautiful weather here and I hope it's the same way there, so you could take the babies out every afternoon.

Love,
Babe

By the end of March, things at Anzio had calmed down a good deal. The weather steadily improved; there were fewer bitter jokes about "sunny Italy." German guns still targeted the beach, but their ammunition was growing scarce, and the rain of shells that had once fallen around the clock had dwindled to sporadic harassing fire. In one sector, German gunners held their fire each afternoon to let GIs play softball. In a ceremony on the beach, thirty-seven foreign-born members of Ciarlo's division were sworn in as American citizens. Three hundred men from his outfit attended a wedding between a first lieutenant and an army nurse. The bride cut the cake with a trench knife. At still another ceremony, Ciarlo and two hundred other men from his outfit were awarded the combat infantry badge. "I will send it home as soon as I get a chance," Babe wrote, "because I don't like to wear stuff like that."

Boredom had become a new enemy. The men bet on mule races, fashioned stills from gasoline cans and copper tubing scavenged from wrecked planes, tuned in Axis Sally to hear the big-band hits she played between propaganda messages, and bitched among themselves about the officers, politicians, and other big shots who'd sent them to Anzio and then kept them there. "As the boys say here," Ciarlo wrote home, "the more war bonds you buy, the longer the war lasts."

IN MID-APRIL, BACK IN THE STATES, Quentin Aanenson finally received his orders: he was to sail for England and be prepared to take part in the coming invasion. Before he could leave for overseas he had some business to attend to. "We were very much aware of the fact that ours was a deadly calling," he remembered. The office of the judge advocate was aware of it, too, and required every pilot to have a will drawn up and signed in the presence of three witnesses. "The three pilots who witnessed my will," Aanenson remembered, "were all dead in six months."

Then he went to see Jackie. He had some ground rules he wanted to lay down. "I'd like to make a deal with you," he said. "I will come back and survive this war if you will agree that while I'm gone you will not date any one guy more than three times."

"I don't know where in the world he came up with that," she remembered. "I never did understand it. But the rule was, I couldn't have over three dates with any one fella. He explained it

that I wouldn't get too familiar with them in three dates. And if I couldn't have any more, it couldn't go any further. And it surely worked."

She gave him a ring for good luck before he said goodbye, and as added protection he promised to whistle the first few bars of the "Army Air Corps Song"—"Off we go into the wild blue yonder"—every time he took off. Then he headed home for ten days' leave.

I went up to Luverne, to see my parents, my brothers and sisters. And it was a very difficult time, because I knew that we'd been assigned to fly this terribly dangerous type of combat mission. So when I was leaving and saying goodbye to my mother and dad, we went to the train station to catch the midnight train. My sister Mavis was with me, and I took her aside and we walked down the platform a ways and I told her what my assignment had been and that the odds were pretty great that I would be killed. So I told her to be very much aware of this possibility and that she should be prepared to help my parents.

At Boston in early May, Aanenson boarded the USS *Brazil*, bound for Liverpool. He was on his way to Atcham Field, a redistribution center north of London, where he was to receive a few days of last-minute training before D-day. When he got there, he found letters from Jackie Greer waiting for him.

May 17, 1944

I'm reading the news before turning to the funnies these days. Saw yesterday where they're going to use a lot of P-47s to escort our bombers during the invasion. I wish I could go with you on your first mission. I'd love to dig myself a little hole right behind your seat, crawl in before each of your take-offs, and whistle that bar of the Air Corps song with you.

June 4, 1944

Your cablegram arrived about an hour ago and now I'm so happy! Nelwyn and I spent the day in Zachary. . . . We went horseback riding. As we rode through the pastures, P-47s flew over as thick as flies. Beautiful afternoon, P-47s, etc.—suppose you know who that adds up to. Then, riding home, my thoughts were of you. No one was talking—the music on the radio was too good for that—and as I looked at the full moon, I could picture you so many places. Suppose I've spent more hours thinking of you today than any other day since you left, if it's possible.

There were now nearly a million and a half Americans encamped in southern England, so many that some local citizens called it

ON THE WAY

Conditions belowdecks were crowded and claustrophobic. Thousands became seasick. The stench grew overwhelming. There were no showers for enlisted men. Tempers frayed. "We'll win this damn war," one GI wrote to *Yank,* "but I can't face that trip back."

As Allied troops held on at Anzio and Cassino, hundreds of thousands of American troops were boarding transports at New York (left) and other points of embarkation, on their way to England and the imminent invasion of Normandy. Luxury liners were enlisted as troopships. Second Lieutenant Gardner Botsford found himself aboard the *Queen Mary:* "Since there were not nearly enough cabins to hold all the troops on board—thirteen thousand soldiers, plus one thousand in crew and staff—less conventional dormitories had been created from the barbershop, the hairdressing salon, the dress shop, the newsstand, the dog kennel, the wine cellar (empty), the gym, the squash courts; even the enormous ornamental fish tank on the reception deck had a resident soldier. And still there was not enough room."

"occupied England." It took 398,666 prefabricated huts, 279,204 tented camps, and 115,590 requisitioned British buildings just to house and provide services for them all; 4,500 new cooks had to be trained to feed them. And the Americans were not alone. There were fourteen British and three Canadian divisions, as well as Poles and Frenchmen. Millions of maps were printed up for soldiers to carry with them, along with a million pamphlets telling GIs how to get along with the French.

More than 15 million tons of supplies had been unloaded at British wharves, 320,000 kinds of items, "from locomotives to dental fillings," one soldier wrote: 450,000 tons of ammunition, 137,000 vehicles, 124,000 hospital beds, and numberless coffins, stacked and ready at a supply depot in Dorchester. One hundred and seventy miles of new railroad track had had to be laid to help move it all around. "I stood on a bridge one day," remembered an Englishman who'd been nine years old then, "and saw the largest train I had ever seen pass slowly by, packed with tanks. I thought it would go on forever." Tree-shaded country lanes were lined with mines and shells and miles of wire, all covered with corrugated iron to keep off the spring rain. Farmers' fields became vast parking lots for trucks, tanks, and artillery pieces that seemed to stretch all the way to the horizon.

Everyone knew D-day was imminent. Only a few knew where or when. All letters intended for overseas were now opened and read. Diplomats from neutral nations were forbidden to send or receive uncensored communications. No diplomat or diplomatic courier from any nation except the United States and the Soviet Union was permitted to enter or leave the country. Mollie Painter-Downes, a British journalist writing for the *New Yorker*, described the universal air of anticipation.

> *Living on this little island just now uncomfortably resembles living on a vast combination of an aircraft carrier, a floating dock jammed with men, and a warehouse stacked to the ceiling with material labeled "Europe." It's not at all difficult for one to imagine that England's coastline can actually be seen bulging and trembling like the walls of a Silly Symphony house in which a terrific fight is going on.*

In Luverne that spring, editor Al McIntosh also sensed that big things were about to happen.

An English family goes about its daily chores in a coastal village despite the tanks and jeeps and other invasion vehicles that have turned the narrow street beyond their garden wall into a parking lot.

AL McINTOSH'S WAR
December 1943–March 1944

DECEMBER 15, 1943. "One of our bombers is missing!" How often we've heard that phrase used over the radio and we've thought how that ominous sentence must strike cold terror in the hearts of every mother and father who is wondering where "he" is tonight.

The grim import of that laconic summation of an aerial raid struck home this week when Mr. and Mrs. George Nelson received one of those dread messages Sunday morning:

"The Secretary of War desires me to express his deep regrets that your son, Second Lieutenant Darwin G. Nelson, has been reported missing in action since December 1 in the European area. . . ."

We think Darwin Nelson is (and we are deliberately using the present tense because we have a strong premonition that somehow the big strapping youngster made it down to earth all right) one of the most vivid personalities we've ever encountered. Polite . . . and then some . . . about every tenth word was "sir" . . . And he had a grin on him that was about as powerful a radiance as a locomotive headlight. . . .

If you remember, it was just a bit over two months ago that he gave Luverne a roof rattling salute as he power dived his big Fort over the business district in an eardrum-blasting "hail and farewell." . . . We've often thought what he was thinking of as he circled several times low over the family farm south of town. . . . And his final gesture as he waved goodbye to "the folks" was to do a little bombing on a small scale as he dropped clothing and belongings that he could not take with him.

DECEMBER 30, 1943. We'll tell you the little story behind the want ad in this issue of a black Labrador dog with some white

marking at its throat that has been lost in Luverne. D. J. Ahrendt of Jasper came over Christmas Day to visit his mother, Mrs. Dora Ahrendt. . . .

In the evening when the family was ready to return the dog was nowhere to be found. Ahrendt searched the town in vain. And this isn't any "newspaper exaggeration" when we say that he is heartbroken over the loss.

You see that dog belongs to his son, Sgt. Duane Ahrendt, a paratrooper now in Italy. The son entrusted the dog, his pal, to his father for safekeeping during his absence. Now you can understand why the father is so upset . . . so if by chance you know of a stray Labrador you can be a "swell person" if you'll just call Mrs. Ahrendt. You'll make several people very, very happy.

JANUARY 13, 1944. If we should have such poor judgment as to even hint that somebody in Canton, S.D., is a dog thief we know that Andy Johnson, editor of the *Canton News,* would immediately give vent to screams of outraged civic pride. So we won't say it [but] it seems that a Canton man who had friends in Jasper happened to notice a black Labrador with a Jasper dog license was aimlessly wandering the streets there. The Canton man notified Jasper friends who knew of the Ahrendt loss. To say that there was a very happy reunion at Canton, of dog and Ahrendt, is gross understatement.

JANUARY 20, 1944. Here's the best news of the week! There's real joy at the George Nelson home this week. Because there is new hope that their son, Lt. Darwin G. Nelson, may be alive. . . .

Tuesday, they received a telegram from the Foreign Broadcast Intelligence of the

Federal Communications Commission which reads as follows:

"The name of Second Liutenant Darwin Nelson has been mentioned in an enemy broadcast as a prisoner in German hands."

MARCH 2, 1944. The middle aged man, his shoulders bent just a bit more that morning under a crashing blow of sudden grief, came out of the Western Union office clutching a yellow piece of paper, and walked over to where we were talking on the sidewalk.

"I was just coming down to your place but maybe you'd care to look at this now if you want to," [he said] and he handed over the telegram with shaking fingers.

It was one of those "we regret to inform you" type of messages, the kind that hundreds of Rock County parents live in terror of, day and night.

We copied down the text of the official telegram. What could we say? Absolutely nothing. . . . Nothing, no matter how much you mean it, can ease the heartache the slightest bit. . . . He tried to be so casual, to choke back any word that might reveal the depth of his emotion.

But I thought then—I wish that some of those people who like to say so patronizingly "you folks out here in the Midwest don't have the slightest idea there is a war on" could have looked at the tear-reddened eyes of Herman Wiese, Sr., that morning.

If they had—they never would utter such slander again.

MARCH 30, 1944. Been complaining lately about life's hardships have you?

Maybe you'd like to trade places with some of the boys—for instance Sgt. John Wahlert just back from Italy. One night not very far from Cassino shell concussions knocked Wahlert out of his foxhole three times, tossing him from 10 to 15 feet each time. But he was so exhausted he'd crawl back to the hole, usually filled with four inches of ice water, and drop off to sleep despite the continuous roar of artillery fire.

Outwardly, things haven't changed here. The lilacs are out in full bloom. . . . The countryside was never greener. At night there are a million stars . . . winking in the . . . sky with a couple of million bull frogs parked along the edges of the bank—full ditches croaking a mighty chorus.

But things are different.

Staffs of daily newspapers all over the country are on alert in case the invasion breaks. . . . Key executives don't stir very far from a telephone day or night. The belief is that the long-awaited flash will come sometime after 11 p.m. but before 5 a.m.

THE MEN STILL CROWDED TOGETHER AT ANZIO were anticipating something big, too. "By the look of things this war isn't going to last much longer," Babe Ciarlo wrote home on April 16, "and then I and the rest of the fellas will be home to be a civilian. . . . Something is bound to happen soon."

At the end of the month, the men of Ciarlo's division were pulled back to rest—and get ready for the big battle they knew was coming. Ciarlo had been on or near the front line for more than three months. He had seen all of the fighting that had taken place at Anzio, had taken part in some of it, but never said a word about any of it in his letters home.

"It was always the upside," his younger brother, Tom, remembered.

You see in the newsreels or you read in the paper about different battles. But you don't actually put Babe in that position because he's always telling you how everything is fine, everything is no problem. At one point, as a matter of fact, my mother had my aunt write a letter in Italian that she sent to Babe. "When you get to Rome, we have relatives over there. When you get there, show them these letters and they'll treat you well." And at the time, you think, "Well, yeah, he's going to be going to Italy. He's going to go to Rome and he's going to see his relatives." Can you imagine that? You think about it now and it's so unreal.

April 30, 1944
Dear Mom and Family:
This afternoon I might go swimming in the Tyrrhenian Sea. The salt water will do me good. . . .
Last night I received about ten letters. . . . I'm glad to hear that the house was filled with flowers [for Mother's Day] and that you all got a gift for Mom. Don't worry about my money situation, because there isn't anything to spend it on here in Anzio. . . .

Well, I had my dinner and guess what. I had—pork chops, about a dozen of them. I'm getting to be a chow hound.

May 9, 1944
I'm glad that you are going down to the beach with the babies and I hope Mom goes down with you because it'll do all of you good. I won't be with you this year, but I'll guarantee you I'll be there next summer. That's a date . . .
I'm all right. Nothing ever happens here. I guess it's like Waterbury, dead. . . . I figured out just what I'm going to do after the war and when I get home. I'm going to loaf for a while and then I'm going to work and the next spring I'm going to get a car, not bad, eh?

As always, he was keeping the most pertinent facts to himself. By May 9, he and his outfit were undergoing intensive training for the projected breakout. Day after day, Ciarlo and his buddies practiced capturing fortified buildings and destroying tanks and pillboxes; clearing mines and laying communications wire; hand-to-hand combat and bayonet drill.

Meanwhile, south of Anzio on the evening of May 11, the final assault on the Gustav Line got under way with a barrage from 1,660 guns. Instead of still another chain of piecemeal assaults, General Alexander had ordered a massive coordinated attack concentrated on just twenty-five miles of the enemy's line. This time, the Fifth and Eighth armies—fourteen divisions, almost three hundred thousand men—would go forward together, and the British, not the Americans, would be responsible for the cen-

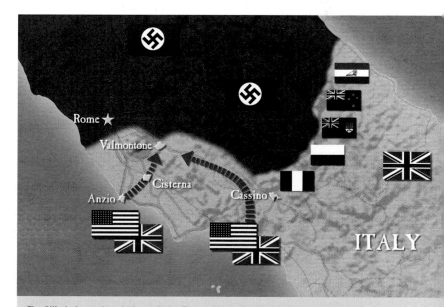

The Allied plan to break through the Gustav Line and destroy the German army; thanks to General Mark Clark, the reality would be very different.

tral drive into the Liri Valley. Clark's men were expected to fight their way up the coast. Suspicious always of British motives and uncomfortable unless he was in the spotlight, Clark saw this as an insult, a British attempt to snatch the glory and honor of taking Cassino from him and his men. He was convinced that Alexander intended to have the Eighth Army take Rome as well.

The Germans held for a time. But over the next few days, French colonial troops on the left of the Liri Valley managed to work their way around behind them and then climb down into the valley itself. Poles, eager to avenge what the Germans had done to their country, attacked the ruins of the abbey. Nearly one thousand of them fell on the slopes of the mountain, but the Germans refused to be driven off it until May 18, when British troops outflanked both the ruined town and the ruined abbey, ending all hope of resupply or reinforcement. The following day, the Germans finally abandoned their positions and began retreating northward, with the Eighth Army in pursuit.

From Anzio, Babe Ciarlo continued to reassure his family.

May 18, 1944
Well, I guess you read the news about the Cassino front breaking. . . . Everything is looking good and we get good news from every front. I know it can't last much longer.

May 19, 1944
Today we had a little rain, but it wasn't bad at all, because it cooled us off. We had beer again today and I gave my share to the fellas, because I don't like beer.

Mom, how are you getting along, fine I hope and keeping happy always. I'm doing good, and always happy, because I know you're okay.

On May 20, the commander of Ciarlo's G Company and that of every other company in the 15th Infantry received written orders reminding him that in the coming battle the "recovery and evacuation of bodies" would be his responsibility.

[Collection points for corpses were to be] clearly designated by map coordinates (i.e., road junctions; house along road; bridge; or other prominent terrain features). . . . Bodies having no identification tags will be, if humanly possible, identified by the unit with the man's name and organization written on a piece of paper and inserted in one of the uniform pockets. Absolute identification is imperative.

That night, Ciarlo and the rest of the men at Anzio could see the distant flash of guns to the south. The Germans and their pursuers were drawing closer.

The following evening, May 21, two days after Babe Ciarlo assured his mother that he still didn't like beer, General Clark ordered his forces at Anzio into action. They were to break out of the beachhead, fight their way inland, block both highways to Rome, and link up with the approaching Allied armies at a crossroads town called Valmontone, where they hoped to encircle the German army and destroy it.

A gray blanket of smoke was laid down to obscure the men's movement, but there could have been little doubt among the Germans as to what was about to happen. As the men of the 3rd Infantry started inland at dusk, the enemy heard the division band blaring its signature tune. Some of the marching men joined in.

I'm just a dog-faced soldier with a rifle on my shoulder,
And I eat a Kraut for breakfast every day.
So feed me ammunition,
Keep me in the 3rd Division,
Your dog-faced soldier-boy's O-Kay!

Ciarlo's 15th Regiment helped spearhead the fighting that began the following morning, shooting its way into the ruined village of Cisterna it had come so close to taking four months earlier. His company alone flushed more than one hundred enemy soldiers from the caves in which they'd been living since January.

Men belonging to Babe Ciarlo's 15th Regiment of the 3rd Infantry (left and above), wounded during the battle for Cisterna, May 23, 1944

By the morning of the twenty-fifth, Cisterna was in Allied hands, and with the rest of Lucian Truscott's VI Corps, the 3rd Division was driving hard toward Valmontone. Then, suddenly and without consulting General Alexander, Mark Clark abruptly changed course: he ordered it to block Highway 6 while the rest of Truscott's corps—two thirds of the men under his command—were to abandon their original objective, wheel northwestward, and race for Rome instead. Clark later said he'd never believed the Germans really could have been trapped at Valmontone, but his decision to defy orders and reduce his forces there helped insure that they were not. In the end, the Allies let their enemy escape to fight another day, just as they had in Sicily the previous year. Clark's motives for defying his superior were at least as much personal as strategic: he wanted to beat the British to Rome, to see himself and the Americans dominate the headlines before the world's attention turned to the Normandy invasion that was now just days away. Meanwhile, the Germans continued to retreat toward the Gothic Line, north of the Italian capital, the same line Allied planners had initially believed they should have taken themselves six months earlier.

The British—and many of Clark's American subordinates—were appalled at what he'd done. Ward Chamberlin was now in command of Platoon C—his friend Bob Bryan had been killed by a shell during the final fight for Cassino—and following along behind a South African regiment as it pursued the enemy. His memories mirrored the disillusionment felt by a good many of the men with whom he had served in Italy.

When we finally did break through, we didn't even beat the German army then. There wasn't a lot to show for all that [fighting in Italy], all those casualties, all those terrible things. The only thing we did from a larger perspective was to keep a number of German divisions occupied there that otherwise could have gone to France or could have gone to Russia or somewhere else. But there wasn't a lot to show for it. It was horrible.

ON SUNDAY AFTERNOON, JUNE 4, 1944, Olga Ciarlo was in her mother's living room in Waterbury, Connecticut, writing a letter to her brother in Italy. It was his twenty-first birthday. The radio was on.

The Fifth Army threads its way into Rome, June 4, 1944. "We were woken by trucks moving through the street," one jubilant Roman citizen remembered. "At first I thought that it was the Germans, but then I heard American accents. . . . By dawn people were lining the steets. I cried."

Dearest Babe:

It is now about 3:15 in the afternoon and it's a beautiful day. . . . We just had news a little while ago and our American forces are in Rome. Gee that's swell. I do hope it's over soon. . . .

The news is on again Babe. The Allies have passed the city limits in Rome but they're not doing any fighting. Gee, I don't have to tell you anything. You know everything from beginning to end. Babe, try to tell us a little more about you. Where you are and what you are doing. We do hope everything is all right with you. Remember always to take good care of yourself.

Well Babe, today is your birthday and we do wish you a happy one. May all your wishes and dreams come true and let's hope that you'll be home for your next birthday. I'm sure you will be. It won't be long now. We'll have the biggest party you've ever seen. Just keep your chin up. You're 21 years old and what a man. We're all so proud of you, especially Mom. There's not a minute that goes by that she doesn't think of you. We all miss you and pray so hard for this war to end so you can come home. In the other day's paper it said that 100 soldiers from Italy came home on furlough, so it won't be long now that you'll be coming home. What a day that will be. . . .

Yesterday we received two letters from you. . . . You said you sent home $30.00. We didn't receive it yet, but it will get here soon. Mom is going to put it in the bank for you Babe, so that when you come home you can have everything you want. You can buy your car and all your new clothes. . . .

Well Babe, I guess I've said enough for now. Love from all. Take good care of yourself and write as often as you can. . . . May God bless you and keep you safe. Our thoughts are always with you.

Your loving sister,
Olga

Twenty-two days later, a telegram from the War Department would arrive at the Ciarlo home. Babe was dead. He may have been wounded as early as May 23, as his battalion struggled to take Cisterna during the first few hours of the Anzio breakout. Nine hundred and ninety-five men from his division were lost that day. Hundreds more were killed or wounded during the four days that followed, some the victims of friendly artillery fire, more than one hundred others strafed and bombed by American P-40 fighter planes whose pilots mistook their advancing countrymen for retreating Germans. Fighting for the ruined village of Artena, Babe's regiment lost seventy more.

Whenever Babe was hit, however he was wounded, he died in or near Artena on May 27, nine days before his sister began her birthday letter to him. Among the belongings found in his pockets were two rosaries, his driver's license, a wallet with sixteen photographs of family and friends, a blood-stained letter, and one dollar and sixty-one cents in cash.

Olga Ciarlo happened to be out with friends at a sewing club the evening the telegram came.

After I got off the bus, I see all these lights lit, which is very unusual that my mother would have all these lights lit through the dining room, living room, kitchen. And the closer I got to my house, lights were all over the place and I can hear people talking, and as I went up the front stairs, I can hear my mother screaming, crying, my aunts, uncles, everybody was there. And I didn't know what had happened, so my aunt called me aside and told me what had happened. Well, it was a terrible night.

Babe's younger brother Tom came home late that evening, too. "When I approached the house, I could hear screaming and yelling," he remembered.

When I got upstairs and found out what happened, of course, it came as a complete shock to all of us because we thought everything was fine. Babe said everything was fine. He's coming home soon and it would be great so—to tell you the truth—I just went to my room. I closed the door and that's where I stayed with all the screaming and the yelling, you know how the old Italians were, when they had a death in the family.

The news spread through the neighborhood. A friend called Anne DeVico. She was crying. DeVico asked what was wrong. "Babe Ciarlo was killed." "I said, 'Oh, my God,' " DeVico remembered. "He was always so happy and jolly and then I'm thinking, 'He's not coming back.' And it was terrible because you started to realize that this isn't just going over there and winning the peace and then coming back. They're not coming back. Some of them aren't."

Ciarlo's mother refused to believe her son was gone. There had been some mistake. She was sure of it. "She was a disaster," her daughter remembered.

We would be getting the newspaper and my mother would look at pictures and she'd say to me, "There's Babe. That's Babe." And I'd say, "Gee, no, Mom, that's not Babe." "No! You have to write to them. You have to." I don't know how many newspaper offices I wrote to, questioning the name of that boy that was in that picture, because my mother always thought it was Babe. But it never came to be.

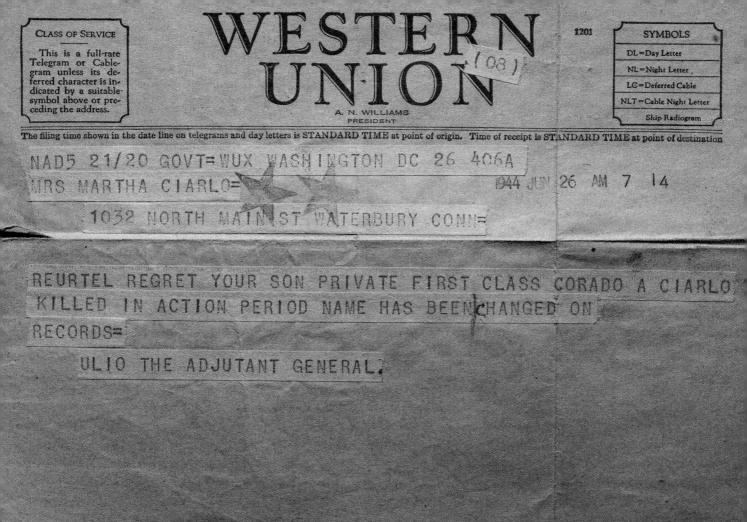

WESTERN UNION

CLASS OF SERVICE

This is a full-rate Telegram or Cablegram unless its deferred character is indicated by a suitable symbol above or preceding the address.

A. N. WILLIAMS
PRESIDENT

1201

SYMBOLS

DL=Day Letter
NL=Night Letter
LC=Deferred Cable
NLT=Cable Night Letter
Ship Radiogram

The filing time shown in the date line on telegrams and day letters is STANDARD TIME at point of origin. Time of receipt is STANDARD TIME at point of destination

NAD5 21/20 GOVT=WUX WASHINGTON DC 26 406A

MRS MARTHA CIARLO=

1032 NORTH MAIN ST WATERBURY CONN=

1944 JUN 26 AM 7 14

REURTEL REGRET YOUR SON PRIVATE FIRST CLASS CORADO A CIARLO
KILLED IN ACTION PERIOD NAME HAS BEEN CHANGED ON
RECORDS=

ULIO THE ADJUTANT GENERAL.

THE COMPANY WILL APPRECIATE SUGGESTIONS FROM ITS PATRONS CONCERNING ITS SERVICE

PRIDE OF OUR NATION

ON SATURDAY, JUNE 3, 1944, at 3:49 p.m. Eastern War Time, American radio and newspaper offices received the news the country had been waiting for: "Associated Press. FLASH: Eisenhower's headquarters announced landings in France." Broadcasters raced to microphones. Within a minute, some five hundred stations had broken into regular programming with word that D-day was here. At New York City's Polo Grounds, the Giants and the Pittsburgh Pirates stopped playing while nine thousand baseball fans stood in prayerful silence. People rushed to church in cities and small towns. Less than two minutes later, another bulletin came in over the wire: "Bust that flash." The invasion had not yet begun: a tearful twenty-two-year-old British teletype operator confessed that it was all her fault: she had been practicing her typing and somehow her practice tape had made it into the transmitter. It took hours to disentangle American telephone traffic as those who hadn't heard the second announcement placed anxious calls to friends and family members.

People did their best to get back to normal that weekend. It was the wedding season, and the Sunday women's pages were filled with loving detail about bridal veils, floral displays, and maids of honor, just as they had always been, though a careful reader would have noticed that most of the grooms seemed to belong to some branch of the service. In Sacramento, the river for which the town was named experienced the heaviest salmon run in years. In Mobile, Miss Jacquelyn Kuffskie received special recognition at the Murphy High School graduation ceremony for having completed eleven years of schooling without missing a single day. The Waterbury Shriners were about to open their ninth annual charity circus, its proceeds earmarked for the Zindah Grotto's Keep 'Em Flying Fund, which provided free cigarettes for local boys and girls in uniform. And in Luverne, where spring had come earlier than usual, Al McIntosh found room in his weekly column to report that a local gardener had already harvested a tomato the size of a quarter.

But in the back of everyone's mind, hope continued to combine with dread. In spite of the progress that had been made, everything that had happened so far in the war seemed a mere preliminary. The Japanese empire had begun to shrink, but its rulers seemed determined to defend to the death every island

they still held. The Germans were falling back before the Red Army and Rome had been taken, but Hitler's grip on western Europe could not be broken until Allied troops finally crossed the English Channel and opened the long-awaited second front. Everyone understood that sometime very soon, thousands of sons and fathers and husbands would be called upon to gamble their lives for the sake of victory.

The Germans were on edge, too. Hitler understood the vital importance of holding on to the western edge of his empire. "In the East, the vastness of the space will, as a last resort, permit a loss of territory, even on a major scale, without suffering a mortal blow," he'd told his generals the previous year. "Not so in the West! If the enemy here succeeds in penetrating our defenses on a wide front, consequences of staggering proportions will follow within a short time." To keep that from happening, hundreds of thousands of slave laborers and POWs and German soldiers had been put to work constructing the Atlantic Wall—nearly three thousand miles of fortified gun emplacements, radar and observation towers, and bunkers that stretched from Norway all the way south to the frontier of neutral Spain.

Field Marshal Erwin Rommel was now in command of the Channel defenses. The war, he believed, would be "won or lost on the beaches," and he had done everything he could to insure that Allied troops would never reach them. The waterline was seeded with six million mines and half a million obstacles—angled wooden stakes, steel gates and jagged tetrahedrons fashioned from welded steel girders—all heavily mined and intended either to blow up landing craft or tear their bottoms out. Rommel called the result a "zone of death."

Seasick GIs aboard a landing craft bound for Normandy (opposite) seek fresh air and shelter from salt spray atop army supply trucks. Meanwhile, the wry sign above greeted newcomers to Tarawa.

The Germans expected the invasion to come near Calais, the closest French port to Britain, in part because Allied Intelligence had managed to convince them that a vast army, commanded by George Patton, was being readied to attack them there. There was no such army; thousands of tanks and guns and landing craft, assembled near Dover and duly reported to the enemy, were made of rubber by movie set designers. The elaborate hoax was one of the most important Allied Intelligence feats of the war. Instead, commanders planned five coordinated landings along a forty-five-mile stretch of the Normandy coastline between the Cotentin peninsula and the Orne River.

The U.S. First Army, under General Omar Bradley, would assault "Utah" and "Omaha" beaches on the western flank. British and Canadian units of the British Second Army were to fight their way ashore at "Gold," "Juno," and "Sword," then move swiftly inland some seven miles to take the town of Caen, with its

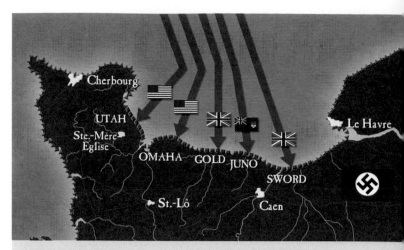

While the Allies prepare to assault five beaches in Normandy (above), Field Marshall Erwin Rommel (below, third from left) inspects German defenses along the shore of Pas-de-Calais, where he has been led to believe his forces are most likely to be attacked.

Just before D-day, P-51 fighters, freshly unloaded from American ships—and with wingtips detached to ease their passage between buildings—are trucked through Liverpool, on their way to a British airbase from which they will help provide cover for the coming invasion.

important airfield and its command of roads that led through mostly open countryside to Paris, just 120 miles away.

When the go-ahead was given, the assault was to proceed in three phases.

First, paratroopers would be dropped behind the beaches in the dead of night to confuse the enemy and seize the roads and bridges that led inland from them to prevent the Germans from bringing up reinforcements.

Then, wave after wave of warplanes were to batter German defenses, destroying the enemy emplacements that overlooked the landing beaches.

Finally, a massive flotilla was to ferry thousands of British, Canadian, and American troops to their assigned landing points.

The invasion was set for Monday, June 5, but bad weather closed in late on the third, and Eisenhower ordered it put off for twenty-four hours. Further delay could have meant disaster. It would be two weeks before the tides off Normandy were low enough to land again, and there would then have been too little moonlight for the paratroops to locate their targets. And the Germans had a new weapon—the pilotless V-1 rocket—and some fifty secret sites from which to fire it. If Eisenhower waited too long, the Allies feared, Hitler might use it to destroy the gathering invasion force before it could get under way. Morale and secrecy were at risk as well. Tens of thousands of men were already riding out the storm aboard the ships that were to ferry them to France. Late on the fourth, a British meteorologist on Eisenhower's staff told him the weather was likely to improve at least a little over the next thirty-six hours. Eisenhower decided he could wait no longer. "OK," he said. "Let's go." The invasion of Europe would take place on Tuesday, June 6—D-day.

Phase One really began just before dark on the evening of the fifth as thirteen thousand young men of the U.S. 82nd and 101st, and the British 6th Airborne divisions, all bent nearly double by the weight of their parachutes and combat gear, began filing onto 882 C-47 transport planes at airfields all over southern England. As his plane taxied into position for takeoff, one private in the 82nd lifted the little blackout curtain that covered his window and peered out.

> *Along each side of the runway were . . . hundreds of people, lined up two and three deep. United States and RAF ground personnel, British army girls, cooks, bakers—and no one moved. They just stared at our plane. Without moving, they seemed to offer a profound salute—and perhaps a blessing or prayer. We could feel—I know I could—the spirit of all those people with us as the pilot released the brakes and the plane surged forward.*

They began taking off shortly after ten o'clock and flew above the Channel in compact nine-plane V formations, lit only by the dim blue lights that tipped their tails. Behind them, in a slow-moving line that eventually stretched three hundred miles, streamed hundreds more C-47s, many of them towing British-made gliders filled with more men and the vehicles and weaponry they would need once they were on the ground. The planes flew just five hundred feet above the Channel to elude German radar, rose to fifteen hundred feet to evade German antiaircraft guns on the Channel Islands, then swooped down again to seven hundred feet as they neared the French coast and got ready to loose their eighteen-man "sticks" over the Norman countryside.

Most of the men of the British 6th Airborne dropped on target behind the easternmost beaches, reassembled, and before dawn had achieved their objectives, destroying a massive German battery at Merville and seizing bridges across the Caen Canal and Orne River to keep German tanks from mounting a flanking counterattack along the coast.

Behind the western beaches, the men of the 101st and 82nd Airborne were less fortunate. Their main objective was to seize the inland sides of four causeways that led from Utah Beach into the countryside. But the narrow neck of the Cotentin Peninsula proved hard to hit from the air. German antiaircraft fire targeted

American infantry crowd into Higgins boats during a rehearsal for D-day, somewhere on the English coast. "Again and again," an officer recalled, "we loaded onto landing craft that pitched and rolled out into the Channel and then roared landward to drop the ramp over which we lumbered to flounder through surf to the beach and go through the assault drills."

Aboard a C-47 transport, men of the 82nd Airborne Division prepare to unhook and jump into Normandy. As his turn came to step out into a night sky lit up by tracer bullets, one man said to himself, "Len, you're in as much trouble now as you're ever going to be in. If you get out of this nobody can ever do anything to you that you ever have to worry about."

the slow-moving planes. Low-hanging clouds blocked the moonlight and obscured the landing zones. Paratroops fell helplessly into the sea or drowned in fields and river valleys flooded by the Germans. Some were blown from the sky as tracer bullets set off the explosives they carried. Still others were dropped so low their parachutes had no chance to open: they hit the ground, one man remembered, with "a sound like ripe pumpkins being thrown down against the ground."

Paratroops of the 101st Airborne found themselves scattered over an area twenty-five miles long by fifteen miles wide. Most were lost. Of the 6,600 men who dropped that night, only a little more than 1,000 had reached their reporting points by dawn. Twenty-four hours later, their commander had located less than half his surviving men. But they managed nonetheless to secure all four exits from Utah Beach.

Elements of the 82nd Airborne drifted down in and around the little crossroads town of Sainte-Mère-Église. The Germans shot them up at first, but they regrouped, took over the town, and held it against repeated counterattacks. The fight was still on at around eight-thirty that morning when the glider carrying Dwain Luce, now a captain, approached the landing zone. A survivor of the invasion of Sicily and the landing at Salerno, he was part of the 320th Glider Field Artillery Battalion, and he was late: his first glider had crashed in England when its nylon towrope snapped, and it had taken time to find and load a second one and get it into the air.

We had been in combat before, and we knew kind of what we were getting into. But we knew this was the big bang, and it was kind of worrisome, you might say. I mean, anybody who says they weren't scared either wasn't there or they're lying. You're getting in that glider and not knowing where you're going to land or what you're going to be met with. Those things go through your mind, but you have to learn to accept it and make the best of it and try to maintain a little sense of humor.

Gliders were silent—ideal for clandestine landings behind enemy lines—and capable of ferrying equipment and vehicles too heavy to be dropped in any other way. But they were also fragile, covered with flammable fabric, hard to control; and in some landing zones, Rommel had placed forests of sharpened twelve-foot poles wired to trip mines intended to rip gliders apart, impale the men, and blow up anyone who managed to get out alive.

Inexperienced towplane pilots, wary of antiaircraft fire, flew erratically that morning. More than half the twelve hundred gliders missed their drop zone. Scores of glider pilots and passengers were crushed when vehicles and artillery pieces slammed forward during crash landings. Even for those who reached their target safely, Luce recalled, landing could be an ordeal.

The problem was that when the pilot of that glider was cut loose, he was on his own and he had to have enough speed left to get over those trees, but then when he got over them, he had to get down. So instead of landing slow, we landed at the highest rate of speed. I remember I was sitting up next to the pilot and I leaned over his shoulder and looked and when we dove over those trees we were doing over a hundred and ten miles an hour and I thought, "This is no speed to land." But it was too late to change. That's why so many of the gliders crashed.

Once he'd managed to extricate himself from his glider, Luce found himself right in the middle of combat.

I fortunately did not land in front of any of those antitank guns, which were vicious. I had a friend that landed in front of one and he was cut in half, and those are things I don't like to think about or talk about. But there was some guy up on a hill above me trying to disrupt my life, and it wasn't a pleasant experience.

The Germans held the high ground southeast of Sainte-Mère-Église and were fighting hard to regain control of the vital causeway that ran from Carentan to the port of Cherbourg. The fighting was confused. There were no established lines. At one point, the men of Luce's squad found themselves firing two howitzers simultaneously in opposite directions because they were "more or less surrounded," he recalled. "It was kind of like cops and robbers to a degree, because you were all mixed up in there with them. I mean, they wasn't on one side and we were on the other. We were all like scrambled eggs. But we got it straight." Despite the confusion, the Americans held their ground, continued to block the causeway behind Utah Beach—and waited for the assault force to come to their rescue.

The airborne landings alerted German commanders to the fact that something was happening, but they couldn't agree on just what it was. They doubted that a full-scale invasion could be launched in such bad weather, and most continued to be convinced that when it did come, Calais, not Normandy, would be the target. No one wakened Hitler or Rommel—who had gone home to Germany to celebrate his wife's birthday. Finally, Field Marshal Gerd von Rundstedt, the German commander in the West, ordered two panzer divisions to move up to the Normandy coast just in case. But within the hour, Hitler's chief of operations, General Alfred Jodl, angrily countermanded his orders: no such change in plans could be made without the Führer's approval.

During the initial drop and the days that followed, 2,499 American airborne troops were lost; so were 1,500 airborne Britons. But Allied troops were on the soil of western Europe at last, and the next phase of the invasion was already under way.

Shortly before midnight, Quentin Aanenson had been awakened at an air base north of London and told to get into his flight gear and meet with other fighter pilots in the briefing room. They were barely awake as they took their seats, Aanenson remembered.

But we knew it was something serious. We could tell by just the atmosphere. There were two or three briefing officers up at the front. They had a large map that was covered, and as we took our seats and they pulled the curtain back, they said, "Gentlemen, this is it. The invasion of France has begun." I remember the feeling that I had, that I can't believe I'm actually here. And so with that we prepared ourselves for what we were doing, and we took off in the dark on that first mission over Normandy.

At 4:30 a.m., Aanenson and his squadron set out for France as part of the flight of eleven thousand warplanes—Lightnings and Lancasters and Liberators; Mosquitoes and Mustangs; Spitfires and Thunderbolts and Typhoons and Flying Fortresses—assigned to bomb and strafe German defenses before the first troops reached the coast. "As we approached Normandy," Aanenson said, "we were coming in at about eight thousand feet, and there was a mixture of some clouds, but we could see down into the Channel, and it was impossible to understand, really, what we were seeing. There were ships everywhere."

Down below, the largest fleet ever assembled—more than 5,300 vessels—carrying more than 175,000 men—was streaming across the Channel: battleships and troop transports and tugboats; cruisers and barges and rusty freighters; gunboats and hospital ships and converted ocean liners; ships filled with ammunition and ships equipped to lay down screens of purple smoke; plus a flotilla of more than two thousand landing craft to ferry men and supplies to the beach, most of them flat-bottomed Higgins boats with hinged prows that could disgorge troops fast and then back away, allowing men to land on almost any kind of coast.

"The best way I can describe this vast armada and the frantic urgency of the traffic," Ernie Pyle reported, "is to suggest that you visualize New York Harbor on its busiest day of the year and then just enlarge that scene until it takes in all the ocean the human eye can reach, clear around the horizon. And over the horizon there are dozens of times that many."

H-hour for the Americans was 6:30 a.m. On Utah Beach, drifting smoke that hid the target, the loss of three guide boats to mines, and strong tidal currents combined to bring the first landing craft carrying the men of the 4th Infantry in to shore more than two thousand yards south of the spot chosen by D-day planners. Some wanted to redirect the reinforcements coming in behind them to the original target. But among the first men ashore was the assistant division commander, fifty-seven-year-old Brigadier General Theodore Roosevelt, Jr. The eldest son of one president and the fifth cousin of another, he took charge right away. "We'll start the war here," he said, and, armed only with a pistol and a walking stick, he signaled for the landing craft to keep coming. German positions were quickly overrun. Of the 23,500 men who went ashore at Utah Beach that day, there were just 197 casualties, 60 aboard a single landing craft. By late morning, Roosevelt's most serious problem was directing traffic as American tanks roared off the beach and onto the four causeways airborne troops had captured just hours before.

"We were back there, and we didn't know for sure what was going on on the beach," Dwain Luce remembered.

We knew that it would hold if we got our job done. And we also knew that if the beach didn't hold, we would probably be left there. We would be abandoned. They couldn't get us out. So naturally, it was of great interest to us to get our job done. One of the things I will always remember with a great deal of emotion is that first tank that came through. Because when that first tank came through, I knew the beach had held and I knew help was on the way.

Coming ashore half an hour after the Americans, British troops would take Gold and Sword almost as fast, aided in part by an array of ingenious mechanical contrivances U.S. commanders had dismissed as impractical, including Sherman tanks var-

iously modified to clear minefields with flailing lengths of chain, hurl flame as well as shells into German positions, and drop big bundles of logs into antitank ditches so that they and other tanks could roll across them.

Canadian troops took Juno, too, although 90 of their 306 landing craft were destroyed by German obstacles and one in nineteen of the fifteen-thousand-man invading force was killed. By nightfall they had managed to fight their way seven miles inland.

But neither the British nor the Canadians were able to extend their beachhead into Caen. The Germans in and around the city would hold out for more than a month, denying the Allies access to the open countryside they had planned to use to race toward Paris and forcing them to inch their way inland instead, through terrain that offered every advantage to the enemy.

For the Americans of the 1st and 29th Infantry divisions waiting off Omaha Beach in the darkness that morning, almost everything was about to go wrong. Omaha is a gently curving natural amphitheater, dominated by 130-foot bluffs pierced by five "draws," or gullies, each with its own road or cart track leading up to the plateau. At roughly six miles across, it was the broadest of the five invasion beaches—and the deepest, with more than three hundred yards of exposed beach at low tide. It was also the most strongly defended on June 6. Thirteen fortified strongpoints, reinforced with steel and concrete and equipped with 50-, 75-, and 88-millimeter artillery pieces, overlooked the five draws and were situated to provide overlapping fields of fire. Each was surrounded by antitank and anti-fire ditches, and interspersed among them were batteries of artillery, antitank guns, mortar pits, armor-piercing howitzers, and rocket launchers, as well as eighty-five machine-gun nests—all well concealed, reinforced, and interconnected by a maze of camouflaged trenches, subterranean barracks, and command posts. Because of the tall cliffs and curving waterline, guns fired lengthwise from the heights at either end of the beach could cut to pieces anyone brave or foolhardy enough to try to come ashore.

Naval Ensign Joseph Vaghi was aboard Coast Guard LCIL88 (Landing Craft, Infantry, Large), tossing in the waves some eleven miles offshore. The flat-bottomed, three-hundred-ton vessel had twice been under fire, ferrying troops onto beaches in Sicily and Italy, but none of the men she was now carrying toward the Norman coast had yet heard a shot fired in anger. Vaghi was part of Company C of Navy Beach Battalion 6 and assigned to be a beachmaster on Omaha that morning. It would be his task to use flags, blinkers, and a megaphone to help

Joseph Vaghi (seated at right) and his four brothers in uniform

get men, vehicles, and supplies belonging to the 16th Infantry Regiment of the 1st Infantry Division safely ashore on the central "Easy Red" segment of the beach—and to help set up emergency aid stations once they got there. A big, strapping college football player from Bethel, Connecticut (just up the road from Waterbury), Vaghi had gone home to say goodbye to his family before heading overseas that spring. Both he and they had known he was headed for England and likely to play a part in the coming invasion, he remembered.

It was very difficult, because I had two other brothers already in the service and my poor mother, she knew all of us were going to go eventually. And, as it turned out, we all did go, all of us were in the service. And that was kind of rough. But when I was leaving, she had her chin up, you know. She spoke in Italian. She spoke English very well, but she said all of the sentimental things in Italian. She said, "Mio caro figlio, Dio sia con te. . . . Non dimenticare mai tuoi genitori." [My dear son, God be with you. Never forget your parents.]

LCIL88 had a coast guard crew of 33 and room for some 140 "passengers"—the 45 men of Vaghi's platoon, plus a platoon of amphibious engineers with whom they had trained and who were meant to hit the beach at the same time. Vaghi played poker in the wardroom with several other officers until he grew tired of it. Around four o'clock in the morning he went topside. It was still dark, he remembered, but "everywhere you looked you saw ships—ships, ships, ships."

Somewhere nearby, Staff Sergeant Walter Ehlers of Manhattan, Kansas, and his twelve-man squad from Company L of the 3rd Battalion, 18th Regiment, 1st Division, were battling seasickness aboard another LCIL, which also served as company headquarters. They weren't supposed to be there. When their battalion boarded at Weymouth, England, there hadn't been room for them in the boat assigned to carry the rest of their company, so at the last minute they'd been ordered to sail with the headquarters staff.

Ehlers and his older brother, Roland, had joined the army together shortly before Pearl Harbor. They had had a strict religious upbringing. "When we were growing up," Walter recalled, "I told my mother one time that I hated my sister. And she said, 'Well, son, you don't hate anybody,' and she washed my mouth out with soap. And said, 'Now, remember this. You don't hate anybody. Never use that word again.' *Hate* was probably the worst four-letter word she could think of."

Walter had been just nineteen in 1941, and at that time in Kansas a man had to be twenty-one before he could wear his country's uniform. His father agreed to sign a waiver allowing him to go, but his mother refused unless he first promised he'd be "a Christian soldier." He told her he'd do his "very best." Later, he recalled, "whenever there were temptations, I could see those tears in her eyes, and I didn't want to dishonor her." Whenever he went into battle, Walter made sure his mother's photograph was in his pack.

He and Roland had originally served together in K Company of the 3rd Battalion. "We had a pact between us," Walter recalled.

Since we would be fighting as brothers, we knew that the other guys might suspect that one of us might want to cover the other or if one of us got wounded we would stop our fighting to go protect the other or something. So my brother and I made an agreement that we wouldn't do that, because we knew that there were other men's lives on the line.

Their own lives had been on the line many times. At the battle of El Guettar, in Tunisia, K Company helped hold an important hillside position against panzer troops, suffered 60 percent casualties, and earned a Distinguished Unit citation. The brothers had narrowly escaped death from misdirected American artillery and airpower in North Africa, as well, and had battled their way together across Sicily. Soon after they got to England, the company commander had taken them aside. First he advised them to double their life insurance coverage from five thousand to ten thousand dollars, because the upcoming landing was likely to be a bloodbath. Then he said he was going to have to separate them because of what had happened to the five Sullivan brothers, who had all died

Walter Ehlers

Canadian infantry, part of
the multinational Allied
force heading toward
France, June 5, 1944. An
American officer remem-
bered the view from the
deck of his ship that day:
"Vessels of all shapes
and sizes, towing barrage
balloons as if in some
gigantic, colorless
carnival procession,
were before, behind, and
to either side—part of
the fleet of some five
thousand streaming out
in long columns from
southern England."

199

when their ship went down off Guadalcanal. General Marshall no longer wanted brothers to serve in the same outfit when there were likely to be heavy casualties. Ronald would remain in Company K, but Walter would have to train a whole new squad as part of Company L. The brothers didn't argue, Walter recalled. "I only went to L Company. That's a sister company in the same battalion. We were close together enough for visiting places in England and things like that. So it didn't bother us there."

Joe Vaghi, the Ehlers brothers, and all the other Americans of the 1st and 29th divisions who had spent up to a week riding the swells while waiting to storm Omaha Beach had been given a great many reassurances by their commanders. Only some six hundred enemy troops were in position to defend the beach, they were told, and most of them were former prisoners of war, captured on the eastern front, with little enthusiasm for battle. In any case, navy guns and Eighth Air Force bombers were going to blast enemy positions to smithereens before the assault boats got anywhere near the shore, and any defenders left alive were sure to have been "neutralized," left too addled and traumatized by the shelling to man their weapons before the landing parties overwhelmed them. Twenty-four teams of army and navy demolition engineers would reach the beach first to blast sixteen safe paths through the thicket of mined German obstacles. A phalanx of sixty-two modified Sherman tanks—each fitted out with an inflated canvas-and-rubber shroud that enabled it to float and twin propellers that allowed it to move through the water under its own power—was to precede the infantry onto the beach as well. They would provide cover, roll over barbed wire, and use their 75-millimeter cannon to complete the destruction of enemy strongpoints. Finally, by the time the men themselves came ashore, they would find the beaches covered with bomb craters, which would provide shelter against any defenders who happened to survive.

Not one of these promises was kept. There were twelve hundred enemy troops waiting along Omaha Beach, not six hundred, and half were German veterans of the Russian front. The roar of the naval shelling that was supposed to pulverize their positions nearly deafened the men in the landing craft. "The concussion seemed to want to pull your clothes off," one man remembered. The rumble of the big shells made another think that jeeps were somehow hurtling over his head. But it lasted less than forty minutes, smoke and terrain obscured targets, and little actual damage was done.

General Bradley professed to be unconcerned: Allied airpower would more than make up for the shortfall. As the first landing craft continued to move toward the beach, more than 450 bombers roared in over Omaha. From fifteen miles out, Walter Ehlers watched them come. "We never saw so many planes in our life. The sky was black with planes—bombers and fighters and planes pulling gliders. Wave after wave. And we thought, 'Wow, with all this going on, there ought not to be anything left by the time we get there.' "

But the cloud cover was thick, and pilots, who had orders not to risk hitting American landing craft, did not dare release their bombs until they were well inland. Not one hit the beach; only a few hit German gun positions; far more Norman cattle were killed than enemy soldiers. There would be no seaside craters in which infantrymen might find protection. (Bradley had never wanted craters, in any case, for fear they would have kept vehicles from moving inland.)

Then, nearly half the demolition engineers sent in to destroy the German obstacles were killed or wounded by enemy shells, most of them within the first thirty minutes. Instead of the sixteen paths to the beach they were meant to create, they managed just five and a half. Twenty-seven of the thirty-two self-propelled tanks intended to provide support for the 1st Division were launched in choppy water six thousand yards out at sea. The waves quickly loosened or ripped apart their canvas floats and sent them to the bottom, carrying most of their crews with them. The thirty-two tanks meant for the 29th Division's half of the beach were ferried all the way in to shore but got little farther than the surf line, where they sat, exposed to enemy mortar and shell fire, while the men huddled inside peered through periscopes in search of something to shoot at.

The shelling had not done much damage to German positions, but here and there it had set the grass atop the bluffs on fire. Drifting smoke masked the landmarks navy coxswains had carefully memorized. A strong eastward current was running, too, and as the first Higgins boats came close to shore most found themselves hundreds of yards from where they were supposed to land. The men—most of whom had had no sleep and all of whom were stiff and out of shape after a week at sea in cramped quarters—were also wet and cold, seasick and scared. Waves came over the sides of some boats. Men bailed desperately with their helmets. At least ten landing craft were swamped. Scores of men, burdened with equipment, struggled to stay afloat, screaming for help as other boats wallowed past them. Coxswains were forbidden to stop and pick them up. Many drowned.

Terror intensified. As his landing craft shuddered to a stop one soldier asked another, "Mac, when a bullet hits you, does it go through?" His friend had no time to answer. The men kicked down the landing ramp and found themselves in what one sur-

The ramp falls and infantry step off into the surf at Omaha Beach. Ahead are tank obstacles and barbed wire—and hidden German defenders, about to open fire.

vivor called "a new world." The Germans along the bluffs had largely held their fire until that moment. Now machine-gun fire ripped through many men before they could step onto the ramp. Scores more were hit in the water. Two companies were obliterated before they could reach the sand. Some wounded men made it to the waterline, then lay helpless amid the seaweed as the tide rose slowly over them.

Those who managed to push past the dead and dying in the shallows found they had nowhere to go. Some scrabbled at the sand and shale, trying to dig foxholes. Others huddled together behind wrecked landing craft or German obstacles. Many had lost their weapons in the water and could not even fire back. The Germans concentrated their fire on such groups to do as much damage as possible.

One demolition engineer felt a machine-gun bullet tear through his buttock, then watched, fascinated, as bullets from the same burst spattered the sand leading away from him for eight feet or so, then pierced a friend's canteen. "I can still see to this day," he remembered, "a stream of water the size of a lead pencil come out."

Another man, shot through the spine, began immediately to apologize. "I'm not goldbricking, lieutenant," he said. "My legs won't move. Help me get up and I can get one of the bastards." After a shell struck nearby, hurling sand and men and weapons into the sky, another private remembered finding "a big chunk of bloody meat in my lap." Stunned, he asked his sergeant what it was. The sergeant didn't know. "Does it belong to you?" he asked. "I told him I didn't think so," the private said, "but I was so scared I wasn't really sure."

A second wave of frightened men soon began coming ashore—and stalled behind the remnants of the first. "Except for

The photographer Robert Capa, on assignment for *Life* magazine, went ashore at Omaha Beach with a rifle company of the 16th Infantry Division that morning, as part of the second wave. Despite the furious fire that met him the moment the ramp went down and made him shake "from toe to hair," he managed to take 106 photographs—three appear on the previous pages—and then get them back to England by nightfall.

In this full frame of one of Capa's images, frightened GIs, struggling through the surf, take what cover they can find behind beach obstacles and disabled vehicles as German fire pours down upon them from the bluffs above. Back in England that evening, an inept darkroom assistant ruined all but ten of Capa's negatives. They constitute the sole surviving close-up record of the struggle at the shoreline.

one tank that was blasting away from the sand," one of the newcomers remembered, "the crusade in Europe was, for all practical purposes, disarmed and naked before its enemies." Another soldier remembered the first things he saw as he stepped onto the beach.

The single-file ramps of a smoldering LCI were filled from beach to deck with soldiers who had been killed wholesale in the act of debarking. They were sprawled on the ramps two and three deep, those on the bottom oblivious to the weight of those on top. At another point I could not avoid running through an instep-deep pool of blood that seeped from the head wound of a dead sailor. . . . As I came around the end of a stalled tank I found myself staring, horrified, into the chest cavity of a mutilated corpse. It was cut diagonally in two from the left armpit to the bottom of the right rib cage. The upper part, along with the viscera, was nowhere to be seen; the lower part, all too visible, was lying prone before me, naked except for brown GI shoes that identified it as being recently part of a U.S. soldier. The bowel contents streaked out on the sand behind, demonstrating progressive states of digestion.

Some men lost touch with reality. A tanker remembered a soldier sitting at the waterline with his back to the enemy, apparently no longer able to register what was happening around him, "throwing stones into the water and softly crying as if his heart would break."

Around 7:35, LCIL88, carrying Joe Vaghi's platoon, approached the beach, part of the third wave to go ashore. "As we were going in I had no fear," he remembered.

We prayed as a platoon, we prayed together and said, "Well, it's God's will they want us to go over there and get this devil off the thing. We're going to do it. We know what to do, and we're ready." And that was it. I wasn't scared, only because I had not experienced this before.

We had all simulated landings. But this was for real. We knew that we would be fired upon. And we saw the tracers coming toward us. And we saw people fall. And we saw people being hit and yelling for help. If it were not for the good training we had—and I cannot stress that enough: train, train, train, train, train—we couldn't have made it. You can't overdo training. Because that's sort of a buffer between reality and the capacity of your mind to absorb what's going on.

After finding a bit of precious cover, an American machine-gunner on Omaha Beach begins returning fire.

A. J. Liebling, a journalist writing for the *New Yorker,* also happened to be aboard LCIL88. She came in fast, he wrote, and as she did, shells were exploding on the beach ahead and sending spray high in the air, and "there was a shooting gallery smell in the air." To the left an empty landing craft was grounded and in flames. Another came into view, also burning. "A number of men who had evidently just left her were in the water," Liebling wrote, "some up to their necks and others up to their armpits, and they didn't look as if they were trying to get ashore. Tracer bullets were skipping about them and they seemed perplexed."

Then Liebling felt the LCIL ground. Coastguardsmen winched down the twin ramps. The coxswain, wearing his helmet and swimming trunks, stepped off first, holding the guideline in his hand. A shell blew him apart. The men stepped off right after him. Vaghi had asked for the honor of leading his platoon onto the beach, so "they went off that way," the skipper told Liebling, "Vaghi running out ahead as if he was running out on a field with a football under his arm." Moments later, an antitank shell tore through the starboard bow of the LCIL they'd just left, killing one of the four men who'd lowered the ramps and mangling another.

Somehow, everyone in Vaghi's platoon managed to make it onto dry land. "Once we got on the beach all of us, without exception, knew what we had to do," Vaghi said. "Our objective was to get into the dune line and then start controlling activities on the beach." First they had to get there, running across three hundred yards of sand and shale, all of it exposed to enemy fire. "It's a long, long way to go," Vaghi remembered, "but as it turned out, all of my men—all of them—got up to the dune line."

Choked with shattered and burning equipment and crowded with more and more desperate men unable either to retreat or to move forward, the dune line provided little protection from the fire pouring down from the escarpment. Joe Vaghi did what he could to bring order out of his little piece of chaos, directing his men as they tried to clear a path, helping to set up an aid station for the wounded and the dying. "I was bending down," Vaghi recalled. "There was a corpse on a stretcher. Somebody wanted the stretcher, and they were going to roll the body off, and I said, 'No, let's move him over, because I want to keep this avenue, this area clear.' And as I bent down this shell hit." It hurled a truck into the air. When the truck came down, it crushed one of Vaghi's men to death and slammed into Vaghi's right knee. He was knocked unconscious. "When I came to, my clothes were on fire," he recalled. He beat out the flames, struggled to his feet, and went back to work, scrambling to remove grenades and gasoline cans from a burning jeep before they could explode and kill the wounded men lying all around him.

You know what to do because your instinct tells you. But there are other times you calculate what you have to do. I was trying to help this young boy who was moaning for help, and I went over and said, "Hold on a minute, I'll get you a doctor." That was not instinct. That was something I responded to. And the poor guy died.

At about the time Vaghi and his platoon reached Omaha, Walter Ehlers—still aboard the 18th Regiment's headquarters LCIL at the lowering point some twelve miles offshore—began to overhear reports of what was happening onshore. "I heard the officer say, 'Well, they're pinned down on the beach . . . and they've requested more troops immediately.'" The 3rd Battalion wasn't due to go ashore for some hours yet, but when an empty Higgins boat, back from the beach, came alongside, Ehlers and his squad were ordered to clamber down into it and start in. It took well over an hour to get there. "They told us they were pinned down, so we expected something, but not the chaos that we found when we finally got there," Ehlers remembered.

About a hundred yards out we hit a sandbar. So we asked the pilot of the boat, "Is this as far as it's going?" And he says, "As far as it can go." So he lets the ramp down and we rush out the front, and we go in the water and it's clear up to my neck. And the little sergeant I had, second-in-command in this squad, it was over his head. I had to drag him along. I got him so his feet touched the sand, and he could get his head above water and we waded in.

No one else in Ehlers's squad had been in combat. Their first instinct was to try to dig in on the beach. He wouldn't let them, and instead led them toward the bluff. Somehow, no one got hit. Nearby, men of the 16th Infantry Regiment of the 1st Division and the 116th Regiment of the 29th were jumbled up together. "We'd hear somebody say, 'Come on, Sixteen, let's go,'" Ehlers remembered. "We'd hear somebody on the other side say, 'Which Sixteen?' And I thought, 'Wow, this is chaos!' Now, here I am, out here with my squad. I don't have anybody to report to. I'm not even with my company, because I'm coming in ahead of time." He could see two pillboxes ahead of him. Machine-gun tracers streamed from each. A beachmaster appeared. Ehlers asked him where to go. "Just follow that passage made by guys that already cleared the mines," he said, "because if you go to right or left, you'll be in a minefield." Ehlers led his squad up the passage until German fire and whorls of barbed wire made it impossible to go any farther.

At around ten o'clock that morning, the German commander at Omaha telephoned his superiors to report that in his area, at least, the invasion had been stopped. Landing craft of all sizes and kinds were still coming toward the shore, but the waterline was so crowded with dead and wounded men, burning vehicles and ruined vessels, that it was difficult to find places to unload them; below him, thousands of Americans continued to huddle together, helpless, on the shale. At about the same time, reports filtering out to General Bradley aboard his flagship, the USS *Augusta,* far offshore, were so alarming that he considered halting further reinforcement of Omaha and redirecting the rest of his force to Utah instead.

But by then, individual Americans had already begun to improvise. Offshore, the commanders of nine U.S. destroyers (and three British ones) defied orders and risked ripping the bottoms from their ships to bring their vessels within a thousand yards of shore so they could use their batteries of five-inch guns to pound German pillboxes and gun emplacements. And up and down the beach, officers and enlisted men alike began taking their survival into their own hands. "They're murdering us here!" one wounded officer shouted to his men as machine-gun bullets roiled the shale around them. "Let's move inland and get murdered there instead!"

With the Germans continuing to block the gullies that led off the beach, GIs had to hurl themselves at the bluffs in between them, hoping to clamber to the top and then attack enemy strongpoints from the side and rear. Here and there, individuals got to their feet and started forward. Small groups began to follow. Joe Vaghi helped organize one of them.

At one point, this officer came up to me and saw that I was a navy beach master and I had a power megaphone, and he said, "Tell these guys to get the hell off the beach." They're all army people. So I said, "Got orders here from so-and-so that you're to get the hell off the beach now. And do it without delay." So this one soldier got up and put a bangalore torpedo [an explosive charge at the end of a long, extendable tube] under the barbed wire, blew a gap in it. Then he said, "Come on, follow me." And he led the way, and then they all got up and started to run through it.

Some yards up the beach, Walter Ehlers and his squad took action, too. Two demolition men, also armed with bangalore torpedoes, were trapped with them. Ehlers asked them to blow the wire blocking their advance. They said they couldn't: every time they tried to get close enough, Germans firing down at them from the trenches along the bluff drove them back. Ehlers asked exactly where the enemy bullets were coming from. The men

weren't sure, but they pointed in what they thought was the general direction. Ehlers ordered all twelve men in his squad to provide covering fire. The two demolition men raced forward. A German bullet killed one before he could detonate his charge, but the other managed to slide his torpedo beneath the wire and blow it apart. Ehlers and his men rushed through the gap. "It was probably the biggest thing I ever did in my life, to get all twelve of those men off the beach," Ehlers remembered.

> *We went up, and apparently there weren't any mines on the other side of the wire, because we went right up the hill into the trenches at the top. We were chasing the Germans then. We captured four of them and sent them back down. And then we got behind the pillbox, and what we didn't kill escaped, because they were running from us.*

Germans had begun running from others, too, and filing out of their strongpoints with their hands in the air. At one-thirty, General Bradley would receive the message: "Troops formerly pinned down on beaches Easy Red, Easy Green, Fox Red advancing up heights behind beaches." As the day wore on, combat engineers managed to clear more safe boat paths through the shallows. They bulldozed new exits from the beach, too, and

Survivors: both the stunned GI shivering on the shale above, and the battered man below, who seems only half aware of the medic who is tending to him, belonged to the 16th Infantry, 1st Division, and were trapped beneath the bluffs overlooking the Coleville draw at Omaha's eastern end.

started to build a road that men and vehicles could follow. By day's end, men of the 1st and 29th divisions would be more than a mile inland.

In less than twenty-four hours, the Allies had torn a forty-five-mile gap in Hitler's Atlantic Wall. More than 150,000 troops were on French soil, and more men, equipment, and supplies were coming ashore every hour.

Many survivors were in shock, unable to comprehend what they'd just been through, unsure of what they'd accomplished. Over the next few days, Private Andrew A. Rooney, a correspondent for the army newspaper *Stars and Stripes*, interviewed survivors. "Most of them thought it had been a disaster," he remembered.

All they saw was dead friends. Guys drowning in the water, and dead people around them. And back in the London headquarters they were calling it a great victory, a great success. It didn't look like a success to the guys who were there fighting it. But it turned out it was in fact a success, and the guys who were up close and saw it firsthand were wrong, and the people who had the grand view of it were right.

Far fewer Allied troops had died than Allied planners had expected, but D-day still had been the bloodiest day in U.S. military history since Antietam. Some 2,500 American soldiers lay dead on and behind the beaches. Thousands more were wounded or missing.

Roland Ehlers was one of them. His brother, Walter, was resting behind Omaha with his exhausted squad when his old Company K came plodding past. Roland should have been with them. He wasn't. Ehlers pulled the first sergeant aside and asked where Roland was. The sergeant said he didn't know; he'd been reported missing. Ehlers wasn't sure what to do.

I figured he wasn't missing, I figured he was either wounded or in a hospital and they just didn't have a record of it, because that happens a lot in combat. I thought about looking for my brother, but then when we looked down there were so

By the end of D-day, men and vehicles and supplies were already streaming inland from Omaha; within ten days, 278,000 troops and 15,000 vehicles would be put ashore on this beach alone. "Looking from the bluff," Ernie Pyle would write, the Allied armada "lay thick and clear to the far horizon of the sea and on beyond. Its utter enormity would move the hardest man." Two German prisoners stood on the bluff, too, under guard, and gazing out across the water. "They didn't say a word to each other. They didn't need to. The expression on their faces was something forever unforgettable. In it was the horrified acceptance of their doom. If only all Germany could have the rich experience of standing on the bluff and looking out across the water and seeing what their compatriots saw."

many things down on the beach, it would be like trying to find a needle in a haystack. Besides, Roland and I had a pact that if one of us fell in combat, we would not stop to take care of each other. We said we'd leave it up to the medics, and that's what we did.

It would be weeks before official word reached him of what had happened to his brother.

He got killed as he was coming down the ramp on his LCI. His whole squad got wounded or killed. I cried like a baby when I heard. I would have rather come back without my arms and legs than to come back without my brother. That's what it meant to me. I never saw him die. That stayed with me for over fifty years. I had nightmares about that. He'd come back every night. And he'd be all neatly dressed, and smiling like he usually does, and we'd have a conversation. First thing, he'd disappear. Or I'd go to do something and he's gone.

IN LUVERNE, AL McINTOSH WAS SOUND ASLEEP in the early morning hours of June 6 when the telephone rang.

When we stumbled . . . down the hall to answer . . . we made a mental note that it was shortly before 3 a.m. We picked up

the receiver, thinking it was Sheriff Roberts calling to say that there had been an accident. Instead, it was Mrs. Lloyd Long, playing the feminine counterpart of Paul Revere, saying, "Get up, Al, and listen to the radio, the invasion has started. . . ."

We sat by the radio for over an hour listening to the breathtaking announcements. . . . And then we went to bed—to lie there for a long time, wide-eyed in the darkness— thinking, "What Rock County boys are landing on French soil tonight?"

Americans woke up on June 6, 1944, to newspaper headlines and the briefest of radio bulletins: "Under the command of General Eisenhower, Allied naval forces, supported by strong air forces, began landing Allied armies this morning on the northern coast of France." It was the news they'd hoped to hear. But there were few further details, no live radio reports from the beaches. No one knew precisely where their sons and brothers and fathers had landed or how those landings were going.

In Philadelphia, the mayor gently tapped the Liberty Bell for the first time in more than a century. In New York, traders on the Stock Exchange observed two minutes of silence and then went back to work, sending the Dow Jones average soaring 142 points to a new high for the year. Major League Baseball canceled all its games. Everywhere, church bells rang, calling people to prayer. They knelt or bowed their heads in factories and schoolrooms and public parks.

In Waterbury, special masses were said at the Church of the Immaculate Conception. There were prayer services at Temple

D-day dead from both sides, prepared for temporary burial in a field just behind Omaha Beach

LITTER

On the morning after D-day, Ernie Pyle, the Indiana-born war correspondent whose devotion to ordinary GIs in North Africa and Italy had made him their favorite reporter, waded ashore on Omaha Beach. American infantrymen, tanks, and other vehicles streamed past him, moving toward the front, already several miles inland.

Pyle went for a long walk along the beach. He saw wreckage everywhere—smashed trucks, burned-out jeeps, upended tanks, half-submerged landing craft. He'd expected to see all that.

But there is another and more human litter. It extends in a thin little line, just like a high-water mark, for miles along the beach. This is the strew of personal gear, gear that will never be needed again, of those who fought and died to give us our entrance into Europe.

Here in a jumbled row for mile on mile are soldiers' packs. Here are socks and shoe polish, sewing kits, diaries, Bibles and hand grenades. Here are the latest letters from home, with the address on each one neatly razored out—one of the security precautions enforced before the boys embarked.

Here are toothbrushes and razors, and snapshots of families back home staring up at you from the sand. Here are pocketbooks, metal mirrors, extra trousers, and bloody, abandoned shoes . . . torn pistol belts and canvas water buckets, first-aid kits . . . I picked up a pocket Bible with a soldier's name in it. I carried it half a mile or so and then put it back down on the beach. I don't know why I picked it up, or why I put it down. . . .

Two of the most dominant items in the beach refuse are cigarettes and
writing paper. Each soldier was issued a carton of cigarettes just before he started. Today these cartons by the thousand, water-soaked and spilled-out, mark the line of our first savage blow.*

Writing paper and air-mail envelopes come second. The boys had intended to do a lot of writing in France. Letters that would have filled those blank, abandoned pages.

Always there are dogs in every invasion. There is a dog still on the beach today, still pitifully looking for his master. He stays at the water's edge, near a boat that lies twisted and half sunk at the water line. He barks appealingly to every soldier who approaches, trots eagerly along with him for a few feet, and then, sensing himself unwanted in all this haste, runs back to wait in vain for his own people at his own empty boat. . . .

Bodies and parts of bodies still littered the beach Pyle was walking, as well, but Pyle was decorous in describing them for readers back home.

The strong, swirling tides of the Normandy coastline shift the contours of the sandy beach as they move in and out. They carry soldiers' bodies out to sea, and later they return them. They cover the corpses of heroes with sand, and then in their whims they uncover them.

As I plowed out over the wet sand . . . that first day ashore, I walked around what seemed to be a couple of pieces of driftwood sticking out of the sand. But they weren't driftwood. They were a soldier's two feet. He was completely covered by the shifting sand except for his feet. The toes of his GI shoes pointed toward the land he had come so far to see, and which he saw so briefly.

A member of a Graves Registration Company carefully letters the name of a dead GI onto the burial bag that every man who came ashore carried in his pack.

Israel and Beth El Synagogue, and on the town green as well. In Sacramento, workers at the Pacific Fruit Express Cannery prayed for the safety of one hundred former employees now in the service. In Mobile that day, no liquor was sold, and at the railroad station young women walked up and down the platforms holding up the morning newspapers so that traveling soldiers could read the headlines.

Luverne was excited that morning, too, Al McIntosh reported, but characteristically reserved.

The invasion news came to Luverne, quietly. There were no whistles, no sirens . . . no demonstrations. Not much was said. The coffee shops were filled almost to standing room as the 10 o'clock news approached. [Sioux Falls] Argus-Leader "extras" were grabbed up like hotcakes and eagerly scanned. There were sober faces on the men as they listened to the news but there was a smile of exultation when they heard that the Allied forces had penetrated ten miles inland.

One mother dropped in the coffee shop. She shook her head and pushed the cup of coffee placed in front of her aside. "I just want to listen to the radio," she said. Her boy, by all the odds, was "there." One didn't have to be psychic to know what was in her mind—or her heart. The prayer that she was uttering right then as she listened to the announcer was multiplied a thousand times and more in Rock County countless times during the day.

In Baton Rouge, Jackie Greer got off a letter to Quentin Aanenson.

June 6, 1944
Well, D-Day is here at last. I wish you could see how Baton Rouge is taking it. The first news came in the early morning, and someone took it upon himself to call every phone in the book, I think. Mrs. Garon [a neighbor] waited until close to 5:00 a.m. to wake us up, but from that minute on, sleep was almost impossible. . . .

Radios are blaring in every office [at Harding Field] that's lucky enough to have one. Both chapels are having services. . . . Quent, when they first woke me with the news, I heard the radio say, "Ladies and gentlemen, this is D-Day." So sleepy was I that my first thoughts were that the war was over and I could stay at home and celebrate. Then I remembered that D-Day was the invasion and that all America had been asked to pray, so I slipped out of bed and knelt in prayer for a few minutes. I prayed for all the boys over there, but mostly I prayed for you.

That evening, the whole country gathered around their radios to hear President Roosevelt say a prayer for all the men who'd gone ashore in France.

Almighty God: Our sons, pride of our nation, this day have set upon a mighty endeavor, a struggle to preserve our Republic, our religion, and our civilization, and to set free a suffering humanity. Lead them straight and true; give strength to their arms, stoutness to their hearts, steadfastness in their faith. They will need Thy blessings. Their road will be long and hard, for the enemy is strong. He may hurl back our forces. Success may not come with rushing speed, but we shall return again and again; and we know that by Thy grace, and by the righteousness of our cause, our sons will triumph.

FAR OUT IN THE PHILIPPINE SEA that same evening, aboard the light cruiser USS *Montpelier*, Seaman First Class James A. Fahey was busily writing down the day's happenings on one of the loose sheets of paper that made up the journal he kept in his duffel bag against naval regulations. "At 6:30 P.M. this evening," he noted, "the announcement came over the loudspeaker that the Allies landed in France. Everyone gave a big cheer when they heard this. I won $40 from the boys because some time ago, I bet the invasion would come off about the middle of June."

Fahey was from Waltham, Massachusetts, the youngest of four orphaned children. His brothers, John and Joe, had been in the navy at Pearl Harbor when the Japanese attacked—and had been spared. James had signed on the following year and was assigned to the *Montpelier*. "It was a great feeling as I staggered up the gangway to the ship with my sea bag in one hand and the mattress cover loaded with blankets, mattresses, etc., over my shoulder," he'd written then. "At last I have a home—and a warship at that." He had hoped to see action at sea, and as a member of a gun crew he had not been disappointed. The *Montpelier* shot down Japanese planes and sank Japanese ships off Guadalcanal, bombarded Japanese defenses at Munda, and survived an enemy bomb and two torpedo hits off Bougainville.

James Fahey

A week or so after hearing the news of D-day, Fahey and the men of the *Montpelier* were preparing again for battle. She was a part of Task Force 58, the strike arm of the vast U.S. Fifth Fleet, moving toward the next American objective in the Pacific: the Marianas, a chain of volcanic islands the Americans wanted to transform into advance naval bases and from which U.S. long-range B-29 bombers could begin to attack the Japanese home-land, just 1,200 miles away. The fleet's three most important targets in the Marianas were Guam, Tinian, and Saipan, where a combined force of marine and army troops would land after four days and nights of shelling by the *Montpelier* and her sister ships.

Fahey noted in his journal:

We fired the 5 & 6 inch guns [at Saipan] from Wed. morning at 3 A.M. until Saturday morning at 7 A.M. We did enough bombarding to last us a lifetime. . . . There are an awful lot of sore ears, the cotton and ear plugs are no good. In the daytime we fired low and point-blank, but at night we fired higher and further into the shore. Hollywood could get some great pictures. It was just like a movie. Big alcohol plants were blown sky-high, assembly plants, oil storage plants, ammuni-tion dumps. . . . Thick smoke miles high was all over the island. I never saw anything like it before, it was like the great Chicago fire. . . .

The men on the 5 and 6 inch guns had a rugged time. . . . The deck of the mounts and turrets was covered with their perspiration, they looked like ghosts when it was over. If they did lay down to get some rest the concussion and noise from the guns shook them up and made sleep impossible. . . . We had a candy bar for breakfast, two cookies and an apple for dinner and at night we did not have very much either.

Among the marines of the 4th Division waiting to go ashore once the guns fell silent was Corporal Alvy Ray Pittmann, a Mis-sissippian who'd been working as a carpenter alongside his father at Mobile's Brookley Field when he decided to join the marines. By now he had already had more than his share of com-bat. During the battle for Namur in early February—part of the Kwajalein campaign, which ensured Allied control of the Mar-shall Islands—enemy bullets had rattled off the sides of his land-ing craft, he'd seen his own battalion commander fall with a bullet through his brain, and he'd nearly been killed himself when a blockhouse he helped blow up turned out to be filled with Japanese bombs that killed twenty of his fellow marines. But Namur had been like most of the Central Pacific islands the marines had encountered: occupied almost entirely by Japanese soldiers and small (its total area was less than a square mile).

Alvy Ray Pittmann

Saipan was different. It was five miles wide and fourteen miles long and encompassed several kinds of terrain: a 1,600-foot peak, sheer cliffs, swamps, jungle-covered hills filled with caves and cut by deep ravines, and a flat plain covered with sugarcane. It was defended by more than thirty thousand Japanese troops, but it was also home to some-where between sixteen thou-sand and twenty thousand civilians, including Japanese citizens and conscripted Korean laborers, as well as descendants of the Chamorro and Carolinian people who were the island's original inhabitants.

Pittmann was to land in the first wave, part of a sixteen-man demolition team assigned to destroy enemy strongpoints wher-ever they were found, using explosives, grenades, flamethrowers.

You never think about getting hurt yourself. You think about maybe some of your buddies are going to get hurt. And you wonder who it's going to be. I mean, I really didn't ever think about getting hurt myself. Of course, when slugs start bounc-ing off your amtrac [amphibious tractor] going in, you know it could happen.

Once again, the naval bombardment had looked spectacular from out at sea but had failed to eliminate the island's defenses. Concentrated Japanese mortar and artillery fire from positions

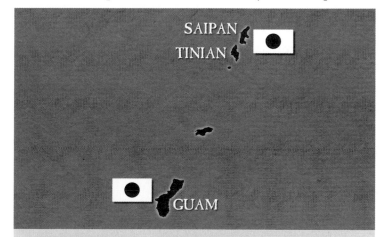

As Allied forces fought their way inland in Normandy in mid-June of 1944, U.S. Marines in the Pacific assaulted Guam, Tinian, and Saipan in the Mari-anas chain.

hidden in the shoreline cliffs rained down among the men fighting to get onto the beach. Casualties were heavy—more than 1,500 men—and, as Pittmann remembered, the fighting was sometimes close-in.

A Jap jumped up and grabbed one of our men. What the enemy would do is grab someone and hit his grenade on his own helmet [to trigger it] and then hold the grenade between them so they would both be killed. The marine grabbed the Jap, pinning both his arms so he could not start the fuse of the grenade. And they were dancing around, and somebody else went up and shot the Jap in the head with a forty-five. We called that boy "Dancer" from then on, because it had looked like they were dancing. He later got killed on Tinian.

By evening, twenty thousand marines were ashore, enough to break up three counterattacks that night, one of them led by massed enemy tanks. The next morning, they began pushing farther inland as waves of landing craft filled with army and marine reinforcements streamed in behind them toward the beaches.

The Japanese considered the Marianas vital to the survival of their empire. If the islands fell, no Japanese city would be safe,

D-day on Saipan, June 15, 1944: The soaked uniform worn by the marine scrambling across the sand suggests he may have been aboard one of some twenty amtracs destroyed by Japanese shelling before they reached the shore. The newly developed armored amtrac beached at the shoreline behind him seems to have been stopped by enemy fire as well. The marine wounded in the neck at the right made it a few yards inland before he was hit.

and supply lines to their remaining outposts in the South Pacific would be severed. But the commander in chief of the Japanese fleet, Admiral Toyoda Soemu, thought he saw opportunity as well as danger in the U.S. assault on the islands, a chance to destroy both the American land forces—still struggling their way inland on Saipan—and the American fleet offshore. He directed Vice Admiral Jizaburo Ozawa, commander of Japan's First Mobile Fleet, to steam northward from his base off Borneo, send waves of carrier- and land-based warplanes against the American ships, then reinforce the Japanese garrison on Saipan. "The fate of our empire rests on this one battle," said Admiral Soemu. "Everyone must give all he has."

But the Americans—who had intercepted Japanese coded messages and knew they were coming—bombed the nearest enemy airfields to minimize danger from land-based warplanes

Advancing marines take cover amid enemy dead on Saipan. The Japanese defended the island with particular ferocity because it was the first outpost of the prewar Japanese empire to come under attack. "Because the fate of the Japanese empire depends on the result of your operation, inspire the spirit of the officers and men," the chief of the Imperial Army General Staff radioed the island's commander in the name of the emperor, "and to the very end continue to destroy the enemy gallantly and persistently, thus assuaging the anxiety of our Emperor." The commander radioed Tokyo his thanks for the emperor's well wishes. "By becoming the bulwark of the Pacific with ten thousand deaths," he said, "we hope to requite the imperial favor."

and sank seventeen of twenty-five enemy submarines that tried to slip in among their warships. Then hundreds of carrier-based planes took off to engage the Japanese. The two-day Battle of the Philippine Sea would be the greatest carrier contest of the Pacific war, nearly four times as big as Midway. From the beginning it was clear the Americans now had the edge. Their pilots were better trained than the enemy's. Their planes—mostly Hellcat fighters—were better now, too, and they had twice as many of them. The Americans lost 29 planes the first day, but they shot down at least 273 enemy aircraft while U.S. submarines sank two Japanese carriers, one of them Vice Admiral Ozawa's flagship. Those who took part in the one-sided contest on June 19 remembered it as the Great Marianas Turkey Shoot.

Late the following day, American spotter planes located the rest of the crippled enemy fleet some 275 miles away. Within twenty minutes, 216 U.S. warplanes swarmed off the carrier decks to attack it, even though darkness was falling and fuel was likely to run out before they could return. The Americans destroyed sixty-five more Japanese planes, sank another carrier, and badly damaged three others, then started for home.

Meanwhile, James Fahey noted in his journal, the sun went down.

The time dragged as we waited to hear from our pilots, everyone kept his fingers crossed hoping for the best. It was like waiting in the death house for a pardon. . . . Then something never before done in wartime happened, all the ships in this huge fleet put their lights on, and flares were dropped into the water. . . . This would make it easier for our pilots to land, and if they did hit the water they could be saved.

Eventually, the men on deck heard the drone of approaching planes. In the end, only twenty failed to return. Eighty more were lost within sight of the fleet, sputtering into the sea or crashing on the carrier decks. All but forty-nine of the pilots and crewmen were recovered. The American forces on Saipan could continue their struggle to take the island without fear of enemy reinforcement from the sea.

Meanwhile, what remained of Vice Admiral Ozawa's fleet limped toward the horizon. Only 37 of the 340 carrier planes he'd begun the battle with could still fly, and three of his five carriers were at the bottom of the Philippine Sea.

The naval disaster was only one in a series of setbacks that struck the Japanese in the summer of 1944. The American invasion of the Marianas, a U.S. raid on the steel center of Yawata by U.S. B-29s based in China (the first strike on the Japanese home islands since the Doolittle raid in 1942), and the Japanese failure to take the Burmese outpost of Imphal from the British would combine to force Prime Minister Hideki Tojo to submit his resignation to the emperor. His replacement as prime minister, General Kuniaki Koiso, vowed to fight on, even though the War Journal of Imperial Headquarters had privately concluded that "we can no longer direct the war with any hope of success. The only course left is for Japan's 100 million people to sacrifice their lives by charging the enemy to make them lose the will to fight." From then on, Japan would be fighting for what it considered its honor, rather than for victory.

IN EARLY JUNE, the Japanese-controlled Manila *Tribune* had carried a series of stories that kindled fresh hope of liberation among the internees at Santo Tomas. First came word of the fall of Rome, then the news of D-day—FOE INVASION BEING WIPED OUT BY GERMANS, read the headline—finally an account of fierce fighting for a Japanese airfield at Biak, an island off the northern coast of Dutch New Guinea, the closest battlefield yet to the Philippines. At reveille on June 8, the camp's disk jockey played the World War I anthem, "Over There," with its promise that "The Yanks are coming."

A few days later, the Japanese refused to allow internees to read the *Tribune* anymore. "It would appear there is difficulty in handling the news," one internee noted in her diary. Regardless, word of what was happening elsewhere in the world continued to swirl through camp from other sources. When it was falsely reported in July that a plot by some of Hitler's generals to kill him had succeeded, the wake-up song played over the loudspeakers was "Ding-Dong, The Witch Is Dead."

As Axis prospects worsened, so did the lives of the Japanese captives at Santo Tomas. Lieutenant Abiko, the commandant's officious and often brutal right-hand man, ordered internees to construct barbed-wire barriers in and around their compound and to put up a wall made of dense mats of woven bamboo to keep friends and family outside from so much as waving at them. When the Internee Committee protested, arguing that the Geneva Convention forbade forcing prisoners to undertake such labor unless the result would benefit them, the commandant responded once again that the Geneva Convention did not apply to Santo Tomas; the Japanese military made the rules, and internees must abide by them or face the consequences.

All U.S. and Philippine currency was confiscated, replaced by nearly worthless Japanese-printed bills the internees called Mickey Mouse money. Captives could no longer supplement their diets or replenish their supplies. "Daddy is now out of tobacco," Sascha Weinzheimer noted in her journal. "He dries papaya leaves on the roof and smokes that. People use anything to roll their cigarettes. Some even use pages from the Bible because the paper is [so] fine."

The Japanese cut the food ration again, too. By July, the average male captive at Santo Tomas had lost thirty-one pounds, the average woman almost eighteen. Half the children were severely underweight. Nearly everyone had some telltale sign of malnutrition: emaciation, failing vision, edema, beriberi. Filipino doctors and nurses were no longer permitted inside to help with the sick.

An overworked nurse remembered her ongoing frustration:

One of the cruelest things the Japanese did to a group of desperately hungry people was to refuse to accept the carts of food that were sent to our camp by Manila organizations. Day after day, fruit, vegetables, and eggs were sent in pushcarts, which were left standing outside the gates while representatives of charitable organizations pleaded with the Japs to permit them to give us the food. But our benevolent jailers told them that we had sufficient food, and we sadly watched them wheeling away the carts. For this cruelty and falsehood, we hated them.

The strain of it all was beginning to tell. There was more thievery in camp now, more squabbling. "There are spies in here who run and tell the Japs things against internees," Sascha wrote.

The most awful one is a woman who looks like a mummy. We all know she has gotten many into trouble. One of Dad's best friends, Stu Barnett, was taken to [the prison at Fort] Santiago. We all blamed this woman.

There are many others, especially ones who work for the Japanese, like Mr. M. when he tried to get extra chow from the line and Dad wouldn't give it to him. Then he said, "We have a way of fixing you guys." "We" meant the Nips, of course. Then Dad said, "Oh, yeah! Well, we have a way of fixing guys like you, too."

Every day I hear of some person doing strange things. A Catholic priest did a mortal sin by going around with a lady, then falling in love with her, acting so mushy in front of everybody that he was kicked out of the church.

Mother was sitting in the clinic yesterday morning waiting for the doctor. She admired a lady's bracelet and touched it. The lady pulled her hand away, then took it off and put it in her pocket. She thought Mother was trying to steal it.

I heard a husband and wife fighting loudly. She yelled at him, "If I hadn't married you, I wouldn't be in this camp now!"

Later that summer, fearful that the weakest prisoners would begin to starve to death, the Internee Committee would agree to distribute the last of the small reserve of tinned meat they'd obtained from the Red Cross and managed to keep aside for emergency use. They did so reluctantly, knowing that if they weren't freed by October, there would be no more protein to fall back on.

In fact, there was then still not even a timetable for freeing the Philippines. Some in the navy argued that the war in the Pacific would end faster if they bypassed the islands altogether in favor of driving the enemy from Formosa and then attacking the Japanese home islands from there. MacArthur threatened to resign. To adopt any such plan, he declared, would be to "admit the truth that we had abandoned the Filipinos and would not shed American blood to redeem them; we would undoubtedly incur the open hostility of that people; we would probably suffer such a loss of prestige among all the peoples of the Far East that it would adversely affect the United States for many years." At a hastily called conference at Pearl Harbor in July, Roosevelt seemed to side with the general, in part because he feared that in the upcoming election voters might hold him responsible for forsaking the Filipinos. But it would take another month for the Chiefs of Staff to set the date for an American landing on Leyte: December 20, more than eight weeks after the last of the camp's reserve protein supply was sure to run out.

"I've seen a lot of hard times," Mrs. Sanders, the formidable woman who had defied the commandant of Santo Tomas during his inspection tour a few months earlier, told a friend that August, "and I tell you that I can see we're moving into the hard, hard times."

NOT LONG BEFORE D-DAY, John and Glennie Frazier of Fort Deposit, Alabama, had received a telegram from the War Department. Their son, Glenn, had been missing in action for two years—ever since the fall of Bataan in May of 1942—and since nothing had been heard from him in all that time, he was now officially presumed dead.

Frazier's parents refused to believe it. "I'm sure if anybody can make it," his father said, "my son can." He was right. His son was still alive, still a Japanese prisoner, though he had now been moved to Tanawaga, a new camp just south of Osaka.

There, Frazier and his fellow captives toiled as slave laborers alongside hundreds of Japanese criminals and kidnapped Koreans at a gigantic bay-front construction site, carving three massive dry docks for submarines out of a hillside and then lining them with stone. They worked at it from dawn until after dark six days a week, digging and rolling carts filled with rocks and dirt down narrow-gauge tracks to barges that dumped the refuse

A VERY DIFFERENT COUNTRY

Before Pearl Harbor, most Americans had believed their country self-sufficient. The war quickly taught them different. Japanese conquests in the Far East cut off the sources of 97 percent of America's supply of crude rubber. German U-boats preyed on the tankers that carried 95 percent of the oil used on the East Coast. Washington imposed strict rationing on both commodities: pleasure driving was banned; automobile tourism died; homeowners shivered as fuel oil was cut back.

Food was in short supply, as well: sugar, coffee, meat, and more. "There were shortages of everything," Paul Fussell remembered.

This week it might be rubber bands. Next week it might be condoms or cigarettes or toothbrushes. It's really not hard to imagine if you think of contemporary America with everything enjoyable missing. That includes automobiles, washing machines, full-strength beer, hamburgers, hot dogs. And everybody ostentatiously cheerful all the time because they'd been told that their morale was important. That's what it was like. It would melodramatize things to say that life was a struggle even on the home front. But it was to a degree, in minor matters, at least.

For adults like the man below using his ration card to buy a few gallons of gas, rationing could be an irritant. But for younger people, like Jim Sherman of Luverne, whose ration book appears at the right and who had never known life without it, even the most harrowing recipes housewives were forced to come up with to feed their families could still spark fond memories. "My mother used to deep-fry Spam," he remembered. "I'm sure some people could not look at a piece of Spam now at all. But that was our major source of meat. And I still like it."

4 939|692 BB
UNITED STATES OF AMERICA
OFFICE OF PRICE ADMINISTRATION

WAR RATION BOOK FOUR

Issued to _James R. Sherman_
(Print first, middle and last names)

Complete address _503 N. City_

LUVERNE   _MINN._

READ BEFORE SIGNING

In accepting this book, I recognize that it remains the property of the United States Government. I will use it only in the manner and for the purposes authorized by the Office of Price Administration.

Void if Altered _Jimmy Sherman_
(Signature)

It is a criminal offense to violate rationing regulations.

OPA Form R-145

STAMP NO. 1 · STAMP NO. 2 · STAMP NO. 3 · STAMP NO. 4
RATION STAMP NO. 5 · 6 · 7 · 8
RATION STAMP NO. 9 · 10 · 11 · 12
RATION STAMP NO. 13 · 14 · 15 · 16
RATION STAMP NO. 17 · 18 · 19 · 20
RATION STAMP NO. 21 · 22 · 23 · 24
RATION · RATION · RATION · RATION

How to make your points go farther...

SPAM BIRDS

SPAM BIRDS
Wrap thin slices of Spam around your favorite stuffing, fasten with toothpicks, brown in a hot oven. Serve with garden peas, fried candied sweets. Lunchbox hit: let your defense worker take to the plant a couple of big hearty Spamwiches spread with mustard or relish.

NO BONE, NO WASTE, NO SURPLUS FAT to take precious points when you buy Spam. Serve it cold, serve it hot—get full point value either way, because Spam cooks quickly with scarcely any shrinkage and there's a use for every bit of left-over. Scarcities compel careful choosing—get something good, something the family likes—Spam!

DON'T BLAME YOUR GROCER WHEN HE'S OUT OF SPAM—a large share of the available supply is going to the armed forces, according to a letter from Cpl. Harley McGuiness, Hormel man now somewhere in Africa: "No matter what part of the world you go to, Hormel products are in all out use to fill the boys up and they really are treats to eat."

COLD OR HOT... SPAM HITS THE SPOT!

HORMEL GOOD FOODS SPAM

Every American was issued a book of ration stamps. "On the back of each one was written, 'Do not buy unless absolutely necessary,'" Katharine Phillips of Mobile remembered.

We did without during the Depression, so doing without these commodities really was not hard. We didn't mind rationing. It meant we were helping the boys. Recipes were adjusted according to what you could get. You could get very little white flour so you had to switch to rye flour or barley flour or oat flour. The recipes for cakes were all adjusted to no sugar, and very little fat or shortening of any sort. So to have a birthday cake was a real treat, because it meant they had to save everything to make one cake. Meat rationing became almost funny. The recipes that came out in the newspaper to help you stretch your meat were truly terrible. Things like liver loaf. In one you made a white sauce, and you cut up Vienna sausage and put in a can of green peas, and you served that over a waffle.

The unifying spirit of sacrifice was not universally shared. An illicit market in commodities and counterfeit ration stamps soon flourished all across the country. According to one estimate, one-quarter of all wartime retail business transactions involved "Mr. Black." "If somebody had been eating a lot of steaks," Jim Sherman of Luverne recalled, "you kind of wondered where did they get their meat? Then you remembered they had a brother who farmed out south of town and they were butchering out there. But I don't know that we necessarily called that black market."

"FDR had to clamp on industry an excessive profits tax," Paul Fussell remembered. "That would be unthinkable now. Making too great a profit was thought to be rather wicked while your boys were being machine-gunned in New Guinea. So, people who made a lot of money had to apologize for it or else give a lot of it away. And that made it a very different country."

out at sea and then returned for more. The private contractor in charge of the project was paid by the amount of earth moved and the number of stones cemented into place, so his foreman— whom the Americans called Hitler—constantly urged the starving men to move faster.

The treatment Frazier and his fellow prisoners received was similar to what they'd encountered before: frequent and often inexplicable beatings, inadequate clothing, filthy conditions, and meager rations (which were halved for anyone too weak or ill to work). Frazier and another prisoner once came to blows when a sympathetic old Japanese woman slipped a bag of parched beans through the fence and the man to whom she gave it refused to share it. In the scuffle, Frazier fell and reopened the bayonet wound in his knee.

It started getting infected and it finally got gangrene, and Dr. [George] Campbell, who was our American doctor in there, had nothing to treat me with except iodine. So I would hold a cup to catch all the blood and the stuff that came out of my knee, and he'd cut it open with a pocketknife and poured pure iodine in there to kill the gangrene. They were thinking about taking my leg off. I told Dr. Campbell I'd just rather die than to have my leg taken off. So he fought it and we won. But at one point, there was only a space in the back of my leg about an inch and a half across where the flesh was just like normal flesh. The rest of it was decayed. I could open that wound up and see my bone.

Frazier's knee eventually healed, and he went back to work at the project site, where he and his friends continued to do all they could to sabotage the Japanese war effort. They loosened blocks, so that a submarine under repairs slid into the bay upside down. They let carts filled with earth slip downhill, smashing the carts ahead of them, twisting the tracks, forcing delays. And once they managed to jam so many heavily laden carts onto a dock that it collapsed under the combined weight. "That's when we found out what real beatings were all about," Frazier remembered. "Every man got it."

MORE THAN TWO WEEKS AFTER D-DAY, below the hundred-foot cliff called Pointe du Hoe at the western edge of Omaha Beach, bodies were still washing up onto the sand, and because the Graves Registration crews had moved inland with the advancing troops, no one was gathering them for burial. Finally, men from Quentin Aanenson's fighter squadron decided to do the job themselves. They retrieved the corpses with long poles, heaped them with gasoline-soaked driftwood, and set them ablaze. A few days later, Aanenson looked down from the bluff and saw that the problem still had not been solved. "More bodies were rolling in the surf," he remembered, "as the English Channel continued to give up its dead."

Aanenson now belonged to the 391st Fighter Squadron of the Ninth Army Air Force and had just moved across the Channel to new quarters: Advanced Landing Strip A-1, between Pointe du Hoc and Omaha. The hastily constructed five-thousand-foot airstrip was made of steel mesh that loosened with time; the fliers who had to contend with its unreliable surface called it chicken wire. They lived in five-man tents and ate their K rations and reconstituted stew and watery powdered eggs in an apple orchard swarming with bees. A battery of 90-millimeter antiaircraft guns stood in the woods nearby to deal with night attacks by enemy planes. There weren't many. The worst hazard was falling shrapnel from the American guns. The Allies had already made themselves masters of the skies over Normandy. The Luftwaffe had been able to muster fewer than one hundred planes to fend off the D-day invasion; Allied fighters now outnumbered theirs eight to one.

But the work that Aanenson and his fellow pilots in the U.S. Ninth and First Tactical Air Forces and the British Second Tactical Air Force were called upon to do nearly every day in support of the men engaged on the ground was both exacting and terribly dangerous. It was traditionally performed in three phases. First, fighter-bombers ranged ahead of the men on the ground, taking out surrounding airbases from which enemy fighters might otherwise rise to interfere with an Allied advance.

Then, to isolate the enemy positions about to be attacked still further, they were sent in to destroy bridges, railroads, and highways and to bomb and strafe any enemy forces that tried to use them to reach the battlefield. That was what Aanenson was doing the first time he knew he had actually killed anyone.

We caught a group of Germans that were on a road in an area where there were no trees, and so there was no place for them to hide. And we caught them before they could really get off the roads and run toward the ditches. And I remember the impact it had on me when I could see my bullets just tearing into them. We had so much firepower that the bodies would fly some yards. And as I was doing this I was doing it knowing I had to do it. That it was my job. This is what I'd been trained to do, and I dealt with it fine. But when I got back home to the base in Normandy and landed, I got sick. I had to think about what I had done. Now, that didn't change my resolve for the next day. I went out and did it again. And again and again and again.

Premission briefing for Quentin Aanenson's 391st Fighter Squadron in Normandy; Aanenson is the fourth man from the left in the second row.

Squadrons like Aanenson's constituted aerial artillery batteries. The pilots saw themselves as hunters. The radio call sign for Aanenson's outfit was "Foxhunt." When the lead pilot was ready to roll over and start the dive toward his target, he radioed, "Foxhunt, Red Leader, Tallyho!" Each of the four planes in his flight would follow suit: "Foxhunt, Red, Two (or Three or Four)—Tallyho!" The Germans on the ground saw the Thunderbolts as hunters, too, and came to call their incessant attacks "steel weather."

Finally, fighter groups were called in to hit enemy troops and destroy enemy strongpoints that stood in the way of the Allied advance.

German antiaircraft fire was a constant menace, directed at the attacking planes from tanks and truck convoys, even railroad cars, as well as from the conventional batteries that lined airstrips and protected positions in the field. Tactical air strikes had to be swift, accurate, and often perilously close to the ground. Planes stalled, slammed into one another, disintegrated

in explosions their own bombs had set off. One pilot never forgot swooping down to hit a railyard, flying through a dense cloud of smoke and flame, and seeing the steel wheel of a boxcar spinning high above his wing. Eighty-five men from Aanenson's 366th Fighter Group would be killed in action before the war in Europe was over.

"We would be sitting around our tent area in the apple orchard in Normandy," Aanenson remembered.

And we would discuss just how much they would have to pay us to get us willing to do what we had just done that day. Now, you have to remember, this was way back there when this figure I'm about to mention meant something, which it doesn't anymore—but we agreed first that we might do it for $1,000 a mission. Less than ten days later—our losses had gone up heavily—we decided that we wouldn't consider

doing it for less than $10,000 a mission. And I think that it went off the radar screen in value before the end of July, because there's no way that you can be mercenary enough, that they could pay you enough, to do what we were doing on a volunteer basis.

Under fire, American infantrymen struggle to solve the riddle of how to fight among the Norman hedgerows: "We were rehearsed endlessly for attacking beach defenses," wrote Charles R. Cawthon, a captain in the 29th Division, "but not one day was given to the terrain behind the beaches, which was no less difficult and deadly. This is hard to understand, for the planners had current aerial photographs showing the maze and its problems, and the written record of fighting there goes back at least as far as Julius Caesar."

The ground combat Aanenson and his fellow pilots were there to support was proving more challenging than planners had expected. There had been some progress since D-day, but it had come painfully slowly and at great cost. Nearly a million men were now ashore. The five Allied beachheads were linked together along a sixty-mile front that was twenty miles deep in some places. The U.S. First Army had seized Carentan, cut off and cleared the Cotentin peninsula, and captured Cherbourg, but it had taken three weeks and more than twenty-two thousand casualties to do it, and when the GIs marched into the port city on June 30, they found its facilities so badly damaged by the enemy that Allied supplies could not be landed there for nearly three months. Meanwhile, the Germans had unleashed their "Retaliation" weapon, lobbing the first of more than nine thousand two-ton V-1 rockets across the Channel. Hitler hoped they would force the evacuation of London and weaken the British will to win. More than 2,500 of them would hit the British capital, killing 5,775 Londoners that summer, destroying some twenty thousand homes and damaging eighty thousand more. At the eastern end of the beachhead, two British attacks on Caen

had yielded British casualties high enough to alarm the high command (after five years of war, Britain was running out of men) but had done nothing to open the most direct route to Paris—and seven panzer divisions would eventually be stationed in the area to keep it blocked.

If further advances were to be made in Normandy, they would have to come in the American sector, through the farm country the French call the *bocage*. At first, it reminded Ernie Pyle of "the rich gentle land of eastern Pennsylvania," but it was as unforgiving as it was lovely, quilted with small, irregularly shaped fields walled off from one another by hedgerows—waist-high earthen ramparts, out of which grew tall, centuries-old hedges that turned them into natural fortifications and made it all but impossible to see from one field into the next. Drainage ditches flanked each hedge, and here and there the tops of the hedgerows arched all the way across the sunken wagon tracks that ran between them, turning shady paths into dark tunnels inside which men and vehicles could face ambush at any time from almost anywhere.

One answer to the hedgerow challenge: Late in the battle for the *bocage*, Sherman tanks newly fitted out with steel prongs chew their way into an enclosed field.

The Germans took advantage of all of it. In one area that measured just two miles by four, there were four thousand such fields; each became what Pyle called "a separate little war," fought mostly by companies of riflemen. Sherman tanks could not break through the hedgerows, and when they tried to roll over them, they exposed their unprotected underbellies to deadly fire. Major General Lawton Collins, commander of VII Corps, said Normandy was the worst place to fight he'd seen since Guadalcanal.

The battle in the *bocage* was "a slugging match," Bradley complained, with no knockout in sight. Progress was measured in yards—and casualties. Unarmed C-47s—cargo planes stripped down so that as many litters as possible could be lifted aboard—carried the worst hit to hospitals in England, less than an hour away, then turned around and came back for more. Emily Lewis, who had been tending to wounded bomber crews in Britain, now found herself caring for her charges from just behind the battlefield. "All those wounded soldiers," she remembered.

They were scared to death. Really frightened half out of their minds. I hugged them. I was teary-eyed. It makes me cry to think of it. Got them on my plane. Talked to them. Some of them were so unnerved that I just had to put my arms around them and hold them. I was twenty-three, and they were twenty-two, twenty-one, twenty-four, eighteen. It was just terrible, but it had to be done.

One day, Quentin Aanenson thought he'd leave his airstrip for a look at what life was like for the men inching their way among the hedgerows just a few miles away. Armed with an M-1, he managed to make it up to the front, where he struck up a conversation with some infantrymen as they strolled along what he thought was a safe road. Suddenly, German 88 shells began falling around them. Aanenson dove into what he thought was an empty foxhole and landed on top of a rotting German corpse. "My right hand and right arm went right through him," he remembered. "The shelling continued for about ten minutes. I stayed right there. I didn't move. Maggots were crawling all over me. The stench was terrible. Only when I was trying to crawl out did I realize I had been holding the dead German by his spinal column."

On the Fourth of July, Al McIntosh addressed one of his newspaper columns to local boys who found themselves overseas.

We've had a couple of letters from boys out in the South Pacific asking for more of those columns describing how life

"goes on" back in Rock County. . . . Well, this is being written the evening of the Fourth of July . . . the . . . quietest Fourth that Rock County has spent in many a decade.

First, people hung out their flags either at their home or their place of business. You never saw so many flags being displayed in Luverne. Then about noon they headed for [the] park down by the river under the big trees.

Some, with their elders, were busy in a softball game. The old timers drifted over to the horseshoe pitching headquarters and as far away as the highway you could hear the familiar "clink" of the shoes hitting the steel peg.

We said the Fourth was a . . . quiet day. There wasn't excitement—no speeches, no parades, no band music. Everybody spent the day quietly—but they were all thinking of you [boys]—and hoping and praying that this would be the last Fourth of July you'd spend away from home.

"The enemy is burning and bleeding on every front at once," Winston Churchill wrote that week to Joseph Stalin, whose country had suffered the most at the hands of the Germans, "and I agree with you that this must go on to the end." In the East, the Red Army encircled twenty-eight German divisions in Belorussia, killed 40,000 men when they tried to fight their way out and took Minsk, and with it more than two thousand tanks and 150,000 prisoners; 57,000 captives would be marched through the streets of Moscow as its citizens jeered and cursed.

In Normandy, British planes dropped twenty-five hundred tons of bombs on Caen, beginning a third attempt to take the city from the Germans. When it was over, two thousand French civilians had been crushed or blown apart and the Germans had withdrawn to new defensive positions just south of what was left of the city. Meanwhile, Bradley ordered the U.S. VII, VIII, and XIX Corps to begin to battle their way south side by side, seeking a way out of the hedgerows. Their path was eased at least a little by Sergeant Curtis Culin, Jr., an inventive New Jersey National Guardsman, who showed that when Sherman tanks were fitted out with sharp prongs fashioned from Rommel's beach obstacles they could slice right through the matted roots of the hedgerows. Rifle squads were no longer on their own. The Germans would lose some forty thousand men in the next two weeks. Bradley would lose just as many. "The whole battle is one tremendous bloodbath," said a veteran German corps commander, "such as I have never seen in eleven years of war."

British troops survey what little is left of Caen after weeks of Allied bombing and shelling.

"IT RAINED FOR A WHILE THIS MORNING," James Fahey noted in his shipboard journal on Independence Day.

The Press News said that in the first couple of weeks [of fighting on Saipan] over 6500 Japs were killed. There is a very strong odor from the beach. It smells like burnt flesh. Yesterday and today our artillery on the beach gave the Japs an awful pounding. Today is the fourth of July and a good way to celebrate it is by killing Japs.

With the Japanese fleet wrecked and no hope of rescue or reinforcement, Saipan's defenders burrowed into caves and pillboxes, prepared to keep fighting until they were destroyed. "Your Japanese soldier is probably the toughest soldier that fought in World War II—other than the marines," Ray Pittmann said.

You surround one, he's going to keep fighting. In Germany, you surround fifty thousand Germans and they'd surrender. Or Italians, they'd surrender. But you surround one Japanese and he's going to keep fighting right on. He's going to keep firing until you kill him. And they're just good soldiers, they're tough soldiers, and they had one thing in mind—it's killing you. With the Japanese fighting like they did, it'd make Americans kill everything that moves. If it moves in front of the lines, you shoot it first and then ask questions later.

The airfield and the southern half of the island had been cleared by now, and both marine divisions plus the 25th Infantry Regiment had begun a slow, agonizing march toward the north, trying to keep from killing Japanese civilians while flushing Japanese troops from caves and gun emplacements, and bracing for dangerous but seemingly suicidal banzai attacks. "When we'd hear the Japanese talking and drinking and clanking bottles and everything, we knew there was one coming," Pittmann recalled.

They'd get drunk first. They'd come at us and we had machine guns set up in crossfires every which way. They'd have to get through the crossfire before we started shooting, but then some of them would get through. I had one that came at me with a bayonet and I shot him in the face, and I was lying in the foxhole and he fell in the foxhole with me. And bled all over my pants. And the bayonet went down between my arm and my chest. That nearly got me and him dead.

Before dawn on July 7, the enemy launched a final charge. More than three thousand Japanese—some forced from their hospital beds and barely able to walk, many armed only with clubs and rocks and shovels—attacked the American lines and came close to breaking through before three 10th Marine

On Saipan, a marine reassures a Chamorro mother and her children that they can safely surrender.

artillery battalions firing at almost point-blank range blew them to pieces. Bulldozers buried all but a handful the next morning. It was the largest banzai charge of the Pacific War—and one of the last.

Saipan was officially declared "secured" three days later. In almost four weeks of fighting, 16,525 Americans had been killed, wounded, or reported missing, the costliest battle in the Pacific to date. Among them were several black marines who had finally been permitted to fight. "The Negro marines are no longer on trial," said the marine commandant. "They are marines, period."

Almost thirty thousand Japanese soldiers were dead as well. Most of the Koreans and the native peoples who had lived on the island before the Japanese occupied it had surrendered. So had several thousand Japanese noncombatants. But in the final days of fighting, some four thousand Japanese civilians, mostly terrified women and children, had fled to the island's northern tip, a high plateau called Marpi Point. The military had convinced them that it was their duty to kill themselves rather than fall into the hands of the cruel Americans, and the handful of Japanese solders who still survived were prepared to shoot them if they hesitated. Japanese American interpreters with bullhorns pleaded with the civilians to give up. But more than a thousand were either killed by Japanese troops or chose suicide. "When we got down to the end of the island, they were jumping off the cliff," Ray Pittmann remembered.

They thought we'd kill them and eat them. Stuff like that. It's just a Japanese mentality. They don't want to get captured. But in one area of Marpi Point, some of the Japanese troops went down to the beach area instead of going over the cliff. They were swimming out to sea. So we decided, well, they're going to die anyway, we might as well shoot them. So we set up there shooting at them, slugs hitting around them, and sometimes somebody would hit one. But it was a long shot trying to hit their head.

On Sunday morning, July 16, James Fahey wrote, church services were held on the deck of the *Montpelier*. It was a warm, sunny day, but "it was the first time I ever went to church services and saw dead bodies floating by. . . . It is nothing to see men,

women and children floating. . . . There must be thousands of Japs in the waters near Saipan. The ships just run over them."

The Americans would go on, within days, to take Tinian (where Ray Pittmann would win the Bronze Star for removing mines in the face of continual Japanese fire) and then Guam, the first U.S. possession to be recaptured from the Japanese. Each battle cost American as well as Japanese lives, and each took its toll on the men who survived. Pittmann had lost almost fifty pounds by the time the navy took him and his surviving comrades off Tinian.

They lowered the nets down in the boat and picked us up and set us on the deck and we got out. 'Course, the Navy people

A jeep carrying a wounded marine speeds along the west coast of Saipan, past a bulldozer gouging out a ditch for some of the Japanese dead left behind after the final, futile banzai charge on the island, July 8, 1944.

An exhausted marine momentarily at rest in the ruined town of Garapan, known as "the Tokyo of Saipan" before it was leveled by the war

stayed way away from us. We thought they was afraid. But they really wasn't afraid. We hadn't had a bath in six weeks. And I know we smelled awful. We couldn't smell each other, but the Navy could smell us. And so we took showers, and they became friendly with us then.

But it was what had happened on Saipan that continued to haunt the victors. "Do the suicides of Saipan mean that the whole Japanese race will choose death before surrender?" the journalist Robert Sherrod asked after witnessing what had happened at Marpi Point. "Perhaps that is what the Japanese and their strange propagandists would like us to believe." That was precisely what Japan's rulers wanted both their own people and their enemies to conclude. Japanese civilians would soon be ordered to undergo universal military training so that they could resist the invasion their rulers now feared could not be stopped. At the same time, Saipan helped convince Allied commanders, already planning their next moves toward the Japanese home islands, that the only way to overcome a people willing to die rather than admit defeat would be to destroy it.

THE FALL OF ROME JUST BEFORE D-DAY had boosted Allied morale, but it had not ended warfare in Italy. The Allies had failed to destroy the German army, and as it retreated northward Field Marshal Kesselring continued the delaying tactics that had frustrated his pursuers for so long. His men fell back from one defensive line to the next in carefully staged withdrawals, buying time until the autumn rains began again and he could settle into the Gothic Line, the well-fortified defensive chain in the Appennines north of Florence where he hoped to hold out all winter, his hand strengthened by the arrival of eight fresh divisions.

The British Eighth Army followed him through central Italy while Mark Clark's Fifth Army continued to advance along the western side of the peninsula. Among those in closest pursuit were Japanese American troops. Some were brand-new to combat. Others had already seen far too much of it. But it had not been easy to persuade the military to give any of them a chance to show what they could do. Eisenhower's staff had initially rejected the whole idea, but early on Clark had said that he was happy to "take anybody that will fight," and the 100th Infantry Battalion, made up of draftees from Hawaii, had already become one of his favorite units. Temporarily attached to the 34th Infantry, they had fought their way across the winding Volturno River three times, hurled themselves against German positions along the Gustav Line, endured forty days of fighting at Anzio, and lost more than 950 men—so many that they came to be called the Purple Heart Battalion. The unit's brilliant example persuaded the army to send the 2nd and 3rd battalions of the 442nd Regimental Combat Team, still training at Camp Shelby, Mississippi, to join it in Italy.

Sergeant Tim Tokuno, a Sacramento Valley farmer's son, who had been drafted before Pearl Harbor and then volunteered for the 442nd, was granted fifteen days' leave to say goodbye to his parents in the Topaz relocation camp.

As I entered the compound the MP captain stopped me and said, "Sergeant, have you got any liquor in your bag?" I said, "Yes, I have a fifth of whiskey to take to my folks." The captain shook his head and says, "Sorry, sergeant. No liquor allowed in camp. Hell of a war, isn't it?" And I says, "It sure is, captain. Look, you got machine guns on all four corners, with live ammunition, and you got the guards patrolling the perimeter, and here I'm going into combat with my folks behind barbed wire," I said. "It is a hell of a war."

In early June, two-thirds of the 442nd and what was left of the 100th had joined forces at Civitavecchia, north of Rome. The 100th was now meant to replace the 442nd's 1st Battalion (which had stayed behind to help train new Japanese American draftees), but because of its distinguished record during nine months of fighting, it was allowed to keep its original name in this new combination. Japanese Americans would go forward together as the 442nd Regimental Combat Team. At first, it was not a happy marriage: the veterans from Hawaii distrusted the green newcomers, who were mostly from the mainland, and they resented being swallowed up by another unit.

Tim Tokuno

On the night of June 25, they were all gathered in an assembly area near the village of Belvedere. A motorized SS battalion held a hill north of town that overlooked the road to Sassetta. The 2nd and 3rd battalions of the 442nd were assigned the task of driving them off it. The 100th was to remain in reserve.

Private First Class Robert Kashiwagi of the 3rd Battalion's Company K, who'd grown up on a farm just outside Sacramento and had volunteered from the camp where he and his family were interned at Amache, Colorado, remembered the last campfire before he and his unit moved toward their first battle.

Our company commander stood up, and we just looked up to him, because he was such a huge, very stern military individual. And when he got up in front of us Japanese Americans he says, "We're going under fire and the very first one of you guys that turns your tail and runs the other way," he says, "I'm gonna shoot you." I says, "Oh, that's something you don't ever say to a Japanese, because that's very derogatory."

At around eight-thirty the following morning, the two battalions started toward the German positions. Like newcomers to any battlefield, each man came away with his own first impressions. Susumu Satow of Sacramento would be charged with laying telephone wires between his mortar platoon and a forward observation post under fire that day, but his most vivid memory was of something he saw along the roadside before the shooting began.

Because of our action, there were two Germans, young men, killed in action on the side of this hill, and that affected me pretty bad. Because they were nineteen years of age—about—they were the same age as me. And I thought to myself, "Gee. If this was stateside, we could have been going to school together." You know. And so emotionally that affected me at that time. That was my first bad experience of the war, to see a young man, even though an enemy, dead. Still recognizing their youth. And that this shouldn't be happening. And so that hurt me.

Sergeant Daniel Inouye from Honolulu, in the first platoon of E Company, 2nd Battalion, on the left of the advancing force, recalled how naïve he'd been.

I was then assistant squad leader. I was a three-striper. I felt very important, eighteen years old with three stripes. But in our first battle it was almost comical, because we stood in formation, just like the book said. The scouts are out and then the BAR comes up and the riflemen on the side, and we were walking up forward with our bayonets on. Looked magnificent. But after that it became bloody.

German tanks opened fire with 88 shells. The newcomers hit the ground. "We burrowed as close to that warm earth as we could get," Inouye remembered, "suddenly aware that death was flying overhead and crashing down on every side." One shell laid bare the brain of Inouye's best friend from premed school. Another shell landed in battalion headquarters and killed Captain Ralph Ensminger, the company commander from Honolulu who had always understood that his men faced not one but two enemies: the Germans and those among their fellow citizens who doubted their loyalty. Inouye was so stunned by the two deaths, he remembered, that afterward he was unable to shed a tear for nearly a decade—and so angry that killing would come easily to him.

"The 442nd was shaken by its first bloodletting," Inouye said. "Units that had lost their leaders floundered momentarily." Then the veterans of the 100th were sent in to help. In three hours, they encircled the town, destroyed the German battalion—and won for themselves a Presidential Unit Citation.

The Caucasian captain who had insulted the men of Robert Kashiwagi's company by saying he'd shoot them if they flinched had also found himself in combat for the first time that day, and hadn't done as well as they had. "An artillery shell killed his first sergeant, his runner, and a radio man, all in front of his eyes," Kashiwagi remembered. "He was just shaking and turned completely white and was not hardly able to walk. They almost had to lead him out."

The men of the 442nd continued north along the road toward Sassetta. It was on this march that Daniel Inouye killed his first man.

I was leading a little reconnaissance patrol, to see what the area looked like. And as we were walking I happened to glance up at the next hill and I saw this German. He was sitting there. And so I signaled the men and they all quieted down and I said, "That's mine." I very deliberately got my rifle and set the sights, got the wind, and just squeezed the trigger and bang!

You would think that at that moment, after killing a human being, you would feel a little remorseful. I felt pleasure. And the men applauded. "You were terrific, Dan." That was the early times in the war. And we were taught to kill the enemy. He was not a good person. He was the evil person. So you felt you had accomplished something. And that haunts me, because before I became a soldier, I sang in a choir. I was a Sunday school teacher. And "Thou shalt not kill" was real to me. And here I was, killing someone and not feeling remorseful.

For three bloody weeks, the 442nd kept moving. It drove the Germans off Hill 410, fought its way across the Cecina River, and took Castellina. Along the way, Inouye was given greater responsibility.

I was now in charge of three squads and a total of forty-one men, and I began to realize why this was done. If you're an engineer, you're selected to be an officer because you know mathematics and logarithms and all of that. If you're an artillery officer, I suppose they'd select you because you know something about trajectory and physics. Why would they select someone for an infantry officer? Well, he has to know how to read the maps and the compass, but he has to know how to kill. That's a horrible thought. I won't tell you how many men I killed. But there are some who count sheep, so they tell me. But there are times in my life when I count men. And that's a terrible thought, because I'm certain the average person, if he or she ran over a cat, you'd never forget that. So how in the world can you forget killing a man?

But even Inouye sometimes found it hard to do as he was ordered.

This one experience was so bad that I had to see the chaplain. We had just attacked a farmhouse where we thought there was a machine-gun nest. We just blew it up with a bazooka, and I ran up there and sure enough, there were three Germans, two dead and one alive. He was leaning against the wall, and he spoke in German. And I don't speak German. And he was saying, "Kamerad, Kamerad." And he had his hands up to surrender. Then, all of a sudden, he stuck his

Men of the 442nd enjoy cigarettes and coffee and weeks-old newspapers in Livorno, at the end of their first campaign in Italy.

hand into his jacket. And the only conclusion I could reach instantaneously was that he was going for a gun. So, almost instinctively I reacted and I hit his face with the butt of my rifle. And his hand flew out and in his hand was a bunch of photographs. He wanted to show me pictures of his wife and his children. That's war.

The 442nd fought so well and so hard in the drive toward the Gothic Line that when Mark Clark led his men into the important port city of Livorno in full view of the cameras that accompanied him everywhere, he insisted that the Japanese Americans march right behind his jeep. "They were superb!" said General Marshall. "They showed rare courage and tremendous fighting spirit. Everybody wanted them." Reports of their courage made the old stateside suspicion about their patriotism seem more and more absurd. Pressure to close the internment camps and allow

those still living in them to go home and resume their old lives built steadily within the Roosevelt administration. But FDR himself refused to act. The fall elections were coming up, and he did not wish to alienate white voters on the West Coast.

Racist feeling had not disappeared. When the Sacramento newspapers reported that three nisei who had once lived in the city had been killed in Italy in a single week, someone pasted the clipping to a postcard and mailed it to Sacramento state assemblyman Chester Gannon, chairman of the Committee on Japanese Problems, with a note saying, "Here are three Japanese who will not be coming back to California." Gannon or someone in his office sent it back to the sender with an unsigned message, "Glory! Hallelujah! Hallelujah! Hallelujah!"

On August 5, 1944, Japanese American Boy Scouts raise the flag at a memorial service for the first six nisei soldiers from the Amache Internment Center to have been killed in action. Fifteen hundred friends and family members attended.

WHY WOULD WE WANT TO ESCAPE?

On June 5, 1944, the day before the Allied invasion of France began, the 4-H Club Building on the fairgrounds at Fairmont, Minnesota, some eighty miles east of Luverne, had begun to be put to a brand-new use. It had become a camp for some 135 German prisoners of war who were to be employed at the Fairmont cannery at eighty cents a day, part of a national program to provide substitutes for workers in essential industries. Like most of the 400,000 other German POWs in stateside camps, they were fed and housed well and had the opportunity to learn English.

The prisoners at Fairmont looked and acted like many of the young Minnesotans who had gone off to war. Two girls were soon caught inside the fence. They were ushered out of the camp under armed guard:

"It just isn't policy," the commanding officer said, "for anything in skirts—or slacks—to come waggling feminine figures around [prisoners]." But local women did not stay away and prisoners were soon slipping out to see them so regularly that they learned to park outside and honk twice to let them know they were available.

One prisoner was asked if he didn't want to escape.

"Escape?" he answered. "Why would we want to escape?"

A Minnesota soldier, fighting in France, came across a Fairmont newspaper that told of the interest women were showing in the German prisoners back home and wrote to complain.

I gave up EVERYTHING that makes life worthwhile to do my part to stop these Germans from destroying worthwhile things and look at the sympathy being shown those barbarians back there. If only those who are carrying on flirtations and making personal contact with those prisoners would stop long enough to visualize the hardships we are encountering in subduing these barbarians, they might at least understand why such things irk the soldiers who are guarding them from their fox-holes. . . . The prisoners you are slipping food to and also flirting with, took the food and lives of helpless and innocent families who love the same kind of life and freedom . . . you and I do.

German captives at a prisoner-of-war camp in Tennessee salute the German army flag.

ON JULY 15, QUENTIN AANENSON'S THUNDERBOLT barely made it back to Airstrip One from a dive-bombing mission. The right wing was so badly torn by flak, he had feared it would fall off before he was on the ground. The next day, he took the time to write a note to Jackie Greer.

Almost every pilot I know over here has some sort of a good luck charm or ritual he goes through. . . . Before every mission, as I'm climbing into the cockpit I whistle the first bar of the "Air Corps Song" and kiss the ring you gave me. It seems to do the trick, because I'm still flying. Johnny Bathurst carries one of his baby shoes with him. One of the other fellows recites a little poem.

Aanenson would need all the good luck he could get over the next weeks. The men on the ground continued to grind their way south toward Saint-Lô. On July 18, what remained of it after six weeks of Allied bombing and German shelling finally fell to the Americans. Ninety-five percent of the town was rubble. "We sure liberated the hell out of this place," one GI said.

British, American, and Canadian forces had suffered 122,000 casualties since D-day—and had inflicted almost as many on the Germans. But now Bradley was ready to break out of the *bocage* and send his armor roaring through the German lines into the open countryside. First he called for some three thousand Allied warplanes to blast an opening. The operation was called Cobra and set for the twenty-fourth. Bradley's requirements were very specific: the warplanes were to carpet-bomb a three-and-a-half-mile by one-mile rectangle on the southern side of the road between Périers and Saint-Lô. Bad weather forced a cancellation at the last minute, but some 1,600 bombers had already taken off from England by the time the order to abort the mission was given, and nearly seven hundred tons of bombs were dropped on what the pilots thought was the target area. It had been marked by red smoke, but an errant wind blew it back over the American lines; the bombs killed 25 men of the U.S. 30th Infantry and wounded 131 more.

The operation was rescheduled for the following day. Bradley insisted that the planes parallel the road this time rather than again fly across it over the heads of his own men. The air commanders refused: to do so, they argued, would expose their bombers for far too long to antiaircraft fire from the guns that lined the road. Bradley felt he had no alternative but to agree.

The 366th Fighter Group led the attack. Quentin Aanenson's Thunderbolt was the eighth plane over the target. "I remember," he said, "that after we did our dive-bombing and pulled off the target, that for probably ten minutes we flew in heavy concussion

from the airplanes—the endless row of airplanes—coming in behind us, dropping their bombs. The world was shaking."

Down below, Ernie Pyle was watching from a battered French farmhouse with officers of the 4th Infantry Division.

The first planes of the mass onslaught came over a little before ten A.M. They were the fighters and dive bombers. Our front lines were marked by long strips of colored cloth laid on the ground, and with colored smoke to guide our airmen. We stood in the barnyard of a French farm and watched them barrel nearly straight down out of the sky. They were bombing about half a mile ahead of where we stood.

They came in groups, diving from every direction, perfectly timed, one right after another. Everywhere you looked separate groups of planes were on the way down, or on the way back up, or slanting over for a dive, or circling, circling, circling over our heads, waiting for their turn. They came in groups, diving from every direction, perfectly timed one after another. . . . The air was full of sharp and distinct sounds of cracking bombs and the heavy rip of the planes' machine guns. . . .

And then a new sound gradually droned into our ears, a sound deep, all-encompassing, with no notes in it—just a gigantic far-away surge of doomlike sound. It was the heavies, coming on with a terrible slowness . . . in flights of twelve,

Expectant GIs watch the sky over Normandy as Operation Cobra begins, July 25, 1944. After almost six weeks of struggle in the *bocage,* the massive bombing was meant to blow a path through the enemy lines and allow the Allies to advance toward Paris at last.

three flights to a group and in groups stretched out across the sky. Maybe these gigantic waves were two miles apart; maybe they were ten miles. I don't know. But . . . I thought it would never end. What the Germans must have thought is beyond comprehension.

Their march across the sky was slow and studied. I've never known a storm, or a machine, or any resolve of man that had about it the aura of such a ghastly relentlessness. You had the feeling that even had God appeared beseechingly before them in the sky with palms outward to persuade them back they would not have had within them the power to turn from their irresistible course. . . .

We spread our feet and leaned far back trying to look straight up until our steel helmets fell off. . . . And then the bombs came. They began up ahead as the crackle of popcorn and almost instantly swelled into a monstrous fury of noise that seemed surely to destroy all the world around us.

The bombs continued falling for an hour and a half. The bright day grew dark with smoke, Pyle remembered, and the steady roar seemed to fill "all the space for noise on earth." Then, again, the wind shifted. The red smoke began to move toward the American lines. So did the bombs. "We dived," Pyle wrote.

Some got in a dugout. Others made for foxholes and ditches. . . . I was too late for the dugout. . . . I remember hit-

Moments after the photograph on the preceding page was taken, frantic men of the U.S. 30th Division struggle to save their friends, buried by misdirected American bombs. For the sake of morale back home, when this photograph first appeared in the newspapers it was miscaptioned "After German shelling, Yanks dig out men buried in foxholes."

ting the ground flat . . . and then squirming like an eel to get under one of the heavy wagons in the shed. . . . The feeling of the blast was sensational. The air struck you in hundreds of continuing flutters. Your ears drummed and rang. You could feel quick little waves of concussion on your chest and in your eyes.

It was the worst American friendly-fire incident of the war. American bombs killed 111 American infantrymen that day and wounded nearly 500 more. Most belonged to the 30th Division, the same unit that had suffered all the casualties the day before. Their desperate fellow soldiers struggled to free them from the earth into which they'd been blasted. Lieutenant General Leslie J. McNair, commanding general of the Army Ground Forces, who had crossed the Channel to observe the bombing, was hurled sixty feet; when his body was found, it could be identified only by a fragment of collar with three stars. He was the highest-ranking U.S. casualty of the war.

The bombing also blasted and burned and blew apart at least a thousand German troops and mangled many times that number. Some maddened men shot themselves rather than endure more of it. Massive tanks were tossed into the air and landed upside down. Bradley followed up the bombing with some fifty thousand artillery shells. "My front lines looked like the face of the moon," the German commander remembered, "and at least seventy percent of my troops were out of action—dead, wounded, crazed, or numb."

Two days later, on July 27, the First Army broke through the enemy lines south and west of Saint-Lô and rolled out at last into the broad countryside beyond the hedgerows. For weeks, the Americans had felt fortunate to gain a thousand yards a day; soon they would be covering up to seventy miles in the same amount of time.

Operation Cobra and its immediate aftermath proved to be disastrous for Quentin Aanenson's squadron. Flak downed one flier on July 24. Two more were shot from the sky on the twenty-sixth. There were two missions on the day of the breakout, each with orders to attack "anything that moved on the German side of the lines": tanks, trucks, artillery, flak guns, infantrymen. In the morning, they destroyed two tanks and several trucks. "I was flying with Second Lieutenant Paul Bade," Aanenson remembered.

He was the element leader, and I was on his wing. We were at about a thousand feet over the trees. And suddenly I saw him start into a dive, a gradual dive. There was no sign of enemy fire. There were no tracers. We had no exploding flak around us. But they must have been firing flak without tracers, and

BOMBER! BOMBER!

For Jim Sherman of Luverne—shown at the right above, listening to his mother read the news from the front and below, armed with a wooden machine gun—the war was a source of constant excitement. He and his two brothers battled the Japanese in their backyard, helped their parents tend the family's Victory garden, and watched newsreels at the Palace: footage of Tarawa seemed "mysterious and exciting," Sherman remembered, but D-day made little impression because until the war was over he and his friends didn't understand "the extent of it."

Every weekend uniformed men on leave from the army air force base at Sioux Falls, South Dakota, thirty miles to the west, visited Luverne by bus and train. Most stayed at the Manitou Hotel and drank at the Brass Rail in its basement, he remembered. Jim Sherman and his friends quickly learned to hang around just outside the doors.

They would have some girl they'd met at the bar and they'd want to take her to the park or the fairgrounds. And so, we'd rent them our bikes for a buck. And when these guys would bring them back, they'd say, "Are you going to be here next weekend? I'd like to buy or borrow your bike again." It was big money to us, a whole dollar.

At Thanksgiving, Sherman remembered, his father invited any servicemen stranded in town home for a turkey dinner. "We always listened to the Army-Navy game. I had two uncles in the Navy and so I was cheering for the Navy. And all these soldiers, they're cheering for the Army. If the Navy scored, I'd jump up and down and they'd grab me and wrestle me to the floor. You didn't think of these guys as being monarchs or anything. They were obviously quite a lot older than I was but you just felt close to them."

When one of their Thanksgiving guests married a local girl, the reception was held in the Sherman parlor, and the Shermans made two bedsheets into a honeymoon nightgown for the bride. Fighter pilots in training at Sioux Falls were strictly prohibited from flying low over Luverne, but sometimes one would defy orders.

If some guy was dating one of the local girls and he was flying one of these P-47 Thunderbolts, he would come zooming right down Main Street—200, 300 feet over the city, waggling his wings so she'd know who it was. The windows would rattle and people would get all upset. But I don't think it ever stopped them.

The bombers went up a lot, too, and we were all excited to see them—big Liberators and B-29s, flying out of Sioux Falls. If we heard them coming, we'd say, "Bomber! Bomber!" and everybody'd run out the back door and we'd look up and watch them. We had a cocker spaniel named Rinky. We'd say "Bomber! Bomber!" And Rinky'd head for the back door just as fast as he could. It got so that all you had to say was, "Bomber! Bomber!" whether or not there were any planes coming over, and Rinky—he's gone. And one time, my mother had just waxed the kitchen floor and we said, "Bomber! Bomber!, and Rinky goes tearing out to the back door, his feet just churning away like crazy, falling down, trying to get out.

he must have been hit or his controls had been hit. And he started to go down. I was close to him. I pulled up so our wings overlapped and saw him desperately trying to disconnect everything—his oxygen hose, his radio hose, his seatbelt—and bail out. But he was already too low. But in that instant while I'm overlapping with him and he knows—in his mind he knows he's dead—he looked over at me and glanced at me for just a minute, and then crashed into the trees. I had pulled off just enough so I wasn't caught in the explosion. He knew he was dead. And I remember so many times thinking about that. He was an only son. His mother lived in, I believe, Richmond, Virginia. And I remember thinking, "She does not know that her son was killed today."

That afternoon it happened again. Captain Jack Engman's plane was so riddled with flak that, as the squadron flew back over the American lines, he radioed the other pilots that he was going to bail out and would see them back at the base. "He jumped clear and we circled him. But his chute wasn't opening. . . . He just kept falling—and we kept screaming for him to pull the ripcord. He fell eight thousand feet, and we could see his body actually bounce several feet in the air when he hit the ground." The next day, Aanenson and some of the others went looking for Engman. They found his body in a village churchyard to which French farmers had brought it, wrapped in a sheet, and buried him there.

On the twenty-eighth, two more men were shot down and captured. Five days later, another pilot was killed. Nine men lost in ten days: "We grieved for them," Aanenson remembered.

That is, the day they were killed we talked about the circumstances and we packed up their things and maybe at the officers' club that night if we went in there we might talk a little bit about what the angle of the flak had been so we could try to avoid certain approaches on targets. But then we never talked about them again. It's just as if they did not exist. Yet the killing we did haunted us all the time. We thought about—or I did, I can't speak for the others—but it was the killing, the numbers.

On August 3, 1944, the law of averages almost caught up with Aanenson himself. He'd been flying air support for American troops near the Norman town of Vire.

I was flying the Tail-End Charlie position, which means the last one in the line of flight. It's the most vulnerable position because that's the one they'll start with first. And suddenly the eighty-eights and twenty-millimeters started coming up in heavy amounts and I heard this roar through my airplane,

and fire came into the cockpit . . . all in an instant. My airplane was shaking, and so I tried to bail out. I tried to push the canopy back, but a piece of flak had come up through the glide and so I couldn't get the canopy fully open. The fire was still coming at me, and so I put the plane in a dive because we'd always discussed that we didn't want to die by burns. I was only at four thousand feet. And that move, literally, saved my life because the air pressure changed and so the flames were sucked out through that opening in the canopy and that fire died out. My plane, they told me, looked like a comet—it had so much fire and flames behind it. So I was able to get back to the base. I expected any minute for it to explode.

I would stall if my speed dropped below one hundred and sixty miles an hour, so I landed back at the base at one-seventy. I didn't know that one of the twenty-millimeters had come up through my left wheel well, and I had a flat tire there. So when my wheels came down and I hit the runway, there was a jerk. I'm doing one-seventy miles an hour, then that jerk. I lifted the wing off a little bit, but then the landing gear collapsed on one side, I was still going about a hundred miles an hour, and I was spun around by the force. My shoulder harness on the right broke loose. The left one held. I was spun around and the back of my head hit the gunsight. And so I was unconscious. Then a couple of enlisted men pulled me out and took me to the medical tent. I had a dislocated shoulder, which they had to slam back into place. And I had burns above my shoe tops, up to my knees, so they had bandaged them.

A photographer from the British magazine *Picture Post* happened to be on hand when Aanenson's plane finally spun to a stop. He hurried to the medical tent and stood by until the handsome young pilot's burns had been bandaged before speaking to him. "Then he asked me if I thought I was up to walking over to the airplane so he could get a shot," Aanenson remembered. "And I thought, 'Well, I can try.' So I got my flight suit back on and they drove me over there in a jeep, and then he had me get in front of the airplane and walk away from it."

In the *Rock County Star-Herald* a month later, Al McIntosh would note a remarkable coincidence.

Lt. John Stavenger, bomber pilot now in England, has decided it's a mighty small world after all. He hadn't hardly landed before he bumped into Lt. Howard James of Luverne.

Then, he leisurely settled back and read an English magazine. He looked at one big picture of a wrecked plane. . . . The picture carried the caption: "The man who was lost returns to base. . . ." The pilot in question was none other than Lt.

Quentin Aanenson of Luverne. His family knew nothing of the incident. . . . And the picture showed the Luverne youngster walking away from his wrecked plane as blithely unconcerned as if he'd just bought a nickel's worth of candy.

Lieutenant General George Patton had played only a phantom role in the invasion so far, as the commander of a mythical army meant to mystify the Germans about where the Allies were going to land. But after the breakout at Saint-Lô and the capture of Avranches, the gateway to Brittany and southern Normandy, he was given a real army of his own and made the most of it.

The terms military historians routinely apply to the movement of armies are often a source of amusement, if not irritation, to the men actually forced to take part in them; soldiers on the ground rarely feel they are "driving" or "sweeping" or "dashing" anywhere. But during the first week and a half of August 1944, the armored columns of Patton's newly created Third Army did all those things. From Avranches, they seemed to spread everywhere at once: west across Brittany to seize the battered port at Brest, southwest to isolate German coastal garrisons at Lorient and Saint-Nazaire, southeast to capture Nantes, Angers, and Le Mans.

After more than six weeks of bloody, hedgerow-by-hedgerow combat, one correspondent wrote, "suddenly, the war became

fun. It became exciting, carnivalesque, tremendous." That was how Patton himself saw it from the backseat of his jeep—three oversized stars fore and aft—as he raced ahead of one or another of his columns, a Michelin map open on his lap. "Just look at that," he shouted to an aide as they roared past the still smoldering evidence of an attack by one of the Thunderbolt squadrons that ranged ahead of his army "like hawks seeking prey": fields on fire, burning tanks, charred enemy corpses. "Could anything be more magnificent? God, how I love it!"

The Germans were reeling. Ever since D-day, most of Hitler's field commanders had wanted permission to pull back to the German border. The Führer would not hear of it. He had demanded Field Marshal von Rundstedt's resignation when he seemed less than enthusiastic about German prospects in France. Now, instead of ordering a withdrawal, he directed the new commander, Field Marshal Günther von Kluge, to mount an immediate counterattack westward along a narrow corridor between the See and Sélune rivers. Its object was to recapture Avranches and seal off the American army in Normandy and Brittany. "We must . . . strike like lightning and turn the enemy front from the rear," Hitler insisted; it was a "unique, never-recurring opportunity."

It was madness. Six battered, ill-prepared mechanized divisions dutifully began moving westward during the night of August 6–7 and got nowhere. The U.S. 30th Infantry Division stopped them near Mortain. Bradley rushed in reserves. In five days of fighting, American gunners and fighter-bombers destroyed nearly one hundred enemy tanks and sent the Germans fleeing eastward through the *bocage.*

Then, on August 15, some 550 miles to the south, thousands of American and Free French troops began to fight their way ashore between Cannes and Toulon, on the French Riviera: the German grip on southern France was now in jeopardy and Allied supplies could begin to be unloaded at Marseilles and other nearby ports. The following day, Hitler reluctantly agreed to pull what was left of his armies out of Normandy.

Meanwhile, the British and Canadians had finally broken through the enemy lines at Caen. The Allies saw a chance to encircle and annihilate the retreating Germans. The U.S. First Army would pursue them from the west. The British Second and Canadian First armies would squeeze them from the north, while Patton's Third Army was ordered to wheel sharply north from Le Mans and come at them from the south. If all went well, Patton and the Canadians would close the circle and cut off their retreat between Falaise and Argentan.

At that point, in one of the most controversial decisions of the war, Bradley ordered Patton to halt. A number of explanations were later given: the Third Army's rapid pace had overstretched its supply lines; Bradley feared that if the Canadians got too close to the Americans, they might accidentally fire into each other's lines; part of the battlefield the Americans would have occupied was assigned to Montgomery, and he had issued no invitation to move into it. In any case, the Canadians advanced slowly, and some forty thousand Germans were able to slip away before Canadian and Polish troops finally closed the gap and Allied fighter squadrons and artillerymen could begin what became a three-day slaughter. London *Daily Express* correspondent Alan Moorehead, who visited the battlefield afterward, reported what happened when the shells began falling near the little village of Saint-Lambert.

The horses [that pulled many of the German guns] stampeded. Not half a dozen, but perhaps three hundred or more. They lashed down the fences and the hedges with their hooves, and dragged their carriages through the farmyards. Many galloped for the banks of the river Dives, and plunged headlong with all their trappings down the twelve-foot banks into the stream below, which at once turned red with blood. Those animals that did not drown under the dragging weight

of their harness, or die in falling, kept plunging about among the broken gun-carriages, and trampled to death the Germans hiding under the bank. The drivers of the lorries panicked in the same way. As more and more shells kept ripping through the apple trees, they collided their vehicles one against the other, and with such force that some of the fighter cars were telescoped with their occupants inside.

At some places for stretches of fifty yards vehicles, horses and men became jammed together in one struggling, shrieking mass. Engines and broken petrol tanks took fire, and the wounded pinned in the wreckage were suffocated, burned and lost. Those who were lucky enough to get out of the first collisions scrambled up the ditches and ran for cover across the open fields. They were picked off as they ran.

Parts of two German columns tried to get across a narrow bridge at the same time. A cluster of shells turned men and vehicles alike into a blazing barrier that blocked the men and machines trying to follow in their wake.

I suppose there were about a thousand German vehicles of every sort lying out in the fields behind. All these came under fire. The Germans made no attempt to man their guns. They either huddled beneath them, or ran blindly for the futile cover of the hedges.

They ran in the direction of the fire, shouting that they had surrendered. They gave up in hundreds, upon hundreds. There was no fight left in them any more, and now, here, you can see what is left of the battle in the warm mid-day sunlight. It is exactly like those crowded battle paintings of Waterloo and Borodino—except of course the wreckage is different. Every staff car—and I suppose I have seen a hundred—is packed with French loot and German equipment. There is a profusion of everything: field-glasses and typewriters, pistols and small arms by the hundred, cases of wine, truck-loads of food and medical stores, a vast mass of leather harness. Every car is full of clothing, and every officer seems to have possessed a pair of corsets to take home.

Moorehead made his way to what was left of a Norman farmhouse. It was full of armed Germans, he reported, but they were so traumatized that no one had bothered to strip them of all their weapons. Further resistance from them was unthinkable.

Over at the hospital it is far worse. The dead and the wounded lie together. Living or dead there is not much difference in the appearance of the men. Many hours ago life ceased to count for anything at all. The wounded keep dying, but quietly, so that one is not aware at any given moment of just how many are surviving. . . .

Outside, a Canadian soldier is mercifully going round shooting wounded horses with a Luger pistol. It would be equally merciful if he did the same for those enemy patients who are beyond hope and too weak to cry any more.

At least ten thousand Germans died in the Falaise pocket (the survivors called it the *Kessel,* or cauldron). Two thousand horses were killed, too. So many dead men and dead animals lay along the cratered, cluttered roads that the pilots of Allied spotter planes hundreds of feet above the battlefield were nauseated by the stench; so many that after the shooting finally stopped, General Eisenhower wrote, "it was literally possible to walk for hun-

dreds of yards at a time, stepping on nothing but dead and decaying flesh."

Once again, Quentin Aanenson's squadron had been among those called in to do the killing.

I had caught a bunch of Germans in double-tandem trucks. They were just massed in there, and I was the only one that was firing—my wingman's guns had been jammed—and the effect on me was that my right hand quit working. After I pulled off that and I was on the way home, I couldn't grip with that hand. So I had to put my left hand over on top of the stick to maintain it and go and land with that. When I'd have these nightmares in years after the war, many years after the war, if it was one relating to that mission or missions like that, when I'd get up in the morning and go out to the kitchen, Jackie would be there—she was usually up before me, and she would have had the coffee made—and she could tell when I walked in that my right hand wasn't functioning right. She'd pour a cup of coffee, not say a word. She'd hand it to my left hand. Never a word said. We just went on.

All across France, the Germans were now in retreat. An Allied Intelligence report declared their army "no longer a cohesive force, but a number of fugitive battle groups, disorganized and

Carnage in the Falaise pocket: A German master sergeant remembered what it had been like to run the three-day Allied gauntlet. "Never-ending detonations—soldiers waving to us, begging for help, the dead, their faces screwed up but still in agony—huddled everywhere in trenches and shelters, the officers and men who had lost their nerve—burning vehicles from which piercing screams could be heard—a soldier stumbling, holding back the intestines which were oozing from his abdomen—soldiers lying in their own blood—arms and legs torn off—others, driven crazy, crying, shouting, swearing, laughing hysterically."

AL McINTOSH'S WAR
June 1944–August 1944

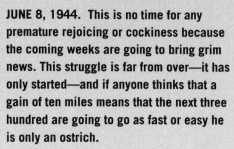

JUNE 8, 1944. This is no time for any premature rejoicing or cockiness because the coming weeks are going to bring grim news. This struggle is far from over—it has only started—and if anyone thinks that a gain of ten miles means that the next three hundred are going to go as fast or easy he is only an ostrich.

There's a War Bond Drive starting next Tuesday. Rock County has a big job cut out for it.

But Ned Brown, county chairman, is gambling on the patriotism of you Rock Countians. Ned is starting the campaign where the last one left off—without a single meeting of any of the workers.

"I don't feel like calling a county meeting . . . ," he said. "That's an awful lot right now when most everybody is busy with their farm work, asking them to take off hours to come to a meeting."

Here is the way Ned looks at it—the workers have been thru four previous campaigns—they know their job and what has to be done. . . . With a man having so much faith in the people of Rock County, we can't afford to let them down. Just remember this . . . it's "better to buy bonds than to wear them."

JUNE 22, 1944. Mrs. Andrew Brekke, Beaver Creek, reports that her son, Cpl. Elmer D. Rollag thinks enough of war bonds that he has bought his 12th $50 bond. He's been with the army engineers in the southwest Pacific two years and of that time 16 months was spent on Guadalcanal.

Kind of puts a lot of people to shame doesn't it?—considering that a corporal doesn't make any "defense wages."

JULY 20, 1944. Somehow, the gossip "grape vine" had heard that there was a telegram coming through after 6 PM last Friday for Mr. and Mrs. Ray Lester of Magnolia. Ray Lester heard about it and his heart was heavy.

He started walking down the street—on the way he met "Scotty" Dewar, the depot agent.

"Which one is it?" asked Lester—because there were four boys to worry about in that family. After being told [it was Kermit] he went sorrowfully home to break the news to his wife.

It must be a hard job handling those death messages. Dewar had known Kermit since babyhood—it was more than he could do to carry that message to the home—he left it in the Lester box at the post office. And the family understood why.

And it was a gracious gesture that was made at the dance in Magnolia that night. When the crowd heard the news—the dance was halted immediately out of respect to the memory of that fighting Marine [who died on Saipan].

AUGUST 3, 1944. Rock County's service honor roll, bearing the names of 1,065 men and women who claim Rock County as their home or their birthplace, has been completed on the north side of the city hall. Seal Van Sickel of Hawarden, Iowa, did the art work.

The honor roll, one of the most beautiful seen in this section of the country, was sponsored and erected by the Rock County Post 2757 Veterans of Foreign Wars, and paid for by voluntary contributions received by the post from the public. Of the 1,065 persons in service, 29 are young ladies. . . . Gold stars have been placed before the names of seven men who have been killed in action, ordered while in the service. Room still remains to add at least 60 more names, the artist stated.

AUGUST 17, 1944. Wartime travel restrictions have made campaigning a real handicap for office seekers. Hitch-hiking through Minnesota are Byron E. Allen, Democratic-Farmer-Laborer candidate for Governor, and A. F. Nellermoe, DFL candidate for congressman from this district.

A meeting of DFL party members had been arranged for Tuesday night but by the time the 11 p.m. bus arrived the chilly evening had caused most of the party faithful to drift on home.

A couple of real, personable fellows, they did the best they could Wednesday morning, shaking hands up and down Main Street, to meet as many as possible before keeping an engagement in Pipestone.

AUGUST 31, 1944. W. F. Baack, who farms west of Luverne, nearly fell out of his chair the other night when he looked at a picture from France in the Sioux City Journal and saw the beaming face of his former hired man [now an infantryman] who was being enthusiastically kissed by a French couple.

even demoralized, short of equipment and arms." Allied planners had assumed the enemy would stop and hold along the Seine, allowing their pursuers to rest and resupply before resuming battle. Then Eisenhower had hoped to mount a two-part assault on Germany itself, aimed at destroying its industrial heart: in the north, Montgomery was to send the Canadian and British troops of his 21st Army Group through Belgium to seize the coal mines and industrial cities of the Ruhr Valley, while Bradley's 12th Army Group crossed Belgium and Luxembourg south of the Ardennes Forest, then drove through Metz and the Saar basin to Frankfurt-am-Main.

But now, as the Germans fled across the river instead of fighting for it, and with the Allies about to plunge right after them, a new plan was needed. Supply lines were threatening to snap. It wasn't a matter of scarcity: hundreds of thousands of tons were being unloaded on the Normandy beaches every week. The problem was getting supplies to the front, more than three hundred miles away. The Allies were meant to be in control of seven ports by the time they reached the Seine. In fact, the Germans had garrisoned Dunkirk, Calais, Boulogne, and Le Havre, as well as the ports in Brittany; only Cherbourg was in Allied hands, and its badly damaged facilities were still being rebuilt. The French railyards remained in ruins, smashed by Allied planes before D-day. Not even the heroic, twenty-four-hour-a-day effort by the mostly African American truck drivers of the "Red Ball Express" could keep up with the relentless demand. Each division required five hundred tons of matériel a day.

Montgomery suggested a solution: instead of trying to mount twin attacks, he called for a single "really powerful and full-blooded thrust" by the British Second and U.S. First armies through the lowlands into the Ruhr and then onward "toward Berlin." Such a northern drive by "a solid mass of some forty divisions" under his command, he argued, would be "so strong that it need fear nothing." But for it to work, Patton's columns farther south would have to be halted.

Eisenhower, who was to take official field command of all the Allied armies in France on September 1, did not agree. A single thrust was always subject to a flanking attack. He wanted to have "more than one string to our bow"—several armies moving in parallel columns against Germany along a "broad front." But because there were not enough supplies on hand to support both assaults, he was willing to give temporary priority to a limited northern drive by Montgomery's forces and to order Courtney Hodges's First Army north of the Ardennes to protect the British right flank.

If all went well, Montgomery's troops would overrun the last of the platforms from which V-1 rockets rained down on Greater London and destroy what was left of the German Fifteenth Army, which had been awaiting the attack on the Pas-de-Calais that never came. But above all, success would secure the big Belgian port of Antwerp and greatly ease the problem of supply. Montgomery, who privately believed Eisenhower's "ignorance as to how to run a war . . . complete," was bitter that his grand plan had not been adopted. Bradley and Hodges were against dividing U.S. forces; George Patton complained that if *he* were given the supplies, his Third Army could drive eastward through Metz and be in Germany in ten days. But Eisenhower had made his decision: Antwerp would make everything worthwhile.

Since D-day, telegrams from the War Department had been arriving on doorsteps all across America at a rate inconceivable just a year earlier. Mrs. Augusta Niland of Tonawanda, New York, received three of them. One son had died on Omaha Beach, a second at Sainte-Mère-Église; a third was missing in action in Burma. A fourth son was hastily pulled out of the line so that at least one of her boys would be sure to survive the war. Twenty-eight men from the tiny town of Bedford, Virginia, had landed on Omaha Beach; nineteen had died within the first fifteen minutes, and three more died fighting in Normandy.

Private First Class James Donohue and Staff Sergeant Frederick Smith, both Army Rangers, were also lost on June 6, the first of ten boys from Waterbury, Connecticut, to be buried in France. On August 10, 1944, in his weekly column, Al McIntosh noted Rock County's first loss on European soil.

> *Here is one of life's tragedies. Mrs. Henry Smook went over to Sioux Falls with her youngest boy, Harold, 17. It wasn't a shopping expedition or a long-planned day of fun. She had gone with her youngest son to give her consent to his joining the navy.*
>
> *She didn't know that while she was there a telegram had come to her home in Luverne telling her of the death of her son in France, Private First Class Herman Smook.*

The Germans continued to flee, the roofs of their vehicles heaped with tree branches in the faint hope they would be seen from the air as just part of the landscape. Since D-day, they had lost some 240,000 men. An additional 200,000 had surrendered. Fifty-seven German divisions had tried to stop the Allies in June; by the end of August, just ten remained intact as fighting units. Allied casualties were appalling, too: 256,000 soldiers and airmen killed, wounded, captured, or reported missing.

Countless French villages had been pounded into dust and at least nineteen thousand French civilians had been killed. But most of France was free, and on August 25, Paris itself was liber-

ated. Eisenhower had initially hoped the city could at least temporarily be bypassed: he feared the Germans would put up a "helluva fight" for it, overstraining his supply lines and slowing the Allied drive toward Germany. But then the people of the French capital had risen up to overthrow their occupiers. Rather than see them crushed, he agreed to let Free French forces lead the way into the city, with Americans from the 4th and 28th divisions following in their wake.

Parisians poured into the streets to greet them. "I have seen the faces of young people in love and the faces of old people at peace with their God," one correspondent wrote. "I have never seen in any place such joy as radiated from the faces of the people of Paris this morning." Old women in black waved Allied flags and shouted "*Merci! Merci!*" Young ones clambered onto jeeps and tanks to hug the unshaven GIs who had helped to free them. Private "Pepper" Martin of Luverne sent word back to his family that he'd been in one of the first American units to enter Paris: "Well, Ma," he wrote, "to tell you the truth, you just can't imagine what it was like. . . . They say that there are six million people in Paris, but I don't believe them because I was kissed at least by five million girls—and I mean beautiful girls."

Quentin Aanenson, also from Luverne, saw the same scene from a very different vantage point.

We were flying a mission near Paris. The Germans were retreating on one side, and the Americans and French were coming in on the other. And as I pulled off my strafing run and turned back—I turned back over the city because there wouldn't be any German flak guns there—and as I looked down there were just thousands of people jamming the streets of the Champs-Élysées around the Eiffel Tower and the Arc de Triomphe and I realized that I was seeing something that was basically the culmination of why we were there. And it was so thrilling and exciting that I went down very low. I circled the Eiffel Tower, and I just enjoyed the thrill of seeing this happening that had been an objective—or one of the accumulating objectives—that was so meaningful in showing we are winning this war. The good guys are going to come out ahead.

The U.S. 28th Infantry Division strides along the Champs-Élysées in Paris, August 29, 1944. Free French forces and Resistance fighters had freed the city after five years of Nazi rule, but the Americans were welcomed as liberators, nonetheless. "A physical wave of human emotion picked us up and carried us into the heart of Paris," one captain recalled. "It was like groping through a dream." The dream was shortlived; by nightfall most of these men were back at the front.

FUBAR

AS THE ALLIED ARMIES SPED ACROSS France in the last weeks of August 1944, Quentin Aanenson's 366th Fighter Group moved with them, first to airstrip A-41 at Dreux, thirty miles west of Paris, then to A-70, a former German base near Laon, nearly one hundred miles northeast of it. Enemy bombers had come and gone from there during the Battle of Britain, but American bombs had recently cratered one of its two runways and badly damaged its hangars. Wrecked German equipment was strewn across the surrounding landscape just as it was all across northern France, abandoned by the battered, disorganized enemy now staggering back toward Germany, trying to avoid being hunted down by fighter-bomber squadrons like Aanenson's.

He and two of his closest friends, Johnny Bathurst and Ray Beebe, managed to turn their tent at Laon into a remarkably comfortable home. They scrounged up planks for flooring, located a wood-burning stove, installed a real door that would help keep out the worsening cold, and used a steel helmet on a single-burner gas stove to boil eggs and the occasional elderly rooster obtained from a local farmer.

They named their warm dwelling Duffy's Tavern, after the weekly CBS radio comedy about a Brooklyn workingman's bar whose motto was "Where the elite meet to eat," but Aanenson and his fellow pilots often spent their evenings in front of the fireplace in the officers' club, still more comfortably furnished courtesy of the departed Luftwaffe. It was there, between missions, that Aanenson wrote the letters Jackie Greer longed for back in Louisiana. He and she did their best to exchange letters every day, each trying to keep the other's spirits up till they could be together again. Jackie also did all she could to understand where he was and what he was going through. She remembered:

Following that war was the best history lesson I ever had. I got a big map, and every day I'd get crayons out. Every day. Certain colors meant this group is here. Certain colors meant they'd moved there. And I kept up with that war. I learned more about Europe than I had ever learned at school. It was very important that I stay with it.

Aanenson got letters from Jackie's mother, too. "If it were possible for you to get two glimpses of Jackie each day," she told him, "I think what the two of you would enjoy most would be the run in from the car in the afternoon to her mailbox, and when she's kneeling by your picture at night as she says her prayers." Those images, Aanenson remembered, "brought everything [back home] very close," and when it came time for him to be assigned his own Thunderbolt—until then he'd flown whatever P-47 happened to be available—he gave it one of his nicknames for his Southern-born girlfriend, "Rebel Jack."

"It's awfully cold in France today," he wrote her on September 3. "The autumn winds are beginning to whistle around our tent, and the leaves are getting a little nervous. Like Germany, they know they'll be falling soon. Only the leaves will be missed."

That week, everyone seemed to think the Germans would be falling soon. "Militarily," Dwight Eisenhower's chief of staff, General Walter Bedell Smith, assured reporters in London, "this war is over." The British army's Chief of the Imperial General Staff, Field Marshal Sir Alan Brooke, told Churchill that the Nazis would surrender before the end of autumn. In Washington, General Marshall began planning for the winter redeployment of troops from Europe to the Pacific, and the War Production Board started canceling military contracts. Post exchanges were ordered to halt any further holiday packages for the men on the European front. No room was made for winter clothing in the supply trucks heading east from the Normandy beaches, either; the men wouldn't be needing it. A Gallup Poll showed that nearly three out of four Americans thought the war in Europe would be over by Christmas.

For anyone who read a newspaper, it was hard to draw any other conclusion. In

The three stars in the window of the Oswego, New York, house on the opposite page signal that three men who lived there are in the service. "Duffy's Tavern," Quentin Aanenson's improved tent (above), kept out the cold near Laon, France. Aanenson's tentmate Johnny Bathurst leans on its salvaged door.

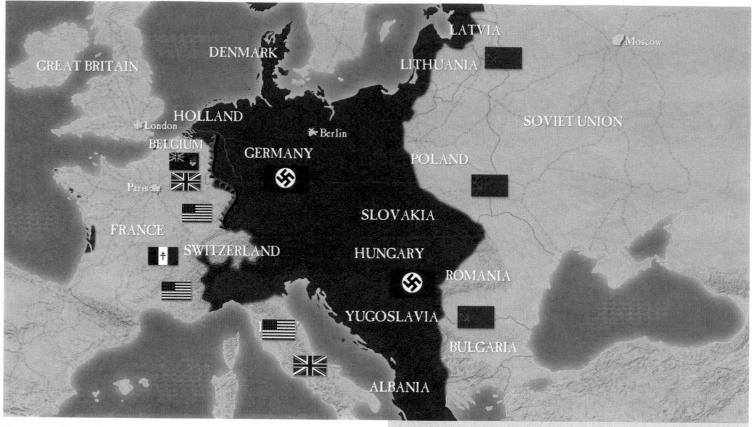

the East, the Red Army was moving steadily westward along a twelve-hundred-mile front: nearly every inch of Russian soil had now been recovered from the Nazis, and from north to south, Soviet columns were pushing their way into Finland, Estonia, Latvia, Lithuania, Poland, Slovakia, Hungary, Romania. Meanwhile, in western Europe, more than 2 million Allied troops were now ashore and five Allied armies had driven farther eastward in three months than D-day planners had expected them to go in eleven. The thrust into Belgium mounted by Montgomery's Canadian and British forces covered 250 miles in six days, overran the remaining flying-bomb sites, and on September 4, the day after Quentin Aanenson predicted a German collapse to Jackie Greer, captured the port of Antwerp. Meanwhile, Courtney Hodges's U.S. First Army had captured twenty-five thousand weary Germans near Mons and begun racing across Belgium; George Patton's Third Army had crossed the Meuse, and his patrols had reached all the way to Metz on the Moselle; and Alexander Patch's Seventh Army, made up of American and French troops, was moving fast up the Rhone Valley from the Riviera to link up with Patton and create the solid Allied front Eisenhower continued to insist upon.

"The August battles have done it and the enemy in the West has had it," an official Supreme Headquarters Allied Expeditionary Force (SHAEF) Intelligence report declared. "Two and a half months of bitter fighting have brought the end of the war in Europe within sight, almost within reach." Since June 6, the Germans had lost 1.2 million men on the eastern and western fronts; a quarter of a million more remained bottled up in besieged French coastal cities. Of the 2,300 tanks and assault guns that had defended France, just 120 had made it safely back across the Seine. The Allies were advancing with some 2,000 tanks, while the Germans had just 100. Only 572 German aircraft were still flying, while some 14,000 remained at the disposal of American and British commanders.

The only real question now seemed to be which army would be the first to break through the line of reinforced-concrete pillboxes, natural barriers, and belts of pyramidal antitank "dragon's teeth" that guarded the approaches to Germany for nearly four hundred miles from just below Arnhem in the Netherlands all the way south to Switzerland. Hitler called it the West Wall. (The Allies called it the Siegfried Line, after a London music-hall hit from early in the war, which promised British Tommies would one day hang out their washing on it.) It was a forbidding sight. One of the pilots from Quentin Aanenson's fighter group, forced to fly back and forth over it to raid targets in the Ruhr Valley,

A section of the jagged West Wall, behind which the Germans would soon feverishly prepare to defend their homeland

compared it to "a long, ugly scar on the earth's surface." But in late August and early September, the West Wall was far less formidable than its name implied or than it looked on a map or from the air. It had been built in the late 1930s to intimidate France and the Low Countries, not as a last-ditch defense line for the Fatherland, and had long since fallen into disrepair. The Germans had lost the keys to some pillboxes; farmers stored beets and potatoes in others; as late as the first week of September, no mines or barbed wire guarded the approaches; and steel gates had yet to be installed to close off the roads that ran through it.

"The defeat of the German armies is now complete," Eisenhower wrote, "and the only thing needed to realize the whole conception [of moving directly into Germany along a broad front] is speed." But that same week, the Allies finally began to fall victim to their own success. One by one, the armies moving eastward sputtered to a halt, out of gas—and nearly everything else. Patton's Third Army had set the pace: five hundred miles in twenty-six days. But it alone needed between 350,000 and 400,000 gallons of fuel per day to keep going. With enough gasoline, Patton told one newspaperman, "I'll go through the Siegfried Line like shit through a goose." Without it, he could go nowhere. Neither could anyone else. And the priority given to Montgomery's northern drive had not yielded the results Eisenhower had hoped for. Antwerp had been taken, but the inland port alone, even with its twenty-six miles of wharves, could provide no solution to the supply problem. The Germans still held the mouth of the Scheldt River and the sixty-mile estuary that stretched between the North Sea and the Antwerp docks. Not a jerry can of gas could get through until they were cleared out, and Montgomery, now a field marshal, had failed to give anyone

THE RED BALL EXPRESS

The convoy of two-and-a-half-ton trucks (left) is taking a ten-minute break to rest and change drivers. At checkpoints like the one above, military policemen totaled the supplies moving past them and kept truckers on the right road.

"My men can eat their belts," General Patton said, "but my tanks gotta gas." Nothing was more important to the Allies than getting fuel and supplies from the Normandy beaches to the armies advancing across France. The Red Ball Express was organized by the Quartermaster and Transportation Corps in late August of 1944; its name derived from a railroading term for priority freight. In less than three months—operating around the clock, wearing through some forty thousand tires, struggling to keep sixty feet apart and move no faster than twenty-five miles per hour in order to avoid pileups—they delivered more than 412,000 tons of ammunition, food, and fuel. Three out of four of its drivers were African American. Theirs was a remarkable accomplishment—but in the end it would not be enough to keep the armies moving.

the order to begin that arduous and bloody process; instead, he'd sent his troops to take the ports of Le Havre, Boulogne, and Calais, all of which the enemy wrecked before surrendering. Even Montgomery, who rarely second-guessed himself (or praised anyone else), would later admit this had been "a bad mistake on my part." Nor were his forces able to stop some sixty thousand men of the German Fifteenth Army from slipping across the Scheldt and escaping into northern Holland over the next three weeks. Just as they had in Sicily and Italy and at the Falaise Gap, the Allies had allowed large numbers of Germans to escape destruction and prepare to fight again. Under the Fifteenth Army's protection, the enemy began using Dutch as well as German sites to launch a second "retaliation" weapon against Antwerp and England, the silent V-2 rocket. Some nine hundred of them battered the Belgian port over the next few months, and more than a thousand fell on England—an average of five a day for a time—killing 2,700 civilians.

Early in the war, employing language they would never have used in front of their mothers or wives back home, American GIs had coined words for the chaos in which they often found themselves—and the miserable judgment of some of the commanders who sent them there: *snafu,* for "situation normal, all fucked-up," and *fubar,* for "fucked-up beyond all recognition." The autumn of 1944 would provide more examples of each on both sides of the globe than even the most cynical and war-weary among them could have imagined.

Hitler was prepared to concede nothing to the Allies. Pale and trembling now, convinced by his close call with assassination that he was surrounded by traitors, he nonetheless clung to the belief that victory could still be his. The Allied drive would have to stop eventually; its supply lines were simply too long. When it did—and with the help of "fog, night, and snow"—he planned to mount a surprise counterattack through the Ardennes, the forested hills of Belgium and Luxembourg through which the Germans had attacked twice before, in 1914 and 1940, with the intention of recapturing Antwerp and hurling the Allies back into the sea.

Meanwhile, as Hitler worked feverishly to rebuild and rearm his forces for the surprise assault, his generals were ordered to hold at the West Wall in what one of them called a "fight-and-die manner," especially in those areas the Allies were most likely to hit hard: along the Dutch border, at the Moselle River, and in the Vosges mountains to the south. Hitler ordered up ten new panzer brigades, each fitted out with forty of the new Panther and Tiger tanks German factories continued to produce. Despite the relentless Allied bombing that regularly blasted the roofs

from German defense plants and battered what remained of its cities, production of some weapons was now four times as great as it had been two years before. All men from sixteen to sixty were called up to serve in the armed forces. Nonessential civilian jobs were eliminated. Policemen and postmen became soldiers. Sailors and fliers, deprived by the Allies of ships or planes, were transformed overnight into infantrymen. Convalescing soldiers were called back to the front, including a "stomach battalion" made up of men who had to be fed a special diet because they suffered from duodenal ulcers, and an "ear battalion" of ex-soldiers whose hearing had been damaged by shellfire. The most able-bodied new recruits were formed into twenty-five fresh divisions of Volksgrenadiers, or "people's infantry." The oldest were put into one hundred "fortress battalions" assigned to garrison the West Wall. "We began to collect extraordinary prisoners," Alan Moorehead noted, "nearsighted clerks who had left their desk jobs three weeks before; men with half-healed wounds, even cripples and children of fifteen and sixteen. It was a makeshift, hotch-potch army . . . put in simply to hold the gap . . . to fight for time while the German generals reorganized on a sounder basis. [But] little by little a crust was formed."

Every day the Allies delayed, the German crust thickened a little more. Montgomery tried again to argue that he should be allowed to lead a single "full-bodied thrust toward [the Ruhr] and Berlin." When Eisenhower again resisted, the field marshal proposed a daring alternative: a two-part airborne assault called Operation Market Garden. First, a "blanket" of American and British airborne troops would be dropped behind German lines to seize river and canal bridges along a sixty-mile two-lane highway that led from the Belgian-Dutch border through Holland to Arnhem on the Lower Rhine. Then, armored elements of the British Second Army were to race along it, cross the Rhine, wheel around the north end of the West Wall, and drive southeast across the German border and into the Ruhr basin. For the plan to succeed, everything had to go perfectly—and quickly. On September 10, Eisenhower gave the go-ahead. It was another great gamble, but if it succeeded, the war could end in weeks. "I not only approved of Market Garden," he would say later, "I insisted on it." D-day was set for September 17. The Allies had just a week to get ready.

DURING THAT WEEK, EVENTS ELSEWHERE further fueled Allied optimism. At around 6:05 p.m. on the eleventh, Staff Sergeant Warner H. Holzinger, leading an advance unit of the U.S. First Army, waded across the Our River south of the city of Aachen and stepped into Germany itself, the first foreign soldier to stand

Before General MacArthur could begin his campaign to liberate the Philippines, he wanted the Japanese airstrip on the island of Peleliu taken.

on German soil since the time of Napoleon. The following day, Roosevelt and Churchill began meeting with their top military advisors at Quebec. With victory in the West apparently so near, they discussed plans for how postwar Germany should be dealt with and refocused their attention on the war in the Pacific. There was good news from that quarter as well. With the victory off the Marianas in June and the big Japanese naval base at Truk cut off from support, the whole of the western Pacific was now open to attack. But Allied planners still remained wary of Japanese airpower in the region, and before Douglas MacArthur's forces made their scheduled landing on Mindanao, the first and southernmost of the large Philippine islands, in late October, it had been thought best to capture the enemy-held islands on its eastern flank: Yap, the Talauds, and the Palaus.

Last-minute preparations were already under way for all three assaults when an almost giddy message from Admiral William Halsey, commander of Allied naval forces in the South Pacific, reached Admiral Nimitz on September 13. For the past three weeks, Halsey reported, planes from his fast carriers had been methodically attacking Japanese bases all over the region, destroying some 489 enemy aircraft, most of them on the ground, without encountering any serious opposition. The enemy's "non-aggressive attitude" was "amazing and fantastic," he said; he urged that all three preliminary landings be abandoned and that MacArthur skip Mindanao altogether and proceed instead directly to Leyte, in the heart of the Philippines. Nimitz agreed to almost everything Halsey suggested: Americans would land on Leyte, not Mindanao, on October 20—two

months ahead of schedule—and he was happy to cancel the Yap and Talaud operations as well. But he insisted that the invasion of Peleliu in the Palaus go forward. The island was small, just five miles long and less than two miles wide. It had an airfield and might prove useful as a staging point for future operations in the region. Besides, the preliminary bombardment was already under way.

"We're going to have some casualties," Major General William Rupertus, commander of the 1st Marine Division, had told his unit commanders before they set out for Peleliu, "but let me assure you, this is going to be a short one, a quickie. Three days, maybe two." Rupertus was so convincing and seemed so confident that thirty of the thirty-six correspondents authorized to sail with his marines chose to cover other landings likely to yield more casualties—and more headlines.

By the evening of September 13, a naval Fire Support Group—including five battleships with fourteen- and fifteen-inch guns firing explosive shells—and wave upon wave of carrier-based aircraft dropping 500-pound bombs and napalm had taken half-hour turns pounding Peleliu for two straight days. Together they had blasted to rubble nearly every trace of human habitation and burned away most of the foliage that had blanketed Umurbrogol Mountain, in the northern section of the island. Invasion plans had called for a third day of shelling and bombing, but that evening the officer in charge told his superiors he had "run out of targets" and called it off. No one objected. Three marine infantry regiments—some nine thousand assault troops—were already in place offshore aboard a flotilla of LCTs (Landing Craft, Tank). The landing was set for the morning of the fifteenth, two days before Operation Market Garden was to begin in western Europe.

One of those about to face combat for the first time was twenty-year-old marine Private Eugene Sledge of Mobile. It was hard to sleep the night before the landing, he remembered.

> I thought of home, my parents, my friends—and whether I would do my duty, be wounded or disabled, or be killed. I concluded that it was impossible for me to be killed, because God loved me. Then I told myself that God loved us all and that many would die or be ruined physically or mentally or both by the next morning and in the days following. My heart pounded and I broke out in a cold sweat. Finally, I called myself a damned coward and eventually fell asleep saying the Lord's Prayer to myself.

Sledge was Sid Phillips's best friend from high school, and if it had been up to him, Sledge wouldn't have been in the service at all. While still on Guadalcanal back in the fall of 1942, Phillips wrote his parents to tell his friend that "I want him to take four years of college without stopping and to join nothing . . . not even the Boy Scouts or the Salvation Army." But Sledge was the grandson of Confederate officers and determined to go to war. Bookish and frail as a child, he had been taught to fish and hunt by his physician father. He was a freshman at the Marion Military Institute that December, studying to become an officer, when he decided to sign on as a private in the marines instead, "prompted," as he said, "by a deep feeling of uneasiness that the war might end before I could get overseas into combat."

Eugene Sledge (left) and his older brother, Edward, a second lieutenant in the army, who told him "life would be more beautiful" for him in the service if he, too, became an officer.

In the late spring of 1944, he and Sid Phillips had a surprise reunion. By then, Phillips had been stationed in the Pacific for more than two years. He had survived Guadalcanal and Cape Gloucester and had hoped to be sent to Australia, with its plentiful beer and friendly girls, until he got his orders to go home. Instead, the 1st Marine Division had been sent to Pavuvu in the Solomons, a remote island infested with rats and scuttling land crabs, reeking with the smell of rotting coconuts, and so small that when the men drilled, one outfit had to march clockwise and the next counterclockwise to keep from blocking the only road. "War is mostly boredom," Phillips remembered.

Telling lies, stealing from some other outfit if they've got something better to eat than you have, and just making the best of a thousand bad situations. It's going to rain. You're going to get wet. It's going to get too hot. It's going to get too cold. I mean, you're always uncomfortable in the service. There are times when you're so bored that you just feel like you'll go crazy, because it's just not very entertaining to be stuck in a jungle with nothing to do day after day after day except dig holes in the ground and pile the dirt up and all.

Sitting on his cot one hot afternoon, Phillips was surprised to look up and see his old friend.

I saw him coming down the company street looking intense. I recognized him and ran out in the company street and screamed his name. And we ran and beat on each other and embraced and rolled around on the ground. People thought we were fighting, and a big crowd gathered. But then I introduced him around, and it was just a great day.

Sid Phillips soon got his orders to go home, but he worried about Sledge, just as he did about every newcomer to the battlefield.

He had come in as a replacement, and I was being rotated home because I had been overseas over two years. I certainly did think about what he was facing, because it was all bad. Every campaign was bad. Some were a little quicker and a little worse than others. Some were fought under worse conditions than others, but they were all bad. And I knew he was going to face some hard times.

Not long after Sledge got to the Pacific, he began keeping a journal, slipping tiny sheets of notes between the pages of the small New Testament he carried so that no one else would know what he was doing. Years later, those uncensored notes would be turned into a harrowing memoir, *With the Old Breed at Peleliu and Okinawa.* "The awesome reality that we were training to be cannon fodder in a global war that had already snuffed out millions of lives never seemed to occur to us," he wrote of his early days in the U.S. Marine Corps. "The fact that our own lives might end violently or that we might be crippled while we were still boys didn't seem to register. The only thing that we seemed to be truly concerned about was that we might be too afraid to do our jobs under fire."

He was about to find out. At around six-thirty that morning, two days before Operation Market Garden was due to begin, the men of Gene Sledge's Company K, 3rd Battalion, 5th Marines, filed down a ladder to the tank deck of their LCT and clambered into one of several amtracs waiting to be launched. Then the big bow doors swung open, the tractor's engine coughed into action, its treads caught on the ramp, and Sledge and his comrades slid down onto the sea and into bedlam. The sound of the shells and warplanes roaring overhead was so loud that men huddled next to one another had to scream to be heard. Sledge's outfit was part of the second wave. Before it reached the island it would have to crawl its way across a broad coral reef. As the first wave of amtracs reached the reef Japanese shells began to scream down among them. Huge geysers erupted. Beyond them, Sledge recalled, "the beach was . . . marked along its length by a contin-

Men of the 5th Marines cling to the beach at Peleliu as the island's defenders—who were supposed already to have been eliminated—open up with mortar and machine-gun fire. "Son of a bitch," a company commander said. "The beach is lousy with the bastards." His lips and tongue were "dry as sandpaper," he would remember. "Black vapor and the pungent odor of gunpowder . . . seeping from the earth helped to clog my throat. Sweat was rolling off the end of my nose."

uous sheet of flame backed by a thick wall of smoke. It seemed as though a huge volcano had erupted from the sea."

One member of Sledge's company hung over the side, vomiting. Sledge was nauseated, too, he remembered, "and feared that my bladder would surely empty itself and reveal me to be the coward I was." A lieutenant offered him a fortifying drink from a pint of whiskey. He refused it: "Just sniffing the cork under those conditions might have made me pass out." His amtrac made it to shore untouched by enemy fire, crunched its way a few feet onto the sand, and stopped. An NCO shouted, "Hit the beach!" Sledge vaulted over the steep side, stumbled, fell, got up again, ran a

few yards, and took what cover he could find just beyond the beachline.

Shells crashed all around. Fragments tore and whirred, slapping on the sand and splashing into the water a few yards behind us. The Japanese . . . machine gun and rifle fire got thicker, snapping viciously overhead in increasing volume. . . . The world was a nightmare of flashes, violent explosions, snapping bullets. Most of what I saw blurred. My mind was benumbed by the shock of it. . . . Up and down the beach, a number of amtracs . . . were burning, Japanese machine gun bursts made long splashes on the water as though flaying it with some giant whip. . . . I caught a fleeting glimpse of some Marines leaving a smoking amtrac on the reef. Some fell as bullets and fragments splashed among them. . . . I shuddered and choked. A wild desperate feeling of anger, frustration, and pity gripped me. It was an emotion that always would trouble my mind when I saw men trapped and was

Men of the 5th Marines start across the Peleliu airstrip in the face of deadly fire. "We were exposed," Eugene Sledge remembered, "running on our own power through a . . . shower of deadly metal and the constant crash of explosions."

unable to do anything but watch as they were hit. . . . I turned my face away and wished that I were imagining it all.

Men from three marine regiments—the 1st, the 7th, and Sledge's 5th, more than five thousand men—went ashore side by side on the western side of the island and quickly discovered that two days of bombardment had done little damage to Peleliu's carefully prepared defenses, an interlocking warren of some five hundred fortified caves and gun emplacements concealed within the island's ridged spine. Some shielded single snipers; others, outfitted with sliding doors of armored steel, were large enough to shelter big guns, a dozen tanks, or up to a thousand men.

The Americans would lose 1,200 men by nightfall, but there was no seawall to block their progress, as there had been at Tarawa, so most who made it ashore unhurt got beyond the beach. Sledge and his regiment managed to make it all the way across the narrow island before nightfall, though no one slept for fear that Japanese infiltrators would slip into their lines and slit their throats.

It was the darkest night I ever saw. The overcast sky was as black as the dripping mangroves that walled us in. I had the sensation of being in a great black hole and reached out to touch the sides of the gun pit to orient myself. Slowly the reality of it all formed in my mind: we were expendable! It was difficult to accept. We come from a nation and a culture that values life and the individual. To find oneself in a situation where your life seems of little value is the ultimate in loneliness.

The next morning, Sledge's regiment was ordered to assault enemy positions on a slope they called Bloody Nose Ridge, overlooking the airfield from the north. Naval and artillery shelling and bombers from the carriers offshore blasted the hillside while the marines waited in the sun for the signal to charge across the exposed gravel airstrip to attack the high ground. The temperature reached 105 degrees. There was no shade. The only water available, hauled up from the beach in five-gallon cans, turned out to be fouled by diesel oil. Some men collapsed from heat exhaustion before the signal came.

As the marines—four battalions, 1,800 men—finally got the order to move forward, Sledge wrote, the enemy opened up from above with everything they had.

I clenched my teeth, squeezed my carbine stock, recited over and over to myself, "The Lord is my shepherd, I shall not want. Yea, though I walk through the valley of the shadow of death, I will fear no evil, for Thou art with me. . . ."

The ground seemed to sway back and forth under the concussions. . . . Chunks of blasted coral stung my face and hands while steel fragments spattered down the hard rock like hail on a city street. . . .

The farther we went, the worse it got. . . . It seemed impossible that any of us would make it across. . . . To be shelled by massed artillery and mortars is absolutely terrifying, but to be shelled in the open is terror compounded.

Sledge somehow made it across the airstrip and took what shelter he could beneath a charred bush. He was "shaking like a leaf," he wrote, but took comfort from the fact that a veteran of the fighting on Guadalcanal who was crouched nearby was shaking, too.

Over the days that followed, the marines learned that Japanese tactics had changed since Guadalcanal, Tarawa, and Saipan. Banzai charges were now largely a thing of the past. Instead, Peleliu's 10,500 defenders were prepared to contest every inch of the island from deep within their hillside strongholds. They would have to be blasted or burned out of them, one at a time.

Willie Rushton, also from Mobile, was in the thick of the fighting on Peleliu. He wasn't supposed to be. His African American 11th Depot Company was meant simply to unload supplies and ammunition. But he and some of his friends had petitioned their officers before the landing to be allowed to fight and had been promised they'd at least be permitted to carry supplies to the front and carry back wounded marines. In the end, there was little room for such fine distinctions. "We were right there where the fighting was going on," Rushton recalled. "They was just knocking us off, and we came forward. It didn't make no difference whether you was black or white or whatever. They didn't care when you got into combat."

Exhausted marines at the end of a day's combat on Peleliu

Fifteen members of Rushton's company were hit. Rushton was one of them, wounded by shrapnel from a Japanese mortar. He was carried to a hospital ship offshore, the only wounded black man aboard. After his wounds were treated, he asked if he could have a haircut. The ship's barber refused.

He told me, said, "I can't cut your hair." So a couple of white marines asked him, said, "Why can't you cut his hair?" Said, "You don't have to give him no style, just cut his hair off. All he wants is some of that hair off his head." So he said, "No, I can't cut his hair."

Then the captain of the Red Cross ship came down there and told that barber, said, "I'm telling you for the first and the last time. I don't care who comes on this ship, if he's an American soldier, whether he's black or white, or whatever, I want you to cut his hair, you know, just cut his hair." He said, "Don't ever make a remark like that anymore."

Willie Rushton got his haircut. The battle for Peleliu continued.

Like Sid Phillips, Eugene Sledge had been trained as a mortarman, and during his time on Peleliu his twelve-man mortar section helped fire hundreds of rounds in support of the rifle companies that ranged ahead of them. But again and again they were called upon to pick up rifles themselves and, when necessary, help carry out the wounded as well. When the regiment was seen to be taking additional fire from a tiny nearby island called Ngesebus, Sledge and his battalion were sent to silence it. They fought their way onto still another beach and were told to set up their mortars just beyond a pillbox. Grenades tossed in through the ventilators were supposed to have killed all the enemy troops inside it. They had not. Neither did repeated carbine shots fired at point-blank range. The trapped Japanese responded by hurling grenades through the openings. The marines hugged the ground. Sledge, closest to the door, was ordered to look inside. He did, and a machine-gun burst just missed his head. The marines dropped in more grenades. The Japanese threw two of them back, wounding an American. A flamethrower and an amtrac armed with a 75-millimeter gun were called up. Before they got there, several Japanese bolted out the door and were cut down. The amtrac lumbered into place and fired three armor-piercing shells at the pillbox, blowing a hole four feet in diameter through the walls.

Someone remarked that if fragments hadn't killed those inside, the concussion surely had. But even before the dust had settled I saw a Japanese soldier appear at the blasted opening. . . . He drew back his arm to throw a grenade at us.

My carbine was already up. When he appeared, I lined up my sights on his chest and began squeezing off shots. As the first bullet hit him, his face contorted in agony. His knees buckled. The grenade slipped from his grasp. . . . I had just killed a man at close range. That I had seen clearly the pain on his face when my bullets hit him came as a jolt. It suddenly made the war a very personal affair.

There were still more enemy troops inside. Sledge and the rest of his section poured rifle fire into the pillbox until the man carrying the flamethrower and tanks on his back filled with seventy pounds of jellied gasoline got there. "He pressed the trigger. With a *whooooooooosh*, the flame leaped at the opening. Some muffled screams, then all quiet."

The next day, a hidden Japanese artillery piece fired from only a few yards away terrified Sledge and his company and tore through the rifle company on their right. The gun was silenced. Men from Sledge's oufit who had rushed to help the wounded eventually drifted back with ashen faces. One man recalled trying to get a mutual friend onto a stretcher. "We knew he was hit bad, and he had passed out," the marine said. "I tried to lift the poor guy under his shoulders and he [pointing to the other mortarman] lifted his knees. Just as we almost got him on the stretcher, the poor guy's body came apart. God! It was awful!"

"Everyone groaned and slowly shook their heads," Sledge wrote. Peleliu was supposed to have been taken in three days. Two weeks had now gone by, and victory was nowhere in sight.

I felt myself choking up. I slowly turned my back to the men facing me as I sat on my helmet, and put my face in my hands to try to shut out reality. I began sobbing. The harder I tried to stop the worse it got. My body shuddered and shook. Tears flowed out of my scratchy eyes. I was sickened and revolted to see young men get hurt and killed day after day. I felt I couldn't take any more. I was so terribly tired, and so emotionally wrung out from being afraid for days on end that I seemed to have no reserve strength left.

In the end, Sledge did find the reserve strength needed to pull himself together. He and his outfit returned to Peleliu, where they were sent to help clear Umurbrogol. "The terrain," he wrote, "was so unbelievably rugged, jumbled and confusing, that I rarely knew where we were located. Only the officers had maps, so locations meant nothing. One ridge looked about like

Near Peleliu's northern end, army tanks and Eugene Sledge's marine battalion move together into the valley the men called the "Horseshoe" to clear the Japanese from their hillside emplacements.

another, was about as rugged, and was defended as heavily as any other." The men gave their own names to the anonymous crags and ravines riddled with caves: Death Valley, China Bowl, Five Sisters, Wild Cat Bowl, Five Brothers, Baldy Ridge, the Horseshoe, and the Knobs. All sense of "time and duration" deserted him, Sledge remembered, as it deserted many others who were left to fight too long. One day, one firefight, one terror-filled night, seemed just like the next. But certain sounds and sights would always remain with him.

Each morning just before sunrise, when things were fairly quiet, I could hear a steady humming sound like bees in a hive as the [bluebottle flies] became active with the onset of daylight. They rose up off the corpses, rocks, refuse, brush and whatever else they had settled on for the night like a swarm of bees. Their numbers were incredible.

During [a] lull the men stripped the packs and pockets of the enemy dead for souvenirs. This was a gruesome business, but Marines executed it in a most methodical manner. . . . The men gloated over, compared, and often swapped their prizes. It was a brutal, ghastly ritual the likes of which have occurred since ancient times on battlefields where the antagonists have possessed a profound mutual hatred. It was uncivilized, as is all war, and was carried out with . . . savagery. It wasn't simply souvenir hunting or looting the enemy dead; it was more like Indian warriors taking scalps.

·　　·　　·

While I was removing a bayonet and scabbard from a dead Japanese, I noticed a Marine . . . dragging what I assumed to be a corpse. But the Japanese wasn't dead. He had been wounded severely in the back and couldn't move his arms. . . .

The Japanese's mouth glowed with huge gold-crowned teeth and his captor wanted them. He put the point of his kabar [knife] on the base of a tooth and hit the handle with the palm of his hand. Because the Japanese was kicking his feet and thrashing about, the knife point glanced off the tooth and sank deeply into the victim's mouth. The Marine cursed him and with a slash cut his cheeks open ear to ear. [He put his foot on the sufferer's lower jaw and tried again. Blood poured out of the soldier's mouth.] I shouted, "Put the man out of his misery." All I got for an answer was a cussing out. Another Marine ran up and put a bullet in the enemy soldier's brain and ended his agony. The scavenger grumbled and continued extracting his prizes undisturbed. . . .

·　　·　　·

A survivor of the fight for Peleliu: "Boy! That was terrible," one marine veteran said after leaving the island. "I ain't never seen nothing like it"—and he had seen some of the worst fighting on the western front in World War I. "I'm ready to go back to the States. I've had enough after that."

At first glance, the dead [enemy machine] gunner appeared about to fire his deadly weapon. He still sat bolt upright in the proper firing position. . . . Even in death his eyes stared widely along the gun sights. . . . The crown of the gunner's skull had been blasted off. . . .

As [a rifleman and I talked], I noticed a fellow mortarman sitting next to me. He held a handful of coral pebbles in his left hand. With his right hand, he idly tossed them into the open skull of [the dead] Japanese machine gunner. Each time his pitch was true, I heard a little splash of rainwater in the ghastly receptacle. My buddy tossed the coral chunks as casually as a boy casting pebbles into a puddle on some muddy road back home; there was nothing malicious in his action. The war had so brutalized us that it was beyond belief.

·　　·　　·

There were certain areas we moved into and out of several times as the campaign dragged along its weary, bloody course. [In many such areas] I became quite familiar with the sight of some particular enemy corpse, as if it were a landmark. It was gruesome to see the stages of decay proceed from just killed to bloated, to maggot-infested rotting, to partially exposed bones—like some biological clock marking the inexorable passage of time. On each occasion my company passed such a landmark, we were fewer in number.

Sledge and the rest of what was left of the 1st Marine Division would finally be taken off the island after six weeks of combat, replaced by the U.S. Army's 81st Infantry Division. By then, Japanese resistance was largely confined to an area measuring less than four hundred by five hundred yards, but it would nevertheless take another month of fighting before the Japanese commander finally radioed his superiors that "all is over on Peleliu" and killed himself; a handful of Japanese would go on fighting on the island until April of 1945.

Some ten thousand enemy soldiers died defending Peleliu. More than twelve hundred Americans died taking it from them, including twenty-year-old Private First Class John D. New, who had grown up in Mobile just across town from Eugene Sledge, and who had hurled himself onto a Japanese grenade, saving the lives of two friends but losing his own, a selfless act for which he was awarded a posthumous Medal of Honor. An additional 5,274 Americans were maimed or missing. Out of the 235 men in Sledge's company, only 85 left the island without physical wounds.

And in the end, there had been no tactical need for the island for which so many of Sledge's friends had died. He wrote:

> As I struggled upward (onto the troopship) with my load of equipment, I felt like a weary insect climbing a vine.
>
> I stowed my gear on my rack and went topside. The salt air was delicious to breathe. What a luxury to inhale long deep breaths of fresh clean air, air that wasn't heavy with the fetid stench of death. . . . But something in me died at Peleliu. Perhaps it was a childish innocence that accepted as faith the claim that man is basically good. Possibly I lost faith that politicians in high places who do not have to endure war's savagery will ever stop blundering and sending others to endure it.

ON SUNDAY MORNING, SEPTEMBER 17—two days after Eugene Sledge and the 1st Marines hit the beach at Peleliu—1,481 C-47 transports and 478 gliders began taking off from twenty-four British airfields in two great streams, escorted by more than 1,200 fighters. Operation Market Garden had begun. Twenty thousand paratroopers were on their way toward Holland. The largest airborne operation in history had been organized in just seven days—and it showed.

Three airborne divisions were taking part. The most experienced paratroopers—the American veterans of the 82nd and 101st Airborne—had been assigned what would likely be the most easily gained objective: taking and holding the bridges in or

near Eindhoven and Nijmegen along the sixty-mile road that led from the Belgian border to Arnhem. The least experienced, the British 1st Airborne, had been given the most difficult task: capturing the farthest target, the highway bridge over the lower Rhine at Arnhem, then holding it for four days until the twenty thousand vehicles of the armored British XXX Corps could drive up the road to relieve it and then rush on into Germany. To further complicate things for the British, plans to drop them as close as possible to their objective had been canceled by the air-transport commander, who declared the danger from flak too great and the terrain too soggy for gliders or the vehicles they carried. The paratroopers would now have to land some seven miles west of Arnhem instead and then fight their way into town. And because there were too few planes and gliders available to ferry everyone to Holland in a single drop and the air command refused to try two drops in a single day for fear of exhausting pilots and risking aircraft, the full complement of men and supplies would not be on the ground anywhere for at least three days. The Germans might be surprised by the first flight, but they would surely be waiting for the second and third, while the British at Arnhem would be forced simultaneously to defend their drop zone on the north side of the Rhine and take and hold the all-important bridge. To make things still worse, Allied code breakers had discovered that two SS panzer divisions were camped for rest and refitting in and around Arnhem. Dutch Resistance fighters confirmed the fact; so did aerial reconnaissance photographs. The Allied commanders in charge, still convinced that the German army was in disarray, dismissed all the

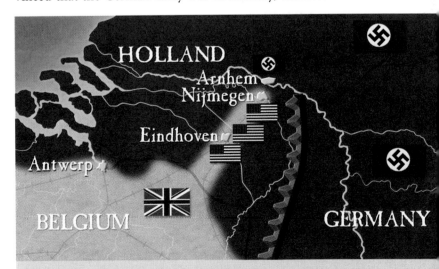

Operation Market Garden, General Bernard Montgomery's daring plan to shorten the war by driving through occupied Holland, demanded close, continuing coordination between the American and British paratroopers who were to seize and hold bridges at Eindhoven, Nijmegen, and Arnhem and the British armor that was expected to race up the road that connected them—and on into Germany.

Market Garden gets under way: Below at a British airbase, a jeep backs into a Waco glider for the flight to Holland; and, above, men of the 82nd Airborne float down near the Groesbeek ridge, not far from the Dutch border with Germany.

evidence. When Eisenhower suggested to Montgomery that the plan be changed to allow one of the two American airborne divisions to be dropped at Arnhem to strengthen the British hand just in case, Montgomery declined the offer. They wouldn't be needed.

For the Americans, things went reasonably well, at least at first. The 101st Airborne took four bridges near Eindhoven by nightfall, and when the Germans blew up a fifth, the Americans began rebuilding it right away. The 82nd had a tougher time, but it managed to capture two more bridges, occupy the Groesbeek ridge that overlooked the Nijmegen area, and send a patrol into town to probe the defenses of the main highway crossing over the Waal River.

But for the British at Arnhem, everything went wrong from the beginning. The towropes on more than thirty gliders broke, destroying the fleet of armored jeeps meant to speed men to the bridge before the stunned enemy could react. Three battalions had to set out on foot instead and lost four precious hours. Crowds of jubilant Dutch citizens, offering apples, pears, and kisses to their liberators, further slowed the advance. The Germans, who were now armed with a copy of the Market Garden plan, inexplicably carried into battle by an Allied officer in whose wrecked glider it was found, reacted with remarkable efficiency and speed. Makeshift units harassed the advancing Britons until panzer troops could move to block them. Only one British battalion—some six hundred men with a single antitank gun—made it to the bridge. It captured the northern end, tried twice without success to seize the southern end as well, and then took up defensive positions in nearby buildings and waited for the reinforcements its men were sure must be on the way.

"Actually, except for the Rhine bridge at Arnhem, the bridges were not so difficult," Captain Dwain Luce of Mobile remembered. "We were so far back we surprised them, you might say. And there were not yet heavy concentrations of troops in those areas. Oh, we had a fight. And they moved people in in a hurry. But we took those bridges." Luce's 320th Glider Field Artillery Battalion would join the fight around Nijmegen on its second day. So many pilots from his unit had been killed on D-day, in June, that there weren't enough trained pilots to go around for this operation. "I was senior man. I'd never flown a plane, so naturally I rode copilot," Luce remembered with a grin.

We got over the North Sea, and that pilot had a parachute on, and we didn't carry parachutes because we needed the weight for other things. I told him, "Look, you might as well take that parachute off, because you're not leaving here without me." And I said, "Now, if you get your ass shot, who's going to land this thing?" He says, "You are."

I said, "Well, give me the controls. Let me see if I can learn how to fly in the little time we've got." So he flipped the controls over to me, and after I started flying, man, I was up and down and in and around. I had an old Polish sergeant in the back of the glider, and he ran up, I remember, and he said, "Captain Luce, I didn't get sick until you started driving."

Anyway, we got in and the air force had cleaned out a route for us to go in where they had shot up the antiaircraft guns. Because we were sitting ducks. We went slow, you know. But we didn't have all these navigation instruments in those days, and our flight got off-line. And we went over an antiaircraft outfit, and if you want excitement, get in a glider behind a plane when that towplane starts taking evasive action. You're back there like the tail of a kite and it's rather exciting, and they were knocking us around pretty bad. And that towplane called back—we had a telephone wire between us, and it was my job to cut the thing loose when we landed—and the pilot of the plane says, "Cut loose. Cut loose." I said, "This isn't the right place." I knew from studying my maps that we

were not where we were supposed to be. And he said, "I don't care if it's the right place or not. You cut loose or I'm going to cut you loose." I said, "Okay, big boy, go get a warm shower in London." I hit the release button and we went down, and we went through a few things we weren't supposed to go through. It was a crash, not a bad crash, but we crashed.

Luce's glider and several others in his formation came down some five miles southeast of Nijmegen, dangerously close to the German border and within several hundred yards of the enemy antiaircraft battery that had been firing at them. German soldiers rushed toward them. "They came to get me and the people around me," Luce remembered, "but I didn't see it that way." There was a brief firefight. The Germans backed off. "They didn't want us as much as we didn't want to go with them."

Luce and his men had to figure out where they were and then try to make their way to their rendezvous point near the Grosbeek ridge.

I had never been to Holland before, and there were no street signs to tell us where we were. But Holland is flat, and you could see a long, long way. I saw a few buildings, and a church steeple a ways off, and I thought I knew where that was on the map I had. My pilot and the pilot of the other plane did not agree with me, but I told them, "Look, dammit, either you keep your mouth shut and go with me or go in your own direction. You have thirty seconds to make up your mind."

The pilots stuck with Luce. He left a sergeant in charge of twenty-two men who had survived from his glider and several others that had come down off target, and crept toward the nearest sign of human habitation, a farmhouse with an attached barn. He slipped into the barn, found no one, then moved toward the door that led into the house. He heard nothing but sensed that someone was on the other side of the door and thought of pushing it open and tossing in a grenade, just in case. Something made him simply raise his rifle instead. The door swung open. A Dutch woman was standing there, holding out a glass of fresh milk. They had trouble communicating at first. He kept asking her and her family if they were Dutch. They thought he was saying "Deutsch"—German—and indignantly shook their heads. They eventually got things straight, looked at Luce's map, and confirmed his position.

At least he now knew where he was. The next thing was to find his unit. Luce returned to his men, ordered them to gather up whatever they could carry from the wrecked gliders, and set out toward the northwest. The most direct route seemed to lie across open fields, but he did not want to risk being seen and so led his

party into the dense forest, instead. Darkness fell. They kept going until they stumbled onto a road with a stone road sign. Luce didn't dare so much as light a match to read it by for fear of drawing enemy fire, but he set up a position nearby for his men to rest and stood guard until dawn allowed him to get a better fix on where they were. What he found was not reassuring: somehow they had wandered into Germany, and as they made their cautious way toward the American lines they had to leave the road and hide several times so as not to be seen by the enemy troops being trucked back and forth along the front. By day's end, Luce and his men had managed to link up with their outfit. For leading them to safety, he would be awarded the Bronze Star.

Everyone was now waiting for the armored British XXX Corps to come up the corridor, but so far it was nowhere to be seen. German shelling and the traffic jams the damage caused on the narrow road forced the endless column to stop and start, over and over again. By the time its lead tanks reached Eindhoven, late on the eighteenth, the corps was already more than a day behind schedule. The British had to wait there overnight while engineers strengthened the rebuilt bridge the enemy had blown, so that tanks could roll across it. It took two more days—until the evening of the twentieth—for the 82nd Airborne to seize the Waal River crossing at Nijmegen with help from British armor.

The Americans, who had suffered heavy losses, assumed the column would now rush onward. Arnhem was only nine miles away, after all, and the situation there was desperate. British attacks intended to relieve the dwindling force struggling to hold the northern end of the bridge had all failed. Fog, mist, and rain prevented help from the air. The weather cleared briefly on the twentieth, but only half of the aircraft that left England managed

The British Guards armored column (left) made painfully slow progress up the highway to Arnhem, where British paratroopers (below) were already dying.

to reach their target. Most supplies fell into enemy hands. Polish paratroopers, dropped on the opposite side of the Rhine, were shot from the sky by the Germans waiting below. The ferry that was to have carried the survivors across the river was sunk. That evening, the men at the bridge in Arnhem were forced to surrender. By then, the rest of the airborne troops, who had tried repeatedly to rescue them at the bridge, were in need of rescue themselves: trapped on the northern bank of the river west of town, running low on ammunition, without heavy weapons, and under constant shelling from three sides.

Despite the situation at Arnhem, the British armored column at Nijmegen did not move north that night. The arrow-straight road ahead was built high above the flat farmland on either side. Tanks passing along it would be silhouetted against the sky like targets at a shooting gallery. Before they risked it, their commanders wanted to wait until British infantry coming along behind could catch up with them. They would not resume their advance until nearly noon of the following day.

AT AROUND NINE-THIRTY on the morning of September 21, 1944, Sascha Weinzheimer, her mother, and a family friend were in the family shanty at Santo Tomas when Mrs. Weinzheimer heard a distant unfamiliar hum.

"That's a different sound," she said. "Can't you hear it?"

"Oh, I suppose it's just the Nips," her friend answered. "Nothing excites me anymore. Not until they come in the front gate."

Mrs. Weinzheimer stepped outside. The sky was blue and cloudless. Just moments earlier, seven Japanese fighters had been lazily practicing maneuvers overhead. Now they were gone. The sound was loud and growing louder. "Look! Look!" she shouted. "There are hundreds of them!" Sascha ran outside. The sky was filled with planes roaring in from the northeast and northwest, swooping low and racing up and away again: American dive-bombers. Parts of the city beyond the walls—airfields, barracks, docks, warehouses—rocked with explosions. There had been air-raid drills over the past few weeks, and internees had been encouraged to dig trenches in which to huddle in case of Allied air attack. But this was the real thing.

" 'Planes! Planes! Planes!' Everyone was screaming and pointing up at the sky," Sascha wrote. "Oh what a sight! We thought we were dreaming." The air-raid siren sounded. Antiaircraft guns began firing. Shrapnel rattled down all over the compound, breaking windows, slicing through the roofs of the internees' shanties. Mrs. Weinzheimer shoved Sascha and her brother and sister under a mattress for protection, but Sascha climbed out again to get a better view. "Everyone seemed to feel that OUR

boys and OUR bombs couldn't hurt us. This went on for two hours. . . . No one seemed to realize any danger. They were just so happy."

To celebrate the internees' first glimpse of American forces since the fall of Bataan, Sascha's mother opened one of the four tins of meat she had managed to hoard for her family and served it for supper that evening. As they ate their meal and the children took turns licking the fat from the empty tin, the western sky glowed red from fires U.S. bombs had set off along the waterfront. The next morning, the wake-up song played over the camp PA system was "Pennies from Heaven." Shortly after breakfast, waves of American planes returned to bomb targets in Manila for a second time, driving all the internees to take shelter inside the big towered main university building. Watching one anxious Japanese sentry rush past with a sprig of leaves tied to his helmet to camouflage it from the air, one woman laughed out loud. "Only God can make a tree," she said.

The planes would not return again for almost a month. Rumors of landings flew. "Daddy said as long as there were only fighter planes so far they must come from airplane carriers at sea, and until we saw the big babies up there they hadn't landed yet on any island," Sascha wrote.

We always wondered how the Nips would treat us when we started bombing THEM, whether they would be more generous and give us more chow so that we would do the same for them later—or be so mad that they would be meaner and take more away from us. Now we know! Cut in rice again!! Less vegetables coming in camp!! Can't do this and can't do that!!

Internees were forbidden to look up during air raids; Lieutenant Abiko saw to it that those caught doing so were dragged out into the open, tied to poles, and made to stare at the glaring sun for hours at a time. He also insisted everyone in camp line up in two rows for roll call morning and evening—and sometimes in the middle of the night as well. No one was excused, no matter how young or frail. No one was allowed to sit. When roll call ended, everyone had to bow from the waist to express "gratitude" to their captors. When some proved reluctant, Abiko forced them to attend bowing "classes" under his supervision.

When the Japanese began bringing stores of fuel and ammunition into the camp in the hope that American bombs would not reach them there, the Internee Committee formally protested: using a civilian camp for military purposes was a violation of international law. The indignant commandant answered their letter with one of his own: "Your letter is an insult to Imperial army, it does not hide behind internee." But trucks

The Weinzheimer family shanty at Santo Tomas, painted by Madeleine Wooten, a teenaged fellow internee. The banana tree to its left "didn't last long," Sascha remembered, "as we gradually chopped it up to eat. My mom cooked it with curry powder. It filled us up but the stalks played havoc with our intestines."

tem. And then I'd go on. But the kids would cry, you know, they'd grab their throat, or they'd grab their belly, and go up to my mother and that probably was a very bad thing to see your kids do."

Some children, including Sascha, stopped going to school; it burned up too much energy. When her hunger pangs became too great, her mother gave her a piece of rock salt to suck or a garlic clove to chew. As food became still more scarce it also became of more obsessive interest, she remembered.

We'd lie down in bed in our shanty. I had a mattress on the floor. My mother and my father and my sister had one mattress, and my brother had another small mattress. And we'd lie there—we had to go to bed early because of blackouts— and talk about what we were going to have on our birthdays, what dinner we were going to have. If I said I was going to have pork chops and potatoes and ice cream and cake, my sister and brother said, "Oh, me too!" because they didn't know what potatoes and pork chops and ice cream and cake were, so they'd say, "Me too!" And then they'd ask, "What's a pork chop?" So then you knew you'd been there too long.

kept bringing potentially lethal cargo into the compound every night, and new orders were issued for internees to bow still lower, to treat their captors with still more "respect."

Rations were slashed again. Many women now weighed less than one hundred pounds. Camp doctors saw 100 to 150 fresh diet-related cases a week. People pulled weeds and ate them, boiled canna lily bulbs, chewed banana stalks, and made salad out of hibiscus leaves until the doctors warned they only worsened the chronic dysentery from which many internees already suffered. Some women used cold cream for cooking oil. Women—even the "nicer ones from Manila," Sascha's mother said—sometimes fought physically with one another over sweetpotato peelings from the camp kitchen. When internees told the camp's supply officer of their desperate need for protein, he urged them to eat the dogs and cats that wandered through the camp. Some did. One man—tall and thin, Sascha noted, with a disconcerting habit of constantly licking his lips—was known as "the cat eater" because of the number of pets he was believed to have devoured.

Children may have suffered most from the scarcity of food. "When I'd get bouts of really severe hunger—it comes over you like waves—I'd do something to distract myself," Sascha remembered, "like drumming on the side of the shanty, or making noise, or even screaming a little bit. Just to get it out of your sys-

ON SUNDAY MORNING, SEPTEMBER 24, a cold, blustery rain drummed steadily down onto the roof of "Duffy's Tavern," Quentin Aanenson's tent near Laon, as he wrote a letter to Jackie Greer back home. It had been raining off and on for days now, grounding the 336th Fighter Group and further complicating the Market Garden disaster that was still unfolding less than two hundred miles to the north.

Such miserable weather I have never seen! It's raining cats and dogs and the wind is doing its best to push our tent down. Johnny [Bathurst] and I are both wrapped around our little stove to keep from freezing to death. The only trouble is that we have to keep stuffing it with wood. I hate to think of what winter will be like.

Received four letters from you today along with one from Mom. It certainly is good to be getting mail from you all again—especially when the letters are so sweet. I still save all your letters so I have quite a stack now. If the war lasts a long time I'll have to start sending them home. . . .

We managed to locate four eggs this evening, so pretty soon now we'll be having a little lunch. Want your eggs "sunny-side-up"? I'll have mine boiled please. I hope you'll appreciate our invitation. We walked three miles in the rain to get these eggs.

Nijmegen and its bridge across the Waal, captured intact by American and British forces after a fierce three-day battle

The fate of a lot of American and British paratroopers is being decided up in Holland tonight. They've been going through hell now for a week, trying to hold until the British Second Army could reach them. If contact isn't made soon, there sure won't be many paratroopers left to save. May God help them!

Time to boil these eggs—then hit the sack.
Goodnight, my love—
Quentin

The American paratroopers about whom Aanenson expressed concern were still defending the road they now called Hell's Highway, but it was already too late for the British and Polish forces at Arnhem. By the previous evening, fewer than three thousand of them remained confined to an area less than a thousand yards wide and two thousand yards deep. German armor rolling south across the Arnhem bridge had helped prevent the XXX Corps from ever reaching them. A two-hour cease-fire had been arranged to allow the British to remove their wounded; some five hundred were carried out of basements and ruined homes and turned over to German medics. Then the shelling

had resumed. On Monday morning, Montgomery ordered what was left of the 1st Airborne Division to begin withdrawing across the Rhine as best it could.

Market Garden had failed. There would be no rush into the Ruhr Valley, no quick end to the war in Europe. Seventeen thousand Britons and Americans and Poles had been lost, more casualties than the Allies had suffered on all the landing beaches on D-day. August's swift victories in France had produced unseemly competition among British and American commanders; the September disaster in Holland now yielded recriminations. One British officer sought to blame the luckless Poles for the debacle. American paratroopers, who would now have to continue to safeguard the hard-won corridor for weeks without armored vehicles or heavy guns, blamed the British XXX Corps for setting a too stately pace up the corridor; much was made of the fact that its tankers could be seen stopping for tea each afternoon. "We were supposed to be there four days," Dwain Luce remembered, "and Montgomery was supposed to come up and relieve us after we took the bridges. But that damn Montgomery didn't get to us. We got our bridges, but we didn't get our Montgomery." (Some British survivors of the long siege at Arnhem felt the same way: "Have a nice drive up?" one asked the first tanker he saw.) For his part, an unrepentant Montgomery pronounced the battle of Arnhem "ninety percent successful" because the paratroopers had captured all but one of the bridges assigned to them. But the bridge that had really mattered was the last one, and the highway that had cost so much blood and effort finally led nowhere. "We were told in briefings that the war in Europe would end with the successful conclusion of Operation Market Garden," one American veteran of the campaign remembered, but "the Germans kicked our Allied asses good in less than a week."

Aachen, September 1944: "Every building was damaged or destroyed," correspondent William Walton wrote. "Not a window remained.... For the first time, the people of Germany were joining the long lines of Europe's refugees.... None of the politicians and generals and strutting youths were in that procession. It was only the very old, the very young and helpless, moving past their ruined homes through the blasted streets of Aachen in poverty and fear."

To the south, Allied commanders continued to conduct cautious probes of the German defenses. Without adequate supplies there was little else they could do. In early October, the Canadian I Corps was finally ordered to begin clearing the Scheldt estuary; it would take nearly two months and cost thirteen thousand casualties before the last German was killed or captured, the waters were cleared of mines, and supplies finally could begin streaming through Antwerp unimpeded.

Meanwhile, the U.S. First Army attacked the West Wall toward Aachen, the city where Charlemagne and thirty-two subsequent rulers of Germany had been crowned. A preinvasion bombardment by 432 planes, meant to blast a hole through the German defenses, nearly obliterated a Belgian village and failed to hit a single pillbox. The newly recruited middle-aged Germans who had been rushed to the West Wall to man its bunkers and pillboxes put up unexpectedly fierce resistance. "I don't care if the guy behind that gun is a syphilitic prick who's a hundred years old," one GI from the U.S. 3rd Armored Division said. "He's still sitting behind eight feet of concrete, and he's still got enough fin-

gers to press triggers and shoot bullets." It took nine bitter days of battle to encircle Aachen and another week of fighting through the rubble before the Allies could claim to have captured their first major German city. By then, there was almost nothing left of it. W. C. Heinz, a correspondent for the New York *Sun*, remembered how the ruins looked and smelled: "The fronts of the houses just fell out into the streets. It was the start of the autumn rains . . . so the hills of rubble, wet by the rain, smelled of plaster and charred wood and of the disintegrating bodies underneath."

At the same time, some eighty miles farther south, in Lorraine, the Third Army tried repeatedly to seize Metz and get through to the West Wall and the Saar Valley beyond it. But the ancient town—which had not been captured since the time of Attila the Hun—was shielded by thirty-five forts, including a formidable modern citadel, Fort Driant. Patton was still low on fuel and ammunition. The fort's massive walls resisted bombs, artillery, explosives. The steady rain turned the landscape to goo. "I hope that in the final settlement of the war . . . the Germans retain Lorraine," a frustrated Patton wrote to the secretary of war, "because I can imagine no greater burden than to be the owner of this nasty country where it rains every day and where the whole wealth of the people consists in assorted manure piles." On the night of October 12–13, he reluctantly withdrew his forces.

A few nights later, Quentin Aanenson wrote another letter to Jackie.

Sweetheart—
Received three not too recent letters from you today—#156, #159 and "?" dated September 30th. All three were sweet, just like you. . . .

I can hear the heavy bombers going over as I write this. That means some part of Germany is going to catch hell tonight, but it also means that some of those boys up above are going to die soon. . . .

My missions will be building up quite slowly from now on because of the winter weather. We're grounded a lot even now, and the worst is yet to come. I'll try to keep you up to date on the number of missions I do fly, though.

When Aanenson failed to do so, or the mail was unaccountably slow, Jackie worried. "It appears that no one is getting mail from their men overseas," she would write him later that month.

Makes me feel some better about the situation—misery loves company. The other morning Bubber [her mother] heard the young lady next door, screaming, crying, and saying she

wished she were dead. Today we found out what her trouble was—no mail. We'd already figured she'd gotten a telegram from the War Department. When I don't hear from you, or I get to feeling unusually lonely, I get off to myself and have my little cry. No one knows about it—much less the whole neighborhood. But the whole block will hear me when you walk in through the door!

ON THE WET, FOGGY MORNING OF OCTOBER 15, some 175 miles southeast of Aanenson's base at Laon, three U.S. infantry battalions began moving through an evergreen forest toward the little town of Bruyères, in the Vosges Mountains. From a distance the men looked just like any other GIs, weapons in hand, bent under the weight of their packs, eyes fixed intently on the woods ahead of them where Germans were thought to be waiting. But they were shorter than their fellow Americans—their average height was five foot three—their radio communications were sometimes conducted in a pidgin dialect neither the enemy nor some of their counterparts in other outfits could decipher, and many were from Hawaii and already shivering from the unaccustomed cold. The Japanese American 442nd Regimental Combat Team was going into action in a new theater of operations, attached to a new division under an untried commander.

The mid-August landing on the French Riviera by the U.S. Seventh and French First armies had gone spectacularly well; the German coastal defenses had so easily been breached that Bill Mauldin pronounced it "the best invasion I ever attended." And during the following two months, the Allies had opened up badly needed port facilities at Marseilles and Toulon, cleared the enemy from southern and southwestern France, taken nearly ninety thousand prisoners, and pushed the Germans back more than 360 miles toward their own border. But like the Allied armies in Normandy, they eventually outran their own supplies, wore out vehicles, and wore down men. Also like the Allied armies to the north, they'd been unable to trap and destroy all the Germans fleeing before them. By late September, the Allies had reached the foothills of the Vosges. Steep, wooded, and nearly trackless, the mountains barricaded the German border so successfully that no invader had ever made it through them. There, Hitler had ordered what was left of two German armies— the First and the Nineteenth—to stand and fight.

Three veteran American divisions—the 3rd, 45th, and 36th— were assigned the task of battering their way through them in an operation called Dogface. The 36th was known as a hard-luck division because it had twice been badly mauled in Italy, first during the landing at Salerno and again when it was torn nearly to pieces trying to cross the Rapido below Monte Cassino; by mid-October it had been under fire for two exhausting months. Its new commander, Major General John E. Dahlquist, was a big, anxious Minnesotan with a lot to prove—to himself and to his superiors. He had never commanded troops in combat before the August landings—he was best known in the army for reorganizing its postal system—and twice during the drive north from the beachhead, the corps commander, General Lucian K. Truscott, Jr., had come close to removing him for causing delays

and failing to drive his men hard enough. Dahlquist determined to act from then on in such a way that he could never be accused of anything like that again. In the early fighting in the Vosges, he would insist on action before anything else, and when his impulsiveness led him to make costly mistakes, he would call upon the veterans of the 442nd to rectify them.

In September, the nisei had been pulled from the ongoing battle in northern Italy and rushed to France, still wearing their summer uniforms, to bolster the 36th Division. Once considered a "problem" by the army, the 442nd was now seen as a problem solver, to be called in when others failed. Two of its battalions—the 100th and the 2nd—were trucked up from Marseilles to the front. Private Robert Kashiwagi of Sacramento and the 3rd Battalion arrived by train, aboard the kind of narrow-gauge boxcars

Burdened by heavy packs and rain-soaked coats, men of the 442nd Regimental Combat Team advance along a muddy forest track toward Bruyères in the Vosges Mountains, France, October 14, 1944.

World War I doughboys called forty-and-eights, because each could hold forty men or eight horses. The car in which Kashiwagi rode had no toilet, and the train made no scheduled stops, he remembered, so the men hacked holes in the corner of the car with their bayonets.

Sergeant Daniel Inouye of the 2nd Battalion remembered that his first look at the Vosges gave him an almost instant "sense of nightmare."

Gale winds had been driving the autumn rains into our faces, and when they died down, an eerie fog rolled across the broken land. . . . Ahead, curving toward the German border, lay a series of mountain towns—Bruyères, Belmont, Biffontaine, La Houssière—fiercely defended by the enemy from long-prepared positions, and with armor and artillery that was perfectly suited to that rocky, precipitous land.

The village of Bruyères and the four hills that overlooked it would be the 442nd's first target. A railway line ran through the

Chow time for the 442nd: The initial antagonism between nisei from Hawaii and the mainland had long since been smoothed over. "By now we have come to know our mainland 'kotonks' very well," one Hawaiian wrote home. "We have identified with them and they with us. We are united in a common cause."

town; so did a road that led through the mountains to Saint-Dié, Strasbourg, and eventually Germany itself. The Japanese Americans were to lead the assault with the weary men of the 143rd Regiment coming along behind. General Dahlquist assured the commander of the 442nd, Colonel Charles W. Pence, that the Germans had already abandoned the hills army maps denoted as A, B, C, and D. In fact, as reconnaissance patrols quickly discovered, the thickly wooded slopes were all heavily mined and still concealed hundreds of well-dug-in Germans with automatic weapons. When a company belonging to the 100th Battalion, edging its way toward Hill A, radioed back to headquarters that it was coming under intense mortar, artillery, and tank fire, Dahlquist refused to believe it. The nisei were "a bunch of damn liars," he bellowed over the field telephone; the hills could be taken easily—just get going. That exchange set a pattern that would continue for the next three weeks: the general insisting that his men keep moving forward while ignoring their on-the-spot warnings of what was likely to happen if they were made to do so. "The battle we were fighting was a different battle than Dahlquist was fighting," recalled Captain Young Oak Kim, the 100th Battalion's Korean American intelligence officer. "We came to the conclusion that we're in trouble—not because of the Germans but because we have a commander who doesn't believe what we're telling him."

The general wanted his men to advance ten kilometers by dark; German fire limited them to less than 150 yards. Most of the nisei were veterans of the fighting in Italy, but the Vosges presented fresh challenges. In the mountain warfare they'd mastered, the Germans had fought hard but then fallen back from one defensive line to the next. In these mountains, they would stay put and counterattack whenever they could. And they had perfected an artillery technique ideally suited to killing and maiming men in an evergreen forest: the tree burst, shells specially fused to explode in the treetops, showering the men below with dagger-sharp shards of wood as well as shrapnel. Private Susumu Satow of the 2nd Battalion remembered trying to convince a young replacement—an old friend from his Sacramento neighborhood named Chester Abe—that he needed to roof his slit trench with logs as protection. Abe just smiled and said, "When your time is up, your time is up." Moments later, a tree burst killed him.

The fighting went on for three days. Rain filled foxholes. Casualties mounted. Dahlquist hectored the men at the front by field telephone so harshly and so constantly that at one point Captain Kim pulled out the wire between headquarters and his position. The general then turned up at the front, issuing contradictory orders and exhorting the men to move forward. "General

Dahlquist was a very strict general," Satow recalled. "It seemed to me that he was trying to push the 442nd too hard, too far, telling us to 'Advance, advance,' you know. He was hard in that way. I really didn't have any respect for him."

By nightfall on the eighteenth, the 100th Battalion had taken Hill A, the 2nd Battalion had captured most of Hill B, and the 3rd Battalion had begun working its way from house to house in Bruyères itself. One German prisoner, baffled by the GIs who now held him at gunpoint, decided that they must be "head-hunters from the South Pacific accustomed to jungle fighting"; French villagers were baffled by them, too, and could agree only that they were tough and *"très, très, petits."*

When the town seemed safely in American hands, Dahlquist asked that the 3rd Battalion reenact the battle for the newsreels. Its commander protested that his men were too tired for such foolishness, so relatively fresh troops from the 2nd Battalion were hurried in to go through the motions of battle while the cameras ground. The enemy still held hills C and D, and it would take two more days before they could be driven off them.

Dahlquist then insisted that the 100th Battalion push farther into enemy territory and seize another heavily defended hill overlooking the village of Biffontaine. The men slipped through the German defenses and captured the ridge so swiftly that the battalion found itself cut off from the rest of the 442nd. Dahlquist then ordered them off the hill again with orders to take the village below it, even though it had no tactical importance. The Germans immediately occupied the hilltop the nisei had abandoned and then surrounded the town. The 100th beat back repeated assaults before elements of the 2nd and 3rd battalions could reach them and help secure the village.

On the evening of October 24, the 442nd was relieved by the 141st and the men were trucked to a newly organized rest area near Belmont. After nine days and nights of combat in cold rain, without a change of clothes or a real meal or a night's sleep, and having endured the loss of scores of friends, the filthy, exhausted men of the 442nd were glad it finally seemed to be over, at least for a few days. Clean uniforms, hot food, and hot showers were waiting for them.

ON OCTOBER 20, 1944—the day after Quentin Aanenson heard bombers heading for Germany, and five days after the men of the 442nd first went into combat in France and Eugene Sledge and his fellow marines were finally pulled from the line on Peleliu— U.S. Army forces began landing in the heart of the Philippines, at Tacloban on the island of Leyte. Four hours later, Douglas MacArthur himself boarded a landing barge and started in

toward the beach. He wore a crisply starched uniform and the sunglasses and soft cap that had become his trademark, and he was eager to step ashore and redeem the pledge of liberation he'd made more than thirty months earlier. Then, fifty yards out, the barge ran aground. Landing craft were still burning around them, bullets snapped overhead, and when the harried harbor-master heard about the general's potential embarrassment, he was unmoved. "Let 'em walk!" he said. Muttering under his breath while photographers clicked, MacArthur and his companions, including Sergio Osmeña, the new president of the Philippines, stepped knee-deep into the surf and grimly waded ashore. MacArthur feared that his return to the Philippines had been insufficiently dignified, until he learned what a dramatic impression photographs of his landing made in newspapers around the world.

He wandered up and down the sand for a time, ignoring intermittent fire from snipers concealed in the tops of palm trees. An aide heard him murmur, "This is what I dreamed about." The signal corps set up a mobile-radio hookup for him on the beach. "People of the Philippines, I have returned!" he said. "The hour of your redemption is here. . . . Rally to me. Let the indomitable spirit of Bataan and Corregidor lead on. . . . Let

Return to the Philippines, October 20, 1944: General MacArthur splashes ashore at Leyte in what he would describe as "a full moment for me"; Philippine president Sergio Osmeña wades at his left.

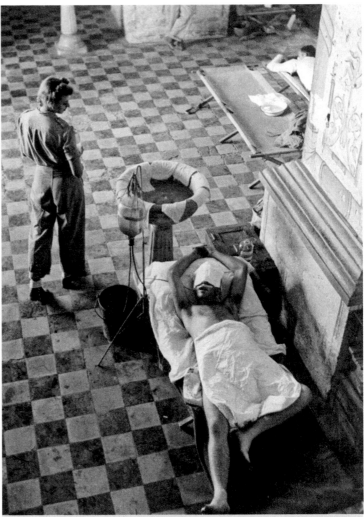

Struggle for Leyte: Within hours of the landing, coastguardsmen (opposite), balanced precariously on an improvised sandbag jetty unload supplies from one of more than twenty LSTs moored off the beach near Tacloban. A few days later, an army nurse (above) keeps an eye on one of her wounded American charges in a church that has been turned into a makeshift hospital.

every arm be steeled. The guidance of Divine God points the way. Follow in His name to the Holy Grail of righteous victory."

Filipinos did rally to MacArthur, strewing his path with flowers, rushing up to embrace him and shake his hand. But months of hard fighting lay ahead. And within a few days, in the waters off Leyte, the Japanese navy would make one more effort to win a "general decisive battle" that would reverse their fortunes in the Pacific. Three strike forces were sent to attack the U.S. Third and Seventh fleets and cut off the American beachhead. The three-day contest was the biggest naval battle in history and the worst Japanese defeat of the war. Four enemy carriers went to the bottom; so did three battleships, six heavy cruisers, four light cruisers, and eleven destroyers. As Halsey radioed to Nimitz, the

As these images make clear, the American naval victory in the Battle of Leyte Gulf came at a high cost. The crew of the light cruiser USS *Birmingham* (left) struggles to put out fires aboard the fast carrier USS *Princeton*, hit by a 550-pound Japanese bomb. It crashed through her flight deck and exploded among six torpedo planes on the hangar deck below, setting off their deadly cargo. The wreckage of one of the destroyed planes can be glimpsed through the smoke in the photograph below. No amount of water could douse the fires, and when they reached the magazine the resulting explosion killed or wounded nearly every member of the crew left aboard—and destroyed the *Birmingham*, as well. Three hundred and thirty seven men died. The nine American officers and enlisted men whose shrouded bodies are about to be tipped into the sea for burial (above) were killed by a kamikaze that hit the carrier *Intrepid*.

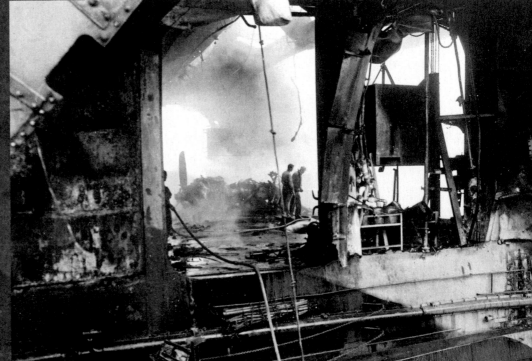

Battle of Leyte Gulf had "beaten and routed and broken" the once proud enemy fleet; Winston Churchill called it "a brilliant and massive victory."

But despite their defeat, the Japanese had managed to land more men on the west coast of Leyte; it would be two more months before the Americans could move on to Mindoro, the next big island in the Philippine chain—and still longer before they could land on Luzon and liberate Manila. And during the contest at sea, American sailors had witnessed new and troubling evidence of Japan's resolve to keep fighting, no matter the odds: twenty-four volunteer enemy pilots had been willing deliberately to crash their planes into the decks of carriers in hopes of setting them ablaze. They were called *kamikazes*—Japanese for "divine wind."

The internees at Santo Tomas did not see the photographs of MacArthur striding ashore, nor did their increasingly anxious captors tell them about the landing. But the news came the following morning anyway, when the announcer at wake-up call ended his daily greeting with "You know, folks, it's better Leyte than never." "How happy we all were," Sascha Weinzheimer wrote. "Everyone was sure there would be landings all over the islands right away." Her father continued to caution patience. "The slower they do it," he said, "the better it is done, and not so many of our boys and Filipinos will be killed."

Glenn Frazier, still a prisoner of war near Osaka, Japan, knew very little of these developments. He sometimes heard the dim rumble of what he believed to be big American bombers flying too high to be seen, on their way to targets elsewhere in the Japanese home islands, and as he and his fellow prisoners were marched past newsstands on their way to and from their waterfront work details they cast an occasional surreptitious glance at the front pages of the Japanese papers on display. They couldn't read the headlines, Frazier remembered, but "once in a while we would see a map where it showed the navy battles were coming closer. And that was encouraging for us. But it was still a question as to how we were going to get out of there. Because we had no idea of any way to get out except an invasion of Japan. And if we had an invasion of Japan, we knew we were dead."

IN WESTERN EUROPE, the enforced stalemate that followed Market Garden, the struggle for Aachen, and the failure at Metz did not mean that fliers like Quentin Aanenson were idle. Since D-day the men of the 366th Fighter Group had flown so many missions amid such constant tension that they sometimes had to be lifted from the cockpit when they got back to the base, and the flight surgeon thought it best to have himself or one of his assistants drive from plane to plane, jump up onto the wing, and pour each pilot a restorative shot of whiskey. Whenever the bad weather cleared even slightly, the men were expected to find and try to destroy enemy targets despite the thickening flak that made such missions more rather than less perilous as the days dragged by. "As the Germans retreated," Aanenson explained, "they were able to take all of their flak guns and most of their artillery with them. So we were facing a larger number of flak guns for the amount of space than we had been dealing with before. It was a terribly brutal time for us."

It was also frustrating. A member of Aanenson's outfit, returning from a three-day leave, asked another pilot what had been happening while he was away. "Oh, the same old crap," his friend answered. "We bombed a railroad track, shot up a train, and probably scared some Germans, but nothing worthwhile."

Meanwhile, American pilots continued to be killed. After missions during which men died or came close to dying, some fliers drank too much, Aanenson remembered. Some couldn't stop talking; others wouldn't talk at all. And a few collapsed. Shortly after taking off, one pilot was heard radioing for help: "Foxhunt leader, this is Foxhunt Red 4. My eyes are crossed, and I can't uncross them." The strain of trying not to miss seeing anything while flying in formation—checking instruments, keeping the proper space between his plane and the others, scanning the ground for antiaircraft guns, watching out for fighters attacking from above or below or from either side—had evidently caused the muscles in one of his eyes to cramp, doubling his vision. The squadron leader ordered him back to base, where, by closing one eye, he managed to get safely down. His vision soon returned to normal, but his nerves had been shattered. A few days later he failed to dive on a target, and that evening, while visiting Duffy's Tavern, he suffered what Aanenson remembered as "an emotional breakdown": he pulled a .45 and threatened to kill his friends. A fellow pilot felled him with a plank, and he was sent home to the States in a straitjacket.

Later, two of Aanenson's closest friends were killed in front of him within seconds of each other. One of the three original occupants of Duffy's Tavern, Second Lieutenant Ray Beebe, was shot out of the sky as he started to dive on a target. First Lieutenant Richard Curtis parachuted safely to the ground after his plane was hit, only to be shot there by the Germans. First Lieutenant Richard "Red" Alderman, an old friend with whom Aanenson had gone through training, moved into Duffy's Tavern. So did another young flier, who was killed so soon thereafter that Aanenson never learned his name. He, in turn, was replaced by First Lieutenant Gus Girlinghouse.

Airmen work to remove an unconscious pilot from a P-47 Thunderbolt that has survived a spectacularly awkward landing on a makeshift airstrip in France.

One evening Aanenson, now a first lieutenant, and Johnny Bathurst were sitting in the officers' club unwinding after an especially difficult mission. As they relived the day's litany of close calls, Bathurst pulled a Saint Christopher medal from his pocket and tied it to the zipper tab on Aanenson's flight jacket. It would help keep him safe, Bathurst promised. Ever since D-day, Aanenson had faithfully performed his own good-luck ritual each time he swung into the cockpit, whistling the "Army Air Corps Song" and kissing the ring Jackie Greer had given him. Now he would remember to touch his friend's medal as well.

On the evening of October 26, Robert Kashiwagi was standing in a long line outside a tent set up to house a field shower at the Belmont rest center. He and his friends from the 3rd Battalion of the 442nd were about to enjoy their first hot shower since landing in France. A German shell arced into the clearing and hit the tent. Two men were killed, and several more were wounded. There would be no showers. Kashiwagi was "disgusted," he remembered, but found a muddy rainwater pool so that he could at least wash his feet and replace his socks with the dry ones he always carried inside his helmet to prevent trench foot.

More bad news followed. Dahlquist had canceled the 442nd's rest period. While they had been mopping up at Bruyères, he had rushed the 1st Battalion of his 141st Regiment farther into the mountains along a wooded ridge that overlooked the village of La Houssière and the road to Saint-Dié. Again veteran officers had warned him that the woods were full of Germans. Again he had insisted that the enemy had moved on and exhorted his men to pick up speed. The 275 men of B Company led the way, moving so far so fast that they lost contact with the rest of the battalion. The Germans attacked them from both sides, trapped them on top of a hill, and set up roadblocks augmented with automatic weapons to block the forest track behind them. The Americans dug in as best they could and radioed for help. For two days, the 2nd and 3rd battalions of the 141st had tried to break through to them without success.

Dahlquist's career had once nearly been ruined by being too hesitant; now it was threatened again, this time by his heedlessness. To rescue the trapped men who came to be called the Lost Battalion—and to restore his own reputation—he ordered the 442nd to return to the wooded slopes right away.

"We went back into battle with a mean frame of mind," Robert Kashiwagi recalled. To him and the other weary Japanese Americans it seemed an unfair assignment: they'd done everything Dahlquist had asked of them at Bruyères and Biffontaine and suffered heavy losses caused, at least in part, by the general's own interference and impulsiveness. And when they subsequently learned why they were being ordered to return to the front, they were doubly angered: Dahlquist had created this mess, too, so why couldn't his own men sort it out?

The 442nd reentered the forest before dawn on the twenty-seventh, moving toward the men trapped some five miles to the east. A French partisan led the way, but it was so dark, Kashiwagi remembered, that each man in his Company K had to hold on to the straps of the backpack worn by the man ahead of him. When one man stumbled, the whole company staggered to a stop. The three battalions moved along abreast at first, with the 2nd on the left, the 100th on the right, and Kashiwagi's 3rd in the center. Germans seemed to be hidden everywhere along the forest trails and to be firing down on them from every ridge and summit. Fog prevented air support. Tanks couldn't maneuver on the narrow forest tracks. If the Lost Battalion was to be rescued, the infantrymen of the 442nd would have to do the job.

They covered two miles the first day. Here and there, they passed "Americans dead in their foxholes," one man from the 2nd Battalion remembered, soldiers from the 141st who had been killed trying to break through to their comrades. "They were all over the place," he said. "They couldn't do it, so we had to go in." Another nisei, from California, was unimpressed by the rescue effort made by the 141st. "We found one bunch of them hiding in a cave," he remembered. "And there was one guy in there from Salinas. He said, 'Hey, you can't do what that guy wants you to do. They'll butcher you.' I said we knew that already."

On the second day, while the 2nd Battalion veered northward to drive the Germans off a hill that commanded the valley through which the rest of the 442nd was moving, the rest of the men endured the worst artillery barrage they had yet encountered—and managed to eke out another mile in spite of it. General Dahlquist, disappointed at what he saw as their slow pace,

radioed the 442nd's commander to "get the men out there crawling, and get the Krauts out of their holes."

Convinced that there was a feeling of "failing futility" among the troops, he was back at the front the next morning, October 29, when the 442nd began fighting the most celebrated battle in its history. It began when the 3rd and 100th battalions fought their way through another artillery barrage and broke through a mined roadblock at a place the men called the Crossroads. Dahlquist raced from place to place during the fighting, exhorting the men to keep attacking. He kicked one GI out of his foxhole. "Hey, you," he told another, "you're going to die anyway. Charge that machine gun." He gave an artillery unit a set of coordinates that would have sent shells into the midst of the Lost Battalion itself had the officer in charge not tactfully altered them before firing. Lieutenant Colonel Alfred Pursall, the big, bluff commander of the 3rd Battalion, challenged him directly: when Dahlquist urged him to have his men fix bayonets and charge into the enemy guns, Pursall refused. Those were *his* boys, he said, and only he would decide whether or not ever to give such an order.

Early that afternoon, the spearhead of the rescue mission, three companies from the 3rd Battalion—I, B, and Robert Kashiwagi's K—found themselves fighting their way up a narrow forested ridge with steep drop-offs on either side. Just over a mile away, the surviving men of the Lost Battalion were huddled in their foxholes. To reach them, the nisei would have to make it past seven hundred Germans. Tank and mortar and machine-gun emplacements were hidden among the trees. A flanking attack failed. Dahlquist ordered an all-out frontal assault.

A tank led the way, struggling up the slope while firing into the trees. The Germans responded with a wall of fire. "I had never seen men cut down so fast, so furiously," one survivor recalled. Some were reluctant to leave the limited shelter that simply lying flat afforded them. "We were stuck because the terrain was steep," Robert Kashiwagi remembered, "and so we were on our own like a cowboy-and-Indian type of battle." One soldier never forgot listening to a wounded friend calling out in Japanese, "Mama, it hurts, it hurts."

At about that time, Pursall lumbered to his feet, waved his .45, and shouted, "Okay, boys, let's go!" All across the ridge, the men rose and began charging up the hillside, cursing, firing from the waist, hurling grenades. "We just decided we were just going to

Nisei soldiers struggle up a forested hillside. "Orientation by compass is vital throughout the Vosges," an intelligence report warned, "where paths winding through wooded areas cause even people who know the sector to lose their way."

Wearing newly issued winter coats, survivors from the 442nd on parade before the general whose folly had shattered their ranks, November 12, 1944.

rush them," Kashiwagi recalled, "and shoot at anything that moved and make as much noise as we can. We just went hog-wild crazy, and we were mad at everybody, and we were ready to kill anything that there was." Private Barney Hajiro knocked out two machine-gun nests and killed two snipers all by himself. By nightfall, the 442nd was just over a thousand yards from the Lost Battalion.

The following day—the sixth since the men of the 141st had been surrounded and the fourth that the 442nd had spent fighting its way toward them—a scout from I Company, PFC Matsuji "Mutt" Sakumoto, spotted a Caucasian GI among the trees ahead of him. The GI shouted with joy. More men from the Lost Battalion came out of the woods behind him. "You guys need a smoke?" Sakumoto asked. The GIs were clapping one another on the back. "I'm glad to see you Japs," one of the rescued men said

to Kashiwagi when he came up. The nisei wasn't offended: "I know he didn't mean it. It just came out that way."

Just 230 men of the Lost Battalion survived their time on the hillside. The 442nd had lost some 400 trying to get to them. I Company had started into the forest with 185 men; just eight walked out unhurt. K Company had begun with 186; only 17 emerged on foot. "But even then General Dahlquist wasn't through," Kashiwagi remembered. "He wanted us to keep on pushing to Germany, to keep pushing the Germans back." The following day, Kashiwagi's squad was again in the lead when they made contact with the enemy. A mortar shell hit his right hand. "I knew it was a mortar because I saw the fin that opened up my fingers," he remembered, "and I told my buddies, 'You know, I have to go back and get this sewed up, because I'm going to bleed a little bit.' And so I started to walk back to the battalion aid station." An artillery shell burst above him, sending a shard of shrapnel into his left foot. He hopped toward the nearest foxhole and asked another GI to cut off his boot and see "if my foot was

A squad leader from the 2nd Battalion of the 442nd. By the time this photograph was taken in early December, the 442nd had been awarded five Presidential Unit Citations in less than a month, an achievement unmatched by any other army unit of its size during the war.

ber 12 when General Dahlquist told Lieutenant Colonel Virgil R. Miller, now commander of the 442nd, to have the whole regiment assemble for his formal review. When Dahlquist saw how thin the ranks were, he was indignant. He'd asked that *all* the men be present, he said to Miller. Where were the rest of them? "That's all that's left," Miller said. Until that moment, Dahlquist had evidently not understood the scale of the sacrifice he had demanded of the 442nd. In less than a month, 1,940 men—well over half the regiment—had been lost. The next day, the general ordered everyone who was left in the 2nd and 3rd battalions back into the line for four more days before finally permitting them to rest.

The 442nd would spend the next four months in the south of France, patrolling the mostly quiet border with Italy, replenishing its ranks with Japanese American replacements, and awaiting new orders.

The bitterness the survivors felt toward General Dahlquist continued to smolder. Years later, at a review at Fort Bragg in North Carolina, Dahlquist—who had been promoted to four-star general and eventually became commander in chief of the Continental Army Command—again encountered Lieutenant Colonel Gordon Singles, who had commanded the 100th Battalion in the Vosges. He offered his hand. "Let bygones be bygones," Dahlquist said. "It's all water under the bridge, isn't it?" The colonel saluted—but he would not shake the general's hand.

While the 442nd was still fighting in the Vosges, twenty-year-old Paul Fussell, a newly minted second lieutenant in the 410th Infantry Regiment of the 103rd Infantry Division, had been bivouacked at Épinal, at the foot of the mountains. He was a college boy from Pasadena, California, fresh from nineteen months of training that had taught him more about himself than it had about anything else. "I learned a vast amount," he remembered.

Because I had come from the upper middle class I'd never met anybody who worked for a living except the maid we had. And all of these kids, high school boys, some not even in high school yet, came from working-class families. And I suddenly began to realize, good God, I've missed most of what life is about. And that was a great, instructive educational experience for me.

But the main thing it did was to show me what I really was underneath. That I was athletic. I could do all these athletic things that I'd never done before: climbing over eight-foot walls and marching thirty miles with a big pack in the summertime with people fainting everywhere from heat stroke and so on. I survived that and I almost enjoyed it, it was fun:

still attached." It was, but badly damaged. With three other wounded men, he was lifted onto an evacuation jeep. It started back. Fragments from another shell blew out a tire. More shells began dropping along the muddy forest track. The driver panicked. Kashiwagi told him to keep moving.

The jeep slipped and slid its way back to a field hospital, from which Kashiwagi was eventually flown to England for treatment. So he was not present on the snowy parade ground on Novem-

Paul Fussell's army identification card

taxing yourself, seeing what you could do, how long you could last. I also learned how not to make an ass of myself in front of other people. But they didn't at all prepare us for what combat is. Nothing could have done that.

Fussell had told his parents that he felt "very confident and safe" as he went off to war. "It looks like the Germans are on their last legs," he wrote. "Bets are being made here that the European war will be over in six weeks." The giddy reception he and his fellow soldiers had received during their first few days in southern France had added to his buoyancy. As the division had moved northward up the Rhone Valley, young women had appeared along the road, waving and passing out bottles of wine.

Eventually, he and the rest of the men of Company F were ordered to the front, to a forested hillside overlooking Saint-Dié, the town toward which the Lost Battalion had been heading when it was surrounded by the Germans. They were to relieve an exhausted company that had been engaged with the enemy for weeks. He recalled,

We relieved them at nighttime, and everybody got lost. It was an entire screwup. We went to sleep right where we were, and the promise was that we would renew the relief in the daytime. When I woke up, I saw things all around me that I had tripped over in the dark. They were corpses, German corpses left lying there by the unit we were relieving. There were American troops of this unit who had been killed, too. And they were a short distance off, but the unit had had the decency to cover them with pine branches that they had hacked off the trees. Later I learned that two of the officers in my battalion, young second lieutenants like me, had been so

shocked to behold these dead Americans that they left, and were never seen again. I couldn't imagine such behavior from anybody. I realized, good God, it's possible to be that scared. It's possible to throw overboard all of your promises about being a decent officer and abandoning yourself entirely to fear.

Fussell was determined never to betray the fear that grew rather than diminished as the fighting went on. "I was never worried that I couldn't survive morally," he remembered. "I knew how to cover up cowardice. That's one thing you learn. Especially if you're leading troops. You cannot indicate that you're scared, too. You have to treat them as if being scared was a minor business: 'Come off it. Let's go.' I learned how to do that, all right."

Not long after he arrived, the company commander told him to take three or four men to an abandoned farmhouse that stood between their position and where they thought the Germans might be concealed, several hundred yards away. There, he was to climb to the second floor and scan the woods for signs that an attack was coming.

"What should I do then?" Fussell asked.

"Well, I don't care what you do," the captain answered. "If you want to surrender, you can do that. If you want to be killed, you can do that. If you want to try to get back unhurt, you can do that. But give us warning." Fussell started for the farmhouse.

On my way down there, I came across two German kids lying on their backs. They'd been killed the day before. And they were so young I couldn't believe it. I thought they were between maybe twelve and fourteen years old. Now, at the end of the war, of course, the Germans were absolutely scraping the bottom of the barrel: old men who could hardly walk and kids from late grammar school. These kids had little uniforms on. They were wearing caps, not helmets. And each had been shot through the head. They had their eyes open. And the blue, bluish-red brains of one were coming out his nostrils. And the other one, his bluish-red brain was coming out just from under his cap, just displacing his cap as he wore it. And that really gave me a jolt. It was my introduction to some painful facts. This war is serious. We are going to kill people regardless of their age as long as they're wearing German uniforms, and they are going to try to kill us. And many of us are going to be killed and wounded, and there's no way out of it.

In the end, the Germans did not attack. They burned the village of Saint-Dié instead and melted into the forest beyond it. The Americans followed, the fighting continued through the mountains, and day by day Paul Fussell learned more about combat, about himself, and about the men he was being asked to lead.

Just outside an enemy-occupied town called Nothalten he and several other officers and NCOs joined a twelve-man reconnaissance patrol that came under fire from two Germans crouched in a trench just fifty yards away. Fussell and the rest ducked down behind a bush-covered mound. The Germans kept firing. Someone needed to do something, Fussell remembered, but no one seemed sure just what. The captain in command asked if anyone had a grenade. No one did. He ordered a soldier with a BAR to lay down fire. The soldier, reluctant to lift his head, said the weapon was "jammed" and began stripping it down, "ostentatiously looking for the cause of the stoppage . . . blowing into the weapon's interstices to dislodge fictive dirt particles." The captain cursed him. German bullets continued to thwack into the far side of the mound. "Did one of the lieutenants resolve the situation with a crisp and brave [Fort] Benning decision?" Fussell asked. "No, none did anything but lie there and hope."

Finally, a lieutenant named Abe Goldman muttered, "Let's get those sons of bitches," and started crawling forward with his carbine. Fussell remembered:

He was from Princeton, and most of the people I fought with were from the south and Texas and Oklahoma and had never seen a Jew in their lives. But this Jewish kid, Abe Goldman, who should have been—in the view of most of the other soldiers—in the drygoods business or in accounting or a dentist or a surgeon, was very enthusiastic. He knew what had happened to the Jews. He probably was the bravest one in the whole platoon of forty men. And that's why he got himself shot.

As Goldman reached the crest of the mound and peered over it, a German bullet gouged a long, bloody gash the length of his back. He slid back down the hill, bleeding badly but still breathing. "Once I had seen him and what he did," Fussell said, "I realized that the anti-Semitism of the whole battalion of a thousand men that I was in was appallingly impolite, misplaced, wicked. The fact that out of twelve people, Abe Goldman was the only one that crawled forward and risked his life changed a lot of minds."

Fussell managed to crawl with Goldman to the rear, then send in a squad with a bazooka and grenades to flank the two Germans and kill them. Afterward, Fussell recalled,

I was very hungry, probably from the experience, so I opened a K ration, which contained a small can of yellow cheese, and

ate that. Years later, I asked one of my sergeants, "What's the worst thing I ever did in your view?" He said, "Eating that piece of cheese covered with the blood of Lieutenant Goldman. How could you have done that?"

OVERCONFIDENCE AND EGOMANIA, carelessness, national pride, and personal ambition, had all helped undermine the Allied cause during the disheartening autumn of 1944. Sheer stupidity seems to have accounted for the long nightmare that unfolded in the Hürtgen Forest. It began five miles southeast of Aachen, just inside the German border—fifty square miles of dense, undulating pine forest through which ran two narrow ridges occupied by farm fields and small villages. Beyond it lay the Roer River, and beyond that was the Rhine and the city of Cologne, which were the real targets of Courtney Hodges's First Army.

Just inside the forest's edge, several big dams controlled the Roer's downstream flow. So long as they remained in enemy hands, any Americans who managed to make it across the river could be drowned or isolated and then annihilated on the opposite shore. In September, when the First Army initially crossed the German border nearby, the dams were only thinly defended. Had they been taken then, the drive to the Rhine might have succeeded months before it finally did. But Hodges and his staff failed to grasp this basic fact, though army engineers did their best to make it clear to them. Instead, fearful of a future attack on

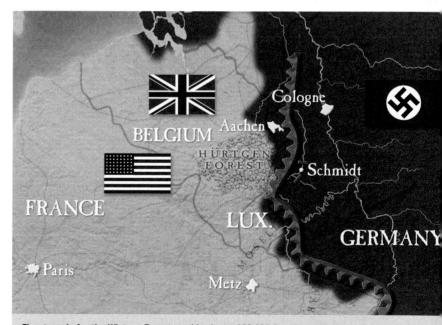

The struggle for the Hürtgen Forest would exhaust 120,000 American troops, cost 24,000 American casualties—and yield little tangible result.

their right flank and convinced that the Germans were still reeling, they resolved to clear the whole forest and seize the high ground above the river.

The Hürtgen would prove a horrific place to fight. A writer for *Yank* reported:

> *The firs are thick, standing dismal and dripping at the approaches to the Cologne plain. The bodies of the firs begin close to the ground, so that each fir interlocks its body with another. At the height of a man standing, there is a solid mass of dark, impenetrable green. But at the height of a man crawling, there is room, and it is like a green cave, low-roofed and forbidding.*

It was so dense and dark and perpetually shrouded in dank fog, one general remembered, that "upon entering it, you want to drop things behind to mark your path, as Hansel and Gretel did with their bread crumbs."

The West Wall twisted through it, two parallel belts of pillboxes and log-and-dirt bunkers several miles apart and virtually invisible among the trees. The American commanders who planned the battle knew almost nothing about the terrain and never came to see it for themselves. They failed to understand that the Allied strengths that had helped win earlier victories— air power, artillery, and mobility—would be of little use beneath the forest canopy: fog and almost steady rain grounded fighter-bombers, targets were almost impossible to spot from the air or from the ground in any case, and vehicles quickly bellied-down in mud.

In early October, the 9th Division had been sent into the Hürtgen Forest with orders to take Schmidt, a village on the far side of the Kall River valley that sat astride three roads. The division lost 4,500 men in three weeks and moved less than three miles; at one point, the regiment was losing a man and a half for every yard it gained.

At the end of the month, the 28th Infantry Division was ordered into the forest to relieve the 9th and mount a new offensive. Originally a Pennsylvania National Guard unit, it had fought its way across Normandy, paraded down the Champs-Élysées past cheering Parisians, then swept across Belgium and Luxembourg; it now included in its ranks replacements from all over the United States. Second Lieutenant Tom Galloway from Mobile was one of them. He had been a nineteen-year-old senior

Dwarfed by evergreens, alert for the sound of incoming enemy shells, men of the 28th Infantry Division move warily through the Hürtgen Forest near the German-held town of Vossenack.

at Auburn University when he entered the army. He attended Officer Candidate School, where he studied mounted artillery, hauling guns with horses, before becoming a forward observer, trained to accompany the lead platoon of an attacking infantry company and call in artillery on enemy targets. More than sixty years later, he could still remember his place in the OCS roll call: "Galoogly, Galloway, Gamble, Gardner, Gantham, Ginsberg . . ." Not long before the battle began he'd

Tom Galloway

been assigned to the 105th Field Artillery Battalion of the 109th Field Artillery. "The Hürtgen Forest was the worst," he said.

And you haven't heard much about it because it was just a mess-up. There was no reason to go through the forest, but the generals kept wanting to go through it. And you'd put a division in there and chew it up. And they'd pull it out and put another division in and chew it up. The man I replaced got shot. And it just wasn't too good to think what happened to him. But then you've replaced him.

As his division filed into the dark forest, the filthy, hollow-eyed survivors of the 9th Division whose foxholes they would be occupying stumbled past them toward the light. Grisly reminders of what had happened to them were everywhere. Thousands of treetops had been blown off by shell bursts. Newcomers were advised to remain standing and hug the tree trunks when they heard shells coming, in the hope that their steel helmets would provide at least a little protection; lying flat only made them bigger targets. The pine needles that blanketed the forest floor disguised trip wires and five different kinds of mines, including the ones GIs called Bouncing Bettys, which sprang into the air and went off at groin height. Here and there, bits of gear and clothing hung from scarred and splintered trees, marking spots where the mines had gone off.

The second battle began on November 2. The three regiments of the 28th Division were given different tasks. Galloway's 109th, on the left, was to take the heights above the town of Hürtgen. On the right, the 110th set out for a village called Raffelsbrand. In the center, the 112th had the most demanding assignment: capture the little town of Vossenack, clamber down one side of the

Kall River gorge, climb up the steep opposite bank, and take two more villages, Kammerscheidt and Schmidt. The 112th succeeded in achieving all three of its objectives by nightfall, but after that, all three regiments ran into trouble. Galloway's outfit was halted by mines and artillery; the 110th was stopped, too; and the day after Schmidt fell, the Germans took it back again.

The fighting would go on for nearly two weeks. "The days were so terrible that I would pray for darkness," one private said, "and the nights were so bad I would pray for daylight." Roads were impassable: in some places the enemy had felled as many as two hundred trees across them so that they were inextricably tangled together, then mined and booby-trapped the massive obstacle, and zeroed in artillery, so that as soon as GIs started trying to clear it, they could open fire. Sight lines were often so short that rifles were useless. GIs could not see one another, let alone the enemy. Men appeared and disappeared between the trees "like wraiths," one war correspondent noted. "If anyone . . . said he knew where he was," an officer said, "he was a damned liar!" (The man who said it was dead within days.) German artillery worked its way systematically from one American position to the next. One officer counted fifty shells that fell around him in ninety seconds. Some men were killed by such barrages, another officer remembered, "because they were so tired that they were only able to scratch the outline of a foxhole in the dirt." German tanks trapped men in their holes, grinding their way toward one to blast its occupants at point-blank range, then waddling to the next and blowing the men trapped there to pieces.

"It rained most of the time," W. C. Heinz remembered, "and the water ran into the holes, and the men slept in it and got pneumonia and trench foot. Then the first snow came, wet snow and wind-driven, and it fell on the men and into their food and into their coffee, and it plastered their helmets and the sides of the ambulances so that, through it, the red crosses showed pink." There were no real battle lines. No "tide of battle" ran one way or another for very long. "We were all mixed up," Galloway remembered.

Sometimes you were firing backward and sometimes you were firing forward. You didn't have any food after you'd been up there a couple days and you're cut off. One evening I asked the sergeant with me, "Didn't we pass a knocked-out tank down the way?"

And he said, "Yeah."

I said, "Go down there and see if they don't have some K rations on them."

He came back, he said, "The Germans are using it."

As tanks try to maneuver their way up a narrow hillside road toward the fighting in the heart of the Hürtgen (above), a steady stream of wounded men are carried back down the same slope.

Give you another example—the medics. There was only one building [a log aid station within the Kall River gorge] that I know about there. And both the German and the American medics were using it. They were just bringing in all the wounded, and both sides were using that one building.

Entire companies broke and ran under the persistent shelling. Even officers with drawn pistols could not stop them. Scores of men shot themselves in the foot or hand rather than endure any more. Hundreds more collapsed psychologically, sat staring into the distance as if no battle raged around them. Ernie Pyle called it "the accumulated blur . . . the hurting vagueness of being too long in the lines."

Just a month earlier, the office of the U.S. Surgeon General had sent Eisenhower a study by two soldier-psychiatrists who had found that "there is no such thing as 'getting used to combat.' . . . Each moment . . . imposes a strain so great that men will break down in direct relation to the intensity and duration of their exposure. Psychiatric casualties are as inevitable as gunshot and shrapnel wounds." Any soldier who survived more than two hundred days of combat was likely to collapse. On average—

American artillery crews load and fire rocket launchers, hoping they will find targets among the thickly planted trees.

throughout the war and in both the American and the British army—for every five men wounded, one died and another broke down emotionally.

Many of the men who emerged from the forest, one correspondent recalled many years later, "did not talk. They just sat across the table or on the edge of your cot and looked at you very straight and unblinking with absolutely no expression in their faces, which were neither tense nor relaxed but completely apathetic."

"There just was no place to get protection," Tom Galloway recalled.

The Germans had it all mapped, and you had to go down the firebreaks. And, of course, they would have guns at those firebreaks. It made it bad. I recall one morning, I went in with the battalion. And by nightfall, the sergeant major came to me and told me I was the only officer they had left. And that's out of a battalion *[of six hundred men]. It just chewed people up.*

Another morning, he watched a fifty-man platoon vanish into the fog and later followed their progress over the radio.

That afternoon, the battalion commander radioed [the platoon leader] and asked him how many men he had. They had chocolate, and he wanted to wait for darkness and then send up chocolate bars. He said, "We got one for each man, how many you want?" He said, "Send me five." He only had five men left out of his platoon. You just lost folks like mad in there.

The officers of every rifle company in the 28th Division were killed or wounded; most had not yet celebrated their twentieth birthday. Lieutenants had only a 17 percent chance of surviving for two weeks in the forest.

"I spent a whole day watching them pick up dead Americans," W. C. Heinz recalled.

The lieutenant [in charge of the detail] was twenty-three years old and wore silver-rimmed eyeglasses, and he had six men and two jeeps. They lifted them onto the stretchers into the trailers behind the jeeps. When the trailers were full, they pulled the tarpaulins over them. It was raining, and on the ride back the rain ran in rivulets off the tarpaulin, and the men said they didn't mind it so much anymore. They said that at first they were always picking up friends, but now they seldom found anyone they knew. At the collecting point they took them out of the trailers and stacked them between the trees, and the people from Quartermaster would take them from there in the trucks.

On November 10, fresh troops began relieving what was left of Tom Galloway's division. Of the roughly fifteen thousand men who'd entered the Hürtgen Forest with him, only some seven thousand were able to leave it under their own power. "The men were just all beat up," Galloway said of himself and his fellow survivors. He had not himself been wounded, but he hobbled painfully from trench foot, and his face bore cuts and scratches from the tree bursts that had caused so many casualties in the struggle for the forest.

You'd been in that mess. You'd been under that strain. You just were glad to get out of there. Probably the prettiest sight that I saw over there was coming out of the forest, up on a hill, and looking down. It had snowed and the whole forest, these were big fir trees, and they were all pretty with snow on them. I couldn't decide whether the scene was pretty or I was so glad to get out of there that it made it look so pretty. But I do remember that.

He and his battered comrades were eventually sent some thirty miles south to rest and recover in the Ardennes, a quiet forest where Allied commanders thought nothing much was likely to happen.

On November 16, less than a week after the 28th Infantry began moving out of the Hürtgen Forest, General Courtney Hodges ordered an attack by eight divisions of the First and Ninth armies across a twenty-five-mile front at the forest's northeastern edge, aimed at finally breaking out into the open and driving on to the Roer. Late the following morning, the relentlessly wet, foggy weather over Belgium lifted just enough for Quentin Aanenson and fifteen other pilots from the 391st Fighter Squadron to be ordered into the air in support of the men moving forward on the ground. Their first target was the enemy-held town of Hürtgen. They dropped their five-hundred-pound bombs on its center, then split into groups of four and went in search of further prey. They found it, shooting up four horse-drawn vehicles filled with troops, strafing a German staff car and two trucks, and sending a German motorcycle and its rider spinning off the road.

Then they came upon the big turreted Renaissance castle of Merode. It was an otherworldly scene, Aanenson recalled. Flashes from the big guns on the ground reflected off the dark, low-hanging clouds. The sky was filled with flak. Two P-47s, piloted by Aanenson's tent mates, Red Alderman and Gus Girlinghouse, roared in low; the men spotted several camouflaged tanks parked beneath the trees, and when no one fired at them, they wheeled around to have another look. They came in at just one hundred feet above the ground this time. By then, two

MISSING IN ACTION

Staff Sergeant John Soden of Waterbury had married Virginia Fleming just before Pearl Harbor. They had a daughter, born while he was in training, and he had been home to see her just once before leaving for Europe in the summer of 1944. He served in France with the 80th Infantry Division of Patton's Third Army, and one day volunteered to lead a patrol across the Moselle River. He was wounded and carried to a barn, where he was to receive treatment. A German shell hit the barn. A few days later, Virginia Soden

got a telegram regretting to inform her that he was missing in action. She wrote to him right away.

September 22 1944

To My Dearest Husband & Daddy Write Soon, I miss you.

Dearest John
Just a few lines in hopes you are well and safe wherever you may be. Well, darling, I received a telegram

from the War Dept. saying you are "missing in action," since Sept. 6. It was a shock and you know how I feel so I won't be able to write much except I pray to God you will be OK and be back soon. As I don't know what I'd ever do. But you're coming home darling. I keep praying for you. . . . I'm just about worried sick over you. I hope in a few days I'll get word of your safety and that you'll be home real soon. And we'll enjoy life like we were supposed to be entitled to. . . .*

Well sweets your daughter is OK. I still kiss her every night for her daddy. But the poor little dear doesn't know what it's all about. She's so like you darling in every respect. The check you sent for $40 came. Thanks a million darling. Every little bit will help for our future, right?

Well John, I can't seem to write anymore, except I still love you more than ever. I pray you'll be safe and home soon. (I'm so lonesome for you). In hopes I'll hear good news soon from you and soon as I'm worried so darling.

Everyone here extends their best regards, and good luck darling and take care of yourself as you've got lots to come home for. Remember the things we are going to do when you get home? ("Just we three.") God Bless the swellest, dearest hubby and daddy in the world.

Your wife,
Virginia

A month or so later, a second telegram arrived. John Soden's status had officially been changed from missing to dead. Virginia's younger brother remembered that after she read it, his sister let out "an unearthly howl."

AL McINTOSH'S WAR
September 1944–November 1944

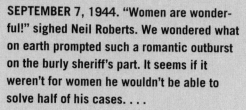

SEPTEMBER 7, 1944. "Women are wonderful!" sighed Neil Roberts. We wondered what on earth prompted such a romantic outburst on the burly sheriff's part. It seems if it weren't for women he wouldn't be able to solve half of his cases. . . .

Here's the story behind the recent pick up here of a soldier from Jackson County who had been A.W.O.L. for three months. The soldier who had been hiding couldn't resist sending word to his wife who was working at Worthington to meet him here. The Jackson sheriff got a tip to that effect so he and Roberts met the bus. They spotted the woman getting off the bus and followed her west a block on Main Street. Suddenly, out of nowhere, seemingly, appeared a man in overalls. The meeting place had been prearranged for it was the A.W.O.L. chap. . . . The two sheriffs pounced on him and it wasn't long before he was in army custody.

SEPTEMBER 21, 1944. The selective service contingent that left last week got to say their farewells twice in one day, but the postponement of their leaving was a trying experience for everybody—the prospective army men, their families, local draft board officials and Ike Johnson, depot agent.

The men said their goodbyes as the 3:30 bus piled in and started to get on board. The driver already had a load and said he knew nothing of any selective service contingent to be taken to Windom. The driver, Ike, Mrs. Nora Campbell all got busy on the long distance phone. Something had slipped between state headquarters and the bus line and the special bus that should have been here had never come. A bus showed up finally from Windom at 12:30 p.m. to pick them up.

When the delegation were taking their routine physicals again one examining doctor took a look at Bill Nath's feet and asked "have you ever been here before?" Bill said "Yes." The doctor took another look, scratched a big red cross all over his chart and waved him on his way home.

• • •

Case Van Engelhoven was hunched at a desk at the elevator this week, one ear glued to the radio and one eye cocked at a map of Holland. . . . It seems the American parachute invasion of Holland at Nymegehen was taking place just five miles from where his parents, brothers and sisters live.

• • •

We're not going to have the front office windows at the *Star-Herald* washed (yes, we do have them washed from time to time) until we take the present display out. There are so many finger and nose prints made every day that window-washing would be a losing battle. Causing the interest are two captured German machine guns, one of the heavier field type and the other a typical "tommy gun" type. They were sent back by Lt. (j.g.) Bob Haakenson as a gift to Ensign Warren Schoon. Leave it to that amazing entrepreneur Haakenson to acquire a couple of guns like that and get them back. He'll probably be shipping robot bombs next. Fred Herman yielded to that suppressed desire that burns in the heart of every youngster and climbed into the window and played with the guns, aiming the tommy gun at all the apartment windows across the street.

• • •

Usually eggs produce either an omelet or a baby chick, but an egg produced a correspondence friendship for Janet Horrigan. One day down at the Worthington Creamery plant she wrote her name on an egg and placed it in a crate of eggs. Monday she received a letter from Pvt. Kenneth Chartier now in Italy. Chartier, whose home is in Watertown, Mass, wrote that the camp cook had given him the egg with Janet's address. Chartier said he'd been overseas 20 months [and] had been in on the invasion of Italy.

OCTOBER 12, 1944. A kind-hearted California woman sent Mrs. Mike Ormseth of Canby a picture the other day. That doesn't sound like much, but it was the most welcome picture ever received in that home. It showed a group of five American soldiers who are being held prisoners by the Japs and Russell Ormseth (a brother of Norm of Luverne) was one of the group. . . . Russell looks very thin, otherwise "not too bad," although those that know him say he looks older. But when they stop they recall that it's nearly five years since he left home. Russell, a Marine, had been in China, then was taken prisoner at Guam. . . .

NOVEMBER 23, 1944. This last Hallowe'en will always be an unforgettable one for John Michael. Seems that young John was out with his pals tipping over "you know whats" and had the misfortune to fall into the seventh one.

• • •

Seems there is a slight disagreement between certain clergymen and the VFW and American Legion posts as regards the handling of military funerals. The ministers object to the firing squad volleys as being too hard on the grieving families. The veterans say that it isn't a military funeral without the firing squad and they can't take part unless it is a military funeral in every sense of the word. Personally we don't think anything is harder on the emotions than the blowing of "taps." We noticed in the coffee shop the other morning when "taps" was heard on the Armistice Day program from Arlington, that several of the local toughies (who like to boast of how hard-boiled they are) were furtively wiping away the tears that suddenly sprang to their eyes.

German prisoners captured by the U.S. 9th Division during the December drive to the west bank of the Roer.

German flak wagons were ready for them. Each plane was hit twice, once as it approached and again as it passed by. One crashed into a stable, setting it on fire. The other burned in a field. Both pilots died. So did Lieutenant Rufus Barkley, Jr., the squadron's youngest man: he had seen the tanks, too, dove to strafe them, and was hit by flak fired from the drawbridge of the castle. His plane crashed and exploded just inside the forest.

Aanenson's own plane was hit twice. His radio went out. His engine lost power, and his controls were damaged. He flew as best he could back across the American lines, spotted an unfinished airstrip, and managed to get his plane down safely. When he got back to his base, he found himself listed as missing in action on the pilots' board. It also recorded the deaths of Barkley, Alderman, and Girlinghouse.

Within three weeks, Aanenson had lost four friends.

That night was the worst night of the war for me. It's the only time I remember breaking down and crying. Johnny Bathurst and I, who were the survivors in Duffy's Tavern, decided that we couldn't deal with that anymore. After we had packed up the footlockers for Red Alderman and Gus Girlinghouse and written to their families, we quit making friends, new friends.

The battle to take the Hürtgen Forest would not end for three more weeks. Tom Galloway's 28th Division had been followed by the 8th, the 1st, the 4th, the 83rd, and the 5th Armored. Even when all three corps of the Ninth U.S. Army had finally fought their way to the west bank of the Roer, none dared cross it and move toward the Rhine, because the enemy still controlled the dams that would have made such a crossing suicidal. By then, more than thirty-three thousand American soldiers had been lost. So many died to take those fifty square miles of empty forest, and those who lived spent so much time desperately digging for their own protection during the battle, that despite the best efforts of men like the young lieutenant with whom W. C. Heinz rode, there were relatively few burials. When the snow melted the following spring, hundreds of bodies and parts of bodies would still litter the forest floor.

THANKSGIVING FELL ON NOVEMBER 23 IN 1944. Defense workers in Mobile and Waterbury remained on the job to help "speed the day of victory." At noon, servicemen at McClellan Field in Sacramento were serenaded by the glee club of the 4909th Aviation Squadron. And in Luverne, the local Lutheran church held separate services in English and in German. The Commander in Chief, just reelected for an unprecedented fourth term, carved a ceremonial turkey for polio patients at Warm Springs, Georgia.

At Santo Tomas, Sascha Weinzheimer and her family did their best to celebrate Thanksgiving, too:

> We had half a can of Spam, cooked one extra cup of rice and got enough talinum from our garden for a salad with three whole garlics chopped up in it. We thank God we are all together and not really sick like so many people in here are. . . . As usual, we talked about our next Thanksgiving. . . . Buddy wouldn't know what a turkey was anyway, but I still remember what good food we always had.

Rumors of imminent rescue continued to sweep through Santo Tomas from time to time, raising hopes, then dashing them, but there had been no more signs that the Americans were coming. MacArthur's army was still 350 miles away, still struggling to capture Leyte.

In Europe, morale among Allied troops was said to be sinking. The men at the front, like their commanders, had expected the war to be nearly over by now. To help lift their spirits, Eisenhower declared that every man in the European theater should have a turkey dinner for Thanksgiving, no matter how hard it was to organize. In the Hürtgen Forest, a major in the 8th Infantry went all the way up to the division commander, begging that no such dinner be served to his men. When they gathered around to eat, he said, German artillery was sure to zero in on them. But the division commander had his orders. The cooks were already on their way. The major was right. When his men grouped themselves around canisters of hot turkey, the enemy opened fire. As many as ten at a time were blown apart. The major would survive the war but was never able to face a turkey dinner again without weeping.

Two days after Thanksgiving, Quentin Aanenson's 366th Fighter Group moved east again, to a new airbase, named Y-29: a narrow landing strip between groves of fir trees near Asch, Belgium, northeast of Aachen and the Hürtgen Forest and not ten minutes from the front line. From their new tents, the men could hear the guns going night and day. The pilots took turns, two at a time, keeping their planes warmed up in case of a sudden German air attack. Aanenson himself had survived the loss of friend after friend; had endured two bad fires in his plane; was haunted by the fear that he had at least once mistakenly fired on Allied troops; and had himself almost been killed by misdirected American flak, which nearly ripped his plane apart, and then had nearly died again when his plane hurtled toward its target so fast his controls froze. (When he managed to pull out of his dive at six hundred miles per hour, blood vessels in his eyes burst and blood trickled from his ears.) Through all of it, his anchor to sanity remained the belief that Jackie Greer would marry him when he got home. On December 5, 1944, the impact of all that Aanenson had seen and experienced overcame him, and he wrote her a very different kind of letter from those he'd written before.

> Dear Jackie,
> For the past two hours I've been sitting here alone in my tent trying to figure out just what I should do and what I should say in this letter in response to your letters and some questions you have asked.
> I have purposely not told you much about my world over here, because I thought it might upset you. Perhaps that has been a mistake, so let me correct that right now. I still doubt if you will be able to comprehend it. I don't think anyone can who has not been through it.
> I live in a world of death. I have watched my friends die in a variety of violent ways. Sometimes it's just an engine failure on takeoff, resulting in a violent explosion. . . . There's not enough left to bury. Other times, it's the deadly flak that tears into a plane. If the pilot is lucky, the flak kills him. But usually he isn't and he burns to death . . . as his plane spins in.
> Sometimes they bail out and die when they don't jump clear of the tail. I've watched close friends be killed in their parachutes by the German gunners, or have their chutes catch fire so they just fell helplessly to their death.
> Fire is the worst. In early September, one of my good friends from Luke [Army Air Field in Arizona] crashed on the edge of our field as he was attempting to land after a mission. As he was pulled from the burning plane, the skin came off his arms. His face was almost burned away. His nose, ears and

An American P-47 burns out of control at a temporary airstrip in Normandy.

lips were gone. He was still conscious and trying to talk. You can't imagine the horror. . . .

Three weeks ago, one of my Harding Field friends—you met him and his wife once—crashed a few miles from our field when we were trying to get home from a mission. As soon as we landed, Johnny [Bathurst] and I got a jeep and drove to the crash site. We shouldn't have—he was so crushed we couldn't find much of him. His head was torn off and was lying near the wreckage. We didn't know what to do—we didn't want to leave it there because a couple of dogs were sniffing around it. . . .

So far I have done my duty in this war. I have never aborted a mission or failed to dive on a target no matter how intense the flak. I have lived for my dreams for the future. But like everything else around me, my dreams are dying, too.

In spite of everything, I may live through this war and return to Baton Rouge, but I am not the same person you said good-bye to on May 3rd. No one could go though this and not change. We are all casualties. In the meantime we just go on. Some way, somehow, this will all have an ending. Whatever it is, I am ready for it.

When he finished his letter, Aanenson folded it up and put it away in his footlocker. Mailing it home would only have been cruel to the woman he loved and hoped to marry—if he made it through what was still to come.

THE GHOST FRONT

THE VILLAGE OF BOCKHOLZ was nothing more than a cluster of snow-dusted stone houses set back above the Our River, which separates Luxembourg from Germany. But when Second Lieutenant Tom Galloway and the other veterans of his 105th Field Artillery Battalion reached it in late November of 1944, after weeks of sleeping in rain and snow in the Hürtgen Forest, it seemed something like paradise. "They let us move into the houses," where it was warm and dry and safe, Galloway remembered. He and two other officers were quartered inside the biggest residence in town, complete with a walled garden; its original occupants, the village priest and his housekeeper, continued to live there, too. Galloway's frostbitten feet healed; so did the cuts and scratches on his face. His most onerous duty now was censoring his men's mail. "It was just about as boring as you could get," he remembered. "I do recall that I just didn't read one fellow's letters to his girlfriend. It was ten pages every day! He was only writing his wife about a page."

Galloway's 28th Infantry was one of just four divisions assigned to hold a line that wound its way for some eighty-five miles along the West Wall from Monschau, Germany, on the Belgian border in the north, to Echternach, Luxembourg, in the south. Two of those divisions—the 28th and the 4th, just below it—were still recovering from combat. The 106th and the 99th, above the 28th, were newcomers to combat being gently introduced to what one former GI called "the milder elements of infantry warfare": observing, patrolling, supplying. All told, there were some eighty-three thousand men in place, far too few to provide much more than a picket line. The 28th Division alone had a twenty-mile stretch to cover, most of it organized around a handful of village strongpoints scattered along the north–south road they called Skyline Drive, which overlooked the Our. The men pulled back from their outposts at dusk to escape the bitter nighttime cold, leaving the wooded banks on both sides of the river a no-man's land, warily patrolled by squads from both sides.

No one thought the Germans capable of a serious new offensive anywhere, and certainly not in the rugged forested region, called the Ardennes, that blanketed much of Belgium and Luxembourg and stretched into France as well. Ernest Hemingway, covering the war for *Collier's,* thought the region's densely wooded hills and deep-cut rivers resembled "the illustrations for Grimm's Fairy Tales only a lot grimmer." Martha Gellhorn, his wife and fellow correspondent, thought the landscape looked like "scenery for a Christmas card: smooth white snow hills and bands of dark forest and villages that actually nestled."

But whatever its aspect, what action there might be was expected to come elsewhere. Just above the northern edge of the Ardennes, Courtney Hodges had finally begun an assault by the 2nd and 99th divisions on the dams that controlled the crossing of the Roer. To the south, George Patton planned a new Third Army push into the Saar basin, to begin on December 19, supported by General Alexander Patch's Seventh Army, which had now fought its way through the Vosges. But it was clear to everyone that no Allied army would be crossing the Rhine any time soon; that even with Soviet forces advancing through Hungary toward the Austrian border, the war in Europe was unlikely to end before spring. "Between our front and the Rhine a determined enemy held every foot of ground and would not yield," General Omar Bradley remembered. Since August, the Allies had learned through bitter experience that the Germans could still mount an effective defense, but they still did not believe that

Before the storm: a lone GI patrols in the Ardennes (opposite page) while his fellow soldiers on a three-day pass (above) line up for billet assignments at their division's rest center in Clervaux, Luxembourg.

another full-scale enemy offensive was possible. The German army, said Bradley's chief of intelligence, "is [even] thinner, more brittle, and more vulnerable than it appears" and suffering so many casualties—some three thousand a day—that at any moment simple attrition could bring about its collapse. Whatever reserve units the Germans might be able to cobble together would be needed to resist Allied pressures elsewhere up or down the line.

Later, Bradley would bravely maintain that the decision to stretch the American lines so thin in the Ardennes had been "a calculated risk." In fact, it had been an unavoidable one. Since September, the U.S. Ninth, First, and Third armies alone had suffered 134,182 battle casualties and lost nearly that many more men to fatigue, exposure, and illness. Only half those men had been replaced, and there were now simply not enough troops to cover in adequate strength the entire line from Holland to Switzerland. Some section of it had had to be slighted.

The thousands of young Americans who were stationed in the Ardennes during the fall and winter of 1944 knew little and cared less about questions of grand strategy. They just relished the comparative tranquillity of the Ardennes. "Lucky guys," one veteran shouted to a newcomer, "you're coming into a rest camp." General Hodges's First Army headquarters was spread out among casinos and handsome old hotels in the once fashionable Belgian resort town of Spa. GIs on three-day passes hunted deer and wild boar in the forests, bowled or boxed or went to the movies at Malmédy, Saint-Vith, or one of ten other official rest areas in Belgium and Luxembourg. Marlene Dietrich entertained the troops. Frankie Frisch, manager of the Pittsburgh Pirates, toured the front with two of his players, signing baseballs for eager fans in uniform. Life was so uneventful that the men began calling the Ardennes the Nursing Home and the Ghost Front. "Because it was a quiet area and nothing was going to happen," Tom Galloway remembered, "I fired twenty-five howitzer rounds a day into Germany. I'd go up in the morning and fire just one at a time. Just to let them know we were there."

Some eight miles to the northeast of Galloway's comfortable lodging, where Private Ray Leopold of Waterbury, Connecticut, was stationed with the 3rd Battalion of the 112th Regiment, things were mostly tranquil, too. "We were located at the junction of three countries," he remembered. "You could stand with one foot in Luxembourg, a second foot in Belgium, and you could spit into Germany." In fact, Leopold was himself in Germany, on the east side of the Our near the hamlet of Sevenig, where the American line looped around to encompass enemy pillboxes that had been taken in September and held ever since.

"It was a nice, secure place," Leopold recalled. He was twenty-eight (older than most of his fellow GIs), the son of a Jewish immigrant from Latvia, and he had been a mortgage broker when he was drafted. He'd begun combat as a rifleman but had become a medic after a sniper wounded him when he carelessly got up to stretch after a night of guard duty. The bullet buried itself in his left thigh. The medic assigned to his outfit had been killed two days earlier, so he crawled to his dugout and began to care for his own wound, using a German medic's kit he'd picked up on the battlefield and employing the rudiments of first aid he'd learned as a scoutmaster and Red Cross volunteer back home.

I did the probing. I found the bullet about three inches deep within my thigh. I took hold of the bullet and, since the bullet is spinning when it hits you, I knew enough to turn it in the opposite direction while slowly pulling the bullet outward. In about a minute, minute and a half, I had extracted the bullet. I had to debride the area. I had to cleanse it thoroughly, and I had to make it as antiseptic as possible. I put a butterfly bandage on it so that it could get a bit of air. I went to the battalion aid station two days later. Captain De Marco saw the wound. He said, "Your medic's dead. Who did this?" And I told him that I had done it. "Ah!" he said, "I've got a good proposition for you. How would you like to be a combat medic?"

Leopold was reluctant at first. He knew that medics suffered proportionally higher casualties than riflemen. But he agreed and never regretted it. "In retrospect, I'm very glad I became a medic," he said. "It was the opportunity to do something warm, genuine, and human in a morass of—what should I call it? It's surely the opposite of morality, decency, and warmth." He would find plenty to do in the coming days.

In the second week of December, there began to be signs that something unusual was happening in the forests across from the American lines. Civilians reported growing numbers of German troops. At night, GIs sometimes heard the far-off whine of motors. Tom Galloway noticed something, too: men coming back

Ray Leopold

from night patrols across the river said that "some mornings there was no snow on the roads in Germany, which meant there was traffic on those roads at night. I reported it, but I didn't put any significance to it. Certainly, Intelligence didn't put any significance to it."

Allied Intelligence remained unconcerned. Enemy troops were simply being shifted up or down the line in response to American probes, they said. It was obvious to them that a German offensive in the Ardennes in midwinter could never succeed, and they were comforted by the conviction that the German commander in the West, Field Marshal Gerd von Rundstedt, must share that opinion. He was a professional's professional, after all, too cool and cautious to undertake any task he did not believe likely to bring success.

They were right about that: Von Rundstedt privately thought the idea of an offensive "nonsensical," and "absolute madness." But he was not really in charge. Hitler was, and since August he had been planning to hit the Allies hard where they least expected it. Hidden beneath the trees in an assembly area three miles deep, three great German armies were gathering: the Fifth, Sixth, and Seventh Panzers, with 200,000 men, 1,800 tanks, and 1,900 guns and Nebelwerferen, the six-barreled rocket artillery pieces whose shrieking shells GIs called Screaming Meemies.

Hitler had convinced himself that a swift strike by this massive force could still turn the war around, and he had managed to keep secret the details of the plan he called Operation Autumn Mist from all but a handful of his commanders. He imposed radio silence to insure that Allied code breakers heard no hint of what was coming. Overcast skies and dense low-lying fog kept Allied spotter planes grounded. Cook fires were made with charcoal to keep smoke from betraying the men's presence. Bundles of straw scattered across country roads muffled the hooves of the horses dragging up the big guns.

"Our enemies are the greatest opposites that exist on this earth," Hitler told his generals when he finally revealed his plans. "Ultra-capitalist states on one side, ultra-Marxist states on the other; on one side a dying empire and on the other side a colony, the United States, waiting to claim its inheritance." The coming attack, he said, would "bring down this artificial coalition with a mighty thunderclap." His armies were to race out of the forest, overwhelm the outnumbered Americans, storm across the Meuse, bypass Brussels, and race all the way to Antwerp to choke off Allied supplies and trap the British and Canadian armies—and they were to do it all in just six days. Then, with the Allied front in the West shattered and its forces without hope of resupply, reinforcement, or retreat, he hoped to refocus his commanders' attention on stopping the oncoming Russians and force

Hitler's scheme to reverse his fortunes in western Europe called for a lightning armored strike from Germany through the Ardennes Forest to take Antwerp and split the Allies in two.

Stalin to make a separate peace. Everything would depend on surprise and speed.

Like von Rundstedt, most of Hitler's commanders thought the plan folly as soon as they understood what he expected of them. SS-Obergruppenführer Josef "Sepp" Dietrich, commander of the Sixth Panzer Army, which was meant to spearhead the attack, was especially caustic.

> All Hitler wants me to do is to cross a river . . . and then go on and take Antwerp! And all this in the worst time of the year through the Ardennes when the snow is waist-deep and there isn't room to deploy four tanks abreast, let alone armored divisions. When it doesn't get light until eight and it's dark again at four and with re-formed divisions made up chiefly of kids and sickly old men—and at Christmas.

In addition to the problems posed by distance and weather and terrain, the Germans faced another obstacle: they now had access to so little fuel that tanks and other vehicles would have to go into battle with just enough gasoline to move for three days; if they failed to capture enough Allied fuel on the way to their objectives, they would simply have to stop. The generals urged less ambitious plans, meant merely to bloody the U.S. First Army. But Hitler was immovable. Preparations for the offensive continued beneath the thick evergreen canopy. It was to begin before dawn on Saturday, December 16. Despite his doubts, von Rundstedt issued an Order of the Day on Friday evening, meant to inspire the men he was sending into battle.

CIVILIZED BEHAVIOR

"To me, the real heroes of the war are those who very seldom got medals," Dan Inouye of the 442nd Regimental Combat Team remembered. "They're the medics. Whenever a man gets injured, he very, very seldom calls out for his sweetheart or his mother. First thing he calls out is 'Medic!' And whenever that word is heard, the medic rushes over, just dodging bullets. That takes guts. He doesn't capture anyone, he doesn't kill anyone. So very seldom does he get a medal for bravery."

Medics were paid ten dollars less per month than the men they struggled to save. Many were conscientious objectors, unwilling to take lives but willing to risk their own lives to save others. Before they left the States they were sometimes ridiculed as "pill-pushers" and worse. But "overseas it became different," one remembered. "They called you 'Medic' and before you knew it, it was 'Doc.' I was nineteen at the time."

Like the men they tended, medics learned to improvise in combat. During the Bulge they kept morphine and plasma inside their shorts to keep them from freezing. In the Pacific, some dyed the red crosses on their helmets green in the belief that enemy snipers singled them out. And everywhere, they were forced to make awful choices, as medic Ray Leopold from Waterbury remembered:

If you're in a firefight and you see a party that is wounded in a way that you know he cannot survive, you must pass him by even though he may be calling to you for help, and you must doctor somebody whose life you potentially can save. It's a terrible decision you have to make to pass somebody by who is in need of comfort, but is not going to live. It's never pleasant to do the work of a medic. But it's one of the essentials of civilized behavior.

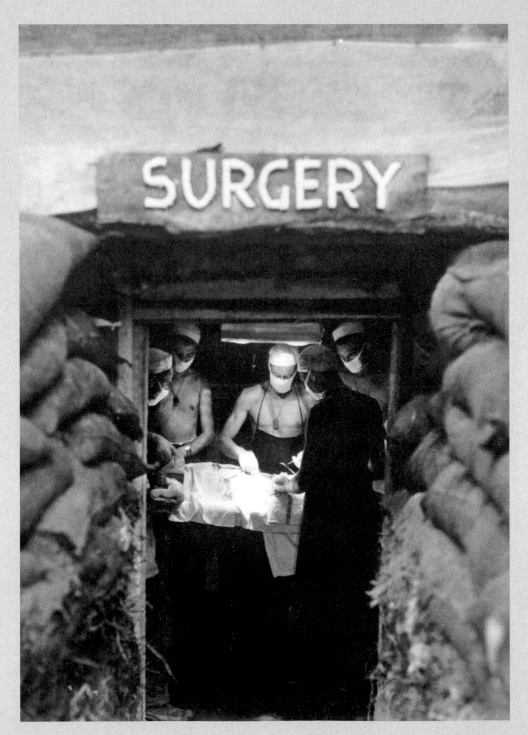

Whether sandbagged against Japanese bombs on Bougainville (left), administering plasma to a man who might have died without it on Saipan (top right), or pinned down by the same machine gun that wounded a GI in need of rescue in France (bottom right), medical personnel exhibited extraordinary resourcefulness—and extraordinary courage—throughout the war. "The medic could do more with less . . . than anyone," a wounded veteran recalled.

Soldiers of the Western Front! Your great hour has arrived. Large attacking armies have started against the Anglo-Americans. I do not have to tell you more than that. You feel it yourself. WE GAMBLE EVERYTHING! You carry . . . the holy obligation to give everything to achieve things beyond human possibilities for our Fatherland and our Führer!

At five-thirty the next morning, Tom Galloway and his house mates were asleep at Bockholz when there was an explosion just outside. The officers dressed quickly. A German shell had landed in the garden. "The Battle of the Bulge broke right there," Galloway remembered, "and as I say, when they fired the first round, it darn near hit me. From then on, it got worse."

From the German side of the Our, scores of glaring spotlights lit up the low-hanging clouds, which bounced their light downward to illuminate the battlefield. The roofs of Hosingen, the village that stood between Bockholz and the river, were silhouetted against the light; beyond them and to the north, Galloway could see hundreds of Germans swarming toward the Americans, some in gray greatcoats, others in white uniforms suited to fighting in snow. "We thought they had lost their minds," he remembered. "They were supposed to be beaten. We were there resting up, and we weren't disturbing them. They weren't supposed to disturb us either. They came barreling over there, hit the infantry along the river first, of course, and then us."

The captain commanding Galloway's battery took the eastern end of Bockholz and ordered Galloway to take charge of defending its west side. Germans were now pouring into the town, firing as they came. The captain was hit. So was the first lieutenant. The first sergeant ran up to tell Galloway what had happened and then asked him for orders. "I knew we were in trouble when the sergeant was asking me, a second lieutenant, what to do," he remembered. "They never asked second lieutenants anything. I said, 'I'm going home to Alabama. You can stay here and figure this out. See you later.' "

In fact, Galloway went nowhere. Instead, he took charge, ordering his unit to move a howitzer into place on the east side of town in the hope that they would be able to fire it at point-blank range into the advancing Germans. The enemy overran it before he could load and fire. Galloway and the rest of the battery fought on as infantrymen. "You just had waves of Germans coming at you," he recalled. "We had one machine gun going, just mowing them down. They'd keep coming right down the road. Right into that machine gun. But there were waves of them."

At midmorning, four U.S. tanks turned up and helped take the guns back. Battery C kept firing "sporadically" for the rest of the day and into the night, Galloway remembered.

The one thing I'd worried about before I got over there was whether I would know what to do at the right time. And of course that came home to roost with me, because at one point the first night of the Battle of the Bulge, there I am trying to figure out tactics. And to be perfectly honest, I'd figured, as a junior officer in the artillery, I'd be a forward observer and I didn't have to worry about tactics too much. And as it ended up, here I am in charge and thinking to myself, "Why did you sleep through tactics?"

Similar scenes were taking place along much of the eighty-five-mile line that day. The German infantry's task was to overwhelm American strongpoints and then seize the east–west roads needed by the massed armor that was waiting for the signal to advance.

German patrols were already in place around the position held by Ray Leopold's outfit near Sevenig before the artillery barrage began. They had filtered silently into the draws on either side of it where the Americans had never quite finished the barbed-wire entanglement meant to keep them out. They surprised one platoon at breakfast, killed its commander, and captured two company kitchens before they were driven off at nightfall. "Nobody able to sleep and no hot meals," one GI noted when things had at least momentarily quieted down. "This place is not healthy anymore."

Leopold went to work, doing his best first to patch up wounded Americans and then the twenty or so wounded Germans they had managed to capture over the course of the day. "As I was doctoring the shoulder wound of a young German approximately twenty-four years of age," he recalled, "he turned to me—and in a voice completely accent-free—said, 'Is it permitted to talk to you?' "

I said, "Yes, what's on your mind?"
He said, "Where are you from?"
I said, "I'm from the United States."
"Where in the United States?"
"The Northeast," I said.
"Where in the Northeast?"
I said, "I'm from Connecticut."
"Where in Connecticut?" He was persisting.
I said, "I'm from Waterbury, Connecticut."
"Ah, yes," he said, "Waterbury, at the junction of the Naugatuck and Mad rivers."

German troops scavenging for supplies abandoned by retreating Americans during the first hours of the attack through the Ardennes. The man in the background has scared up two jerry cans filled with precious Allied gasoline.

Now, you have to know a bit about the area. The Naugatuck is a fairly substantial river. But the Mad River is a little stream that you can jump across without any trouble. Anyone who knew this . . . I was puzzled.

I said, "How did you possibly know that?"

He said, "I was in training for the administration."

"The administration of what?"

He said, "The administration of the Territories."

My blood went cold. I couldn't imagine that Hitler, in his wildest imagination, not only had Europe in his grasp, but also figured that he would control America.

The medic wanted to know more. Hitler had foreseen an eventual war with the United States as early as the 1920s, but it was impossible to tell whether the wounded officer was serious about his training or just trying to frighten his captors about what would befall them once Hitler won the war. Before Leopold could ask more questions, they were interrupted by what he remembered as "the impossible": enemy searchlights that revealed a long, rumbling column of Mark VI tanks emerging from the forest to the northeast along a footpath so narrow it was hard to imagine two men walking along it side by side.

As the Germans attacked in the Ardennes on the morning of the sixteenth, Dwight Eisenhower, newly promoted to the rank of five-star general, was attending his valet's wedding at his Versailles headquarters. Generals Bradley and Hodges were visiting a Belgian gun maker to order a pair of custom-made shotguns. General Montgomery was playing golf at Eindhoven in Holland; convinced that the Germans could no longer "stage major offensive operations," he planned to go home for Christmas unless the war "becomes more exciting."

German artillery had cut telephone communications, and headquarters were far from the front, so it was not until late afternoon that Allied commanders began to get fragmentary reports suggesting just how exciting the war had suddenly become. "If the other fellow would only hit us now!" Bradley had said a few days earlier. "We could kill more Germans with a good deal less effort if they'd only climb out of their holes and come after us for a change." He got his wish, but both he and Hodges initially dismissed the offensive as a localized "spoiling attack," meant merely to lure the Americans away from their assault on the Roer River dams. Eisenhower ordered the 7th Armored Division from the Ninth Army and the 10th Armored Division from Patton's Third Army to move in to protect the northern and southern flanks of the Ardennes line just in case, but it would be another twenty-four hours before he understood the enormity of what was happening.

The columns of German armor that began breaking through the Americans all along the line the next morning began to clarify things. The Battle of the Bulge—named for the forty-mile salient the enemy had begun to carve into the American line—would be the biggest battle of the war on the western front.

On paper, things still seemed to be going according to the German plan. In the north, Dietrich's Sixth Panzer Army was hitting the Americans below Monschau, hoping to make quick work of the green 99th Division, then hurry west to cross the Meuse near Liège and race on across the flat Belgian plain to Antwerp. Hitler expected the Sixth's advance elements to reach there no later than Wednesday.

Meanwhile, the Fifth Panzer Army, commanded by General Hasso von Manteuffel, was intent on breaking through the center of the line held by the 106th and 28th infantry divisions (where Ray Leopold and Tom Galloway were already under fire), so that it could move on quickly to take the two rail and road hubs at Saint-Vith and Bastogne, which controlled movement in the Ardennes, and then sweep on to establish its own beachheads across the Meuse at Namur and elsewhere.

At the same time, to the south, General Erich Brandenberger's misnamed Seventh Panzer Army (it consisted of four infantry divisions without tanks and with few vehicles of any kind) was crossing the Our to set up a defense line to protect the German flank against American counterattack.

The Germans had achieved the surprise that was the first prerequisite for success. For the first time since D-day, stunned American soldiers would find themselves falling back, hunted by the enemy instead of hunting him. And the winter weather that Hitler had hoped for continued to hold: for eight days there would be no serious air support for the GIs on the ground.

But the speed Hitler insisted upon would prove harder to achieve. German engineers were slow getting bridges across the Our. German tankers sat for hours in traffic jams, breathing blue gasoline fumes, burning precious fuel. Snow and mud, narrow roads and difficult terrain, would make life hard for the retreating Americans, but they also slowed the advancing Germans. So, eventually, did the extraordinary tenacity of otherwise ordinary GIs.

Maps of the Battle of the Bulge seem straightforward enough: unambiguous arrows denote the movement of armies, meticulously dotted lines trace positions that shift neatly from one point to another, and tidy numbered symbols are meant to show just where each unit was at a given moment. But military maps invariably mislead. There would be nothing unambiguous or meticulous or tidy about the struggle for the Ardennes.

Early communiqués called the situation "fluid." In fact, it was chaotic, "a nightmare of bewilderment," one newspaperman wrote. As the enemy came on—blasting through hastily organized roadblocks, pouring past the Americans, pushing them back or flowing around them—cooks and typists and bandsmen and truck drivers and other service personnel, some of whom had never so much as visited a rifle range, found themselves in combat. Adding to the bewilderment were thirty-six English-speaking German commandos in four-man teams, wearing American uniforms and riding in captured American jeeps. Organized by Otto Skorzeny, the man who'd rescued Mussolini from his Allied captors in 1943, they snipped telephone wires, removed or altered road signs, misdirected traffic, and spread rumors of overwhelming German triumphs just over the horizon. Their unsettling presence, Bradley would write, forced "half a million GIs . . . to play cat and mouse with each other every time they met on the road." New passwords were issued each morning and rigorously enforced by sentries. An American gen-

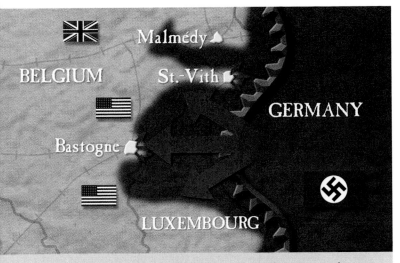

The initial phase of the German offensive (above) seemed to go more or less as Hitler had hoped. But before his columns could push toward the Moselle, he wanted Bastogne and Saint-Vith taken from the Americans. The SS officer below consults his map at a crossroads thirteen kilometers from Malmédy; the signpost points the way to a U.S. ordnance depot, a potential source of precious supplies.

eral was locked up when he placed the Chicago Cubs in the American League; Bradley himself would have trouble when an MP insisted that the capital of Illinois was Chicago, not Springfield, and again when Bradley couldn't remember that the bandleader Harry James was Betty Grable's latest husband.

In many places there were no "American lines" to which the retreating men could repair; there were only areas, one correspondent wrote, "where the Germans weren't [and] where the Americans were scattered about the landscape." Anxious officers in the rear had a hard time keeping up with what was happening. A visitor to one regimental headquarters found the commanding general playing the piano to steady his nerves. When a junior officer radioed from a besieged village for tank destroyers, the colonel who answered insisted on knowing how many tanks were on the scene and how far away they were. "Well, colonel," the young officer said, "if I went up to the second floor, I could piss out the window and hit six." Some officers acted like traffic cops, trying to get the clogged roads free of abandoned vehicles and frightened men. Others simply ran away. One said he had to go and "see about ammunition"; another abandoned his men in order to "plan alternate positions."

In the end, "the fighting, the holding and the winning would have to be done by the guy in the line," one correspondent wrote. "We were not really retreating," recalled a platoon sergeant whose battalion had been broken up by the initial assault, "but simply doing our best to stay out of the enemy's way until we could figure out what was happening and what we could do about it. Dodging and praying—fighting only when necessary—we looked for any friendly unit we could hook up with." He finally found such a unit but not before he was forced to spend two days hiding in the woods, helplessly watching German armor roll past.

> After a while, the squeaking of the tank tracks really got to me. I was so close that, had I had one, I could have touched the armored giants with a fishing rod as they passed. Eventually, one of my riflemen took a shot at a panzer, but the next tank in line fired a shell in our direction as if to say, "Get the hell out of the way." Luckily he couldn't get his barrel down low enough to do more than frighten us. All this time we stayed hidden in the trees and bushes or burrowed down in the snow. Somehow we convinced ourselves that if we couldn't see them, they couldn't see us. I'm sure they knew we were there, but they were more interested in keeping to their schedule.

No one was more interested in keeping to that schedule than the commander of the Sixth Panzer Army's advance guard. Lieu-

tenant Colonel Joachim Peiper was an ardent young Nazi whose 1st SS Panzer Division had earned the nickname the Blowtorch Battalion for the enthusiasm with which it had burned villages and butchered civilians on the eastern front. Determined to lead the way to Antwerp, he was so angered by the slow pace with which the infantry was clearing a path for his twenty-five-mile column on the morning of December 17 that he ordered the foot soldiers to clamber up onto his vehicles and roared westward out of the Losheim Gap to blaze his own trail. Warned that German mines lay ahead, he plowed right through them rather than wait to have them cleared. Five tanks and five other vehicles were disabled, but he kept going.

Around one that afternoon, at a crossroads just south of the Belgian town of Malmédy, his lead tanks spotted trucks carrying the 140 men of Battery B of the 285th Field Artillery Observation Battalion on their way to Saint-Vith. The Germans knocked out the first truck and the last, shot up those in between, then nudged the wreckage off the road and continued on. The GIs who survived the attack surrendered. As he hurried away Peiper leaned out and shouted at the captives, "It's a long, long way to Tipperary!" More than one hundred prisoners were prodded into a field and bunched together, hands in the air. Moments later, an SS officer raised his pistol and shot two of the prisoners, one of them a medic. Other Germans opened up with rifles and machine guns. The Americans crumpled into the snow. SS men walked among them, kicking each man; those who stirred or moaned were shot in the head. At least eighty-three died, but about a dozen managed somehow to stagger into the woods and eventually reach American outposts.

By then, the Germans were in the process of overwhelming the last U.S. strongpoints along the border. In most places there were simply too many of them attacking with too much firepower to be halted altogether. But GIs were doing everything they could to slow them down, to keep them from achieving their objectives before reinforcements could reach the battlefield. Rumors of what came to be called the Malmédy Massacre only added to the desperation with which they fought. Ray Leopold's outfit had been driven back across the Our when he first learned of it.

Archie Costran was the first sergeant. He came up to me within an hour of getting word of what had happened at the Malmédy Massacre only [a few] miles away from us. He said, "Ray, why don't you do what I'm doing. Take your dogtag with the big letter 'H' on it, wrap it around your hand, put your glove back on. If by chance you're ever forced to surrender," he said, "as you raise your hand, throw the glove together with the dogtag into the snow and step on it." He said, "If you are captured and identified as Jewish, from what we know that has happened just a short distance away, you will not live."

Fortunately, we never confronted a situation that I had to throw my glove and dogtag into the snow, but it is true that, for twelve days, my hand had the dogtag wrapped around it.

Leopold's concern was not just for himself. He now feared that anyone captured by the Germans might be killed, and when some of the exhausted men around him, struggling to stay on their feet in the cold, began to develop high fevers, he worried that they would collapse and fall into enemy hands. His own medical supplies were running out when he came upon an abandoned German medic's truck. "The driver had been killed and was sitting behind the wheel frozen," he remembered. "The engine had burned, but the supplies in back were untouched." It was a court-martial offense to dispense German medications to American troops, but when he found bottles of tablets of an unknown medication whose label indicated that it contained quinine—a known fever-reducer—he stuffed as many bottles as he could into his pouches anyway. He tested two tablets on a German POW with a fever of 103. When the prisoner's temperature quickly dropped to 99, he handed them out to some one hundred GIs from his own unit and others who now found themselves fighting alongside them. "They apparently worked," he remembered with satisfaction, "because I don't personally know of anybody who in the twelve days we were surrounded did surrender."

Out of the hundreds of skirmishes and firefights, random encounters and full-scale tank battles that made up the Battle of the Bulge, several struggles would stand out. Toward the northern end of the front, a single platoon immobilized an entire German battalion for a full day, and remnants of the 99th and 2nd divisions—outnumbered more than five to one—managed to hold on to Elsenborn ridge and keep open the vital road behind it so that American reinforcements could get through. Some twenty miles to the south, the Germans trapped two regiments of the inexperienced, ineptly led 106th Infantry atop a snowy

plateau; somewhere between eight thousand and nine thousand Americans would eventually surrender there, the largest number to lay down their arms since the fall of Bataan. And for several crucial days, the 7th Armored Division and elements of other units would keep the enemy from capturing the six roads that came together at Saint-Vith.

But for most Americans it would be the protracted battle for Bastogne, some thirty miles south of Saint-Vith, that came to symbolize the Ardennes struggle. "We all knew they were holding out there," Katharine Phillips remembered, "and we were all cheering them on." Seven roads spread out from the center of the little market town, including the east–west highway best suited for supplying the German drive to the Meuse. Hitler was determined that Manteuffel's Fifth Panzer Army take it right away, and by midday on the seventeenth, three armored columns were fighting their way toward it. Eisenhower was no less determined to deny them the town and called in the 101st Airborne Division to help hold it.

The 101st was still more than a hundred miles away, in Mourmelon, France, recuperating from the Market Garden fiasco. Until it could reach Bastogne, the Americans would have to block the roads leading toward it with what some of the men

A truck crowded with men from the 101st Airborne moves toward Bastogne past a line of vehicles hurrying the other way. "You'll never stop 'em, boys," a major shouted from a retreating jeep. "We're going to have a try at it, sir," a paratrooper shouted back.

On the icy road to Bastogne, a Sherman M-4 tank grinds slowly past a gun carriage that has slid down into a ditch.

involved began to call the Snafu Division, cobbled together from a combat command team of the 10th Armored, the 705th Tank Destroyer Battalion, and scattered elements of the 28th Infantry Division, including what was left of Tom Galloway's battery. "We'd drop back and fire," he remembered. "Drop back and fire. And at that time, I didn't know it, but apparently we were trying to protect Bastogne. I had never heard of Bastogne. I didn't know there was such a place."

The men of the 101st Airborne didn't know there was such a place either, and they were not pleased to be awakened and told they faced a nightlong ride in open trucks through the bitter cold to get to it.

Private Arthur Mayer of Company A, 1st Battalion, 327th Glider Infantry, may have been among the most displeased. He was a big-city boy from Chicago's South Side and a college man (he'd volunteered from the University of Michigan), the son of Jewish parents serving alongside a good many men from the rural South, a free-thinker and a determinedly free spirit: during training he'd grown so weary of hearing that there were no atheists in foxholes that when his turn came to dig his own, he jumped into it as soon as he'd finished and announced, "There, now you've seen one."

He had just rejoined his outfit a few days earlier after weeks in a hospital in England, recovering from machine-gun wounds suffered shortly after D-day. He'd been hit in the arm and leg after rescuing two men from drowning in the Douve River behind Utah Beach, an effort that had won him the Bronze Star. His colonel had welcomed him back with reassuring words: Mayer needn't worry about getting involved in any more serious combat, he'd said. "The war's over."

Arthur Mayer

There was no time fully to outfit the men before they boarded the trucks. Some had no weapons. Most were without gloves or winter clothing. The icy wind numbed the men's faces, fingers, and feet. A relative of Mayer's had recently sent along a box of twenty-four chocolate bars. As the roofless truck lurched and rattled through the night, its headlights picking up frightened refugees and retreating soldiers who shouted, "Run! They'll murder you," Arthur Mayer crouched at one side in the back, quietly eating all the candy bars, one after another; he'd been in battle before and wasn't sure when he'd get real food again.

The 101st got to its assembly area, southwest of Bastogne, early the following morning and began to set up a perimeter in the snowy fields. Within an hour of their arrival, the Germans choked off the last road into town.

Tom Galloway never made it to Bastogne. On the nineteenth, he was sent out in a jeep with three other men to scout one of the roads leading toward it from the east. He radioed back that he had spotted enemy soldiers approaching. They were still a ways off. The officer in charge asked him to find out if they were really Germans or just reluctant Polish conscripts known to be attached to the enemy army and likely to be less formidable in combat. He got down from his jeep and crept forward to have another look.

I had to get right up by the road so I could hear. And I could hear them speaking—sprechen zie Deutsch. So I went back and got in my jeep. I had to go down that same road the patrol was on, but I figured with the machine gun on the jeep that I could scatter them. But I didn't do anything but make that bunch of Germans mad. There was a whole lot more Germans in the road when I got back there than they had before. So I had to back up. I got to a house and got inside and they brought a tank up and shot that house up pretty bad. I only had four people, and we had to give up.

You never think you're going to get caught. You think, "It's not going to happen to me." The worst part of it is trying to figure out how to get caught without getting shot, because you're dealing with people you've been shooting at. And you hope they're not going to shoot you. And in my case they didn't.

Galloway was taken to the village of Mageret, newly captured from the Americans. He was treated well enough there, he remembered, even given a deck of cards to while away the time.

Maybe a week after I was captured, I was sitting on the church steps and this German officer came up and he was artillery. And he could tell I was artillery: You had your brass on your collar. When I had been in Luxembourg firing over into Germany, I thought I knew where the German forward observer was. So I didn't shoot where he was, and he didn't shoot where I was. This officer asked me, "Were you the forward observer over there?" I said, "Yeah." He was the fellow

I'd avoided shooting at. He went and got me food, and he spoke better English than I did. He had been to school in England. He came home and just got caught up in the war just like I was. So he and I had old-home week, sitting there on the church steps. I was glad to see him. I have no idea what his name was.

A day or two later, Galloway would join some ten thousand other captured Americans on their way to POW camps inside Germany.

On the morning of December 19, the same day Tom Galloway fell into enemy hands at Mageret and about the time Arthur Mayer and the 101st Airborne were digging in around Bastogne, Eisenhower met with his generals at Verdun, where more than a

American prisoners rounded up during the first days of the Battle of the Bulge

quarter of a million men had died during the most prolonged battle of the First World War. His lieutenants were understandably grim-faced when he got there. The situation had steadied some, but the 28th Division had been broken and the 106th was within hours of being destroyed; Peiper's tanks, refueled from a captured American depot, were driving hard toward the Meuse; advance elements of the Fifth Panzer Army were sweeping westward between Bastogne and Saint-Vith; and Americans back home were stunned that a victory that had seemed so close to being won seemed once more to be in question. Burt Wilson, then a delivery boy for the *Sacramento Bee*, remembered how he and many of his customers felt that week.

One of the nice things about being a Bee *boy is I got to read the paper every day. And for me the war was that little square map on the front page where it showed wavy lines moving in some direction and the next day you'd see them move a little more. Arrows pointed here and there where different armies were going. And then, all of a sudden, there was this bulge in the map that was going back the other way. And, my God, what's happening here? Are we losing now that we're this close?*

Eisenhower remained unshaken. He would have "only cheerful faces" at his table, he insisted; the German offensive should be seen "as one of opportunity for us and not of disaster."

George Patton needed no pep talk. "Hell," he said, "let's have the guts to let the sons of bitches go all the way to Paris. Then we'll really cut 'em off and chew 'em up."

"No," Eisenhower said. "The enemy will never be allowed to cross the Meuse." To insure that they didn't, he made two key decisions that day. First, since Bradley's Twelfth Army headquarters was in Luxembourg, at the southern end of the Ardennes line, and the Germans had cut such a broad swath through the American forces, it was impossible for him to keep up with fast-breaking events in the north. Therefore, Eisenhower temporarily awarded the U.S. First and Ninth armies to Montgomery. Bradley and other U.S. commanders were appalled. The field marshal was delighted and immediately deployed his XXX Corps along sixty miles of the Meuse to block potential crossings. Eisenhower also directed Patton to rush his three armored divisions north to relieve Bastogne and begin a counteroffensive from the south. Patton eagerly agreed: he would disengage his army from the Saar front on the twenty-second, wheel it ninety degrees to the left, and then move some 133,000 tanks, trucks, and other vehicles one hundred miles northward over a handful of snowy roads, he promised—and he would see that it was all done in seventy-two hours.

Meanwhile, at Bastogne, Arthur Mayer and the other men of the 101st Airborne, exposed to artillery and mortar fire, encircled and in constant danger of being overwhelmed, would have to hold on. Medical supplies were running out. Ammunition was dangerously low. "If you see four hundred Germans in a hundred-yard area, you can fire artillery at them," the garrison commander, Brigadier General A. C. McAuliffe, told a junior officer. "But not more than two rounds." He was only half-joking. The weather was still too bad for resupply from the air, and no one could say precisely when Patton's men would arrive.

The men of Mayer's squad soon faced a small crisis of their own. Their foxholes were not far from a farmhouse where the farmer's wife had proved willing to aid the Allied cause by baking big round loaves of bread every day for the boys, whose diet otherwise consisted of cold K rations. But after a few days she ran out of yeast. No yeast, no bread. Since Mayer alone knew the French word for the all-important ingredient—*levure*—he was sent into Bastogne, under fire, to try to find some. He ran the whole way, he remembered. German shells arced overhead. Some crashed into the rubble-strewn streets nearby. He found a tiny grocery, ducked inside, and asked for the yeast. The grocer gave him a stick of something. "It looked like butter to me," he remembered, "and I wasn't sure I'd picked up the right stuff." He had. He made it back safely, and by evening he and his buddies had more warm wheels of fresh bread to keep them going.

Shortly before noon on the twenty-second, four Germans carrying a big white flag approached the 327th Glider positions. Two were officers who asked in English to see the American commander; they had a message for him. A sergeant tore the flag into pieces to make blindfolds and led two of the emissaries to his regimental commander, Colonel Joe Harper. Harper took their message to General McAuliffe.

"What did they want?" he asked.

"They want us to surrender."

"Aw, nuts," McAuliffe said.

The German message was peremptory and patronizing. The Americans had two hours to surrender, it said. If they failed to do so, "one German artillery corps and six heavy A.A. battalions are ready to annihilate the U.S.A. troops in and near Bastogne. . . . All the serious civilian losses caused by this artillery fire would not correspond with the well-known American humanity."

There were no such "A.A. battalions." McAuliffe had no intention of giving up anyway, but he had a hard time thinking of a suitable written response.

"That first remark of yours would be hard to beat," an aide finally told him.

McAuliffe agreed and scrawled his response:

22 December 1944
To the German Commander
NUTS!
The American Commander

The German emissaries were puzzled: "Is the reply affirmative or negative?" one asked.

"It is decidedly not affirmative," said Colonel Harper. "If you finish this foolish attack, your losses will be tremendous."

The Germans were escorted to the road that led back to their lines. "If you don't understand what 'NUTS!' means," Harper reiterated as he removed their blindfolds, "in plain English it is the same as 'Go to Hell.' And I will tell you something else: If you continue to attack, we will kill every goddamned German who tries to break into the city."

The Germans saluted. "We will kill many Americans," one said. "This is war."

"On your way, Bud, and good luck to you," Harper said. Later, he wondered why he'd added those last words. He certainly hadn't meant them.

The next morning dawned bright and clear for the first time in weeks, and at around noon the blue sky over Bastogne was filled with U.S. C-47 cargo carriers. Hundreds of red, yellow, and blue parachutes drifted slowly down, bearing 144 tons of medicine, food, blankets, ammunition, and other supplies. At the same time, U.S. Thunderbolts attacked German columns wherever they found them out in the open. But the same clear weather that made resupply and air attacks possible also allowed two flights of Luftwaffe planes to bomb the town that evening, burying thirty-two wounded men in the rubble of their improvised hospital; it also brought still greater cold, which froze the ground and permitted German tanks to move into position to launch new attacks on Christmas Day. "The finest Christmas present the 101st could get would be a relief tomorrow," McAuliffe told VII Corps headquarters by telephone. "I know, boy," General Troy Middleton said, "I know."

IN MANILA, SASCHA WEINZHEIMER was looking forward to Christmas, though her life and those of her family and her fellow internees seemed to be spiraling steadily downward. "I am making a few gifts for Buddy and Doris and bookmarks [for my friends]," she wrote. "Mother said it was best to forget it this year but we can't on account of the little kids. She told them because of the antiaircraft guns in Manila, Uncle Sam told Santa to keep away . . . and leave his gifts . . . for [them] in San Francisco."

U.S. aircraft were bombing Manila almost daily now, and when their target was the nearby Grace Park Airfield, the ground shook and the family's shanty swayed. The Weinzheimers still spent their days together there, but for safety's sake, Sascha and her mother and siblings had all resumed sleeping in the main building; her father remained behind to keep a protective eye on the family's few remaining belongings.

The Japanese had grown more and more agitated over the past weeks. There were more roll calls, more unannounced inspections. Food supplies continued to dwindle, though internees could hear the voices of street vendors just beyond the gate selling delicious Philippine breads made from rice flour. "If anyone still has a watch, fountain pen, or cigarette lighter," Sascha noted, "you can trade them with the sentries when it is dark at night for rice or sugar, which they steal from the Japanese storeroom." Some parents, she continued, urged their children to beg the Japanese for food.

There is one little girl three years old. She goes out every day and hugs the sentries around the knees and says, "Nice Japanese, I like you. Give me candy. Give me sugar." One day a sentry didn't like it and pushed her off. Her two older brothers always stand around waiting for her. Then they take the stuff to their mother. Sometimes she gets a banana or a few peanuts or a rice cake. This little girl's father was killed at Cavite by a Japanese bomb before she was born. Mother and Dad think this is awful and would beat us kids if we ever tried it. "Starve first, kids, but don't ever do that."

"When you stop and think how hard our boys are fighting for us," Sascha continued, "I guess we can take it, too. But just a little more rice would be all I can ask for. We always picture Opa and Oma [her grandparents] on their farm in California. If they only knew how hungry we are, they would be very sad. I guess even when we tell them they will never, ever believe it." On his farm in the Sacramento Valley, Sascha's grandfather Ludwig Weinzheimer had continued to blame himself for having left his sons and their families in the Philippines, and he had tried again and again to contact them through the Red Cross and the State Department.

Around midday on Christmas Eve, Sascha's father walked her to the main building. In the fierce heat, the whole camp shut down for a three-hour siesta. On their way inside, he was told that a Red Cross telegram had arrived for him. "It was from my grandmother," Sascha remembered, "and it said my grandfather had passed away eight months prior. And we were just getting it. He stood there and cried, and then walked me up to my room. Later, everybody told us that my grandfather died of a broken heart."

In spite of everything, her parents did their best to celebrate the holiday that evening. Sascha's father got her to take the two younger children for a walk while he turned their rocking horse into firewood with which to cook Christmas dinner—"hamburger," made by mixing the family's last can of corned beef with boiled mashed roots and mint leaves. They fashioned a Christmas tree out of a palm branch stuck in a dirt-filled tin can, too, and lined up with the other prisoners for a special treat: two tablespoons of jam and one bite of chocolate. Sascha thought it all delicious, even though "there were tiny white worms in the chocolate."

That night, another American plane could be heard overhead. Leaflets fluttered out of the dark sky.

The Commander in Chief, the officers and men of the American forces of liberation in the Pacific, wish their gallant allies the people of the Philippines the blessings of Christmas and realization of their fervent hopes for the New Year

Christmas 1944

Japanese guards frantically gathered up as many leaflets as they could. Lieutenant Abiko warned that any internee caught with a copy would be severely punished, and he confiscated all the typewriters in camp so that no more could be made. But everyone heard about them nonetheless. Sascha's mother wept with joy. Clearly, the Americans really were coming closer. The race between rescue and slow starvation might still be won.

"A CLEAR, COLD CHRISTMAS," General Patton confided to his diary on December 25, "lovely weather for killing Germans, which seems a bit queer, seeing Whose birthday it is." His tankers would kill a good many Germans that day, but they could not make it all the way to Bastogne. Stiff resistance and bad roads slowed them down. At dawn the next day, eighteen German tanks and two infantry battalions launched an assault northwest of the town that came within a mile of McAuliffe's headquarters before the men of the 101st managed to rebuild their line and destroy the tanks and scores of the foot soldiers who had attacked alongside them. The Germans withdrew, leaving behind wrecked vehicles and big clouds of black, oily smoke. The exhausted Americans prepared for the next assault.

Shortly before dusk the following day, Arthur Mayer was just trying to keep warm in his foxhole southwest of Bastogne when he spotted, far across the snowy fields, three enormous tanks barreling toward the town. He was sure they must be German. "Christ," he said as he ducked back down, "fucked again!"

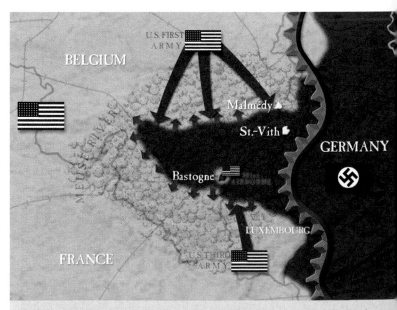

Hitler's dream of destroying the Allies in the west dissipated as Bastogne held and his columns were halted before they could cross the Meuse.

This time he was wrong. They were American Cobra King tanks, brand-new forty-ton Shermans, belonging to Colonel Creighton Abrams's 37th Tank Battalion, the advance guard of Patton's relief force—a day late but welcome nonetheless. "Gee, I'm mighty glad to see you," General McAuliffe told the first tanker he saw. More tanks soon shot their way into town. Bastogne was no longer surrounded, but Hitler continued to insist it be taken, and the men of the 101st Airborne would remain in their foxholes, fighting off repeated enemy assaults for three more weeks.

Meanwhile, the German offensive was failing all over the Ardennes. Americans had already stopped Joachim Peiper's SS Panzers. Everything had begun to go wrong for him not long after his column murdered the Americans near Malmédy. GIs denied him further fuel by turning some 124,000 gallons of gasoline into a wall of flame. U.S. engineers blew bridges before he could cross them and at one critical point fooled him into thinking that he faced overwhelming odds when only a single company actually stood in his way. American armor and artillery destroyed many of his tanks. Finally, he had had to abandon the rest of his vehicles and start back toward Germany on foot.

The 2nd Panzer Division, which had swept past Bastogne, reached the outskirts of Celles—almost within sight of the Meuse—before it was battered into submission over three days by American armor and flight after deadly flight of British Typhoons and American P-38s in what the exultant U.S. commander on the ground called "a great slaughter." Other German thrusts were similarly blunted and blown apart.

During a jeep ride through what she called "breathtaking scenery," Martha Gellhorn witnessed the sort of damage now being done to the Germans all through the region.

The Thunderbolts had created this scenery. You can say the words "death and destruction" and they don't mean anything. But they are awful words when you are looking at what they mean. There were some German staff-cars along the side of the road: they had not merely been hit by machine-gun bullets, they had been mashed into the ground. There were half-tracks and tanks literally wrenched apart, and a gun position directly hit by bombs. All around these lacerated objects of steel there was the usual riffraff: papers, tin cans, cartridge belts, helmets, an odd shoe, clothing. There were also, ignored and completely inhuman, the hard-frozen corpses of Germans. Then there was a clump of houses, burned and gutted, with only a few walls standing, and around them the enormous bloated bodies of cattle.

The road passed through a curtain of pine forest and came out on a flat, rolling snowfield. In this field the sprawled or bunched bodies of Germans lay thick like some dark shapeless vegetable.

In most respects, Hitler's great wager had failed. The German offensive had come nowhere near Antwerp, had never even reached the Meuse, but it had at least temporarily divided the Allied top command, just as its author had hoped it would. Montgomery wrote to Eisenhower again, demanding that he be

Fighting back: GIs reload their M-1s after a firefight that left two Germans sprawled in the snow.

Infantrymen move cautiously from tree to tree in the snow-filled forest (left), then dig in for the night: "If there's one thing all of us remember, it's how damn cold it was," one veteran said. "It was . . . with you all the time. . . . God, it was rugged."

granted field command of all the Allied forces. Eisenhower saw the letter as an attack on his leadership and that of Bradley and his other American lieutenants. Only an abject written apology kept the field marshal from being fired, and when he went on to hold a London press conference that falsely suggested he'd seen the German attack coming and was personally responsible for having stopped it, Churchill himself felt called upon to declare before the House of Commons that in this case it was to American and not British homes that "the telegrams of personal losses and anxiety have been going. . . . Care must be taken not to claim for the British army an undue share of what is undoubtedly the greatest American battle of the war, and will, I believe, be regarded as an ever-famous American victory."

"Now," George Patton noted in his diary, "we are going to attack until the war is over." He and the other commanders were eager to begin a counteroffensive aimed at pinching off the enemy salient and trapping the German forces at its western end, where they could be destroyed. Their hope was that the U.S. First Army would attack from the north while Patton's Third Army fought its way up from Bastogne. The trap would be complete when the two armies met at the village of Houffalize. But Montgomery, still in command of the battered U.S. First Army, refused to order it into action until it was fully reinforced. Bradley and Patton resolved to move anyway. The 11th Armored Division, newly arrived from Brittany and without any combat experience, was picked to lead the attack.

On December 30, Private First Class Burnett Miller from Sacramento found himself among the newcomers being readied for battle at a snowy assembly area near Neufchâteau, southwest of Bastogne. "We went over to [Europe] to have a great experience," he remembered, "and all of a sudden we were about to have more of an experience than we had really reckoned on. We were scared to death." Miller, the only child of a prominent businessman, had enlisted from Santa Clara College and taken part in the Army Specialized Training Program at Monterey, hoping to become an officer in the Engineer Corps. When the army abruptly canceled the program, he was

Burnett Miller

sent to the 11th Armored as a lowly private instead and—"typical of the army," he said—underwent training for desert warfare, though the battle for North Africa had long since been won.

Now he was about to go to war in snowdrifts. "I remember the first night," Miller said.

Our vehicles became almost inoperable. We dug in on a hill, and it was very difficult digging foxholes in this frozen ground. And that night there were tracer bullets all over, lots of artillery, and it was very, very scary.

The next day we mounted up in half-tracks to go down to someplace, I don't remember exactly where. From then on it was mass chaos. Nobody knew where they were going or what they were doing at the front. I'm sure at headquarters there were perfectly decent plans. And the maps showed things. But we men didn't have maps. The officers had maps, and I'm not sure they knew where we were either.

The battalion commander ordered his men to take a hill, another man from Miller's battalion recalled.

We moved out from the road in basic training fashion, leaps and bounds and rushes, everything according to the book. We charged across the open ground and up the hill until we were ordered to stop. We were attacking the wrong hill. The Krauts were not up there. Somebody had made a mistake. I was told later that the tank commander yelled to our battalion commander and asked him if he felt qualified to lead his men. His reply was "I guess not."

Burnett Miller witnessed what happened next.

I was in a hole, and our battalion commander in a light tank came whizzing past and hit a rut. He'd been standing up, and the top of his tank fell down on top of him, and the next thing I know the tank stops and a Red Cross jeep came out and they pulled him out from the bottom of the tank, which is where they got out from these things, and took him away, and that was the end of our battalion commander.

The injured man's replacement was an untried and overwrought young major from West Point, who issued orders in a shrill voice and liked to wave his .45 around. He led them toward their next objective, Miller remembered.

We were fired on immediately. And bailed out of these half-tracks and started running through the snow to get some kind of cover. Everybody was extremely frightened and confused. But you were really better off when you were moving someplace, doing something, moving fast, diving into holes in the

THE INFANTRY

It had been raining for days. You were coming back from the front and you knew where you were going, and you knew where you'd been, and you came around a turn in the road. It was the turn in the road that made it so sudden because all at once you were meeting the infantry face to face, and the rain had turned to hail.

The infantry was like it always is, two thin, long lines, one moving along each side of the road. It was two long, thin lines as far as you could see and then it was faces looking into yours.

Your jeep had slowed down again so others could pass it between the lines, and you looked out again to the right, and faces looked into yours. There was one face and then another face, and there were ten feet between them, and they kept on coming. There were rifles slung over shoulders and packs on backs. There were red hands and water and brown eyes and blue, but all the faces looked the same.

There were round faces and long faces and rough faces and smooth, and they all looked the same. They all had the same expression because they had no expression at all, because the one looked into yours and was gone and the other took its place, and it was that way for a mile. . . . [And] when you had passed them the jeep went faster because you knew where you were going, and you knew where you had been. When you had gone many miles it started to snow, and you still saw the faces of the infantry, because the infantry never knows where it must go.

W. C. Heinz, *New York Sun*

Riflemen of the 101st Airborne, moving toward new positions near Bastogne

More than 16 million Americans served in the armed forces during the war. Fewer than a million ever saw serious combat. The infantry represented just 14 percent of the troops overseas. But wherever they were sent—North Africa or the Pacific or western Europe—infantrymen bore the brunt of the fighting and suffered seven out of ten of the casualties.

Those who lived endured hardships for which no amount of training could have prepared them because, as Paul Fussell remembered, combat was simply "unthinkable." "The highest officer that one saw daily was one's own company commander, a captain," he recalled.

Except for a major, or a lieutenant colonel who ventured to show himself now and then, usually to chew us out for something, I never saw a higher officer at all. No general ever appeared. No full colonel ever

appeared. We recognized that that had to be it. They couldn't be killed because otherwise there'd be nobody in the battalions to make the attack orders we had to carry out. I got rather bitter about that. It just sort of festered. They knew nothing about what the fight was really like because they were a half-mile back. And that was heaven—half a mile away from the line.

Now, soldiers are fond of saying, the back is anywhere where anybody is working behind you. Just five yards behind you, that's back of the line. People whose business was to fire mortars had to be back of the line and in concealment and they had to have high ground in front of them so the enemy couldn't see what they were doing. Although we liked them, we were a little contemptuous of them,

too. They were worse than machine-gunners from our point of view. If you were a machine-gunner, at least you had to show yourself at some point and that was a terrible risk and you had to be pretty brave not to run away when you were doing that. But you could be cowardly and be a very good mortarman.

For the most part, men on the front line had only one another to depend upon. "The best way an infantryman could protect himself overnight," medic Ray Leopold of Waterbury recalled, "was by digging a slit trench—a

break in the earth so that three quarters of your body is below the level of the ground—and then getting together with your buddy back to back so that your buddy protects your rear, you protect his. This is what we called being 'asshole buddies.' You're as safe as your buddy can make you by being able to see what you cannot see."

Leopold would eventually forget the names of most of the little Belgian towns where he tended the wounded, but he never forgot the cold, the worst cold in Europe in a quarter of a century.

Our captain told us that we had to hold our position, had to stay exactly where we were overnight. And while we were going to have guards, and most of us would still be awake in any event, we should catch some sleep if we could. We lay down on the pine needles. The temperature must have been somewhere between ten degrees and zero. My breath was directed downwards into the pine needles. When I woke up I remember trying to lift myself up but the moisture in my breath had frozen my overcoat to the ground. I tried to

get up and couldn't immediately. So I got up and gave it a strong yank and tore my overcoat. That was how strong that ice bond was between me and the earth.

"The weather was so terrible," one officer recalled. "It was white when you looked down, white when you looked up, white when you looked out that way." Many men shivered in light uniforms; winter clothing, woolen socks, and waterproof boots did not reach the front until mid-January. M-1 rifles froze; when firefights broke out, desperate GIs urinated on the moving parts to get them working again. Ground fog and snow sometimes made it hard to see more than a few feet. Drifted snow quickly exhausted men who tried to move through it more than a few yards.

"You had no possessions at all," Paul Fussell remembered.

You would cut everything down to the simplest because you had to carry

everything. So when we were marching from one horror to another, I had shoepacks on because the ground was always wet or frozen. I had two pairs of woolen socks. In my pockets I carried a couple of boxes of K rations. I never had a toothbrush at all. I didn't take a shower for six months. I always had plenty of cigarettes; they were free in the army if you were out on the line where you were sort of tempted to smoke. There were always leaves if you didn't have toilet paper. But each box of K rations had toilet paper in it as if it had anticipated the whole process of alimentary support. I had a sleeping bag which I carried with a rope over my shoulder like a tramp. And that's all I had. No change of underwear at all. No change of clothes at all for months. Everybody smelled terrible, but since we all did, you didn't notice it. Those who could grow beards, did. I didn't shave yet, except once a week.

snow, trying to avoid getting shot at. The worst time was when you were sitting in a hole and artillery shells were coming in.

The following day, December 31, Miller's Company C moved with Company B toward the enemy-held village of Chenogne, a group of stone houses along a single street. It was only Miller's second day in combat, but he would receive the Bronze Star for an incident that took place during the course of it. The citation, signed by Major General Holmes E. Dager, commander of the 4th Armored Division's Combat Command, lauded him for having "without regard for personal safety moved forward over open and rolling terrain, under enemy observation, destroyed a machine gun and captured the entire crew of thirteen men."

Miller's own account of what happened—he called it "my hero story"—was considerably less high-flown.

We were making an attack on [Chenogne], which was being held by the Germans. Our platoon split up, and another fellow and I got lost. And we were going down a hedgerow and we got pinned down by a machine gun. And this took quite a while. We worried around and worried around and then, when the machine gun quieted down, we decided, well, the village has probably been taken by the rest of the platoon, so we'll go there. So very carefully we were going down a road, keeping close to the hedgerow, and I looked over it and in a sort of a hole were thirteen Germans putting a machine gun back together. They looked up and saw me and my buddy and threw up their hands and surrendered. But we realized that the village had not been taken. So we turned around and started across a field back to where we had come from. And at that point, the Germans in the town saw us and started lobbing mortar shells. This of course was unnerving to us, but it bothered our new prisoners just as much, and they started running toward our lines in the village that we had come from. And we could hardly keep up with them. It looked like we were chasing them. And when we were getting close to the village, we were getting worried that our men would start shooting at them, so we started yelling to protect them, "No, they're surrendering! They're surrendering!"

When we finally got to the village, the officers came out and said, "This is marvelous! You've done a marvelous job." One said, "Would you take them to division headquarters, because they need to interrogate them. They're really looking for information on these people." So we got in a half-track, and I went with thirteen prisoners and a driver back to division headquarters, and there they said I was a real hero. This

was "fantastic!" they said, and then I realized how little contact headquarters have with the front lines, because they asked me, "Well, what's going on up there?" "Where are you?" "Can you show us on the map where you are?"

The following day was New Year's. Hitler, still somehow convinced his defeat in the Ardennes could be turned into a victory, launched two new attacks. "By no means am I entertaining the thought that the war will be lost," he said. "I have never in my life known the word *capitulation*." In what he called "the Great Blow," he sent most of what was left of his Luftwaffe into the air to attack Allied bases in Belgium, Holland, and northern France. They did serious damage, but by evening some three hundred German planes and 235 trained pilots had been lost—and the Führer was left with only the semblance of an air force with which to defend the Fatherland. The same day, he launched Operation Nordwind, sending eighteen divisions against the thinly stretched U.S. Sixth Army in Alsace, at the southern end of his West Wall. His hope was that his columns would break through the American lines there, link up with German troops still holding on in and around the city of Colmar, cut off Strasbourg, and lure parts of Patton's Third Army away from Bastogne.

The 103rd Division, in which Paul Fussell served, held part of the threatened line. The Germans—"clad in white camouflage suits and wearing white-painted helmets, supported by white tanks," Fussell recalled—attacked in swirling clouds of snow. The startled Americans fell back. Some ran. The snow stopped eventually, but the temperature fell to twenty below zero. For two weeks, the Americans, including the 103rd Division, would be forced to give ground, fighting through two-foot drifts with the Germans right behind them. Vehicles and tanks slid off icy tracks. One creative GI in Fussell's unit scattered upside-down dinner plates across a road in hopes that once enough snow had sifted down onto them German tankers would think them mined and be forced to pause, however briefly.

Finally, Fussell wrote, the Americans took up positions on the south bank of the Moder River, huddled together in shallow holes engineers had blasted out of the frozen ground and roofed with railroad ties, leaving only a narrow slit through which to "watch the Germans on the other side of the river getting ready to attack us. The only entrance was through a slippery slide at the rear which became increasingly nasty because there we had to throw out our excrement, deposited first on a spread-out K-ration carton. To appear outside the hole in daylight was to be shot instantly. . . ."

"We were all afraid," Fussell recalled.

And at that point, a little ASTP boy—a boy who had come to the infantry from the Army Specialized Training Program— sought me out. I said, "What do you want?" and he said, "I want to tell you that I'm not going to fire my rifle when we're attacked. I'm not going to fire it, I just can't." See, he expected to be sent back. And he was shocked when I said, "I don't give a fuck whether you fire your rifle or not. That's your business, not mine. I don't care. I rather hope you don't fire it because you'll be easier to get rid of that way." And he burst into tears and fled. But I heard no more about not firing his rifle.

Fussell and his men continued to shiver and to take turns peering through the opening below their roof, trying to stay alert for the fresh onslaught they knew would come.

American attitudes toward the enemy differed greatly between the Pacific and the European theater. "Brutish, primitive hatred [was] as characteristic of the horror of war in the Pacific," Eugene Sledge would write, "as the palm trees and the islands." For the most part, Tom Galloway recalled, GIs in Europe did not share that hatred.

I don't think that the animosity was there like with the Japanese. We all kind of came from the same roots, when you get right down to it. Certainly you'd shoot a German. But it was not because you were mad at them. It was just that that was your job. And that was it. They had the same job you did. Those people—a bunch of them, anyway—didn't want to be there any more than we did. And they got drafted in and they were doing their job and we were doing ours. And some of them were just as likeable as could be when you got to know them.

But there were exceptions to the rule. Chenogne, the Belgian village Private Burnett Miller had prematurely thought safely in American hands, had finally fallen to the men of the 21st Armored Infantry Battalion on New Year's Day. The two-day fight to take it had been costly. Every haystack seemed to hide a weapon. Each house and outbuilding had been turned into a fortress. Men fell, writhing in the bloody snow. Cries of "Medic! Medic!" seemed to come from everywhere. Only U.S. tank and artillery fire from behind saved the green, frightened troops from disaster. "We actually retreated back up onto a hill," Miller remembered, "dug in, and spent that night in a big snowstorm, and we were wet, and I thought, 'Boy, I don't think we can make it.'" Another GI remembered being so tired that night that he could no longer stand, and sitting in the snow instead, chipping away at the frozen earth between his legs. His buddy lay down next to him and said he'd just as soon die there as underground.

The battle for the village began again at dawn and went on for most of the next day with more deaths, more wounded men, more terror. Finally, "artillery and tanks came in and sort of leveled the houses," Miller continued. The men were angry, exhausted, grieving. Their excitable new battalion commander had told them before the fighting began that they were to take no prisoners, and they took him at his word. When a German medic stepped out of a wrecked and burning house waving a Red Cross flag, GIs shot him. Several more unarmed Germans followed. They shot them, too. "A ring of bodies was forming around the doorway," a man from the company adjacent to Miller's remembered. Then a group of terrified women and children came out of the building. The men held their fire. But later, as the Americans moved from house to house in the ruined town, Miller remembered more German troops appeared with their hands in the air.

They finally surrendered, and they came out and were lined up, and per usual no one knew what was going on. It was confusion. [The battalion commander] lined them up and said, "I want you to shoot 'em." And I was horrified. Quite a few of us were horrified. And I went to him and told him, you know, that this was against all international law and humanity.

The frozen corpse of a German officer

Then my good buddy grabbed me and said, "This nut'll shoot you. You better quit. Knock this off."

A hastily assembled party of Americans led some twenty-five Germans into a snowy field out of sight of the enemy in the woods beyond the village and shot them. Afterward, Miller wondered what could have made a commander order such a thing.

I've rationalized that the Germans had massacred a group of Americans at Malmédy and maybe he'd gotten wind of this or something. But it was a terrible thing to see, and I talked to a lot of my buddies who had shot these guys, and they were horrified, too, after it happened.

You can't comprehend doing that under any circumstances. But, you know, people do change in war. When you've seen people killed every day and people maimed every day, pretty soon you become hardened, very hardened. I once stayed in a hole for an hour and a half or something like that—it seemed like that, anyway—with a dead German. And it's kind of an eerie feeling. But you were so worried, really, about yourself that you didn't think too much about it. I remember I was not affected when a good friend of mine was killed and run over by a tank, and it was an awful horror, and I was shocked that it didn't bother me very much. But about a week after the war ended, I saw an automobile accident and I got sick, as I normally would have before the war. I went from being terribly, terribly tough to being normal.

Miller's battalion commander was not alone in refusing to take prisoners in the Ardennes. Word of the massacre at Malmédy had inflamed American troops, though the full extent of it was not understood until the scene of the crime was retaken more than a month later. Accounts of other butcheries committed by German troops further fanned the flames: eleven black artillerymen murdered at Wereth; nineteen POWs said to have been slaughtered at Honsfield, fifty at Bullingen; more than one hundred Belgian civilians slain at Stavelot. SS men were the most common targets of American wrath. One officer apologized to General Bradley for having allowed four of them to reach his POW cage intact. "We needed a few samples," he explained. "That's all we've taken, sir."

IN MANILA, ON THE NIGHT OF JANUARY 8, an American plane once again dipped low over Santo Tomas to drop a leaflet. It, too, was addressed to the people of the Philippines. "MacArthur has returned," it said. "General MacArthur will tell you over the radio in proclamation and leaflet exactly how and when you can help. Watch closely for these instructions."

Sascha Weinzheimer's hopes soared: "Gosh! Maybe soon we can sing 'God Bless America' out loud! Maybe we can see our flag flying again! What a thrill it will be when our first boys come through that gate! Mother says we fought this war, too, like soldiers."

That morning, some 140 miles north of Santo Tomas, almost a thousand American ships filled Lingayen Gulf. The first wave of Americans came ashore at about ten o'clock, landing on the same beaches the Japanese had assaulted more than three years earlier. At two in the afternoon, a small boat brought MacArthur and his staff toward shore. This time the Seabees had created a crude pier for the general to step onto. He refused to use it, preferring to wade through the surf instead so the photographers could get more dramatic pictures.

The almost daily bombing in and around Manila intensified—"exciting and thrilling and convincing," one internee called it. Rumors of imminent liberation coexisted with fears of starvation. Sascha kept track of what was happening around her.

JANUARY 12. Carroll Grinnell, Chairman of the [Internee] Committee and our good friend, and three other Americans were taken out of Camp today. No one knows why or where. Uncle Carroll did a great deal for the Internees these last three years and we hope he will be rewarded some day. [Grinnell and his companions were murdered and their bodies dumped in a mass grave in Manila.]

The wood-chopping crew is busy cutting up almost everything in sight for the camp stoves—even tearing up the roof, benches and tables of the dining shed. They aren't useful any more because most of the people who ate there are too weak to leave their beds to go outside to eat. It is sad to see people, even us, watching our little plants grow and pulling them out to eat before they are ready. People are dying every day from starvation. Fred Fairman and Mrs. Everett yesterday. We have such a short time to go—what a pity they couldn't hang on to life just a while longer. Mother weighs only 73 pounds—she used to weigh 148—and Dr. Allen says she has to stay in bed from now on because she can't walk. My knees don't work so well when I walk.

JANUARY 17. Buddy's favorite expression is, "Let's talk about food." He has a favorite suit too which he calls his "Gate suit." He's been taking this suit out almost every day for months, putting it on the bed and saying, "I'll put my Gate things right here Mummy, so I can be ready." All of us have some-

thing saved to wear out the Gate—Doris a ribbon, me a pair of brown socks. All of us except Daddy who has been bare-footed now for six months. "I don't need a thing for the gate except two good legs to walk out with," he said. He works very hard for us chopping wood, fixing beds, doing the laundry, besides working in the Central kitchen most of the day and night. We pray he will keep well even if he is so thin.

JANUARY 28. Nothing special happened outside of bomb-ings, fires and explosions. . . .

People are so hungry they will do anything. Some fathers we know even take food from their kid's share and we know of three Daddies who cry loud in front of their kids even because they [are] so hungry. A little boy was carrying his mush from the line to his shanty when two men tried to grab them away from him. The Nips are still bringing in big legs of meat and plenty of rice for themselves. They want us to die—how awfully wicked they are. . . . Right this minute those awful soldiers are yelling at their bayonet practice—yelling as if they are really killing our soldiers. Mother thinks they do that to get us down.

"Hunger had become a living thing, like cancer," another Santo Tomas diarist noted. "It ate into our bodies and minds. We thought of nothing but food and hate." That hate focused with special intensity on Lieutenant Abiko. His superiors had actually done more harm to the internees than he had, since it was they who issued the orders to reduce rations, impose humiliations, mete out punishments. But Abiko had carried out those orders with obvious enthusiasm and frequent brutality. To the internees he symbolized everything they loathed about their imprison-ment. On February 1, he was present and in charge when Japa-nese soldiers led a carabao into the compound and butchered it for themselves to eat while hundreds of inmates stood in a silent circle, hoping for some of the leavings. When their captors had carried its skinned carcass off to their kitchen, an internee remembered, "men, women, and children rushed to the spot, and like voracious dogs they clawed around the blood, entrails, dust, and grit, searching for tail, ears, hooves, or anything that resembled food."

"This morning Auntie Bee [a family friend] came to visit," Sascha Weinzheimer wrote that same day. "She works in the hos-pital. She says the doctors expect seven more to die today—all from starvation." The Japanese tried to talk Dr. T. D. Stevenson into putting some other diagnosis on their death certificates. Stevenson said he could not do such a thing and was locked up for his honesty.

AMERICAN ANXIETY OVER WHAT HAD HAPPENED in the Ardennes was easing now, Burt Wilson remembered, as the lines on the front-page maps of the Sacramento paper he delivered each morning "started moving again the right way and we thought, 'Well, it's only a matter of time now.' "

For the men actually fighting to recapture the ground they had lost in December, inch by frozen inch, things did not seem quite so clear. The trap Bradley and Patton had hoped to spring failed. The First Army did not begin to edge south until January 3 and then was unable to make more than a mile or two a day. By the time the twin forces linked up at Houffalize, on January 16, most of the Germans the Americans had planned to cut off within the Bulge's tip had fought their way out of it.

Meanwhile, the winter worsened, Burnett Miller remem-bered.

We always had frozen feet, because our shoes were really very, very poor for keeping out snow. We went into combat in the Bulge in the same overcoats we'd gone to London in, big, bulky, miserable things that would get wet. Pretty soon we were looking for German prisoners or German dead because they had nice bunny-fur jackets that were just terrific, not only comfortable and warm but white and cam-ouflaged.

Some fifteen thousand GIs were disabled by frostbite; gangrene forced the amputation of fingers, toes, feet. Arthur Mayer devel-oped a mild but painful case. One day he was ordered to accom-pany two young prisoners—maybe fourteen or fifteen years old, he recalled—back to the POW cage behind the American lines. They walked fast. Trench foot made it painful for him to keep up. Finally, he remembered, more in irritation than anything else, he said, "*Ich bin ein Jude*—I am a Jew." The boys panicked and broke into a run. Other GIs opened fire. "Both of them were shot," Mayer recalled. "I didn't mean to do that. I don't know if they died."

Even those who managed somehow to keep their feet dry, protect themselves against the deadliest cold, and find a way to sleep for at least a couple of hours a night were exhausted by the effort. "It was very, very difficult for anybody who was much older than we were," Miller recalled.

We had a fellow in our outfit who was 30 or 31, and it was just a nightmare for him. Just sitting in a hole hurt him. He'd just get up out of a hole no matter how dangerous it was if there was a fire and go stand by the fire just to get warm. And one morning after he'd done that he told us, "You know, I could

PERSONAL PINUP

Every day during the war, Dolores Silva, above, a Portuguese American farmer's daughter from the Sacramento Valley, wrote to her high school sweetheart, Norman Greenslate, below right. He was an engineer in the 389th Division and she worried constantly that he might be killed or wounded, even when she went to the movies. "You kept track of the war either by newspaper or by the *Movietone News*," she remembered.

This standing invitation to Betty Grable was issued on Guadalcanal.

When we saw those newsreels you were always looking for a familiar face, looking to see if there was somebody that you knew. And, one time, they showed this battle and I saw this one fellow, he had been wounded or he was killed and he was lying on a road in this town. I didn't know where the town was. I just got a side view of his face and he looked just like Norman. And I about fell apart. I just went to pieces and I had to run out into the lobby to compose myself. It looked just like him. It was very traumatizing. And I finally got my composure. I went back in and then I found out that it was in Italy and he was still in England.

Later, Greenslate took part in the Battle of the Bulge. Dolores was determined to wait for him and wanted to be sure he would wait for her, as well.

They had a lot of pinup girls. Betty Grable had a picture of herself in her bathing suit. She's glancing back over her shoulder. And it's a back view and, oh, it was gorgeous. And then there was Rita Hayworth. She was in a negligee and she was kneeling on a bed, and that was very sexy. And the boys liked to have a pinup picture. So I said Norman's going to have his own pinup picture. That was the first time that the two-piece bathing suit came in. And I had one that laced on the side. You could either wear it low, if you had enough nerve to do it, or you could wear it all the way to the top. Well, anyway, I put it on and went out in the back yard and I gave my mother my camera and I says, "Here. Take a picture. I want to send it to Norman. I'm going to be his pinup girl." So, I sent him this little picture just big enough to put in his wallet. And he carried that through the war with him and he said that he received a lot of comments from his buddies when they saw that picture. They looked at him and they looked back at the picture and they looked at him again and said "What does she see in you?" He got the biggest kick out of that. I had a picture of him on my desk (below), one that he took in France and I especially liked and so I had that on my desk. So, I was with him and he was with me.

Men suffering from minor wounds and frostbite at a crowded evacuation hospital in Huy, Belgium. The survival rate for Americans wounded in the European theater was the highest in the history of warfare. "We were convinced," one lieutenant said, "that the army had a regulation against dying in an aid station."

hear Germans on the other side of the fire. They were getting warm, too."

The Germans now held the villages GIs had seized from them in September. To take them back again, the Americans had to fight their way from one to the next across frozen fields. One infantryman recalled how it was to take part in such an attack.

We started out. Then there came the long, wild screams and crash of German artillery, and then the double line, thin-looking without overcoats, indistinct in the swirling snow, wavered and sank down flat, then struggled up and went on, heads bent against the wind. This was "jumping off," this cold, plodding, unwilling, ragged double line plunging up to their knees in snow, stumbling, looking back.

Men sometimes reoccupied foxholes they'd been forced from just a few weeks earlier. Some towns changed hands four times, and at least 2,500 civilians died in the crossfire. Thousands more cowered in cellars as one side or the other destroyed their homes above them.

On average, the Americans suffered two thousand casualties every day. Burnett Miller was one of them: an artillery shell tem-

porarily deafened him, damaged his equilibrium, and gave him what he remembered as "a tail wound" that required a series of painful injections of penicillin. He recuperated in a head-wound ward, he remembered. "It was horrible. I was lucky because I could only hear rushing noises. The poor fellow in the bunk next to me had had his eyes blown out and fortunately I couldn't hear much. It was a horrible, horrible thing and fellows were dying all the time. You could only tell that because they'd come in and get them, put them in a bag and take them out." When Miller rejoined his unit three weeks later, it had made very little progress on the ground. "I'm well and as happy as can be expected," he wrote to his parents. "I'd like to get drunk as the devil right now. But so would everyone else I talk to. I guess the feeling is universal in the E.T.O. [European Theater of Operations]. Our main prayers are with the Russians [advancing from the east] . . . however I've kept my optimism to a minimum."

German prisoners of war forced to carry the frozen body of an American from a snowy field in the Ardennes, February 1, 1945. In the previous thirty days alone, the United States had lost almost forty thousand men.

"A frontline soldier was immensely well informed," one officer recalled, "if he knew the name of his company commander, who had just arrived the day before to replace the other one who had lasted only a week." Most enlisted men were replaced by high school boys who had been rushed through six weeks of cursory training and often died before anyone learned their names—and who were then replaced by still more frightened, anonymous newcomers.

"I had a friend who claimed he was sent into the Battle of the Bulge with six weeks' training and a new rifle," Katharine Phillips recalled. "He said if he had not been shooting squirrels all his life, he would have been completely lost. But Greylap was put on the front lines. He said he shot the Germans like he would squirrels, and that was it."

As the men battled their way back toward the West Wall again, the men from Graves Registration followed along behind, harvesting the dead. Many drank heavily to stave off the cold and blunt the impact of what they had to do. Men who'd died recently could be handled with relative care. But those who'd been killed earlier in the fighting had frozen solid and had to be slung into the trucks and stacked like grotesque tree limbs after a winter storm. More than a million men would take part in the Battle of the Bulge before it was over, and more Americans would be lost in it than had been lost by both sides at Gettysburg: twenty thousand dead; sixty thousand more wounded, captured, or marked as "missing." Still, by the end of January, the Allies had managed to regain all the ground they'd given up. More than eighty thousand Germans had been lost to Hitler's cause, and thousands more cold, miserable enemy troops were stumbling back into Germany, terrified whenever they emerged into the open that American fighter-bombers were somewhere nearby.

From a tangle of frozen corpses a Graves Registration officer and his men seek to separate out the Americans.

By then, Operation Nordwind in Alsace was also collapsing. The attack across the Moder that Paul Fussell and the 103rd Division had been expecting had finally begun with a terrifying artillery barrage on the morning of January 25. "We cowered at the bottom of the hole," Fussell recalled, "dreading a direct hit and dreading equally a German attack during the barrage, which would catch us utterly unprepared to repel it." The shells stopped for a moment. Then the crack troops of the SS 6th Mountain Division—full of schnapps, Fussell remembered, and cursing as they came—crossed the river and ran right into American machine-gun and artillery fire. Corpses lay scattered across the snow. Those Germans who did make it through the line were killed or captured or driven back again.

The German operations Autumn Mist and Nordwind had failed. It was time for the Allies to resume the vast assault the enemy offensive had interrupted. Eisenhower now had nearly 4 million men in place along four hundred miles of the German border. But his forces had still managed to punch just one forty-mile hole through the West Wall, near Aachen. Beyond the fortified line—at distances ranging from twenty to ninety miles—was the Rhine, the broad, fast-flowing river that was everything to the Germans: moat, mythic symbol, waterway to the North Sea. Between the West Wall and the river, hundreds of thousands of enemy troops were still in place, ordered by Hitler to hold the west bank at any cost; withdrawal across the Rhine, he told his generals, was "unthinkable."

Montgomery argued yet again for the chance to lead a single drive into northwest Germany. His plan reflected Churchill's hope of capturing the North Sea ports of Bremen and Hamburg before the Soviet army, now momentarily paused just forty miles from Berlin, could overrun them. But Montgomery's plan also called for all American forces not under his command to stay put while he went forward. Bradley and Patton were infuriated. They blamed Montgomery for having been too slow to take Caen after D-day, for the Market Garden fiasco, above all for trying to take credit for the victory their men had just won in the Ardennes. Bradley threatened to resign if the field marshal was given command of any more of his forces, and had to be reassured by Eisenhower that he was still in charge of the Twelfth Army. The hardest part of his job, Eisenhower confided in a letter to General Marshall, was "arranging the blankets smoothly over several prima donnas in the same bed."

Actually, Montgomery's plan never stood much chance of being adopted. British power and influence were waning. Three out of four of the men under Eisenhower's command were American; so were 12,500 of the 17,500 Allied aircraft he could call upon. Washington wanted the European war over with as quickly as possible so that it could turn its full attention to the Pacific, and Eisenhower continued to believe that multiple attacks along the entire front would be the fastest means to that end. But he also remained understandably wary of an enemy whose ability to resist he and his lieutenants had so badly underestimated in December. Before any of his armies tried to cross the Rhine, he wanted the whole length of its west bank cleared. "The more Germans we kill west of the Rhine," he told Montgomery, "the fewer there will be to meet us east of the river."

Eisenhower outlined a series of carefully staggered attacks all along the Allied line. Montgomery's British and Canadian armies were to begin the movement toward the Rhine on February 8 with Operation Veritable. They would be joined on their southern flank two days later by the U.S. Ninth Army, once it had crossed the Roer. To make that crossing possible, Courtney Hodges's First Army was to undertake Operation Grenade, finally capturing the dams that should have been the primary Allied target at the beginning of the battle for the Hürtgen Forest, three months earlier.

Meanwhile, American commanders to the south would not be required to remain static. Instead, they were to go on the "aggressive defensive," a deliberately vague phrase they were free to define as loosely as they liked. But once Montgomery reached the Rhine, Bradley's First Army was to begin Operation Lumberjack and drive toward the Rhine from the Ardennes. As soon as Bradley got there, in mid-March, it would be the turn of General Jacob L. Devers's 6th Army Group, the southernmost Allied force; he was to move across the heavily industrialized Saar basin to the Rhine in an operation code-named Undertone. In the interim, Devers was also to clear the last of the Germans from the Colmar pocket. By the end of March, if all went well, the Allies would be ready to cross the Rhine into the heart of Germany. On February 2, at a meeting on the island of Malta, Eisenhower was given the go-ahead by the Combined Chiefs of Staff.

THE FOLLOWING DAY, SATURDAY, FEBRUARY 3, 1945, at about five in the afternoon, Sascha Weinzheimer and her father, sister, and brother were standing in the long chow line at Santo Tomas (her mother remained too weak to leave her bed) when ten American planes roared in just above the treetops. One dropped a small dark object onto the patio of the main building. It was a rolled-up pair of pilot's goggles. Wrapped inside was a brief message: "Roll out the barrel. Santa Claus is coming Saturday or Sunday." The whole camp began to buzz, she remembered. "It was like throwing a rock at a beehive and having it come alive."

"There is no doubt that the boys are nearer," one diarist had written the day before. "There have been extra-heavy demolition reports and fires." There had been still more fires and explosions since then, but the internees' hopes had been raised and dashed so often over the past months that no one could be sure it wouldn't all die down again. The airborne message seemed full of real promise.

Darkness fell over Santo Tomas. There was now no power. Internees had to find their way around by flashlights and candles. They could see tracers and fires and shells landing far beyond the compound walls and they could now hear rifle and machine-gun fire as well. But they also heard a strange sort of rumbling they hadn't heard before. "We were rushing back and forth," Sascha remembered. "People were saying, 'Gee! Isn't this a different thing!' The Brits were saying, 'Oh, it's the Brits! The Brits are coming! They're here! The Limeys are here!' And the Americans said, 'Don't be silly. This is the Americans coming.'"

Then, just before nine o'clock, two umbrella flares erupted overhead, lighting up the lawns. A grenade flashed. Then a tank crashed through the front gate and someone called out, "Hello, folks. We're Americans." Four more tanks followed.

A great cheer went up. "People went crazy," Sascha remembered.

You'd think the war was over. My mother was bedridden, at seventy-three pounds. She'd always said, "Now, let's always keep one item to wear when our boys come in." She had a half-used lipstick, and so when my father picked up my mother and ran out of the shanty, she says, "Wait! Wait!" He couldn't understand why. She says, "Go back." So she reached underneath her mattress and pulled out her lipstick and put it on. Then she said, "Now I'm ready for my boys."

The internees spilled out onto the lawn, one of the tankers remembered, "waving, shouting, screaming, weeping." One woman couldn't get over how tall and healthy all their rescuers seemed, like "young giants," she said. A small boy was frightened

Hours after their liberation, jubilant Santo Tomas internees still fill the entrance hall (opposite) and crowd the windows of the Administration Building (below) to see and talk with their rescuers. "People were hugging them, kissing them and crying," Sascha Weinzheimer remembered. "Mother said to one, 'May I please just touch you?' They all seemed dazed, too . . . they didn't realize so many Americans were here."

Internees savor army rations. "The Army is feeding us now—and how!" Sascha wrote. "Sugar, milk, bread, butter, spam, and oh, such good things. Chocolate bars, gum, and cigarettes for all. With all the food we had, many internees were griping because they didn't get enough, just as if it wouldn't last."

by them at first; the only American soldiers he'd ever seen had worn World War I–style tin hats, and he feared that these helmeted strangers must be Nazis. They were part of a flying column of some seven hundred men belonging to the 2nd Squadron, 8th Cavalry Regiment, 1st Cavalry Division, dis-

patched ahead of the advancing army by General MacArthur himself to free the Americans being held at all three sites on the city's northern edge: Santo Tomas and Los Baños internment camps and Bilibid prison. Word of what the enemy had done to 150 U.S. POWs on the island of Palawan in December had provided the impetus for the mission: rather than allow them to be rescued, the Japanese had burned most of their prisoners alive and hunted down and shot all but a handful of the rest.

The internees broke into "God Bless America." "I have never heard it sung as it was sung that day," a correspondent reported. "I have never heard people singing 'God Bless America' and weeping openly. And I have never seen soldiers—hard-bitten youngsters such as make up the First Cavalry—stand unashamed and weep with them." Part of the reason for the soldiers' tears was the sight of so many emaciated, ragged, frail-seeming men, women, and children, some of whom reached out to touch them as if to reassure themselves that they were real. The men handed out all the K rations and chocolate bars and cans of fruit they happened to have in their pockets. Some inmates simply dropped to the ground and began to eat.

Two internees emerged from the education building, asked by the commandant, Lieutenant Colonel Hayashi, to help negotiate safe passage out of the compound for himself and his men. The commandant and several subordinates, including the hated Lieutenant Abiko, followed in their wake. Soldiers relieved two lieutenants of their swords without incident. But when Abiko's turn came to be disarmed, he clawed at a pouch that hung from his shoulder. It held a grenade, and he evidently planned to detonate it, killing himself and as many of the Americans who surrounded him as he could. The commander of the rescue team snatched a carbine from one of his soldiers and shot Abiko four times. He collapsed, moaning. Furious internees surrounded him, kicking and spitting and slashing at him with knives. Women leaned down to stub out cigarettes on his flesh. They eventually dragged him by his feet into the annex clinic, leaving a bright smear of blood across the steps and along the hallway. When he was lifted onto a table, his grenade fell out onto the floor. A soldier carefully carried it outside in his helmet. Dr. Stevenson did what he could for the wounded man. Just released from the jail to which he'd been sent because he'd refused to falsify the death certificates of his fellow internees, Stevenson said he had a duty to try to save his captor's life. Abiko was carried to a bed in a nearby women's dormitory, but when its owner turned up, she rolled him off onto the floor. She did not want the pig to die in her bed, she said. His corpse was left in a stairwell for a day so that everyone could have a look at him. Sascha was among those who filed past it. "The prisoners had him positioned with

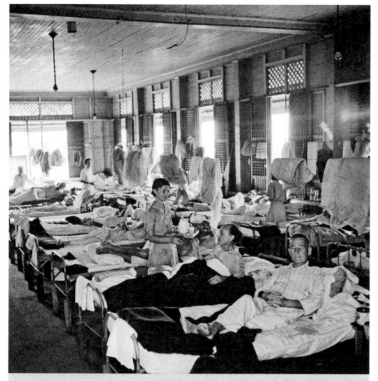

Life photographer Carl Mydans, who took these photographs, had himself been an internee in the early months of the war. "Three years of Jap militarism left its mark on our people," he wrote, "and many of them, like withered plants, will not begin to perk their heads up again until nourishment restores the vitality which humans have to live." The hospital (above and lower right) was filled with starving men and women when Mydans visited it, and shanties (right and bottom left) still crowded the administration building's courtyard.

Teenage internees try to look their best for their liberators: "Such nice young fellows the GIs are," Sascha Weinzheimer wrote. "Every single one seems so wonderful." The men of the 1st Cavalry felt the same about those they'd rescued. "It sure is good to see American women," one said. "It makes me feel almost like I'm home again."

his boots facing the rising sun, which was a disgrace in their Japanese beliefs," she recalled. "It felt good."

Meanwhile, the commandant and the other officers had slipped back into the education building. There, he and sixty-five of his men barricaded themselves for two days, holding some 240 men and boys hostage until the American commander agreed to have the Japanese escorted safely through the gates. As they left, some of the children ran after them, shouting, "Make them bow, boys! Make them bow!"

On February 7, General MacArthur himself visited Santo Tomas. It was Sascha's twelfth birthday.

MacArthur came in for twenty minutes, greeted the prisoners, and left. And as soon as he left, the Japs started shelling the camp. A lot of internees were killed. A lot of soldiers were killed. And it was just one of those wild things: blood everywhere, and stretchers, and people running.

An American soldier and two Sisters from the order of the Daughters of Charity help dazed women and children out of the ruins of Intramuros, the old walled city of Manila where the Japanese had made their final stand.

Sascha and her family spent two days crouched in a kitchen storeroom, sustained by a birthday cake her mother had made for her. Twelve internees and two GIs were killed by mortar rounds the first day; six more people would die before the Americans located and destroyed the enemy mortars.

The internees tried to adjust to freedom. "We're eating and eating," an internee wrote. "K-rations—boy what good chow!" Sascha wrote. "The soldiers were tired of it and hardly ate anything. We gobbled it all." The Red Cross arrived with food, medicine, and current magazines, *Time* and *Life* and *Liberty*. "It is bewildering," one internee wrote after leafing through their glossy pages, "to try to realize that they refer to the world we should have been living in."

The battle for Manila would go on for a month. Most of the city was destroyed. A thousand Americans died. So did sixteen thousand Japanese soldiers—and nearly one hundred thousand Filipino civilians, some hit by American artillery, many slaughtered by their retreating captors. "Manila," said General Robert Eichelberger, commander of the Eighth Army in the Philippines, "has ceased to exist, except for some places that the Japanese thought were not worth defending or where our American troops got in by surprise."

Afterward, a friend of the Weinzheimers drove them through what was left of city they had loved.

[Major] George Woods took mother, Dad, and [me] through Manila in a jeep to see the ruins. . . . We had heard how badly Manila was destroyed, but until we saw it with our own eyes, we couldn't believe such a thing could happen. . . . The whole city—nothing left! Taft Avenue, the Boulevard, everything in ruins. The odor from the dead was awful, and whenever we stopped the big green flies were all over us.

American troops, fighting to complete the recapture of Luzon before moving on to free other Philippine islands, soon came upon what was left of Camp O'Donnell, where so many Americans and Filipinos had died in the weeks that followed the surrender on Bataan. The nipa shelters that had once housed thousands of sick and starving men had collapsed. Jungle had overgrown the mass graves. A Graves Registration Unit began the grim business of opening them and trying to identify remains. In one, they discovered a dogtag with Glenn Frazier's name on it. Believing he was likely to die in Japanese hands, Frazier had deliberately left it there back in 1942, in the hope that Americans would find it one day and be able to tell his parents what had happened to him.

Eventually, an officer knocked on the Frazier family's door in Fort Deposit, Alabama. It was now clear that their son was dead, he told Frazier's parents. He had the dogtag with him as proof. They were now entitled to an insurance payment of ten thousand dollars.

"Well," Mr. Frazier asked, "if I take the ten thousand dollars and he's not dead, what happens then?"

He'd have to give it back, the officer answered.

"Well, you just keep it, because I'm sure if anybody can make it, my son can make it. And if he's dead, then I'll come back to you and get the ten thousand dollars."

Meanwhile, their son, still a prisoner of war in Japan, had been moved twice over the past few months. First he'd been housed in a camp near the industrial city of Kobe, where he labored in a graphite factory and talked incessantly with a southern-born friend of "what we were going to cook and eat when we got back home. Even a bowl of chitlins sounded good at this point." Then he'd been shifted to Tsuruga, southwest of Tokyo on the coast of the Sea of Japan. There, despite frequent beatings by two guards they nicknamed The Emperor and Sir Shit Bird, he and his fellow prisoners continued their "disrupt on purpose by accident" style of sabotage: bursting bags of rice and beans they were ordered to unload and at least once managing to drop railroad ties on one of their captors.

ON FEBRUARY 4, 1945, the day after Sascha Weinzheimer and her family were liberated, Roosevelt, Churchill, and Stalin began a week of talks in a dilapidated czarist palace near Yalta, on the Black Sea. Roosevelt was weary and ill. Churchill was tired, too. The Soviet premier was triumphant: his armies had now overrun Romania, Bulgaria, Hungary, Poland, and East Prussia and were closing in on Berlin itself, while Eisenhower's forces had just begun working their way toward the west side of the Rhine.

Many of the decisions made over the course of the three leaders' deliberations concerned the shape of the postwar world. Stalin's determination to hold on to those sections of eastern and central Europe that his armies had taken back from the Germans had not weakened since the Teheran conference two years earlier, and the Americans and British still had neither the resolve nor the capability with which to try to change his mind: the official Big Three communiqué issued from Yalta, promising free elections and reaffirming "the right of all peoples to choose the form of Government under which they will live" was largely a formality. Defeated Germany was to be carved into four occupation zones (American, British, French, and Soviet), with Berlin going to the Soviets. Stalin also agreed to join the newly constituted United Nations, provided that the USSR had a veto as a member of the Security Council and was awarded two extra votes in the

Churchill, Roosevelt, and Stalin at Yalta

General Assembly (for the "republics" of Ukraine and White Russia).

Two decisions made that week would directly affect the course of the still unfinished war. American commanders dreaded what they would have to face once they could turn their undivided attention to the Pacific: Guadalcanal, Tarawa, Peleliu, Saipan, Leyte, Luzon, and all the other costly landings they'd made since 1942 had only strengthened their conviction that an invasion of the Japanese home islands might take at least two more years and cost countless American lives. If Stalin could be persuaded to make good on his promise to enter the Pacific war once Germany was defeated, FDR believed, even the militarists who ruled Japan might see the hopelessness of their cause and make a bloody invasion unnecessary. To win the Soviet premier's commitment, and without consulting his Allies, the president was willing to make several concessions to him, including the Kurile Islands and recognition of Mongolia as a Soviet satellite. When Fleet Admiral King, chief of Naval Operations, heard that Stalin had agreed to come into the war against Japan, he was jubilant. "We've just saved two million Americans!" he said.

But before they could proceed together against Japan, the Allies had to complete the conquest of Germany. To that end, the Russians wanted to improve coordination between their armies advancing on the ground and the British and American bombers that now controlled the skies overhead. They asked for a designated "bombing line" beyond which Allied aircraft would not bomb without consulting Soviet commanders to prevent inadvertent attacks on their own troops. More important, they

A heap of Dresden's dead, only a fraction of the 6,865 corpses of men, women, and children waiting to be doused with gasoline and set on fire in the city's Old Market after the Allied bombing raids of February 13 and 14, 1945

wanted to stop Hitler from reinforcing the eastern front. "Air action," a Soviet officer said, can "hinder the enemy from carrying out the shifting of his troops to the east from the western front, from Norway and from Italy." He wanted the American and British air arms to step up their assaults on railroad stations and marshaling yards in the hearts of cities. As an example, another Soviet officer suggested, "we want . . . the Dresden railway junction bombed."

The American and British air chiefs needed little urging. German oil plants continued to take top priority; enemy armor could not move without it. But German cities already ran a close second, and a day or two later, the Targets Committee of the British Air Ministry sent new recommendations to SHAEF, Bomber Command, and the U.S. Strategic Air Force Command: "The following targets have been selected for their importance in relation to the movements of Evacuees from, and of military forces to, the Eastern Front." Berlin was first on the list, though it had already been bombed more than three hundred times and had been hit again just a few days earlier, killing some three

thousand people. Dresden, in the heart of Saxony, was second. It had been bombed just twice and remained largely undamaged, a lovely medieval city, which some called Florence on the Elbe, that had been a favorite among British tourists before the war. Thousands of German refugees were now streaming through it each day, in flight from the oncoming Russians; German troops were moving through it, too, headed in the other direction.

On February 13 and 14—Shrove Tuesday and Ash Wednesday—nine hundred British and American bombers hit Dresden in two waves, dropping incendiary bombs in hopes of deliberately setting off the sort of firestorm they had first achieved accidentally in Hamburg nearly two years earlier. They succeeded. At least thirty-five thousand civilians were burned or blown apart—or robbed of oxygen as they huddled in basements and bomb shelters.

The bombing of Germany went on, battering oil facilities, defense factories, roads, and railways—and more cities: Pforzheim, Würzburg, Essen, Dortmund, Potsdam. In March alone, Allied warplanes dropped sixty-seven thousand tons of bombs on Germany, almost as many tons as they had dropped in the preceding three years combined. By the middle of the next month, the Allied air chiefs would call a halt. There were no more targets. By then, 593,000 German civilians had been killed by Allied bombing. Most were women. More than 100,000 were children.

AMERICAN B-29S COULD NOW REACH JAPAN, too, from Saipan and Tinian. Roughly halfway between them and the Japanese home islands lay the tiny volcanic island of Iwo Jima. It was an eerie, otherworldly place, barely eight square miles of volcanic ash and rubble, reeking of sulfur, without safe drinking water. But it had an airstrip from which Japanese fighters rose to harass U.S. bombers as they flew to and from their targets. American commanders wanted the island taken to eliminate that threat and turn the island into a safe haven for crippled U.S. bombers as well.

For seventy-two straight days, American bombers pounded Iwo Jima with some six thousand tons of high explosives. Three more days of relentless navy shelling followed. Then, in the early morning of February 19, 1945, the 4th and 5th Marine divisions started going ashore. Most were veterans of earlier struggles—Saipan, Tinian, Peleliu. The first men to climb up the steeply terraced beach met little resistance and began to think this landing would be different, that for once the preinvasion bombardment really had knocked out the island's defenses. But it had not. As soon as the beaches were sufficiently crowded with men and equipment, the Japanese began hitting them with what marines called flying ashcans, mammoth mortar shells that blew victims and parts of victims one hundred feet into the air. The men killed on the beaches of Iwo Jima "died with the greatest possible violence," wrote the veteran correspondent Robert Sherrod. "Many were cut squarely in half. Legs and arms lay fifty feet from any body."

Some twenty-one thousand Japanese soldiers were hidden within a virtually impenetrable network of mutually supporting tunnels and bunkers and gun galleries. Their commander's instructions to them were brutally clear: "We would all like to die quickly and easily, but that would not inflict heavy casualties. We must fight from cover as long as we possibly can. . . . Each man will make it his duty to kill ten of the enemy before dying." The ghastly, claustrophobic struggle to dislodge and destroy the island's defenders would last more than a month and be among the most savage of the Pacific war.

Ray Pittman of Mobile, now a sergeant, directed a demolition squad through the entire campaign. His first task was to find and disarm or detonate mines, but by the time he reached the beach there was so much shrapnel mixed in amid the sand that the mine detector wouldn't work. A mortar round soon tore apart

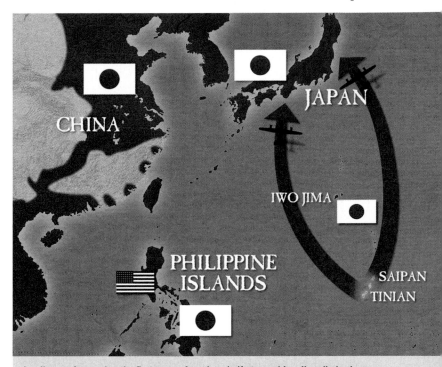

Landing craft carrying the first wave of marines knife toward Iwo Jima (below), February 19, 1945. More than six thousand marines would die before the island was taken. Their sacrifice permitted bombers to make emergency stops on the flight between their bases on Saipan and Tinian and the Japanese cities that were their targets.

Iwo Jima: while navy shells explode on Mount Suribachi in the background (left), riflemen of the 5th Marine Division inch their way up the beach's black volcanic sand; a chaplain (above) gives communion during a lull in the fighting; and a war correspondent finds a temporary sanctuary in which to bang out a story.

his closest friend, with whom he'd fought on Namur, Saipan, and Tinian. Pittmann took his dead friend's prized Colt .45 and put it in his pack, where it deflected a bullet that would otherwise have killed him. He repeatedly went forward under fire to blow up Japanese strongpoints. "You'd crawl up to their pillbox," he recalled. "You could hear them talking inside. I always wished that I could speak Japanese so I could tell what they were saying. But we'd stop their talking." Afterward, he had to clean human flesh as well as ash and concrete dust from his face, hands, and helmet. Pittmann won a second medal on Iwo Jima; and despite the loss of friends, the horrors he endured, and his own bewilderment that he had been spared, he would always consider "being in the 4th Marine Division and being in the four battles that I was in and coming through all of them all right one of the greatest experiences I ever had."

In the end, the Japanese sacrificed virtually their entire garrison on Iwo Jima. Their mission had been to take as many American lives as possible before they gave up their own. They succeeded in killing 6,821 marines, five times the number of dead on Guadalcanal or Saipan, one third of all the marines killed in the Pacific. Among them were Private David Harris of Luverne, Sergeant James Albert Chambliss of Mobile, Corporal John B. Zwanch of Waterbury, and Private Zera Richards of Sacramento. Twenty-seven Medals of Honor were awarded to those who fought on Iwo Jima; thirteen had to be given posthumously. Of the sixteen men in Ray Pittmann's squad, only he and two others emerged from the battle unhurt. American bombers were now free to attack the enemy's cities at will while the American buildup continued for the invasion of Okinawa, the far larger island that would serve as the springboard for the final invasion of Japan.

IN THE LAST WEEK OF FEBRUARY, as American soldiers continued to close on the Rhine and American marines struggled to end Japanese resistance on Iwo Jima, a group of eager young marine pilots boarded a Liberty Ship at San Diego and set out on a six-thousand-mile journey across the Pacific. Twenty-year-old Captain Sam Hynes from Minneapolis had been concerned that they might be too late. He and his fellow pilots had followed the progress of the European war in the newspapers, he remembered, but "we were much more interested in our war than in

In a shell crater on the Iwo Jima beach, a wounded marine awaits evacuation while holding on to a precious souvenir—the piece of shrapnel that inflicted the "million-dollar wound" that will take him out of combat.

other people's wars. If we followed any war, it was the Pacific war, and we followed it because we were worried that they'd finish it before we got there. We didn't want them to be too successful too soon."

Hynes had enlisted because "it had been impossible not to," he recalled.

Sam Hynes and his father

Because a current was established in the society so swift, flowing toward war that every young man who stepped into it was carried downstream. It's not a moral force, it's a physical force. You have to imagine what it was like to be a teenaged, lower middle-class kid in Minneapolis in 1941. Chances for excitement were fairly limited. You could drive a car fast, you could get drunk, you could take a girl out and try and get somewhere and fail. That's local excitement. But to have an exciting life—it was hard to imagine what an exciting life would be. And then suddenly you could be a pilot or a submariner or an artilleryman or any damn thing, but it was something exciting and it was something adult. All of a sudden, you could just choose to be an adult by writing your name. . . . I write my name and now I'm potentially a combat fighter pilot, an ace. Or I'm the commander of a submarine going into Tokyo Bay. These are incredible opportunities. They're melodramatic, exciting, like the movies. And you might do it. So that's terrific. It has nothing to do with patriotism. It has nothing to do, really, with who the enemy is. It's the opportunity to be somebody more exciting than the kid you are.

His older brother, Chuck, had entered the service the day after Pearl Harbor. His father, a veteran of World War I, had tried to sign up then, too—and was rejected because he wore false teeth. "What do they want me to do?" he asked when he got home. "Bite the Japanese to death?" Sam had wanted to join up then as well, but at seventeen was too young. He finished high school, spent the summer working in a Seattle defense plant, then entered the University of Minnesota as a freshman. But it wasn't long before he tried to enlist in the marines, hoping to become a pilot. "I was a very independent kid. I wanted an independent war. And I was attracted, therefore, to the idea of flying my own plane, myself, and attacking, myself, and deciding when to let the bomb go, myself." The recruiter took his name and told him to go back to college until he heard from the marines. He hadn't wanted to wait.

My friends were going. One of them was already a marine fighter pilot. That was unendurable for me, to be a college boy and him to be a marine fighter pilot. So I felt I had to accelerate this somehow, and I went into the recruiting office and there, to my astonishment, was an old friend of mine at the desk. And I said, "I've got to go." And as I talked to him it got more and more intense. "I've got to go. I've got to go. I'm out of money. Everyone else is going." And he went to the corner of the room where there was a great pile of files and fingered down to the bottom, pulled one out, and put it on top. And said, "You'll get your orders next week. Don't tell anybody."

And I went out and it was like that moment at the beach when you climb the ladder of the diving board up to where you usually dive off and then keep going to the one where you might jump off, and keep going still until you get to the very top where you've never jumped off before, and then you step up to the edge and jump. I felt that I was in empty space. Something had happened to me that had never happened before. And that I had done it. You know, as a kid, you don't have an opportunity to determine your life very often. Your parents do that for you. Your teachers do that for you. But I'd just made a decision that was going to change my life forever. And it did.

"I left Minneapolis for the service on a dank, wet, cold March Minneapolis evening," Hynes continued.

My father drove me to the station in the car that he almost never let me drive as a kid, downtown past all the places that had been the stations of my childhood, to the Rock Island Railroad station—the depot, he called it, "down to the depot." And we got out of the car and walked into the station. It was dark. The long platform was dark with hanging arc lights at a distance, so that as you walked it was dark light, dark light, dark light. And at the far end was a navy yeoman with a clipboard and a gathering of young men or boys around him. And we stopped and my father shook my hand. It seemed very strange to me that my father and I were on hand-shaking terms. Then he turned around and walked back to the entrance, dark light, dark light, dark light, and out into the street and he was gone. And I turned to the yeoman and went up and said "Present" when my name came up, and I was in the navy.

Hynes began his training on the campus of North Texas State Teachers College at Denton, rooming in a women's dormitory and taking his first flying lessons in a Piper Cub flown from a meadow from which sheep had to be driven before he could take off or land. He would undergo further training at Athens, Georgia; Memphis, Tennessee; Pensacola and Deland, Florida; and three bases in California—sixteen months during which he grew both as a pilot and as a person.

Growing up is a series of tests, motivated partly by curiosity, about what it's like to do things that grown-ups do that you've never done before, and partly, a series of tests of your readiness to be an adult. By passing the tests, you earn admission to this class of people that you think all know what they're doing and are adults.

Learning to fly is a series of tests, too, but as an eighteen- or nineteen- or twenty-year-old kid, you're at the same time still going through the other set of tests. You're finding out what it's like to be drunk. You're trying to pass the test with girls—when you really don't know what to do when you get there. You're trying to live independently. You're trying to act independently. You'd be trying to pass those tests whether you were in military training or not. On top of those are the tests about soloing an airplane and doing your first loop and dropping your first bomb and so forth.

By the time he and his friends found themselves aboard their pitching, tossing Liberty Ship, Sam Hynes had passed every test with which he'd been presented—he had learned to live on his own, mastered the dangerous art of flying torpedo-bombers, married the sister of a squadron mate—and was eager to face combat. For a young man from Minnesota, the Pacific was a revelation. "You got a sense of what a huge space you were going into. This was not going to be like Europe, where there was land all around and everything had names. This was going to be nameless, empty space, with little dots of land in between."

The ship took them as far as Honolulu, where they steamed slowly past Pearl Harbor, saw the superstructures of sunken wrecks projecting above the water, and thought about the men still trapped beneath them. They sampled sweet Hawaiian drinks that yielded near-instant hangovers, too, and swam at Waikiki ("nothin' but Amarillo with a beach," said a disappointed flier from Texas). It took three days of island-hopping flights by transport to get them to the battle zone: Johnson Island, Majuro, Kwajalein, Eniwetok, Guam, and finally Ulithi, a coral atoll of some thirty islands that was the chief staging area for Operation Iceberg, the coming invasion of Okinawa. "Ulithi was huge," Hynes recalled. "The anchorage was miles across, and it was covered with ships of all sizes, carriers, battleships, destroyers, cruisers—I'd never seen so many ships. It was like seeing all the power in your corner. And there wasn't any power in the other corner." The assault, scheduled for the first of April, was to be so vast that forces scheduled to take part were being readied simultaneously at American bases all across the Pacific, from the West Coast to the Marianas, the Philippines, Espíritu Santo, and Guadalcanal.

Hynes and his friends moved into the neatly laid-out tent city the men called Officers' Country on the tiny, triangular island of Falalop. Life there seemed unreal, he wrote.

> The sun was always warm and the breeze was always an ocean breeze. Wherever the island came to an end there was a spotless coral beach, with a lazy surf breaking. Wherever you stood on the island and whatever direction you looked, the sea was always in the background, at eye-level because the island was so low, a winking blueness behind everything. On the sand among the tents, coconuts lay waiting to be opened and eaten. It was like Eden.

The newcomers' first duties were not especially demanding: daylight patrolling against enemy submarines that might slip into the lagoon to disrupt the anchorage, and bombing and strafing airstrips and docks on the bypassed island of Yap, where Japanese gunners still sometimes fired at overflying planes. Even though one member of the squadron was shot down not long after it got there, Hynes remembered, Ulithi seemed a "pastoral, innocent place, a long way from the real war" being waged a thousand miles away on Iwo Jima and in the Philippines. The real war would soon come much closer.

QUENTIN AANENSON OF LUVERNE had not flown any P-47 missions during the Battle of the Bulge. Poor weather had kept his unit grounded until Christmas Eve, and he'd been in his plane on the runway, ready to go that day, when a jeep drove up and its driver handed him new orders. He was now to help direct close air support for the U.S. Army's VII Corps from what he assumed would be the safety of the ground. (The next day both the Thunderbolts he'd been flying and had named in honor of Jackie Greer, the *Rebel Jack* and the *Rebel Jack II,* were shot down and their pilots killed.) Safety on the ground had proved only relative. Most often Aanenson worked behind the lines, fielding requests radioed in from spotter planes and forward observers, then relaying target coordinates to the pilots overhead. But he also sometimes operated from frontline tanks, one of which was blown up by a German .88 moments after he and the crew leaped out and rolled into a ditch.

By the third week in February, he was stationed in a battered castle at the northeastern corner of the Hürtgen Forest, near the seventeen-mile stretch between Linnich and Duren where the 8th Infantry Division was still trying to force its way across the Roer. Operation Grenade was fourteen days behind schedule by then, because the First Army had failed to capture the biggest of the Roer dams before the Germans blew up the spillway, turning the river into a mile-wide lake. It had taken thirteen days for the waters to recede again, Aanenson recalled, and now the Americans in eight-man assault boats, battling both a swift current and heavy enemy fire, needed all the help they could get.

> I was calling in my fighter planes, and there was just a tremendous amount of requests coming in, when suddenly an .88- or a 105-millimeter artillery shell came through an opening in the wall of the castle and exploded about thirty feet from me. I was partially shielded because there was a stone column there, but the explosion took the top of the head off an enlisted man who was about fifteen feet from me, and it threw blood, tissue, brains, everything, all over me and my maps. It created a lot of havoc, but I had fighter planes that were in the process of their dive, so I had to keep working. They carried the man who had been killed out and a couple that had been wounded. And then, while I was still working, calling in the fighter planes on targets, they came over and cleaned the brain tissue out of my hair and off my leather flight jacket and off my maps, and we just continued on.

More than half a century later, Aanenson would learn that he had been quartered that week in the same Merode castle his squadron had attacked back in November, when his own plane had been badly damaged and his tent mates Red Alderman and Gus Girlinghouse had been killed. Their unmarked graves had both been within sight of the ruined room in which he'd continued to call in strikes against the enemy.

All along the line, Allied armies were now nearing the Rhine. Operation Veritable was almost over; the British XXX Corps was within three miles of the river. By February 25, the U.S. Ninth and First armies had finally crossed the Roer. While the Ninth moved north to link up with the British, the First prepared to move against the ancient riverside cathedral town of Cologne. Rundstedt asked for permission to begin withdrawing to the other side of the river. Hitler refused at first; retreat, he said, "would only mean moving the catastrophe from one place to another." But on February 28, he finally, reluctantly agreed to begin pulling troops back—with strict orders to destroy every bridge behind them. Allied troops fighting their way to the Rhine at Kalkar and Wesel, Oberkassel and Neuss, and elsewhere over the next few days watched helplessly as bridge after bridge collapsed into the water. The buildup of supplies for the crossing of the Rhine had been exceeded only by that for D-day, and the advancing armies carried with them more than six thousand river craft of every imaginable kind, along with everything they would need to build more than sixty bridges of their own. But it was sure to be slow and bloody work under deadly fire.

"The war news is good again tonight," Quentin Aanenson wrote Jackie Greer on March 3. "The Ninth Army has reached the Rhine . . . and the advances on other sectors are also good. I sure

Braced against German fire, trying not to see the water roiling on either side or the dead GI sprawled ahead of them, infantrymen of the Ninth Army rush across the Roer, February 23, 1945. Nearly three hundred U.S. engineers were lost that day, but they managed to throw nearly twenty-four bridges across the flooded river.

wish we were across that river, though. Unless we can capture one of the bridges, we're sure going to have a job on our hands."

On March 6, Hodges's First Army reached the ruins of Cologne to find that its bridges, too, were gone. But the next afternoon, some thirty miles to the south, advance elements of his III Corps slipped into the little resort town of Remagen and were amazed to see that the 1,069-foot Ludendorff railroad bridge still spanned the river. The Germans set off two explosive charges that damaged it but failed to knock it down. A U.S. infantry platoon rushed across to seize it and the steep cliff that overlooked it. Engineers ran with them, destroying the wires linking sixty more demolition charges that had somehow not gone off. (For failing to bring down the bridge at Remagen, four German officers were hanged and Rundstedt was replaced by Alfred Kesselring.)

Courtney Hodges telephoned Bradley with the news.

"Hot dog, Courtney," Bradley said. "This will bust 'em wide open. Shove everything you can across." Montgomery was not scheduled to mount the main Allied attack at the northern end of the line for two more weeks, but this unexpected breakthrough altered everything. Five divisions were rushed to Remagen and began streaming across the river into Germany past a crudely lettered sign that read CROSS THE RHINE WITH DRY FEET—COURTESY OF THE 9TH ARMORED DIVISION.

Three days later, on March 12, those waiting in trucks for their turn to cross the river at Remagen included a brand-new infantry platoon made up wholly of African Americans. There was nothing remarkable in that. Segregated black units had served all through the war in Europe. Black engineer battalions had built airbases in Britain, and black members of the Quartermaster Corps unloaded supplies on the Normandy beaches. Black truck drivers had manned the Red Ball Express. Black Graves Registration squads had buried the dead. Black infantrymen had fought on Elsenborn Ridge and guarded bridges across the Meuse. Black artillery units and black tankers had helped defend Bastogne.

But this platoon was different. It was not going to be temporarily attached to one regiment or another, as had been the practice before, but was to become a full-fledged part of one—the 5th Platoon, K Company, 394th Infantry Regiment, 99th Infantry Division—just as soon as it could find its new company, dug in and under fire somewhere on the steep slopes across the river.

Among the soldiers waiting to cross was Waymon Ransom from Detroit, the eldest of six children of a widowed and often absent mother. He'd been working the night shift at a print shop

Fifth Platoon, K Company, 394th Regiment, 99th Infantry Division: Waymon Ransom is seated third from the left in the front row.

This opportunity to volunteer will be extended to all soldiers without regard to color or race. . . . In the event that the number of suitable Negro volunteers exceeds the replacement needs of Negro combat units, these men will be suitably incorporated in other organizations so that their service and their fighting spirit may be efficiently utilized.

Practicality, not progressivism, had brought about the change. The unexpectedly savage winter warfare had seriously depleted the pool of infantry replacements immediately available to Eisenhower. He had already stripped junior officers and trained infantrymen from the fresh divisions waiting in England and needed still more. The top command rejected a straightforward plan to send individual black soldiers to the front to fill out white units for fear it would encourage civil rights groups to push harder for full integration of the armed services. Integrating by unit was thought less likely to stir up controversy and threaten the status quo.

Forty-five hundred African Americans volunteered. Half joined one of thirty-seven sixty-man rifle platoons, each to be commanded by a white officer and attached as a "5th platoon" to an existing white company. Some who signed on were eager to demonstrate that they could fight as well as any white man. "We had a point to make," one member of Ransom's platoon said. "We knew damn well we could perform." Others had simply grown bored performing monotonous and often menial work far behind the lines. And some, like Waymon Ransom, didn't really volunteer at all. Back in the States, he'd once asked to join the infantry, and the ancient piece of paperwork that request created was enough for his commanding officer to have him transferred out of his unit and into a rifle platoon. He was not alone: a good many men were similarly "volunteered" by officers eager to get rid of them. "I would say more than half of us signed the payroll with an X," Ransom remembered. "And I don't think much of anybody among my friends was in a hurry to go fight anybody."

As Ransom's 5th Platoon waited for the signal to start across the narrow pontoon bridge U.S. engineers had just built south of the battered Ludendorff span (which would collapse a few days later), its commander, Lieutenant Richard Ralston, was talking with another officer, Ransom remembered.

Ralston's saying that we're supposed to be going in the line to a quiet sector so "we can break 'em in on how it is." But this guy's saying, "There ain't no quiet sector. These people in Company K that you're going up to, nobody's quite sure whether they're there or not. They're having a real tough go with the Germans."

when the war began, and it had made little impression on him at first. "So far as why we were fighting—if you'll pardon my French—I didn't care whether white folks killed each other or not." And when he'd been called before his draft board in 1942, he recalled, "I went down there to get declared 4F, or at least a deferment so that I could get a better job." But he'd failed at that and found himself part of the segregated army. He trained in Georgia—where he once rode a train for two days without anything to eat because the Jim Crow railroad restaurants would not accept army meal tickets from black soldiers—and was then assigned to a black labor battalion, the 377th Engineers SEP. ("SEP" officially stood for "Separate," but the men said it meant "Shovel and Pick.") The battalion eventually shipped off to England, where blacks and whites went on leave on separate nights to avoid fistfights and worse. Ransom became a surveyor, helping to build bases for white infantrymen preparing for the Normandy invasion. By the time his battalion got to Utah Beach, thirty days after D-day, "there were so many people on the beachhead, it looked like it was about to sink," he remembered. For the next six months, the 377th cleared mines, repaired railroads, and rebuilt bridges for the Third and Seventh armies. Ransom rose to sergeant, though he was, as he himself said, "a smartass," unwilling always to knuckle under to the white officers in charge.

He and his outfit had been at reveille in a Third Army rest area near Dijon one morning in late December when the company commander read out a letter from General Eisenhower. In order to "destroy the enemy forces and end hostilities in this theater without delay," it said, he had now resolved to make room on the front lines for able-bodied men currently enrolled in service units.

THE FIRST ACROSS THE RHINE
CONSTRUCTED BY
• 291 ENGR C BN
• 988 TDWY CO
• 998 TDWY CO
THE LONGEST TACTICAL BRIDGE BUILT

As the trucks rumbled slowly across the river German dive-bombers flew overhead and German shells arced toward the miles-long line of men and vehicles waiting to cross behind them. "Somebody is shooting big stuff down here into the water," Ransom remembered thinking. "Oh, my God, this is the Rhine, and we're gonna be on the other side of it. This doesn't look good." When they did reach the other side, Ransom noticed six dead Germans lying along the shore with their feet in the water: "Fresh-killed Germans. Somebody had just killed them, and I began wondering just how deep this bridgehead was. It couldn't be as deep as some people were saying."

It wasn't, and what was left of nine German divisions had been ordered to keep it from growing any deeper. As the men of the platoon climbed down from the trucks, shouldered their weapons, and set out up the steep hillside in search of the outfit to which they'd been assigned, the sight of black infantrymen startled some of the first white troops they met along the way. Some jeered: "Hey, Sambo! You guys would be better at night fighting. What're you doing up here during the day?"

The men kept moving. Every so often a German bullet snapped nearby—just "to whom it may concern," Ransom remembered. They entered a forest. Somewhere inside it, Company K was said to be pinned down and fighting for its life. A machine gun opened up. A German mortar round landed nearby. While one squad provided covering fire, Ralston hurried the other two forward; mortarmen couldn't pinpoint anybody who was moving. A shell burst overhead, and fragments blew off the top of the head of one of Ransom's friends. The exposed brains looked like "bloody oatmeal," Ransom recalled; this was "a hell of a way to learn while doing." Despite the shock, the men of the 5th Platoon managed to knock out a machine-gun nest and a flak gun and send several dozen prisoners back to the rear. They kept climbing until they were just below the crest of the bluff, five hundred feet above the Rhine.

When we got up there, the first thing I remember is a white guy looking out of a hole, asking, "Who are you guys?"

"We're looking for K Company."

"Well, you're here. Get yourself a hole quick. Don't stand up. If you stand up, somebody'll get you."

A radioman at work beside the brand-new treadway bridge that paralleled the captured railroad span across the Rhine at Remagen. Some among the British engineers thought the boastful placards routinely put up by their American counterparts in questionable taste.

I think their first reaction was they were glad to see anybody. And before the night was over they was really glad to see anybody. And the next day, "Hey, we're here."

Somebody said, "I saw you guys come up, thought I was going blind slow." I said, "Yeah, yeah, yeah." But from there on out I don't recall us having any one-on-one difficulties.

Before they could scratch out shelter for themselves, a sergeant ordered Ransom and five others to return to the forest and see if they could locate Company B. They were met by a volley of German fire. One of Ransom's friends, a street kid from Maryland, fell with a bullet in his thigh. "They got me in the same place they shot me in Baltimore!" he shouted. Another man dragged him to the rear.

The rest of the patrol did their best to dig in. "I'm sitting at the base of a stump," Ransom remembered.

I'm trying to dig a hole. I have my rifle leaning up beside the tree. I had the safety on the rifle. And I hear something jingling, sounded like sleigh bells. I says, "What the hell is this?" And there'd be a bunch of jingling and then it'd stop and then it'd move forward again. And I says, "Well, it's right close."

The sound was coming from a link belt of machine-gun bullets dangling around a careless German soldier's neck. The German was now no more than fifteen yards away.

So I let go of the shovel and I'm reaching for the rifle and I see this German step from behind a bush. And he looks at me like he doesn't believe it. I'm lifting the rifle. He's got an automatic rifle of some sort and he starts to swing it across to fire. I beat him to the move, and pow! *He just keeps on turning and falls and lays there. He made his move, I made my move. I beat him. He's dead and I'm still sitting here. And from then on I was a seasoned infantryman.*

On March 15, a little over one hundred miles south of the spot on the eastern bank of the Rhine where Waymon Ransom and the men of the 5th Platoon were being introduced to combat, the final offensive in the series that was meant to complete the clearing of the west bank of the river was about to get under way. The target for Operation Undertone was the three-hundred-thousand-square-mile oblong bounded by the Saar, the Moselle, and the Rhine. Within it, two German armies manned the last bastions of the West Wall. George Patton, whose own broad definition of "aggressive defense" had allowed his Third Army to drive through the enemy defenses in the Ardennes, then wheel south and storm across the Moselle in record time, would now attack them from the rear, while fourteen divisions of Patch's

U.S. Seventh Army and the Algerian 3rd Infantry would push into the industrialized Saar basin from Alsace along a forty-mile front from Saarbrücken to Karlsruhe.

"This was the attack that was advertised as ending the war," Paul Fussell remembered.

The whole Seventh Army, which had sort of been resting in winter quarters for months, was going to go into action again. And we all lined up and went into skirmish line attack against the Germans. We had to clear that part of the land that came to the Rhine so that it could be crossed for the final ground-war effort going into Germany. And this was sort of the end for me, because I had been leading the same men for months and I had sort of had enough of it. But nobody knew that except me.

Second Lieutenant Fussell's battalion was to attack across a narrow river in the center of the 103rd Division's sector and capture the little German-held town of Gundershoffen. He had been in combat now for four months. "When you come on the line," he remembered, "you are very brave, because you know nothing. And it's easy for you to perform pseudo-brave gestures and procedures. You have a reservoir of courage when you arrive, and each time you get badly frightened, a little of it diminishes until you don't have any left. And that is the worst moment."

H-hour was 6:30 a.m. A fifteen-minute seven-hundred-gun artillery barrage preceded the assault. When it was over, Fussell ordered his men forward; although he felt no more frightened than usual, he remembered that his mouth was dry and he had a hard time getting his breath.

We attacked through a smokescreen so thick that you didn't know where you were. It was a bizarre thing. It was a ground-warfare technique from the First World War. But we did it anyhow. And there were dead Germans all the way along. They were stepping on mines and blowing their feet off. My people were relatively untouched.

Fussell and his men made it across the river—though he would later be unable to remember just how they did it—and moved quickly through what was left of a small town on the far bank after the intense shelling. Indignant chickens flapped through the smoking rubble. Dazed and deafened German soldiers staggered about, hands in the air—"crying, cringing, gibbering." Some wore GI wool trousers, captured from a U.S. supply depot during the Battle of the Bulge.

The battalion's next objective, Fussell recalled, was to clear "a compact woods maybe a half-mile wide and a mile long." To assemble for the assault, the men first had to scramble up

The Seventh Army reaches Saarbrücken in late March of 1945. Even the most battle-hardened GIs were astonished by the damage Allied air raids had already done to German cities.

and over an elevated road embankment under concentrated machine-gun fire. Fussell sent several men ahead. They all made it to the other side. But when his turn came he found himself frozen, a victim of what he later realized had been "sheer unofficer-like terror." A lieutenant colonel told him to pull himself together and get going or he'd be in serious trouble. "Thus rebuked," he wrote, "I took a deep breath, climbed up the embankment, scuttled across the asphalt where the machine-gun bullets were striking off sparks, and tumbled, unhit, down the embankment on the other side."

He and his men charged into the woods—and into machine-gun fire directed from trenches and dugouts hidden among the trees. "The Germans had been preparing that position for months, probably since Normandy," Fussell remembered. It was the fiercest combat he had ever faced.

On my left, I remember I was lying on my stomach, trying to keep as low as possible to avoid this machine-gun stuff that was going on about an inch above my head—so close I could feel the heat of the bullets as they passed by. One of the replacements, who'd never impressed me much because he was rather fat and clumsy, kneeled up and he was aiming at a machine gun some distance from us. And before he could get a shot off, they hit him with three bullets. And I saw only his back. I didn't see his face or anything else but out of his back there flew little clouds of what looked like dust. But they were blood, bits of tissue, and pieces of cloth uniform. About three of these came at me, and then he collapsed and that was the end of him. I knew he'd been hit in the center of the chest.

Almost at the same moment, on Fussell's right, one of his squad leaders was shot through the mouth.

He and his men kept moving through the trees. More enemy soldiers were now trying to surrender, but others fought on, and the Americans were not always careful to draw distinctions between the two. "We did all the shooting," one member of Fussell's company recalled. "They did all the dying."

When they reached the far end of the woods, they found a line of earth-and-log bunkers in which German troops had been living until that morning. Fussell climbed on top of one of them to rest and decide what to do next. With him were the lieutenant in charge of the company machine guns and Platoon Sergeant Edward K. Hudson, who was perhaps Fussell's closest friend in the army. When he'd first joined his platoon back in the States, Fussell remembered, "I was very young and preposterous giving orders." His men had been openly contemptuous. Hudson, who at thirty-one was eleven years older than Fussell, had helped change all that: "He defended me . . . and helped me work with them, and [by the time we got into combat] we had reversed positions and I could give him orders that were plausible and he could obey them in a plausible way."

Suddenly, off to the left, a German gun began firing systematically along the fringe of the forest. The shells came closer with each blast, bursting high in the air, each one louder and more frightening than the last. Fussell's men dove for cover, shoving each other aside to get inside one or another of the former German dormitories. A wounded man screamed, "They blew my legs off! They blew my legs off!"

Fussell stayed where he was on the exposed roof of the bunker. He'd been accused of cowardice that morning, he recalled, and didn't want to be seen as "ostentatiously prudent a second time." Because he remained out in the open, the lieutenant and Sergeant Hudson remained there, too. Each made himself as small a target as possible and hoped for the best. The shells methodically marched toward them. Finally, one exploded above their heads. "It was the loudest sound I'd ever heard," Fussell recalled. The lieutenant was killed. So was Sergeant Hudson, huddled so close to Fussell that the two men's elbows were touching. "They were killed absolutely instantly, which was a nice thing," Fussell recalled. "They didn't have to suffer."

Fragments from the shell plunged deep into Fussell's back and thigh. Almost half the men who made up what was left of Company F would be lost that day: fifty-five killed or wounded. A medic did what he could for Fussell in the field. A train carried him back to the 236th General Hospital in Épinal, the same town where he and his men had begun their war four months before. From there, he wrote a letter meant to reassure his worried parents.

Dear Mother and Dad:
As you may have already learned from the official telegram, I have been slightly wounded. A piece of shrapnel hit my right thigh, between the knee and the hip, but did not break the leg. Another piece hit my back, on the left side, but didn't go in very far. Both have been removed. I am now sewed up, no bones were broken, and I feel OK. They were really very slight wounds, and nothing at all to worry about. . . .

I should be up and walking around shortly, and enjoying these white sheets and nice beds. I'm in a general hospital. . . . It is luxurious, to say the least. Don't worry.
Love,
Paul

But Fussell himself was worried. His wounds would heal, he knew, but he now blamed himself for the death of his friend and his fellow officer. "The Germans were not to blame, nor the war," he would write. "It was all my fault for, afraid of giving more evidence of being a confirmed coward, I hadn't run for the entrance of the bunker when the shelling started. They would have followed and would still be living. Turning over and over these convictions and images, I gradually loosened emotionally and bawled like a small boy."

On March 16, the day after Paul Fussell was wounded, Iwo Jima was officially declared "secure" and the Red Army broke through to the Baltic, southwest of Königsberg. Operation Undertone would succeed quickly. Some German units fell back toward the Rhine almost immediately. Others fought stubbornly and were overwhelmed. Patton's twelve fast-moving divisions ripped at them from a dozen different directions, took tens of thousands of prisoners every day, and killed so many men that even the general found the carnage hard to bear. On March 20, the survivors began fleeing across the Rhine.

On March 24, Montgomery was due to launch Operation Plunder, the northern offensive that had originally been intended to lead the way across the Rhine. Its commander had drawn up his plans with what the official U.S. Army history would call "the majestic deliberation of a pachyderm." American commanders continued to think him too slow. Bradley had been delighted when his forces crossed the river before Montgomery got started, and on the afternoon of the twenty-third he received a phone call from George Patton at Oppenheim, south of Mainz, with more good news:

"Brad, don't tell anyone but I'm across," he said.

"Well, I'll be damned. You mean across the Rhine?"

"Sure am. I sneaked a division over last night. But there are so few Krauts around there they don't know it yet. So don't make any announcement—we'll keep it a secret until we see how it goes." But the temptation to upstage Montgomery on the eve of

AL McINTOSH'S WAR
December 1944–March 1945

DECEMBER 7, 1944. Some time ago L. Roy Fodness wrote us from a foxhole. . . . This time he writes from the lap of luxury. But he is afraid the soft life is getting him down.

"I've located in a friendly French family's home and they gave me a bedroom with a real honest to gosh bed in it, with an inner-spring mattress, feather ticks and clean white sheets. I had a heck of a time getting used to it but after the third night I mastered it. I don't think the change from sleeping on the ground was good for me, because I caught a terrible cold. In fact I stayed in bed all day today and the people of the house brought me hot soup."

DECEMBER 14, 1944. Because Nick Stavenger's eyes were a bit misty when he pulled a telegram out of his pocket and handed it to me yesterday morning I couldn't help thinking "bad news." But those weren't tears of sadness . . . they were tears of joy for he had received the finest Christmas present in the world.

The telegram dated from Bradley Field, Conn., read as follows:

"On my way home, will wire arrival time later, Johnny."

Second Lt. John Stavenger has been flying a B-24 over Germany from a base in England.

DECEMBER 28, 1944. We've always had strong belief in our hunches and we always had a hunch that Jarnet Johansen [of Hardwick], who had been reported missing in action as of September 27, would sooner or later be reported a prisoner of war in Germany. So it was a double shock when the word came Wednesday morning that the Hardwick boy is now reported as having been killed in action, September 27,

because it's hard to believe when you've kept in close touch with a boy to realize that you're never going to get any more letters from him.

FEBRUARY 5, 1945. When John Bosch was in Luverne last Friday he happened to stop and count the gold stars on the Honor Roll board and said "There are now 20 gold stars." He didn't know it then, but the 21st star would be that opposite the name of his own son, Pfc. Everett Bosch, who was killed on Luzon. The message telling of his son's death was handed Bosch when he reached his home at Steen that afternoon.

Here is a coincidence Steen residents talked about. Pfc. Everett Bosch and S/Sgt. Jay Aykens entered the army the same day. They were together in training camps during their entire stay in the states but when, after 18 months, it came time to receive overseas assignments, Bosch was sent to the Pacific theatre and Aykens to the European battle zone. Mr. and Mrs. Bosch received word Friday of their son's death. On that same day, Mr. and Mrs. P. D. Aykens received word that their son, Jay, had been wounded in action for the third time, on the western front.

MARCH 1, 1945. The men overseas, in England and in Europe, are getting their *Star-Herald* again. But it was pretty bad about the time of the Battle of the Bulge. Everything but munitions, food and supplies was sidetracked and none of the papers got thru for a while. But Lt. Davis, John Conover, Major Matty Jensen and a dozen others send word that the [papers] are coming thru all right now.

MARCH 8, 1945. We didn't know it till this week, but among the overjoyed American

prisoners freed in Manila were two Rock County residents, Mr. and Mrs Arthur H. Riss, formerly of Steen [where he was once the mail carrier]. "Mrs. Riss and I," he writes, "were mere walking skeletons when General MacArthur's boys rescued us on Feb. 3. We could not have stood it much longer. . . . It will be a slow climb back to health and strength [and] I shall be anxious to get back to good old Minnesota and its invigorating climate."

• • •

Monday morning Louis Haroldson got up early to take his daughter, Lois, down to the train so that she could get over to Sioux Falls. The day before had been the birthday of his son Berdell, who has been with the navy in the Philippines. Haroldson was wondering where and how Berdell had spent his birthday. The train rolled in. Haroldson picked up his daughter's grip and carried it down to the coach door. Who should jump down but the son just back from the Philippines. Was that unannounced and unexpected reunion at the depot a happy one? You know it was. Berdell had a ten day leave when his ship docked on the west coast. He didn't even take the time to wire because he knew every minute counted if he was going to get two or three days at home and dashed for the nearest bus terminal.

MARCH 22, 1945. When you lug home the shrapnel-punctured steel helmet you were wearing when you were wounded and all your wife has to say, after greeting you, is "It will make a lovely flower pot"—then that's an anti-climax. That's the remark that Lt. Le Roy Fodness is now teasing his wife about and he says he really is going to give her the helmet to use as a flower pot. He wants a new one. . . . He was wounded in Germany Dec. 18 [during the Battle of the Bulge]. Jesting about his wounds, Fodness said, "if it had been anywhere else but in the head I might have been seriously wounded . . . but with my head nothing could really get hurt."

his long-awaited offensive quickly proved irresistible. Patton placed a second call: "Brad, for God's sake, tell the world we're across. . . . I want the world to know Third Army made it before Monty." An hour or so later, Bradley's headquarters announced that elements of the Third Army had crossed the river and done so "without benefit of aerial bombing, ground smoke, artillery preparation, and airborne assistance." Montgomery's massive assault—which would get all the land and air support Patton hadn't waited for—would be masterfully executed but anticlimactic.

"I really believe this is one of the outstanding operations in the history of war," Patton noted in his diary. The following day, he stalked onto a pontoon bridge and started toward the opposite shore. Halfway across, he stopped. He'd always wanted

General George Patton makes good on a pledge.

to "piss in the Rhine," he said—and in full view of his men he did.

There were now some ninety-two thousand American prisoners of war housed in more than fifty camps scattered across Germany, all of them presumably equally deserving of liberation. Yet within hours of crossing the Rhine, Patton asked that a full-fledged combat command from his 4th Armored Division—three thousand men and fifty tanks—prepare immediately to race forty miles behind the German lines to the town of Hammelburg and rescue a particular group of officers confined there in Oflag XIIIB. His commanders objected. Their men were exhausted from weeks of combat; German resistance was still fierce; the POWs at Hammelburg would be freed with all the others in the course of the overall Allied advance. Patton backed off, but not very far. He ordered a far smaller task force to take on the mission: sixteen Sherman tanks, twenty-seven half-tracks, three self-propelled guns, and 307 officers and men under the command of Captain Abraham Baum. Puzzled aides wondered why Patton seemed so intent on this objective. He wanted to outdo Douglas MacArthur, he told one; this raid would make the much-publicized rescues of Americans in the Philippines "look like peanuts." He told others he feared that the Germans were about to kill all their POWs. But he never told Captain Baum the real reason he and his men were being asked to risk their lives: Patton had learned that his daughter's husband, Lieutenant Colonel John Waters, who had been captured two years earlier at Kasserine Pass, was among the officers held at Hammelburg, and the general wanted him freed right away. On the evening of March 26, Baum's task force set off into German-held territory.

Tom Galloway of Mobile was a prisoner at Hammelburg, too. It was the third camp he'd endured since his capture, just outside Bastogne. He'd been sent first to Stalag 2A, north of Berlin, then imprisoned at Stalag 4 in what was then West Prussia until the approaching Red Army forced its abandonment.

American personnel who fell into German hands were treated far better than were those unlucky enough to be captured by the Japanese. Less than 2 percent of American POWs failed to survive German captivity; more than 40 percent of those captured in the Pacific died. (German treatment of Soviet prisoners was a different story: some 5 million Red Army troops were captured over the course of the war; fewer than a million would live to see its end.) But, as Galloway remembered, the treatment he and his fellow prisoners got was bad enough.

There were about forty of us in Ia room. And for heat, each man got a lump of coal a day, which is forty lumps of coal for a big room, and so that didn't help much. Your food was little or nothing. I probably lost about fifty pounds in just a few months. I mean, you're not eating. You'd get a watery bowl of soup for lunch and a watery bowl of soup in the evening. But it wasn't much. And every so often you'd get a piece of bread. That helped, but it just wasn't enough. Hunger was just foremost in everybody's mind.

You had no bath facilities or anything like that, but again, it was so cold you didn't need a bath. We had no recreation and no facilities for recreation. I think we had one book, as I recall, that everybody read every so often. I recall that I drew a map of the United States just for something to do, probably the sorriest map you ever saw.

If there wasn't an air raid on, you could walk a little. But you couldn't walk far. About fifty steps and you were done for. We were just too weak. So we couldn't have played any games or anything if we'd had facilities—which we didn't have.

One day, Galloway remembered, "a skinny, dirty fellow came up to me and said he heard I was from Mobile. It was Herndon Inge, Jr. He and I were raised about eight blocks from each other." Inge was a second lieutenant, too. He also had been captured in the Ardennes, and he shared his fellow Mobilian's hatred of the pervasive cold. "You were just cold all the time," he remembered. "I went three months without ever taking my clothes off. You stayed in your clothes twenty-four hours a day. You took your boots off, and you'd tie them to your bunk at night, because they might get stolen."

The senior American officer at Hammelburg had a small crystal radio set hidden in a bucket. Nightly BBC broadcasts reported the general progress of the war, and by the third week of March the men knew that the Americans were coming closer. But, Galloway remembered, "you couldn't get too excited about anything, you were too hungry." He was attending Mass, presided over by a Jesuit priest in one of the barracks, when

all of sudden a round came flying in there. And we didn't know what was happening, and we all hit the ground. The altar was a table that had a sheet hanging over it down to the floor. I don't know where the priest got a sheet, 'cause we didn't have sheets. Anyway, after the round, we started getting up and looking around, and we couldn't find the priest. But in a minute or so, that sheet raised up and his head stuck out from under that makeshift altar. So we broke up Mass. And everybody went back to their respective barracks.

It had taken the Baum Task Force forty-eight hours to shoot its way to the gates of the prison camp. They had been attacked repeatedly, had lost both men and vehicles along the way, and were now firing on the adjacent camp, which housed Serbian captives whose gray coats the Americans had evidently mistaken for German uniforms. Lieutenant Colonel Waters was one of several men who volunteered to go forward and get the Americans to stop shooting. As they advanced toward the tanks a trigger-happy German guard shot Waters in the buttocks, tearing away the lower segment of his spinal column. Gravely wounded, he was carried back into the compound, where a Serbian doctor began tending to his wounds. Patton's son-in-law would not be rescued this day.

"Two big Sherman tanks broke through the double barbed wire, trailing the wire and uprooted fenceposts," Inge recalled; "the pavement in the street cracked under the tank's weight." The prisoners rushed through the opening, cheering and embracing the tankers. "Everybody was jubilant over the fact that at last we were going to be taken to good food," Galloway remembered.

But there were some 1,300 American officers in the camp, and there was room for no more than 250 in and on the vehicles Captain Baum still had with him. Inge decided to clamber onto the deck of the lead tank with five or six other men and try to hang on among the jerry cans of gasoline and clusters of 76-millimeter shells already stored there until they made it back to the American lines. The tanks began to roll as soon as it grew dark. "As we moved out the cold wind blew in my face," Inge recalled, "and I had an exhilarating and wonderful feeling of freedom. We thought we were going to have breakfast the next morning. But it didn't happen that way."

The Germans were already closing in. Within two hundred yards, the American column came upon a heap of logs blocking the way. As the tanks and other vehicles labored to turn around

Herndon Inge, Jr.

in the narrow road, Inge remembered, a German Panzerfaust rocket "whooshed by my head like a deadly Roman candle and exploded in the woods. I felt the heat and clung on for dear life." As soon as he could, he jumped down and ran to a less-exposed half-track farther back. He stayed with it until dawn, when the column came to a halt and the senior officer among the liberated prisoners told them they were free to continue on with the task force but he was going

to walk the eleven miles back to Hammelburg under a white flag. Inge and most of the other prisoners stumbled along in his wake, exhausted by their all-night ride under fire in the cold wind.

Within a few minutes, they heard explosions. German infantry and tank-destroyers with 90-millimeter guns were attacking what was left of Baum's task force. Every vehicle was eventually smashed or burned or captured. At least twenty-five men died. Many more were wounded. Those who survived were added to the prison roster at Hammelburg. The raid had been a fiasco. Patton would never admit what his real motive had been, but he did write that his failure to insist upon sending a full-scale combat command team to Hammelburg had been the only thing he regretted during the whole course of the war. "Otherwise," he said, "my operations were to me strictly satisfactory."

Most of the prisoners for whom the task force had had no room had decided to stay within the compound, too weak to strike out on their own. But some, like Tom Galloway and two of his best friends, had set out cross-country on foot.

We got to the Main River and found the bridges guarded because the task force had come in over one of those bridges. If we were going to get away, we had to swim. I could swim, and I turned to my two accomplices there, my buddies, and can you imagine, of all the people in camp, I picked the only two that couldn't swim. So things didn't look too good. I could have gotten them across if my strength had been built up, but it wasn't.

Galloway and his friends backed away from the river without being seen and looked for shelter from the cold, steady rain that had begun to fall just outside the little riverside town of Gemunden. "We had passed a farmhouse the night before," he recalled.

Now, over there, most of the farmers lived in the villages and went to the farm during the day. Here was a separate farmhouse with barns, outbuildings, and a small chapel. It was Good Friday, the Friday before Easter. And that part of Germany, Bavaria, was mostly Catholic—as a matter of fact, I thought it was all Catholic. So I told my friends, "Look, at three o'clock on Good Friday, they're going to be in church and we're going to go in there and get in that barn that we saw last night and get out of this weather." Well, we broke across the field just as fast as we could go and ran in that barn. And I think we hit the only Protestant family in that part of Bavaria. They were all in the barn. So our luck ran out at that point.

The three escapees decided it would be best just to make their way back to Hammelburg. It took them most of the day, Galloway remembered. The prison camp stood atop a long hill.

We'd been walking along, and just at the foot of the hill a German staff car pulled up. And we thought, "Oh, God, we're in for it now." There was an officer sitting in the back. And he says, "How you boys doing?" And we said, "We're tired." And he said, "Well, come on and get in. Let me ride you up the hill." It was the colonel in charge of the prison camp, and he rode us up the hill in his staff car. And we thought that was a little unusual, but we appreciated it.

Galloway and his companions didn't get much rest. That same evening, they and all the other able-bodied American prisoners—those who'd escaped as well as those who'd stayed behind—were marched together to the railroad station and loaded into boxcars. As the train rattled south toward the Bavarian Alps, one prisoner remembered, he heard the most terrifying sound he'd ever heard: an American P-47 flying in low to strafe the train. Bullets from eight .50-caliber machine guns fired simultaneously splintered the roof of the car. The brakes shrieked. The train lurched to a stop. Guards and prisoners alike jumped down and sought cover wherever they could find it. "You just tried to get away from the train," Galloway remembered.

I went out a window and down an incline and across to where there was a little bridge over a road. I slid under there, and there were two or three German soldiers under there that gave up to me. They thought the Americans had landed or something. They wanted to surrender to me, and I didn't want them. I explained to them that I wasn't in any position to take them captive. And I left them, and as far as I know, they're still under that bridge, because when the shooting was all over they rounded us up—rounded me up, anyway—and put me back on the train.

The train jerked back into motion and continued on its way, but with the doors of each boxcar left open this time in case the Americans came back and everyone had to jump for their lives again. It rolled slowly through the ruins of Schweinfurt, the ball-bearing center that had cost the lives of so many American fliers two years earlier, and eventually slid to a stop in Nuremberg. It was the middle of the night. There were no lights. The men could hear air-raid sirens. Allied bombers rumbled overhead. There were explosions and fires in the distance. The city had yet to suffer the Allied shelling that would finally pound most of it into dust, but it was already badly damaged by repeated bombings. Guards marched them through the blasted streets, picking their way among hillocks of rubble in the dark.

They had an early-morning breakfast of bread and soup in a little park in the shadow of the vast Zeppelin Field where each summer two hundred thousand of Hitler's Nazi followers had rallied to hear him excoriate his enemies and describe the world the Germans would one day rule as the Master Race. Afterward, the guards hurried Galloway and some twenty-five other prisoners out of the battered city, toward the south, away from the Allied armies that now seemed to be advancing everywhere in Germany.

A WORLD WITHOUT WAR

ON THE MORNING OF MARCH 27, 1945, Americans listening to the Blue Network heard a breathless Los Angeles broadcaster named Gil Martyn announce "electrifying news": President Roosevelt and his cabinet, he said, "are preparing for word of victory." A few minutes later, the wires carried an International News Service bulletin: "Eisenhower says Germans quit." Neither story was true. FDR had merely asked his cabinet to remain in Washington during the upcoming inaugural meeting of the United Nations at San Francisco; Eisenhower had said only that "the German army as a military force on the western front is a whipped army. But that does not mean a front cannot be formed somewhere where our maintenance is stretched to the limit. I am not writing off this war." Both stories were corrected within minutes: "There has been no suggestion from any Washington official that any armistice announcement is imminent."

The false news report that had preceded D-day the previous spring had kindled hope as well as trepidation. This one engendered only disappointment. The American people were weary of the war. They had been at it for three years and three months now. They still wanted to win—more than 90 percent believed the Allies should accept nothing less than unconditional surrender from any of their enemies—but they also wanted their boys home, an end to rationing, a world in which no one needed to scan the casualty lists every day in fear of finding names they knew. And when they looked at the news from the battlefield, it still sometimes seemed as if things were getting worse, not better. In Europe, all the arrows on the front-page maps were going in the right direction again and victory did seem to be creeping closer: the Red Army was just fifty miles east of Berlin, while in the west six great Allied armies were storming

As wounded Staff Sergeant Arthur Moore (opposite) celebrates victory in Europe in New York City, May 7, 1945, an Arlington, Virginia, man continues to tend his Victory garden.

through the enemy heartland between the Rhine and the Elbe. But 20,325 American boys would die in battle by the end of March, more than in any other month since the United States entered the war. In the Pacific, Allied forces were still hundreds of miles from the Japanese home islands; the fury of the fighting on Iwo Jima seemed to signal that the worst might still lie ahead, and American commanders fretted that a war-weary public might have neither the patience nor the stomach for it. General Marshall worried privately that victory in Europe might signal a "great impatience" and "great letdown" just as his forces were "approaching one of the most difficult periods of the war."

A few hours after the Blue Network embarrassed itself so badly, Al McIntosh began typing up one of his seasonal editorials addressed to Rock County boys serving overseas. The snow was finally gone, he wrote.

You should be able to shut your eyes, wherever you are, and imagine what everything looks like. . . . The lawns are turning green again . . . and everywhere you drove in Luverne Tuesday night you could see people starting to work out in their yards. Seed catalogs are favorite reading right now. Everybody, papa, mama, and the youngsters, are out raking lawns. And wherever you go there is the pungent smell of bonfires made from the leaves and dead grass. And, of course, the youngsters are busy poking at the bonfires with sticks. You see a few kites but very, very few. There is a shortage of string.

But if the boys were wondering how things were back home, "today, most of the folks back home have been wondering how things are going 'over there,'" he continued.

Today started off with a big mistake caused by an overenthusiastic radio broadcaster who got the idea that a "Victory" flash was coming up in a few minutes. To tell you the truth, it didn't cause much of a flurry on Main Street. People have had tentative dates for victory before and have seen their hopes dashed . . . so they've . . . made up their minds to keep their heads down and keep working until there is no doubt of victory any more.

It would be a lie, though, if we didn't say that the main topic of conversation wasn't "how long will it take?" Common attitude is "it might happen tonight, but it will probably take another six weeks."

And don't get the idea that the folks back home think it's a "grand waltz." They know the fighting is brutal and costly . . . and that lots of our best boys have been lost in victory drives before. They are praying and hoping that the struggle, for your sake, will be mercifully short.

JAPAN'S RULERS WERE DETERMINED that the struggle would be neither merciful nor short. In retrospect, their defeat seems to have been certain. "It was certainly clear by the time I got to the Pacific who was going to win," Sam Hynes recalled. "It was just how long it would take and what the casualties would be." The Japanese fleet had never recovered from the disaster in Leyte Gulf. American warships now prowled Japan's coastal waters, sinking merchant shipping more or less at will; American B-29s based in the Marianas had begun Operation Starvation, systematically mining each Japanese port to bar the raw materials required by battered industries and cut off the imported food the civilian population needed simply to survive. And the cities were burning. Major General Curtis E. LeMay had brought to Japan the same sort of firebombing that had reduced German neighborhoods to cinders. It began March 9 when 334 B-29s roared in low over Tokyo and dropped hundreds of thousands of seventy-pound napalm bombs in a carefully orchestrated grid pattern meant to insure total destruction. A quarter of the city—constructed largely of pine, paper, and bamboo—burst into flame. Perhaps one hundred thousand people were, as LeMay said afterward, "scorched and boiled and baked to death." In the next ten days, the Americans hit Nagoya, Osaka, Kobe, Nagoya again. Some Allied commanders believed that the deadly combination of bombing and blockade would eventually force Japan to surrender without ever having to mount a costly invasion.

But the generals and admirals who made up Japan's war council continued to see things differently. They still had a formidable army of nearly 3 million men, a population still fiercely loyal to their emperor, and all the advantages a mountainous landscape could afford to the forces defending it. They also still ruled vast territories and millions of conquered people that might be used as bargaining chips in negotiating a settlement short of surrender. By refusing to consider giving up, they believed, they could convince the Allies to mount a full-scale invasion of the home

Searchlights pinpoint a B-29 above Sakai, a suburb of Osaka, Japan. Hundreds more drone overhead, unseen. Each of the bright calligraphic flashes is an incendiary. In five separate raids, Osaka would be virtually obliterated.

islands—and then, by making that invasion as costly as possible, could eventually persuade the bloodied invaders to settle for a peace that would keep their emperor in power.

To achieve that goal, they developed Ketsu-Go (Decisive Operation), a new three-part defense plan for the homeland: massive forces would be deployed to destroy any Allied beach-head before it could be extended more than a few miles inland; Japanese forces on land, at sea, and in the air were to employ suicide tactics against the enemy; and the civilian population, transformed into a Patriotic Citizens Fighting Corps, was to fight and die alongside them. All men aged fifteen to sixty and all women from seventeen to forty were expected to enlist in Volunteer Fighting Units. Those without modern weapons drilled with knives lashed to bamboo spears. One woman who had been a high-school girl then remembered being issued an awl, with instructions to plunge it into the abdomen of any enemy soldier she saw. "Even killing one American soldier will do," her instructor said.

The fury with which Japanese forces had defended the tiny island of Iwo Jima had been meant in part to provide Americans with a taste of what they could expect if they dared to invade Japan itself. The fierce defense of Okinawa—sixty miles long and eighteen miles wide, about the size of New York's Long Island and only three hundred miles from Kyushu—would be intended to drive that lesson home.

For weeks, the largest Allied fleet since D-day—nearly 1,500 U.S. and British vessels, so many that one Japanese soldier

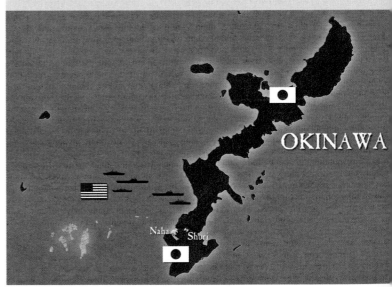

As the Allies prepared to land on the west coast of Okinawa (below), Japanese civilians, like the women above, drilling with bamboo spears in a schoolyard, were preparing to resist an Allied landing in the home islands even if it cost them their lives.

onshore said he couldn't tell what color the sea was because of all the ships covering its surface—had fired 2.3 million shells onto the island. But there were still scores of Japanese airfields within reach of the Allied warships and enemy bombs, and kamikaze attacks took a heavy toll among them.

On March 31, Midshipman Maurice Bell of Mobile was still serving as a gunner aboard the heavy cruiser USS *Indianapolis* when she was targeted for destruction.

I looked up to my right and there was one small cloud up there, and just as I looked up I saw a plane come out of this cloud, a Japanese kamikaze plane. The very instant I saw him up there he must have spotted our ship, because he turned into a dive and was coming straight down. It looked like he was coming straight to the very spot where I was sitting. A gunner started firing at it with a 20-millimeter, and you could see the tracers hit the plane. It actually bounced off the ship, but the motor and the bomb went through the deck. Went through Number Three mess hall, and right down there was three or four or five men sitting at the table eating. It killed all of them. And the bomb went all the way through the ship into the water and then exploded back up through. They said that hole was large enough to drive an eighteen-wheeler through.

Nine sailors died; twenty-nine were wounded. The *Indianapolis* began limping toward Ulithi to have her hull mended and would eventually be dispatched all the way across the Pacific to Mare Island, near San Francisco, for further repairs.

Meanwhile, sixty thousand Americans were to go ashore side by side the following morning: the 6th and 1st Marine divisions and the 7th and 196th Infantry divisions. Ensign Joseph Vaghi, the beachmaster who'd led his men onto Omaha Beach running like a high school football player and had since recovered from the wounds he'd received there, had volunteered for the Okinawa landing. Aboard his transport the night before, he and his men had listened to swing music played by one of several female enemy radio propagandists whom Americans in the Pacific conflated into the single voice they called Tokyo Rose. "Here we are, going into Okinawa," Vaghi recalled, "and Tokyo Rose is telling us, 'OK, GI Joes, we know you're coming, we're gonna give you an Easter party when you land. We'll be there waiting for you.' Well, that really sent shivers up and down one's spine."

Aboard another transport, Private Eugene Sledge heard similarly grim warnings from the commander of his battalion: the 1st Marine Division could expect to lose eight out of ten men before they got off the beach, he'd said. But when the naval barrage ended, shortly after sunrise, and the amtracs started knifing toward the landing beaches on the western side of the island, only a few scattered enemy shells splashed into the water among them. A correspondent compared the landing to "a fierce, bold rush by cops, hunting gunmen, into a house that suddenly turned out to be only haunted."

"It was quiet," Vaghi remembered. "You could just walk ashore. I couldn't believe this." Sledge and the men of his outfit couldn't believe it either and were so relieved that, as they unloaded their gear and started inland, they sang Glenn Miller's popular hit "Little Brown Jug."

They were pleasantly surprised by the terrain, too. It was "pastoral and handsomely terraced," Sledge remembered, "like a picture postcard of an Oriental landscape. The weather was cool . . . and there was the wonderful smell of pines, which reminded me of home. It was such a beautiful island. You really could not believe that there was going to be a battle there."

At first, there really wasn't one. American tanks and infantry hurried inland across the patchwork of farm fields and captured two airfields so fast and with so little difficulty that a hapless Japanese fighter pilot landed at one of them moments after it fell into American hands. A journalist noted:

He brought his neat little green fighter down gracefully and taxied to a stop near what had been the Japanese operations office. In five seconds his plane was full of holes of every caliber from every gun around the airstrip. Appreciating that the situation was unfavorable, the pilot got out of the plane with his revolver drawn and was immediately full of holes himself.

"I'm sorry the boys were so damn impulsive," the marine commander said afterward. "He would have been a good prisoner."

By April 4, the Americans were eight to thirteen days ahead of schedule. The marines encountered plenty of terrified Okinawan farmers and their families—nearly half a million of them lived on the island—but, except for an occasional sniper, the enemy seemed nowhere in sight. The marines moved north to clear the central and northern parts of the island. Sledge and his friends kept asking one another, "Where the hell are the Nips?"

The army was about to find out. It turned south, and discovered some hundred thousand enemy troops waiting for them within a succession of rocky ridges that ran from one coast to the other. Seventy-six thousand belonged to the Japanese Thirty-second Army; twenty-four thousand were conscripted Okinawans. Their commander, Lieutenant General Mitsuru Ushijima, based in a fifteenth-century fortress called Shuri Castle, had adopted what he called "sleeping tactics": concealing most of his men within a network of trenches, caves, gun emplacements, and hundreds of ancient tombs, impervious to anything but a direct hit. "Do your utmost," Ushijima told his men as the first Americans approached. "The victory of the century lies in this battle."

On April 6, Japan loosed a new tactic against the Allied fleet offshore: not single kamikazes now but flights of hundreds at a time, dropping out of the sky to attack. The Japanese called them

Floating Chrysanthemums. "Kamikazes just poured at us, again and again," a sailor remembered. "It scared the shit out of us. . . . We'd get warnings about half an hour before they appeared, and the waiting was scary, too."

The journalist John Lardner, caught in the open in a little army messenger boat, captured the feeling of helplessness such flights could inspire.

The first warning of sudden visitors was an arm of anti-aircraft fire which shot up from a ship close by, to be joined immediately by other arms darting from every direction. Riding the apex of this cone of fire was a two-motored Japanese plane. Its purpose became obvious when the pilot went into a clean deliberate dive instead of making for higher, freer spaces. Three ships loomed off our port bow—a white hospital ship, a gray transport, and an LST—and one of them was

Within thirty seconds of each other on the morning of May 11, 1945, two Japanese kamikazes slammed into the crowded flight deck of the carrier USS *Bunker Hill* off Okinawa. A minute or two later some thirty planes and twelve thousand gallons of fuel exploded. Nearby vessels surrounded the wounded ship, wreathed in smoke and steam (opposite), and did what they could to help her crew douse the flames raging above and below deck.

his target. They followed him, groping and clutching. I could see slugs swarming around him, and red tracer bullets, and this made me realize how close he was—able to look down our personal throats in our personal small boat, if he cared to, and read the linings of our stomachs. I grabbed my helmet, put it on and ducked behind the bulkhead. The others did the same. The coxswain had given up purposeful steering by now, having no idea which way to run, and we bounced around aimlessly and watched the wild race between a man intent on

his destiny and guns that tried to forestall him. In spite of the plane's speed, it was an unequal race. Halfway down, a trimming of fire suddenly crept over the fuselage, and a moment later the plane twitched in its course just enough to make us doubtful about what its target was. Then the plane hit the water, skipped once, like a flat stone, and broke into pieces. We still couldn't tell which ship it was that the pilot had chosen for his altar of destruction. He crashed between the hospital ship and the transport and a couple of hundred yards from us, but we did not note such points specifically until after we had picked ourselves off the bottom of the boat, to which we had dived to avoid the fragments of plane flying over our heads.

The Flying Chrysanthemums kept coming. By the end of the next day, they had sunk eleven ships, seriously damaged twenty-two more, and killed 367 sailors.

On April 8, the Japanese sent into battle most of what remained of their once mighty Second Fleet: the battleship *Yamato*, the biggest warship on earth, along with a single cruiser and eight destroyers. The men aboard were also on a self-destructive mission: their orders were to lure American carriers away from Okinawa so that kamikazes could do their deadly work undisturbed by American interceptors, then beach themselves on the island and die fighting the Americans onshore. "Okinawa was surrounded by carriers with navy fighters," Sam Hynes remembered, "and when they heard the *Yamato* was coming, they swarmed in like flies around something sweet. And everybody got a shot at it. It was the biggest shooting gallery in the history of the war." Three waves of American torpedo-bombers sank the *Yamato,* six of her escorts, and 4,250 of the men aboard them before they got anywhere near the island.

The *Yamato* and its escorts were gone, but the Floating Chrysanthemums would return nine times over as many weeks. The Japanese would lose some 7,800 aircraft, piloted by thousands of young men, many of whom were barely trained enough to get off the ground. But they sank or crippled some four hundred ships. Nearly one out of five U.S. Navy casualties suffered during the war would come off the coast of Okinawa: 9,731 men.

THE STUBBORNNESS AND BRAVADO of Japan's rulers in the face of apparently hopeless odds continued to bewilder and frustrate Allied commanders. They weren't certain of what Hitler and the remnants of his regime might do either. Germany's fate also seemed sealed, but the Nazis continued to issue orders their adversaries considered mad. Old men and teenaged boys, some riding bicycles with Panzerfausts attached to the handlebars as if they were fishing rods, were still being hurried to the front. Any *Burgermeister* who surrendered his village to the advancing

Allies was to be hanged or shot. Everything that might be useful to the enemy was to be destroyed upon withdrawal: bridges, factories, offices, autobahns. When Albert Speer protested that such wholesale destruction would threaten the "elemental survival" of the German people, Hitler no longer seemed to care: "If the war is lost, the people will be lost, [and] it is not necessary to worry about their needs . . . for the nation has proved to be weak, and the future belongs entirely to the strong people of the East. Whatever remains after this battle is in any case only the inadequates, because the good ones will be dead." Defeat was the fault of the German people, not their Führer.

Events in Europe were now moving so fast it was difficult even for Allied headquarters to keep track of it all. Six Allied armies were rapidly executing what one correspondent called "a series of vast loops and encirclements" aimed at overrunning western Germany and tearing apart what was left of the enemy's forces. In less than a month, Bradley's First and Ninth armies would systematically destroy what was left of German Army Group B in

Only a few feet above the tossing sea (opposite page), a severely wounded sailor is swung by a system of pulleys, called a breeches buoy, from the *Bunker Hill* to the light cruiser USS *Wilkes-Barre*. Despite the terrible damage done to her, the *Bunker Hill* survived, though 393 members of her crew were killed or reported missing and 264 more were wounded.

Souvenir-hungry GIs were not always deterred by the kind of warning signs painted on these German storefronts or by the presence of armed military policemen pledged to enforce them.

the Ruhr pocket and capture more than three hundred thousand prisoners—so many of them packed so close together that one U.S. pilot flying overhead momentarily mistook them for a "dark plowed field."

Two side-by-side armored divisions set the pace for Patton's Third Army: the 4th and the 11th, in which Private Burnett Miller of Sacramento still served. During March the divisions had raced from Luxembourg through the Siegfried Line to the Rhine in two long columns. Miller and his fellow infantrymen rode together in a seemingly endless line of half-tracks. Sherman tanks ranged ahead. Mobile artillery rumbled along behind. As the column approached a village it would pause, coiled along the road, until the town's frightened citizens hung sheets from their windows as a sign of surrender—either voluntarily or when forced to do so by tanks, artillery, and aircraft that had been called in at a moment's notice. Most enemy troops had fled. Here and there, remnants of German units tried to make a stand; but, as another man in Miller's outfit remembered, the war was now "very one-sided."

As they moved through one village after another—past what one soldier remembered as "white flags and eyes peeping from behind lace-curtained windows"—GIs quickly learned the joys of "liberating" enemy property. They usually began by ransacking local Nazi Party headquarters. Pistols were popular souvenirs. So were jeweled Nazi daggers, Leica cameras, Zeiss binoculars, leather flight suits, German helmets. "When the center of a town and business district was to be searched," a member of Burnett Miller's outfit remembered, "men would volunteer for perhaps the first time in their lives. Taverns and *Gasthauses* were always searched thoroughly, and the beer sampled carefully." The men filled their pockets with canned goods, bottles of cognac, eggs, all meant to make the evening meal of C rations more palatable. "At one time or another," a soldier from the 11th Armored remembered, "a GI's conscience would ask him whether it was right to take such things, and he would often think to himself how much he would hate to have such things happen to his home and city. But these thoughts would usually be dismissed with 'Hell, it's German, isn't it?' "

Burnett Miller had survived fierce combat outside Bastogne, had lost friends to the enemy, and been wounded himself, but he still had developed no special animosity toward the Germans. "We had had lots of training films showing us how bad the enemy was, how evil and so forth," he remembered, but like many GIs, he'd heard about the false propaganda that had been disseminated about the enemy during the First World War—babies skewered on bayonets, Belgian nuns ravished—and was determined not to be fooled again.

We were all quite cynical about these films. We thought it's an awful lot of propaganda and baloney. We didn't think we were fighting to save the world, but we thought that it was our country against that country and that country had been the aggressor. And the Japanese, their allies, had started us in it and we had to win. It was that simple. We didn't believe in the brand of evil that they were propagandizing.

Nothing he'd seen so far had made him alter that opinion.

"Dear Mom and Dad," he wrote during one momentary pause on the way to the Rhine.

We are now living in another small German village, not as modern as the last, but very quaint. The people, as usual, are overly nice and well treated by us. We eat their preserves and some of the fellows are souvenir hunters extraordinary, but that's about as far as we go. Of course, when we can find a short snort, which is rare, we don't hesitate. . . . Yes, it's quite different being an invader than a liberator. I like Germany very much. It seems a cleaner and fresher country than the others I've seen. It reminds me of the good ol' U.S. in parts. It's hard for me to realize that these people are our enemies and the hated huns.

A couple of weeks later, he wrote again.

We are living in another German village now, and it is very much like all the rest. Many pictures of German soldiers of three wars all over the walls. The people very coolly tell of how this one was killed in France, that one in Austria and so on. You cannot understand why they do not learn their lesson from all this sorrow.

The 11th Armored Division crossed the Rhine at Oppenheim on March 28. The first towns through which they passed on the other side—Oppenheim and Darmstadt—had already been flattened by Allied bombs. When Germans tried to stop them near Fulda, they paused just long enough to watch American artillery and what infantrymen called the "glamour boys" of the Ninth Air Force set the town ablaze, then hurried on. At Oberhof on April 3, German snipers pinned down Burnett Miller's C Company in a wooded area for a time, but the men of B Company got down from their half-tracks, one of them remembered, quickly deployed, "and really woke up the countryside. . . . Everyone was firing." Surviving Germans fled into nearby houses. A grenade hurled through the window of one killed several. Several more were cut down when they fled another house.

The 11th Armored had now reached deeper into German territory than any other unit, and things were getting even easier.

"Seemed as though the farther into Germany we went," the soldier from B Company recalled, "the less resistance we encountered."

The Third Army may have been spurred on by its commander's special vehemence. "Tell those boys just to go hightailing it along," Patton said. "I think this war is over . . . and I want my men to be up front, to share the glory." But there were scores of shifting fronts now. German resistance was cracking everywhere. Late one evening, not long after his 28th Infantry crossed the Rhine, medic Ray Leopold from Waterbury was walking alongside a railroad embankment on his way back to quarters with some fresh medical supplies when he glimpsed a man with a German helmet and a rifle on his shoulder just across the tracks. As a medic, Leopold carried no weapon. He knew he had to do something:

Without thinking—I didn't do much thinking at this point—I yelled out in German, "Hande hoch!" The German was a wise man. He threw his rifle down and raised his hands. I ran up quickly with a fountain pen in my hand, and shoved it into his back. He could not tell a pistol from a fountain pen. He kept his hands up. I told him in German to turn left and start marching. Now, this is a rather unusual thing in that I was a medic. And according to the Geneva Convention, no medic can carry any firearm, cannot carry a pistol, cannot carry a rifle, cannot exercise the use of a killing instrument. I don't know how deadly a fountain pen is, but that was the instrument that took the prisoner. I walked him into headquarters and turned him over to the authorities. He asked my permission, in German, if he could keep his gold watch. And I said as far as I was concerned yes he could, but I didn't think that the others would allow him to keep it. At which point one of my men said, "You're damned right he isn't going to keep it." The German protested, "That's from my dead father." It didn't mean anything. The young GI had himself a beautiful gold pocket watch, and the prisoner now had something that was probably more precious to him. He was through with the war.

As the American and British armies moved farther into enemy territory they began to uncover some of the Reich's darkest secrets, to witness firsthand the nature of its industrialized barbarism. They were comparative latecomers. There had been credible reports since the summer of 1942 that the Nazis had turned from persecuting and "resettling" Jews to systematically murdering them; that December, the Allied powers had issued a formal condemnation of Hitler's "bestial policy of cold-blooded extermination." But as late as 1943, most Americans either believed that reports of mass killings in Europe were greatly exaggerated or had no opinion about their accuracy, one way or another. In July of 1944, while the Western Allies were still fighting through the Norman hedgerows, the Red Army had come upon the Lublin-Majdanek concentration camp in Poland. The camp was virtually empty. All but a few of the inmates had been driven west on foot, among the growing numbers of slave laborers and prisoners of war and intended murder victims the Germans sought to hide from the advancing Allies. But the Russians found gas chambers, a warehouse filled floor-to-ceiling with abandoned shoes, and a crematorium containing human ashes, all that remained of tens of thousands of Jews, non-Jewish Poles, and Soviet prisoners of war who had died of starvation and neglect or had been murdered there. Over the weeks that followed, the Red Army overran three more dismantled killing centers: Belzec, Sobibor, and Treblinka. Still, as late as December of 1944, most Americans thought these reports from the easternmost reaches of the Nazi empire overstated and did not believe that either gas chambers or camps intended for mass murder could really exist.

Human bones and skulls unearthed by Soviet troops at Majdanek, the first death camp discovered by the Allies, on the outskirts of Lublin, Poland

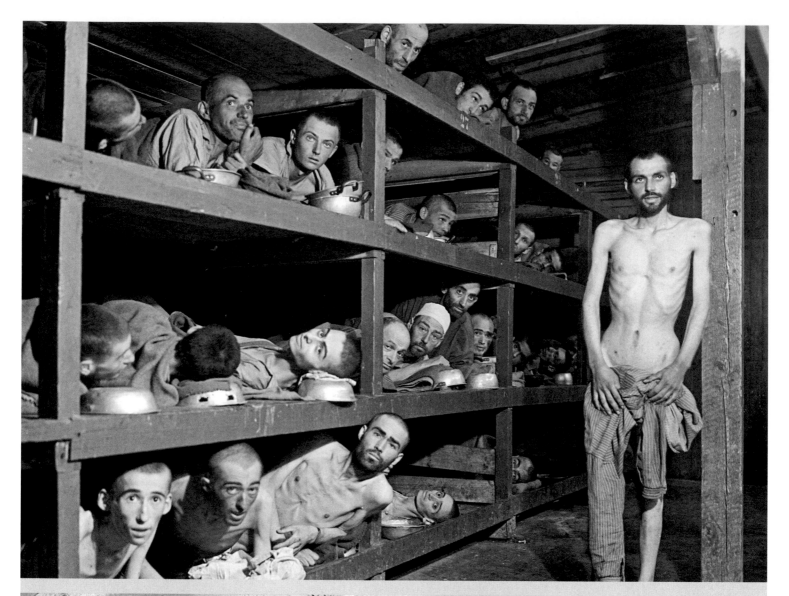

The horrors of Buchenwald appalled even the most battle-hardened of the Americans who liberated them. The bodies of most of the fifty-six thousand persons murdered here by the Nazis were disposed of in crematoria like those at the left, discovered by the men of the Third Army. Generals Patton, Bradley, and Eisenhower (opposite) watch as prisoners demonstrate the torture many of them had undergone. The seventh man from the left in the center tier of the Buchenwald barracks (above) is the future Nobel laureate Elie Wiesel. "You were our liberators," he would later write, "but we, the diseased, emaciated, barely human survivors were your teachers. We taught you to understand the Kingdom of Night."

"Where atrocities are concerned most Americans are skeptics," a correspondent for the Washington *Post* wrote. "They have to be shown." Beginning in April 1945, they were. On April 4, the 2nd Infantry Division captured the pretty little town of Hadamar, and with it, a big hilltop hospital. When Ray Leopold's outfit passed through the town a few days later, he climbed the slope to see it. "The *Burgermeister* described the building as an insane asylum," he recalled. "We went up there and found that, true, they did have an insane asylum there, at least initially." But since 1939 it had been something else: one of six institutions scattered across Germany in which Nazi doctors carried out the Führer's conviction that the State had a duty to snuff out the lives of all those he deemed "unworthy of life" in the interest of "racial hygiene." Only retarded or malformed infants had been killed at first in the Nazi "euthanasia" program, then older children, juvenile delinquents, crippled and senile and mentally ill adults, prisoners of war—some fifteen thousand men, women, and children at Hadamar alone. Hidden in the cellar was a tiled gas chamber disguised as a shower; alongside it were an operating room in which medical experiments had been performed on living people and a crematorium for doing away with the evidence. Starving, disoriented inmates still occupied many of the beds.

"I really can't tell you what I saw at Hadamar," Leopold recalled.

It affected me profoundly, and I think all the men who were with me at that time were equally affected. I felt that it was too bad that I was forbidden by the Geneva Convention to kill. I felt that this was the most horrible human experience that had ever been visited on the face of the earth. I think the horror is still with me. I think there's no apology that can ever atone for what I saw.

Worse sights were to come. Some two hundred miles to the east, near the town of Gotha, the 4th Armored Division reached Ohrdruf, a subcamp of Buchenwald. Again, the SS had marched away most of its 11,799 inmates before they could be liberated. But hundreds of prisoners, too weak or ill to walk, had been shot and left where they lay. A few days later, on April 12, Generals Eisenhower, Bradley, and Patton all came to see the camp. Bodies still sprawled everywhere. Before they fled, the SS ordered hundreds more dug out of the ditches in which they'd been buried

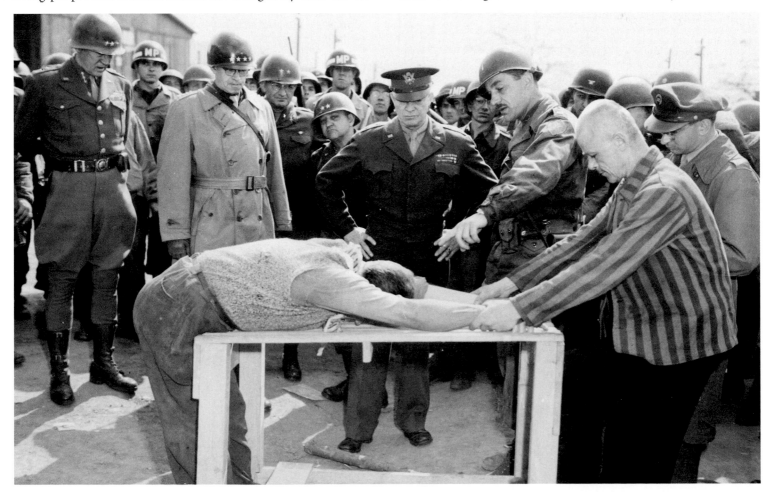

and frantically tried to burn them on a giant grid fashioned from sections of railroad track. It had failed to do the job: charred skulls and bones littered the ashes beneath the grid. The stench was overpowering. Patton stepped behind a barracks to vomit, then refused to enter a room crowded with the naked corpses of men who had starved to death, for fear he would again be sick in front of his men. Eisenhower, his face dark with anger, turned to a nearby GI and asked, "Still having trouble hating them?" He insisted on seeing everything himself, he cabled Marshall, so that he would be "in a position to give firsthand evidence of these things if ever, in the future, there develops a tendency to charge these allegations merely to 'propaganda.'"

AS AMERICAN TROOPS BEGAN TO WITNESS for themselves the horrors of the Nazi regime, Sascha Weinzheimer, her family, and some other survivors of the Santo Tomas internment camp were aboard an American transport, the USS *Admiral Capps*, part of an American convoy zigzagging at last toward home. The coast guard crew spared no effort to make them comfortable, and the former internees did their best to get used to the comparative luxury even a warship could provide.

"When we came to the ship's dining room we could hardly believe our eyes!" Sascha noted in her journal. "Long tables with white table cloths, glasses—not cups—white plates, *two* spoons, *two* forks . . . [and] what chow! Ice cream and red apples, too!" The children peered into the water on the lookout for mines, played poker and pinochle with wounded GIs, jitterbugged to music provided by a coast guard quartet, and sneaked peeks at the movie actor Gig Young, who was serving aboard as a pharmacist's mate. Having a number of lively children like Sascha and her siblings roam the decks of a warship was a novelty for the crew as well, and one coastguardsman published some verse about it in the ship's newsletter.

Look here, little man, let's get this thing straight,
Reach some understanding before it's too late.
I'm just a G.I. and I work on this ship
While you're an American kid on a trip.
I work on the boat and you're the boat's guest,
So nothing's too good for you, even the best.
A stateroom, clean linen, a deck up above,
All the chow you can eat of the kind that you love—
After three years of rice, Lad, you rate a good break,
So fill up your belly with ice cream and cake.
But look, my young fellow—don't go quite so fast.
You've got our ship's discipline lashed to the mast.
The deck crew is jittery, Skipper is wild,
The stewards are suffering, mess cooks are riled.
The mischief you're into, you and the others,
I should think would be the death of your mothers;
You've marked up the bulkheads with crayons and chalk;
You've kept us from duty with incessant talk,
Greased all the handrails, with butter I think,
Splashed all the bedsheets with fountain pen ink,
Built bonfires in places where powder is stored—
You've just about driven morale overboard.
Now don't get me wrong, Pal, we're friends, you and me.
You remind me of my boy, whom I'm longing to see.
But hold it, Lad, hold it! You're one up on the Japs,
You're raising all Hell with the Admiral Capps.

They reached San Francisco harbor early in the morning on April 8. "It was foggy," Sascha recalled.

We went up on deck just as we were going under the Golden Gate Bridge. It was about nine o'clock in the morning, but the tip of the bridge—this golden tip—was sticking out with the sun breaking through. And then we cruised slowly in, past Alcatraz, and then docked, just as the sun was coming over the hills. And to me that will always be a beacon. That Golden Gate Bridge was a wonderful salvation for us.

The Weinzheimers on their way home from the Philippines at last, after what Sascha called "nine weeks of eating"

Their widowed grandmother and other relatives and friends were waiting at the dock to greet them. "We looked at these people as if we were in a trance," Sascha remembered. "They looked like a million dollars and we were in sloppy, ill-fitting GI khaki issue. They smelled clean and crisp. . . . The women had hats with veils . . . and some with fur coats."

The family checked into a downtown hotel. "Look at this," Sascha's father said as he called room service. "I never thought I'd be dialing a phone again." They dined on steaks and potatoes and ice cream. Afterward, Sascha's little brother, Buddy, spent hours turning the water on and off, on and off. He'd never seen faucets before.

After a couple of days, the Weinzheimers thought they'd go shopping for clothes to replace their khakis. But before they could set out from their hotel, they were told that everything was closed and would remain closed for the next three days. It was Friday, April 12. The radio newscaster John Daly, his crisp familiar voice uncharacteristically shaky, had just broken into regular network programming:

> *We interrupt this program to bring you a special news bulletin from CBS World News. A Press Association has just announced that President Roosevelt is dead. The president died of a cerebral hemorrhage. All we know so far is that the president died at Warm Springs in Georgia.*

" 'Oh No!' Those two simple words seemed to be the most common expression heard when people learned of the sudden passing of President Roosevelt," Al McIntosh reported from Luverne.

> *We just didn't believe the news when we heard it. But later, when we walked back to the newspaper and into the Associ-*

New York subway riders learn of President Roosevelt's death, April 12, 1945.

Mobile shipyard workers (above) listen to a radio broadcast describing the president's funeral cortege in Washington (left) as it passes along Pennsylvania Avenue past mourning crowds.

ated Press room and read some of the bulletins streaming out of the racing teletypes, then we believed. Outside stood J. D. Coon, the Republican leader well known here, staring at the bulletin in the [Sioux Falls] Argus-Leader *window. His face was drawn and haggard and you could almost see a suggestion of tears in the attorney's eyes. "It's tragic," he said, and walked away. . . .*

Norman Johnson, manager of the local telephone exchange, said that beginning at 4:45 and continuing for an hour, the flood of telephone calls . . . was so heavy that six telephone operators were working at full speed to keep up. The rush, which lasted for an hour, was the biggest of any in any recent year, perhaps in history, Mr. Johnson said, and he added, "It gives us some idea what we can expect when V-day arrives."

The country was stunned. There had been rumors about the president's health for some time, always indignantly denied by the White House. In fact, he'd been suffering from congestive heart failure for well over a year, though only he and a handful of others had known it. "We can all tell you where we were when we heard that Roosevelt had died," Katharine Phillips remembered.

We didn't realize Roosevelt was sick. They had kept all that from us, so, like Pearl Harbor, it came as a complete shock. President Roosevelt was really the binding force for the United States. Everyone looked to him for leadership. He had led us out of the Depression, so we felt that certainly he could lead us through a war. And when the news came, it was a terrible blow to the entire country.

Children felt it, too. FDR's death seemed "catastrophic" to twelve-year-old Burt Wilson of Sacramento. "Now, the thing was, my parents were Republicans and hated Roosevelt, but I loved him. And most of us kids loved him, I believe, because he was the face of America that was saying, 'Hey, things are going to be OK.'"

FDR had been president for so long, more than a dozen years, four years longer than any other man, that most of the young men and women serving overseas could not remember an America without him. They had not universally admired him. He and his wife had been the targets of sometimes savage GI jokes. Men crouched in foxholes in Europe or struggling for possession of some Pacific island whose name they barely knew had often mocked him for having once promised never to send American boys into foreign wars, and some never understood why he had insisted on defeating Germany before turning America's full attention to Japan, the enemy that had struck the first blow against the United States. But they had voted for him in overwhelming numbers in 1944 nonetheless, and were badly shaken by his loss. Many could not recall Vice President Harry Truman's name, but their chief concern, Eugene Sledge remembered, was "how he would handle the war. We surely didn't want someone in the White House who would prolong it one day longer than necessary."

Sam Hynes was stationed on Saipan with his torpedo-bomber squadron when word of Roosevelt's death reached him.

I was standing outside a quonset hut looking across the little strait between Saipan and Tinian. There was a loudspeaker above my head on the wall that was used to make announcements, and I heard a voice say, "President Roosevelt is dead." He had been for us the only president we knew. I was eight years old when he was elected for his first term. So he was a much larger than life person and a person for whom we all felt love, I think. He was our leader, but he was also, in some way, our friend. I felt a great sense of loss. More than that, I thought, how will we go on fighting the war when our Commander in Chief is dead?

Ray Leopold was in central Germany with the 28th Infantry when he heard the news on Radio Luxembourg. His first reaction was that the report was Nazi propaganda, he remembered: "But word went up and down the line: 'You know, it's possible that it might be true.' 'No, no, not a man like Roosevelt.' Roosevelt was our rock."

Word also spread fast through the hospital ward at Épinal, where Paul Fussell was still recovering from his wounds. "We were all very sad," he remembered, "less about his leaving than about the irony of it. If he'd held on for a few weeks more, he could have seen the success of what he had done."

Earlier that month, the Japanese American troops of the Regimental 442nd Combat Team had moved into new positions at the western end of the Gothic Line in the Appennine mountains of northern Italy. Mark Clark's climb up the Italian peninsula had stalled. In the summer of 1944, he'd lost nearly a third of his force to the struggle for western Europe. Then winter weather had sheathed the slopes in ice. To help get his spring offensive started, he'd personally requested that the 442nd be brought back from France and attached to the badly battered all-black 92nd Infantry Division. The men of Dan Inouye's platoon were resting between assaults when they got word of Roosevelt's death. FDR had signed the order that interned the families from

which some of them had come. But he had also provided them with the opportunity to prove their loyalty on the battlefield, and once he'd been reelected in 1944, he had agreed that the camps could close, that internees might go home and try to rebuild the lives that his decision to round them up had so brutally interrupted. It was the latter Roosevelt the men of Inouye's outfit chose to remember.

When we got the word, the men in my platoon—I have no idea what happened in the rest of the regiment—took out their bayonets and started putting them on.

I said, "What's happening here?"

They said, "Well, I think we've got to do this one for the Old Man."

A few moments later the men rose up. They were not ordered to move. They just stood up and started attacking, and I think on that day we covered about ten miles. And the commanders couldn't stop us. I remember radio calls coming in from the company commander: "What in the hell are you doing? You're not supposed to be attacking."

I says, "Captain, you can't stop them." They were all moving forward for the Old Man, a man they had never met.

The fighting went on. That same evening, General Eisenhower took George Patton aside and gave him still more stunning news. He had decided that neither British nor American forces would try to take Berlin. That task would be left to the Red Army. He had already informed Stalin that its capture would be left to his troops. It was a purely pragmatic political decision. Eisenhower's closest armies were still more than 120 miles from the German capital; the Soviets were now less than 30 miles away. The Nazis were sure to defend Berlin with special ferocity, street by street, house to house. Bradley believed taking it from them would cost him one hundred thousand men. (It would eventually cost the Russians roughly three times that many.) And it would burden the Americans with caring for the hundreds of thousands of German refugees, displaced persons from captive nations, and prisoners of war who now clogged the roads. Beating the Soviets to the city would have been a largely symbolic act, in any case; the prize would have had to be turned over to them because, under the agreement made at Yalta, Berlin lay within their zone of occupation. Then, too, Eisenhower remained wary of the enemy's ability to counterattack. Allied Intelligence, which had underestimated the German ability to resist in December, was now warning him that enemy forces were gathering for a final stand in what would turn out to be a mythical "Alpine Redoubt," somewhere in southern Germany.

Eisenhower ordered the First and Ninth U.S. armies to halt at the Elbe to await the arrival of the Red Army, while Patton's Third Army was to turn southeast and drive toward Austria and Czechoslovakia to deal with those phantom armies.

QUENTIN AANENSON WAS HOME ON LEAVE when Roosevelt died. He had been in more or less continuous combat since D-day—ten ghastly months, during which he'd killed men and seen friends killed and come close to collapsing from despair. He expected to find himself in action again soon, in the Pacific this time, and he badly wanted to see Jackie Greer before going back overseas. Her letters had been his anchor to sanity.

She was eager to see him, too.

Always there would be something in the back of my mind. He might not come back. It could happen. But then I just wouldn't believe that. I prayed for him to come back, and I just felt that my prayers would be answered. One day I was walking down the street and I saw a wedding dress in a window. So I went right in and I bought that dress and shipped it to my mother and I said, "Have this ready for me. I'm going to need it."

Aanenson began talking about marriage almost the first moment they saw each other, he remembered. "Jackie and I had to discuss what to do because I was going to be going back to the war. I didn't want to face the idea that she could end up being a widow in a couple of months. But the more we talked about it, the more we decided, let's get married now."

"When he came back, the first night, we were in the living room and he formally proposed to me," she recalled.

And for some reason, I got shy. And I couldn't quite make myself say yes. I don't know why, because I'd been saying yes for eleven months. And when I hesitated and couldn't quite say yes, he said, "Well, now, just make up your mind." Or something like that. And I said, "Yes." But the funny part was the door right near my chair was closed. And on the other side of that door was my bed with that gorgeous wedding dress spread out all over it. And I thought later, "If I hadn't said yes and he had walked out. . . ." I didn't tell him about that until after we were married.

Aanenson took his fiancée home to Luverne to meet his family. While they were there, Ben Pelstring, the president of Nelson Brothers Department Store, the largest retail firm in southwestern Minnesota, invited them to be the guests of honor at a dinner with several other prominent citizens and their wives at his three-story turreted home, which occupied an entire block on Estey Street. Al McIntosh was one of the guests. It didn't go as well as might have been expected. People peppered Aanenson with questions about what it was like to be in combat. They wanted war stories. He couldn't bring himself to tell any. The memories were too raw. "There are casualties in war that never show up as casualties," he remembered.

Quentin Aanenson and Jackie Greer at their wedding, April 17, 1945

They're internal casualties. We all changed. We went out as a bunch of kids. Wars are fought by kids. And we came back—looked maybe the same, a little older—but inside we were so different. They thought we were just odd, I guess: "What's happened to Quent? What's wrong?" And I was feeling that nobody knows, nobody understands, and I am not good enough with words to be able to tell them.

Finally, Aanenson asked to be excused. He stepped into the bathroom to splash water on his face. When he came back out, McIntosh was waiting. He'd sensed what was wrong. "Quentin," he said, "I apologize." There would be no more questions about the war.

Quentin and Jackie returned to Baton Rouge, where they were married at the First Methodist Church at eight o'clock in the evening on April 17.

IT WAS CLEAR NOW THAT THE WAR IN EUROPE really was drawing to a close. Burnett Miller and the 11th Armored Division were moving fast. "It was the type of warfare for which we had been trained," a member of his outfit remembered, "fast and furious." Between April 10 and 14 alone, they traveled fifty miles and captured 115 towns and eight hundred prisoners. On the afternoon of the fourteenth, they pushed their way into Bayreuth, meeting only token resistance from snipers who seemed more eager to flee than fight. "It was quite a nice place," Miller wrote to his mother, "famous for its Wagner Festival which I don't think will be held this year. The place is a shambles." A third of the town had disappeared under Allied bombs.

A Red Cross ambulance creeps across a provisional bridge at the tail end of an 11th Armored Division column moving through Lunebach, Germany. The town is empty, its dwellings leveled by the Eighth Air Force.

Two antitank infantrymen dash across an open square in Kronach, Germany, April 14, 1945. Civilians have draped sheets and towels from their windows as a sign of surrender. But, as the burning ammunition trailer and the speed at which the men are moving show, sporadic military resistance continued.

It was there, a few days later, that Miller reluctantly shot the only man he was ever certain he'd hit in five months of fighting.

There was a river that split the town in half. We'd moved down to the river and we were in a little bar, and over our radio it came through from way up in back of us that there was a squad of Germans coming down the road right outside. And we watched them. They came down and they went into a building across the street. And we really didn't want a big fight. Pretty soon, one came out and came down and looked at the bridge that had been blown and then trotted up the road a couple of blocks, and we thought, well, the squad up there will pick him up. But pretty soon he came trotting back, so we realized there was no squad there.

So everybody said, "Why don't you shoot him?" "No, you shoot him."

I ended up having to shoot him. He flew up in the air, and the next thing I knew there were two of us out there nursing him and dragging him back. And then the rest of his squad came out from across the street and surrendered.

That's the only one I'm ever sure I shot. I shot at lots and lots of things. But you were shooting at smoke. You were shooting at where you could see machine-gun fire coming from. You were shooting at tanks, which was useless. You never knew what you were doing. This was the only case where you could really see somebody, and nobody really wanted to do it. Here he was. And he was doing no harm. And he was really just trying to retreat. But we couldn't think of any other way to do it.

In the Appennines there were rumors that the war would soon be over but few signs of letup so far. Germans still held the high ground; Americans still struggled to drive them off it. "Our company commander, like all other company commanders of the regiment, called his officers together," Daniel Inouye recalled. "He said, 'The war is ending. The Germans are giving up. They're now sending messages to negotiate. So it's obvious the war is over. But we cannot let down the pressure. Because if we do, the war will be prolonged. So keep it up.' "

Inouye continued: "It's a horrible thing, knowing the war is going to end and you have to keep urging your men to go forward." On April 21, his platoon was one of three ordered to try to take a high rocky ridge called Colle Musatello. Inouye felt unusually anxious that morning. Ever since the battle for Bruyères, he had carried with him in his jacket two silver dollars. Both had been twisted by a bullet that might otherwise have killed him, and he had come to consider them his good-luck charms. This morning he could find neither his jacket nor his coins. "I saw the platoon leader of the next platoon," he recalled, "and I said, 'I think today's my day.' He said, 'What are you talking about?' I says, 'This is the day I'm going to get banged.' Sure enough."

Things went well at first. He and his men moved up the slope so swiftly he had to use his radio to call off the American artillery blasting the hillside up ahead for fear his own men would be hit. Then machine guns opened up from three different positions, pinning him and his men to the rock face. If they lay there too long, Inouye knew they would be killed. He pulled a grenade from his belt, rose to his feet, and started toward the nearest machine gun. "As I was going up I suddenly felt someone punching me on the side. That's what I thought it was. A bullet had gone right through my abdomen. Came out just about a quarter inch from my spine." Inouye fell, struggled back to his feet, then ran forward, pulling the pin and hurling the grenade. The log bunker in which the machine gun had been hidden exploded in dust and dirt and splinters. When its dazed crew staggered outside, Inouye killed them all with a long burst from his tommy gun. The other two machine guns kept firing. He hobbled farther

up the hill and silenced the next one with two more grenades. His men charged up toward the third but had to take cover before they reached it. Inouye stayed on his feet, staggered toward it, and pulled the pin on yet another grenade. But this time, as he raised his arm to hurl it, a German soldier swung his rifle-grenade up and fired from just ten yards away. The grenade smashed Inouye's right elbow and nearly severed his arm. Somehow, with his left hand, he pried his dead fingers from the live grenade and threw it.

Then, according to the men and according to my company commander, I went berserk. I had a Thompson submachine gun and with my left hand started approaching the last machine-gun nest, just firing into it with the blood splattering out, and it was a horrible sight. And finally I got hit again on my leg and I kept rolling down the hill, and that was the end.

German prisoners of war were pressed into service to carry Inouye back down the hill. He was given so much morphine at the aid station that later, when surgeons at a field hospital began to amputate his shattered arm, he had to endure it without anesthetic. The pain was so intense, he remembered, "that dying didn't seem like such an awful idea."

I ended up receiving seventeen whole blood transfusions. Before they gave you the blood, they showed you the bottle, and on that bottle was a label that had the name, rank, serial number, and the unit. And so, here is someone with some fancy name, Thomas Jefferson Lee, serial number, 92nd Division. Now, 92nd Division was the unit that we were attached to in the last battle, made up of African Americans, and all of the bottles I saw were from the 92nd Division. So I must have had seventeen bottles of good African American blood. And so here I am.

Two days after Inouye's arm was destroyed, German resistance in the nisei sector ended. Nine days after that, the enemy in Italy would surrender. Recuperating in an army hospital, Inouye found himself in the same ward with a farmer's son from Kansas named Robert Dole and a young lawyer from Michigan named Philip Hart. All three were gravely wounded; all three would go on to serve their country as members of the United States Senate. Fifty-five years later, Daniel Inouye would receive the Medal of Honor for his heroism under fire.

"The Germany in which we found ourselves traveling at the end of April presented a scene that was almost beyond human comprehension," wrote Alan Moorehead. He was accompanying

British troops as they moved across northern Germany, but the scenes he saw were being repeated everywhere.

Her capital was lost and almost razed, and [there was] nothing to give that ash-heap significance beyond a name, a history and the presence of a lunatic who was about to make his last gesture to a colossal vanity—his death. Around us fifty great cities lay in ruins. . . . Many of them had no electric light or power or gas or running water, and no coherent system of government. Like ants in an ant heap the people scurried over the ruins diving furtively into cellars and doorways in search of loot. . . . Everyone was on the move, and there was a frantic ant-like quality about their activity. Life was sordid, aimless, leading nowhere. Every house in every unbombed village was stacked to the roof with city refugees living on soup and potatoes. . . . Ninety per cent of the country's industry was at a standstill. No trains ran. Every family was bereaved or broken up. A very large part of the population was simply wandering on the roads with the millions of [foreign slave laborers]. And to these was now added the German army itself. A mass flight from the Russians toward the Elbe and the Anglo-American lines began. Officers stripped off their uniforms and begged or stole civilian clothes from the nearby houses. Mass fear had gripped them so greatly that when aircraft appeared in the sky the shout went up: "The Russians! The Russians!" and the mob would break out in panic across the countryside.

Panic was justified. The men of the Red Army, advancing relentlessly westward, showed no mercy. "You are now on German soil," they'd been told as they crossed the border. "The hour of revenge has struck!" Each regiment was encouraged to keep its own "revenge score." One battalion carried with it across eastern Germany a hand-lettered poster that read: WE ARE NOW GETTING OUR REVENGE FOR 775 OF OUR RELATIVES WHO WERE KILLED, FOR 909 RELATIVES WHO WERE TAKEN AWAY TO SLAVERY IN GERMANY, FOR 478 BURNT-DOWN HOUSES AND FOR 303 DESTROYED FARMS. The Soviets looted and burned villages and gang-raped hundreds of thousands of women, often with the full approval of their officers. When their bleeding, beaten victims in Königsberg begged to be put out of their misery, the rapists were indignant: "Russian soldiers do not shoot women," one said. "Only German soldiers do that." Thousands hid from them in cellars and attics. Millions more fled before them onto the German roads.

On April 23, Burnett Miller and the 11th Armored Division were approaching the Austrian border. Over the first three weeks of the month, Allied armies had discovered more than one hundred camps, including Buchenwald, Nordhausen, Flossenbürg, and Bergen-Belsen. No one who saw them could doubt any longer the monstrous nature of the regime with which they had been at war. Now it was Miller's turn.

As his division passed through a wooded area just outside the city of Cham, the men began to notice bodies crumpled here and there along the roadside. Some had clearly been shot. Others seemed to have died from exhaustion or malnutrition. All were dressed in filthy black-and-white-striped uniforms. "We had heard about concentration camps," Miller recalled. "We still didn't know whether to believe it or not, and all of a sudden we found bodies strewn along the road. They were in horrible condition, just terrible." The column slowed, then stopped. The road ahead was blocked by thousands of living skeletons wearing the same uniforms, slave laborers from Flossenbürg being driven along by their SS guards. The column backed up a bit, then drove around them and into Cham. Thousands more prisoners crowded the central square. "Some were dying," Miller remembered; "some were trying to steal food." The SS men had run away.

We actually saw a guard move into a house, and we chased him in. He was an officer, and he was trying to change out of his uniform into civilian clothes. He turned to us and said in a Brooklyn accent, "Hey, you guys, do you know what you're doin'? I know your country well," which was a startling thing. I think he was a colonel, and we took him as a prisoner and tried to escort him outside. I don't know where we were taking him, but the prisoners who were out there tore him apart. Just killed him right there.

The column kept moving, but a few days later, Miller found time to write another letter to his parents. Like most GIs, he'd been careful to keep out of his letters anything he thought might unduly disturb them. What he'd seen on the road into Cham now made that impossible.

April 28, 1945
Dear Mom & Dad,
*   I haven't had a chance to write for some time now as we've been quite busy. We again have made a big jump and if every-*

At Nordhausen, a subcamp of the Dora-Mitelbau concentration camp, where slave laborers too weak and ill to be of any further use to the Reich were simply allowed to die of starvation, Third Army troops discovered the bodies of some three thousand of them. Some had been killed when Allied bombers mistook their cement barracks for a German munitions depot.

one keeps making jumps like ours the main resistance should weaken in a few weeks. . . .

For the first time in my life I feel a real hate for anything as large as an organization, or should I say "way of life" (philosophy). Our last drive was a night-mare. No one who has not seen such a terrible thing can imagine it possible. Our column fell on the trail of a column of humans being driven from a concentration camp away from us, and we over-ran and freed these people. Many who could not keep up were shot on the road. More died from starvation. Those who were left hardly resembled men. Their crimes were refusing to become slaves and being born Jews. I would not tell you these unpleasant things but that you should know what we are fighting for.

I'll write soon.

Love,

Burnett

By then, American and Soviet forces had linked up at Torgau on the Elbe River. Germany had been overrun. Word had come that Italian partisans had shot Mussolini and his mistress and hung their corpses upside down from a girder above a gas station in Milan. The next day, Soviet troops began assaulting Berlin itself. On April 30, as Russian troops fought their way into the Reichstag, the symbol of German power, Hitler and his closest aides huddled beneath the rubble in their bunker, less than half a mile away. That afternoon, he named Admiral Karl Dönitz to succeed him, then shot himself in the mouth. Only his most fanatical followers continued to fight on.

THE NEXT DAY, MAY 1, turned into a nightmare for Eugene Sledge and the men of the 1st Marines. The battle for Okinawa had not been going well. The marines had cleared the northern and central parts of the island by mid-April, but in the south, the army had been unable to blast the Japanese from their positions within the limestone ridges around the walled town of Shuri. "The stuff has hit the fan down there, boys," a sergeant told Sledge's Company K. "The Nips are pouring on the artillery and mortars and everything they've got." The entire 1st Marine Division was to move south right away, into positions on the right of the American line occupied till then by the exhausted men of the 27th Infantry Division.

They started south in trucks, one marine remembered, and soon became aware of "a grumbling on the horizon, which turned into a thumping, then a drumming, then a rumbling, and then an enormous thudding, as though Fafner and Fasolt, the giants in *Das Rheingold,* had been let loose." As the sounds of battle intensified, they drove past tent cities that housed thousands of service troops, acres of ammunition and supplies covered with camouflage netting, heaps of empty brass shell cases, and hundreds of shell craters that marked a prolonged and vicious artillery battle. Then, "at some unmarked spot," Sledge wrote, "we stopped and got off the trucks. I was filled with dread." Shells tumbled and howled overhead as the men of K Company formed a single line and started forward.

A column of men approached us on the other side of the road from the 106th Regiment, 27th Infantry Division, that we were relieving. Their tragic expressions revealed where they had been. They were dead beat, dirty and grisly, hollow-eyed and tight-faced. . . .

As they filed past us, one tall, lanky fellow caught my eye and said in a weary voice, "It's hell up there, Marine."

I said with some impatience, "Yeah, I know. I was at Peleliu."

He looked at me blankly and moved on.

Ahead of the marines was a low, gently sloping ridge where Company K was to go into the line. The noise was deafening now. "Keep your five-pace interval—don't bunch up," an officer bellowed. Shells began bursting between them and the ridge. They ran toward it. Five-pace intervals were forgotten. As they scrambled forward, trying to avoid the shells now falling among them, they met more of the soldiers they were relieving coming the other way. The Japanese, delighted to find so many confused targets out in the open, filled the air around them with machine-gun and rifle bullets. Men screamed for medics and stretcher bearers.

A navy corpsman does what he can for a marine emotionally overcome by weeks of combat on Okinawa. The marines alone would suffer more than fourteen thousand cases of battle fatigue during the battle for the Shuri Line.

THE DIFFERENCE

The war correspondent Ernie Pyle had left the European front in September of 1944, shortly after the liberation of Paris. By then, he'd lived alongside American GIs for three years, from North Africa, through Sicily and Italy, and all the way across France. "I've been immersed in it too long," he told a friend as he left for home. "The hurt has finally become too great."

But he couldn't stay away. He was back, living in foxholes and interviewing marines on the island of Ie Shima, on April 17, when a Japanese machine-gunner shot him in the head. Among the papers he had with him was an unfinished column, evidently intended for publication after the war in Europe had officially ended. He had planned to be with the GIs as they landed on Okinawa.

And so it is over. The catastrophe on one side of the world has run its course. The day that it had so long seemed would never come has come at last. . . .

This is written on a little ship lying off the coast of the Island of Okinawa, just south of Japan, on the other side of the world from [the] Ardennes. But my heart is still in Europe. . . . It is easy for us to forget the dead. Those who are gone would not wish them-selves to be a millstone of gloom around our necks.

But there are many of the living who have had burned into their brains forever the unnatural sight of cold dead men scattered over the hillsides and in the ditches along the high rows of hedge throughout the world.

Dead men by mass production— in one country after another—month

Ernie Pyle (fourth from left) and a marine patrol take time out for a smoke on Ie Shima, April 6, 1945. Eleven days later, he was dead.

after month and year after year. Dead men in winter and dead men in summer.

Dead men in such familiar promis-cuity that they become monotonous.

Dead men in such monstrous infinity that you come almost to hate them.

These are the things that you at home need not even try to understand. To you at home they are columns of figures, or he is a near one who went away and just didn't come back. You didn't see him lying so grotesque and pasty beside the gravel road in France.

We saw him, saw him by the multiple thousand. That's the difference.

The marines plodding toward the camera are headed for the front on Okinawa; those marching away from it have had enough—at least for a time.

Sledge reached the ridge and flung himself down, panting from exertion and fear. Then, as the shelling intensified, he and the rest of Company K did their best to dig in. Peleliu had taught him what to expect now, so he no longer worried that his fear would paralyze him. He could distinguish in the chaos the sound and impact of one kind of shell and then another: fifty-millimeter knee mortar shells yielded small puffs of sooty smoke, high-velocity antitank-gun shells hit with a *whiz-bang*, slower-moving 75-millimeter shells shrieked as they came in, and the earth shook whenever the "big stuff" landed from the enemy's 105-millimeter howitzers.

News spread that two of Sledge's friends had been killed coming across the field, one a nineteen-year-old married newcomer, the other a veteran who had fought on Cape Gloucester and Peleliu before coming ashore on Okinawa. "Many men were superstitious about one's chances of surviving a third campaign," Sledge would write. "By that time one's luck was wearing thin." As darkness fell and they huddled in their fresh foxholes eating cold C rations, word of still more deaths and more woundings reached them. "They were just the first of what was to grow into a long tragic list before we would come out of combat fifty hellish days later."

IN EUROPE, THE GERMAN COLLAPSE was accelerating. On May 1, the same day Sledge arrived at the front on Okinawa, the 82nd Airborne reached the Elbe. "We were with the British Second Army," Dwain Luce remembered.

It wasn't bad. The food was awful, but on a cold night, the brigadier had the right to break out a dram of rum. The little old ladies in this country probably didn't approve of it. But we did. And then we made that last river crossing, and I'll always remember we were pushing ahead and the colonel sent me back in a jeep to do something and come right back, and when I came back I ran into the curb with the jeep and, lord, here comes—looked like to me—the whole German army. I thought to myself, "Man, I've got myself in a mess." Then I saw what it was. They'd quit. And I didn't know it. They had some camp followers with them. It was the German Twenty-first Army that surrendered to us up there. They just threw up their hands. And the women in the houses you passed by were on the front porch crying, and the end had come. It was something to see.

The 82nd Airborne took 144,000 prisoners that day. By then, commander General James Gavin had set up his headquarters at Ludwigslust in the handsome palace of the grand duke of Mecklenburg, which overlooked a little green park in the center of town. He was puzzled to discover that within moments of his arrival the mayor and his wife and grown daughter had all hanged themselves. The next day he learned why. Just north of town, his own men as well as units of the 8th Infantry Division came upon Wöbbelin, a subcamp of the Neuengamme concentration camp, where some fifty thousand slave laborers who had worked in German armament factories had died over the course of the war. More than one thousand unburied corpses were found at Wöbbelin, along with four thousand men who barely clung to life. There was no food anywhere and little water, and there was evidence of cannibalism.

On May 8, Dwain Luce remembered, "we made the German people in that community go get two hundred of those bodies and had a burial in the park right in front of the castle." While he and some seven hundred members of the airborne division looked on, the U.S. Army chaplain who presided over the services spoke directly to the crowd, made up of captured German officers and citizens of Ludwigslust. He paused after each sentence so that his words could be translated into German.

The crimes here committed in the name of the German people and by their acquiescence were minor compared to those to be found in concentration camps elsewhere in Germany.

Here there were no gas chambers, no crematoria; these men of Holland, Russia, Poland, Czechoslovakia, and France were simply allowed to starve to death. Within four miles of your comfortable homes four thousand men were forced to live like animals, deprived even of the food you would give to your dogs. In three weeks, one thousand of these men were starved to death; eight hundred of them were buried in pits in the nearby woods. These two hundred who lie before us in these graves were found piled four and five feet high in one building and lying with the sick and dying in other buildings.

After the bodies were laid to rest, each grave was marked by a cross or a Star of David so that no one would ever forget what had been allowed to happen there. "These people in this country who say it didn't happen?" Dwain Luce remembered many years later. "It happened. I saw it. I know."

When the U.S. 8th Infantry and 82nd Airborne reached the Wöbbelin concentration camp near the town of Ludwigslust, they found some 3,500 starving inmates (above). A thousand more lay dead and unburied. U.S. commanders insisted the townspeople first view their corpses (right, above) and then carry 200 of them to the town square for a public burial on May 8, 1945 (right, below).

Cheering inmates of the Mauthausen concentration camp greet the lead tanks of the 11th Armored Division, May 5, 1945. Political prisoners among them had prepared the welcome sign in several languages. "There was a surge of people who were in fairly good condition begging for food," Burnett Miller remembered, "and we were giving them what food we had—concentrated food—and in some cases it overwhelmed their systems and actually killed them." Touring the camp, Miller saw heaps of corpses and ovens filled with ash. "It was a horrible, horrible experience. And then we came—at least I came—to think, well, this effort has been worthwhile."

It would be years before the grim statistics of Nazi rule could even be approximated. But when Hitler took power in 1933, there had been some 9 million Jews in Europe. By 1945, roughly two out of three of them were dead and thousands of Jewish communities had been wiped from the face of the earth. Hitler's regime had also been responsible for the deaths of nearly 2 million non-Jewish Poles, more than 4 million Soviet prisoners of war, as well as hundreds of thousands of handicapped people and political opponents, homosexuals and Gypsies and Jehovah's Witnesses and slave laborers from all the countries it had conquered. And the Americans in uniform who helped to end that regime had a new appreciation of what they had accomplished. Paul Fussell remembered:

On D-day morning, Eisenhower had distributed to the troops a general order. Everybody read it. He said, "You are about to

embark upon a great crusade. . . ." At first none of us could believe it was anything like a crusade, because we were playing dice and we were thinking about girls all the time and getting as drunk as possible. It wasn't like a crusade. There was no religious dimension to it whatsoever. But when they finally got across France and into Germany and saw the German death camps, they realized that they had been engaged in something like a crusade, although none of them called it that. And it all began to make a kind of sense to us. I'm not sure that made it any better—it may have made it worse—to

Amid the ruins of the German capital, a German officer subsists on C rations: "Nothing is left of Berlin but memories," a Soviet officer wrote. "I would never have believed that a great city could be reduced to mere rubble. It seems so strange, after four years of gunfire, now not to hear a single shot around us."

see that the war was actually conducted in defense of some noble idea.

On May 7, the day Dwain Luce watched the dead of Wöbbelin being buried at Ludwigslust, German General Alfred Jodl, representing Hitler's chosen successor, Admiral Dönitz, signed the documents of unconditional surrender at SHAEF headquarters at Reims. Moments later, the Supreme Allied Commander sent a one-line telegram to the Combined Chiefs of Staff: "The mission of this Allied Force was fulfilled at 02:41 hours, local time, May 7, 1945. Eisenhower." The war in Europe was over. The Reich Hitler had said would endure for a thousand years had lasted less than a dozen.

Burnett Miller wrote home again that day. He was now helping to guard the last of the concentration camps to be liberated, Mauthausen, where scores of men and women were still dying from malnutrition and disease every day.

May 7, 1945
Dear Grandma,
We heard yesterday that peace was coming within twenty-four hours. It was hard to believe, but as we have not been fired on for four days, it must be so. Our reaction to the announcement was odd. We all tried our darnedest to be terribly gay. Some jumped up and down a few times, others fired a few shots and, of course, a few bottles were opened, but it lasted no more than half an hour. Things were very quiet, and we moved into the same old routine. I guess the great joyousness will not come naturally until we're home again and with those we love.

THE FIRST HOME-FRONT REACTION TO THE NEWS from Europe had been remarkably cautious, too. An overzealous Associated Press reporter named Edward Kennedy had his army credentials canceled for having sent out the news before SHAEF Publications officers gave him official permission to do so. Many Americans worried that it might be still another false rumor. The whole country seemed to fall silent the following morning as people listened first to President Truman and then to Prime Minister Churchill confirm the good news over the radio. There were parades in some cities. Church bells pealed everywhere. But even then the reaction was more subdued than it had been on Armistice Day in 1917. Then peace in Europe had meant peace everywhere; now a second victory would have to be won in the Pacific. In Mobile, where an extra edition of the *Register* was headlined RIOTOUS JOY PREVAILING, some thirteen thousand ADDSCO workers quietly kept at their jobs. "Say a prayer, buy a

bond, and go to work," the president of the chamber of commerce said. "Our boys in the Pacific need you to keep up the steady stream of ships from Mobile." In Sacramento, the state government lifted a midnight curfew so that bars and cardrooms and bowling alleys could remain open into the early morning hours for the first time since Pearl Harbor. In Waterbury, shops and factories also stayed open and Mrs. T. F. Weeks, who had seven sons in the service, told a reporter for the *Republican* that she wouldn't allow herself to get too excited until she knew each and every one of them was safe; three were in Europe, but four remained in the Pacific.

"Unlike New Yorkers, who whooped, hollered, and tore up tons of paper to throw in the streets," Al McIntosh reported from Luverne, "the news here was greeted with quiet dignity and reverent restraint."

> *One by one, the flags blossomed out on Main Street and store by store the employees quietly filed out and the business places were locked up for the day. . . . [But there] was no shouting, no hilarious display of any kind. Most everybody went home. There was quiet exultation over the fact that a great victory had been achieved, but that rejoicing was tempered by the sobering knowledge that there was another great war yet to be won.*

But everywhere on every downtown street in America that night, the official brownout that had eliminated all unnecessary lighting came to an end, and the defeat of Hitler was hailed by a rainbow of neon, selling cigarettes and cafés, restaurants and rooming houses and double features at the movies.

THREE WEEKS BEFORE PATTON'S THIRD ARMY crossed the Rhine, General Patton had written General Marshall, asking to be given a command in the coming invasion of Japan. "I am of such an age that this is my last war," he wrote, "and I would therefore like to see it through to the end." It is safe to say that Patton's eagerness for additional combat was not shared by most of the other officers and men who'd struggled to liberate Europe. Lieutenant Paul Fussell got the V-E Day news in southern France, where he was still recovering from his wounds.

> *I was delighted. I remember I drank a warm can of beer that I had been saving for some months. I had it under the sheets on my bed. And I somehow got somebody who had a beer can opener and I drank that can of beer to celebrate the fact that it was all over. But then I realized that for me it wasn't all over, because very soon I was going to be shipped across*

France, ready to reenter the war on the other side of the world against the Japanese.

Among the men already fighting in the Pacific, the European victory did not resonate as it did elsewhere. "The Japanese were not going to fight any less hard because Hitler was out of it," Sam Hynes remembered. "I suppose there was a certain satisfaction that we'd beaten that lot. And could now turn our attention entirely to the other lot. But aside from that, I don't think, there was much excitement."

Hynes and his torpedo-bomber squadron were based on Okinawa now. They'd spent two weeks on Saipan and three days on Iwo Jima—"a blasted, charred heap of sand, as littered and abandoned as a public beach after the Fourth of July," Hynes recalled—before finally joining the battle in the third week of April. They were stationed close enough to the fighting that Hynes could hear the sound of guns—"a distant rumble, like a trolley-car passing late at night"—and could see from the entrance to his tent the battleships offshore shelling Japanese positions in and around Shuri. There were frequent air raids and an occasional artillery shell as well. In the month that followed their arrival, Hynes and his squadron mates would fly more than one thousand combat missions, going after torpedo launchers, gun emplacements, submarines, dropping supplies to the Americans and propaganda leaflets behind enemy lines. Hynes lost friends, shot from the sky, victims of their own errors, or simply reported missing somewhere over the featureless sea. But the battlefield below remained remote, distant. Never once in all that time did Hynes see a live enemy soldier.

> *Terrible things happened at Okinawa. But a man in an airplane above the battle doesn't see the terrible things. What I saw was drifting smoke, explosions, shells coming in from the battleships offshore. The targets we were diving on were usually rather small scale. A cave that had a gun in it. What might be a Japanese emplacement or supplies or something like that. Or just bombs ahead of the advancing line of the troops. You saw destruction: the town of Naha, the capital of Okinawa, had a single wall standing. Of all the buildings, just one wall. You see that and you can imagine the devastation, but you don't exactly see it. You don't see the dead civilians who died in their thousands. You don't see the dead Japanese. You don't even see your own dead. I dropped some bombs on buildings that blew up, and if there was anybody in them, I suppose I killed somebody. I don't know. I'd like to think I didn't. But that's what I was being paid for, was to kill people.*

Marines on Okinawa listen with a notable lack of excitement to the news that the war in faraway Europe has finally ended.

Down below, Eugene Sledge and the marines were fighting a very different kind of war. From the second of May until the fifteenth, the 1st Marine Division inched its way toward Shuri, helping to blast and burn the enemy out of their hiding places one ridge, one village, one gulley at a time: the Awacha Pocket, Dakeshi Ridge, Dakeshi Village, Wana Ridge. The men's initial reaction to victory in Europe, Sledge remembered, had been " 'So what.' Nazi Germany might as well have been on the moon.... We were resigned only to the fact that the Japanese would fight to total extinction, as they had elsewhere, and that Japan would have to be invaded with the same gruesome prospects."

It rained. Tanks and amtracs stalled. Shelling was continuous. Marines had to stumble through the mud under fire, carrying heavy crates of ammunition and supplies. "Unlike at Peleliu," Sledge wrote, "we got numerous replacement lieutenants. They were wounded or killed with such regularity that we rarely knew anything about them other than a code name and saw them on their feet only once or twice." Mail somehow made it to the front lines. It was good for morale, Sledge remembered, but one letter

had the opposite effect on him. He'd learned to greet the death of fellow marines with dry eyes, but a letter from home reporting that his spaniel, Deacon, had been killed by a passing car reduced him to tears.

Every two or three days, Sledge's outfit would be relieved to rest and then sent back up to the front again.

I found it more difficult to go back each time we squared away our gear to move forward.... With each step toward the distant rattle and rumble of that hellish region where fear and horror tortured us like a cat tormenting a mouse, I experienced greater and greater dread. And it wasn't just dread of death or pain, because most men felt somehow they wouldn't be killed. But each time we went up, I felt the sickening dread of fear itself and the revulsion against the ghastly scenes of pain and suffering among comrades that a survivor must witness.

The increasing dread of going back into action obsessed me. It became the subject of the most tortuous and persistent of all the ghastly war nightmares that have haunted me for many, many years. The dream is always the same, going back up to the lines during the bloody month of May on Okinawa.

On May 14, the 1st Marine Division entered the Wana Draw. In front of them was Shuri itself. To their left was Wana Ridge. A rise they dubbed Half Moon Hill loomed on the right. All three hid enemy positions from which relentless fire was directed down at them. They stood seven days of it without complaint. Then rain began to fall again, more than a foot of it in a week. Shells filled the air, too, fired by the Japanese, by Americans on the ground, and by U.S. Navy warships offshore—so many for so long that Sledge's head pounded with pain all day and all night.

On May 23, his outfit moved again, to the center of the Shuri Line, this time just below the slope called Sugar Loaf Hill. It was a matter of pride with the marines that no dead comrade was ever left on the battlefield. But during this phase of the fight for Okinawa, "because of the deep mud, the able-bodied could scarcely rescue and evacuate their wounded. . . . Regrettably, the dead had to wait," Sledge wrote.

We slogged along through a muddy draw around the base of a knoll. On our left we saw six Marine corpses. They were lying face down against a gentle muddy slope where they apparently had hugged the deck to escape Japanese shells. They were "bunched-up"—in a row, side by side, scarcely a foot apart. They were so close together that they probably had all been killed by the same shell. Their browning faces lay against the mud in an even row. One could not even imagine the words of fear or reassurance that had been passing among them as they lay under the terror of the shelling. Each clutched a rusting rifle, and every sign indicated that those tragic figures were new replacements, fresh to the shock of combat.

Rain continued. The draw became a lake of mud. Nothing ever dried. The men developed mysterious fungal sores, malaria, amoebic dysentery, a crippling condition called immersion foot, and hundreds of cases of combat fatigue, which left men catatonic or hysterical. A correspondent watched two medical corpsmen dragging a third toward the rear as he screamed over and over again, "They'll get every one of you! They'll get every one of you!"

A marine with a tommy gun fires a burst at a hidden Japanese sniper during the furious struggle for Wana Ridge.

Sledge wrote:

We realized quickly that any time any of us moved out of our holes, the shelling began immediately. Every crater was half full of water, and many of them held a Marine corpse . . . [and] everywhere lay Japanese corpses. . . . The scene was nothing but mud; shell fire; flooded craters with their silent rotting occupants; knocked out tanks and amtracs; and discarded equipment—utter desolation. . . . The ever-present smell of death saturated my nostrils. It was there with every breath I took.

Artillery shells uncovered half-buried Japanese corpses and tore dead marines into pieces. The ceaseless rain washed maggots and feces into foxholes. There was no relief from any of it, day after day.

If a Marine slipped and slid down the back slope of the muddy ridge, he was apt to reach the bottom vomiting. . . . I saw more than one man . . . stand up horror stricken as . . . fat maggots tumbled out of his muddy dungaree pockets, cartridge belt, legging lacings and the like. We didn't talk about such things. They were too horrible and obscene even for hardened veterans. . . .

Nearly three thousand Americans would die before Sugar Loaf Hill was finally taken, as many per square foot as anywhere else in the war.

In late May, the Japanese finally began a carefully staged withdrawal from the Shuri Line, slipping back ten miles or so to their last refuge, another series of ridges at the island's southern tip. It would be three more weeks before its last defenders were killed and their commanders committed suicide. By then, 92,000 Japanese soldiers and at least 100,000 Okinawan civilians were dead, many of them buried within the tombs and caves in which they'd hidden. Thousands killed themselves rather than surrender. Of the 235 members of Eugene Sledge's Company K who had landed on Okinawa, just 26 emerged unhurt; of the 254 men brought in to replace those who had fallen, only 24 remained. In the end, more than 12,000 Americans died and 60,000 were wounded, one-third of all American combatants, the worst losses of the Pacific war. Among the dead were Private First Class

A frightened Okinawan boy surrenders to the Americans. "The civilians were in terrible shape," one marine recalled, "wounded, starving, terrified."

J. J. McCarthy of Waterbury, Sergeant Jeff Fleming of Sacramento, Private First Class Lowell Reu of Luverne, and Private Ernest Roy of Mobile.

AS THE ALLIES PREPARED to move on to the Japanese homeland itself, still more terrible losses seemed inevitable. "Ugly rumors circulated that we would hit Japan next," Sledge recalled, "with an estimated casualty figure of one million Americans. No one wanted to talk about that." Sam Hynes heard the rumors, too.

We were told that in the invasion of Japan we would be the first land-based single-engine bombing squadron. To be in on the invasion of the Japanese home island. That would be heroic stuff. We all felt that. But at the same time, by then our sense of the strangeness of the Japanese opposition had become stronger. And I could imagine every farmer with his pitchfork coming at my guts, every pretty girl with a hand grenade strapped to her bottom. Everyone would be an enemy.

A two-part plan for the Allied invasion of Japan was already in place: on November 1, a vast U.S. amphibious force, larger even than D-day's, was to assault Kyushu, which would, in turn, act as the staging area for a second decisive assault on the rest of the home islands to be mounted four months later, on March 1, 1946. Insane as it may seem in retrospect, Japan's military rulers hoped the Allies would try to make good on these plans. They continued to believe that a prolonged, bloody battle on their own soil could force the Allies to agree to a peace that would leave their emperor on his throne, themselves immune from outside prosecution, and their country free of occupying troops.

Allied preparations for the invasion continued, but planners grew increasingly uneasy as they learned through deciphered diplomatic and military messages that many of the assumptions on which they'd based their initial plans had been badly wrong. Since New Year's Day, the Japanese had nearly quadrupled their forces on Kyushu, from 150,000 to 545,000, and more than doubled their men under arms throughout Japan to nearly 2 million. Some 5,350 airplanes readied for suicide attack awaited the invasion fleet; so did 6,200 single-crewman suicide boats. Estimates of U.S. invasion casualties varied, but it was clear that tens of thousands—and perhaps hundreds of thousands—would be lost. And if the civilian deaths on Saipan and Okinawa were any guide, so would hundreds of thousands—perhaps millions—of ordinary Japanese citizens. If the emperor was willing to sanction the "sacrifice [of] twenty million Japanese lives in a special [suicide attack]," promised the founder of the

Okinawa, May 1945.

kamikaze corps, Admiral Takajiro Onishi, "certain victory" could still be won.

All but a handful of Americans at home wanted nothing less than unconditional surrender by the nation that had dared attack Pearl Harbor; a third of them wanted the emperor himself executed as a war criminal. But their impatience for an end to fighting had also continued to grow. More than six out of ten U.S. casualties had been incurred over the past eleven months. Americans were freshly appalled by the number of lives lost on Iwo Jima and Okinawa, and lived in dread of what was still to come. Three out of four Americans had expected demobilization to begin the moment peace was signed with Germany, and Congress had insisted that the armed services be reduced immediately by a million men. Thousands of seasoned officers and men had already been sent home from some divisions, beneficiaries of a complex system that awarded different numbers of "points" to servicemen depending on factors as various as how many decorations they'd won and how many children they had.

Truman approved the initial invasion of Kyushu, but he also expressed his hope that some way could be found to prevent "an Okinawa from one end of Japan to the other." His administration looked hard for alternatives to invasion. It intensified the blockade of Japanese ports and the razing of Japanese cities. The navy methodically sank supply ships that entered Japanese waters: by the end of the year, Tokyo citizens would be struggling to subsist on fewer than a thousand calories a day. Meanwhile, American aircraft bombed and burned sixty-six Japanese cities, killing at least 300,000 Japanese civilians, injuring 1.3 million, and leaving 8 million more without homes. The Fifth U.S. Air Force printed a pamphlet meant to reassure any of its bomber pilots who might feel uneasy about the damage they were doing to ordinary people on the ground. Because the entire population of Japan had now been organized into a citizens' army, the pamphlet said, all of her people had become "a proper military target. . . . THERE ARE NO CIVILIANS IN JAPAN."

Some Allied commanders, General Arnold and Admiral Nimitz among them, still believed that bombing and blockade alone might force Japan to surrender, if they were given enough time. But others argued that time had long since run out. Japan's military rulers continued to ready their forces for Armageddon. Allied prisoners of war were dying every day.

Glenn Frazier, still at Tsuruga, was one of 168,000 POWs remaining in Japanese hands.

When the bombing started in our area, first it was about once every two weeks. Then it was a raid about every week. Then it stepped up. Most of the raids started at night with the B-29s,

and you could distinguish their sound, and all of a sudden you could hear these Zeros up there and the gunfire, trying to shoot them down. They burned out a third of our whole area and killed over three hundred Japanese. It burned out our own barracks that we were in. But it was like a ballgame to us. I mean, we were happy about it. They made rats out of us in the Philippines when we were there, and now our B-29s were making rats out of them in Japan.

We knew that the end was coming. But that did not help our feelings as to what was about to happen. Our lives were going to be sacrificed. If we had an invasion of Japan, we knew we were dead. They issued orders to shoot all prisoners of war the minute American or Allied forces landed on their homeland, so we had basically accepted our fate.

On July 15, 1945, the USS *Indianapolis,* ready to go back to war now that her repairs in California were complete, received orders to pick up a piece of special cargo at Hunters Point. "'Course, we had no idea what the cargo was," Maurice Bell recalled. "There was all kinds of rumors went on aboard ship about what we was delivering. There was one rumor that just flew all over the ship, that we was delivering scented toilet paper to General MacArthur. They picked certain men on the ship to load and unload this and they picked me. So I helped load it."

On July 26, the *Indianapolis* delivered her mysterious cargo to the B-29 base on Tinian. Then she set out for the Philippines, where she was to be fitted out to take part in the coming invasion of Kyushu. Four days later, Bell remembered, disaster struck. "A few minutes after midnight, there was a loud explosion. It knocked me out of my bunk. I didn't know what had happened, and the first thing that went through my mind was that a boiler had blown up." A Japanese submarine had sent two torpedoes into the hull of the *Indianapolis,* cutting her nearly in half. Of the 1,196 men aboard, some 300 were blown apart or burned to death within the first few minutes. The captain ordered the rest—nearly 900 men—to abandon ship. Bell remembered:

I estimate that I was about twenty-five to thirty feet in the air when I jumped. I put my foot against the side of the ship and pushed and started swimming, because I'd been told that the best thing to do is to get away from a ship, because as it went under it would create tremendous suction. So as I pushed with my foot and started swimming, the ship just shot away from me as it was going under.

Within twelve minutes, the *Indianapolis* was gone and her survivors were alone, scattered across miles of empty sea. Many were badly wounded. Some had broken limbs. Able-bodied survivors did what they could for them in the dark, tying together life rafts to fashion floating beds.

Morning brought worse horrors, Bell recalled.

When daylight came, I looked around and all I could see was just the group that I was in. There was probably over a hundred men in that group to start with. Just shortly after daylight, somebody yelled out real loud, "Sharks!" And sure enough, there were sharks swimming all around us. And those sharks would swim around and all of a sudden they would dive in on us and start attacking guys. And you'd see them attack somebody just a few feet from you. And of course, they'd grab them and down they'd go and you'd never see that man again. All you would see then would be the water turning red around them. They attacked us every day, several times a day. Some of the sharks swam three or four feet from me, but none ever touched me.

An intercepted message from the submarine commander, exulting in having sunk the American ship, had been dismissed as Japanese trickery. No one, Bell remembered, was sent to rescue them.

I stayed in the water for four days and five nights. A little over one hundred hours altogether, with nothing to eat or no fresh water to drink. [Some] of the guys just went completely out of their head. Didn't even know where they was at. They would feel that cold water down at their feet and they'd dive down there and drink it, thinking they was back aboard ship and they'd come back up and say, "Come on down below. Come on down to the officers' quarters, there's water fountains down there with ice water all the time."

When a navy spotter plane did finally happen upon the survivors, only 321 men remained alive (four of whom would soon perish from wounds and exposure). Some 880 crewmen died. "Some of the things that I actually went through out there," Bell remembered, "it just seems more like a dream sometimes. I wonder how I made it through that time. I tell everybody now that I were too sour for the sharks to eat."

ON THE EVENING OF JULY 16, the day after the *Indianapolis* set out from San Francisco, President Harry Truman had received the word he'd been waiting for. A few days after assuming the presidency, in April, he'd been told for the first time about the Manhattan Project, the top-secret three-year effort originally intended to beat the Germans at building an atomic bomb. No such device had been finished before the collapse of the Nazi regime, but that morning a test of a plutonium implosion device in the New Mexico desert had proved a spectacular success; heard at a distance of 100 miles and seen up to 180 miles away, it had such potential destructive power that Dr. J. Robert Oppenheimer, the director of the Los Alamos bomb laboratory, was reminded of a line from the Bhagavad-Gita: "Now I am become Death, the destroyer of worlds."

Truman was awed, too. The atomic bomb was "the most terrible weapon in the history of the world," he noted in his diary. But he was also relieved: It could accomplish with one blow what it had taken hundreds of aircraft and thousands of tons of explosives to achieve, and might finally provide him with an alternative to the Kyushu landing and the months of bloody fighting that would surely have followed it.

On July 26, Truman and Churchill, meeting with Stalin at Potsdam on the outskirts of Berlin, once again set forth the only terms under which they would agree to end the war. It called for "the unconditional surrender of all the Japanese armed forces," and warned that Japan's only alternative would be "prompt and utter destruction."

The Japanese chose to react with an ambiguous phrase that could be translated either as withholding comment or killing with contempt. The Allies read it as complete rejection. For most of the members of the six-man Japanese Supreme Council for the Direction of the War—despite the agony the Japanese people were enduring, despite the even greater agony that seemed certain to come—unconditional surrender still remained unthinkable. On the same day that the council dismissed the Potsdam ultimatum, it issued an edict urging Japan's starving populace to harvest and eat acorns.

On August 5, three days after the rescue of the *Indianapolis* survivors, the unknown object the ship had delivered to Tinian was placed aboard a B-29 named for the mother of its pilot, the *Enola Gay*. It was a second atomic bomb. At 8:15 the following morning it tumbled through the bomb-bay doors over Hiroshima. Forty-three seconds later, six miles below the plane but still high above the city, it detonated. In a single blinding flash, forty thousand men, women, and children were obliterated. One hundred thousand more would die within days of burns and radiation.

The White House issued a statement. Hiroshima had been destroyed by an atomic bomb, it said, "a harnessing of the basic power of the universe," because of the intransigence of Japan's rulers: "If they do not now accept our terms they may expect a rain of ruin from the air, the like of which has never been seen on earth."

Some Japanese commanders simply refused to credit what had happened: such a bomb was an impossibility, they said. Others argued that there could not be more than one such weapon. The emperor was disquieted by the reports, and his mother asked that the imperial bomb shelter be deepened, but he did not intervene to end the war.

The news disquieted the guards at the Tsuruga POW camp, too, Glenn Frazier remembered:

They came the next morning and took us in trucks out to an old rice paddy with a machine gun at each corner of it and started us digging. We wanted to know what we was digging in an old rice paddy for. So they finally told us we were digging our own graves. I have to tell you we didn't get much digging done. When you're digging your own grave, you don't dig very fast. Plus the fact that we had paired off in units of three and we were not going to stand there in that rice paddy and let them just shoot us. We were going to try to get a machine gun.

But the order to fire never came. Instead, guards ordered them back to their barracks. Some of Frazier's fellow prisoners wept that night, sure they would have to fight for their lives when dawn came. Instead, over the next few days they were simply told to dig their graves deeper.

On August 8, Stalin made good on the pledge he'd given at Yalta to join the war against Japan, sending hundreds of thousands of troops into Japanese-occupied Manchuria. The Japanese Supreme Council for the Direction of the War continued to bicker over what to do next. Three members now wanted to accept the Potsdam proclamation with only a single proviso: that the imperial system remain in place. But the other three resolved to fight on unless the Allies also agreed not to occupy the home islands or disarm its armed forces or try Japanese soldiers for war crimes.

At 11:02 the following morning, an American plane dropped another atomic bomb on the city of Nagasaki. Some forty thousand more civilians died in an instant. The Americans had no more such bombs and would be unable to produce another for several weeks, but the Japanese had no way of knowing that. Still, the Supreme Council remained divided. That evening, its members called upon the emperor in his air-raid shelter and apolo-

> Japanese civilians stumble along what were once the streets of Nagasaki, the day after it was hit by the atomic bomb. Familiar landmarks have virtually disappeared; only charred corpses remain. "The mystery of the atomic bomb is still sealed," George Weller, the first U.S. correspondent to visit the site, would write. "But the ruins are here in testimony that not only Nagasaki but the world was shaken."

gized for failing to reach a consensus. Hirohito then broke the deadlock. "I swallow my own tears," he said, "and give my sanction to the proposal to accept the Allied proclamation"—provided he be allowed to retain his "prerogatives . . . as a Sovereign Ruler."

In the end, the Allies agreed to a face-saving compromise. Hirohito could cling to at least symbolic power, they said "subject to the Supreme Commander of the Allied Powers." This concession, Secretary of War Stimson explained, was made because only the emperor could insure the surrender of his forces still stationed overseas and thus "save us from a score of bloody Iwo Jimas and Okinawas."

Precisely at noon on August 15, 1945, Glenn Frazier and his fellow prisoners heard an unfamiliar voice echoing from the camp loudspeaker. It was Hirohito himself, speaking directly to his subjects for the first time, employing an archaic form of Japanese only the learned among them could fully understand. An interpreter let Frazier and the other Americans know what he was saying: it was the duty of each of his "good and loyal subjects," the emperor said,

> to endure the unendurable and bear the unbearable. . . . We have ordered our government to communicate with the governments of the United States, Great Britain, and the Soviet Union that our empire accepts the provisions of the Joint Declaration. The enemy has begun to employ a new and cruel bomb, the power of which is indeed incalculable. . . . To continue to fight . . . would not only result in an ultimate collapse and obliteration of the Japanese race, but also the destruction of all human civilization.

The world held its breath. Then, at seven o'clock that evening Eastern War Time, President Truman summoned reporters into the Oval Office.

> I have received this afternoon a message from the Japanese government in reply to the message forwarded to that government by the Secretary of State on August 11. I deem this reply a full acceptance of the Potsdam Declaration, which specifies the unconditional surrender of Japan.

Over the half century that followed the war, the motives and methods of the men who finally ended it have been examined and reexamined to see if there hadn't been some other path to peace than the brutal one they chose to follow. Some of the questions raised may never be answered satisfactorily. But only two mattered to most Americans at the time: Did the bomb shorten the war? And did it save American lives?

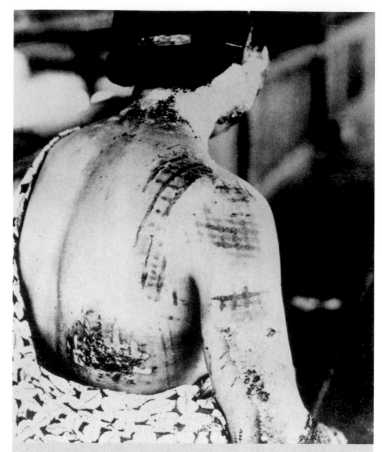

The Nagasaki bomb's flash seared the pattern of this woman's kimono into her flesh and left the family on the opposite page dazed and just hours from death from radiation poisoning. "The atomic bomb's peculiar 'disease,'" George Weller would report almost a month later, "uncured because it is undiagnosed, is still snatching away lives here. . . . The doctors . . . candidly confess . . . that the answer to the malady is beyond them. Their patients, though their skins are whole, are simply passing away under their eyes."

The answer to both questions was yes.

"Everything was set for the landings in Japan," Katharine Phillips remembered. Her own brother Sidney, who had already survived Guadalcanal and Cape Gloucester, had been in officer's training school preparing for it. "So when the atomic bomb was dropped and it ended it so quickly, we were stunned, but rejoiced, our boys would come home. There wouldn't be any more of them killed. So you can never convince anyone of my generation that the atomic bomb was not the greatest thing they ever came up with. Because we'll defy you. It was just finally the end of that horrible war."

To those who had been fated to take part in the Kyushu landing, the bomb seemed, as Winston Chrchill wrote, "a miracle of deliverance." Eugene Sledge was still on Okinawa when word came. "We thought the Japanese would never surrender," he wrote. "Many refused to believe it. Sitting in stunned silence, we

remembered our dead. So many dead. Except for a few widely scattered shouts of joy, the survivors of the abyss sat hollow-eyed and silent, trying to comprehend a world without war."

Nearby, Sam Hynes's squadron marked the occasion in its own distinctive way.

We decided that we ought to make some gesture of celebration. We took off as a squadron in formation and flew out over the fleet in Buckner Bay. And I expected that was what it was going to be: We'd fly over the fleet and then we'd go home and land. And to my astonishment, the man leading the flight signaled for us to go into a column. So we all pulled back, one behind the other, and dove on the fleet. And then, to my amazement, he pulled up and did a barrel roll. Now, a barrel roll in a TBM is like a fat lady dancing. She shouldn't do it. And you're not even sure she can do it. But he did it. And then the next plane did it. And then it was my turn. And I pulled up and pulled it over and all the rubbish and debris in the bottom of the airplane came floating up into my eyes. And the crewmen in the back rattled around a bit, I guess. And then we came out and it was still flying and the wings hadn't fallen off. Then we went back and landed. And I reckon what we were doing was giving death one more chance.

"At that moment I was in a staging area in France," Paul Fussell recalled,

ready to be shipped back to the United States, where I would be retrained a bit and then sent to take part in the invasion of Kyushu. And what I did was to pull the shade on my tent so nobody could approach me and nobody could see me. And I sat there in silence for at least a full day before I could compose myself because my joy was such that I knew I couldn't survive it in public. I would have to make it mine in private. And after a while I was all ready, and then I could come out and cheer and dance around and horse around with the other people. But at first, the relief was such that I was unmanned, almost. I just had to stay away.

"Jackie and I were on the boardwalk in Atlantic City," Quentin Aanenson remembered.

There was an air force redistribution base, and it was from there I would have been leaving to go to Okinawa within the next ten days or so. And when VJ Day came along, it was all of the dreams you've ever had in your life that were good dreams rolled into one. Everybody loved everybody else. I walked along the boardwalk, and every enlisted man I saw I saluted him. You just hugged everybody.

GIs aboard the carrier USS *Ticonderoga* celebrate VJ Day, August 14, 1945. They had been scheduled to take part in the assault on the Japanese home islands that would now never have to take place.

A reporter for the *Sacramento Bee* wrote of how the news came to the state capital.

One moment everything was quiet, and the next moment Sacramento cut loose with the greatest, noisiest, merriest, wackiest, most unrestrained celebration in her history. . . . It was like a dozen New Year's Eves and Fourths of July and Armistice Days, all rolled into an atomic bomb of a celebration. . . .

A sidewalk radio blared the news. . . . A young girl stopped and began weeping. "He's coming home!" she said. "He's coming home!" Then, as the celebration broke around her she dried her tears and joined in the merrymaking.

Sailors, their faces smeared with lipstick, grabbed at pretty girls, collecting kisses as their willing victims giggled and squealed. . . .

[In Chinatown] an ordinance against the use of firecrackers inside the city limits was ignored. This was a victory celebration. As night fell . . . bonfires were started. The benches in Plaza Park provided the fuel.

American fighters fill the sky above Tokyo Bay as Japan formally surrenders aboard the battleship *Missouri*, September 2, 1945.

This time, even the citizens of Luverne were caught up in the excitement, Al McIntosh reported.

Evening meals at most of Luverne's homes were gulped down in excitement. By 7 p.m. revelers were beginning to make their way downtown. . . . GIs from Sioux Falls [soon] took over, snake-dancing and yoo-hooing through the streets. . . . A bunch of high school youngsters piled into a truck and ser-enaded the town with band music. It was a good idea for a while but an impromptu parade of horn-blowing cars soon drowned out the loudest efforts of the musicians. . . . Every girl, pretty or not, was complimented by shrieking whistles of approval from every GI.

Katharine Phillips was at home in Mobile when the news broke.

My daddy was so excited that he ran in the room and he got his pistol from World War One and he filled it and we went out of the front door. And if you go dig around that azalea bush, I know the bullets are still in the azalea bush. He fired six rounds into the azalea bush, brought the pistol back in the house, and said to my brother and me, "Come on, gang, we're going downtown." And he threw Mother in the car and we drove down to the Admiral [Raphael] Semmes statue. And Daddy circled it three or four times, honking his horn. So by the time we left downtown, people were climbing up the Admiral Semmes statue and the celebration had begun. But I've always said my daddy started the celebration for VJ Day.

To keep things from getting out of hand sheriff's deputies and city policemen fanned out across Mobile, closing bars and liquor stores. But thousands of celebrants had stocked up in advance. A man stood at the corner of Dauphin and St. Joseph streets with a quart of whisky, stopping cars and offering every occupant a drink.

VJ Day celebrations at the corner of Ninth and K in Sacramento (top left), on Exchange Place in Waterbury (bottom left), and in New York's Times Square (above), where some 2 million people celebrated far into the night

didn't make any difference if it was the military or what, nobody'd give you a job.

Counselors working for the Veterans Administration were of little help. "Just act normal and you'll feel normal," they assured him. But he didn't. Frazier eventually married, had two children, ran his own trucking business. But the war would not go away.

I hated the Japanese as hard as anybody, I believe, could ever hate. And mine was just deep. I think I was justified in the hate that I had. But it come a time I realized it wasn't affecting them. They didn't even know I existed. They were over there and having their fun. And getting their country straightened out. And here I am over here, I'm hating and hating and hating. And having the nightmares and so forth. I had to get rid of it. I had to throw it off. Because it was just completely destroying me. And I prayed and I was hoping that I could get rid of it. And with my preacher's help, I started on the path of getting rid of it. It was very difficult to get rid of. But I got to the point to where I woke up one morning and I felt a little bit more rested. My war lasted actually another thirty years.

FOR THOSE AMERICANS WHO LIVED through the Second World War—for those whose fathers and sons and brothers were lost or maimed or changed by it in subtle ways outsiders could not see, as well as for those whose only contact with combat was listening to the radio and reading the local paper—it remains to this day simply The War.

"The young men that came home from the war were my neighbors when I was a young married woman, and they continued to live the war," Katharine Phillips Singer remembered.

They married, they established homes. We all lived in a wonderful little neighborhood where the homes were built for the GIs. And every night after we would get the children to bed, we would all gather and the boys would exchange stories. That was the great way of entertaining ourselves. The boy next door to me had ridden with Patton across Europe. The boy across the street went in on D-day-plus-four, hanging on to a machine gun on a half-track, and he said he was four miles inland before he could pry his hands off the half-track. He was scared out of his wits. The boy who lived catty-corner had been a medic, and had survived the battles in Europe. And we would just sit and listen, we wives. We learned more about our husbands and what they did by listening to them

exchange stories than we'd ever known before. But I realize, as I've gotten older, this was a healing for them.

"When I came out of the war, I could not be recognized," Paul Fussell remembered.

I had a terrible time with my family, because they had been reading the Saturday Evening Post *and* Life *magazine all during the war and they thought it was a sort of cheerful game that we won. They knew I was in the infantry, but they thought that was a branch of the service where you did a lot of running, you know, moving, athletic stuff. And they had no idea that it was about close-up killing. That was impossible for my parents even to understand. I had some notes, fairly bloodthirsty, that I had written about the war, and I gave them to my dad afterward and he couldn't finish them. He said, "I can't read this."*

Fussell went on to a distinguished career as a teacher and an essayist. But his subject remained wars and the ordinary men who found themselves called upon to do extraordinary things simply to survive them. "To forget the war would not be just impossible, it would be immoral," he said.

It doesn't get to me very often except when I talk about it, and I seldom do that. It's just something that never goes away. It's something you have to endure the way you endured the war itself. There's no alternative. You can't wipe out these memories. You can't wipe out what you felt at that time or what you knew other people felt. This is part of your whole possession of life. And I suppose it does some good.

Quentin Aanenson never returned to live on his father's farm south of Luverne. He and Jackie instead moved to Maryland. They had three children and he became a successful executive in the insurance business. "I have had a wonderful life," he remembered.

I have a family that just is ideal, and I've enjoyed my life. But the dynamics of war are so absolutely intense, the drama of war is so absolutely emotionally spellbinding, that it's hard for you to go on with a normal life without feeling something is missing. I find there are times when I'm pulled back into the whirlpool. The intensity of that experience was so overwhelming that you can't quite let go of it.

The memorial to Rock County's servicemen that stood for a time at the corner of Cedar and East Lincoln streets in downtown Luverne

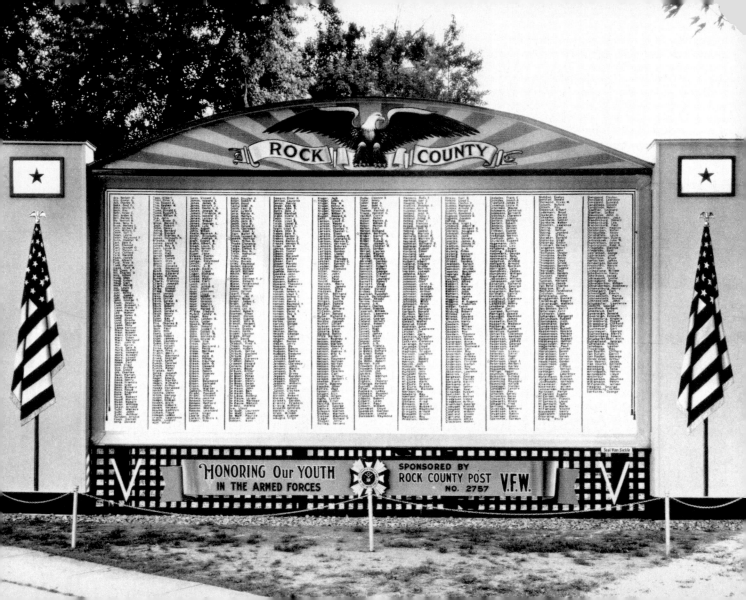

Memorial Day at Magnolia Cemetery in Mobile, 1947

ACKNOWLEDGMENTS

It would be tempting to employ all the metaphors of battle when trying to acknowledge the remarkable people who have worked to put this book and film project together, the necessary credit for superb "generalship," the great respect one has for the "specialist," the unique and sometimes solitary recognition felt among those "recruited" for the great task, the comradeship found in the "foxhole" of this mutual undertaking, the shared "danger" in attempting our complicated objectives, the quiet satisfaction of completion ("victory"), and it would all be true of the "brave" people who volunteered (actually) for this assignment.

But those metaphors would still fail the actual circumstances of our work together, fail to accurately take into account the exhilarating, difficult effort we have been involved in for so many years. Of course we labored without the daily physical threat common to war, and so have another good reason to shed any pretext to that which we have not, not one of us, faced. Still, we have lived the joy of collective work, and at times felt a love for and with each other, a luxury perhaps even soldiers, armored as they are against the possibility of violent loss, never fully experience. We who have headed these projects are grateful for all of this and that gratitude requires careful acknowledgement.

For almost a quarter of century, we have worked with Geoffrey C. Ward, a writer of uncommon sensitivity and eloquence, and he has brought to this project an urgency and thoughtfulness that has helped us to avoid the clichés and platitudes that inevitably cling to most attempts at describing the chaos of war. It is thrilling to enjoy a collaboration that finishes each others' sentences without ego or possession, that anticipates the improvisation necessary to free any endeavor from the pitfalls of preconception, and in the end is willing to give up even the most cherished of literary constructions to serve the larger, sometimes contradictory, demands of book and film. Geoff has done all of this and more, cheerfully getting out of the way of a good story, yet always making those stories better with his careful, direct prose that in the end elevates normal exposition to something higher, more valuable. We treasure this.

Sarah Botstein, our indefatigable producer, did everything, selflessly bestowing her enormous talents on every aspect of the production of the film, offering enormous support and encouragement to each and every one of us who faltered along the way or who needed the sympathetic perspective only an ancient and generous wisdom could confer. She possesses the "four o'clock in the morning courage" that Ulysses S. Grant was said to have had, a courage that could wake him (and Sarah) up at four in the morning with the news that the enemy had turned the left flank, and he (and she) would be as cool as a cucumber. We cannot adequately say how much we cherish this utterly professional association and lifelong personal friendship.

To each of the witnesses who so graciously and generously shared their stories with us—it is literally impossible for us to find the words to express the depth of our gratitude to you. This book and film project could not have happened without your participation, and we are perpetually mindful of our debt to you. Your honesty, decency, modesty, and generosity of spirit have been an inspiration, and we truly feel privileged not only to have known you, but also to have been present as you bore witness to the remarkable lives you have lived.

We are also indebted to Jean Vickstrom McIntosh, who helped us to understand so much about her father, Al McIntosh, a superb writer whose weekly chronicle of the war in Luverne became essential to our effort. We owe so much to the family of the virtuosic memoirist and marine corps veteran Eugene B. Sledge; they championed the project from day one and provided precious family photographs, background information, and critically important introductions to many people in Mobile, without which this book and film would have been dramatically different.

It is impossible to name all of the talented people who participated in this undertaking, especially because each rose far above and beyond the call of duty to do his or her very best work for this enormous and demanding project. Coproducer David McMahon maintained his remarkable equanimity and sense of humor as he left no stone unturned in his tireless search for thousands of exquisite still photographs, without which the book and film literally could not have existed. Coproducer Peter Miller effortlessly managed to wear at least two hats: the breathtaking footage of the war in the Pacific that he discovered literally helped us see those battles as if for the first time, and his utter efficiency in dealing with all matters music-related allowed us to develop a truly magnificent soundtrack. Associate producers Meghan Horvath and Taylor Krauss cheerfully and efficiently accomplished every possible production and postproduction task we asked of them, solved problems before we knew they existed, and truly made our lives better every day.

The tireless Mike Hill and Susan Shumaker provided critical research for us at the early stages of the project, helping us figure out what kind of story we were telling.

Our longtime collaborator, the masterful writer and producer Dayton Duncan, served as consulting producer and guided us at every step of the way. We are particularly beholden to him for suggesting the central idea that has animated this entire project—that we should try to tell the story of the war through the experiences of an American town and its citizens.

The transcendently gifted Paul Barnes, as always the calm at the center of the storm, not only served as supervising editor, but also somehow found the time brilliantly to edit two of our most challenging episodes. Erik Ewers became almost obsessed with the daunting task of editing his three episodes, infusing them all with his singular passion, intensity, and creativity. Tricia Reidy brought her incomparable talent, and an uncanny ability to eschew gratuitous sentimentality, to her two episodes, imbuing them with integrity, grace, and subtlety. Each of their devoted and multi-talented assistants, Dan White, Ryan Gifford, and Paul Docherty, made the film his own in countless ways. We have always relied on cinematographers Buddy Squires, Allen Moore, Jon Else, and Steve McCarthy to create beautiful images in the camera for us to work with—and this time, in dozens of interviews and on location in the U.S. and overseas, they truly outdid themselves.

The narrator of the film, Keith David, kept his cool through hour after grueling hour in the recording studio, refusing to settle for anything less than a perfect reading of every line, and for his ingenuity, command, and magnificent voice, we are truly thankful. Tom Hanks returned to the studio time and again to give voice to the timeless words of Al McIntosh, infusing every syllable with sympathy, intelligence, and humanity. Josh Lucas seemed miraculously to channel the spirit of Eugene B. Sledge, and in his haunting performance seemed almost able to wake the dead. Adam Arkin, Kevin Conway, Eli Wallach, Carolyn McCormick, Bobby Cannavale, Rebecca Holtz, and Robert Wahlberg also graced our film with their singular craftsmanship. Lou Verrico at Full House, as he has for so many years, made sure all of these artists' work was optimally recorded.

That the still photographs in the book and film literally jump off the page and screen is, in large part, thanks to the genius of editors Paul Docherty and Dan White. Dave Mast kept our complicated computer system running smoothly, weathering crisis after crisis. Robert Gold and Valerie Marcus handled all legal matters with aplomb. Ted Alcorn, Kirk Carapezza, Devon Ciampa, Christopher Darling, and Meagan Frappiea kept us superbly organized in the office and in the editing room, and never hesitated to roll up their sleeves to solve a problem. The magnificent team in our Walpole office—Pam Baucom, Brenda Heath, Patty Lawlor, and Elle Carriere—did everything we asked of them and so much more, keeping our finances and our company in perfect order, coping with logistics of every kind, guiding us in our search for witnesses, providing invaluable feedback throughout the project.

Our peerless team of sound editors—Erik Ewers, Mariusz Glabinski, Ryan Gifford, Marlene Grzaslewicz, Jacob Ribicoff, Ira Spiegel, and Magdaline Volaitis—alchemists all, created sound effects, music, and dialogue tracks that literally brought the film to life on screen—and the magnificent sound mixing done by Dominick Tavella at Sound One exceeds anything we could ever have dreamed of. John Dowdell, Peter Heady, and Tim Spitzer at Goldcrest toiled for months to create our gorgeous video masters. John Bair, Nathan Meier, and Vivian Connolly at Edgeworx designed maps that are not only beautiful and timeless, but also able to convey complex information so elegantly. The United States Military Academy's history department provided crucial guidance that enabled us to make these maps as accurate as possible.

Many ingenious people contributed to the film's evocative soundtrack. First and foremost we must thank Wynton Marsalis, who did us the tremendous honor of composing music especially for this project. His work both expressed and amplified the many moods of the film perfectly. The virtuoso musicians who played with him crafted music that never ceased to amaze and delight us, and enriched our film beyond measure. Pianist Jacqueline Schwab, as always, brought new life and feeling to the many tracks she recorded for us. Tom Evered and Leon Botstein provided priceless advice and guidance as we searched the twentieth-century classical repertoire for compositions that would be appropriate for this project, and they directed us to any number of splendid recordings that became instantaneously indispensable in our editing room. We must also thank Gene Scheer for composing such a beautiful song, "American Anthem," which seemed to express all the many themes and feelings of our entire enterprise. We are forever beholden to Norah Jones, who graciously agreed to sing this song for us, and did so with more artistry and understatement than we thought humanly possible.

This project has been profoundly enriched by the contributions of our dedicated and sagacious advisors, James Barker, Lizabeth Cohen, Gerald Early, David Kennedy, Bill Leuchtenburg, Martin E. Marty, Richard Snow, and Roger Spiller, who provided historical perspective, access to archival materials, and most important, a deep understanding of so many diverse aspects of this exceptionally complex subject. Sam Hynes and Paul Fussell did double duty in agreeing to tell their own riveting war stories on camera as well, expanding our horizons exponentially.

In addition to the invaluable Lisa Hartjens who helped us navigate through the incomparable collections at the National Archives in Washington, D.C., we relied heavily on the dedication and knowledge of Polly Pettit, Jim Parker, Holly Reed, Theresa Roy, and Rutha Beamon. We also availed ourselves of the expertise of a small cadre of researchers overseas, including Reiko Sakuma Adrian Wood, and Jane Fish, who helped locate vitally important photographs, film footage, sound recordings. In each of our four chosen towns we benefited greatly from the assistance of archivists and historians who literally made this entire undertaking possible at every stage: James Henley, Pat Johnson, and Dylan McDonald at SAMCC in Sacramento; Dr. Michael Thomason, Elisa Baldwin, and Carol Ellis at the University of South Alabama in Mobile; Betty Mann at the Luverne Historical Society; Marie Galbraith, Raechel Guest, Debra Perugini, Cynthia Roznoy, and Rebecca Slaughter at the Mattatuck Museum in Waterbury. Each of the newspapers in our towns—the *Rock County Star-Herald*, the *Mobile Register*, the *Sacramento Bee*, and the *Waterbury Republican-American*—helped us spread the word about our project in their communities, provided essential access to their archives, photographs, and microfilms, and enthusiastically supported us in many ways.

Throughout the entire project, we relied completely on the dedicated service and expert advice of Joe DePlasco, Dave Donovan, Brian Moriarty, and Cassin Donn at Dan Klores Communications, who did yeoman's service to ensure our film did not go unnoticed, in both the media and the world at large.

Our representatives at William Morris, Jennifer Rudolph Walsh and Jay Mandel, saw the potential in this project from the beginning, and have been steadfast advocates, superb agents, and great friends to us ever since.

To Paula Kerger, John Wilson, and their estimable colleagues at PBS, as well as to our longtime partners at WETA-TV in Washington, D.C.—Sharon Rockefeller, David Thompson, Karen Kenton, Dalton Delan, Craig Impink, and many others—we want to express our great appreciation for everything you did to make this project a reality. Without your support, it absolutely could not have happened.

None of this would have been possible without the financial support of our funders, and we are grateful beyond words to the corporations, foundations, and organizations that have been such committed partners to this project: General Motors, Anheuser-Busch, Bank of America, the Lilly Endowment, the Public Broadcasting Service, the Corporation for Public Broadcasting, the National Endowment for the Humanities, the Arthur Vining Davis Foundations, the Pew Charitable Trusts, the Longaberger Foundation, and the Park Foundation, Inc.

KEN BURNS
LYNN NOVICK

———————

A lot of people were involved in making this book come together. Many have already been thanked by Ken and Lynn, and in every case I share their gratitude.

But as the author of this book's text, I also want to thank Kevin Bourke, Carol Devine Carson, Diana Coglianese, Tita Gillespie, Andy Hughes, Chris Jerome, and Andrew Miller at Alfred A. Knopf for the skill and care with which they helped to bring this book together.

There would not have been a book at all, however, without eight other individuals whom I want to thank individually:

My old friend Ken Burns, whose willingness to undertake important historical missions has again allowed us to fight alongside one another in the same trench;

Lynn Novick, whose seriousness about the subject and empathy for our witnesses suffuses the transcripts that are at this book's heart;

Wendy Byrne, whose unerring taste and love for pictures is evident on every page and whose patience with second-guessing authors remains a source of wonder;

Dave McMahon, who found many of the photographs and then labored heroically to gather them all together as Deadline-Day approached;

Sam Hynes, whose restraint and clear-eyed candor I tried to keep constantly in mind when writing about the war through which he lived;

Roger Spiller, who was kind enough to read the whole manuscript, offering much-needed encouragement (and saving me from countless embarrassments) as he went;

Kathy Hourigan, the professional's professional, who invariably keeps her head when others' have long since toppled off;

and Sonny Mehta, whose commitment to serious writing in general and enthusiasm for this project in particular meant more than I can say.

GEOFFREY C. WARD

BIBLIOGRAPHY

This book is built around from filmed interviews with nearly fifty men and women who lived through the war. But unpublished memoirs by three of them—Sidney Phillips, Sascha Weinzheimer Jansen, and Glenn Frazier—proved central to the story and I want to thank them individually for permitting me to draw upon them. I'm also grateful to Quentin Aanenson for sharing with me both the script for his PBS program, "A Fighter Pilot's Story," and additional materials found on his Web site, http://pages.prodigy.com/fighterpilot/.

For reasons of space, I have not listed here the hundreds of Web sites I consulted in search of wartime memories. But I do want to pay special tribute to the Hanashi Oral History Program of the Go for Broke Foundation. By going to this Web site, http://www.goforbroke.org/oral_histories/oral_histories_hanashi.asp, you can see and hear for yourself survivors of the 100th Infantry Battalion and the 442nd Regimental Combat Team telling their own extraordinary stories.

G.C.W.

Adams, C. C. *The Best War Ever: America and World War II.* Baltimore, MD, 1994.

Alexander, Joseph H., with Don Horan and Norman C. Stahl. *The Battle History of the U.S. Marines: A Fellowship of Valor.* New York, 1999.

Alexander, Joseph H. *Utmost Savagery: The Three Days of Tarawa.* Toronto, 1997.

Ambrose, Stephen E. *Citizen Soldiers: The U.S. Army from the Normandy Beaches to the Bulge to the Surrender of Germany June 7, 1944–May 7, 1945.* New York, 1997.

———. *D-Day: June 6, 1944: The Climactic Battle of World War II.* New York, 1994.

———. *Eisenhower: Soldier and President.* New York, 1990.

———. *The Victors: Eisenhower and His Boys: The Men of World War II.* New York, 1998.

———. *The Wild Blue: The Men and Boys Who Flew the B-24s Over Germany.* New York, 2001.

Anonymous. *A Woman in Berlin: Eight Weeks in the Conquered City: A Diary.* New York, 2005.

Arnold, James R. *Ardennes 1944: Hitler's Last Gamble in the West.* New York, 2005.

Arthur, Max. *Forgotten Voices of the Second World War.* London, 2005.

Asahina, Robert. *Just Americans: How Japanese Americans Won a War at Home and Abroad.* New York, 2006.

Ashton, Paul. *"And Somebody Gives a Damn!"* Santa Barbara, CA, 1990.

———. *Bataan Diary.* Santa Barbara, CA, 1984.

Astor, Gerald. *A Blood-Dimmed Tide: The Battle of the Bulge by the Men Who Fought It.* New York, 1992.

———. *The Greatest War: Americans in Combat, 1941–1945.* Novato, CA, 1999.

———. *The Mighty Eighth: The Air War in Europe as Told by the Men Who Fought It.* New York, 1997.

Atkinson, Rick. *An Army at Dawn: The War in North Africa, 1942–1943.* New York, 2002.

Balkoski, Joseph. *Beyond the Beachhead: The 29th Infantry Division in Normandy.* Mechanicsburg, PA, 2005.

———. *Omaha Beach: D-Day, June 6, 1944.* Mechanicsburg, PA, 2004.

Bando, Mark. *101st Airborne: The Screaming Eagles at Normandy.* St. Paul, MN, 2001.

Bando, Mark A. *Vanguard of the Crusade: The 101st Airborne Division in World War II.* Bedford, PA, 2003.

Baumer, Robert W., with Mark J. Reardon. *American Iliad: The 18th Infantry Regiment in World War II.* Bedford, PA, 2004.

Beevor, Antony. *Stalingrad: The Fateful Siege: 1942–1943.* New York, 1999.

———. *The Fall of Berlin 1945.* New York, 2003.

Bendiner, Elmer. *The Fall of Fortresses: A Personal Account of the Most Daring—and Deadly— American Air Battles of World War II.* New York, 1980.

Bercuson, David, and Holger Herwig. *One Christmas in Washington: The Secret Meeting Between Roosevelt and Churchill That Changed the World.* Woodstock, NY, 2005.

Bergerud, Eric. *Touched With Fire: The Land War in the South Pacific.* New York, 1996.

Bess, Michael. *Choices Under Fire: Moral Dimensions of World War II.* New York, 2006.

Bird, William L., Jr., and Harry R. Rubinstein. *Design for Victory: World War II Posters on the American Home Front.* New York, 1998.

Blum, John Morton. *V Was for Victory.* Orlando, FL, 1977.

Blumenson, Martin. *Anzio: The Gamble That Failed.* Philadelphia, 1963.

———. *Bloody River: The Real Tragedy of the Rapido.* Boston, 1970.

———. *United States Army in World War II: The Mediterranean Theater of Operations: Salerno to Cassino.* Washington, DC, 1970.

———. *Mark Clark: The Last of the Great World War II Commanders.* New York, 1984.

Bologna, Sando. *The Italians of Waterbury.* Portland, CT, 1993.

Bonn, Keith E. *When the Odds Were Even: The Vosges Mountains Campaign, October 1944– January 1945.* Novato, CA, 1994.

Boot, Max. *War Made New: Technology, Warfare, and the Course of History.* New York, 2006.

Boston Publishing Company, eds. *Above and Beyond: A History of the Medal of Honor from the Civil War to Vietnam.* Boston, MA, 1985.

Bosworth, Allan R. *America's Concentration Camps.* New York, 1967.

Botsford, Gardner. *A Life of Privilege, Mostly.* New York, 2003.

Bourke-White, Margaret. *"Purple Heart Valley": A Combat Chronicle of the War in Italy.* New York, 1944.

Bowden, Mark. *Our Finest Day: D-Day: June 6, 1944.* San Francisco, CA, 2002.

Bradley, James. *Flags of Our Fathers.* New York, 2000.

Bradley, Omar N., and Clay Blair. *A General's Life.* New York, 1983.

Braithwaite, Rodric. *Moscow 1941: A City and Its People at War.* Suffolk, UK, 2006.

Brecher, Jeremy, Jerry Lombardi, and Jan Stackhouse, eds. *Brass Valley: The Story of Working People's Lives and Struggles in an American Industrial Region.* Philadelphia, 1982.

Brinkley, David. *Washington Goes to War.* New York, 1988.

Brulle, Robert V. *Angels Zero: P-47 Close Air Support in Europe.* Washington, DC, 2000.

Buck, Anita Albrecht. *Behind Barbed Wire: German Prisoners of War in Minnesota During World War II.* St. Cloud, MN, 2005.

Calvocoressi, Peter, Guy Wint, and John Pritchard. *The Penguin History of the Second World War.* London, 1999.

Cavanagh, William C. C. *A Tour of the Bulge Battlefield.* South Yorkshire, UK, 2001.

Cawthon, Charles R. *Other Clay: A Remembrance of the World War II Infantry.* Niwot, CO, 1990.

Chang, Iris. *The Rape of Nanking: The Forgotten Holocaust of World War II.* New York, 1998.

Clark, Lester W. *An Unlikely Arena.* New York, 1989.

Clark, Lloyd. *Anzio: The Friction of War: Italy and the Battle for Rome 1944.* London, 2006.

Clarke, Jeffrey J., and Robert Ross Smith. *Riviera to the Rhine: The European Theater of Operations.* Honolulu, HI, 2005.

Cogan, Frances B. *Captured: The Japanese Internment of American Civilians in the Philippines, 1941–1945.* Athens, GA, 2000.

Colley, David P. *Blood for Dignity.* New York, 2003.

———. *Safely Rest.* New York, 2004.

Commission on Wartime Relocation and Internment of Civilians. *Personal Justice Denied.* Washington, DC, 2000.

Conant, Jennet. *109 East Palace: Robert Oppenheimer and the Secret City of Los Alamos.* New York, 2005.

Connaughton, Richard, John Pimlott, and Duncan Anderson. *The Battle for Manila.* Novato, CA, 2002.

Connell, J. Mark. *The Ardennes: The Battle of the Bulge.* Havertown, PA, 2003.

Cook, Haruko Taya, and Theodore F. Cook. *Japan at War: An Oral History.* New York, 1992.

Cooke, Alistair. *The American Home Front: 1941–1942.* New York, 2006.

Coox, Alvin. *Japan: The Final Agony.* New York, 1970.

Costello, John. *The Pacific War 1941–1945.* New York, 1982.

———. *Virtue Under Fire.* New York, 1987.

Cowley, Robert, ed. *No End Save Victory.* New York, 2001.

Cowley, Robert, and Geoffrey Parker, eds. *The Reader's Companion to Military History.* Boston, 1996.

Cray, Ed. *General of the Army: George C. Marshall, Soldier and Statesman.* New York, 1990.

Cronenberg, Allen. *Forth to the Mighty Conflict.* Tuscaloosa, AL, 1995.

Crosby, Harry H. *A Wing and a Prayer.* San Jose, 1993.

Daniels, Roger. *Concentration Camps: North America: Japanese in the United States and Canada During World War II.* Malabar, FL, 1989.

Davis, Kenneth S. *Experience of War: The United States in World War II.* Garden City, NY, 1965.

Daws, Gavan. *Prisoners of the Japanese: POWs of World War II in the Pacific.* New York, 1994.

Day, Beth. *The Manila Hotel: The Heart and Memory of a City.* National Media Production Center, Manila, n.d.

Dear, I. C. B. *The Oxford Companion to World War II.* New York, 1995.

Decker, Ken. *Memories of the 384th Bombardment Group (H): Stories of the Men, the Missions and the Machines.* Chenango Forks, NY, 2005.

D'Este, Carlo. *Bitter Victory: The Battle for Sicily: July–August 1943.* London, 1988.

———. *Decision in Normandy.* Old Saybrook, CT, 1994.

———. *Eisenhower: A Soldier's Life.* New York, 2002.

———. *Fatal Decision: Anzio and the Battle for Rome.* New York, 1991.

———. *Patton: A Genius for War.* New York, 1995.

Dickson, Paul. *War Slang: American Fighting Words and Phrases Since the Civil War,* 2nd ed. Washington, DC, 2004.

Dos Passos, John. *State of the Nation.* Cambridge, MA, 1944.

Dower, John W. *Embracing Defeat: Japan in the Wake of World War II.* New York, 1999.

———. *War Without Mercy: Race & Power in the Pacific War.* New York, 1986.

Drez, Ronald J. *Twenty-Five Yards of War.* New York, 2001.

Dupuy, Trevor N., David L. Bongard, and Richard C. Anderson Jr. *Hitler's Last Gamble: The Battle of the Bulge, December 1944–January 1945.* New York, 1994.

Eisenhower, David. *Eisenhower: At War, 1943–1945.* New York, 1986.

Eisenhower, John S. D. *The Bitter Woods: The Battle of the Bulge.* New York, 1995.

Ellis, John. *Brute Force: Allied Strategy and Tactics in the Second World War.* New York, 1990.

———. *Cassino: The Hollow Victory: The Battle for Rome: January–June 1944.* New York, 1984.

———. *On the Front Lines: The Experience of War Through the Eyes of the Allied Soldiers in World War II.* New York, 1990.

———. *The Sharp End: The Fighting Man in World War II.* New York, 1980.

———. *World War II: A Statistical Survey.* New York, 1993.

Escoda, Jose Ma. Bonifacio M. *Warsaw of Asia: The Rape of Manila.* Quezon City, Philippines, 2003.

Essame, H. *Normandy Bridgehead.* New York, 1970.

Fahey, James J. *Pacific War Diary: The Secret Diary of an American Sailor: 1942–1945.* Boston, 1991.

Falk, Stanley. *Liberation of the Philippines.* New York, 1971.

Farrar-Hockley, Anthony. *Airborne Carpet: Operation Market Garden.* New York, 1969.

Feifer, George. *The Battle of Okinawa: The Blood and the Bomb.* Guilford, CT, 2001.

Ferrari, Michelle, ed. *Reporting America at War: An Oral History.* New York, 2003.

Feuer, A. B., ed. *Bilibid Diary: The Secret Notebooks of Commander Thomas Hayes, POW, the Philippines, 1942–45.* Hamden, CT, 1987.

Feuer, A. B. *FDR's Prisoner Spy: The POW Diary of Cdr. Thomas Hayes, USN.* Pacifica, CA, 1987.

Forsberg, Franklin S., ed. *Yank: The Story of World War II as Written by the Soldiers.* New York, 1984.

Fortier, Norman "Bud." *An Ace of the Eighth: An American Fighter Pilot's Air War in Europe.* New York, 2003.

Frank, Richard B. *Downfall: The End of the Imperial Japanese Empire.* New York, 1999.

———. *Guadalcanal: The Definitive Account of the Landmark Battle.* New York, 1992.

Frankland, Noble. *Bomber Offensive: The Devastation of Europe.* New York, 1970.

Freeman, Roger A. *The Mighty Eighth: A History of the Units, Men and Machines of the US 8th Air Force.* London, 2001.

Fussell, Paul. *Doing Battle: The Making of a Skeptic.* Boston, 1998.

———. *Thank God for the Atom Bomb and Other Essays.* New York, 1988.

———. *The Boys' Crusade.* New York, 2003.

———. *Wartime.* New York, 1989.

Gajdusek, Robert E. *Resurrection: A War Journey.* Nortre Dame, IN, 1997.

Gerard, Philip. *Secret Soldiers: The Story of World War II's Heroic Army of Deception.* New York, 2003.

Giblin, Tucker. *The Class of '42: Marines in WWII.* Edina, MN, 2002.

Gilbert, Martin. *D-Day.* Hoboken, NJ, 2004.

———. *The Day the War Ended: May 8, 1945—Victory in Europe.* New York, 2004.

———. *The Holocaust: A History of the Jews of Europe during the Second World War.* New York, 1985.

———. *The Second World War: A Complete History,* rev. ed. New York, 1991.

Glusman, John A. *Conduct Under Fire.* New York, 2005.

Goldstein, Donald M., Katherine V. Dillon, and J. Michael Wenger. *The Way It Was: Pearl Harbor.* Herndon, VA, 1995.

Goodwin, Doris Kearns. *No Ordinary Time: Franklin and Eleanor Roosevelt: The Home Front in World War II.* New York, 1994.

Goralski, Robert. *World War II Almanac, 1931–1945.* New York, 1984.

Gordon, Linda, and Gary Y. Okihiro, eds. *Impounded: Dorothea Lange and the Censored Images of Japanese American Internment.* New York, 2006.

Gordon, Richard M. *Horyo: Memoirs of an American POW.* St. Paul, MN, 1999.

Grant, R. G. *Flight: 100 Years of Aviation.* New York, 2002.

Graves, Ralph. *Share of Honor.* New York, 1990.

Griess, Thomas E. *Atlas for the Second World War: Europe and the Mediterranean.* Garden City Park, NY, 2002.

———. *Atlas for the Second World War: Asia and the Pacific.* Garden City Park, NY, 2002.

Griffith, Samuel B., II. *The Battle For Guadalcanal.* New York, 1966.

Gross, Jan T. *Fear: Anti-Semitism in Poland After Auschwitz.* New York, 2006.

Gunther, John. *The Riddle of MacArthur: Japan, Korea and the Far East.* New York, 1951.

Hamilton, Nigel. *Monty: Final Years of the Field-Marshal: 1944–1976.* New York, 1987.

———. *Monty: Master of the Battlefield: 1942–1944.* Kent, UK, 1983.

———. *Monty: The Making of a General: 1887–1942.* London, 1981.

———. *Monty: The Man Behind the Legend.* London, 1987.

Hammer, Joshua. *Yokohama Burning: The Deadly 1923 Earthquake and Fire That Helped Forge the Path to World War II.* New York, 2006.

Hapgood, David, and David Richardson. *Monte Cassino.* New York, 1984.

Harris, Mark Jonathan, Franklin Mitchell, and Steven Schechter. *The Homefront: America During World War II.* New York, 1984.

Hartendorp, A. V. H. *The Santo Tomas Story.* New York, 1964.

Hasegawa, Tsuyoshi. *Racing the Enemy: Stalin, Truman, and the Surrender of Japan.* Cambridge, MA, 2005.

Hastings, Max. *Armageddon: The Battle for Germany: 1944–1945.* New York, 2004.

———. *Bomber Command.* New York, 1979.

———. *Das Reich: The March of the 2nd SS Panzer Division Through France.* New York, 1982.

———. *Overlord: D-Day & The Battle for Normandy.* New York, 1984.

———. *Warriors: Portraits from the Battlefield.* New York, 2005.

Heinz, W. C. *When We Were One: Stories of World War II.* New York, 2002.

Herf, Jeffrey. *The Jewish Enemy: Nazi Propaganda During World War II and the Holocaust.* Cambridge, MA, 2006.

Hersey, John. *Into the Valley: Marines at Guadalcanal.* Lincoln, NE, 2002.

Hibbert, Christopher. *Anzio: The Bid for Rome.* New York, 1970.

Hirshson, Stanley P. *General Patton: A Soldier's Life.* New York, 2003.

Holland, Robert B. *The Rescue of Santo Tomas.* Paducah, KY, 2003.

Holt, Thaddeus. *The Deceivers: Allied Military Deception in the Second World War.* New York, 2004.

Hornfischer, James D. *The Last Stand of the Tin Can Sailors.* New York, 2004.

Howard, Michael. *Captain Professor: A Life in War and Peace.* London, 2006.

Howarth, David. *D Day; The Sixth of June, 1944.* New York, 1982.

Hoyt, Edwin P. *Backwater War: The Allied Campaign in Italy, 1943–1945.* Westport, CT, 2002.

Huie, William Bradford. *The Execution of Private Slovik.* Yardley, PA, 2004.

Hunt, George P. *Coral Comes High.* New York, 1946.

Hynes, Samuel. *The Growing Seasons: An American Boyhood Before the War.* New York, 2003.

———. *The Soldiers' Tale: Bearing Witness to Modern War.* New York, 1997.

———. *Flights of Passage: Reflections of a World War II Aviator.* New York, 1988.

Irwin, John P. *Another River, Another Town.* New York, 2002.

Jablonski, Edward. *Double Strike:The Epic Air Raids on Regensburg-Schweinfurt, August 17, 1943.* Garden City, NY, 1974.

———. *Flying Fortress: The Illustrated Biography of the B-17s and the Men Who Flew Them.* Garden City, NY, 1965.

James, D. Clayton, ed. *South to Bataan, North to Mukden: The Prison Diary of Brigadier General W. E. Brougher.* Athens, GA, 1971.

James, D. Clayton. *The Years of MacArthur: Volume I, 1880–1941.* Boston, 1970.

———. *The Years of MacArthur: Volume II, 1941–1945.* Boston, 1975.

———. *The Years of MacArthur: Volume III, Triumph and Disaster, 1945–1964.* Boston, 1985.

Jeffries, John W. *Testing the Roosevelt Coalition: Connecticut Society and Politics in the Era of World War II.* Knoxville, TN, 1979.

Jensen, Oliver. *Carrier War.* New York, 1945.

Johansen, Bruce E. *So Far From Home: Manila's Santo Tomás Internment Camp, 1942–1945.* Omaha, NE, 1996.

Jones, James. *WWII: A Chronicle of Soldiering.* New York, 1975.

Jose, Ricardo Trota, and Lydia Yu-Jose. *The Japanese Occupation of the Philippines: A Pictorial History.* Manila, 1997.

Karnow, Stanley. *In Our Image: America's Empire in the Philippines.* New York, 1990.

Keats, John. *They Fought Alone.* New York, 1965.

Keegan, John. *Atlas of the Second World War.* New York, 1989.

———. *Six Armies in Normandy: From D-Day to the Liberation of Paris.* New York, 1994.

———. *The Mask of Command.* New York, 1988.

———. *The Second World War.* New York, 1990.

Kennedy, David M. *Freedom from Fear: The American People in Depression and War, 1929–1945.* New York, 1999.

Kennett, Lee. *G.I.: The American Soldier in World War II.* New York, 1987.

Kernan, Alvin. *The Unknown Battle of Midway: The Destruction of the American Torpedo Squadrons.* New Haven, 2005.

Kerr, E. Bartlett. *Surrender & Survival: The Experience of American POWs in the Pacific 1941–1945.* New York, 1985.

Kershaw, Alex. *The Bedford Boys: One American Town's Ultimate D-Day Sacrifice.* New York, 2003.

———. *The Longest Winter: The Epic Story of World War II's Most Decorated Platoon.* New York, 2006.

Kershaw, Ian. *Hitler: 1889–1936: Hubris.* New York, 1999.

———. *Hitler: 1936–45: Nemesis.* New York, 2000.

Ketchum, Richard M. *The Borrowed Years 1938–1941: America on the Way to War.* New York, 1989.

Knox, Donald. *Death March: The Survivors of Bataan.* San Diego, 1981.

Koppes, Clayton R., and Gregory Black. *Hollywood Goes to War: How Politics, Profits and Propaganda Shaped World War II Movies.* Berkeley, CA, 1990.

Kotlowitz, Robert. *In Their Time: A Memoir.* New York, 1997.

Lamb, Richard. *War in Italy: 1943–1945: A Brutal Story.* New York, 1993.

Laqueur, Walter, and Richard Breitman. *Breaking the Silence: The German Who Exposed the Final Solution.* Hanover, NH, 1994.

Leckie, Robert. *Delivered from Evil.* New York, 1987.

———. *Helmet for My Pillow.* Garden City, NY, 1979.

———. *Strong Men Armed: The United States Marines Against Japan.* New York, 1997.

Leinbaugh, Harold P., and John D. Campbell. *The Men of Company K: The Autobiography of a World War II Rifle Company.* New York, 1985.

Levin, Nora. *The Holocaust: The Destruction of European Jewry 1933–1945.* New York, 1973.

Lewis, Norman. *Naples '44: A World War II Diary of Occupied Italy.* New York, 2005.

Library of America. *Reporting World War II.* 2 vols. New York, 1995.

Lifton, Robert Jay. *The Nazi Doctors: Medical Killing and the Psychology of Genocide.* New York, 1986.

Linderman, Gerald F. *The World Within War.* Cambridge, MA, 1999.

Lingeman, Richard. *Don't You Know There's A War On?: The American Home Front 1941–1945.* New York, 2003.

Lipstadt, Deborah E. *Beyond Belief: The American Press and the Coming of the Holocaust 1933–1945.* New York, 1993.

Lord, Walter. *Day of Infamy.* New York, 1957.

———. *Incredible Victory.* New York, 1967.

Love, Robert W., Jr. *Pearl Harbor Revisited.* New York, 1995.

Lowden, John L. *Silent Wings at War: Combat Gliders in World War II.* Washington, DC, 1992.

Lowman, David D. *Magic: The Untold Story of U.S. Intelligence and the Evacuation of the Japanese Residents from the West Coast During WWII.* Provo, UT, 2000.

Lucas, Celia. *Prisoners of Santo Tomas.* Wiltshire, UK, 1996.

Lukacs, John. *Five Days in London: May 1940.* New Haven, 1999.

———. *June 1941: Hitler and Stalin.* New Haven, 2006.

———. *The Duel.* New York, 1991.

———. *The Last European War: September 1939–December 1941.* Garden City, NY, 1976.

MacArthur, Brian. *Surviving the Sword: Prisoners of the Japanese 1942–45.* London, 2006.

MacDonald, Charles B. *The Battle of the Huertgen Forest.* Philadelphia, 2003.

———. *Company Commander.* Short Hills, NJ, 1999.

———. *The Mighty Endeavor: The American War in Europe.* New York, 1992.

Maeda, Wayne. *Changing Dreams and Treasured Memories: A Story of Japanese Americans in the Sacramento Region.* Sacramento, CA, 2000.

Maki, Mitchell T., Harry H. L. Kitano, and S. Megan Berthold. *Achieving the Impossible Dream: How Japanese Americans Obtained Redress.* Chicago, 1999.

Malkin, Michelle. *In Defense of Internment: The Case for 'Racial Profiling' in World War II and the War on Terror.* Washington, DC, 2004.

Manchester, William. *Goodbye, Darkness: A Memoir of the Pacific War.* Boston, 2002.

———. *The Glory and the Dream: A Narrative History of America, 1932–1972.* Boston, 1974.

Marshall, S. L. A. *Night Drop: The American Airborne Invasion of Normandy.* New York, 1984.

Maslowski, Peter. *Armed with Cameras: The American Military Photographers of World War II.* New York, 1993.

Mason, David. *Breakout: Drive to the Seine.* New York, 1972.

Masters, Charles J. *Glidermen of Neptune: The American D-Day Glider Attack.* Carbondale, IL, 1995.

Mauldin, Bill. *The Brass Ring.* New York, 1971.

McDermott, Kathleen. *Timex: A Company and Its Community: 1854–1998.* Iceland, 1998.

McDonald, Charles B. *A Time for Trumpets: The Untold Story of the Battle of the Bulge.* New York, 1985.

McFarland, Stephen L., and Wesley Phillips Newton. *To Command the Sky.* Washington, DC, 1991.

McGuire, Phillip, ed. *Taps for a Jim Crow Army: Letters from Black Soldiers in World War II.* Lexington, KY, 1993.

McLaurin, Melton, and Michael Thomason. *Mobile: The Life and Times of a Great Southern City.* Woodland Hills, CA, 1981.

McMillan, George. *The Old Breed: A History of the First Marine Division in World War II.* Washington, DC, 1979.

Meacham, Jon. *Franklin and Winston: An Intimate Portrait of an Epic Friendship.* New York, 2003.

Medoff, Rafael. *The Deafening Silence: American Jewish Leaders and the Holocaust.* New York, 1987.

Merridale, Catherine. *Ivan's War: Life and Death in the Red Army, 1939–1945.* New York, 2006.

Messenger, Charles. *The Second World War in Europe.* Washington, DC, 2004.

Michno, Gregory F. *Death on the Hellships: Prisoners at Sea in the Pacific War.* Annapolis, MD, 2001.

Miller, Donald L. *Masters of the Air: America's Bomber Boys Who Fought the Air War Against Nazi Germany.* New York, 2006.

———. *The Story of World War II.* New York, 2001.

Miller, Edward G. *A Dark and Bloody Ground: The Hürtgen Forest and the Roer River Dams, 1944–1945.* College Station, TX, 2003.

Miller, Nathan. *The U.S. Navy: An Illustrated History.* New York, 1977.

———. *War at Sea.* New York, 1995.

Montefiore, Simon Sebag. *Stalin: The Court of the Red Tsar.* New York, 2004.

Moorehead, Alan. *African Trilogy: The Desrt War: The North African Campaign 1940–43.* London, 2002.

———. *A Late Education: Episodes in a Life.* New York, 1999.

———. *Eclipse: An Eye-Witness Account of the Allied Invasion of Fortress Europe in World War II.* New York, 1999.

Morris, Eric. *Circles of Hell: The War In Italy: 1943–1945.* New York, 1993.

Mortimer, Gavin. *The Longest Night.* New York, 2005.

Morton, Louis. *United States Army in World War II: The War in the Pacific: The Fall of the Philippines.* Washington, DC, 1989.

Muirhead, John. *Those Who Fall.* New York, 1986.

Mullener, Elizabeth. *War Stories: Remembering World War II.* New York, 2004.

Murray, Williamson, and Allan R. Millett. *A War to Be Won: Fighting the Second World War.* Cambridge, MA, 2001.

Nalty, Bernard C. *Strength for the Fight: A History of Black Americans in the Military.* New York, 1986.

Nash, Grace C. *That We Might Live.* Scottsdale, AZ, 1984.

Newcomb, Richard F. *Abandon Ship!: The Saga of the U.S.S.* Indianapolis, *the Navy's Greatest Sea Disaster.* New York, 2001.

Newton, Verne W., ed. *FDR and the Holocaust.* New York, 1996.

The *New Yorker* Magazine. *London 1939 to Hiroshima 1945: The New Yorker Book of War Pieces.* New York, 1988.

Nichol, John, and Tony Rennell. *The Last Escape: The Untold Story of Allied Prisoners of War in Europe, 1944–45.* New York, 2003.

Nichols, David, ed. *Ernie's War: The Best of Ernie Pyle's World War II Dispatches.* New York, 1986.

Nordyke, Phil. *All American All the Way: The Combat History of the 82nd Airborne Division in World War II.* St. Paul, MN, 2005.

Norman, Elizabeth M. *We Band of Angels: The Untold Story of American Nurses Trapped on Bataan by the Japanese.* New York, 1999.

Ohnuki-Tierney, Emiko. *Kamikaze, Cherry Blossoms, and Nationalisms: The Militarization of Aesthetics in Japanese History.* Chicago, 2002.

———. *Kamikaze Diaries: Reflections of Japanese Student Soldiers.* Chicago, 2006.

O'Neill, William L. *A Democracy at War: America's Fight at Home and Abroad in World War II.* New York, 1993.

———. *The Oxford Essential Guide to World War II.* New York, 2002.

Overy, Richard. *The Dictators: Hitler's Germany, Stalin's Russia.* New York, 2004.

———. *Why the Allies Won.* New York, 1996.

Parker, Danny S. *Battle of the Bulge: Hitler's Ardennes Offensive, 1944–1945.* Conshohocken, PA, 1999.

Parker, Matthew. *Monte Cassino: The Hardest-Fought Battle of World War II.* New York, 2005.

———. *The Battle of Britain: July–October 1940.* Chatham, UK, 2001.

Parrish, Thomas. *The Submarine: A History.* New York, 2004.

Patterson, James T. *Grand Expectations: The United States, 1945–1974.* New York, 1996.

Penrose, Jane, ed. *The D-Day Companion.* Oxford, UK, 2004.

Perret, Geoffrey. *Days of Sadness, Years of Triumph.* New York, 1973.

———. *There's a War to Be Won: The United States Army in World War II.* New York, 1997.

Perugini, Giuseppe. *From Pontelandolfo to Waterbury.* Benevento, Italy, 2004.

Phillips, Robert F. *To Save Bastogne.* Briarcliff Manor, NY, 1983.

Pitt, Barrie. *The Battle of the Atlantic.* Richmond, VA, 1977.

Polmar, Norman, and Thomas B. Allen. *World War II: America at War, 1941–1945.* New York, 1991.

Porch, Douglas. *The Path to Victory: The Mediterranean Theater in World War II.* New York, 2004.

Prange, Gordon, W. *At Dawn We Slept: The Untold Story of Pearl Harbor.* New York, 1981.

Prange, Gordon, W., with Donald M. Goldstein and Katherine V. Dillon. *Miracle at Midway.* New York, 1983.

Pratt, Caroline Bailey, ed. *Only a Matter of Days: The World War II Diary of Fay Cooke Bailey.* Bennington, VT, 2003.

Prising, Robin. *Manila, Goodbye.* Boston, 1975.

Pyle, Ernie. *Brave Men.* New York, 1944.

———. *Here Is Your War.* New York, 1944.

Rames, John E. *Traces: A Soldier Writes Home.* Gambier, OH, 2003.

Redding, Jack, and Thor Smith. *Wake of Glory.* New York, 1945.

Relief for Americans in Philippines. *Internews: Santo Tomas Internment Campus Health.* New York, 1942.

Reynolds, David. *In Command of History: Churchill Fighting and Writing the Second World War.* New York, 2005.

———. *Rich Relations: The American Occupation of Britain, 1942–1945.* New York, 1995.

Rhodes, Richard. *Masters of Death: The SS-Einsatzgruppen and the Invention of the Holocaust.* Oxford, UK, 2002.

———. *The Making of the Atomic Bomb.* New York, 1986.

Robar, Keith. *Intelligence, Internment & Relocation: Roosevelt's Executive Order 9066: How Top Secret "MAGIC" Intelligence Led to Evacuation.* Seattle, 2000.

Roeder, George H., Jr. *The Censored War.* New Haven, 1993.

Rooney, Andy. *My War.* New York, 2000.

Rosen, Robert N. *Saving the Jews: Franklin D. Roosevelt and the Holocaust.* New York, 2006.

Rubinstein, William D. *The Myth of Rescue: Why the Democracies Could Not Have Saved More Jews from the Nazis.* Padstow, UK, 2000.

Rutherford, Ward. *Fall of the Philippines.* New York, 1971.

———. *Kasserine: Baptism of Fire.* New York, 1970.

Ryan, Cornelius. *A Bridge Too Far.* New York, 1974.

———. *The Longest Day: June 6, 1944.* New York, 1994.

Sams, Margaret. *Forbidden Family: A Wartime Memoir of the Philippines, 1941–1945.* Madison, WI, 1989.

Schrijvers, Peter. *The Crash of Ruin: American Combat Soldiers in Europe during World War II.* New York, 1998.

Sevareid, Eric. *Not So Wild a Dream.* Columbia, MO, 1995.

Shaw, Antony. *World War II: Day by Day.* St. Paul, MN, 2004.

Shaw, Henry I., Jr., and Ralph W. Donnelly. *Blacks in the Marine Corps.* Washington, DC, 2002.

Sheftall, Mordecai G. *Blossoms in the Wind: Human Legacies of the Kamikaze.* New York, 2006.

Sherrod, Robert. *Tarawa: The Story of a Battle.* New York, 1983.

Sherry, Michael S. *The Rise of American Air Power: The Creation of Armageddon.* New Haven, 1987.

Sladek, Karen. *Lucky Stars and Gold Bars: A World War II Odyssey.* Seattle, WA, 2003.

Sledge, E. B. *China Marine: An Ifantryman's Life After World War II.* New York, 2002.

———. *With the Old Breed: At Peleliu and Okinawa.* New York, 1990.

Sloan, Bill. *Brotherhood of Heroes: The Marines at Peleliu, 1944—The Bloodiest Battle of the Pacific War.* New York, 2005.

Smith, Dale O. *Screaming Eagle: Memoirs of a B-17 Group Commander.* New York, 1991.

Smith, J. Douglas, and Richard Jensen. *World War II on the Web.* Wilmington, DE, 2003.

Smith, Larry. *Beyond Glory: Medal of Honor Heroes in Their Own Words.* New York, 2003.

Sonnenfeldt, Richard W. *Witness to Nuremberg.* New York, 2006.

Spector, Ronald H. *At War At Sea: Sailors and Naval Combat in the Twentieth Century.* New York, 2001.

———. *Eagle Against the Sun: The American War with Japan.* New York, 1985.

Stafford, David. *Ten Days to D-Day: Citizens and Soldiers on the Eve of the Invasion.* New York, 2004.

Stanton, Doug. *In Harm's Way: The Sinking of the USS* Indianapolis *and the Extraordinary Story of Its Survivors.* New York, 2001.

Starr, Kevin. *Embattled Dreams: California in War and Peace, 1940–1950.* New York, 2002.

Steinman, Louise. *The Souvenir: A Daughter Discovers Her Father's War.* Chapel Hill, NC, 2001.

Stevens, Frederic H. *Santo Tomas Internment Camp.* 1946.

Stiles, Bert. *Serenade to the Big Bird: A New Edition of the Classic B-17 Tribute.* Atglen, PA, 2001.

Stilwell, Joseph W. *The Stilwell Papers.* New York, 1948.

Stinnett, Robert B. *Day of Deceit: The Truth About FDR and Pearl Harbor.* New York, 2000.

Sulzberger, C. L., and Editors of *American Heritage. The American Heritage Picture History of World War II.* New York, 1966.

Sweetman, John. *Schweinfurt: Disaster in the Skies.* New York, 1971.

Taggart, Donald G., ed. *History of the Third Infantry Division in World War II.* Washington, DC, 1947.

Taylor, Frederick. *Dresden: Tuesday, February 13, 1945.* New York, 2004.

Terkel, Studs. *"The Good War": An Oral History of World War II.* New York, 1984.

Thomas, Evan. *Sea of Thunder: Four Commanders and the Last Great Naval Campaign, 1941–1945.* New York, 2006.

Thomason, Michael V. R., ed. *Mobile: The New History of Alabama's First City.* Tuscaloosa, AL, 2001.

Thompson, R. W. *D-Day: Spearhead of Invasion.* New York, 1968.

Time-Life Books, eds. *World War II.* 30 vols. Alexandria, VA, 1983.

Tobin, James. *Ernie Pyle's War: America's Eyewitness to World War II.* New York, 1997.

Toland, John. *Adolf Hitler.* New York, 1976.

———. *Battle: The Story of the Bulge.* Lincoln, NE, 1999.

———. *But Not in Shame: The Six Months After Pearl Harbor.* New York, 1961.

———. *Infamy: Pearl Harbor and Its Aftermath.* Garden City, NY, 1982.

———. *The Last 100 Days.* New York, 1966.

———. *The Rising Sun: The Decline and Fall of the Japanese Empire, 1936–1945.* New York, 1970.

Tozier, Carolyn D., ed. *Remembering World War II.* Washington, DC, 1994.

Tregaskis, Richard. *Guadalcanal Diary.* New York, 2000.

———. *Invasion Diary.* Lincoln, NE, 2004.

Truscott, Lucian K., Jr. *Command Missions: A Personal Story.* Novato, CA, 1990.

Tuchman, Barbara W. *Stilwell and the American Experience in China: 1911–45.* New York, 1970.

Tuttle, William M., Jr. *"Daddy's Gone to War": The Second World War in the Lives of America's Children.* New York, 1993.

Vandegrift, A. A., and Robert B. Asprey. *Once a Marine: The Memoirs of General A. A. Vandegrift, USMC.* New York, 1966.

Van Sickle, Emily. *The Iron Gates of Santo Tomás.* Chicago, 1992.

Vaughan-Thomas, Wynford. *Anzio.* New York, 1961.

Walker, Stephen. *Shockwave: Countdown to Hiroshima.* New York, 2005.

Waller, Maureen. *London 1945: Life in the Debris of War.* New York, 2004.

Weglyn, Michi Nishiura. *Years of Infamy: The Untold Story of America's Concentration Camps.* Seattle, 2003.

Weigley, Russell F. *Eisenhower's Lieutenants: The Campaign of France and Germany, 1944–1945.* Bloomington, IN, 1990.

Weinberg, Gerhard L. *A World At Arms: A Global History of World War II.* Cambridge, UK, 1999.

———. *Germany, Hitler, & World War II.* Cambridge, UK, 1995.

———. *Visions of Victory: The Hopes of Eight World War II Leaders.* New York, 2005.

Weller, Anthony, ed. *First into Nagasaki: George Weller: Legendary Pulitzer Prize–Winning Reporter.* New York, 2006.

Wels, Susan. *Pearl Harbor: December 7, 1941: America's Darkest Day.* San Diego, CA, 2001.

Wetmore, Clio Mathews. *Beyond Pearl Harbor.* Haverford, PA, 2001.

Wheeler, Keith. *War Under the Pacific.* Richmond, VA, 1980.

White, David Fairbank. *Bitter Ocean: The Battle of the Atlantic, 1939–1945.* New York, 2006.

White, William, ed. *By-Line: Ernest Hemingway: Selected Articles and Dispatches of Four Decades.* New York, 2003.

Whiting, Charles. *48 Hours to Hammelburg.* New York, 1984.

———. *Death of a Division.* Briarcliff Manor, NY, 1981.

Whitlock, Flint. *The Fighting First: The Untold Story of the Big Red One on D-Day.* Cambridge, MA, 2004.

Willmott, H. P. *The Second World War in the Far East.* London, 1999.

Wilmot, Chester. *Struggle for Europe.* New York, 1986.

Wilson, George. *If You Survive.* New York, 1987.

Winkler, Allan M. *Home Front U.S.A.: America During World War II.* Arlington Heights, IL, 1986.

Wohlstetter, Roberta. *Pearl Harbor: Warning and Decision.* Stanford, CA, 1962.

Woodcock, Teedie Cowie. *Behind the Sawali: Santo Tomás in Cartoons, 1942–1945.* Greensboro, NC, 2000.

Wygle, Peter R. *Surviving a Japanese P.O.W. Camp.* Ventura, CA, 1991.

Yahara, Hiromichi. *The Battle for Okinawa.* New York, 1995.

Yellin, Emily. *Our Mothers' War.* New York, 2004.

INDEX

Page numbers in *italics* refer to illustrations.

ILLUSTRATION CREDITS

Where there is more than one credit for a page the images will be listed clockwise from top left.

Maps created by Edgeworx

Archival set-up photography by Paul Christiansen

Abbreviations:

CDND Department of National Defence, Library and Archives Canada

CSU Department of Special Collections and University Archives, The Library, California State University, Sacramento

Getty Getty Images (photographer is listed where one is known)

HBS Courtesy of Scovill Manufacturing Co. Collection, Baker Library, Harvard Business School

IWM Imperial War Museum, London

LOC Library of Congress, Prints and Photographs Division

MM Collection of Mattatuck Museum Arts and History Center, Waterbury, CT

NARA U.S. National Archives and Records Administration

OU Cornelius Ryan Collection, Ohio University, Athens, Ohio

RCSH *Rock County Star-Herald,* Luverne, Minnesota

SAMCC Sacramento Archives and Museum Collection Center

UCB Courtesy of The Bancroft Library University of California, Berkeley

USA The University of South Alabama Archives

WRA *Republican-American,* Waterbury, Connecticut

Endpapers:

Thanks to our eyewitnesses for photographs from their personal collections.

Frontmatter

i: NARA; ii–iii: NARA; v: NARA; vi: NARA; vii: NARA; viii: NARA; ix: NARA; x: NARA; xi: NARA; xii: Alfred Eisenstaedt/Getty; xv: Courtesy Ken Burns; xviii: RCSH; Betty Mann; xix: (both) RCSH; xx: Sacramento Bee Collection, SAMCC; xxi: Burt Wilson; Ralph Shaw Collection, SAMCC; CSU; xxii: HBS; WRA; xxiii: WRA; The Ciarlo Family; WRA; xxiv: (both) Erik Overbey Collection, USA; xxv: Julius E. Marx Collection, USA; Erik Overbey Collection, USA; S. Blake McNeely Collection, USA

Chapter One

xxvi: LOC; 1: Daniel Inouye; 2–3: U.S. Naval Historical Center; 4: NARA; Getty; 5: Sidney Phillips 7: Sascha Jansen; Carl Mydans/Getty; Sascha Jansen; 8: Getty; Glenn Frazier; 9: Melville Jacoby, Courtesy of Estate of Annalee Whitmore Jacoby Fadiman; 10–11: Carl Mydans/Getty; 12: NARA; 13: Office of Communications & Marketing, Auburn University; 14: Getty; AP Images; 15: Hugo Jaeger/Getty; 16: LOC; Carl Mydans/Getty; 17: AP Images; 18: AP Images; 19: NARA; AP Images; 20: Corbis; Sacramento Bee Collection, SAMCC; 21: AP Images; 22: Mobile Press-Register; Getty; 23: Getty; 25: Carl Mydans/Getty; 26: LOC; 28–29: NARA; 30: Military History, Smithsonian Institution; LOC; 31: Sascha Jansen; 32: NARA; 33: Eugene Hepting Collection, SAMCC; 34: NARA; 35: Susumu Satow; 36: LOC; 36–37: NARA ; 39: Getty; 40–41: LOC; 42: Alberto Montilla; NARA; 44: (both) Lowell and Marian DeWolf; 45: (both) RCSH; 46: NARA; 46–53: NARA; 50: NARA; 52–53: NARA; 54–55: Getty; 56: Getty; 57: NARA; 58–59: NARA; 61: NARA; 63: AP Images; 64: RCSH; 66–67: Culver Pictures; 68: Katharine Singer; 69: Getty

Chapter Two

70: LOC; 71: The Ciarlo Family; 73: NARA; 74: Charles Mann; 74–75: Getty; 76: NARA; 77: NARA; 78: NARA; 79: Carl Mydans/Getty; 80: (both) Sascha Jansen; 82: Alberto Montilla; 85: AP Images; 86: LOC; 87: (both) LOC; 88: Emma Belle Petcher; 89: Alabama Dry Dock and Shipbuilding Company Collection, USA; 90: Alabama Dry Dock and Shipbuilding Company Collection, USA; 91: LOC; 92: RCSH; Culver Pictures; 93: HBS; 94: Clyde Odum; 95: John Gray; 96: (both) Alabama Dry Dock and Shipbuilding Company Collection, USA; 98: Robert Kashiwagi; 99: NARA; 100: (both) NARA; 101: LOC; UCB; UCB; UCB; 102–103: UCB; 105: NARA; 106–107: Eliot Elisofon/Getty; 108–109: Corbis; 110: Alabama Dry Dock and Shipbuilding Company Collection, USA; 112: NARA; LOC; 113: Willie Rushton; 114: NARA; 115: Dwain Luce; 116: Getty; 117: Earl Burke; 118: ullstein bild / The Granger Collection, New York; 119: NARA; 121: Earl Burke; The Ciarlo Family; 122: Burt Wilson; Courtesy of Paramount Pictures FLYING TIGERS © Paramount Pictures. All Rights Reserved; Burt Wilson; 125: NARA; 126–127: NARA; 128: NARA; 129: George Strock/Getty; 130: RCSH; 132: Emily Lewis; 133: NARA

Chapter Three

134: Mansell/Getty; 135: Maurice Bell; 136: LOC; 137: NARA; 138–139: AP Images; 140: AP Images; 141: NARA; 142: Leo Goldberg; 143: LOC; 144: MM; 144–145: ® Timex Corporation; 146: LOC; Frederick W. Chesson; 147: Wallace Kirkland/Getty; RCSH; AP Images; 148: (both) Anne Swift; 150: Sascha Jansen; 153: John Florea/Getty; 154: NARA; 156: Ward Chamberlin; 157: IWM NA 10942; 159: NARA; 160–161: ECPAD/France; 162: Corbis; 162–163: NARA ; 164: George Silk/Getty; Corbis; 166: NARA; NARA; LOC; 167: NARA; Printed by permission of the Norman Rockwell Family Agency Copyright © 1943 the Norman Rockwell Family Entities; LOC; NARA   ; 168: Quentin and Jackie Aanenson; 169: NARA; 171: NARA; 172–173: IWM NA 13274; 176–177: LOC; 177: NARA; 178–179: IWM NYT 27347; 180: RCSH; 182: Corbis; 183: NARA; 184–185: NARA; 187: The Ciarlo Family

Chapter Four

188: David E. Scherman/Getty; 189: NARA; 190: Bundesarchiv Bild1011-719-0243-33; 191: Getty; 192–193: NARA; 194: Getty; 197: Joseph Vaghi; Walter Ehlers; 198–199: CDND Photograph by Gilbert Alexander Milne; 201: NARA; 202–203: (all) ROBERT CAPA © 2001 By Cornell Capa/Magnum Photos; 204–205: ROBERT CAPA © 2001 By Cornell Capa/Magnum Photos; 206: NARA; 209: (both) NARA; 210–211: NARA; 212: NARA; 213: NARA; 214: James Fahey and Family; 215: Ray Pittman; 216: NARA; 217: W. Eugene Smith/Getty; 218–219: Corbis; 222: D. L. Hightower/Clayton Historical Preservation Authority Collection, USA; Culver Pictures; 223: Jim Sherman; Reprinted here by permission of Hormel Foods. © Hormel Foods, LLC; Jim Sherman; 225: Quentin and Jackie Aanenson; 226: Fred Ramage/Getty; 227: Fred Ramage/Getty; NARA; 228–229: NARA; 231: George Rodger/Getty; 232: NARA; 233: W. Eugene Smith/Getty; 234: NARA; 235: Tim Tokuno; 237: NARA; 238–239: UCB; 240: Ed Clark/Getty; 241: NARA; 242: AP Images; 243: (both) Jim Sherman; 245: Haywood Magee/Getty; 247: Mémorial de Caen; 248: RCSH; 250–251: AP Images

Chapter Five

252: LOC; 253: Quentin and Jackie Aanenson; 255: NARA; 256–257: NARA; 257: NARA; 260: The Sledge Family; 261: Getty; 262: NARA; 263: Culver Pictures; 265: AP Images; 266: NARA; 268: (both) OU; 270–271: OU; 271: Bundesarchiv Bild 183-R97496; 273: Photograph by David Pratt, Courtesy

Sascha Jansen; 274: NARA; 275: John Florea/Getty; 277: NARA; 278: NARA; 279: NARA; 280–281: NARA; 281: W. Eugene Smith/Getty; 282–283: NARA; 283: (both) NARA; 285: NARA; 287: NARA; 288: NARA; 289: NARA; 290: Paul Fussell; 292–293: NARA; 294: Tom Galloway; 295: (both) NARA; 296: NARA; 297: NARA; 299: James F. Fleming Jr.; 300: RCSH; 301: NARA; 303: NARA

Chapter Six

304: NARA; 305: NARA; 306: Ray Leopold; 308: NARA; 309: (both) NARA; 311: NARA; 313: NARA; 314: FDR Library; 315: NARA; 316–317: George Silk/Getty; 318: Arthur Mayer; 319: NARA; 320: NARA; 323: John Florea/Getty; 324–325: NARA; 325: NARA; 326: Burnett Miller; 327: The Reda Archive; 328: NARA; 329: George Silk/Getty; NARA; 331: NARA; 334: Dolores Greenslate; Dolores Greenslate; NARA; 335: NARA; 336–337: George Silk/Getty; 338: NARA; 340: Getty; 341: Getty; 342: Carl Mydans/Getty; 343: (all) Carl Mydans/Getty; 344–345: Carl Mydans/Getty; 346: NARA; 347: NARA; 348: Bundesarchiv Bild 183-R72624; 349: NARA ; 350–351: Courtesy of USMC Visual Archives, Archives and Special Collections branch, Quantico, VA.; 351: AP Images; NARA; 352: NARA; 353: Sam Hynes; 356: George Silk/Getty ; 357: Waymon Ransom; 358–359: The Robert Hunt Library; 361: NARA; 363: RCSH; 364: unknown; 365: Herndon Inge; 366: NARA

Chapter Seven

368: AP Images; 369: LOC; 370–371: unknown; 372: Tokuku Kikuchi; 374: NARA; 375: NARA; 376: NARA; 377: NARA; 379: Getty; 380: (both) NARA; 381: NARA; 382: Sascha Jansen; 383: NARA; 384: NARA; 385: Alabama Dry Dock and Shipbuilding Company Collection, USA; NARA; 387: Quentin and Jackie Aanenson; 388–389: NARA; 390: NARA; 393: John Florea/Getty; 394: Yevgeny Khaldei/Getty; 395: NARA; 396: NARA; 397: NARA; 398: NARA; 399: (both) NARA; 400–401: NARA; 402: NARA; 403: WRA; Mobile Press-Register; © The Sacramento Bee, 1945; RCSH; 405: AP Images; 406–407: AP Images; 408: NARA; 410–411: NARA; 414–415: YOSUKE YAMAHATA/Magnum Photos; 416: NARA; 417: Yosuke Yamahata, August 10, 1945 courtesy Shogo Yamahata; 418: NARA; 419: NARA; 420–421: Eugene Hepting Collection, SAMCC; WRA; 421: Getty; 423: Rupert L. Frazier and the Frazier Family; 424–425: Culver Pictures; 426: RCSH; 428: The Sledge Family; 429: The Ciarlo Family; 431: Quentin and Jackie Aanenson; 432–433: Erik Overbey Collection, USA

FILM CREDITS

A KEN BURNS FILM

Directed and Produced by
KEN BURNS
LYNN NOVICK

Written by
GEOFFREY C. WARD

Produced by
SARAH BOTSTEIN

Co-Producers
PETER MILLER
DAVID McMAHON

Supervising Film Editor
PAUL BARNES

Episode Editors
PAUL BARNES
ERIK EWERS
TRICIA REIDY

Cinematography
BUDDY SQUIRES

Associate Producers
MEGHAN HORVATH
TAYLOR KRAUSS

Narrated By
KEITH DAVID

With
ADAM ARKIN
BOBBY CANNAVALE
KEVIN CONWAY
TOM HANKS
REBECCA HOLTZ
SAMUEL L. JACKSON
JOSH LUCAS
CAROLYN MCCORMICK
ROBERT WAHLBERG
ELI WALLACH

**Original Music Composed
and Arranged by**
WYNTON MARSALIS

"AMERICAN ANTHEM"
Music and Lyrics
GENE SCHEER
Performed by
NORAH JONES

Assistant Editors
PAUL DOCHERTY
DANIEL J. WHITE
RYAN GIFFORD

Consulting Producer
DAYTON DUNCAN

Board of Advisors
JAMES BARKER
LIZABETH COHEN
GERALD EARLY
PAUL FUSSELL
SAMUEL HYNES
DAVID KENNEDY
BILL LEUCHTENBURG
MARTIN E. MARTY
RICHARD SNOW
ROGER SPILLER

Coordinating Producer
PAM TUBRIDY BAUCOM

Chief Financial Officer
BRENDA HEATH

Associate Financial Officer
PATTY LAWLOR

Assistant to the Director
ELLE CARRIÈRE

Additional Cinematography
STEPHEN McCARTHY
ALLEN MOORE
JON ELSE

Assistant Camera
JIM BALL
SLATER CROSBY
J. C. EARL
JAMIE FITZPATRICK
ROGER HAYDOCK
PAUL MARBURY
STEPHANE PAILLARD
ANTONIO ROSSI
ANTHONY SAVINI
STEPHEN SPEERS

Sound Recording
STEWART ADAM
GERARD BONNETTE
DOUG DUNDERDALE
JOHN HAPTAS
STEVE LONGSTRETH
JOHN OSBORNE
BRENDA RAY
MIKE REILLY
MARK ROY
BOB SILVERTHORNE

Technical Director
DAVE MAST
SEAN HUFF

Production Associate
TED ALCORN

Administrative Assistant
DEVON LAINE CIAMPA

Dialogue Editors
MARLENA GRZASLEWICZ
MAGDALINE VOLAITIS

Sound Effects Editors
IRA SPIEGEL
ERIK EWERS
MARIUSZ GLABINSKI
MAGDALINE VOLAITIS
RYAN GIFFORD

Music Editor
JACOB RIBICOFF

Assistant Sound Editors
DAVE MAST
SEAN HUFF

Sound Post-Production
SOUND ONE

Re-Recording Mixer
DOMINICK TAVELLA

Voice-Over Recording
LOU VERRICO
FULL HOUSE PRODUCTIONS

Digital Image Restoration
DANIEL J. WHITE

Digital Animation
PAUL DOCHERTY

Archival Footage Consultant
ELISABETH M. HARTJENS

Animated Maps and Title design
EDGEWORX
Design and Animation Supervisor
JOHN BAIR
Animation Producers
VIVIAN CONNOLLY
BEN SPIVAK
Animators
NATHAN MEIER
TREVOR SIAS

Video Post-Production
GOLDCREST POST PRODUCTIONS
TIM SPITZER
Managing Director

IQ Pablo HD color correction
JOHN J. DOWDELL III
Director of Imaging Technologies

IQ HD On-Line Editing
PETER HEADY
Senior Finishing Artist

Film Processing
DUART FILM LABS

Music Consultants
LEON BOTSTEIN
TOM EVERED

Additional Musicians
WALTER BLANDING, Saxophone
BILL CHARLAP, Piano
AMANDA FORSYTH, Cello
VICTOR GOINES, Clarinet
CARLOS HENRIQUEZ, Bass
ALI JACKSON, Drums
WYNTON MARSALIS, Trumpet
MARK O'CONNOR, Violin
ANDY STEIN, Violin
DOUG WAMBLE, Guitar

Additional Music Recorded at
FUTURA PRODUCTIONS
Engineered by
JOHN WESTON
Boston, Massachusetts
JACQUELINE SCHWAB, piano

THE SILK ROAD ENSEMBLE with
YO-YO MA
Appears Courtesy of Sony BMG
Masterworks

Additional Research
MICHAEL DOLAN
MIKE HILL
JIM PARKER
MARI MIYACHI
REIKO SAKUMA
SUSAN SHUMAKER

Post-Production Associates
KIRK CARAPEZZA
CHRISTOPHER DARLING
MEAGAN FRAPPIEA

Legal Services
ROBERT N. GOLD
VALERIE MARCUS

Funding Provided By
General Motors
Anheuser-Busch
Bank of America
Lilly Endowment, Inc.
Public Broadcasting Service
National Endowment for
the Humanities
Corporation for Public Broadcasting
The Arthur Vining Davis Foundations
The Pew Charitable Trusts
Longaberger Foundation
Park Foundation, Inc.

A NOTE ABOUT THE AUTHORS

GEOFFREY C. WARD wrote the script for the film series *The War* and is the winner of five Emmys and two Writers Guild of America awards for his work for public television. He is also a historian and biographer and the author of fourteen books, including most recently *Unforgivable Blackness: The Rise and Fall of Jack Johnson*. He won the National Book Critics Circle Award in 1989 and the Francis Parkman Prize in 1990. He lives in New York City.

KEN BURNS, producer and director of the film series *The War*, founded his own documentary company, Florentine Films, in 1976. His films include *Jazz*, *Baseball*, and *The Civil War*, which was the highest-rated series in the history of American public television. His work has won numerous prizes, including the Emmy and Peabody Awards, and two Academy Award nominations. He lives in Walpole, New Hampshire.

A NOTE ABOUT THE TYPE

This book was set in Minion, a typeface produced by the Adobe Corporation specifically for the Macintosh personal computer, and released in 1990. Designed by Robert Slimbach, Minion combines the classic characteristics of old-style faces with the full complement of weights required for modern typesetting.

Composed by North Market Street Graphics, Lancaster, Pennsylvania

Printed and bound by R. R. Donnelley & Sons, Willard, Ohio

Designed by Wendy Byrne

Daniel Inouye

Phillips family

Sascha Weinzheimer and her cousin

Glenn Dowling Frazier (center)

Susumu Satow

Robert Kashiwagi

Willie Rushton

Dwain Luce

Earl Burke (right) with his mother and brother Tom

Ward Chamberlin

Quentin Aanenson and Jackie Greer

Joseph Vaghi

Walter Ehlers

Tom Galloway

John and Virginia Soden

Ray Leopold

Arthur Mayer